THROUGHOUT HISTORY the British Atlantic has often been depicted as a series of well-ordered colonial ports that functioned as nodes of Atlantic shipping, where orderliness reflected the effectiveness of the regulatory apparatus constructed to contain Atlantic commerce. Colonial ports were governable places where British vessels, and only British vessels, were to deliver English goods in exchange for colonial produce. Yet behind these sanitized depictions lay another story, one about the porousness of commercial regulation, the informality and persistent illegality of exchanges in the British Empire, and the endurance of a culture of cross-national cooperation in the Atlantic that had been forged in the first decades of European settlement and still resonated a century later.

In *Empire at the Periphery,* Christian J. Koot examines the networks that connected British settlers in New York and the Caribbean and Dutch traders in the Netherlands and in the Dutch colonies in North America and the Caribbean, demonstrating that these interimperial relationships formed a core part of commercial activity in the early Atlantic World, operating alongside British trade. Koot provides unique consideration of how local circumstances shaped imperial development, reminding us th⸮ ⸮⸮⸮⸮⸮⸮ consisted not only of elites dic⸮ rial growth from world capita⸮

(continued

D1207151

EMPIRE AT THE PERIPHERY

EMPIRE AT THE PERIPHERY

British Colonists, Anglo-Dutch Trade, and the Development of the British Atlantic, 1621–1713

CHRISTIAN J. KOOT

New York University Press

NEW YORK AND LONDON

NEW YORK UNIVERSITY PRESS
New York and London
www.nyupress.org

LIBRARY OF CONGRESS CATALOGING-IN-PUBLICATION DATA

Koot, Christian J.
  Empire at the periphery : British colonists, Anglo-Dutch trade, and the development of
the British Atlantic, 1621–1713 / Christian J. Koot.
    p. cm. — (Early American places)
  Includes bibliographical references and index.
  ISBN 978-0-8147-4883-1 (cl : alk. paper)
  ISBN 978-0-8147-4884-8 (e-book)
  1. Great Britain—Commerce—Netherlands—History. 2. Netherlands—Commerce
—Great Britain—History. 3. Mercantile system—Great Britain. 4. Mercantile
system—Netherlands. I. Title.
HF3518.N4K66 2011
382.0941'09492—dc22

                                                                              2010037510

References to Internet Web sites (URLs) were accurate at the time of writing. Neither the
author nor New York University Press is responsible for URLs that may have expired or
changed since the manuscript was prepared.

New York University Press books are printed on acid-free paper, and their binding
materials are chosen for strength and durability. We strive to use environmentally
responsible suppliers and materials to the greatest extent possible in publishing our
books.

Manufactured in the United States of America
10 9 8 7 6 5 4 3 2 1

To my family

Contents

Illustrations, Maps, and Tables

ACKNOWLEDGMENTS

In the ten years spent working on this project, I have accumulated many debts. As a work of comparative history, this study would not have been possible without the multitude of talented scholars who provided the foundation upon which many of its claims rest; most notably those who labored to translate Dutch documents, collect biographic information, and deeply examine the different locations around the Atlantic rim that are at the heart of this book.

The financial and intellectual support of many institutions was key to completing the research for this book, including the New-York Historical Society, the Gilder Lehrman Institute of American History, the Program in Early American Economy and Society at the Library Company of Philadelphia, the Jacob Rader Marcus Center of the American Jewish Archives in Cincinnati, Ohio, the Gipson Institute of Eighteenth-Century Studies at Lehigh University, and the John D. Rockefeller Library in Williamsburg, Va. (through a Gilder Lehrman Research Fellowship). Additional support came through a Competitive Fellowship Award from the University of Delaware, a Kraus Research Grant from the American Historical Association, and a Colgate University Discretionary Research Grant. A travel stipend from the International Seminar on the History of the Atlantic World at Harvard University helped fund a critical trip to England. The archivists and librarians of the archives listed in the notes who have graciously helped me track down sources are too numerous to name. Especially important have been Bruce Abrahms at the New York County Clerk's Office, Division of Old Records, and Catalina Hannan (who opened the library for me on her day off) at Historic Hudson Valley. I thank these institutions for allowing me to quote from their materials. The staff of Cook Library at Towson University performed yeoman's work in finding me obscure books as I finished writing.

I am fortunate to have spent my graduate years in the History Department at the University of Delaware, where the Hagley Program not only funded my education, but also embraced and nourished this student of the seventeenth century. A Barra Dissertation Fellowship brought me to the McNeil Center for Early American Studies, which Daniel Richter has continued to make sure is the best place to study and write about early America. The participants in center events, especially the Fellows that shared the center with me, have been critical in helping me to focus and sharpen my work. As I have begun to teach, my colleagues have taken over this role. The History Department at Towson University has been particularly encouraging of young scholars and a Faculty Development and Research Committee Summer Research Fellowship provided me the funding and time to complete my revisions.

The scholar who has had the most significant impact upon my work is Cathy Matson. Guiding the project since it began as a seminar paper in 2000, Cathy has continually amazed me with her unparalleled knowledge of the early modern Atlantic economy, her ability to see patterns in shards of evidence, and her penchant for forcing me to deal with big questions. I especially thank her not only for the incredibly careful eleventh-hour reading of the manuscript she offered, but also for her endless enthusiasm, encouragement, and friendship.

Many other scholars have answered questions, offered sources, discussed approaches, read portions of my work, and helped refine the project at various stages. I especially wish to thank Howard Johnson, Stuart Semmel, Matthew Mulcahy, Kenneth Cohen, Zara Anishanslin, Christine Sears, Alan Meyer, Alex Pavuk, Tom Rylko, John Davies, Michelle Craig McDonald, Roderick McDonald, Philip Morgan, April Hatfield, Dennis Maika, and Victor Enthoven. I was fortunate to receive feedback from several distinguished scholars at academic conferences. I thank John J. McCusker, David Hancock, Karen Kupperman, Sean X. Goudie, and David Voorhees. Dan Richter read the manuscript twice, offering a sharp and judicious critique at a critical juncture. The participants in the 2003 Meeting of the International Seminar on the History of the Atlantic World at Harvard University helped me to frame the project in the first place. The editors of *Early American Studies, Itinerario,* and *De Halve Maen* have allowed me to include revised portions of work that appeared first in their journals. And finally, Mike Jarvis and an anonymous reader for New York University Press provided many helpful comments and corrections. All errors, of course, remain my own. I am fortunate to be publishing with NYU Press. Deborah Gershenowitz showed excitement for the project from the moment I contacted her, and she and Gabrielle Begue have speedily guided this book through publication. Martin L. White compiled the index.

On a more personal note, I want to thank my loving family, to whom this book is dedicated, for their tireless support. My mother and father—a historian himself—know all too well the uneven rhythm of research and writing, and together with my brother, Michael (and his family), seemed always to know when to ask how things were proceeding, and when to focus on other matters. It has been many years since the four of us walked the streets of Williamsburg, tramped along Hadrian's Wall in Scotland, and roamed the halls of English country houses, but it was on those trips that I learned to love the past. Thank you. Paul and Kay Van Horn embraced this project along with a new son-in-law and have been unceasing in their support; this year I will need a new resolution on New Year's Day.

I save my greatest debt for last. My wife, Jennifer Van Horn, not only lived with this project daily for the last decade, but also made my work infinitely better with her incisive comments, her probing questions, and her art historian's eye for detail. I thank her for her unceasing encouragement and love.

Introduction

A 1700 engraving of New York City pictures a thriving British port in the midst of a period of rapid economic growth.[1] The harbor bustles with activity. A great vessel, its sails full of wind, glides to join another already lying at anchor. Sailing among these massive seagoing vessels are smaller coastal craft busily carrying goods to and from the quays or perhaps bringing imports from surrounding colonies. The print portrays a vibrant yet orderly landscape; neatly arranged warehouses and countinghouses line the waterfront as tidy rows of homes stretch to the horizon. A serene hinterland fades into the background as a windmill, just visible on the right, suggests the burgeoning economic possibilities of the mid-Atlantic. A contemporary engraving of another English port, Bridgetown, Barbados, presents a similar if more densely populated scene. In this 1695 engraving, a score or more vessels crowd the Caribbean port's carefully labeled wharfs and two large quays. Multistory structures line the shore, dominated by the great storehouses that front each wharf and suggest the economic success of this leading West Indian island as do the close to forty windmills processing sugarcane that are scattered in the surrounding cane fields.

On the surface, these prints present a British Atlantic composed of well-ordered colonial ports that function as nodes of Atlantic shipping. Metropolitan officials would have endorsed such depictions; they could imagine that these views of the ports' orderliness reflected the

FIGURE 1. Thomas Doesburgh, *Nieu Amsterdam, at New Yorck*, engraving, ca. 1700. Courtesy of I. N. Phelps Stokes Collection, Miriam and Ira D. Wallach Division of Art, Prints and Photographs, The New York Public Library, Astor, Lennox and Tilden Foundation.

effectiveness of the regulatory apparatus they had constructed to contain Atlantic commerce. In these sanitized representations, as in the laws that directed imperial trade, colonial ports were governable places where British vessels, and only British vessels, were to deliver English goods in exchange for colonial produce. But if we were able to look closer at these places, to peer at the bills of lading the vessels carried, to examine their origins and cargoes, or to glance in on the wharves and merchants clustered in taverns and countinghouses, we would discover another landscape, this one much less structured and less amenable to metropolitan goals. Instead of well-regulated and accountable shipping, we would find individuals acting improvisationally in the pursuit of personal and colonial profit, undermining the quest for orderly commerce found in imperial thinking. Behind the regularity artists depicted lies another story, one about the porousness of commercial regulation, the informality and persistent illegality of exchanges in the British empire,

FIGURE 2. Samuel Copen, *Prospect of Bridge Town in Barbados.* London, 1695. London. Courtesy of Prints & Photographs Division, Library of Congress.

and the endurance of a culture of cross-national cooperation in the Atlantic that had been forged in the first decades of European settlement and still resonated a century later.

Until recently, the dominant narrative of British Atlantic development, like these port views, obscured the ad hoc cooperative reality of seventeenth- and early-eighteenth-century trade. Concerned principally with the task of explaining the simultaneous development of far-flung settlements, the imperial centers from which they emerged, and the empires they constituted, earlier work tended to center on bilateral connections between colony and metropole.[2] As scholars have shifted direction, increasingly placing the Atlantic Ocean itself, as opposed to European empires, at the center of their analysis, they have discovered the extent to which culture, goods, and entrepreneurial activities flowed across imperial boundaries in a more integrated circum-Atlantic economy than previously perceived.[3]

Collectively, recent work has demonstrated that the perspectives of merchants and planters operating in the seventeenth-century Atlantic were framed not only by European empire building and the competition that resulted, but also by their cross-national connections to one another. This new scholarship has turned our emphasis away from an approach that centers on distinct empires to one that recognizes how settlers built transnational communities around the Atlantic basin as a strategy for commercial success. It has become clear that to fully describe the development of the British Atlantic colonies in the seventeenth and early eighteenth centuries it is necessary to understand them as settlers did, as part of a larger Atlantic community.[4] Much of the recent work on commercial "border crossing," however, describes the activities of distinctive individuals noted for their transnational and entrepreneurial natures. Such a focus has significantly broadened our understanding of the fortunes of individual traders and the complex networks and identities they created but has yet to be integrated into a larger understanding of the economic development of the British Atlantic.[5]

Empire at the Periphery bridges these two bodies of scholarship that, on the one hand, explain the rise of British Atlantic colonies within an empire struggling to fashion its authority institutionally and, on the other, detail the transnational alliances forged in everyday commerce. Primarily focusing on the key transformative period in England's (and then Britain's after the Act of Union in 1707) relationship with its colonies—the years between 1624 and 1713—this work examines how the interimperial colonial communities of the seventeenth century shaped British efforts to create a state-centered and exclusive empire. The English Civil War, a regicide, three "revolutions," and multiple wars with both the Dutch and French required a bellicose government, and overwhelmingly English state builders realized that it was only by harnessing the nation's commercial power (and particularly that of its colonies) that England could meet these challenges. Simultaneously, this new state could further encourage and expand colonial development. Never coherent, sometimes contradictory, and always uneven, seventeenth-century English colonial policy was characterized by the steady efforts of a constellation of interests including courtiers, Parliament, and the "new merchants," to make the Atlantic colonies productive for the rising English state. Using trade laws, new excises, customs reform, administrative reorganization, the navy, and warfare, English authorities worked to transform colonies that were used to self-determination into a more integrated and mercantilist empire.[6]

The major obstacle England faced in harnessing colonial commerce was the prominent role that Dutch merchants played in the carrying trade of overseas English (as well as French and Spanish) colonies. Arriving first in the Atlantic to prey on Spanish shipping, by the 1640s Dutch merchants girded by the United Province's strong financial and economic position transferred the success they found in northern European and Baltic trades to the Atlantic, supplying manufactured goods to a wide constellation of colonies in exchange for colonial commodities which they carried to the Dutch Republic. This dominance brought wealth to Dutch burghers already reaping the benefits of the East India trade even as it frustrated the hopes of mercantilists in Spain, Portugal, France, and above all, in England. In the colonies, Dutch traders were almost universally welcomed not only because they brought needed trade, but also because they constituted another commercial option for often struggling settlers. Those colonists living in the newly planted English colonies of the early seventeenth century were no exception; Dutch traders frequented each of these places almost from their beginning. From the British metropolitan perspective, colonists' trade with the Dutch both made their settlements less beneficial to the emerging English empire and created a distinct colonial culture that threatened to undermine larger national goals. As Cromwell, the Stuarts, and William III would find, however, removing the Dutch and incorporating the English colonies' trade fully within the empire would not be as simple as conquering Dutch colonies (of which there were few) and passing restrictive laws. Instead, it would require changing the commercial habits and culture of colonists. That is, officials could not extend their fiscal-military state across the Atlantic until locals eschewed their cross-national, flexible origins and chose to conform to new imperial standards. The years between 1624 and 1713 were distinguished, therefore, both by new expressions of state power and by the greater realization that mercantilism rested on individual behavior. It would be the willingness of colonists to abandon an earlier cross-national Atlantic community and accept membership in the British empire, presumably on the same terms as those in the metropole, that would ultimately make a mercantilist empire possible.

This book recaptures the process by which a new idea of an exclusive British empire displaced the seventeenth century's interimperial Atlantic community, focusing on the experience of colonists living in three specific places—New York, Barbados, and the English Leeward Islands—who had particularly important connections to Dutch traders. Concentrating on the commercial experience of these individuals, this book investigates how colonists maintained and adapted their extant commercial practices to outside efforts to tame them by asking: Why did British colonists trade with Dutch merchants? What goods did they exchange? How did this trade occur? How did these patterns change over time? What was the impact of commercial regulations on Anglo-Dutch exchange? How did interimperial exchange shape the economic habits of British colonies? And finally, when and why did colonists shift away from Dutch trade?

I argue that, between 1624 and 1713, colonists chose to live in an entangled Atlantic in which pursuing Dutch trade was a regular and important part of their commercial system. The fluid, flexible, transnational, and often illicit character of early British trade both provided material benefit to fragile colonies and also convinced colonists that cross-national trade was the best route to colonial economic success. Over time, colonists' beneficial experience with foreign trade created a commercial culture that clashed with metropolitan attempts to confine trade to imperial channels. Ultimately Anglo-Dutch trade became less important for colonists, and, looking back from the perspective of the late eighteenth-century British empire, it is easy to miss what many have considered a brief and aberrant set of episodes in Atlantic history. To do this, however, is to overlook a rich story. For it is only by examining the way that an exclusive commercial empire replaced a more inclusive one and the reasons for this change that we can recapture the legacy of the earlier era and its importance in understanding how the Atlantic world developed. Government policies alone did not displace the Dutch from their prominent position in English colonies' carrying trades and thus their importance for those emerging places. Instead, local economic conditions, patterns of migration, commodity prices and transnational credit, international developments, and the ways colonists responded to all of these developments were equally responsible. Explicating these early colonists' actions helps reveal that the incorporation of far-flung territories into the British empire was not only the result of economic development and expanding governmental control, but was also a product of colonists' choosing to more fully integrate themselves into the empire; in the process, they gave shape to the British empire.

Many historians of the British Atlantic have acknowledged the complex, confusing, and multinational nature of seventeenth-century colonies, particularly where empires overlapped in such places as the Caribbean and New Netherland/New York.[7] In general, though, most have seen this period (usually restricted to 1620–60) as a short, atypical interlude in the gradual but steady process of empire building in which colonies became more "British" over time. Intent to explain the origins of the integrated mercantilist British imperial economy of the eighteenth century, these scholars have tended to emphasize how certain institutions and merchant networks on both sides of the Atlantic linked colony to metropole, facilitated greater integration of colonists into the imperial project, and thus laid the basis for the maturing eighteenth-century empire.[8] Growing imperial infrastructure, colonial linkages to Britain, and emerging British identity are important to understanding how the empire grew, but also significant were the many strategies colonists deployed as they sought colonial success. Their thousands of individual, now mostly invisible, commercial decisions made over a century helped render the British colonies viable. These efforts entailed the construction of a variety of commercial connections that both extended back to contacts in the British Isles and tied them to foreign traders throughout the Atlantic. Only by evaluating how the merchants and state builders of London promoted the commercial, financial, and legal institutions of empire, and how colonists chose to operate within or outside of that framework can we understand the crafting of the British Atlantic empire in the seventeenth century.[9]

When assessing colonists' decisions to trade with the Dutch during what was often a period of active warfare between the empires, it is tempting to see their behavior as unpatriotic or disloyal. Remarkably, however, few people in England saw it this way. Certainly for many in government there was little tolerance for colonists' collaboration with the Dutch, but illegal trade was more often seen as a product of self-interest than of traitorous intent, even when popular and political rhetoric turned sharply against the Dutch in the 1660s and 1670s. At the same time, colonists usually did not consider their cross-national alliances as detrimental to imperial interests. As scholars of English history have recently shown, cosmopolitanism was engrained in early Englishmen who were able to adhere to narrowly English definitions of self, while at the same time holding broader (and sometimes conflicting) identities that placed them in a multinational Atlantic.[10] As they saw it, pursing Dutch trade was not contrary to larger English aims but was compatible with them. Understanding this cultural conceit is important because it shows that this period was a significant and distinctive phase of colonial economic development that ended only when *colonists* decided it no longer fit their needs. That this transition took a century to unfold indicates the power of an earlier, multiethnic, multi-imperial world and highlights another dimension to the origins of the British Atlantic empire.

* * *

This study takes the colony as its basic unit of analysis, arguing that specific local factors, especially those relating to economic makeup and location, were central in shaping interimperial networks and determining how colonists adapted to new British laws and policies. At the same time, though, these places were woven into a larger Atlantic world in which flows of goods, peoples, and ideas crossed imperial boundaries to profoundly influence the individual makeup of colonies and the empires to which they belonged. Aiming to balance the local and the Atlantic, this work employs a comparative framework. Founded during a ten-year period beginning in 1624, New York, Barbados, and the Leeward Islands all struggled to achieve stability during their first generatiôns. The government officials; merchants, both Christian and Jewish; servants of many ethnic origins; and both free and enslaved Africans who populated these colonies faced persistent challenges of acquiring adequate supplies, cultivating and exporting viable staples, and protecting themselves from indigenous peoples and foreign empires. The political and economic weaknesses that all three places faced spurred interimperial trade, yet each location also retained particular characteristics that shaped its development. These differences allow us to gauge the range of circumstances that made interimperial trade necessary and profitable as well as the varied consequences of reaching out across imperial boundaries.

New York's European population was more culturally diverse than the mostly British European population of the Leeward Islands and Barbados. Before the conquest in 1664, New Amsterdam had a vibrant community of Dutch merchants already engaged in both intercolonial and transatlantic commerce. The arrival of English authority and migrants required the layering of a new population over the existing Dutch community; English merchants and government officials had to integrate themselves with the extant Dutch commercial culture. The situation was different in Barbados and the Leeward Islands. These settlements were founded by the English within a few years of one another and were therefore without a preexisting commercial culture.

Beyond population, the colonies' positions as islands or as part of a continental land mass also helped determine the extent and content of interimperial exchange. Foreign colonies surrounded the Leeward Islands and were near Barbados so that islanders from different states were in close proximity to one another. Among the most important trading centers in the Caribbean were the Dutch colonies of St. Eustatius (in the Lesser Antilles) and Curaçao (just off the northwest coast of Venezuela), and the immediacy of these Dutch shipping centers provided opportunities for cross-national exchange. Like those in the Caribbean, merchants in New Amsterdam, then New York, engaged in trade with surrounding colonies, but their neighbors were mostly English—on Long Island, in New England, along the Delaware River, and in the Chesapeake. Moreover, New Yorkers were more distant from Dutch entrepôts than were settlers in the Caribbean. Finally, differences in the nature of colonial economies meant that each location had a different need for interimperial commerce. As colonies centered around the export of tropical commodities, Barbados and the Leeward Islands depended upon European markets for their production, though the quicker transition to sugar in Barbados meant that Barbadians had a different relationship with Dutch traders than did the mostly tobacco-producing planters of the Leeward Islands. Meanwhile, by midcentury, New York was more economically diverse. Colonists in this mid-Atlantic settlement sent furs and naval stores directly to Europe but also benefited from trade with other Atlantic colonies. Despite the differences in each region's export market, both continued to depend on European manufactured goods for colonists' consumption. Varying social makeups, the colonies' locations, internal economies, and the organization of export trades provide the opportunity to examine how a range of factors influenced relationships between British colonists and Dutch merchants. In the end, the common demand for Dutch trade by colonists in both locations was not merely a result of a particular ethnic bond or a specific staple crop, though these certainly shaped cross-national ties, but rather was the result of their common experience at the edge of a fragile empire.

Organized chronologically, this work moves from the founding of the colonies through the first decades of the eighteenth century. Because of the scattered and incomplete nature of my evidence, however, I have, when appropriate, combined examples from different time periods. For example, when discussing the smuggling techniques that Caribbean merchants employed in the 1660s and 1670s, I have occasionally drawn examples from the decades before and after these dates.

The first chapter introduces New Amsterdam, the Leeward Islands, and Barbados and describes the earliest interactions between English and Dutch adventurers in these places. Located far from the seat of power in a dangerous, chaotic, and tenuous Atlantic, the settlers who built their plantations and businesses in Barbados and the Leeward Islands discovered soon after their arrival in the 1620s that they could not rely on metropolitan connections alone to advance their settlements. Colonists eager for trade quickly learned to build intraimperial relationships with other English settlements, but they also formed advantageous commercial ties with colonists from other empires, most notably Dutch traders. Predisposed toward Dutch collaboration because of decades of military, political, and cultural ties at home, driven by the fragility of their nascent settlements, and attracted by the experience and skills of Dutch merchants already trading there, English colonists incorporated these foreigners into their regular commerce in the first decades of settlement.

Over time, this trade evolved. In the Caribbean, merchants and planters organized their economies around the export of tobacco and the importation of slave labor. Dutch merchants actively participated in this expansion, offering slaves, credit, and supplies in return for tobacco. During these years, English Leeward Islanders produced tobacco superior to that grown by planters in Barbados, generating the most Dutch attention. Meanwhile, in New Amsterdam, Dutch traders established a strategically placed base from which they could organize trade with Native Americans along the Hudson and Connecticut river valleys and with English colonies already established in New England and the Chesapeake. Largely eschewing imperial borders, they established a tradition of pursuing cross-national trade, a practice that endured after the English conquest. By 1650, Dutch traders had established themselves at the center of the carrying trade throughout the region, weaving English, as well as Spanish, French, and Swedish colonies into their commercial networks as they had already done in northern Europe.

As British West Indians learned to cultivate tobacco, and soon sugar, they maintained their interimperial contacts, modifying them to fit new economic and regulatory conditions for as they started to create wealth, they became more attractive to merchants and policy makers across the Atlantic. Determined to capture the profits from now productive settlements and spurred by those like Thomas Mun who argued that England should not be "constantly embracing the Netherlanders as our best Friends and Allies; when in truth . . . there are no people in Christendome who do more [to] undermine, hurt, and eclipse us daily in our Navigation and Trades," English officials enacted mercantilist laws designed to end foreign trade in the colonies and launched three wars against the Dutch Republic.[11]

Ultimately, these efforts would impact colonists' commerce, but for many decades Anglo-Dutch trade thrived on new challenges and opportunities for collaboration that were introduced in the 1640s as the price of tobacco fell, as planters in Barbados turned to sugar, and as the English Civil War consumed England. In New Netherland, the greatest challenge to stable commerce was the arrival of English rule in 1664. The conquest created a crisis for many settlers, disrupting commercial networks that they had relied upon for supplies of manufactured goods and that had provided them markets for reexports. With British trade not yet sufficient to meet their needs (as their fellow colonists in the Caribbean well knew), New Yorkers relied upon their preexisting ties to preserve trade to the Dutch Republic as British officials worked to incorporate the colony into the British empire. Chapters 2 and 3 focus on these parallel stories, concentrating on how colonists, conditioned by their relative stability, their economic organization, and their location, adapted Anglo-Dutch trade to these new circumstances. Though exchanges with Dutch merchants never constituted the majority of colonial trade at midcentury, they were a part of daily life, with colonists continuing to turn to Dutchmen as trading partners both in times of relative stability and to supplement other sources of trade and credit in times of crisis. Colonists' reluctance to abandon Dutch ties testifies to their continued vitality and indicates how, at the periphery, colonial needs and habits often overrode imperial policies. By the late 1660s, it was becoming clear that the creation of a uniform empire and the besting of Dutch rivals had as much to do with transforming the commercial culture of the colonies as it did with removing Dutch traders and ships from the colonies. For now, however, closing off Dutch trade to British subjects remained elusive.

Chapters 4 and 5 trace changes in interimperial trade over the course of the second half of the seventeenth century and analyze how metropolitan policies affected colonists' economic decisions but did not eliminate Dutch trade. These chapters include a discussion of England's assertion of imperial authority, the continued attractiveness of interimperial commerce for colonists, and the kinds of goods or services they desired. Important for these chapters is analyzing how commercial patterns varied between the Caribbean and New York City up until the Glorious Revolution in 1689. That attempts to displace the Dutch had sporadic success depending upon each colony's economic and demographic makeup reveals that efforts to remake the English Atlantic depended as much on local decisions and developments as they did on a coherent vision flowing from England.

The final chapter traces the evolution of interimperial trade during the wars that plagued European empires almost without interruption from 1689 to 1713. The War of the League of Augsburg (1689–97) and the War of Spanish Succession (1702–13) disrupted both transatlantic trade and regulatory efforts, prompting colonists in both the Caribbean and New York to take the initiative in directing Anglo-Dutch trade, shifting the organization and management of interimperial trade to the Western Hemisphere. As they played an increasingly prominent role in guiding interimperial exchange, British West Indians and New Yorkers called on the portfolio of techniques they had developed in the previous century and added new ones, such as the increased use of the Dutch islands of Curaçao and St. Eustatius and Danish St. Thomas as intra-Caribbean transfer points. As both Barbados and the Leeward Islands continued to mature and as ongoing warfare created scarcities in the Caribbean, colonists there found they were able to trade a more diverse array of goods to English, French, and Danish islands, a pattern of commerce that New York City merchants were also perfecting in the same years. In short, this period witnessed diminishing ties to transatlantic Dutch credit and goods, and a thickening of Western Hemispheric connections within the empire. Traders in New York City and the Caribbean were reaching a point of sufficient stability to begin opening new opportunities for themselves and the empire by constructing a linked, though often still interimperial, economy.

When relative peace came to the Atlantic in 1713, colonists found that their situation had changed dramatically. Success in this European war gave significant shape to Great Britain's eighteenth-century territorial and commercial empire and brought an end to the chaotic first century of Atlantic empire building. With more-developed economies, with better access to more capable British traders, and with Dutch merchants weakened by internal economic instability in the United Provinces no longer in a dominant competitive position, many colonists shifted their orientation and decided they had more to gain from metropolitan protection than from cross-national trade. This transition in thinking was hastened by the ongoing migration of Britons to the Caribbean and New York and the maturation of a new generation of colonists with scanty ties to the multinational culture of earlier decades. An epilogue traces these new arrivals and the shifting interests that encouraged colonists to more fully embrace metropolitan articulations of empire, resulting in their active pursuit of trade policies devoted to augmenting an exclusive empire, most notably the Molasses Act of 1733. Some British colonists continued to seek Dutch trade through the eighteenth century, but on balance the colonial economic culture now favored complicity with British imperial goals.

* * *

The regulations that made some interimperial commerce illegal and some of it permissible were in constant flux throughout the period covered by this work. Depending on cargo, destination, ship registration, crew makeup, and official licensure, some colonists' trade with other nations was permitted and some was not. Though complex, this confusion is important insofar as it indicates why colonists smuggled. Not inspired by an inherent desire to flout imperial restrictions, most colonists instead pursued illicit trade because those exchanges were their habit. By the mid-seventeenth century, commerce between English and Dutch peoples in the colonies was well established; it was English law that had changed. From their viewpoint, colonists trading with the Dutch did not usually see smuggling as a crime against "the laws of nature," but as necessary to maintain established patterns of commerce. As Adam Smith remarked, the smuggler was "in every respect, an excellent citizen, had not the laws of his country made that a crime which nature never meant to be so."[12]

Because we have only fragmentary records of illicit trade, scholars will never be able to discover the precise amount of Anglo-Dutch trade in the colonies. Where possible, I have offered quantities of goods traded to the Dutch or numbers of ships engaged in interimperial trade, but I do not intend these statistics to be exhaustive. We can state with certainty only that the quantities of goods British colonists exchanged with Dutch traders contributed significantly to the stabilizing of British colonies in the early years, but in quantity they remained a relatively small proportion of all British colonial commerce. Nevertheless, I hope this book will show that the value of interimperial trade was not simply in its quantities; the absolute value may be beside the point. Even if the total value could be determined, it would not help to answer the question of why colonists participated in this trade and what importance they placed on it. Colonists went to great lengths and took significant risks to trade with Dutch merchants for more than a century, revealing that they believed these ties to be valuable. At the same time, the vast quantity of resources and effort imperial officials expended to halt the Dutch trade reveals how important administrators considered it. Just as the statistical measurement of interimperial trade is virtually impossible, the details of the merchants involved and specific voyages in the Caribbean are so fragmentary that it is rarely possible to follow the career of any one trader or even a group of merchants. In New York City, records are better and the portions of this work concerning that port can be more specific about individual life paths. In general, though, evidence is still scanty, and thus those examples we can reconstruct must stand in for the experiences of others. Nevertheless, as the colonies' commercial culture was made by hundreds of individual decisions, I have tried to illustrate with as much detail as possible those examples we do have. As such, each chapter begins with a vignette chosen to illustrate the chapter's themes and to emphasize how powerful individual choices were in determining how the British empire evolved.

The desire to pursue cross-national trade, and to evade laws to do so, knit colonists together in their quest for individual and, by extension, colonial profits. Colonists viewed interimperial trade as both one of the many commercial options available to them and as a necessity when there were no alternatives. Concerned with personal and local survival and success, these individuals, supported by governors and colonial councils and assemblies, pursued the most advantageous of the options available to them, alternatively obeying, manipulating, and violating imperial policy dependent on each distinct circumstance. What these personal decisions created in the aggregate was the growing belief that local interests diverged from imperial concerns and that they, as locals, best understood the commercial needs and opportunities of their colonies. Thousands of miles from home and struggling to prosper, colonists understood European expansion differently than did subjects and rulers in the metropole. Where British officials and merchants saw distinct empires competing for the world's wealth, colonists often saw an entangled Atlantic community striving to succeed. Recovering this colonial way of seeing and the interimperial networks British colonists constructed reveals how local articulations of empire helped create the British Atlantic.

PART ONE

BEGINNINGS, 1620–1659

1 / Interimperial Foundations: Early Anglo-Dutch Trade in the Caribbean and New Amsterdam

On the evening of September 29, 1632,[1] the governor of the small and struggling English colony of Nevis welcomed a guest to dinner. Since the colony was blessed by abundant supplies of wood and water as well as a "fine sandy bay" that made it easy for "boats to land," Governor Thomas Littleton was accustomed to receiving visitors from a variety of European empires. Their ships not only brought news, diplomatic intelligence, and fellowship, but also trade goods invaluable to the four-year-old colony that constantly feared the return of ravaging Spanish invaders. That evening his guest was David Pietersz. de Vries, a thirty-nine-year-old Dutch captain and trader who was on his way to the small settlement of New Netherland on the North (or Hudson) River but had stopped first in the Caribbean to load salt at the Dutch island of St. Martin. During De Vries's two-day stay, Littleton prevailed upon the Dutchman "to take aboard some captive Portuguese" whom he wanted delivered to the English Captain John Stone at De Vries's next stop, the English colony of St. Christopher.[2] Upon arriving there, De Vries again met with the island's governor, Sir Thomas Warner, and delivered the prisoners—most likely enslaved Africans taken from a Portuguese vessel—to Stone. De Vries and Stone evidently had much to discuss for when the Dutch captain weighed anchor and sailed for Dutch St. Martin on September 2, Stone was on board, leaving his "barge . . . to follow him with some goods" later.[3]

While such friendly contact and economic exchange between a Dutch merchant and an English governor may at first seem surprising—one might expect men acting as agents of competing empires to have had a strained, if not hostile, relationship—their affiliation was far from aberrant. Collaboration between governors, captains, and merchants from a variety of European empires was a regular feature of Atlantic settlement in the seventeenth century. These relationships, based not upon imperial policies and designs for empire, but on shifting personal and familial relations of convenience and benefit, characterized a seventeenth-century Atlantic in which imperial borders were permeable. Though in the vanguards of rival empires, colonists from England and the Dutch Republic found that, in the Americas, success depended on cross-national cooperation. As De Vries discovered in 1632 and on two subsequent voyages, English settlers were particularly welcoming to Dutch merchants who brought goods and services to sustain their colonies in the 1620s and 1630s. Simultaneously, Dutch colonists living in New Netherland, De Vries's destination in 1632, found trade to neighboring English settlements to be a vital component of their colonial success. On the whole, the experiences of English and Dutch peoples in the Caribbean and North America during this early period of colonization taught colonists that survival and success at the periphery required them to rely not on a distant, and often aloof or distracted metropole, but on their own ingenuity in securing trade. These ideas of fluidity and openness created a lasting legacy that complicated the later imposition of rigorous imperial order on British colonial trade.

Explaining the warm reception De Vries received from English governors and merchants requires us first to understand how and why the Dutch trader came to be in the Caribbean. By retracing his circuitous route, we gain a sense of the larger patterns of colonial settlement and economic development that shaped the seventeenth-century Atlantic, as well as the trajectories of Atlantic empire building. Ultimately, these forces created the conditions of opportunity and demand that bound together fledging English colonists and Dutch traders.

Four months earlier, in May 1632, De Vries had begun the journey that took him to the Caribbean, guiding his vessel and its seven crew members away from the small island of Texel, the southwesternmost of the five Wadden Islands, which guard the entrance to the Dutch Republic's great internal sea, the Zuiderzee. Passing through the English Channel into the open waters of the Atlantic, De Vries plotted a complex course determined by the prevailing winds and currents, taking the vessel to the Caribbean before eventually arriving at New Netherland. As he examined his charts and pondered the journey ahead, perhaps De Vries thought of the thriving metropolis fast becoming the trading center of the Western world that he had just left behind. Of course, Amsterdam was not quite the city of golden light, abundant harvests, neatly creased linen, and domestic tranquility depicted in the work of Dutch genre painters, but nevertheless the city's bustling waterfront, rows of gabled townhouses fronting crowded canals, and comfortable temperatures stood in stark contrast to the often empty roadsteads, rough-hewn dwellings bordering muddy lanes, and extreme temperatures that typified many early-seventeenth-century European settlements in the Americas.[4]

In the spring of 1632, Amsterdam's roughly 115,000 inhabitants (10 percent of the country's population) were enjoying a remarkable, if discontinuous, period of growth that was not yet a half century old. During the first two decades of the seventeenth century, the residents of the United Provinces, only recently acknowledged as virtually "a sovereign, independent state" by the Twelve Years' Truce they signed with Philip III of Spain in 1609, began to establish the new Dutch Republic as Europe's trading center. Located at the midpoint of one of the key European trading axes—between the timber and grain that flowed from the Baltic to southern Europe and the Mediterranean goods that traveled back north again—the United Provinces were well placed to grow quickly. A variety of factors including the fall of Antwerp in 1585, the lifting of a Spanish embargo on Dutch ports associated with the Truce of 1609, and the disruptions that the Thirty Years' War caused in much of Europe reinforced the Provinces' geographic advantages and further encouraged the refocusing of Europe's entrepôt trade through the Low Countries. Together with advances in Dutch agriculture, these changes accelerated commerce and craft production, causing the United Provinces' economy to expand dramatically despite being interrupted by a resumption of warfare with Spain in the 1620s. At the center of the commercial explosion was a large population of merchants with the knowledge and credit needed to fuel economic expansion, and connected by commerce and family alliances in the leading cities of Amsterdam, Haarlem, Rotterdam, Middelburg, and Leiden.[5]

A series of financial innovations in capital markets and banking institutions subsequently allowed Dutchmen, led foremost by those in Amsterdam, to exploit new international trading opportunities. These advances enabled merchants to pool resources and to acquire loans at low interest rates of 3.5 to 4 percent (compared with 6 to 10 percent in England), which in turn kept their transaction costs low, encouraged commercial investment, and allowed them to hold goods in the vast warehouses that lined Amsterdam's canals until market conditions were perfect for their sale. Efficient capital markets, combined with low wages and technological advances in shipbuilding, made Dutch shipping competitive throughout Europe and the Americas, where Dutch traders could often offer goods from 30 to 40 percent cheaper than their rivals. Early success fueled future growth, and as Dutch merchants built commercial networks that spanned the globe, they were able to best European rivals by perfecting the acquisition and dissemination of market knowledge. Published in the *prijs courantiers* (price currents) that flourished in Amsterdam or passed trader to trader while they walked the paths of the Bourse, Amsterdam's exchange and the central node of the vast Dutch information network, intelligence about prices, markets, and foreign affairs augmented Dutch merchants' already advantageous positions.

Buttressing these financial advantages were Dutch innovations in industrial production (especially in those industries requiring significant capital investment), large urban communities from which to draw skilled workers, and supplies of scarce materials. Included in this group of industries were fine-cloth manufacture (much of which was centered in Leiden), dyestuff processing, sugar and whale-oil refining, and ceramic production. Specialization in these areas enhanced Dutch wealth and increased export opportunities. As Amsterdam's superior credit and insurance markets attracted more foreign investment and merchants capitalized on low prices to expand their share of Atlantic exchanges, Amsterdam was transformed into Europe's leading trading city and its most vibrant economy. Soon visitors from around Europe were descending on the city, walking beside its "Grafts, Canals, Cutts & Sluces, Moles, & Rivers" and declaring it "the most busy Concourse of Trafiquers, & people of Commerce, beyond any place or Mart in the world." One even claimed that "1000 saile of shippes have been seen at one Tide to goe in and out" of the port. By the time De Vries boarded a barge and departed Amsterdam to meet his vessel in Texel, the city dominated the lucrative Baltic carrying trades, controlled much of the northern fisheries, and was beginning to secure a central place in colonial commerce in the East and West Indies.[6]

De Vries's Dutch predecessors had only recently charted the route he was to now follow: west through the English Channel, then south along the coast of Portugal, skirting the Madeira and Canary islands (one of the last chances to water and reprovision) before catching the southern trade winds that carried ships past the Cape Verde Islands that lay just off the west coast of Africa. Here shipmasters had a choice: they could

MAP 1. The Atlantic in 1650

turn eastward and sail for the Windward and Gold coasts of Africa, or head westward to the Caribbean. Not equipped to load gold or slaves in Africa, De Vries let the warm-water currents and western-blowing trade winds draw his vessel toward Barbados and into the Caribbean Sea.

The first Dutch vessels to cross the Atlantic regularly were warships deployed to harass Spanish shipping during the United Provinces' protracted struggle for independence from the Hapsburgs at the end of the sixteenth century. As the Sea Beggars drove further and further into the Atlantic and toward the Americas, the information and riches they carried back to the Dutch Republic stimulated interest in the potential value of American trade. While formal Dutch activity in the Americas originated with the establishment of the Westindische Compagnie—West India Company (WIC)—in 1621, individual merchants began to send vessels directly to Brazil in 1587 as an extension of Dutch trade with Portugal. These mostly speculative voyages did not result in steady trade, but, combined with the fame of the Sea Beggars, they led several Dutch mercantile companies to establish more regular trade to Brazil after 1600. Although the Dutch were never the most important carriers of Brazilian sugars and brazilwood (a dyestuff), this early involvement with American commerce nonetheless whetted Dutch appetites for direct colonial trade. Meanwhile, Dutch merchants—many of them based in the West Frisian city of Hoorn—had also discovered salt pans on the Araya Peninsula in what is now Venezuela. Eager to sidestep periodic Spanish interference with Dutch trade in Iberia and needing an abundant supply of the preservative for the herring trade, Dutch traders soon flocked across the Atlantic. By the first decade of the seventeenth century, perhaps as many as a hundred vessels a year defied Spanish claims to the region and called at Punta de Araya to load salt. Soon Spanish authorities grew fearful of the Dutch presence, especially as Dutch merchantmen accompanying the salt fleets began to trade with Spanish colonies along the coast. Though the importance of these salt pans would fade once the Twelve Years' Truce reopened Spanish ports to the Dutch in 1609, the discovery of yet another potential benefit of Atlantic colonization helped generate further support for a West Indies trading company. When that company did receive a charter in 1621, the salt trade of Punta de Araya was included.[7]

The founding of the WIC launched a more intensive Dutch commitment to trade in the Americas. Charted as a joint-stock company, the WIC received a monopoly for trade and navigation in the West Indies, but its early priority was capturing Spanish silver fleets. While trading was initially only a secondary goal of the company, its conquest of Portuguese Brazil (1630) gave it direct access to numerous sugar plantations, and soon the WIC was using the colony as a base for exporting sugar, harassing Spanish silver convoys, and trading with Spanish colonies. The leadership of the WIC, the Heren XIX, intended trade from Brazil to be a company monopoly, but the company's inability to meet shipping demand and to halt private trade prompted them to license private merchants to manage the sugar trade. By the middle of the 1630s, about thirty-eight Dutch vessels a year carried Brazilian sugar to refiners in Amsterdam, Rotterdam, and Middelburg.[8]

Coinciding with their acquisition of plantations to produce tropical commodities in the Americas, the WIC entered the gold and slave trades on the coast of Africa. By 1624, the WIC had seized Fort Nassau on the Gold Coast as well as trading stations at Gorée Island and at the estuary of the Congo River. From these outposts, company merchants mainly concentrated on the gold trade until Brazilian producers began to demand additional slaves. This demand initiated new conquests in 1637 against Portuguese slave factories on the Gold Coast, including the important Elmina Castle. Trade from these Dutch forts amounted to about seven hundred slaves a year between 1600 and 1645, a rate that would increase sixfold by the late 1660s. In time, the Dutch would expand their market beyond Brazil and their own colonies to reach those of the Spanish, French, and English. It would be this trade in human cargoes which would especially draw together the Dutch and English in the Atlantic into the eighteenth century, providing the foundation of exploitation upon which both countries built their empires. These three interdependent poles of commercial activity—in Europe, on the African coast, and in the Americas—established the framework by which the WIC could begin to profit from Atlantic commerce.[9]

With footholds along coastlines but little land under possession, private and WIC merchants quickly realized that the way to benefit from Atlantic trade was to carry European and tropical goods. These merchants discovered they could offer manufactured goods, slaves, shipping, and insurance at lower prices than European rivals, and soon they controlled a sizable portion of Atlantic commerce. By the late 1640s, Dutch vessels dominated the transportation of Caribbean sugars to Europe. While the Iberian countries entered an era of internal decline and the English and French struggled to find a profitable economic foothold in the Caribbean, Dutch traders were firmly in control of the economic fortunes of southern Caribbean colonies and Brazil.[10]

In 1632, though, these developments were only just under way as Dutch merchants like De Vries arrived in the Caribbean to investigate future possibilities for trade and settlement. After an uneventful passage in which De Vries and his crew successfully avoided the late summer and early fall hurricanes that made crossing the Atlantic that time of year so dangerous, he sighted Barbados on September 4, 1632. Two days later, De Vries and his mariners arrived safely at St. Vincent, a small island the English claimed but that was inhabited solely by one of the region's indigenous peoples, the Caribs. Pausing only briefly in the "Green Channel" off the coast, De Vries was met by Caribs in small canoes who swarmed the ship and offered "yams pine-apples, and various other West India fruits" to the sailors. After concluding business with the investigating Indians, De Vries steered for St. Martin, one of the small island colonies the WIC maintained in the West Indies, where he planned to join the eighty Dutch vessels that loaded salt from the island's salt pans each year. In the 1620s, the company had established several colonies in the Lesser Antilles including St. Martin, Saba, and St. Eustatius as well as Curaçao, Aruba, and Bonaire, just off the coast of the Spanish Main. Since these colonies were not intended to be places of permanent settlement, but rather bases from which to manage trade with a number of empires,

MAP 2. The Caribbean in the Mid-Seventeenth Century

to prey on the Spanish, to stock provisions, to maintain livestock, and to harvest salt, the Dutch settler populations in the Caribbean were small and consisted almost entirely of employees of the WIC. In the years soon after De Vries departed, these places would take on added significance as the company became more involved in the slave trade to Spanish (and eventually English) colonies. Later still, the WIC would develop two of the better-situated islands—Curaçao and St. Eustatius—into full-scale trading depots with larger, more diverse support networks.[11]

At the same time that the Dutch were constructing their Atlantic empire, English settlers had just arrived to settle the Caribbean, but their presence was still marginal compared to the efforts of the Spanish and Dutch. On his way to St. Martin, De Vries witnessed this infancy first-hand when he decided to call at the English Leeward Islands for water and to make contact with the English. The Leeward Islands lie in the eastern Caribbean, part of a grouping of about forty islands arrayed north to south in an arc from the eastern end of Puerto Rico to Trinidad in the south. Four of these islands—Antigua, Montserrat, Nevis, and St. Christopher—eventually became known as the English Leeward Islands.

Both because the islands did not contain precious metals and because there were few or no native peoples they could put to work, Spanish conquistadores had quickly passed over these places, pausing only to inspect them cursorily and mark them on their navigational charts. Small in comparison to the Greater Antilles, the four English Leeward Islands have an area of only 255 square miles, combined. The islands looked initially unwelcoming to sailors; formed by tectonic activity, they rise steeply from the ocean and have tall, uneven peaks that in Montserrat climb to 3,000 feet. This feature, though, became one of the reasons that the islands offered agricultural promise to European pioneers; the very height of the volcanic mountaintops increases the rainfall they receive, as the peaks force the northeast trade winds to deposit their precipitation. Europeans discovered that this rainfall, while unevenly distributed on the leeward side of the islands, combined with fertile volcanic soil on the lower slopes of mountains to provide fertile ground for tobacco and sugar.[12]

When De Vries arrived at St. Christopher in 1632, the English had only been there for eight years. While the Portuguese, Spanish, and even the Dutch began to explore the Atlantic in the sixteenth century, the English faced the cumulative effects of royal debt, agricultural stagnation, a decline in the woolens trade, specie shortages, and poorly linked regional economies. Those few English adventurers who did venture across the Atlantic in the middle of the sixteenth century generally only succeeded in establishing temporary or quasi-temporary outposts from which to explore or conduct raids. A notable exception were John Hawkins's efforts to compete with Portuguese slave traders on the west coast of Africa in the 1560s. Though unsuccessful in wresting control from the Portuguese, Hawkins's voyages attracted both courtier and merchant support, and worked to unify disparate interests around the potential of Atlantic trade.[13]

The outbreak of naval warfare with the Spanish in 1585 sparked a conflict that continued for nearly two decades and marked a major turning point for English expansion. The war with Spain brought a great number of English privateers, men who carried permits issued by Elizabeth I to harass Spanish fleets, into the Caribbean for the first time. As independently funded adventurers led and financed by a mixture of merchants, adventurers, and warriors, privateers played an important role in galvanizing English interest in the region. The raiding of individuals such as Francis Drake not only brought Spanish bullion to English shores, but also carried tropical goods such as sugar and dyewoods to English consumers. Despite the tumult and chaos of the period, these high-value luxuries awakened elite merchants to the possibilities Atlantic trade and settlement offered, thus fueling future endeavors. A lack of concentrated financial, legal, or state support, however, limited the extent and success of such early projects. Unlike the Muscovy (1555), Levant (1581), and East India (1600) companies, which traded to Russia, the Levant, and the East Indies, English mercantile ventures in the Caribbean did not receive monopoly protection.[14]

An important feature of early English activity in the Caribbean, especially for privateers, was their constant collaboration with the Dutch. Both facing a common enemy in Spain, English and Dutch privateers worked together against what were often more powerful Spanish treasure fleets. For example, the commissions that English privateers based in Providence Island received included language authorizing and encouraging captains to form consortship agreements with Dutch vessels. Under such arrangements, more ad hoc than formal (Anglo-Dutch negotiations in Europe for a joint offensive on Cuba never came to fruition), Dutch and English shipmasters agreed to collaborate in attacking the Spanish silver fleets that carried the riches of the Americas to Seville. Such interactions suggest the common interests that would continue to bring the Dutch and English together in the Caribbean in coming decades.[15]

During the late sixteenth century, English, Dutch, and French privateers ultimately repelled the Spanish from the smaller Antillean islands and onto what became the Spanish Main. At the same time, English merchants began to develop more expansive visions of the potential profits Atlantic colonization could provide. When combined with those pushing to find productive work for England's landless poor and those looking to enhance England's glory, entrepreneurs seeking riches soon launched a number of colonization schemes. Though short-lived, attempts to settle the Wild Coast—that area between the Orinoco and Amazon rivers in South America, also known as Guiana—reflected the efforts of private groups to build plantations useful for smuggling, raiding, and gold prospecting, but also to grow tobacco. Inadequately funded and numbering in the tens, not the hundreds, English adventurers there failed to found effective settlements. Nestled between more powerful

Spanish and Portuguese colonies, competing with the Dutch, and facing resistance from a monarch still trying to court favor with Spain, English adventurers could not challenge their state-supported rivals before the 1620s. Driven not by a wealthy and powerful commercial company, but by entrepreneurs pooling resources, as in the case of the Virginia Company, English colonists soon realized they could not contend with Dutch capital and merchandizing strengths. As an alternative, they developed a different model for settlement based on the production of raw materials to transport back to the mother country, rather than on deriving revenue from multilateral exchanges. The most profitable of these early efforts, Virginia, struggled mightily through its first decade and a half but ultimately proved a success once colonists there made the transition to agriculture.[16]

Looking to avoid Spanish and Dutch competition and convinced that the cultivation of tropical commodities such as tobacco (which the English had been buying from the Spanish colonies of Cumaná and Caracas before its cultivation in Virginia) was a safer path to pursue, English pioneers shifted their attention to the far eastern and southeastern Caribbean, distant from Spanish control and closer to western Europe. Even then, the first islands the English settled in the Caribbean had difficult early histories. The first of these, St. Christopher, was established by a number of adventurers backed by traders who had been involved with the Guiana ventures of the second decade of the seventeenth century. The leading hand behind this venture was Sir Thomas Warner, who had first visited the island on his return from Guiana to England in 1622. Attracting the investment of the London merchants Ralph Merrifield, Maurice Thomson, and Thomas Combes, and taking his lead from royal officials who encouraged (but did not finance) settlement in the Caribbean, Warner planned to cultivate tobacco out of the reach of Spanish squadrons more concerned with Dutch privateers to the south and west. Upon his arrival, Warner almost immediately discovered that despite metropolitan support, lasting settlement would have to be a cooperative endeavor between English adventurers and other European settlers. Recognizing the vulnerability of their small island, the first settlers gave up both ends of the 68-square-mile island to the French in return for a promise of mutual defense. The Dutch on nearby St. Martin also pledged aid in the event of a Spanish attack. Even with such agreements in place, English colonists worried about attacks from the Spanish and from the indigenous Caribs living in Martinique, St. Lucia, Dominica, and Guadeloupe, whom the English and French eventually brutally exterminated.[17]

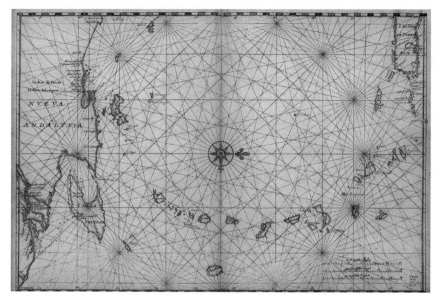

FIGURE 3. Jan Vickenboons, *The Lesser Antilles,* ca. 1650. This map is the kind of chart that De Vries would have carried on his voyage to the Americas, though this example is from slightly later. Courtesy of Geography and Map Division, Library of Congress.

In 1625, the fledgling settlers produced their first tobacco harvest, and upon Warner's return with this to England, he and Merrifield were awarded letters of patent for trade and settlement in St. Christopher, as well as still-unoccupied Nevis, Montserrat, and Barbados. In the next five years, St. Christopher's population swelled as Thomson, Combes, and others sent supplies, settlers, and bound labor to the island. An important early partner of Thomson was Thomas Stone (Captain John Stone's uncle), a retail merchant in London who also traded to Virginia and to the Low Countries. Though St. Christopher was still far from stable, these few adventurers sparked growing interest in the Caribbean, especially when Thomson and his partners returned at least twenty thousand pounds of St. Christopher tobacco to London in 1627. In search of additional arable land, residents of St. Christopher began to migrate to other uninhabited islands even as new arrivals and freed servants settled the rugged interior of the island. Migrants from St. Christopher established Nevis in 1628, and then Montserrat and Antigua in 1632. Soon these islands, too, received investment from England. Rising populations and mercantile attention did not mean that settlers found stability. The decision by Charles I to issue James Hay, the Earl of Carlisle—a Scot and a favorite of Charles's father, James I—a superseding patent for all these islands as well as Barbados in 1627 revealed the precariousness of colonists' situation as previously granted land patents were thrown into confusion. Though these issues were soon resolved, with Warner remaining governor and the London merchants gaining confirmation of their plantations from the proprietor, similar uncertainty over land patents that sometimes discouraged investment would become a distinguishing element of the British islands' early histories.

When De Vries arrived, the Leeward Islands were already producing tobacco and attracting metropolitan attention, yet they remained fragile. Not as initially hospitable to agriculture as St. Christopher, nearby Nevis, Antigua, and Montserrat had small and unstable populations through midcentury that cultivated tobacco and cotton on relatively small plots in the midst of internal and external conflicts. Living interspersed among islands claimed by the French and the Dutch, settlers in the English Leeward Islands spent almost two generations fleeing and then rebuilding their homes after Spanish invasions and local violence. Planters in Nevis, particularly, suffered greatly from their vulnerability to foreign navies and, in 1629, invading Spanish soldiers, who even recruited the English planters' own servants to fight against them. In all, English colonists in the Leewards remained vulnerable, disorganized, and reliant on outsiders to organize the export trade and supply needed goods through midcentury. Nevertheless, with their focus on reaping wealth from the soil of their islands, English colonists had, by 1630, already found the strategy that would make their colonies a success in ensuing decades.[18] After leaving St. Christopher, De Vries shuttled around the eastern fringe of the Caribbean, calling at English and Dutch islands, trading, obtaining provisions, and meeting with settlers. Eventually he set Captain Stone at St. Martin, presumably to organize trade, and departed for New Netherland on November 5.

In almost every port he visited, De Vries remembered encountering English, Dutch, and French vessels, all cycling through the islands in pursuit of their own interests. While De Vries's narrative provides a rare extant first-person perspective, his experiences themselves were not unique. Indeed, his account reflects openly on the variety of intra-Caribbean and interimperial relationships that bound together settlers and merchants from a variety of empires as they worked to build stable communities during the first decades of imperial occupation. Dutch and

English interests were never devoid of tensions, as the persistent warfare between 1652 and 1674 attests; but they also shared close religious, cultural, and political ties. As one historian has recently argued, these connections were so profound that one could say that some Dutchmen and Englishmen had a "shared 'mentality.'"[19] Anglo-Dutch cultural exchange accelerated in the 1560s as Dutch (and Flemish) textile workers fled from the Spanish in the northern Netherlands into England. These men, usually accompanied by their families, helped introduce the New Draperies (worsted and mixed woolens) to England and fostered future cultural exchange. Other Dutch artisans settled in Elizabethan England as well, including those trained in gardening, land drainage, leatherwork, papermaking, brewing, pin production, and metallurgy. Eventually, rising English mercantile and craft interests would come to resent Dutch economic penetration of England, but in the short term, the migration of technically proficient Dutchmen helped advance the Elizabethan and Jacobean economies and bound the two countries together. Meanwhile, English traders as well, especially those belonging to the Company of Merchant Adventurers that managed cloth exports to the Low Countries, migrated to the United Provinces to organize their trade in woolens. In 1635 alone, almost 650 English men and women left London to travel to the Dutch Republic, many of them for business. Such exchanges intensified Anglo-Dutch ties and prompted merchants like William Courteen and Thomas Stone to seek out Dutch involvement in colonial trade in the years to follow. English policy makers also paid close attention to Dutch innovations in finance and national accounting.[20]

The struggle against Spain's European designs also encouraged close diplomatic and military ties during the Dutch Revolt and after. Anglo-Dutch diplomacy flourished when Elizabeth sent an army to aid the Low Countries in their struggle against Spain in 1585, and it flourished again in the 1630s, resulting in the 1641 marriage of Charles I's daughter Princess Mary Henrietta to Prince William of Orange, the son of the Dutch stadtholder, William I. This union laid the foundation for continued Anglo-Dutch cooperation even after the Stuarts were forced from the throne during the English Civil War. Almost forty years later, Princess Mary and Prince William's son, William III, resolemnized those ties when he married his cousin Mary Stuart in 1677, eventually making it possible for William and Mary to replace James II on England's throne in 1689.[21]

Perhaps the most important contribution of Anglo-Dutch exchanges for the Englishmen whom De Vries met in 1632 was the transference of cartographic technology from the Dutch Republic to England between the late sixteenth and early seventeenth centuries. Lagging behind in geographic and mathematic knowledge and without engravers proficient enough to produce precise work, Englishmen relied upon Dutch navigational texts and maps to picture the world. One of the most important of these was the seminal work of the Dutch engraver Lucas Janszoon Waghenaer, an atlas of printed sea charts entitled *Die Speighel de Zeevaert* (1584). Containing detailed textual descriptions of northern European coastlines as well as compass bearings, depth data for shoals, sandbars, tidal variations, and topographical sketches of ports, Waghenaer's guide, called a rutter, was one of the most advanced navigational aides of its time. Published during the Dutch Revolt, the work, and others like it, was vital as Dutch traders expanded their commercial reach throughout Europe. Just four years after it was released in the Netherlands, Waghenaer's atlas appeared in London under the title *The Mariners Mirrour*.[22] In the next half century, Dutch mapmakers continued to progress so that, by the 1620s, they were producing some of the most technically proficient and beautiful atlases depicting the East and West Indies. English cartographers continued to copy Dutch works throughout the century despite English efforts to cultivate domestic cartography.[23] That English mariners carried English reprints of Dutch maps as they traveled the Atlantic indicates how their very ability to develop an Atlantic empire in the first half of the seventeenth century rested upon Anglo-Dutch ties in Europe.[24]

* * *

If De Vries had continued sailing southeast from the Leeward Islands, in a few days he would have reached a lush and green island ringed by white sand, approachable only from the leeward side because of a series of coral shoals, and soon to become the richest colony in British America. The island of Barbados sits at the entry to the Caribbean in a position favorable for trade from every direction. Major equatorial currents and gentle winds combine to carry and blow ships from Europe, West Africa, and eastern South America to the island and enable them to land there easily. Unlike the mountainous Leeward Islands, Barbados sits like "a low-lying bank of clouds on the horizon." Rising gently to the leeward above the three natural harbors—Oistins Bay, Speights Bay, and the largest, Carlisle Bay—are long natural terraces, amply supplied by rain and fertile. Should De Vries have ventured there in 1632, he would have discovered the colony in a situation similar to the Leeward Islands, a condition that barely hinted at the future riches and misery it would offer its planters and the African slaves they soon brought.[25]

The first English arrivals were Simon Gordon in 1620 and John Powell, who stopped at the inviting, forested, and uninhabited island on his return to England from Guiana in 1625. Enthralled with the place's promise, it was Powell's brother Henry who returned to Barbados on the *William and John* with eighty men in 1627 to establish a permanent colony backed by a group of European merchants many of whom had strong ties to the Dutch Republic. Foremost of these was Sir William Courteen, a London cloth trader whose father came from the Spanish Netherlands. Almost immediately after landing his company, Powell departed for a Dutch colony on the Essequibo River in Guiana, where he probably delivered eight men and some trade goods to the Dutch governor (a former associate) on behalf of Courteen. In return, Powell was able to buy the provisions, tobacco, and seeds that the nascent colony needed to survive. Powell's knowledge of this Dutch settlement and his ability to trade are indicative of the fluidity and cooperative status of relations in the early Caribbean. Like Warner's experience in the Leewards, Powell's Guianan voyage exposes the deep roots of Anglo-Dutch ties in the Caribbean, for Courteen's Dutch connections in Europe arranged Powell's Guiana venture and thus made settling Barbados possible. These two elements—a metropolitan environment that encouraged cross-national entrepreneurship and a local situation that demanded it—would foster interimperial trade in the region for decades. It was only as their interests shifted decades later that London merchants and their governmental supporters would come to resent this multinational collaboration.[26]

As in the Leewards, violence, institutional confusion, and the struggle to achieve economic stability characterized the first decade of settlement in Barbados. Here matters were so complex that they merit a lengthy discussion. The main obstacle to smooth development in Barbados was that two rival groups claimed legitimacy as the true government. By the end of 1627, Courteen had sent three ships to the island, and his agents, the Powell brothers, had overseen the building of housing near present-day Holetown and the planting of both corn and tobacco. Meanwhile, more than 4,000 miles north across the Atlantic, as Courteen eagerly awaited news from Barbados, a rival, the Earl of Carlisle, moved to undermine the Courteen faction and won a royal patent for Barbados. Even as Courteen protested to the king and received a rival patent for the same land, Carlisle granted 10,000 acres on Barbados to a merchant syndicate headed by Marmaduke Rawdon. The new partners then quickly agreed to name Charles Wolverton governor of the merchants' land and dispatched him with seventy settlers who were promised a hundred acres each and supplies to establish a profitable settlement.[27]

At first, the two groups of settlers coexisted genially. The Carlisle group began to clear land around what became known as Bridgetown and kept several miles away from the Courteen faction. Soon, however, as the groups competed for scarce resources, tensions arose. Later Wolverton would recount that the Courteen group (which numbered nearly 250 by 1628) had raided his stores, prompting him to conclude that the rival group would try to overrun his party if not confronted. In response, Wolverton ordered them to submit to Carlisle's authority and arrested Governor Powell. In swift succession, both Courteen and Carlisle tried to rearticulate their authority and renamed their own men governors of the entire island. For their part, settlers were virtually paralyzed; they dared not invest heavily in their lands for if their faction lost control of the island, they could potentially lose their land. A measure of stability arrived in 1629, when Charles I confirmed Carlisle's patents, giving him control of the island. Willing to use force and intimidation to ensure obedience, Carlisle's eventual choice of governor, the solider Henry Hawley, pacified colonists and snuffed out rivalries, even as he cheated Carlisle.[28]

Political instability during Barbados's initial decade was reflected in slow population growth. In 1637, there were only roughly 4,000 inhabitants, the majority of whom were young, unfree, white laborers. In 1635, for example, 985 individuals emigrated from London to Barbados. All were servants, with 91 percent of them below the age of thirty and unmarried. During these years, governors distributed almost all of Barbados's arable land—85,000 acres—to 764 planters in unequal quantities. Before they could capitalize on their lands, however, planters needed to clear the dense forests that enveloped the island, a task only possible because of the unfree workers they had imported. A turbulent mix of planters and servants, some often drunk, and all suffering in the tropical heat, made Barbados notorious to contemporaries for its rowdiness, violence, chaos, and poverty.[29]

While Dutch traders had begun to prosper from tobacco and sugar transport, English colonists in Barbados and the Leeward Islands remained vulnerable for years. This disparity, however, helped prompt English and Dutch adventurers to cooperate. In some cases, contacts between individuals from the two empires offered merely the chance to share intelligence or supplies; but at other times, cross-national interaction created more substantial and lasting relationships as was the case in St. Christopher. The colony was slow to recover from the Spanish destruction of the planters' fields and homes in 1629, and trade with passing Dutch vessels helped sustain the intrepid residents. As De Vries recounted in the 1630s, St. Christopher had a steady supply of freshwater, and Dutch vessels, sailing from nearby Dutch St. Martin or on longer voyages, often called there to load water or consumables such as wood and sea turtle meat. In August 1631, for example, thirteen Dutch vessels arrived at the island to water and reprovision, surely selling desperately needed supplies to the English in the process. On other occasions, English colonists allowed Dutch ships to load salt, to buy supplies, or to hire locals to repair their vessels.[30]

In Barbados, too, foreign vessels arriving to reprovision and trade were a relatively common sight, arriving frequently enough that Governor Hawley decided to tax them. In April 1634, he implemented an act requiring that, "all *Dutch, French,* or other strange Ships" that "Anchor here, for Relief, Refreshment, or Trade . . . pay to the Governor Twenty Shillings in Money, or Goods . . . and Seven *per Cent* on all the Goods which they vended, for the Use of the Harbour."[31] Cognizant of the benefits foreign traders provided the nascent colony, the king's Privy Council sanctioned the Dutch trade, confirming colonists' decision to allow Dutch vessels "free ingrees[,] egress[,] and regresse into, and out of all his Majesties [West Indian] Ports, Havens, Roads, and Creekes."[32] While these transactions most likely entailed small amounts of goods, they illustrate the kinds of cross-national relationships which taught colonists that collaboration with other Europeans was necessary for their survival.

The ad hoc contacts with Dutch traders that characterized English colonists' first years of colonization in the Caribbean became more fully elaborated systems of trade after English colonists, imitating their countrymen in Virginia, learned to plant tobacco. Tobacco was a logical choice as a staple not only because of Virginians' success but also because the initial capital investment was relatively low and it required few specialized tools, less land than wheat or corn, and theoretically only a single colonist to produce a harvest. Further contributing to settlers' decisions to plant tobacco was their discovery that the climate and volcanic soil seemed well suited to it. Borrowing technical knowledge from other Spanish and English colonies, as well as Arawak slaves transported from Dutch Guiana, English planters successfully produced tobacco in the Leeward Islands soon after they arrived; by 1630, the crop was already being used to pay poll taxes in St. Christopher.[33] Dutch traders calling to water and sell supplies at the Leeward Islands quickly began to purchase English tobacco, a pattern that sustained Dutch-English commerce for the next several decades. Henry Colt's account of his time in St. Christopher indicates how this interimperial tobacco trade evolved from its ad hoc origins to a regular trade. In 1631, Colt reported that after a visit from several Dutch vessels that had come to water, the "Gouernor of St. Martins" stayed "behinde[,] lodged att my house[,] supt[,] & dyned with me." Ostensibly there to form a temporary alliance to ward off the threat of Spanish invaders, the Dutch governor likely also used the opportunity to convince the English on the island to send their tobacco to Holland for just after hosting the governor, Colt decided to send his ship, the *Alexander*, to Dutch markets, hoping to avoid "ye Custome of 12d lb in England."[34]

Perhaps more important than Colt's avoiding English customs was his opportunity to secure higher prices for tobacco in Amsterdam and to avoid English shippers. As the Thomson syndicate and its London partners—a group of no more than thirty intertwined merchants—expanded their investments in the Caribbean during the 1620s and 1630s, they came to dominate English West Indian markets, cornering access to tobacco exports and controlling the islands' import trade. Independent landholders found themselves under the thumb of distant English merchants, and turned eagerly to Dutch traders who could relieve the London merchants' stranglehold on trade.[35] Sending their tobacco directly to the United Provinces was island planters' main alternative, which in turn gave colonists like Colt entry into Amsterdam's renowned tobacco market. There, technically proficient Dutch producers combined inexpensive, domestically grown leaf with tobacco from the Americas—principally the Chesapeake by the 1630s—to produce the blends favored by most European consumers. Rising demand from a population newly attuned to the drug's effects prompted merchants both in the United Provinces and in the English colonies to seek direct shipments of tobacco from the Leewards (and Virginia) to the center of production, thereby bypassing the Thomson syndicate's less profitable method of reexporting the leaf from England to Amsterdam for processing. In this respect, Colt's decision to trade with the Dutch was not unique but part of a larger trend.[36]

While some planters such as Colt hazarded the risk of freighting their produce to Europe on Dutch vessels and at planters' risk, most English West Indian planters sold their tropical staples under what Richard

Sheridan has labeled the "merchant system." European merchants assembled speculative cargoes and shipped them to the Caribbean for general sale to various islands, often employing a supercargo to disburse the cargo, collect merchants' debts, and assemble freight for the homeward-bound leg of the journey. Middling planters found such exchanges beneficial because, although prices for tobacco exports were lower by this method, they could sell their produce at dockside in exchange for needed European goods and reinvest the proceeds directly into their enterprises, rather than having to bear the burden of shipping the crops across the Atlantic and awaiting later payment.[37]

Given the opportunity to acquire a greater share of the Atlantic carrying trade, Dutch merchants began to call at English islands for tobacco soon after St. Christopher tobacco first arrived in the Netherlands. With a large number of vessels already in the Caribbean and the Leeward Islands strategically located near Dutch islands and along shipping routes through the region, both WIC merchants and some interlopers incorporated these islands, as they had recently done with Virginia, into their commercial orbit. The usual practice was simply for Dutch vessels to stop at the islands as harvests were coming in and to exchange tobacco for European manufactures such as textiles, ceramics (ranging from apothecary jars to plates and mugs to chamber pots), metal goods (including firearms), and provisions such as flour, beer, wine, and cheese. Though direct exchange appears to have been preferred in the early years, on some occasions Dutch traders offered long credit. It was in these types of localized exchanges that Dutch merchants often had an advantage because they offered lower freight charges and cheaper manufactured goods than did their English rivals. One commenter from Virginia insisted, in what is probably an exaggeration, that the Dutch could pay "eighteen pence per pound for tobacco" compared to the "penny a pound" English merchants offered. The precise price difference is uncertain, but colonists perceived that Dutch traders offered better prices, and they eagerly sought the advantage. That English colonists were comfortable consuming Dutch-produced goods is not surprising; decades of trade with the Netherlands and the immigration of Dutch craftsmen to England had made these goods common in England. This was especially true of the tin-glazed earthenwares produced first around the Dutch city of Delft. By the end of the sixteenth century, defltwares dominated northern Europe, and English consumers were long familiar with Dutch forms and designs (which of course mimicked Chinese porcelain decoration) imported from the Dutch Republic or the examples that domestic potters produced in imitation of these. Consuming Dutch ceramics in the colonies, therefore, would simply have been an extension of Englishmen's consumption in England. Never solely consuming Dutch goods or partnering with Dutch traders—English merchants such as Ralph Merrifield, Maurice Thomson, and Thomas Combes were also important in guiding the Leewards' development—English colonists steeped in a cosmopolitan tradition they carried from Europe chose both imperial and interimperial commerce as it suited their needs.[38]

Sometimes Dutch traders stopping at the English islands integrated their purchase of tobacco into a broader set of exchanges ranging over a variety of different places. In 1635, for example, John Winthrop noted the arrival of a "Dutch ship of one hundred and sixty tons" to trade at Marblehead in Massachusetts Bay, carrying "One hundred and forty tons of salt, and ten thousand weight of tobacco" from "Christopher Island" on behalf of a "Capt. Hurlston," a Dutch trader who had lived there for "five years." Here a Dutch vessel and master facilitated commerce between two budding English colonies. Other vessels stopped at the English West Indies for tobacco on their way back to the United Provinces after delivering salted cod they had first bought in Newfoundland to Brazil.[39]

Although at first Barbados's relatively isolated position kept Dutch vessels from landing there, Dutch traders began to arrive more frequently by the middle of the 1630s, when Barbadian planters, such as the island's receiver general of customs for the Carlisle lands, Peter Hay, sold tobacco to Dutch merchants. Informed by the proprietary trustee Archibald Hay that his tobacco was of such poor quality it was hardly worth more than the duties, Peter Hay decided to send it to Amsterdam as an alternative to London. To his dismay, he soon found that even if he shipped his cargo to Holland, bypassing England's six pence per pound duty in the process, he could still not earn a profit. Subsequently, Hay decided it was best to sell his tobacco at Barbados, offering it directly to Dutch traders stopping there who could offer trade goods immediately and bear the risk of freight themselves. In this way, the planter got an immediate return on his production in the form of usable items that he could consume or exchange again. Additionally, by selling directly to a merchant at dockside, Hay was able to ask for a set price and avoid the possibility that his produce could find a poor price in Europe. This was especially important for planters who did not yet know the vagaries of a new and unpredictable market.[40]

Hay was not the only planter that found Dutch traders eager to buy his produce. In 1634, he reported that sixty foreign vessels anchored in

Barbadian waters that year. Subsequent years would reveal more Dutch vessels.[41] For example, in 1637, Thomas Anthony represented the English Barbadian investors William Courteen and Matthew Cradock on a venture to the Americas. Originally bound to Virginia with fifty-six Irish servants, Anthony's vessel arrived in Barbados on January 25, 1637. Finding a ready market, Anthony decided to sell his cargo there. In all, fourteen Barbadian planters bought Anthony's indentured servants, paying between 450 and 500 pounds of tobacco for each worker. Among those who acquired the most servants were Governor Hawley, who bought ten men, and Richard Price (his brother-in-law), who bought ten men and two women. In addition to the 71,000 pounds of tobacco he secured as payment for the fifty-six servants, Anthony also collected an additional 63,436 pounds of leaf, including more than 24,000 pounds from Peter Hay, all of which he carried to the Dutch city of Middelburg.[42]

By the middle of the 1630s, authorities in England had come to realize that Dutch carriers were depriving England of revenue. To capture the taxes from this trade, the king, backed by London merchants eager to maintain their grasp on the colonies' trade, ordered his admirals to force all vessels that did not bring English tobacco to an English port to pay the proper duty before travelling to the ports of other nations.[43] Dispatched to enforce the new policy, the crew of the navy's *Vanguard* soon found numerous violators, including three ships "freighted by Englishmen" in St. Christopher and Barbados who were "minded to goe for Holland."[44] In April 1637, the Privy Council again moved to shore up colonial revenues and halt illicit trade by urging the planters of "St. Christopher's, Barbadoes, and the other Caribbee Islands" to plant less tobacco, pointing out that their focus on that commodity made them too dependent upon supplies "from the Dutch and other strangers" to support the island.[45] Such a situation benefited foreigners, not English subjects, and if duties could not be collected on exports, it damaged the Crown's interests as well. In this respect, the tobacco regulations of the 1630s were a part of fiscal reform designed to capture market share and bolster the treasury of the revenue-starved Charles I, not yet the beginnings of a consistent "mercantilist" system.[46] Whatever the impulse behind their actions, authorities did not have a large enough presence in the Caribbean to stop Dutch merchants from trading there. Moreover, because regulation did little to improve the English market for tobacco or to lower English shipping costs, it did not ameliorate the local conditions that had driven planters directly into the arms of the Dutch Republic.

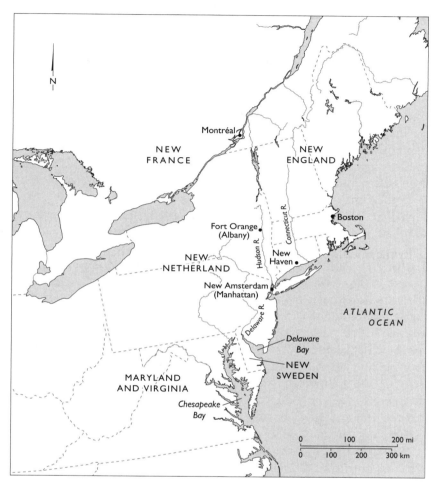

MAP 3. New Netherland and Its Neighboring Colonies in 1650

* * *

Leaving the Caribbean in early November 1632, De Vries sailed north, pausing to explore the South (now Delaware) River and to make contact with the English in the Chesapeake before arriving in New Amsterdam in mid-April 1633. The island of Manhattan (called Manhatoes, Manados, Manahata, and Manahtoes by its Native American inhabitants) was two miles wide and thirteen miles long in 1633. Tucked between two waterways, the North (now Hudson) River and the Helegat (now East)

River, the island extends into a deep bay that is in turn enveloped by a vast continent. Unlike Dutch and English islands in the Caribbean, Manhattan was not simply nearby rivals' lands but instead was surrounded by English settlement to the northeast, to the south, and to the east. Nevertheless, the island itself was defensible. With a stone fort serving both military and commercial functions at its tip and the two rivers intersecting before it, the island formed a triangle that was approachable by land only on one side, and thus the few cannon of Fort Amsterdam offered sufficient defense to the fewer than five hundred people who lived in the roughly thirty wooden or yellow brick houses along New Amsterdam's often muddy, yet orderly, streets.[47]

In the same years that Englishmen first permanently settled St. Christopher and Barbados, Pierre Minuit was establishing a settlement at Manhattan in the name of the WIC. On this northern island, the directors intended to establish a company port and colony they named New Netherland, with the goal of collecting furs from Iroquois and Algonquians living in the interior and serving as a depot for WIC vessels in the Atlantic. Situated at the apex of two rivers, New Amsterdam was well located for both tasks; the waterways provided access to the interior and enabled the easy arrival of oceangoing vessels. The impetus and funding for settlement came not from private individuals, as was the case for the English colonies, but from a company that received significant state financing and monopoly privileges. Only after the company proved it had no interest in settling large numbers of inhabitants in New Netherland did the Dutch States-General grant privately funded patroonships, or estates, to individuals willing to settle the interior.[48]

But with the company still largely in control of the fur trade and the six company farms along the eastern side of Manhattan, New Amsterdam was still economically immature in 1633. The fur trade was to be the focus of the venture, and thus the WIC concentrated its resources on developing outposts along inland waterways and building relationships with Algonquin and Iroquois people. During these early years, some WIC employees also found their way to the Delaware Bay, at the mouth of the Delaware River. Here the WIC established several small seasonal forts from which to trade furs with the indigenous population, though Swedish and Native American opposition kept them from enduring for more than a season or two. While the company held a monopoly on the sale of furs to the mother country, colonists were free to work as trappers and traders, provided they sold their stock to the company alone. Profits were possible for these individuals, but as a monopoly, the

WIC controlled prices and held them below competitive rates, thereby retaining effective control of most aspects of the fur trade. The monopoly on furs and the patroonship system had the effect, then, of restraining economic opportunity in the interior, forcing colonists (mostly former employees) to look seaward, a situation that was largely the inverse of English experience in the Caribbean. For much of the 1630s, resulting tensions between the WIC and the city's small but growing number of private residents stalled economic and social growth.

Soldiers, tradesmen, sailors, and contract laborers for the WIC who remained on the island once their contracts expired became New Netherland's first private residents. Most of them subsisted by finding economic opportunities at the fringes of the company until the WIC abandoned its monopoly on trade in 1639. This shift released constrained entrepreneurial forces both in Amsterdam and in New Amsterdam. From this date on, private initiative and capital became more important in the colony's growth. Whereas WIC vessels trading at New Netherland outnumbered private ventures by two to one before 1639, during the next decade, private and company shipping were roughly equal. By the 1650s, private trade to and from New Netherland outpaced company trade by more than five times.[49]

Most crucial for local residents' expanding economic activity was the permission they received "to build there for themselves ... all descriptions of craft, either large or small, and with such vessels and no others, ascend and descend all rivers, and prosecute their lawful trade and barter, as well as trade therewith along the entire coast, from Florida to Newfoundland," provided they pay a 5 percent duty on their imports. While some colonists moved into the interior fur trade, high duties and competition from company factors and well-capitalized traders connected to Amsterdam-based firms encouraged most colonists to focus on reexporting Dutch textiles, ceramics, and locally produced wampum to New England in exchange for provisions. It was these independent colonists' traffic with their northern neighbors that first indicated the small settlement's promise as a regional entrepôt.[50]

In venturing to New England, Dutch colonists were building on years of contact. Dutch interest in trade there had begun a decade before, when the WIC secretary Isaack de Rasière journeyed to Plymouth to meet with Governor William Bradford. Hoping to exploit ties that were forged when Bradford and other Separatists spent time in the United Provinces, De Rasière proposed a free trade pact between the two embryonic colonies, telling Bradford that if "any goods" come into "our hands from our native countrie [and they] may be serviceable unto you, we shall take our selves bound to help and acommadate you ther with [them]; either for beaver or any other wares or marchandise that you should be pleased to deale for."[51] Though Bradford was suspicious of the company's interest in their economy, he and others began to trade regularly with New Netherland. Bradford noted that after the meeting the two groups had "some profitable commerce togither for diverce years," the Dutch bringing "suger, linen cloth, Holand finer and courser stufes" that they exchanged for "tobacco" that New Englanders had carried from Virginia.[52] Meanwhile, WIC and private merchants both from the Dutch Republic and New Netherland also traded with the Massachusetts Bay Colony. John Winthrop, citing information about Dutch activity gleaned from local vessels that had just returned from New Amsterdam and the presence of numerous Dutch vessels in New England, described the trade as regular: "Our neighbors at Plymouth and we oft trade with the Dutch at Hudson's River. We had [recently] from them about forty sheep, and beaver, and brass pieces and sugar, etc., for sack, strong waters, linen cloth and other commodities." Meanwhile, he also noted that Dutch vessels sometimes transported wheat from Virginia and tobacco and salt (useful for Massachusetts's fishing industry) from St. Christopher to his settlement. On the whole, while the trade between New Amsterdam and English New England remained small in the 1630s, both parties had begun to discover that their proximity provided mutually beneficial opportunities for exchange.[53]

As important as these contacts were, rivalry for access to furs along the Connecticut River sometimes disrupted friendly interimperial relations. When allied Massachusetts and Rhode Island forces launched a war against the Pequots and New Netherland interests along the Connecticut River in an effort to gain control of wampum (small purple and white beads made from seashells and important for trade and which the Pequots produced and received as tribute), the resulting war disrupted peaceful commerce. In the aftermath of what became called the Pequot War (1637–38), the realignment of power in eastern New England meant that the trade between New Netherland and New England took a different shape. Most immediately, it gave English colonists control of wampum supplies, a position that in turn placed them between the Dutch and one of the essential goods necessary to prosecute the fur trade. As a result, the WIC was forced to purchase much of its wampum from New England, and this became the primary commercial connection between English and Dutch settlers in the region.[54]

As the WIC nervously watched encroaching English settlers who gained territory in the Pequot War and as tensions between the colonies became increasingly strained, individuals with interimperial connections who could move fluidly in both communities became essential to maintaining profitable commerce. One of these people was Isaac Allerton. Allerton migrated from England to the northern Netherlands in 1608 as a young man. He stayed there until 1620, worshipping with Separatists who had fled England in the same period. When that group decided to leave for North America in 1620, Allerton went along, helping to plan the venture and sailing on the *Mayflower*. Once established in Plymouth, he quickly rose to prominence, serving as the assistant governor to Bradford and working as a diplomat, explorer, and merchant. Central to his experience in North America was the role he played connecting English, Dutch, and Swedish colonies together, constantly moving along the mid-Atlantic coast and even setting up residence simultaneously in Plymouth, New Haven, and New Amsterdam.

Allerton had arrived in New Amsterdam by at least 1639, and, drawing upon a decade of familiarity with Dutch culture he had garnered as a youth in the Dutch Republic, he quickly integrated himself into the community. From New Amsterdam, he continued to trade with Plymouth and New Haven, supplementing his English alliances with new Dutch ties. In the next several years, Allerton expanded his network, collaborating with other New Amsterdamers including Director-General Willem Kieft, to whom he sold tobacco, and the merchant Govert Loockermans, to whom he sold a vessel in 1642.[55] Soon Allerton became a leading resident, a position that Kieft acknowledged in 1643, when he named Allerton to an advisory board, the Eight Men, designed to give local residents a voice in WIC decisions.[56] In 1643, Allerton was just beginning to build the foundation for a commercial network that would soon stretch beyond New Netherland and New England to New Sweden and to the English and Dutch Caribbean, but clearly, New Amsterdamers' willingness to build on Allerton's connections with New England would remain important and profitable in the future.

Another of the many avenues of interimperial trade that WIC and private New Amsterdam traders utilized was the carrying trade to the Chesapeake. Dutch interest in Virginia tobacco had begun at least by the time captain David Pietersz. de Vries visited there on his voyage. On the morning of May 17, 1635, De Vries arrived off Point Comfort, Virginia, intending to buy provisions and tobacco, but "as it was out of season to obtain tobacco," he "let all of . . . [his] cargo lie [t]here, and gave directions to trade when the crop of tobacco should be ripe," planning to continue on the New Amsterdam and to "return again [to the Chesapeake] . . . [in] September." Perhaps he waited too long, for when De Vries did return he could not find sufficient tobacco to make a cargo. Though De Vries was not satisfied with his Virginia experience, his endeavors neatly summarize the mechanics of early trade between New Amsterdam and the Chesapeake, point toward the opportunities Dutch traders afforded Chesapeake planters, and suggest how the trade benefited New Amsterdam. Kiliaen van Rensselaer, the Dutch founder of the colony of Rensselaerswyck, located north of New Amsterdam on the Hudson River, for example, instructed his representatives to send furs, grain, and barrel staves to Virginia for tobacco. Stimulating to tobacco production and important for New Netherland's entrepôt trade, dozens of merchants followed his lead and journeyed to the Chesapeake each year. Dutch vessels cruising the Atlantic also stopped in the Chesapeake, exchanging Dutch manufactures and provisions for tobacco as they did in the English Caribbean and providing a direct link to Dutch markets and goods for planters eager to gain any advantage they could. Soon factors representing Dutch firms began to migrate to the Chesapeake to manage the tobacco trade. Already in 1632 Dutch commerce was important enough to Virginia planters for them to request a formal pledge from the Crown-appointed Dorset Commission on Virginia to support free trade in Virginia. Though London merchants—led by Maurice Thomson—successfully fought the policy (and won a monopoly for themselves in the process), it is clear Virginians regarded Dutch trade as essential to their economic success.[57]

Metropolitan Dutch interest in the Chesapeake would effectively preclude New Amsterdam control of the trade for most of the 1630s and 1640s, but many New Amsterdam merchants working as agents for Amsterdam or Rotterdam firms traded on their own account in the region. With the trade center of New Amsterdam in close proximity, merchants could use small vessels to ply the bay's waterways, lading tobacco at a number of plantations and carrying it to New Amsterdam, where they also stored manufactured goods and provisions, before exporting the tobacco to Amsterdam. In effect, New Amsterdam merchants pursued the same kind of carrying trade other Dutch merchants employed in the Caribbean, finding a way to profit from the openness of English colonies just emerging in North America. This arena of trade was not the major priority for either the WIC or private Dutch firms based in the United Provinces, which profited most from the slave trade, the West African commodities trade, and, most of all, the Brazilian sugar trade. But for

New Amsterdam merchants, Virginia and Maryland joined New England and Long Island as profitable alternatives for trade when they did not have the capital or goods necessary to traffic on a larger scale.[58] In ensuing decades, this trade would blossom as Dutch colonists built on these interimperial foundations.

Despite conflict with Native Americans and clashes between private and company leadership, New Amsterdam stabilized between 1630 and 1645. During this period, colonists established the trade routes that would sustain the city's next two decades: WIC and private vessels trading at the city brought manufactured goods from Europe, carried furs to Amsterdam, and journeyed back and forth to New England, Long Island, Dutch and Swedish settlements on the Delaware River, the Chesapeake, and—when they were large enough and their owners had enough capital—the Caribbean, exchanging finished products and locally grown foodstuffs for tobacco, sugar, horses, and slaves. But beyond matters of imperial possession, New Netherland differed from the English islands of the West Indies in its role as a trading station. This variation meant that New Amsterdam merchants had a different experience with interimperial trade than did most English West Indians. Residing at a trading nexus, not the port of a staple-producing island, Dutch colonial merchants at New Amsterdam were the ones selling trade goods and buying tropical produce as they sought profitable connections. At the same time, Dutch residents still lived at the periphery of empire, and like English colonists in the Caribbean, depended upon their cross-national commerce for survival. In this regard, these colonists, who in two decades would find themselves living in an English colony, epitomized a colonial impulse to improvise and adapt to rapidly changing circumstances as they stitched together trading careers from the markets the WIC left available to them. In so doing, they laid a foundation of interactions that would endure for decades, ultimately molding New York City's future as an English colony.

* * *

Between 1620 and 1640, English pioneers, merchants, and laborers founded colonies, began to clear the land, and planted their first staple crops in the English empire. The fluid, flexible, and open relationships they forged with Dutch traders from the more powerful empire of the Dutch Republic were indispensable in this process. Dutch merchants brought provisions, seeds, tools, commercial credit, and European merchandise to English colonies in the Caribbean, and carried English produce to Dutch markets. In New Amsterdam, Dutch merchants' similar reliance on the pursuit of interimperial trade helped colonists stabilize their port city, building a legacy of openness for a generation of residents in the process. To live in an English or Dutch colony in North America or the Caribbean in the 1640s meant to live in an interimperial world. For Dutch merchants looking to expand their trade and with English planters eager to benefit from cheaper and more readily available Dutch manufactures and shipping, cross-national alliances were vital to success for all. And at the apex of this imperial intersection were individuals acting not according to some predetermined overarching idea of empire, but behaving as best they knew to support themselves and their communities. In the next decade, changing market, political, and administrative conditions would alter the methods and limit the extent of interimperial trade between English and Dutch colonists in North America and in the Caribbean. Nevertheless, the importance of their early cross-national experience spurred British colonists to vigorously protect their access to Dutch trade as British administrators worked to envelop colonial trade within official imperial channels.

2 / "Courted and Highly Prized": Anglo-Dutch Trade at Midcentury

In 1652, imperial warfare interrupted the collaborative, if competitive, relationship that had distinguished Anglo-Dutch interaction on both sides of the Atlantic since the mid-sixteenth century. Though the execution of Charles I in 1649 infuriated Dutch supporters of the Dutch stadtholder, William II of Orange (himself tied to Charles I by marriage), it was the English Commonwealth government's newfound bellicosity in challenging Dutch commercial superiority that turned most Dutch burghers against England. When treaty negotiations that had initially held the potential of creating a union between the two Protestant powers broke down after the United Provinces refused to give the English trade concessions, enmity increased further and soon the two countries' commercial rivalry erupted into the First Anglo-Dutch War (1652–54).[1] Largely fought in the North Sea and the English Channel, colonists in the Atlantic nonetheless felt the war's effects in the form of disrupted shipping, elevated insurance costs, and scarce goods. In the Leeward Islands, the conflict and the associated pressure from England to strike against Dutch interests provoked English officials there to confiscate the property of the Dutch inhabitants. Included among the estates authorities seized were five warehouses used to stockpile goods in St. Christopher and several more in Montserrat. As they sorted through the contents of these storehouses and the Dutch traders' accounts authorities discovered almost 100 Montserratans, 150 Antiguans, and numerous residents of St. Christopher and Nevis indebted to Dutchmen. In all, Dutch merchants held goods and debts worth almost 280,000 pounds of tobacco valued at more than £2,000 as well as smaller debts denominated in sugar, ginger, and indigo when authorities seized their property.[2]

The presence of these Dutch traders and their warehouses illustrates the ways that interimperial trade had evolved since 1640. A decade earlier, relationships between English colonists and Dutch merchants had mostly been conducted at the water's edge. By 1652, those early contacts had become more fixed, with Dutch traders building warehouses, extending long-term credit, and remaining on the scene to manage trade. For a commercial community used to sending merchants to live in foreign cities to manage trade and for a people used to welcoming "strangers" to their communities, a number of Dutch merchants living, at least temporarily, in the Leeward Islands was not unusual. Instead, it was an expected outgrowth of increased trade and agricultural expansion. But for English officials struggling to affirm and consolidate their hold over infant colonies, the Dutch presence on these English islands was a threat that reaffirmed the Commonwealth's decision to launch a trade war against the Dutch.

The seizure of the Dutch estates in 1652 was a setback for colonists seeking interimperial trade in the English West Indies—as had been the passage of the first Navigation Act (a law designed to stymie Dutch trade in Europe and the colonies) the year before. But to focus on the losses of that year is to miss a larger set of Atlantic transformations that had little to do with metropolitan policy. Certainly from the perspective of Commonwealth leaders the capture of Dutch property was a significant achievement in their new struggle to both integrate the colonies more fully into the English empire and to create a national monopoly over English shipping. But for colonists, these losses, even when combined with the capture of Dutch fleets at Barbados in 1651 and 1655, were less important in causing Anglo-Dutch trade to shift footing in the 1640s and 1650s than were wider Atlantic phenomena such as falling tobacco prices, the widespread adoption of sugar, and the English Civil War (1642–49). The effects of these larger developments, collectively, on local dimensions of island commerce were more important than metropolitan laws.

Though every English Atlantic colony was affected by the changing Atlantic world, each place's physical environment, political situation, and pattern of settlement affected cross-national relationships differently. The early success that planters in the Leeward Islands had enjoyed with tobacco created the deeply engrained ties between planters and Dutch traders that the 1652 inventories reveal. As the English Civil War interrupted overseas trade and as tobacco prices fell, English settlers in the Leewards gravitated even more strongly to Dutch merchants who purchased large quantities of tobacco and offered long-term credit to fund agricultural expansion. Barbadian planters also traded with the Dutch, but since they did not produce a high-quality staple in the 1630s, these interactions remained at the water's edge, leaving English traders as the most important investors of capital. When Barbados's economy expanded rapidly in the mid-1640s, therefore, it was natural for colonists to rely on English capital to fund their construction of sugar works and purchase of slaves, while they also kept their Dutch sources of trade goods. Meanwhile, in New Amsterdam, Dutch colonists capitalized on midcentury disturbances to expand their interimperial ties to the Chesapeake and to the Caribbean, reimagining their place in the Atlantic in the process. Thus, despite the crises of war, cross-national trade in all of these places continued to rise in an environment of mutual convenience. Fragile and poor in 1640, stable and growing in 1660, settlers in the Leeward Islands, Barbados, and New Amsterdam all pursued different strategies according to their local conditions, not imperial mandates.

* * *

The price of tobacco fluctuated widely in the seventeenth century, but in general it trended downward after its peak in the early 1620s. In all, tobacco prices fell a total of 85 percent in value on the London market between 1620 and 1645. When English-American tobacco first reached European markets in the 1620s, the stimulant was still a luxury, available to only a small portion of the public. But as increased production drove the price lower, a larger segment of the population could obtain it. This initial elasticity of demand created a seemingly limitless market that encouraged planters to cultivate new lands and increase their productivity, a combination of factors that produced profits for colonists but ultimately also created a glut in the market that pushed prices downward in the early 1630s.[3]

Planters in the Caribbean quickly felt the effects of falling prices. The Barbadian variety of tobacco had fetched nine pence per pound in 1628, but by the mid-1630s, it sold for only six pence per pound, prompting Barbadians to shift their resources to other staples such as cotton and indigo. In St. Christopher, evidence indicates that the price remained higher, as the quality of leaf was better there. Nonetheless, prices still fell, and as early as 1633, Governor Warner began calling for the cultivation of alternate crops as a way to limit supply and drive prices upward. The failure of these local attempts to control tobacco production prompted a 1639 agreement between Warner and the governor-general of the French Antilles, Chevalier de Poincy, under which Leeward Islanders as a whole agreed to destroy their tobacco and not to plant again for a period of eighteen months.[4] Between 1637 and 1640, tobacco exports from Barbados and St. Christopher to London declined from 124,593 to 66,895 pounds in Barbados and from 263,599 to 138,973 pounds in St. Christopher, a decline of 46 and 44 percent respectively, but these efforts did little to raise tobacco's price.[5]

Declining prices encouraged colonists in Barbados to experiment with new crops, but the Leeward Islands had a different experience. As was the case in Virginia, tobacco planters on these islands, seeing few alternatives, still mainly planted the commodity even as prices slipped, leaving English merchants to conclude that it was "scarce worth the charge in London of carrying tobacco from St. Christopher, Virginia or the Bermuda." Meanwhile, across the Atlantic, the outbreak of the English Civil War forced a readjustment of Caribbean trade. Political instability, violence, periodic naval blockades, and the necessities of mobilizing two armies for war combined with falling tobacco prices to leave few Englishmen with the time or capital to invest in the colonies. Eager to protect their charter rights to land and hoping to remain insulated from destructive warfare, most colonists maintained a cautious neutrality in transatlantic matters, and took firmer local control of their commercial affairs.[6]

To overcome the twin threats of unstable tobacco prices and the lack of English attention, British island merchants and Dutch traders realized they could no longer rely only upon the ad hoc associations that had brought them together earlier, and they began to construct more elaborate interimperial alliances. One strategy Dutch merchants employed was to use Dutch colonies as intermediary ports from which to manage the trade. The Amsterdam partnership of Verbrugge and Son did exactly this throughout the 1640s. Working on commission for the Verbrugges, the New Amsterdam trader Govert Loockermans bought "[St.] Christoffers tobacco," and had it shipped to New Amsterdam. There, Loockermans—who had worked for the family since 1639—combined tobacco with other tropical goods from around the Americas before shipping them to the Verbrugges in Amsterdam. Based in North America, Loockermans was better able than those in Europe to gauge the quality and availability of tobacco and decide on the precise makeup of Europe-bound shipments. Traveling regularly to St. Christopher on behalf of the Verbrugges, Loockermans could also solidify his relationships with traders at the island (though he did not indicate with whom he met), a development that provided the Verbrugges continued access to Leeward Islands tobacco during a turbulent period. For his part, Loockermans earned valuable commissions on both the sale of European manufactures and the purchase of tobacco that he could then invest in his own trade to the South River and New England. Petrus Stuyvesant, the director of New Netherland and Curaçao, also dispatched vessels to trade at the English West Indies on behalf of the WIC. In the early 1650s, he sent both the New Netherland skipper Adriaen Blommert from New Amsterdam "to Curaçao and Aruba, to take in horses . . . which he sold in Antigua," and "Arent van Curler from New Netherland to Barbadoes in the ship *den Jongen Prins van Dennemarquen*" with a cargo of horses for English planters.[7]

English colonists in the Leewards also worked to reinforce their direct ties to the Dutch Republic during this period of transition. In late 1647, the aspiring trader Samuel Winthrop, the youngest son of Massachusetts governor John Winthrop, journeyed from St. Christopher to Rotterdam, where he promptly married a Dutch woman and abandoned his plans to settle in Barbados; instead, he established tobacco plantations in Antigua and St. Christopher, most likely with the help of Dutch connections he made in Rotterdam. In later years, he would utilize these relationships to facilitate trade to the Dutch Republic.[8] Family connections in the Leewards, especially when those families bridged imperial boundaries, were an important development for parties working to regularize their trade and to better take advantage of new prospects.

A related tactic that English planters employed to smooth access to Dutch trade during the 1640s was to allow Dutch representatives to live on their islands semi-permanently, as seen in the 1652 inventories. Whereas in the 1630s, many planters sold their harvests directly to Dutch traders calling there, in the 1640s and 1650s, the presence of Dutch agents at the English Leeward Islands enabled them to play a more active role in the colonial economy.[9] This transition was especially important for Leeward Islanders who lacked capital of their own or who did not have partnerships with metropolitan associates. In these early years, acquiring land was relatively easy, but obtaining the labor necessary to clear the land and the supplies needed to sustain that labor relied upon credit and a steady stream of workers and imported goods. The agricultural cycle required that planters have labor and supplies for planting on hand months before their crops came in, and thus needed extended time to repay their debts. Credit earned in international trade provided this time, especially for the owners of small plantations. While these less wealthy and connected planters—some of them working plots as small as fifteen to twenty acres—had sometimes been able to secure trade credit from Dutch merchants calling there in the 1630s, as their needs expanded and as the price of tobacco fell, continued trade increasingly depended on Dutch merchants taking up residence in English colonies. Located amidst the English planters, these representatives could store tobacco for later transport, could stockpile trade goods, and could offer more extensive credit than could factors who were not on the scene to collect debts.[10]

Though lists of the goods that planters bought from the Dutch merchants resident on the Leeward Islands in 1652 do not survive, in 1642, the receiver general of customs in St. Christopher, William Johnson, noted that the Dutch were able to provide many items inexpensively, including "shewes at 12 [pounds of tobacco] . . . and shirts [,] Cassocks and drawers at the same price." Without Dutch trade, he continued, "the Countrey payes 40 and 50 [pounds] . . . ready tobaccoe for the like" goods. Even more appealing than the price and variety of Dutch goods was that the English colonists could pay Dutch merchants for the goods "upon tyme," or on credit. The English planter Christopher Jeaffreson noted similar advantages that English colonists got from trading with the Dutch, remarking that they "sould cheape," and "allowed a yeare or two for payment." For planters just establishing themselves, ready tobacco was hard to come by and Dutch credit was particularly welcome.[11] Moreover, by building storehouses in nearby colonies, these Dutch agents could purchase tobacco ahead of shipping; when "boats came . . . to the said Island from a Plantacion of ye Dutch at Stasha [St. Eustatius, a Dutch island nearby]" or from the Dutch Republic to load tobacco, the agent would have already assembled the cargo, thereby reducing the ship's time in port and lowering freight costs.[12] Pooling tobacco also meant that Dutch merchants could offer credit to both large and small planters, who in turn guaranteed a steady supply of tobacco to transatlantic captains. Since the easiest way for planters to clear the debts they had amassed was to deliver tobacco, Dutch agents could manage the flow of tobacco to their storehouses by adjusting the amount of credit they offered.[13]

Altogether it is unclear how heavily Dutch merchants invested in the Leeward Islands, but the records of the 1652 seizure give some idea of how widespread that investment was. With hundreds of planters owing

TABLE 2.1

Leeward Island Planters' Debts to Dutch Merchants, 1654/5 (lbs)

	Sugar	Tobacco	Indigo	Ginger
St. Christopher	2,444	89,368	550	1,286
Nevis	39,064	27,516	0	0
Montserrat	1,741.5	43,278	0	0
Antigua	0	119,240	0	0
Totals	43,249.5	279,402	550	1,286

SOURCES: "Moutserrat and Antigua accoumpts, 1654 to 1656," Egerton MSS fols. 54–59, BL; and "Nevis and St. Christopher's Accounts," Egerton MSS 2395, fols. 69–77, BL.

debts to dozens of Dutch merchants, and with numerous Dutch ware-houses stocked with goods, the Dutch presence was significant.

And while it is unclear how much tobacco the Leewards produced by the early 1650s, London port records from 1640 indicate that in that year city traders imported 139,451 pounds from St. Christopher. Even though the decade-long gap in data means that no direct comparison is possible, this figure does suggest that the 280,000 pounds of tobacco planters owed to the Dutch in 1652 was a considerable quantity for the time and place.[14] On the whole, the presence of these merchants and the debts that English planters owed them demonstrate that these Dutchmen played an active role in supplying credit to English settlers, facilitating their commerce, and funding agricultural expansion.

* * *

While colonists in the Leewards enjoyed modest success with tobacco and a combination of Dutch and English trade in the 1640s and early 1650s, Barbados planters struggled as tobacco prices dipped. In response, Barbadians experimented with an array of tropical crops.[15] The first of these was cotton. One visitor to the island in 1631 remarked that "ye trade of cotton fills them all with hope," and another in 1634 noted that cotton was the chief item of trade.[16] Initially, English demand was strong for cotton as textile manufacturers strove to compete with Continental producers weaving their own "fustians" by diversifying the nation's exports, of which woolen textiles still made up 92 percent in 1640. As had happened with tobacco, however, cotton production quickly surpassed consumers' demand, and this, combined with increased competition from East Indian calicoes (printed cottons), drove prices down after 1639. With Barbadian cotton only "of very small value," one resident reported that London "merchants beg[a]n to neglect the supplying of it [the island]."[17] As English interest in cotton flagged many Barbadian planters turned to Dutch buyers already calling at the island who gladly added cotton to the agricultural products they bought from Barbadians. In 1642, for example, the Dutch trader Albert Jocheme and one Captain Heertjies agreed to send Christian Brodehaven of Barbados a yearly shipment of goods worth £400 in exchange for "cotton, &c."[18] Another Dutch vessel returned to Amsterdam with 106,000 pounds of cotton four years later.[19] Meanwhile, other planters began to experiment with indigo, fustic (a dyewood), ginger, and cacao.[20]

Still searching for a leading staple in the early 1640s, Barbadians continued to improve their production of tobacco and cotton, alternating between the two depending on international price swings and demand from merchants who sometimes refused to carry one or the other.[21] Earning sufficient, but not spectacular, profits from these commodities and their experiments with indigo and ginger, planters experienced an export boom. Responding to the growing economy, the disruptions to trade the Civil War caused, and planters' increasing needs for supplies and freight services as exports rose, Dutch merchants intensified their trade at Barbados. By the early 1640s, about five or six Dutch vessels called annually at Barbados, where they soon became, according to the island's first historian, Richard Ligon, an important supplier of needed provisions such as butter and meat. Others agreed, listing "browd-brimd white or black hatts," gold and silver hat tires, "new fashioned shoes," "bone combs," and "whyted osenbridge linen," along with "Wines, Brandywnes, &c" as those goods Barbadians bought from Dutch vessels. The increased pace of Dutch trade at the island corresponded to the beginning of the export boom but did little to change the overall pattern of trade. Most Dutch vessels trading at Barbados still stopped there as they cruised the Caribbean with their captains improvisationally choosing markets and commodities depending on economic circumstances rather than because they had invested in placing agents and warehouses on the island, as was true in the Leewards.[22]

In this same decade, planters also began to successfully produce the first salable harvests of the crop that would define Barbados's early history: sugar. Though they had experimented with it in the island's early years, colonists reintroduced sugarcane at the end of the 1630s. Key in planters' ability to produce palatable muscovado at midcentury were most likely the newly arrived African slaves who had learned the highly technical skills required to process cane in Dutch and Portuguese plantations in Brazil. Once reestablished, the crop flourished. The revolt of Portuguese colonists against their Dutch conquerors in Brazil beginning in 1645 virtually halted the production of sugar in Brazil and boosted the prospects for cultivation in Barbados by driving the price of sugar almost 50 percent higher in just over a year (from .39 guilders per pound in 1645 to .57 in 1646). Not only did the price of sugar rise absolutely; its relative price was even higher because, in the same years, prices for tobacco and cotton fell further, making sugar cultivation even more attractive. By 1649, sugar was the chief commodity used in local exchange; by the mid-1660s, 60 percent of the island was planted with sugarcane, and the crop accounted for 90 percent of the value of all Barbadian exports. Some Barbadians still produced tobacco in the 1660s, but by then it was grown only as a supplementary crop on large plantations or as the main produce of small plantations.[23]

Until recently, scholars have credited Dutch merchants with providing the capital that enabled the Barbadian sugar boom, but work by Russell Menard has provided an important corrective to these earlier accounts. Menard convincingly argues that the expansion of sugar at the island was financed by a combination of Barbadian planters who reinvested profits earned from their diverse range of export crops into sugar and sugar technology and of London merchants attracted to the success local planters had with sugar. Barbados's relative security in the eastern Caribbean, political stability, size and healthy climate, and the immense returns sugar promised further encouraged the transition. Among the most important of the seventy-five London merchants who invested directly in Barbados between 1640 and 1660 was the Thomson syndicate. These "new merchants" were well placed to encourage development on the island because of their experience in colonial trade and because many had also recently begun to experiment with the West African slave trade. As their plantations and capital requirements grew, locals in need of goods gravitated to those who had the connections to meet their demands. In this way, even those colonists who had funded the transition to sugar with their own profits found themselves tied closely to a small number of English merchants whose own political connections would guarantee that English officials would soon pay special attention to what was fast becoming their richest colony.[24]

As had happened with English merchants, the sugar boom began to draw more Dutch traders to Barbados—several of whom valued it five times greater than tobacco in 1647—who preferred sugar over tobacco and cotton after 1645. Nevertheless, the shift to sugar did little to change the nature of Anglo-Dutch trade there. Unlike in the Leewards, where several Dutch merchants lived and built warehouses, most Dutch trade in Barbados remained centered on exchanges at the water's edge even as production expanded. It was not that Barbadians ignored Dutch capital—there are several cases of Dutch traders struggling to collect debts in Barbados and of English planters agreeing to advance contacts to sell their produce to Dutch traders—but with London merchants more eager to buy sugar than tobacco, most Barbadians did not, or did not need, to attract the depth of commercial investment from Dutch merchants as did their rivals planting tobacco in the Leewards.[25] Dutch merchants in turn seemed to prefer the quality of Leeward Island tobacco, the lower capital investment that it required when compared to sugar, and the relative closeness of those colonies to Dutch islands. The investment losses they suffered in Dutch Brazil when they were expelled in 1654 (a process that had begun a decade earlier) further discouraged Dutch merchants from investing in expensive sugar works in foreign colonies.[26] Instead, the as many as fifteen Dutch merchants arriving in Barbados each year by the late 1640s preferred to concentrate on earning profits through the carrying trade, selling provisions, livestock, and dry goods for tropical commodities—now mostly sugar but also tobacco, cotton, and indigo—and reserving their capital investments for other places. These exchanges allowed shipmasters to arrive in Barbados, exchange their cargo of provisions and other manufactures for tropical commodities, and depart the island roughly three months later.[27] Such quick turnarounds would have made the carrying trade especially valuable to Dutch merchants who prized flexibility and wished to avoid having to extend long-term credit and to English planters eager to quickly obtain manufactured goods.

Examining the sources of Barbadian slave purchases further illustrates planters and Dutch merchants' mutual preference for direct exchange as in earlier years. Hand in hand with Barbados's export boom in the 1640s and 1650s came the importation of large numbers of enslaved Africans, a process that the transition to sugar intensified. The best estimates indicate that, in the first two decades of the export boom (1641 to 1660), traders landed about 41,500 slaves in Barbados, or more than 2,000 a year. Since slaves were vital to planters' ability to produce sugar, since they were expensive, and since the Dutch had a well-developed slave trade, we could expect that if Dutch merchants began to extend

TABLE 2.2

Recorded Dutch Slave Imports to Barbados, 1641–1660

	Netherlands	Total	Percent Dutch
1641–45	245	1,366	17.9
1646–50	264	3,175	8.3
1651–55	250	1,058	23.6
1656–60	444	3,365	13.2
Totals	1,203	8,964	13.4

SOURCE: TASTD, http://slavevoyages.org/tast/database/search.faces?yearFrom=1600 &yearTo=1688&mjslptimp=34200.

significant trade credit to planters as they began to produce sugar, it would have been through the slave trade. What we find is that, between 1641 and 1660, only five Dutch vessels landed 1,203 slaves at Barbados, a total of 13 percent of all recorded slave disbursements at the island. Though at first glance significant, including estimated English arrivals in the total lowers the Dutch proportion to 2.9 percent. Anglo-Dutch trade in Barbados continued to be based more heavily on the carrying and provisioning trades.[28]

Indeed, the Dutch carrying trade to the island was significant, as the 1644 voyage of the *Casteel van Sluys* from the Dutch Republic to Barbados with sixty "musquetten" [musketoon] to be sold for 3,300 pounds of tobacco demonstrates. But, in general, Barbadians interactions with Dutch traders during the 1640s did not entail the number of deeply enmeshed credit relationships that characterized Leeward Islanders' involvement with Dutch traders, a pattern which would endure during subsequent years.[29]

The cross-national trade in Barbados and the Leeward Islands that colonists established in the 1640s faced new challenges after Oliver Cromwell and Parliament seized control of the English government in 1649, but that event did little to overturn the trajectory of Anglo-Dutch commercial relations in the short term. Able to remain largely neutral during the English Civil War, the execution of Charles I in 1649 prompted several colonies, including Barbados and Antigua, to reject the Commonwealth and declare for Charles II. In Barbados, as in every colony, local political forces were responsible for the decision. There a small group of elite Royalist planters (led by both longtime residents and newly arrived refugees fleeing England) eager to consolidate their

TABLE 2.3

Estimated Dutch Slave Imports to Barbados, 1641–1660

	Netherlands	Total	Percent Dutch
1641–45	200	11,700	1.7
1646–50	300	14,200	2.1
1651–55	300	5,000	6.0
1656–60	400	10,700	3.7
Totals	1,200	41,600	2.9

SOURCE: TASTD, http://slavevoyages.org/tast/assessment/estimates.faces?yearFrom=1600&yearTo=1688&disembarkation=302.

NOTE: Figures rounded to nearest hundred. Totals calculated by summing raw data and then rounding to nearest hundred.

control over island politics forced Governor Philip Bell from power and worked to punish or expel those who supported the Parliamentarians. When word reached England of the rebellion in Barbados and the associated move by the new holder of the Carlisle patent and supporter of the king, Francis, Lord Willoughby of Parham, to assume the island's governorship, Parliament responded by acting to "reconquer" Barbados for the Commonwealth. Their first step was passing the British Trade Act of 1650, which placed a total embargo on those English colonies in the Americas that had not recognized the triumph of the Commonwealth government.[30]

Intended as a wartime measure, the law also had broader implications. In dictating commercial restrictions for the colonies, the British Trade Act of 1650 set forth the proposition that Parliament had supreme authority over colonial commerce. The next year, the Commonwealth government extended this power, issuing the first of what would be a series of trade laws designed to damage Dutch trade and regain commercial control of its Atlantic possessions by restricting trade with foreigners. Here commercial interests intersected with larger diplomatic goals. With power now firmly in their hands in 1651, Parliament and Cromwell were looking beyond England to shore up and extend the accomplishments of their Revolution. Understanding that a powerful army and navy would be central to English success as they had been in the Civil War, the pacification of the Royalist colonies provided the opportunity to reshape policy there in an effort to harness the colonies' economies for the uses of the metropole. The largest obstacle to colonial control, however, was continued Dutch dominance of Anglo-Dutch trade. When attempts to come to a broader negotiated settlement that included an Anglo-Dutch alliance broke down over Dutch reluctance to accept a smaller share of trade between the countries, the Commonwealth government struck against the Dutch Republic. Supported both by those who saw strategic benefits to better controlling commerce and by the "new merchants" who hoped to consolidate their new trading power through the world, Parliament passed a new trade law and eventually launched a sea war against the United Provinces.[31]

Since the main target of the restriction was the Dutch carrying trade both within Europe and in the Americas, the First Act of Trade and Navigation (1651) restricted English imports to English ships or the European country of their manufacture. From the colonial perspective, the law stipulated that all of the colonies' production that was shipped to England be confined to English vessels. If colonists wished to send commodities to foreign markets in foreign vessels, they could do so, but only in direct exchange for commodities produced in that country. The rules were similar for imports. Goods could come from any country as long as they came directly from the place of manufacture in ships of that country or in English bottoms. At first glance, these restrictions seemed to allow continued trade with the Dutch; they did not. Many of the goods colonists demanded from the Netherlands were not produced there and had simply passed through this entrepôt, meaning much direct trade from Amsterdam would not be permitted. In short, the Navigation Act of 1651 made most foreign trade in the colonies illegal. Because the trade law was intended as just one part of a broader effort to integrate the Atlantic colonies into the Commonwealth empire, Parliament paired it with policies that canceled colonial charters, abolished proprietary rights, named new governors, and eventually dispatched the navy to enforce these new policies. Not yet coalesced into a coherent and fully articulated vision of empire, what all of these policy changes had in common was that they sacrificed local control to the advantage of metropolitan investors and government officials.

As sweeping as their reforms were, the Commonwealth government soon found that their policies were insufficient to remove Dutch traders from the colonies. Eventually, growing attention from England would complicate cross-national trade in the Caribbean, but other than a few spectacular seizures of Dutch ships—including the roughly twenty-five Dutch vessels worth a total of £100,000 that General George Ayscue's

Commonwealth fleet captured at Barbados in 1651—these efforts did not immediately transform colonists' behavior. English efforts to end Dutch trade do reveal, however, how common Dutch trade was; and the unlucky traders whom authorities caught provide opportune evidence for reconstructing much of that exchange.[32] In most of the years between 1650 and 1659, at least ten and as many as thirty (in 1655) Dutch vessels traded in Barbados, with several more doing the same in the English Leeward Islands.[33] With so many traders defying the 1651 act, it is clear that colonial conditions remained more important than metropolitan goals in shaping colonial trade.

Colonial trade with Dutch merchants persisted because of the reputation for superior quality and low prices in the Dutch Republic. The London merchant John Paige (who was an associate of Maurice Thomson and often represented Canary Island wine traders such as William Clerke) actively shipped Barbadian produce to Amsterdam. On one occasion, Paige and Clerke sent Clerke's assistant Henry Hawley from Tenerife to Barbados with a cargo of *vidueno* wines. Once in Barbados, Hawley sold the wine and the small vessel he brought it on, receiving payment in sugar. Learning that the government was preparing a fleet for Barbados to "reduce [the islanders] to obedience," Paige hurriedly sent Hawley notice via Amsterdam that he had only three months to quit the island before the Commonwealth fleet trapped him and his cargo. To Paige's relief, he learned in late March 1651 that not only had Hawley escaped Barbados, but that he would soon be in Amsterdam on the *Meda* with a cargo of "sugar, which came to a reasonable market, worth 7 1/2 stivers per lb."[34] Paige's correspondence does not reveal the precise reason that he and Clerke sent Hawley to Amsterdam, as opposed to England, but one can only assume that they must have found that market more attractive. The ability to find higher prices in Amsterdam, in turn, would enable Clerke and his associates to cover their debts in England and may even have allowed them to buy more goods—or slaves—in return. For those who sold their sugar to Hawley and who were anticipating the arrival of an English blockade, the chance to sell their harvest at high prices despite English intentions must have also seemed quite fortunate.

With a wide network of associates, Paige and Hawley were well placed to manage direct trade with Amsterdam, but other exporters with only tenuous connections also could sell their goods to Dutch vessels stopping at the islands. Governor Searle provided an opening for these vessels despite the new trade law, telling the Council of State that he had allowed "several shipps of war" from "Holland" that had been "near 11 months" off Brazil to take in "wood & water" at Brazil in 1652. War-ships, not merchant vessels, Searle's open policy nonetheless fostered the belief that Barbados welcomed foreign vessels. Several years later, the island's Commissioners of the Admiralty noted the continued arrival of Dutch vessels when they complained that they had been unable to collect "seaven hundred & odd thousands of sugar" due to them for the sale of "prize goods in Sir George Ayscue's time." These prizes were most likely seized from Dutch and other foreign merchants while trading at English islands. Seeking to collect revenues from the arrival of Dutch ships, the Barbadian Council even passed a law in 1652 requiring all "foreign ships that come to trade" to pay a duty of powder at twice the English rate.[35]

In January 1655, Barbados must have recently added to its powder store, for that month an English squadron under the command of Ad-miral William Penn and General Robert Venables entered Carlisle Bay, Barbados, and found a number of foreign merchantmen, all but one be-ing Dutch vessels, that had just recently "Sold all their Goods" in the port. Arriving to recruit Barbadians to join the Western Design, the fleet surprised the Dutch vessels and seized them for the Commonwealth.[36] Over the course of the next eight weeks, various English vessels scouring the Caribbean Sea found more Dutch ships aiming to trade at English colonies. Altogether the English fleet seized sixteen Dutch vessels, just about half of all those recorded as trading in Barbados and the English Leewards that year. Once they secured the Dutch vessels, Penn and Ven-ables ordered authorities to collect depositions from the ships' crews and to produce valuations of the cargoes, all in the goal of claiming their share of the prizes.[37] These documents, never before closely examined, provide an exceptional glimpse of the goods Barbadians demanded from Dutch suppliers and the way that they retained access to foreign mer-chants even in the midst of efforts to strengthen a competitive English state.

The focus on staple production in Barbados provided a difficult chal-lenge for settlers. Since they had to import nearly all manufactured goods and a great deal of their provisions, as well as the equipment to produce tobacco and sugar, English colonists wanted above all to retain access to these goods no matter who brought them to their ports. Therefore, it should have come as little surprise to the English fleet that many of the vessels they saw anchored off Bridgetown had disgorged necessaries for local planters' consumption. One of these merchantmen, the *Greenfoot,* brought Barbadians a typical Dutch cargo of "French wine, Beere, beefe, Brandy, pork, hatts, [and] fine Holland shooes."[38] Other vessels carried textiles, barrel staves, soap, various kinds of wine and liquor, meats, and flour. Finally, one of the vessels carried 240 slaves.[39] Those landing provisions and manufactured goods had come originally from Europe, but had taken a variety of routes to the island. Among the largest of the sixteen vessels was the 240-ton *Brownfish*. This vessel had originally sailed from the United Provinces, departing Texel on April 23, 1654, freighted for Brazil, where it arrived on June 14. But, learning that "Brazile was Lost," and "hearing of ye peace with England, hee [the master] proved on to Barbados, arriveing there ye 19th of July" to sell his cargo of "Beefe, butter, Cheese, beere soape & other provisions."[40]

Another valued item Dutch traders carried to the island was livestock, including goats and horses. By 1655, horses—six of which were needed for each mill—had become indispensable sources of power to drive islanders' sugar mills. While trying to develop efficient windmills to do the work, the animals were in constant demand because, as a member of the Penn and Venables fleet noted, the islanders "destroy so many horses that it begors the planters, a good hors[e] for the mill being worth 50 starling mony." Some horses came directly from Europe, but more often merchants supplied livestock from surrounding colonies. New England, especially, would become an important supplier of these draft animals, but in the 1650s, New Englanders were still just developing this capability. In 1655, horses were so scarce in Barbados that, according to the London merchant Martin Noell, planters had been forced to stop their mills. To fill their demand, islanders turned to Dutch merchants who could supply the horses via intra-Caribbean voyages.[41]

The *Brownfish* had completed such a journey in 1655. First, it had arrived at Barbados to land its cargo of "Beefe, butter, Cheese, beere[,] soape & other provisions" during the month of August. In the process, the master learned that there was great demand for horses on the island, and to exploit this opportunity he departed for Dutch "Carsou [Curaçao] where he loaden and tooke in thirty horses with which he arrived at Barbados" in November.[42] Four other vessels made similar trips, leaving Barbados, or, in one case, St. Christopher, after selling their loads of European goods and heading to Curaçao, where they bought horses and other assorted livestock such as goats and asinegos—a small donkey—with which to return to Barbados.[43] Alternatively, after unlading, the captains of the *White Swan* and the *Black Lyon* guided their vessels out of Carlisle Bay back across the Atlantic to the Cape Verde Islands, where they loaded thirty and twenty-four asinegos respectively for Barbados.[44] Seeing an available market, the masters of these vessels acted opportunistically to seek out intermediate destinations and cargoes. The adaptable and improvisational routes that they collectively pursued represent one of a variety of ways Dutchmen supplied colonial planters with needed goods.

As payment for provisions, dry goods, and livestock, Dutch captains received or were promised primarily sugar or a small amount of coin.[45] It is important to note that the sugar Barbadians provided to Dutch merchants was used primarily as a form of currency to balance accounts. Most of the 5,000 tons of sugar Barbadians exported in 1655 were sent to England in one hundred to two hundred English ships, an arrangement that was already making Barbadians and their English partners wealthy.[46] The relatively small amounts of sugar paid to Dutch merchants, while not part of a principal export arrangement, were nevertheless critical because they allowed planters to purchase necessary supplies in a specie-starved colony. Unlike the tobacco planters in the Leeward Islands who sold large portions of their harvests to Dutch merchants and depended on these men for credit, Barbadians traded sugar to the Dutch to acquire supplies at the water's edge, as their credit needs were largely satiated by London merchants. By holding back sugars from English shipments as payment for Dutch goods, planters were able to ensure that when the opportunity arose, or if they became desperate, they could buy the goods they needed from Dutch traders even while they continued to rely on London as well. Barbadians' varying use of sugar reveals how imperial and interimperial trade overlapped as colonists chose the best way to profit, limit risk, and increase efficiency, voyage by voyage, purchase by purchase.

Meanwhile, Dutch merchants found opportunity in dockside trade as well, seizing the opportunity to satisfy the material demands that Barbados's rapid sugar expansion created without having to devote long-term credit to the colony. Some of these Dutch landings, as the Penn and Venables seizures revealed, had taken multistage routes to Barbados. Three ships stopped at the French island of Martinique, either to trade or gather information, while another stopped at Guadeloupe and at both the English and French sides of the divided St. Christopher.[47] Five others journeyed directly to Barbados from a Dutch port,[48] and one other vessel, the 200-ton *White Swan*, had first gone to Norway from the Dutch Republic, before carrying its cargo of seventy-four horses to Barbados.[49] Similar to the *White Swan*, the 120-ton *Charity*, commanded by Albert Albertson and carrying "28 barrells of porke, [and] some other small parcels of goods," put into Nantes, France, on its way to Barbados, where

Albertson "Loaded 57 butts of Nantes wine."[50] Though traveling directly to Barbados, the masters of five of these vessels, the *Greenfoot*, the *Black Lyon*, the *Peace*, the *King David* of Rotterdam, and the *King David* of Amsterdam, were not explicitly sent to trade at Barbados. Rather, each master was instructed to cruise the Caribbean selling his cargo "where hee would make the best market." [51] In the case of one ship Penn captured outside of Carlisle Bay, the *Peace*, the skipper Herman Barrentson even testified that this order to cruise the Caribbean came not in writing but "by word of mouth from his owners," who wanted him to go to St. Christopher "or any other of ye Caribes" with his cargo of slaves. In what was likely an attempt to convince authorities that he was not trying to trade at Barbados, Barrentson even claimed that the one island he was not to go to was Barbados.[52]

As in the case of Barrentson, at least ten of the captains of the sixteen vessels seized in 1655 served as their own supercargoes and worked without local Dutch agents. Either because they were highly trusted or, as in the case of John Leonards, master of the *King David* of Rotterdam, because they owned a part of their vessels and their freight, the captains were given wide latitude in finding the best markets. Though empowered to make decisions themselves, the masters were not without contacts in the greater Caribbean. Albert Albertson, for example, was in the employ of a group of merchants living in Amsterdam and Hoorn, who instructed him that if he was unsuccessful in selling his cargo at Barbados, he was to go to "St. Eustatiyus where he should expect some [further direction] having one of his owners resident upon that Island."[53]

This strategy of empowering shipmasters as supercargoes, like that of using multilateral trading routes, indicates how Dutch merchants used a variety of commercial strategies in the West Indies—choosing more structured relationships in the Leeward Islands and more flexible trade in Barbados. As earlier captains had done and as colonists had come to expect, Dutch ships regularly called at English islands, offering goods for sale in the form of speculative trade, especially when commercial laws made residency difficult. These speculative arrivals kept relationships between Barbadian consumers and Dutch traders largely short-lived as the two came together for specific transactions. That being said, there was at least one captain in 1655 who did have regular contact with agents residing in Barbados. John Peterson, skipper of the 160-ton *Armes of France*, sailed from Amsterdam to Barbados, via Martinique to deliver a cargo of "beere, beefe, [and] porke" to "Joseph Lewars[,] a Dutchman in this Island [Barbados]."[54]

Other Barbadians had Dutch ties, too. These preexisting kinship and commercial ties—often formed in Europe—reinforced relationships of mutual convenience made in the Atlantic. One intriguing family with strong Dutch connections present in Barbados at midcentury was the Silvester (var. Sylvester) family. Giles Silvester, the family patriarch, was born in England but migrated to the United Provinces with his wife during the first decades of the seventeenth century. By 1640, Silvester, whom authorities still sometimes identified as an English merchant, was arranging for the shipment of Virginia tobacco and cotton from Barbados. It is unclear if the elder Giles ever traveled to Barbados, but at least three of his sons, Constant, Giles, and Nathaniel, did.[55] Most prominent of these was Constant, who established a sugar plantation in the mid-1640s, but also may have helped connect other planters to the markets of the Dutch Republic and to London. As contemporary Robert Nedham noted, "This man, by birth a Dutchman, by profession an Anabaptist, was employed by those of that sect in Amsterdam to follow their trade in these parts [Barbados]." Present in Barbados to pick up a cargo of cotton from Johannes Vriessenburch in 1641 and to establish a plantation for his father, and trading among the Leeward Islands in 1643, by 1644, Constant was back in Amsterdam arranging the shipment of cotton, indigo, and sugar from Barbados to that Dutch city. Nathaniel eventually migrated to Shelter Island on Long Island, where he established a farm and, among other things, shipped provisions to Barbados.[56]

During the late 1640s and early 1650s, the younger Giles was also in Barbados, where he helped to manage his father and brother Constant's sugar plantation. In 1651, he was set to transport "50,000 [lb.] of sugar and 25,000 lb. of ginger" to his father in Amsterdam but "was not permitted to ship" the produce by Barbados's Royalist faction. Shrugging off his earlier setback, in August 1651, Silvester continued to write optimistically about the potential for Dutch trade, informing his father that he "hartily wish[ed]" his father "had sent a small Cargo . . . in any of ye Dutch Shipps" that had recently called at Barbados because "it would have been an excellent business." Though Silvester knew the Commonwealth fleet was on its way to the island, he nonetheless continued to urge his father to try to secure "some Commodities [for shipment] upon bodemery [bottomary]" for he knew the "Dutchmen are made to be gone & to make another Voyage, before ye Coming of ye frygotts." Even with the coming fleet, such a venture was worth the risk, Silvester noted, because for "100 guilders in commodities they [could] make 2000 lb of sugar."[57] Undiscouraged by attempts to shut down Anglo-Dutch trade,

Constant Silvester eventually accumulated a significant estate of nearly 700 acres and 240 slaves on two properties in Barbados.[58] This family, with its English roots and Dutch connections, was well placed to profit from interimperial trade and indicates the ways that connections forged by migration within Europe also fostered trade in the colonies.

There is also some additional fragmentary evidence suggesting that Dutch merchants at least temporarily lived in Bridgetown's mercantile community of about a hundred traders and provided another connection for residents to the United Provinces. A contemporary of the Silvesters at Barbados reported in 1649 that "a great company" of Dutchmen had died at Barbados during an epidemic, but whether they were residents or hailed from ships' crews is unknown.[59] Several years later, "severall of the Dutch Nation" living at Barbados petitioned the governor and council for the "liberty & privilege to convene & meet together on the Sabbath day, for Religious Exercises," a request that the government granted. Meanwhile, Amsterdam notarial records for the 1640s and 1650s indicate that some Dutch merchants had recently been at the island, though again the duration of their stay is unclear. One of these men, Jan van de Loo, was there in June 1650, when a storehouse he had maintained since March of that year burned, destroying his books and papers, cotton and sugar bought from planters, and the textiles, combs, and meat he was storing for local sale.[60] There were also Dutch-speaking German and Jewish residents in Bridgetown. Like the Dutch, German merchants (largely from Hamburg, a city whose traders were tied closely to Amsterdam) also sent representatives to live in Barbados. Hamburg's *Golden Dolphin*, for example, carried the factor Stephen van Schoness to the island from Amsterdam. Upon his arrival, Van Schoness was instructed to trade with "one Paulus Millenburg [a Hamburger] an Inhabitant of this Island [Barbados]."[61] Other merchants from Hamburg, including some Sephardic Jews, resided in Barbados and directed an average of three ships per year from Barbados to Europe between 1644 and 1650.[62] According to the indentured servant Heinrich Von Ucheritz, he obtained passage home through Amsterdam on a vessel coming from Brazil with help from the resident German mercantile community.[63]

Other foreigners traded to Barbados often enough to form at least temporary relationships with local merchants. Frederick Osten, a shipmaster and ship owner living in Hoorn, had sent the *Love* to Barbados in 1654, where it was captured by Penn. When the master of that vessel, Albert Albertson, returned to "Holland [and] out of despaire did hang himselfe," Osten, who had for "along time gone for ye Barbados & traders with the Inhabitants as it is well knowne to many honest merchants there," applied for permission to travel to Barbados, where he could collect those "debts yet oweing to him" in that island."[64] Jacob Dirrickson (var. Derrick, Derrickson) is another of these Dutchmen who spent years moving around the English Caribbean. Listed as one of those living in Antigua when his property was seized at the outbreak of the First Anglo-Dutch War, Dirrickson was in Barbados as early as 1647, and he was back there again in 1659 as the supercargo on a Dutch vessel a group of pirates seized. Still retaining ties in Antigua, he convinced the men to leave him there.[65] Similarly, some Barbadians journeyed to Amsterdam to manage their affairs. One of these men was Thomas Yates. Identified in a 1638 list as owning more than 10 acres of land in Barbados, by 1646, Yates was living in Amsterdam. In that year, he agreed to supply 3,000 guilders' worth of tools and other supplies to John Holmes of Barbados so that Holmes could transform his 100-acre ginger and sugar beet plantation located in St. Lucy's parish into a sugar plantation complete with a mill.[66] Though not as proportionately integrated into Dutch credit networks as in the Leeward Islands, these foreign merchants in Bridgetown or Barbadians in Amsterdam either temporarily or on a more permanent basis provided the islanders there a crucial link to foreign markets, and the personal interaction that travel afforded helped solidify these connections.

The desire to maintain beneficial interimperial commercial relations led settlers to make an extraordinary effort to protect the Dutch traders whom Penn captured in 1655. First, after Searle only reluctantly passed the case on to the local court, for a "tryall at common law" (rather than in an Admiralty court), the suit stalled because no attorneys "could be procured for the state," since all those lawyers in the island had already been "taken up for the strangers [the Dutch]." Eventually the English merchants on the island moved to plead "the state's case" themselves and did so ably, arguing that the vessels should be forfeited because their presence violated both the Act of 1650 and the first Act of Trade and Navigation. Although the state reportedly provided adequate evidence to secure a guilty verdict, the jury found "for the strangers against Parliament and state," a verdict which resulted in "general rejoicing" in the taverns lining Cheapside in Bridgetown. According to Edward Winslow, one of the commissioners Cromwell appointed to advise Penn and Venables, Searle had led the jury to inaccurately interpret the Articles of Surrender that Barbadians had signed with the Commonwealth government in 1651. Thinking that this agreement superseded the Navigation Act, the jury insisted Penn and Venable's actions were illegal, as they had done in earlier cases to thwart the efforts of the Commissioners of the Admiralty to seize foreign trade. The verdict, Winslow wrote, was not a surprise to him because it was clear that in Barbados colonists "generally . . . dote[d] upon the Dutch trade." This favoritism was so complete, Winslow continued, that English merchants found colonists would "give more for a worse commodity to the Dutch, than for a better to themselves [English merchants]." To English authorities and merchants, then, the trial illustrated the preference Barbadians had for the "courted, and highly prized" Dutch merchants and the disdain they had for English traders, whom many considered "great extortioners."[67] Winslow, a strong opponent of the Royalist Barbadians, was most likely exaggerating colonial preferences for Dutch goods. But behind his comments lies an important truth: Barbadians would trade with whomever arrived at their island and could offer better goods, lower prices, and a wider variety of goods regardless of the origin of those ships.

A similar process was at work in the Leeward Islands, where colonists also tried to defend the relationships that tied Dutch merchants and islanders together. For example, in April 1656, the Antiguan governor Christopher Kaynell—urged along by residents—argued that though the Dutchmen's property had been seized, many foreign traders had refused to leave the island. Centering his attack on the Navigation Act of 1651, Kaynell noted that that law's "prohibition of foreigners" to trade had meant the loss of "considerable suppleys," especially for what he called the "Norweesers" living there. Knowing how important this trade had been in earlier years, Kaynell feared that following the law would prove disastrous to the island's economy, and thus he risked disfavor by openly calling for restrictions on foreign trade to be overturned. Initially, the Committee of Trade relented, suggesting that such trade was acceptable, but eventually they reversed course and instead offered to suspend collecting the king's duties as a way to encourage English merchants to trade to Antigua. Whether Kaynell allowed foreign trade when his petitioning proved unsuccessful is unknown, but it is more clear that his colleague Colonel Clement Everard, the governor of English St. Christopher, did. As one informant described to the Council of State in January 1659, Everard was unfit for his post because he "hath suffered the Dutch to Ingrosse the trade of" St. Christopher "contrary to the Acts of this present Parliament" and "the ye Great damage and discouragement of the English Traders."[68] As these governors found, more than a decade of close interaction between planters and Dutch merchants meant that interimperial trade had become a regular part of the Leeward Islands' economic life.

For their part, Dutch colonists endeavored to make sure that their ties to the markets of the English Caribbean remained secure. As early as 1651, a group of Amsterdam merchants trading to the English Caribbean and to Virginia urged the States-General to lobby for the relaxation of the 1650 embargo. After informing the States-General that they yearly brought "a large quantity of sugars, tobacco, indigo, ginger, cotton, and divers sorts of valuable wood" from the English islands, earning a "considerable profit" for themselves and "contributing to the support of several thousand people" in the United Provinces, the merchants offered two reasons for the Commonwealth government to reconsider the law. First, they reminded them that "they ha[d] traded for upwards of twenty years . . . to all the Caribbean islands" and in that time had supplied English colonists with "manufactures, brewed beer, linen cloth, brandies, . . . duffels, [and] coarse cloth." Moreover, they also often rescued English settlers "with food and raiment" from "exteme ruin." Probably referring to their investments in the Leewards, the merchants also argued that since "they must always invest and intrust a heavy capital to" the planters, the embargo would mean that they could not collect "unsold goods and outstanding debts" in the islands.[69] The petition prompted the States-General to instruct their ambassadors to address the situation, but little came of these efforts.[70]

While diplomats in Europe tried to secure continued interimperial trade, and while Barbadians labored to keep the Dutch vessels from being forfeited in 1655, Stuyvesant, the highest-ranking Dutch West India Company official in the Americas, was also working to regularize trade between the two empires in the Atlantic. Operating without the "knowledge and consent" of the WIC directors, Stuyvesant had arrived in Barbados just before Penn and Venables on the *De Peerboom* (The Pear Tree) accompanied by two other Dutch ships. "This man's business" in Barbados, one English official reported, "was to settle a faire trade between the Netherlands and this place [Barbados]; but we spoiled the sport." The presence of the Commonwealth fleet prevented a trade pact, but interestingly the English forces boarded and occupied but did not seize these three Dutch vessels, preferring instead simply to force them to stay at the English island until the fleet launched its assault on Spanish America.[71] This was not Stuyvesant's first attempt to establish formal agreements between English and Dutch colonies in the Atlantic. During the First Anglo-Dutch War, the directors of the WIC had ordered Stuyvesant to propose terms for peaceable trade between New Netherland and Virginia. These long negotiations ultimately resulted in a short-lived formal treaty in 1660 that the Navigation Act of 1660 then almost immediately nullified.[72] In Barbados, too, metropolitan officials quashed the trade agreement, but that the two groups of colonists considered the arrangement at all indicates their mutual reliability and highlights that Barbadian planters were eager to retain access to Dutch trade. The attempted pact also suggests the conflicting signals that colonists of the two empires were receiving from diplomacy in Europe and the associated lack of uniform trade policy within the English empire. For, as Stuyvesant was negotiating with the former avowedly Royalist, and only recently pacified, colony of Barbados, much of the Stuart royal retinue was in exile in the Dutch Republic, where the Oranges and the former English ruling family remained close.[73] With Anglo-Dutch ties still strong in Europe, it followed that they should remain so in the Atlantic.

Barbadians insisted that when parliamentary figures finally forced them to accept the Commonwealth government, the settlement included a clause protecting their right to trade with all "Nations that doe trade, and are in amitye with England," an agreement that the 1651 Navigation Act nullified.[74] Soon thereafter, Barbadians took an extraordinary step to signal Dutch traders that even though trade in 1655 had been disturbed, the island's traders were ready for Dutch trade again. In mid-February 1656, Isaack de Fonseca, a Jewish trader from Bridgetown, arrived in the Dutch island of Curaçao on the *Constant Anna* and submitted a letter on behalf of Searle to the vice director of the WIC, Matthias Beck. The petition stated "that if the Company were to allow free trade to the inhabitants of the Barbados, then the Company would also not be refused the same privileges and freedoms of these islands at the Barbados."[75] After initially rejecting the arrangement, Beck and his council agreed to exchange fourteen horses for 400 pounds of flour, hard bread, beer, brandy, and 600 guilders worth of manufactured goods.[76] That De Fonseca carried a letter from Searle proposing a trading pact between the two colonies further suggests that De Fonseca was sent as Searle's emissary in direct response to Stuyvesant's overtures the previous year.[77]

Neither English nor Dutch, but rather a member of the "Hebrew nation," De Fonseca would have been an ideal intermediary. Though he most likely had lived in a Dutch territory (probably Dutch Brazil) before coming to the English island, Englishmen and Dutchmen would not have considered him to belong to either empire; he, like all Jews, would remain an outsider to most. While such a perspective led to discrimination, marginalization, and suffering, it did mean that De Fonseca could move between the two empires without posing a threat to either. In coming decades, as metropolitan restrictions on trade mounted, Jewish merchants with their international identities would prove critical to the survival and prosperity of both Dutch and English colonies. In 1655, the goods De Fonseca brought to Curaçao further reinforced the purpose of the Barbadian overture. Typically, Barbadians bought provisions from Dutch suppliers, not vice versa. It seems, then, that the precise contents of the cargo were secondary and that De Fonseca was announcing to Dutch colonists that they were ready to trade. Not content simply to await the arrival of foreign shippers, English West Indians also sought out new opportunities by blending interimperial with imperial trade.[78]

Dutch ships continued to arrive in Barbados even though they now risked seizure. Some, like the *Pearl*, which planned to carry £120,000 of merchandise on behalf of Sephardic merchants in Amsterdam to Barbados in 1657, adapted to the new mercantile situation, sailing with both English and Dutch papers so as to avoid seizure in the English West Indies. Other traders, trying to abide by the Navigation Acts, hired English ships like the *Invention of New Castle,* or English captains like William Pestell of London, who sailed the *Pauw* from Amsterdam to Barbados and then planned to take the vessel to Guinea for slaves to be sold in Barbados, or both English captains and English ships such as the *Drie Oijevaars,* skippered by William Arissz of Falmouth.[79] In 1658 alone, at least twelve Dutch vessels called at Barbados. The commander of one English man-of-war, Captain Mings, arrived in Barbados in February 1658 to find six Dutch ships anchored there. Though Mings deftly maneuvered the *Marston Moor* to seize the "Dutch shipps with their ladeing at Barbados . . . trading," he could do nothing about the circumstances that had encouraged their presence.[80] That same year, authorities captured two Dutch slavers after disembarking 253 and 191 slaves, respectively.[81] Undeterred, the next year another Dutch vessel, the *St. George,* "laden with Dutch goods" including horses, brandy, and a "Bayle of French Canvas" was trading at Barbados.[82]

Many of the post-1655 Dutch voyages to the English West Indies resembled cruising voyages that Amsterdam-based merchants had used earlier in the century. Four Dutch merchants, for example, came together to send the English *Invention* to Barbados and the rest of the Caribbean islands. The skipper was then to cruise along the North American coast and to trade with "all other free and unfree places" including Bermuda, Virginia, New Netherland, and New England as he determined best. Once he had fully exchanged his cargo of merchandise for colonial goods, he was to return to Amsterdam. The setbacks of the 1650s aside,

Dutch merchants clearly still believed there were profits to be made from English colonies; in 1660, at least eleven Dutch vessels were back trading at Barbados.[83]

Throughout the 1650s, English colonists and Dutch traders continued to collaborate despite concerted efforts to halt this trade. Though not responsible for funding the transition to sugar and only occasionally extending long-term credit, the number of Dutch ships trading in Barbados between 1640 and 1660 remained relatively consistent, with the export boom attracting more vessels than had called there in the 1630s. As we have seen, the precise number of these is unknown, but it is clear that annually between five and as many as thirty vessels from Amsterdam alone arrived in the English colony each year during these two decades. With a total of between one hundred and two hundred ships a year calling at Barbados, the proportion of Dutch shipping was, though not a majority, significant indeed.[84] Moreover, because the two years in which the highest number of Dutch vessels traded at English Caribbean colonies were those years (1651 and 1655) in which English fleets were present to seize them, it is likely that the overall level of trade in other years was higher than available sources indicate.

As significant as Barbadians believed Anglo-Dutch trade to be to their economy, many metropolitan merchants and officials rejected colonists' claims that they pursued this trade out of necessity, claiming instead that colonists were driven by avarice. The West Indies, they argued, were "well furnished by our own nation with every thing" and that colonists turned to "forraigners" only for things "not of necessary subsistence."[85] Clearly infuriated that locals continued to sometimes choose Dutch over English trade, what metropolitans missed was the unique commercial culture of the Caribbean. Even if English merchants could actually have provided all that planters demanded, as metropolitan traders claimed, it would have made no sense for them to satisfy all their needs from English markets or to, as Barbadians noted in 1651, "deny them [the Dutch] or any other Nation the freedome of our *Ports*" if they brought needed goods.[86] After all, English West Indians lived in a multinational, collaborative Atlantic community and were used to doing business with whoever offered the best prices or the most convenient timing regardless of flag. To restrict themselves to dealing with London merchants would not have fit the colonial interimperial commercial culture that had already developed by midcentury.

* * *

The 1640s and 1650s were also a period of transition for colonists living in New Netherland. Initially the structure of trade in the early Chesapeake, in which a relatively small group of London merchants controlled much of Virginia's and Maryland's trade, limited opportunities for New Amsterdam's merchants to expand their commerce. This situation began to change after 1639. First the WIC relinquished its monopoly on New Netherland's commerce, allowing independent traders to expand their economic reach from the Dutch port to Virginia, New England, and the West Indies. At the same time, mirroring changes in the Caribbean, steadily declining prices for tobacco and the outbreak of the English Civil War provided an entry for Dutch traders operating directly from Amsterdam and Rotterdam. According to one estimate, thirty-three vessels traveled from Rotterdam and Amsterdam to Virginia in 1643–49, compared with just four in the previous six years. With others surely coming from New Amsterdam, the general trend at first was for a larger metropolitan Dutch presence in Virginia's trade. Increased numbers of Dutch vessels also meant that these ships made up a greater percentage of the colonies' total trade. The Dutch trader David Pietersz. de Vries, for example, claimed that of the thirty-four vessels buying tobacco in Virginia in 1643, four of them were Dutch. On his next voyage five years later, twelve of the thirty-one ships were Dutch, with the Virginian Assembly doing much to encourage foreign trade, passing an act explicitly permitting trade in Dutch vessels in 1643.[87]

Within a decade, Parliament's imposition of an embargo on Virginia's trade, together with its authorizing of the first Navigation Act of 1651, and the outbreak of the First Anglo-Dutch War made direct Dutch trade with the Chesapeake more difficult, as the skipper of the Dutch *Goude Leeuw* (Golden Lion) found when his vessel was seized in the James River in February 1652. With ongoing warfare and increased regulations discouraging some Amsterdam and Rotterdam merchants from sending large vessels directly to the Chesapeake, they adapted by chartering nearby New Amsterdam's vessels for Chesapeake trade. Some metropolitan Dutch traders had made this transition in the Caribbean as well, but with New Amsterdam much closer to the Chesapeake than it was to the English West Indies, the practice became more widespread in North America.

For their part, Chesapeake planters welcomed the transition as they had grown accustomed to Dutch commerce. As the directors of the WIC

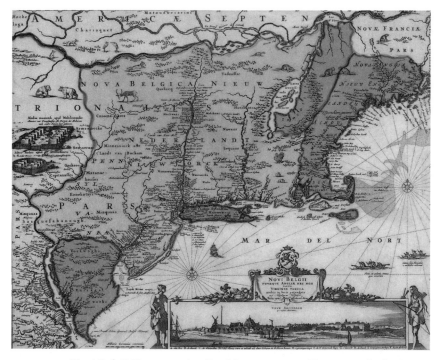

FIGURE 4. *Novi Belgii Novæque Angliæ: Nec non partis Virginiæ tabula.* Amsterdam, 1655 [1685]. This map situates New Amsterdam centrally between the Chesapeake and New England and captures its fortuitous commercial position. Courtesy of Geography and Map Division, Library of Congress.

explained in response to fears that the Navigation Acts would damage this valuable exchange, the Chesapeake–New Netherland trade would continue because "they in Virginia receive from their own nation in England no such goods as they need." This together with the higher tobacco prices Dutch traders offered English planters, they continued, would "induce the Virginians to continue their commercial relations" with New Amsterdam.[88] What the WIC directors left unsaid was that Dutch residents of New Amsterdam needed trade with surrounding English colonies as much as did English colonists. With the fur trade still largely controlled by the WIC and with the transatlantic import trade in the hands of well-capitalized traders from the metropole, locals needed any commercial opening they could find. Exacerbating residents' already weak position was the outbreak of Kieft's War (1643–45), a conflict with Native Americans that threatened to destroy the colony. In this environment, the ability of traders to expand their role in surrounding English colonies would prove vital to the city's continued success.

Active in Virginia as early as the 1630s, New Amsterdam–based merchants, working as representatives of Amsterdam companies and for themselves, were well placed to cultivate trading relationships with Chesapeake planters. A shuttle traffic in tobacco soon developed between the two locations, with Virginian and New Netherland traders bringing small cargoes of tobacco to the Dutch colonial port, where it was warehoused before being shipped to the Dutch Republic. Meanwhile, European manufactures stockpiled in New Amsterdam passed in the opposite direction to Virginia and Maryland. It was in these years that the prominent tobacco-trading Verbrugge family ended its direct trade between Amsterdam and Virginia and instead began to rely upon Dutch and English factors living in New Amsterdam and Virginia to direct their trade. These men, such as Govert Loockermans, soon learned to use "a small fleet of coastal ships built especially to bring 'Virginia leaves' to New Amsterdam" to navigate the bay's intricate waterways.[89]

As Dutch merchants in Manhattan sensed growing opportunity in the coastal trade, they mobilized to win further inducements for trade. Speaking through the Nine Men—an advisory body Stuyvesant established in 1648 to give local residents a voice in civil law—New Amsterdamers, led by Cornelis Melyn and Adriaen van der Donck, appealed to the States-General in Amsterdam for greater local commercial autonomy. Chief among the reforms they advocated were that the WIC allow "returns in Tobacco shipped hence [New Amsterdam], [to] be exempt from all duties." Meanwhile, to bolster exports, Manhattan's merchant community also called for "permission to export, sell, and barter grain, timber and all other wares and merchandise the produce of the Country, every way and every where your High Mightinesses have allies."[90] Partly responding to these petitions and hoping to encourage economic development in the face of increased English competition, the directors of the WIC decided in 1651 to reverse earlier policies and allow "all goods sent there [New England and Virginia] from *New Netherland*" to "pass duty free."[91] It was in these same years that Stuyvesant, responding to constant pleas from the WIC and rising New Amsterdam traders to encourage trade with surrounding English colonies, negotiated the free trade pact with Virginia that served as a model for his efforts in Barbados. He also proposed to John Winthrop that the men work to make sure that all "trafffick trade & commerce" between Massachusetts and New Netherland continue "without molestation or disturbance."[92] To raise

Amsterdam merchants' confidence in the quality of New Amsterdam's reshipped tobacco, the city government worked to regulate the quality of tobacco exported from New Netherland, developing a four-category scale that rated tobacco from good to "not even . . . poor." Such a system both pleased established Dutch traders and, because standardization limited risk for buyers in Europe, encouraged new merchants without metropolitan contacts or reputations to enter the tobacco trade.[93] In all, the efforts of civic government and Stuyvesant cemented New Amsterdam's place as a reliable regional entrepôt.

Prompted by lower taxes, a regulatory system that rated tobacco, and free trade negotiations, many of New Amsterdam's traders began to venture their own vessels to the Chesapeake, bringing textiles, metal goods, wine, meats, and flour to exchange for tobacco and hides that they would reexport to Amsterdam. By the mid-1650s, Manhattan merchants had also begun to import slaves from Curaçao (the two colonies shared a single director-general) to offer to Chesapeake planters desperate for labor.[94] Some merchants such as Nicholaes Boot traveled to Virginia themselves to collect tobacco for transport to Amsterdam. To find sufficient stores, many employed the method used by De Vries two decades earlier, cruising along the Chesapeake's rivers and bays to assemble a cargo. Over time, New Amsterdam traders progressed from waterside exchange to form lasting trading relationships with English planters and middlemen just as merchants had done in the Caribbean.[95] Alternatively, some Dutch New Amsterdamers hired English agents to gather tobacco and send it to them either on their own vessels or on those chartered by English planters. Richard Ary and Co., for example, shipped tobacco from Virginia to New Amsterdam, where they sold it to Loockermans, who often worked for the Amsterdam-based Verbrugge family. At a later date, New Amsterdam's Thomas Wandalls hired the English Ary to take his bark, *The Providence,* to Virginia to collect 1,600 pounds of tobacco due to him from Mr. John Barbar.[96] Likewise, the Maryland planter Samuel Smith was tied to at least two different New Amsterdam merchants, Cornelis Steenwyck and Frederick Gysberts. From these two men, Smith purchased cloth, nails, axes, and other dry goods, and repaid his debts in tobacco that he delivered at New Amsterdam.[97] The involvement of Steenwyck in the tobacco trade is important because it illustrates how appealing the coastal trade was to prominent traders. Steenwyck arrived in New Amsterdam as a member of the WIC and was well connected to the wealthy Amsterdam merchant Gillis Van Hoornbeeck. By 1654, Steenwyck had begun partnering with two fellow

New Amsterdam merchants, Johannes Verbrugge (who was the nephew of Amsterdam's Gillis Verbrugge) and Nicholas Varlet (who was married to Stuyvesant's sister, the widow Anna Stuyvesant Bayard) in the Virginia tobacco trade. One of the Virginia partners with whom these men contracted was James Mill, whom they routinely hired over the course of almost a decade to ferry tobacco to New Amsterdam.[98] Often requiring multiple nodes of contact with European traders, their representatives in New Amsterdam, a Virginian agent, and English planters, the New Amsterdam–Chesapeake trade of the 1640s and 1650s was thoroughly interimperial.

By 1662, this trade drew the ire of the English Council for Foreign Plantations, which decried the practice of planters selling their tobacco "to the plantacôns of the Dutch lyeing contiguous to Delewar Bay and the Manhatoes."[99] Meanwhile, the Council of Maryland noted that it dare not provoke a war with the Dutch at New Amstel (on the Delaware River) because they could not guarantee the support of Chesapeake planters in such a conflict; "the Dutch Trade" was "the Darling of the People of Virginia as well as this Province [Maryland] and indeed all other Plantacons of the English."[100] The close proximity of Dutch colonial ports to Chesapeake plantations and the diffuse nature of English settlement there fostered the shuttle trade and meant that most Dutch traders from New Amsterdam did not necessarily find it imperative to build warehouses in Virginia or Maryland as they had in the Leeward Islands, though they played a similar role in the region's trade. At the same time, this arrangement was difficult for authorities to control.

As New Netherland traders profited from the Chesapeake trade, they also looked to the north and east for other markets. New Englanders were not looking to export tobacco, but rather to import manufactured goods, which Manhattan merchants were well placed to bring them. The struggling colony of Rhode Island formally acknowledged this in 1642, when local officials declared that "the Governour and Deputie shall treat with the Governor of the Dutch to supply us with necessaries, and to take of our commodities at such rates as may be suitable." With transatlantic commerce disrupted, Manhattan merchants found opportunity in New England as they had in the Chesapeake during the 1640s and 1650s.[101]

New Amsterdam merchants traveled regularly to English colonies, which encouraged them to form strong interimperial alliances. In time, colonists thought of these alliances as a single regional network of mutually benefiting peoples, regardless of metropolitan efforts to keep them apart. It is possible to reconstruct in detail the commercial connections of at least one such merchant. Probably born in Bohemia in 1621, Augustine Herrman arrived in New Amsterdam in June 1644 as a representative of the Amsterdam trading firm Peter Gabry & Sons. Quickly he purchased property in New Amsterdam and began to trade on his own account to Virginia, Maryland, New England, and the Dutch and English Caribbean. The Bohemian-born Herrman was a prolific trader between the Chesapeake and New Netherland from the 1640s to the end of the 1660s. Herrman utilized his Amsterdam connections to variously supply salt, horses, slaves, manufactured goods, and lumber to Virginian correspondents, including Anna Varlet Hack (Nicholas Varlet's sister) and her husband, the German-born Dr. George Hack, and worked with Varlet, Paulus Leenderstsen, and Allert Anthony of New Amsterdam. For at least a decade, the Dutch-born Virginia resident Anna Varlet Hack, who traded on her own account, was particularly important to Herrman's success in securing stocks of tobacco, and eventually he married Anna's sister Jannetje, solidifying the two families' commercial ties. Buying tobacco from a wide range of Chesapeake planters, Herrman then transported the leaf to New Amsterdam, where he sold much of it to other New Amsterdam traders such as Joost Van Beeck.[102]

Seeking to stabilize his access to tobacco, Herrman eventually acquired land in Maryland near the Hacks' property along with letters of denization (the legal right to trade as an Englishman) from Lord Baltimore, an accommodation Herrman gained partly through the relationship he established with Baltimore's half-brother Philip Calvert when Herrman served as a Dutch representative in a 1659 boundary dispute between New Netherland and Maryland.[103] Herrman did not remain permanently in Maryland, but instead used his connections to facilitate trade between the two colonies.[104] Eventually Herrman bought land in Virginia and even applied for denization in that colony as well. By connecting resource-starved Chesapeake planters to Dutch markets, and vice versa, New Amsterdam and Chesapeake traders such as Herrman helped build mutually beneficial interimperial alliances that lay a foundation of cross-national commercial cooperation.

As important as coastwise trade was to merchants like Herrman, the 1650s also brought opportunities for New Amsterdam merchants' trade with the Dutch and English Caribbean. Conquered from the Spanish in 1634, the island colony of Curaçao became the Dutch West India Company's major way station for Caribbean trade in the seventeenth century. The colony struggled to survive in its early years, but the Treaty of

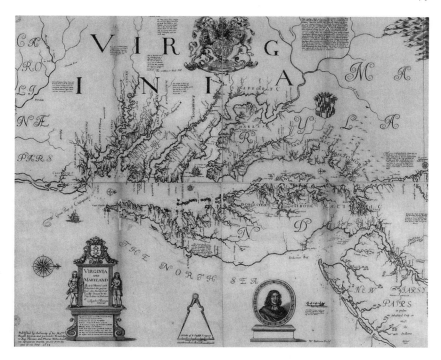

FIGURE 5. Augustine Herrman, *Virginia and Maryland As it is Planted and Inhabited this present Year 1670 Surveyed and Exactly Drawne by the Only Labour & Endeavour of Augustin Herrman Bohemiensis; W. Faithorne, sculpt,* 1673, London. The New Amsterdam trader Augustine Herrman travelled widely enough in the Chesapeake to produce this detailed map. Courtesy of Geography and Map Division, Library of Congress.

Munster (1648) ended the long struggle between Spain and the Dutch Republic and initiated a period of expansion for what was then a mostly deserted island with a good deepwater harbor. After 1662, when Dutch merchants gained a monopoly to supply slaves to Spanish colonies (the *asientio*), Curaçao became the jewel of the Dutch Caribbean as traders there organized a direct trade to Spanish colonies along the northern and northwestern coast of South America. Transatlantic vessels called at Curaçao to disembark their cargoes and pick up goods that had been collected by traders who employed a variety of small vessels to traffic both legally and illegally with the Spanish American colonies. The island's chief port, Willemstad, was soon a cosmopolitan place where "financial institutions were established[,] . . . ships were repaired and fitted out, bought and sold, and sailors were enlisted for voyages to all parts of the West Indies."[105]

Critical to Curaçao's success as a trading depot was the steady supply of foodstuffs and other resources necessary for supporting such a vibrant trading center. From its earliest designs, the WIC had envisioned New Netherland and Curaçao as interdependent, with New Netherland offering a naval base and supplying foodstuffs to the island, and Curaçao reexporting plantation commodities such as dyewoods and salt to New Amsterdam for reshipment to Europe. At first, though, New Netherland struggled to fulfill its role as a provision supplier despite the island government's pleadings.[106] As Curaçao's population swelled, these demands only increased, and to better integrate the two outposts, the WIC brought them under a unified administration (with Aruba and Bonaire) in 1648, though Curaçao retained significant autonomy with its own vice director.[107] These changes worked, and as New Netherland developed during the 1650s and 1660s, New Amsterdam traders such as Johannes Verbrugge, Gerrit van Tricht, Jacobus Backer, and Augustine Herrman established connections with the Dutch island.[108] These connections, and the discovery of how to make the Curaçao trade profitable, endured after the English occupation of New Amsterdam and thus continued to provide an opening for profit through the end of the seventeenth century.

Curaçao, however, was not the only attraction in the Caribbean for residents of New Netherland. New Amsterdam merchants sometimes included English colonies in their trading spheres as the Verbrugges had done in St Christopher. In October 1649, for example, Nicolaas Blancke, supercargo of the *St. Pieter*, sailed from New Amsterdam to Curaçao with a parcel of serge and linen that he exchanged for twenty-four horses at Curaçao. Once there, he discovered an unexpected trading opportunity in the English Leeward Islands and carried the horses to Antigua.[109] Ten years later, Herrman served as the supercargo on the *Niew Amstel*, a vessel that traded between Curaçao and New Amsterdam and included a stop at St. Christopher. Before departing Curaçao for New Amsterdam on May 16, 1658, Captain Jacob Jansen Huys recorded that he carried "twenty-four thousand pounds of dyewood and seven barrels of Caribbean sugar weighing altogether three thousand seven hundred and eighty-nine pounds" on behalf of the company. The vessel also contained smaller shipments from private traders including nearly 4,500 pounds of sugar and 68 pounds of cotton laden at St. Christopher by Herrman for Nicholas Varlet and Company. On his return voyage, Huys also stopped at New Amstel and loaded furs for New Amsterdam.[110] Six years later,

Huys again called at St. Christopher, this time while guiding *De Ver-gulde Vos* between Curaçao and New Amsterdam. Trading on behalf of the WIC, the skipper sold nineteen horses worth 23,660 pounds of muscovado sugar to planters there. *De Vergulde Vos* then carried 5,416 pounds of sugar packed into five half hogsheads, five full hogsheads, one *aem* [40 gallons], one chest, and one pipe to New Netherland.[111] Most likely motivating the organizers of both these voyages was the belief that "Caribbean muscovado sugar can be sold there [New Amsterdam] at a higher price than even in Holland."[112]

Proximity to myriad trading opportunities was one of the chief reasons for the establishment of New Netherland, and residents heralded these opportunities. In his 1656 *A Description of New Netherland*, Adriaen Van der Donck, a legal scholar trained in Leiden who arrived in the colony in the summer of 1641, offered a contemporary view of how the North Atlantic world appeared to New Amsterdam's residents. Van der Donck presents a city poised in prime position to harness the trading potential of the lands that surrounded it. Foremost in his account, Van der Donck noted the many navigable rivers "extending far inland, by which the productions of the Country can be brought to place of traffic." But it was not just the trade with Native Americans in the interior that made New Netherland so valuable. What was vital for the city's success, as Van der Donck indicated, was that the "Country is convenient to the Sea," and was "within four or five days sail" to Canada and New England in the north and to the "South West" was similar distance from "Virginia, which affords . . . a profitable tobacco trade," and Florida. Just a bit farther afield, Van der Docnk continued, were "the Bahamas, and the other Continent & West India Islands, upon which reliance may be made." In the account, part of which is set up as a dialogue between a "New Netherlander" and a "Patriot," the Patriot questions the ability of Manhattan merchants to exploit all these places because "those ports and harbors are shut against us [the Dutch] on every side." Dismissing this pesky detail, the colonist replied that "in New Netherland we have good courage," and thus "we will be able to drive a profitable trade . . . to those places, we have the means, and they cannot easily hinder us," especially since traders could utilize Curaçao, laying within sight of the Spanish Main and close by the rest of the Caribbean, as a way station.[113] Van der Donck's Atlantic, like Herrman's, was a place of virtually limitless opportunity for interimperial trade, where vessels trading from New Amsterdam bringing needed goods at low prices would always be welcome. While there are borders in his account, these are permeable boundaries that European authorities could make solid, especially when locals demanded access to commercially powerful New Netherland merchants. Left unstated were the efforts of English colonists, who worked to attract and trade with Dutch merchants arriving at their colonies.

By midcentury, New Amsterdam merchants had taken advantage of disruptions to English trade, the weakness of English regulation, and growing markets to assemble a trading network that stretched from that city into the interior along the Hudson River, to bordering English colonies to the north and to the south, and finally south across the sea to the Caribbean. In turn, many of these traders were connected across the Atlantic to firms in the Dutch Republic, either directly or through the markets of New Amsterdam. These city merchants' opportunistic responses to the ending of the WIC's trade monopoly and to new opportunities in Curaçao were critical in the port's evolution; but so too were these men's willingness and ability to respond to the markets that larger Atlantic forces created. Ultimately, these early experiences prompted them to force the eventual English conquerors of New Amsterdam to adapt their commercial ideology to this distinct commercial outlook.

* * *

The 1640s and 1650s were decades of adjustment as the English Civil War, falling tobacco prices, the introduction of new crops, rising intercolonial demand for necessary goods, political instability in England, and metropolitan attempts to reshape the English empire forced colonists living in the English West Indies and in Dutch New Netherland to adapt to new situations. Their common experience on the periphery of their respective empires drove Dutch and English settlers alike to realize that their very survival and success depended on creatively maintaining cross-national trade. In the Leeward Islands, planters reacted to larger forces by deepening their relationships with Dutch traders, while in Barbados, colonists who had better access to credit in England increasingly sought out a more flexible system of direct exchange. In both places, colonists defended Dutch trade and clashed with metropolitan officials trying to end it. In New Netherland, colonists experienced the 1640s and 1650s not as a period of challenge, but as one of new opportunities. Nonetheless, these decades were still profoundly consequential as traders there exploited English weakness to expand their cross-national trade. Meanwhile, in England, merchants and statesmen were becoming increasingly frustrated by the detrimental effects Dutch trade was having on their plans for empire. Committed to removing the Dutch and co-opting their commercial networks for themselves, administrators found that trade laws and warfare were ineffective in ending interimperial trade because they could not displace colonists' commercial needs and habits. As war drove the Dutch and English further apart elsewhere, cross-national ties forged during the first three tumultuous decades of settlement and confirmed in the years after would prove vital to continued Atlantic success despite the hardening of imperial boundaries with the ascension to the English throne of another Stuart king in 1660.

PART TWO

ACHIEVING STABILITY, 1660–1689

3 / Mercantilist Goals and Colonial Needs: Interimperial Trade amidst War and Crisis

Burdened by the disruptions in trade that the just-completed Second Anglo-Dutch War (1665–67) had caused as well as the need to provision a larger than usual garrison of English troops and an influx of refugees fleeing the French invasion of St. Christopher, Nevis was on the verge of disaster in the fall of 1668. With many on the island reduced to eating "the hearbs of the soile boyled wth salt only," Governor James Russell received word from the masters of three vessels—two Dutch and one French—who understood "too well" the colony's "wants" that they were willing to offer Nevis "a Supply of Provisions & other refreshments." The only requirement the foreign traders demanded in return was that they be granted "freedom from seizure" so "that they might as freely go as Come." Knowing that violating the Navigation Acts in order to allow foreign traders into Nevis was "a matter of weight," Russell appealed to the island's military commander, Sir Thomas Bridge, and the Assembly for advice. Bridge, a veteran of the English Civil War, objected to the foreign trade, evidently telling Russell that it was unacceptable to turn to their "enemies" for supply. The Assembly, however, decided that "entertainment should be given to" the "offer . . . as . . . [they] knew no other" way to supply the island. Realizing their decision would displease the king, Russell wrote to him admitting that he and the islanders were "Breakers of the Act of trade and Navigation" and "Implor[ing] ye Majesty's Gratious Pardon." The newly installed governor of the entire Leewards, William Lord Willoughby, intervened to defend Russell and urged authorities to consider the "necessity of the occasion" that had made interimperial commerce imperative.[1]

Russell's decision to permit Dutch and French vessels into Nevis in this moment of crisis is evidence of the continued availability and desirability of interimperial trade in the late 1660s. At the same time, it exposes the disjuncture between metropolitan aims and colonial practice. Suffering the effects of England's latest mercantilist war against the Dutch, it made sense for the governor and the island's community to turn to Dutch traders who had been active at his colony for four decades even though such a decision clearly ran counter to English imperial goals. After all, the decision to exclude foreign trade at the island had come not from the colony but from officials in a distant metropole where efforts to crush Dutchmen's ability to interfere with English colonial trade seemed to be a natural response to Dutch commercial dominance.

Articulated first in the 1650s in response to the first Act of Trade and Navigation, the Anglo-Dutch conflict gained new resonance during the 1660s as metropolitan merchants working with and through Charles II and Parliament imposed a series of new trade laws targeting the Dutch that they hoped would harness the expanding empire's commerce for the needs of the expanding fiscal-military state. When these new restrictions combined with a variety of crises—ranging from warfare to hurricanes—threatened colonial success, planter-controlled assemblies, councils, and their governors reacted by working to retain control over their commercial decisions. As William Willoughby had noted in 1668, one of colonists' major complaints with the Navigation Acts was that they were monolithic and did not take the "necessity of the occasion" into account and so limited colonists' options in guiding their own success. For colonists who remained vulnerable to starvation and invasion, the lack of commercial options was a real danger.

The conflict between local custom and metropolitan expectations was an especially pressing issue in 1664, when the English captured New Netherland. Hoping to eliminate the presence of a regional Dutch entrepôt, Charles II also believed that conquering New Netherland would solidify and unify his North American empire, making the whole stronger. But Dutch inhabitants fought to maintain the commercial connections that bound them to the Dutch Republic. In this way, they resembled English West Indians in rejecting metropolitan efforts to shape distant colonies. What English authorities would find in both the Caribbean and New Netherland was that because they failed to appreciate the circumstances behind continued cross-national trade, their very efforts to create an exclusive English empire through laws and warfare actually drove colonists to hold tightly to interimperial connections by creating economic scarcity and instability. Examining colonists' formal (through petitioning) and informal (through the maintenance of Anglo-Dutch trade) responses to new articulations of state control over trade shows the ways an enduring colonial-specific commercial culture that prized openness and free trade competed with new mercantilist ideas. This interimperial culture was one of the key legacies of Anglo-Dutch trade in the seventeenth century. The 1660s were critical years in which Englishmen in the colonies and the metropole worked out their competing, and still evolving, visions of empire.

* * *

When Charles II finally assumed what he regarded as his rightful throne in 1660, he inherited a very different empire than his father had lost. Whereas two decades before the colonies had been sparsely settled and poorly developed, by 1660 they had growing populations that lived on richly cultivated plantations. This development was most notable in Barbados, where the population had risen from an estimated 14,000 residents (nearly all of them white) in 1640 to about 53,300 residents. Much of this increase was associated with the sugar boom. Between 1650 and 1660, planters desperate for ever-more labor capitalized on the continued evolution of the Atlantic slave trade to import more than 3,000 slaves per year so that, by 1660, more than half of Barbados's population was enslaved. Testifying to the brutal conditions slaves endured, these staggering quantities of new arrivals only raised the enslaved population from 12,800 in 1650 to 27,100 in 1660. In these same years, planters perfected the cultivation of sugarcane, learned new processing techniques, and adopted new mill technologies. As Europeans' demand for sugar grew, planters were able to keep pace, doubling their production between 1651 and 1663 and reaping the extra profits that increased sales offered. The Leeward Islands had not achieved the same success or stability that Barbados had by 1660, but planters there were still wealthier than they had been in 1640, especially those few on Nevis and Antigua who had begun to plant sugarcane. With sugar production driving development, by 1660 the West Indies had become the most promising part of the English Atlantic empire.[2]

Not yet expanding as rapidly as it would after 1680 or as quickly as in the West Indies, the English economy nevertheless showed signs of promise by 1660. Though the new king was saddled with debt and was constantly wary of schemes to undermine his government, he ruled over a country primed to grow. Hoping to push England forward and to solidify his authority, Charles II and his councilors worked to found more colonies in the Western Hemisphere and to encourage those already there. Buoyed by a still troubled but expanding domestic economy, a generation of experience in Atlantic trade, and rising colonial demand for manufactures, English merchants, too, found improved opportunities for success in Atlantic trade. Colonial and domestic developments worked together, with English merchants profiting from expanded production in the colonies and colonists benefiting from greater metropolitan investment.[3]

As a means of protecting and extending these advances, a combination of disparate interests united during the 1660s to support policies which could use the power of the government to promote shipping and to secure metropolitan control over the colonies. Supported by merchants looking for state protection, military interests eager to blunt European challengers, a public concerned with the threat the Dutch Republic posed, and a monarch looking to validate and consolidate his empire, Charles II and Parliament passed (or reaffirmed) several new trade laws, chartered the Royal African Company (1660), rejected calls to return the colonies to proprietorships, and prepared to fight for control of the seas. Though not coherent enough to be categorized as "'policy' as distinct from 'decisions,'" and characterized more by pragmatism than by unified theory, the mercantilist steps these communities of interest took in the 1660s were consistent in their aim to strengthen the empire by making "the forraigne Plantations . . . [more] useful to the Trade & navigation" of England. This would never be possible, though, until they eliminated the Dutch from their role as "the general magazine of all Europe" and "the common Carriers of the World." And since most Englishmen agreed, as Samuel Pepys famously quipped to his diary, "the trade of the world is too little for us two [England and the Dutch Republic] . . . one must [be forced] down."[4]

Authorities' mercantilist understanding is most clear in the two new commercial laws Parliament passed, the Act of Trade and Navigation in 1660 and the Staple Act (also known as the Act of 1663). These laws forcefully asserted the notion set forth by the Acts of 1650 and 1651: colonial trade should benefit the state first. These laws mandated that all goods shipped to English colonies from foreign places must pass through England (except horses, which could come from Ireland, and wine and salt, which could come directly from southern Europe) and that certain "enumerated" goods (chiefly colonial produce) be sent first to England, Ireland, Wales, or Berwick before being reexported to foreign ports. In addition to governing the direction of trade to and from the colonies, the Act of 1660 and the Staple Act also reinforced earlier laws mandating that trade between the colonies and England be confined to English or colonial vessels. Merchants and government ministers believed these trade statutes were necessary to capture the invisible profits from freight, commissions, and insurance that the sugar boom generated; to compete commercially with the Dutch; and to raise revenue for the financially strapped monarch.[5] These laws made it clear that, as William Wood phrased it, the "Colonies and Plantations" did not exist for themselves but as "a Spring of Wealth" for England. They "work for us, and their Treasure centers here."[6] If administrators could achieve all of these things and make English shipping competitive with Dutch, then, in the famous words of George Downing, "good night Amsterdam."[7]

Reinforcing this legislation, the Restoration government also moved to better compete with the Dutch WIC's dominance of the Atlantic slave trade by granting a monopoly on West African trade to the Royal African Company (RAC). Replacing two poorly capitalized and ineffective predecessors—the Guinea Company and the Royal Adventurers Trading into Africa—the RAC and the support it received from the Crown and courtiers provided a stable body to govern England's slave trade. From the perspective of those hoping to build an exclusive English Atlantic, domestic control over the slave trade was essential not only because it was among the most profitable transatlantic trades but also because it was essential to supporting the agricultural empire. To leave it in Dutch hands, therefore, was to both allow a vast array of profits to seep beyond the empire and to allow others indirect control over the shape of colonial development.[8]

Coinciding with efforts to increase the scope of English mercantile regulations and to continue their offensive on the Dutch carrying trade, Parliament and the Crown also worked to bring the management of colonial affairs under closer and more efficient control. To correct what metropolitan officials saw as a chaotic and negligent situation, the Restoration government established a series of new committees to oversee the commercial regulation and management of the colonies, including, most significantly, a Council of Trade and Plantations, which sat from 1660 to 1665. Though the Council of Trade and Plantations did not have exclusive control of colonial policy, its formation was another clear sign that the Stuarts intended for colonial affairs to be dealt with from England.[9]

To further ensure the fulfillment of their commercial goals in Barbados and the Leeward Islands, the council followed the lead of the Commonwealth government and advised the king to assume royal control of those islands, stripping Francis, Lord Willoughby, the proprietary patent holder, of his lands and special rights. In order to pacify Willoughby, they named him governor of Barbados and the Leeward Islands but made it clear his authority was derived from the Crown.[10] Finally, the council announced their commitment to stopping illegal trade by making it clear to their governors that they were responsible for enforcing the regulations, recording all ships and their cargoes upon their entering and leaving colonial ports, and returning these lists and all bonds to London promptly. Frequent circular letters sent to all the governors served to remind them of their duties.[11]

As merchants and bureaucrats attempted to reform colonial and commercial policy to preclude Dutch competition in the colonies, some within the government, led by George Downing and the former secretary of state John Thurloe, pushed Charles II to reinforce these laws by going to war against the Dutch. At first able to deflect these exhortations in favor of pursing negotiations, the signing of a Franco-Dutch defense pact in 1662 convinced the king that if he did not act against the United Provinces, England could face an alliance between their three rivals: France, Spain, and the United Provinces. Adding to English fears of a united Europe was the acknowledgment that after a decade, the Navigation Acts had failed to stifle Dutch trade in Africa, the Caribbean, and the East Indies. When Dutch ambassadors renewed their request that England repeal the Navigation Acts, they further enflamed those who had come to believe that the only option to extend English interests and to prevent Dutch commercial hegemony was to use England's superior naval power to strike against Dutch interests. Negotiations, according to Thurloe, were no longer useful because the Dutch were unreasonable, even going so far as to complain that "the English doe fetch and carry their goods themselves, to and from their own Country, in their own ships, and not make use of the Dutch to doe it." When Charles authorized a 1662 expedition against Dutch forts in West Africa, he provoked the Dutch into a devastating response against British interests there. English public opinion quickly turned against "the Hollanders," who many now feared were trying to leverage their economic power into political domination. As the public clamored for war, Charles II relented and in 1664 sparked the Second Anglo-Dutch War (1665–67) by sending a squadron to capture New Netherland. Knowing that the war posed great hazards for their own trade, Dutch leaders, frustrated by English aggressiveness, nevertheless rose to the English bait and retaliated.[12]

Though they played little role in its inauguration, British and Dutch colonists in the Americas suffered from the conflict; not only did the war disrupt transatlantic shipping, but it also led colonists to experience warfare firsthand, with the English capturing New Netherland, the Dutch attacking Barbados, and the Dutch ally France invading St. Christopher, Antigua, and Montserrat. When combined with the effects of new trade laws, the war between the Dutch and British proved potentially disastrous to colonists relishing recent success, and they moved quickly to moderate its effects. Whereas the 1660s were a decade in which the Restoration government moved decisively to remove Dutch trade from the English Atlantic, the same years saw colonists decide they would work just as intently to preserve their Anglo-Dutch ties and to protect local control over the economy. This collective colonial response was only partly a result of the colonies' interimperial economic culture. It was also product of mercantilism itself. As England mobilized to fight Dutch trade through legislation and warfare, in the short run these actions produced trade shortages and economic crises which encouraged colonists to hold tightly to Dutch trade, exactly the opposite effect from what authorities had intended. As had been the case in the 1650s, local conditions and habits would continue to define how English mercantilism worked at the periphery.

In formulating their responses to these new articulations of state power, English West Indians drew upon their early difficult history. This past had taught them that, in order to be successful in the dangerous Caribbean, they needed a commercial policy that allowed adaptation and flexibility. One of the earliest and clearest statements of this developing colonial-economic ideology emerged from the Barbados Council and Assembly's protests of the 1650 embargo and the first Act of Trade and Navigation. Among the most important of these was a pamphlet published in The Hague called *A Declaration Set forth by the Lord Lieutenant Generall and the Gentlemen of the Councell & Assembly occasioned from the view of a printed paper entituled An Act Prohibiting trade with the Barbados, Virginea, Bermudes and Antegoe* (1651). In this work, islanders claimed that they would not abide by the law's restrictions, especially those prohibiting "*all Forraigners . . . from holding any commerce with the inhabitants of this Island.*" Such an expectation was unreasonable, they wrote, because "all the old *Planters* well know how much they have ben houlding to the *Dutch* for their subsistence, and how difficult it would have ben (without their assistances) ever to have settled this place." Moreover, the Barbados Council and Assembly argued, they would not "be so ungratefull to the *Dutch* for former help as to deny them or any other Nation the freedome of our *Ports* and *Protection* of our laws," particularly since the colonists were still "sensible [to] what necessary comforts they [the Dutch] bring us and how much cheaper they sell their *Commodities* to us then our own nation." Relying on their experience with Anglo-Dutch trade, colonists contended that ties to Dutch traders were so fundamental that they could "not imagine that there is so meane & base minded a fellow amongst us, that will not prefer . . . an honorable *Dutch*, before being bound by the regulations of the *Parliament*."[13] Echoing his fellow colonists, Governor Searle explained to the Council of State that, before 1651, "the trade of this island [Barbados] formerly . . . was most of all carried on by the Dutch," but the act had caused "some scarcity & want of commodityes." Several years later, another group of Caribbean planters noted that they had "in their greatest Streights found reliefe and advantage by foreigners." Surely overstating their position for effect, at the heart of Searle's and the planters' claims was the idea that the flexibility which free trade allowed was necessary for colonial development.[14]

In making their argument, the leading planter-merchants of Barbados celebrated the positive consequences of their previous contact with the Dutch, defended their Englishness, and questioned the legitimacy of the Parliament's authority over them. In so doing, they presented the beginning of an evolving colonial position. As locals, this argument held, they could make more accurate decisions about the islands' economic needs since it was *they* who, "with great hazard of *persons* and . . . great *cost* and *charges* . . . setled and inhabited this place," not a distant Parliament, a body in which they had "no *representatives* no *persons* there chosen [by them]." And because they had lived in the colonies, it was only they and "all the old *Planters*" among them who could understand the Dutch contribution to their success.[15] As Carla Gardina Pestana has recently argued, Barbadians combined this sense of local knowledge with "their rights as freeborn English men" to claim the authority "to govern the island and decide its policies."[16] In this early argument, islanders found that by marshaling their political authority, they could call for "free Commerce & Trade both at home & abroad," as was the liberty and freedom of all "true *Englishmen*."[17] By tying their pleas to past experience, West Indians were also highlighting the conservativism of their position. In trying to protect past relationships, they simply wanted to maintain the status quo as they had tried to do during the Civil War. It was Cromwell and the Parliament that were attempting to reshape the Atlantic by displacing colonists' long history of interimperial collaboration.

When confronted with the Restoration government's similar actions a decade later, colonists drew upon their earlier arguments. In the spring of 1661, the Council and Assembly of Barbados explained the effects they feared the new Navigation Act would have on their colony. First, they believed it would reduce the price of their main export. "If all the commodities of the island be by the new Act forced into one market," they wrote, "the result will be a glut, and a still further fall in the value of sugar." Second, islanders warned that confining trade to English vessels would mean that "the prices of servants, negroes, cattle, horses and dry goods" would double, a situation that "would not only be the ruin of the petitioners, but also in a great measure ruin the stock, navigation, and shipping of England, as also to the King's revenue of customs."[18] One sympathizer explained the effect this regulation would ultimately have on the plantations by juxtaposing the current climate and its potentially disastrous economic consequences with that of the 1640s, when settlers enjoyed free trade to the benefit of the English colonies and the empire alike:

In the growth & formerly flourishing condition of the Colonys[,] the Planters in the West Indies, had freedom of Trade with all nations in Amity with England by means whereof they bought the supplyes for their plantations on cheape terms & sent their Sugers & c to the best Marketts, so that . . . the English Planter was able so far to undersell the Planter of Brasill that the colony [Brazil] shrunke in a few yeares from sending 70000 Chests of suger annually into Europe to less than 20000 to the very great decay of the Navigation & Revenue of that [Portuguese and then Dutch] Crowne. . . . [B]ut these priviledges which made the English Colonys flourish so much & proved so destructive to Brasille the English planter is now debarred of by the act of Navigation. . . . [O]ne Cause of the said act seems very grievous for that an English planter or Merchant cannot send an English ship sailed by English Master & Mariners from any part of Europe the freights & c with a supply for his plantations use of the growthe of those Countrys untill that ship hath first returned

into England & there unloaded & paid a Custome for the goods
on board. . . . [But that] Custome doth in no measure accompence
[compensate] his Majesty [for] or Balance the losse he sustaines in
the visible decay of his Colonys neither is the Custome the tenth
parte of the damage the planter sustaines thereby for that the losse
of time the paying a double fraught a double adventure together
with the decay & damage those goods doe sustaine doth infinitly
surmounte his Majesty's duty & no man is the better for this losse.[19]

Evoking the destruction of the colony as the outcome of restrictive
laws, this writer recognized the potential pitfalls that the new acts
of trade created in favoring metropolitan over peripheral interests.
In warning that their effects would make sugar production unprofitable, he suggested the trade regulations might fail to increase national
wealth because they would make sugar scarce by driving up the costs
of planting. Without a steady supply of cheap tropical commodities,
England would not be able to balance its trade with Europe, and the
wealth of the empire would diminish despite a small increase in customs revenues.

Full of rhetorical flourishes and overstated conclusions, petitions such
as this one nevertheless reflected legitimate concerns. After Parliament
passed the first Navigation Act in 1651, many Barbadians had suffered as
some English merchants took advantage of the protected market that the
act created by charging "unconscionable rates" for imports. This price
gouging, according to one settler, gave these English merchants profits as
high as "three for one."[20] Less Dutch competition meant opportunity for
those traders tied most closely to England, but it caused higher prices for
many others, who noted that before the new trade law, "they bought their
Negroes, Horses and other necessaries and provisions cheaper by more
than one halfe of ye present price." Meanwhile, planters continued, confining sugar to English markets had the opposite effect on sugar prices,
forcing them downward. Planters wailed that they had received roughly
thirty shillings per hundredweight for their sugar before the trade laws
and only fifteen shillings for the same quantity by 1661. With English
merchants enjoying both a protected market for trade and shipping services, the Navigation Acts also meant that planters feared they would
face higher transactions costs. This would be especially true on goods
that colonists had previously purchased from the Dutch Republic, on
which colonists now feared they would pay "double fraight [and] double
adventure [insurance]." That these items would now have to pass through

England meant additional port charges and duties that merchants could pass along to colonial consumers.[21]

Meanwhile, even as the state legislated support for English shippers, colonists found that there still "was just not enough authorized shipping in existence to carry all he [the planter] could produce" and, especially, consume.[22] The combined effects of warfare with the Dutch and Spanish in the 1650s left an already underdeveloped English mercantile fleet badly damaged, forcing colonists to turn to foreigners to meet their needs for shipping. One estimate holds that the number of ships calling at Barbados each year actually fell from 400 to 150 following the imposition of the 1651 Act of Trade, resulting in an overall decline of one-third for both imports and exports.[23] In the years after the Act of 1660, colonists experienced a similar problem. Falling sugar prices further decreased trade because they made English merchants unwilling to send goods to the island. "Sugar is at so low a rate," the Council of Barbados noted in July 1661, "that the merchants bring noe Commoditiyes" here but "emptie shipps only to fraight away our Sugar." And since metropolitan merchants held a monopoly on trade, the islanders continued, English merchants "give us what they please [for sugar] . . . [making] us simple planters only the propertie of their gaine."[24] With colonists reluctant to obey laws that benefited England while damaging their own interests, many continued to pursue Anglo-Dutch trade. Partly driven by the desire to avoid new duties and secure more advantageous prices from the Dutch, interimperial commerce was also prompted by the inability of English traders and the state to meet colonial needs.

Beyond their concerns about insufficient shipping and lower profits, planters also complained that the new trade laws would hamper their ability to adjust to local or Atlantic-wide crises. Because the regulations barred direct trade with foreigners, they created a rigid system of commerce in a region that still required flexible and improvisational trade. As wealthy as many had become by the 1660s, West Indian planters still depended on outsiders to provide them with all the necessities of agricultural production and comfortable life. The list of goods they imported was long. It included, "*Servants* and *Slaves*, both men and women; *Horses, Cattle, Assinigoes* [asinego, a small donkey], *Camells, Utensills* for boyling Sugar . . . all manner of working tooles for Trades-men, as, *Carpenters, Joyners, Smiths, Masons, Mill-wrights, Wheel-wrights, Tinkers, Coopers,* & c. *Iron, Steel, Lead, Brasse, Pewter, Cloth* of all kinds, both *Linnen* and *Wollen; Stuffs, Hatts, Hose, Shoos, Gloves, Swords, knives, Locks, Keys,* &c. *Victualls* of all kinds . . . [such as] *Olives, Capers,*

Anchoves, salted Flesh and *Fish, pickled Maquerells* and *Herrings,* [and] *Wine.*"[25] Often undersupplied in times of peace and stability, as Governor Russell had found in 1668, wars and natural disasters had the potential to leave colonies on the verge of collapse. In the wake of these events, colonists did what Russell had in 1668: they pursued trade with Dutch merchants used to calling at their islands regardless of its legality. That they needed to break trade laws—and expose themselves to damaging prosecution if caught—to survive in moments of crisis proved the foolishness of mercantilist laws to colonists.

Although Charles II relaxed some of the conditions of the Navigation Acts during the Second Anglo-Dutch War and the related Anglo-French War (1666–67)—enabling planters to use foreign bottoms to send their sugar to English markets—he coupled such allowances with other restrictive measures including the requirement that ships depart the islands in convoys. These allowances provided security for vessels that did sail, but simultaneously limited and delayed other shipping. Complicating the lack of available resources, war also meant increased insurance and shipping costs.[26] In 1665 and 1666, Barbadians experienced just these effects when the Dutch Admiral De Ruyter invaded Barbados. Though colonists were able to repel the April 1665 attack, they did so at a high cost to shipping and resources. Frustrated with a slow English response to calls for aid and desperate for trade, Governor Francis Willoughby pleaded for the king to allow colonists to trade with whomever could relieve their wants.[27] Two months later, he complained that the people of Barbados still had but a "scantity of bread to put into their mouthes" and that some easement of commercial restrictions was needed.[28] Ignoring these circumstances and Willoughby's pleas for relief from the Navigation Acts, the king and his Privy Council exacerbated already difficult conditions in 1666 when they moved to further protect English ships by mandating that they not travel to the Caribbean, a decision that left colonists to fend for themselves.[29] Six years later, in the chaos of the Third Anglo-Dutch War (1672–74), Barbadians were again desperate for supplies. As William Willoughby noted, "the Island of Barbados doth not furnish of its own growth one quarter of Victualls sufficient for its inhabitants nor any other necessaries for Planting," and since England could not currently satisfy settlers' wants, Willoughy continued, authorities must suspend the Navigation Acts so that colonists could trade with other islands.[30]

In addition to the wars' effects on shipping, they also disrupted economic development by compelling colonists to reorient their energies away from productive work to defending their islands. As one governor explained, war was "very destructive to the planter, who must guard instead of planting."[31] Meanwhile, it was the Dutch, who some believed considered war to be "their heaven and peace their hell," who could still drive trade.[32] With Dutch traders retaining access to relatively cheap credit and the markets of the Dutch Republic, it was they who were able to maintain trade during warfare better than their English rivals, who still did not yet enjoy the same structural advantages. What this meant was that Dutch merchants continued to pursue trade with desperate English West Indians despite the warfare of the 1660s. In effect, England's war with the Dutch created the conditions that encouraged Anglo-Dutch trade.[33]

Making matters worse, Parliament canceled the few exemptions it had issued to the Navigation Acts as soon as the war ended in 1667 and without considering the rebuilding that still remained. Marauding bands of Dutch and French invaders had sacked Montserrat and Antigua (twice), taken St. Christopher (which the French held until 1671), and damaged Barbados with a naval bombardment. The devastation that French invasion caused on Antigua was particularly extensive. The merchant and planter Samuel Winthrop reported that the French forces occupied his house where their commander "possest himselfe of 24 of my slaues, (ye rest escaped,) & most of ye slaues in ye island, destroyed most of my stock, his soldiers plundering ye country round about." Also ruined in the mayhem were many planters' "coppers & sugar works," though most of the colony's houses were spared.[34] The planter Christopher Jeaffreson found a similar situation in St. Chistopher: "The wars here are the more destructive than in any other partes of the world; for twenty yeares' peace will hardly resettle the devastation of one yeares' worth."[35]

Ready access to supplies was thus vital for islanders hoping to rebuild plantations, sugar works, mills, and shipping facilities. Instead, what they found was that virtually the only legal trade available to them was with infrequent and expensive English traders.[36] This situation explains why Russell was so quick to defy the king and allow Dutch traders to land in Nevis in 1668. The simultaneous inability of the English navy to protect Caribbean settlements and officials' adhesion to restrictive policies prompted interimperial trade and created resentment among settler communities whose residents already believed that metropolitan regulations hurt their interests. When they turned to Dutch sources for trade goods, even during the three Anglo-Dutch wars, colonists did not see themselves as acting traitorously, but rather pragmatically; without commerce, their colonies would not be worth fighting for anyway. Dutch trade was, in colonists' view, imperative for their survival.

Natural disasters were a constant threat to island settlements and produced similar effects to wars. In the wake of these crises, colonists needed the same flexibility to find whatever trade they could, prompting many to seek Dutch commerce. On the evening of Saturday, April 18, 1668, a huge fire began in Bond and Bushel's countinghouse in Bridgetown, Barbados. The blaze spread quickly between the closely packed wooden structures and "in the space of two or three houres time burnt and consumed" perhaps as many as eight hundred structures and ignited the "publique Magazine of the island." Before it finally burned itself out, the fire consumed 2 million pounds of tobacco, destroyed unknown amounts of other tropical produce, and "shattered" eighty to one hundred merchants' houses, most which also doubled as warehouses, causing damages estimated between £300,000 and £400,000.[37] Seeking supplies to rebuild, the merchant John Harris "hired . . . the ship *Endracht* to make a voyage" from Amsterdam to Barbados "with timber and other Materials necessary for building," seeking permission from the king only after the voyage was under way.[38] Likewise, a group of Bridgetown's Jewish merchants turned to the Dutch Republic and by late fall were expecting the arrival of the 300-ton *Matthew and Francis* and the 270-ton *Sarah and Mary* from Amsterdam. Unfortunately for the traders, Sir William Temple, ambassador to the States-General, learned of the intended breach of trade laws and alerted English authorities of the ships' plans. When the *Matthew and Francis* arrived in Barbados, Deputy-Governor Christopher Codrington captured the ship but "through some ill management" failed to convict the captain of illegal trade. What exactly caused the "ill management" is unclear, but that the vessel reached Barbados in the wake of a major disaster with a cargo of European goods indicates that perhaps colonists intervened in the case as they had in 1655 so as not to discourage further Dutch trade in a desperate time.[39]

Hurricanes, as unpredictable and devastating as fires, also encouraged interimperial trade. Between 1655 and 1670, at least five severe storms destroyed the islands' infrastructure and left colonists in need of a great number of necessaries. One of these, in August 1666, not only caused extensive damage but also sank Francis Willoughby's vessel, drowning the governor while he was on his way to help Leeward Islanders repel the French invasion. In August 1667, another tempest further devastated colonies already suffering from an ongoing war. Each of these hurricanes—coming during or soon after the already destructive

Second Anglo-Dutch War—sank or damaged shipping, caused flooding that destroyed "almost all their [colonists'] horses, neat [domesticated] cattle, negroes, and other servants," and thus left colonists in need of a great number of supplies.[40] Though few detailed accounts of these storms remain, Sir Jonathan Atkins's description of the effects of a 1675 storm captures the wide-ranging damage hurricanes caused in the seventeenth century. As Atkins described it, the winds and rain the storm produced destroyed not just residents' houses, sugar works, and mills, but also colonists' sugar crops, "corn[,] and ground provisions . . . [that] should have kept their families for 6 months." The extent of the devastation shocked him: "Never was seen such prodigious ruine made here in such a short time . . . there is three churches, about a thousands houses [and] most of the mills to the Leeward throwne down, 200 people killed some whole Families buried under the ruins of their houses. It came with such a torrent of Raine . . . [that] beat downe all afore it unroofing . . . all their worke houses and storehouses and so letting in the wett to their sugars. . . . I must confesse I never saw a more amazing sight."[41] Compounding colonists' suffering, hurricanes and fires did not even produce a financial windfall for those whose crops did fortuitously survive because these disasters rarely drove up the price of sugar, which was set in Europe.[42]

Behind colonists' anxiety over the damage and shortages that wars, fires, and hurricanes caused was the constant specter of slave rebellions. Though there were no documented large-scale rebellions in the English Caribbean during the 1660s, colonists nevertheless feared that slaves would capitalize on the opportunities these disruptions created to rebel. Moreover, in both Barbados and Antigua, planters blamed runaway slaves, some living as maroon communities in inaccessible parts of the two islands, for stealing food and creating further shortages. As conditions worsened and planters grew desperate for trade, these worries increased. Not coincidently, it was in the crisis of 1668, for example, that Barbadians passed new restrictive slave laws designed to prevent an uprising.[43] A decade later, Governor Atkins connected the natural disasters to slave uprisings, ordering the execution of thirty-five slaves in the wake of the 1675 storm that ravaged Barbados.[44] One of the more brutal single acts of violence in Barbados during the seventeenth century, Atkins's actions can be partly explained by the vulnerability that Barbadians felt when cut off from European trade.

The disturbances that war, scarce shipping, natural disasters, and fear of slave uprisings wrought reinforced English West Indians' belief in the benefits of free trade. With open ports, they argued, they could quickly turn to foreign merchants to sustain their plantations without having to wait for special exemptions. Such flexibility would aid the empire by enabling them to maintain shipping no matter the circumstances. One notable test of this evolving economic ideology occurred in 1666 and 1667. Prompted by the difficulties they had endured during the Dutch and French wars, the natural disasters of the decade, and in observation of their "duties to Let yor Majesty know wherin we may be best secured & Encouraged . . . against . . . ye present watchfull Enemy," Barbadians, Leeward Islanders, and their governor lectured the king and his representatives about the advantages of free trade and the damage trade restrictions caused his empire. Because "these Westerne Isles haveing for some late yeares been debarred" of free trade the assemblymen of Barbados argued, "the Planter hath been reduced to a meane state, his courage brought Low, his Labour not recompensed, [and] most much impoverished." The result, they continued, was that these conditions have given "occasion to the Enemy" to "Advance . . . their trade and Interest" and have thus further forced the English to resort to inferior commerce, which they linked to "being forced to fish with French Netts."[45]

Conditioned by their own experiences to subscribe to a theory of empire building that rested on colonial autonomy in determining trade policy, colonists also drew upon the ongoing metropolitan debate over the proper role of state regulation in organizing national economies and the degree of commercial freedom permissible in empires. Most seventeenth-century economic theorists agreed that the rational pursuit of material gain through risk was justifiable and necessary. Such an understanding developed as thinkers began to postulate that national wealth (that is, economic success) could come only through the search for private wealth and not from a commitment to community welfare.[46] Where free trade supporters and regulating interests disagreed was over the system in which this private initiative should function. Writers such as Pieter de la Court in Amsterdam and William Petty and Gerald Malynes in London argued that the free trade (though Dutch trade was far from free) model used in the United Provinces was superior because it encouraged the maximum number of traders to take the risks of commerce and thus drove prices downward. Supporters of this position premised their arguments on an elaboration of the mechanical model of the circulatory system that earlier writers had borrowed from the study of human physiology. Building on the idea that money was the "blood of trade," authors drew evidence from the Dutch example to extend the metaphor, urging policy makers to eliminate state-constructed blockages in the flow of money and capital.[47] Together, increased trade and efficient trade were the keys to economic success: they enhanced individual and thus national wealth. Ignoring or missing the extent of local regulation in the United Provinces, these theorists argued that the extent of Dutch commercial hegemony abroad was all the evidence needed to see the veracity of their position.[48]

To make the argument that open trade was best for the colonies and the empire, West Indians deployed free traders' arguments in their own interests, selectively adapting components as needed. For example, when the Barbadian Assembly asserted that the Navigation Acts damaged their productive capacities because they restricted competition and drove up the price of their supplies, they were echoing the important anonymous work *A Discourse Consisting of Motives for the Enlargement and Freedom of Trade*. In this free trade pamphlet, the author heralded the idea that low prices could lead to enhanced profits through the increased pace of commerce. For their situation, planters and island merchants extrapolated, the same low prices on imported goods would speed the flow of exchange and consumption, in turn spurring the drive to produce more for export, resulting in higher profits for themselves and those in the metropole.[49]

Predictably, however, while planters pushed for lower prices for imports, they rejected low prices for exported sugar. Inexpensive sugar might be good for metropolitan merchants and consumers, but for those on the periphery, lower English prices meant planters could not profitably operate their plantations. The resulting disincentive to produce sugar, colonists pointed out, would eventually cause both the ruin of his majesty's plantations and, since lower production meant less trade, the decline of English wealth. A better path to imperial prosperity would be to permit settlers the freedom "to trade to their best convenience and profit," even if that meant utilizing foreign markets.[50] This contention echoed the writings of Roger Coke, who criticized the Navigation Acts for restricting the total volume of commerce. He contended, "Without question our Plantations and Ireland too would have been much increased by a Free Trade, more than by this restraint and by like Reason the Trade of England too would have been much more and the Nation much more enriched."[51] Even those who favored government regulation in most cases, such as Sir William Petty, conceded colonists' argument that the Navigation Acts hurt planters by raising their costs. In his now famous *Political Arithmetick*, Petty, in advocating for more uniform governance throughout the empire, wrote, "It is a Damage to our *Barbadoes,* and other *American* Traders that the Goods which might thence immediately, to several parts of the World, and to be sold at moderate Rates, must first come into *England,* and there pay Duties, and afterwards (if at all) pass into those Countries wither they might have gone immediately."[52]

The solution to the problem of high import prices and shipping costs, and low export prices for sugar, Barbadians maintained, was to allow them the freedom to "export . . . ye Comodities here produced to any place in amity with England, soe ye Same be Shipped in English bottomes" after paying "your Maties Customes . . . here or in England." Writing in the aftermath of two hurricanes and a French invasion, it is little surprising that colonists concluded, "free trade . . . [is] the Best . . . meanes of Living to any Collony." Such a compromise would foster colonial commerce by encouraging more efficient trade while not "prevent[ing] the increase of his Majesty's shipping and navigation."[53]

The inhabitants of Montserrat, Antigua, and St. Christopher all added their voices to those emanating from Barbados, complaining that, as Francis Willoughby summarized, their islands were "hard pinched by the acts of trade and navigation," unlike "when there was a free and open trade." With the high price of English textiles and provisions, and English freight rates and insurance fees rising rapidly, islanders attempted a compromise. They offered to use English ships and to pay duties—in essence accepting imperial goals to encourage English shipping and industry—if they also received permission to send their produce to whichever market they preferred.[54] Framed in relation to the burdens of protectionism and agreeing that a wealthier empire was their goal as well, English West Indians prized open trade for the competitive environment it created, rather than as a solution to avoiding English trade altogether. In other words, colonists valued access to Dutch trade because it made economic sense to maintain the commercial patterns that had been so crucial in the colonies' early decades, but they were not proposing disloyalty to the English empire's central commercial objectives.

It was not only planters and colonial-based merchants who proposed modifications to imperial regulation. Governor Francis Willoughby, following the lead of other colonists, requested that those found in violation of the trade laws in Barbados not be carried to England for prosecution but be "tried before the courts of record here."[55] Though his exact motivation for this proposal is not known, the events of six years previous when Penn and Venables struggled to prosecute the Dutch traders they apprehended suggest that violators received more lenient treatment in the islands than in England. Next, only a month after his September 1663 arrival in Barbados, Willoughby wrote to the king, suggesting that if "his Majesty would grant them some privileges which the Act of Navigation doth debar them," the colonists might agree to increase the mandated 4.5 percent duty on all commodities produced in the island.[56] The privileges to which Willoughby referred were most probably those for which islanders had begun calling in May 1661, namely the right to send their sugar directly to foreign ports after they had paid the proper duty locally. The Council for Trade found such a compromise an affront to their regulatory powers and ignored Willoughby's repeated appeals.[57]

Willoughby continued to advocate for planters both in Barbados and on the Leeward Islands during the 1660s. In September 1664, for example, he forwarded to the king the three petitions from the Councils and Assemblies of Antigua, Montserrat, and St. Christopher complaining about the Navigation Acts and calling for free trade discussed above.[58] Two years later, in a letter warning of the impending loss of St. Christopher, Willoughby lectured the king that "free trade is ye life, increase & being of all Collonys." But because metropolitan administrators had lost sight of this fact, the people of "Barbadoes & ye rest of ye Caribee Islands" did "not [have] Clothes sufficient to hide their Nakedness, nor food to fill theire bellies."[59] Linking the loss of one of the king's colonies to the miserable economic condition of the residents, Willoughby suggested that the two were directly related. By not allowing free trade, the royal government was on the verge of losing one of its colonies and was failing in its obligation to its satellites. In making this claim, the governor reminded the king that the Navigation Acts were doubly binding. The king and the colonists had reciprocal responsibilities: islanders were to follow the rules, and the king would then provide for his subjects.[60] If the king had failed in his duties, why should they abide by his laws?

In praising the achievements of the purportedly free-trading Dutch Republic during the 1660s and 1670s, colonists were working in sharp contrast to English public opinion. Writing in the aftermath of the London Fire (1666), which some blamed on Dutch agents, and the Dutch naval victory at Medway (1667), leading critics like George Downing frequently attacked not just Dutch commercial dominance, but the unjust and villainous ways Dutch merchants had achieved it. Comparing the Dutch to the Spanish, English pamphleteers and poets made sure that their countrymen did not forget "the bloody and inhumane butcheries" the Dutch had committed against the English to win their success, none of these being more infamous than the 1623 Dutch massacre of Englishmen at Amboyna in the East Indies.[61] The Dutch, according to much of the English public, were like "a Serpent . . . that at length might devour" England.[62]

To English colonists, the Dutch example meant something different. Not more inherently predisposed to be sympathetic to the Dutch than those in England or unpatriotic toward England, colonists' tied Dutch achievements to their own colonial experience. When they asserted, "that an open Market renders the most plenty and best penny worth to any Citty or Countrey . . . so doth free trade render the Best . . . meanes of Living to any Collony," settlers were drawing upon the arguments of free traders celebrating Dutch policies for more than solely academic or opportunistic reasons.[63] Rather, in colonists' lived reality for four decades, they had overcome the instability and vagaries of colonial life by building cross-national alliances. But, beginning in 1651 and more vigorously with the Restoration government's assault on the Dutch carrying trade, the metropole had changed the rules, provoking the leading planter-merchants who controlled the Assemblies of Barbados and the Leeward Islands to greet mercantilism with their own principled call for free trade. For a group of anxious colonists trying to survive the damaging effects of war, natural disasters, and new commercial regulations by resorting to trade with the Dutch, free trade was not a luxury. Instead, it was critical for their, and by extension the empire's, very survival to form beneficial commercial relations regardless of imperial boundaries.

* * *

Colonists in New Netherland also experienced the shock waves that the Restoration government's assault on Dutch trade sent throughout the Atlantic. The English conquest of New Netherland in late summer 1664 provoked a major cultural, social, and economic reordering that would continue into the eighteenth century. While the conquest did not produce the acute immediate fears of starvation that mercantilist policies brought about in the Caribbean, the imposition of English rule nevertheless disrupted existing commercial networks and threatened the economic health of the city and surrounding regions. Realizing the danger the conquest posed to their economic interests, Dutch inhabitants of newly christened New York worked to moderate the impact of new laws by maintaining their Dutch commercial ties. In so doing, they deployed many of the free trade arguments that those in the Caribbean used, modifying them to fit a different cultural and economic situation.

Carried out in 1664, the plans for the conquest of New Netherland had begun as early as 1661, when the Council for Plantations started to receive complaints that Dutch traders from New Netherland had come to dominate commerce throughout English North America. The close access the Dutch colony provided to the Chesapeake, one observer noted, gave Virginians the opportunity to sell "greate quantities of tobacco to the Dutch," an activity that cost the treasury "tenne thousand pounds per annum or upwards." Meanwhile, in New England, other officials reported that Dutch traders carried 100,000 furs a year out of the English colonies. According to Samuel Maverick, a New Englander and the eventual royal commissioner for New England, English losses caused by Dutch possession of the colony extended to the British Caribbean because the geographic position of New Netherland made it "Commodious for commerce from and wth all p[ar]ts of the West Indies." Soon the ministry agreed: with the Dutch believing that "all the world were New Netherland" and that they should have a free right to trade where they pleased, there was no way to enforce the Navigation Acts. So, with the Dutch and English already fighting on the west coast of Africa, a large faction of his advisers calling for war, and a financially plagued brother eager to take up his land, Charles decided to act. In March 1664, he officially issued a patent for New Netherland to his brother, James, the Duke of York, and allowed him to quickly dispatch a fleet of four vessels and three hundred soldiers under the command of Colonel Richard Nicolls to capture the Dutch colony. Along with the English wars in Ireland and Cromwell's attack on Jamaica, taking New Netherland was a somewhat rare effort to strengthen England's Atlantic commercial empire through direct territorial conquest. That the Crown took such an extreme step to eliminate the Dutch colony underscores how great a threat it posed to English control of Atlantic commerce.[64]

On August 16/26, 1664, the roughly 1,500 inhabitants of New Amsterdam watched Nicolls's four English war ships "crammed full with an extraordinary amount of men and warlike stores" anchor just beyond the reach of Fort Orange's guns. With insufficient powder and few provisions, the small Dutch garrison of about ninety soldiers on the southwest corner of Manhattan had little chance to successfully defend the fort.[65] Yet Director-General Stuyvesant remained defiant, reminding Nicolls of Dutch sovereignty over the place and refusing to surrender. While the two men exchanged posturing letters, Nicolls sent Connecticut governor John Winthrop to try to convince the inhabitants of New Amsterdam to capitulate. As the governor of a frequent trading partner, Winthrop had an interest in resolving the matter peacefully as well because Connecticut residents often purchased manufactured goods from the Dutch city in exchange for naval stores, wampum, and agricultural products. Hoping to avoid bloodshed, Nicolls had entrusted Winthrop to offer favorable terms on his behalf in the hope that they would placate Dutch settlers.[66] After the meeting between Stuyvesant, his council, two residents, and Winthrop, many mercantile-inclined New Amsterdamers signed a petition favoring a quick surrender at Nicolls's generous terms. After several days of negotiation with the colony's residents, Stuyvesant relented. On August 27/ September 7, the rival commanders met in New Amsterdam, where Stuyvesant came "to terms with the enemy."[67]

With the surrender completed, Nicolls occupied Fort Orange and re-named the port New York City to honor the colony's new proprietor. Hoping to pacify the residents and incorporate the colony into the English empire, Nicolls and his fellow occupiers offered residents "Articles of Capitulation" that followed the terms Winthrop had first presented to the Dutch. Negotiated by a group of six merchants on the Dutch side and Nicolls on the English, the "Articles of Capitulation" protected the property of the WIC, secured colonists' freedom of worship, enabled the practice of partible inheritance to continue, and offered Dutch inhabitants freedom from being "prest to serve in Warr, against any Nation whatsoever." The pact also guaranteed continued Dutch immigration, and Dutch traders enjoyed the right to "send any sort of merchandize home in vessels of their own Country," while "all Shipps from the Netherlands, or any other place, and Goods therein, shall be received here, and sent hence after the manner for which formerly they were, before our coming hither for Six Monthes next ensuing."[68] Nicolls acknowledged that such a provision was contrary to "the laws of England," but assured the Crown that his larger purpose was "to Encourage the Inhabitatants" and to raise customs revenues, goals that would benefit the larger empire.[69] Finally, the agreement offered Dutch residents temporary denization. This privilege allowed residents most trading rights reserved for native-born Englishmen and provided a path for permanent denization. To Dutch traders in New York City, the ability to trade as Englishmen combined with their traditional access to Dutch commerce placed them in a fortuitous economic position, allowing unfettered trade to many places in two empires. Despite these benefits, however, the large Dutch firms that had controlled New Amsterdam's trade soon withdrew their investment, robbing the city of needed goods and capital.[70] Without a steady supply of quality, inexpensive European goods for regional trade, city traders grasped tightly to their Dutch connections, meaning Nicolls's victory did little to quickly change the city's commercial patterns.

Not even two months after the city had been newly christened New York, the shipmaster Jan Pietersen Poppen guided the *De Hope* out of Manhattan bound for the Caribbean as he had numerous times before when the colony had been a Dutch one. Still working in the employ of the WIC, Poppen's galliot—a small, single-masted vessel—carried a pass from Nicolls and the supercargo Balthazar Stuyvesant, in addition to a cargo of 1,150 pounds of salted meat, 166 schepels of peas, and 75 schepels of wheat. After trawling the Caribbean islands and stopping briefly at St. Christopher, Poppen anchored in Curaçao on December 6, 1664, and delivered his most prized cargo: the news that the English had captured New Amsterdam.[71] Eager for more information about the Dutch invasion and anxious to send a folio of papers to Petrus Stuyvesant, Vice Director Matthias Beck prevailed upon Poppen to return to New York City the next April. Along with the WIC documents and private papers for Balthazar Stuyvesant, Poppen also conveyed one barrel each of sugar and salt, a parcel of lemons, "two ports of sweets," a hammock, and 434 conch shells to Manhattan. In return for these goods, Beck asked the elder Stuyvesant to send him, at his earliest convenience, "a suitable mast for one of the Company's barks," measuring "fifty-seven feet long and thirty-seven inches thick."[72] That Beck would expect a cargo in return for those things sent on *De Hope* suggests that perhaps he had not yet realized that losing New Amsterdam would interrupt trade between the two colonies. At the very least, it represents Dutchmen's continued optimism that the mid-Atlantic city would continue to play its former role as a regional trading center.

Unfortunately for Poppen and Beck, English authorities seized the galliot as it entered New York's harbor in the late fall of 1665. Poppen appealed the detainment of his vessel, but to no avail; the Court of Admiralty ruled that the vessel was "a lawful Prize, for that she hath (contrary to his Majesty's laws and Ordinances) now in a time of Warr, been in a Dutch Port and hath taken in goods there and traded for and with the King's open and professed enemies." In an interesting twist, though, the court allowed Poppen to repurchase his vessel from the colonial government for £117. As a bonus, the vessel was now considered a "free vessel to goe or come trade or traffick in any port" since it had been made an English prize.[73] This designation was important for Poppen, who had instantly turned his Dutch-built galliot into an English vessel fit for legal trade, at once not only helping himself and any other investors, but also Governor Nicolls, who badly needed commerce for his new colony. Unfortunately, the auction records do not indicate if Poppen raised the funds himself, or if New York contacts such as Stuyvesant invested in the repurchase of *De Hope*. In coming years, Poppen, now a denizen of the city as well, continued to trade to Curaçao, obtaining a 1670 permit from Governor Francis Lovelace to trade there in another vessel, the *Trial*.[74] In this manner, three legal instruments—the auction and repurchase of a Dutch ship, denization, and a governor's pass—came together to incorporate Poppen and the networks that connected him to Dutch colonies into English New York's trading sphere and to provide the commerce the city so badly needed.

While he was permitting Poppen to leave New York and then facilitating the Anglicization of his vessel and his trade, Governor Nicolls wrote to English authorities about the colony's dire situation and the reverberations that could be felt along the entire settled North American coastline: "In discharge of my duty I cannot but repeat over againe the importance of employing merchants shipps with a great proportion of merchandize. . . . [O]therwise His Majesty's expences in reducing them [Dutch inhabitants] will not turne to any account. . . . It is a business of great concern to His Majesty that some considerable merchants should joyne their stocks and dispatch here that may arrive in March or April at the furthest."[75] Eight months later, New York had still not received a vessel from England. "We have had no ship or the least suppliers directly out of England, since the surrender," Nicolls complained, and the situation "hath brought the soldiers and planters into very great wants of meane necessaries."[76] In November 1665, colonists remained desperate, prompting Nicolls to plead: "[M]y reputation lyes at stake to the Country having so often (in confidence of a supply) assured the Inhabitants of the care which was takes for their releife; who depending thereupon are now left naked to the rigour of the winter. . . . I must humbly therefore beseech Your R. Highness to dispatch a speedy supply hither before we fall into extremeties."[77] What had begun as a crisis that threatened the city's regional trading sphere had developed into a situation that endangered the very survival of English North America. By 1666, Nicolls was convinced that it was not just New Yorkers who would starve in the coming winter, but the residents of surrounding colonies. "[S]ome such like Overture for trade must be accepted," he told the Earl of Clarendon, for without commerce not only is "the Colony . . . ruin'd," but since New York was the "key to the whole Countrey," the larger empire would be doomed as well.[78] Nicolls's dire predictions notwithstanding, neither the English government nor English merchants headed his calls; in Nicolls's first eight months as governor, no English vessels called at the city.[79]

Without trade goods from England, New York merchants and Nicolls realized that the colony's survival depended upon their ability to place local needs above regional ones, to defy English laws, and to reinvigorate trade with the Dutch Republic. As a result, just months after taking control of the city, Nicolls began giving permission for merchants to freight vessels to the Dutch Republic, knowing that they would not return within the six-month exemption to the Navigation Acts that was included in the Articles of Capitulation. The first ship, the *Eendracht* (Unity) of Amsterdam, carried passengers, almost a hundred beaver pelts for Jan Baptiste van Rensselaer, Chesapeake tobacco to clear accounts in the Netherlands, and a great amount of correspondence from Dutch inhabitants to their families and business partners in Amsterdam.[80]

Soon other vessels—controlled, and sometimes owned, by the same members of the local trading community that had pressed Nicolls to grant passes in the first place—were making the voyage between New York and the United Provinces and back again. Among the most active in late 1664 and 1665 were the wealthy Dutch trader Cornelis Steenwyck and the established Huguenot Jacques Cousseau.[81] Meanwhile, some Amsterdam merchants continued to risk sending trade goods to the English colony. One group, led by Amsterdam's Jan Baptiste van Rensselaer and Abel de Wolff, dispatched the *Eendracht* for New York, where Nicolls permitted it to enter the port. Steenwyck and Cousseau's *Hopewell*, too, made another round trip with Nicolls's approval, arriving in New York in 1666 with merchandise freighted by several Amsterdam merchants. Cousseau quickly sold the cargo that included blankets, duffels, linen, hats, and distilled liquors, and the *Hopewell* departed again for Amsterdam that summer.[82] Perhaps the best example of optimism for continued Anglo-Dutch trade is the voyage of the *D'Oranje Boom* (Orange Tree). In 1667, this Dutch Republic–based and –owned vessel received permission from Nicolls to carry tobacco and furs on behalf of New York and Amsterdam–based traders. Supported by the Amsterdam firms that had dominated trade to New Netherlands since the 1640s (the Verbrugge, Van Rensselaer, Van Hoornbeeck, and De Wolff companies) and leading ethnically Dutch Manhattan traders (Federick Philipse and Steenwyck), the venture signaled mutual confidence in continued Anglo-Dutch commerce.[83] In short, Nicolls initiated legal cross-national trade, and merchants of both sides of the Atlantic used their commercial networks to defeat metropolitan goals for the colony.

Mirroring the efforts ten years earlier by Stuyvesant and other Dutch colonists to build a stable trading relationship between Barbados and

Dutch colonies, some Dutch residents also tried to make Nicolls's occasional permits for Dutch trade more lasting. By the spring of 1666, Nicolls had become convinced that English merchants were too ill-equipped to provide the commerce New York needed to prosper, and he began to call for a more permanent arrangement by which the Dutch inhabitants could trade with their former correspondents in the Dutch Republic. Because the commerce of local merchants was "interwoven with their correspondents and friends in Holland," he reported to his superiors, the English were going to have to "graunt them [local traders] some extraordinary infranchisement" in trade.[84] In Nicolls's view, the only way to produce a stable government was to maintain an active economy, and in immediate post-conquest New York City, allowing trade with the Dutch was the most efficient way to obtain the goods needed to sustain regional commerce.

Extending their attempts beyond the governor, New York's Dutch traders also pressed the Duke of York to allow them more regular access to Dutch commerce. To make this claim, colonists built upon earlier calls for Dutch trade based on desperation to make a more sweeping argument that rested on their interpretation of the Articles of Capitulation they had signed in 1664. Though the English understood this document to have granted colonists a six-month exemption to the Navigation Acts so that residents could complete already initiated ventures, many New Yorkers believed article 6 of the document gave them the ability to continue trading with the Netherlands indefinitely. The article read: "It is consented to, that any people may freely come from the Netherlands, and plant in this Country, and that Dutch Vessells may freely come hither, and any of the Dutch may freely return home, or send any sort of Merchandize home in Vessells of their own country."[85] From the perspective of Dutch residents the agreement was a binding contract protecting and rearticulating the privileges of self-governance and commercial control they had obtained when they received a municipal charter in 1653. For their part, English officials saw it as an agreement to manage the transition from Dutch to English rule, and thus as a temporary measure allowing the conquered to settle outstanding debts or to return to their original homes with their property.[86] These divergent interpretations persisted in the coming years as Dutch residents demanded that their acceptance of English rule be grounded upon English recognition of their right to pursue free trade. In two petitions submitted on behalf of New York City's Dutch population in 1667, former Director-General Stuyvesant protested residents' inability to send commodities to the United Provinces as he believed the treaty allowed. After quoting the text of the sixth proposition, Stuyvesant proceeded to demand that "Dutch Subjects . . . be allowed ye benefitt of a free trade, as hath been granted them by ye 6th Article whereby ye Planters may be furnished wth some necessaries, not to bee had from other parts." Calling attention to English merchants' inability to satisfy New Yorkers' needs, Stuyvesant and the other members of the "Dutch Nâcon" insisted that freedom of trade to the United Provinces be absolute and that it was in the English occupiers' interests to allow the Netherlands trade "Since the Trade of the Beaver . . . hath allwayes been purchased from the Indyans, by the Comodities brought from Holland." The difficulty English had in supplying the kinds of trade goods that Native Americans demanded would force them to "the french of Canida . . . [who] will in turn divert the Beaver Trade." Because, Stuyvesant added, "noe shipps from England are resolv'd to visit there parts," the only way to hold on to their Indian trading allies was to allow trade with the Netherlands.[87] If Dutch residents could be accommodated with sufficient trade from the Dutch Republic, they would become invaluable partners in English efforts to defeat competing French interests.

Stuyvesant and his Dutch allies in the city also feared losing their foothold in the Chesapeake. Their worry had begun with the passage of the Navigation Acts a decade earlier, an obstacle Dutch New Netherlanders had overcome, but their lack of easy access to direct transatlantic shipping after 1665 renewed this concern. Without manufactures from Europe, New Yorkers struggled to compete with New Englanders, who also drew tobacco from the Chesapeake to ports such as Boston and Newport. As new members of the English empire, Dutch New Yorkers had recently received legitimatization for their Chesapeake trade, and they were not ready to relinquish their position simply because English merchants being "blowne up with large designes, but not knowing the knacke of tradeing," could not supply them.[88]

New Yorkers' pleas for a resumption of the Netherlands trade combined with the failure of English traders to bring sufficient goods eventually convinced London authorities to allow three Dutch ships a year to trade between New York City and the Dutch Republic. A royal proclamation would permit this trade for seven years beginning with the end of the Second Anglo-Dutch War.[89] Hoping to take advantage of this opportunity, Steenwyck and Stuyvesant used their influence to purchase the three royal permits for 1668. They then again joined with the Dutchmen Jan Baptiste van Rensselaer, Abel de Wolff, and Gillis van Hoornbeeck as well as Amsterdam partners Jacob Benturi and Cornelis Jacobsz to form a trading company reconnecting the two cities. As another sign of their belief in the long-term future of such ventures, the company built the 120–ton *Juffrouw Leonora* specifically for the New York–Amsterdam trade; the other two vessels they acquired, the *Posthoorn* and the *Nieuw Jorck*, were English vessels with English masters and English crews.[90]

Despite bright prospects, the new partnership, financed with ƒ6,000 of initial capital, operated for only one year and just three ships sailed. Departing the Dutch Republic in the spring of 1668 with manufactured goods and livestock, the three company ships arrived in New York City in time to successfully purchase furs that summer.[91] On their homeward voyages, however, English customs officials stopped the vessels and declared their cargoes illegal. The masters who held permits granting them permission to trade between the two empires were shocked. Unbeknownst to them, the Board of Trade had reversed its decision and revoked the permits, concluding that such traffic would "have an unhappy influence by opening a way for forrainers to trade with the rest of his Majesty's plantations" in North America.[92] If New Yorkers were able to purchase "linen, Shooes, Stockins, Cloaths, and other Comodities" from the Dutch, English traders argued, then these goods would find their ways to "Virginia, Barbadoes and New England," and "in a short time" the "principle part of the plantations trade" would be "lost" to the English.[93] For Dutch New Yorkers, this was precisely the point. Access to sufficient supplies of high-quality goods at prices they could afford was necessary for them to maintain their trade to surrounding colonies. For the Amsterdam merchants, the Board of Trade's reversal devastated what they had hoped would have been a profitable arrangement, and they dissolved their company.[94] In the end, Charles II decided that the intertwined interests of English merchants trading to New York and of the rising state were paramount to the needs of the colony and its residents.

In response to the decision to revoke the permits, New Yorkers modified their tactics. In 1668, the mayor and alderman of New York petitioned the Duke of York directly, asking for "a free trade from this porte [New York City] to Holland and from Holland to this [place in Dutch ships] . . . which is not denied to any of his Majesty's Subjects, touching in some porte in England as they come from Holland, and payenge his Majesty's Customes." Such permission was necessary, they reminded James, because their trade depended on inexpensive, high-quality Dutch-made goods that could not "be so well made in England."[95] This, they argued, was the secret to encouraging more trade and thus economic growth and revenue. By compromising with the Duke of York and agreeing to the payment of duties like their fellow colonists in the Caribbean, New Yorkers took an important step, accepting royal authority but also signaling their intention to negotiate. As key to the province's success, they claimed a voice in shaping the province's future.

This particular petition offers additional insight into how the parties negotiated tensions between colonial and imperial interests. The trade New Yorkers requested was a modification of already existing forms of legal Anglo-Dutch trade. If carried on English (or colonial) vessels, organized by Englishmen (or denizened foreigners), and if the voyage included a stop in England to pay duties, it was legal. What New Yorkers wanted was an extension of these rules, allowing them to employ Dutch vessels while still stopping in English ports and paying duties—a quasi-legal trade typically undertaken as a partial solution to restrictive imperial laws. Colonists could still trade with the Dutch empire, benefiting themselves and New York in the process. Meanwhile, English authorities could maintain their trade laws and capture some invisible profits for English traders.

On one hand, the Board of Trade's 1668 decision to cancel official permits for Dutch trade convinced most Amsterdam-based merchants to withdraw from their transit trade to English colonies and look elsewhere for opportunity. On the other hand, authorities' entertaining of colonists' petitions and the government's allowance of Dutch trade signaled enterprising colonial merchants that all Anglo-Dutch trade was not frowned upon, and if they were willing to conform with metropolitan laws regulating the practice, then there were profits to be made. Some interpreted the implied loophole broadly. For example, Oloff Stevensen van Cortlandt, Nicholas de Meyer, Jacques Cousseau, and Frederick Philipse's wife, Margarita Hardenbroeck, simply carried on as if their trade were legal, sending *De Koningh Carel* (King Charles) from Amsterdam to New York and back (with former governor Richard Nicolls on board) in 1668. In the decades that followed, New Yorkers would continue to find similar way to prosecute Anglo-Dutch trade.[96]

Between 1664 and 1668, there were about three to four clearances per year from the Dutch Republic to New York, or vice versa. In particular, 1668 was especially active, with eleven combined arrivals from and clearances to the Netherlands. During the same period, there is only one vessel recorded as having traveled between New York and London, though without records of all ships calling at New York in these years, it is unclear how many English vessels arrived there after coming from

New England or other colonies. On the whole, the volume of Dutch trade in the first four years after the conquest was only slightly less than the six to eight voyages a year typical during the last five years of Dutch rule. In their largely successful adaptation of their commercial patterns to fit English rule, New Yorkers learned important lessons about their power to continue to shape their trade despite imperial mandates. Future years would test this conclusion, but, recalling the lessons of the late 1660s, New Yorkers would continue to find ways to adapt.[97]

* * *

The conquest of New Netherland interrupted development with results similar to wars or natural disasters in the Caribbean, and colonists in New York had grasped their older connections tightly to survive the difficult times, defying authority when necessary, ignoring ongoing Anglo-Dutch warfare, and adapting to new circumstances just as their compatriots in the islands had. Though "necessity" meant something different to colonists in New York than it did in Barbados and the Leeward Islands, trade with Dutch merchants was important in all three places. London officials rarely comprehended the particular circumstances that prompted interimperial commerce, and they became increasingly frustrated with what they saw as self-interested colonists. On one level, they were right since colonists did pursue free trade because it brought prosperity, pushing prices for tropical commodities upward and those for imports downward. But London officials did not see the greater meaning of these actions. As hurricanes, fires, and wars demonstrated, success in the seventeenth century was fragile, and this fragility led colonists to resist metropolitan control of trade because it endangered colonial success. For those standing in the charred remains of Bond and Bushel's countinghouse or outside the walls of the newly rechristened Fort James in 1668, illegal trade was about colonial communities' survival as much as it was strictly about individuals' profits. So, for many years to come, new and old British colonists continued to seek Dutch credit and goods, replicating some of the patterns of trade they had used previously, and crafting new ways to operate beyond the power of regulatory authorities. In the process, settlers negotiated their relationship with the metropole and helped to determine its economic structure.

4 / Local Adaptations I: Anglo-Dutch Trade in the English West Indies

In October 1680, the surveyor for His Majesty's Customs at Falmouth, Samuel Hayne, was in Cornwall, England, when he learned that "a great Ship," the 300-ton *Experiment*, "had been cleared there [Falmouth] from *Barbadoes* for *Amsterdam* without Unloading her whole Cargo." Racing to Falmouth to investigate the situation, Hayne arrived after dark, but was pleasantly surprised to receive an invitation to dine at the home of a local notable, Sir Peter Killigrew. Unsure why he had been extended such a generous offer, Hayne soon discovered that the invitation was a ruse designed to distract him: while he had been dining with Killigrew, the ship's master, Henry Sutton—who had advance knowledge of Hayne's presence—was "*hunting about for his men to get them on board, in order to set Sail immediately for* Amsterdam." Realizing the deceit, Hayne hurried to seize the *Experiment*, refusing bribes of fifty guineas and "the best Horse Sir *Peter* [Killigrew] had," in the process.

Upon boarding the *Experiment* to interrogate the crew, Hayne found that the hold contained "one hundred Butts and upwards" of sugar, three hogsheads of tobacco, and parcels of ginger and fustic, all of "which were never Landed, taken out, or removed," from the ship according to law. As he continued to investigate, Hayne found something even more intriguing. Though Sutton and Bryan Rogers had entered the goods on behalf of two English Jewish merchants (Antonio Gomesera and Antonio Lousada), Hayne discovered that the hidden goods possessed thirty-five different marks, indicating the ship carried many men's produce.

Unfortunately, Hayne did not enumerate—or could not identify—the various owners beyond several Barbadian Jews including Aaron Barscoe, Abraham Barasse, Emanuel Rodrigo, and Lewis Deus (Dias). Nevertheless, the number of marks indicates that a large number of Barbadians, a group that included non-Jews as well, were trying to deceive customs officials and had intended to direct their commodities directly to the Netherlands. By using Sutton's and local traders' names and bribing English officials, those Amsterdam traders involved in the venture, including Jacob Baruch Lousada, David Baruch Lousada, and possibly Isaac de Mercado—all men with family ties in Barbados—almost succeeded in bringing British sugar to Amsterdam duty-free. For his part, Hayne suffered for his diligence. According to his later claims, Kiligrew and his Jewish partners tried to ruin Hayne because he had interrupted their business, promising him that they *"would make me Rot in Prison, that I must never expect to come out thence till Death."*[1]

The account of the *Experiment* and its cargo is instructive in what it says about how interimperial trade had evolved since the 1660s. On the surface, of course, the incident indicates that Dutch trade still thrived; more than thirty planters and merchants in Barbados had been willing to hazard their sugars to Amsterdam rather than to London. Also enlightening is the manner in which both colonists and their metropolitan contacts conducted this trade. Taking their cue from the openings for legal trade that metropolitan restrictions provided, they employed an English vessel and an English captain to carry their cargo and instructed Sutton to sail the *Experiment* to Amsterdam by way of England, touching at Falmouth to declare the cargo and pay duties according to law. Not content to fully obey the law, however, the traders combined their legal trade with illegal aspects: obscuring the number of merchants involved with the cargo, concealing a huge portion of the cargo so as to avoid duties, and bribing the appropriate officials to make sure their vessel could pass without a problem. These acts of subterfuge neatly summarize both the strategies shippers in the Caribbean pursued to avoid mercantilist restrictions and the difficulties authorities had in fully controlling colonial trade.

At the same time, that a portion of the *Experiment's* cargo bound for Amsterdam was legal—it had been properly landed and duties had been paid—and that some was illegal is also important as it reflects a larger facet of the political economy of cross-national trade. Blending legal and illegal trade together, colonists' behavior showed how arbitrary they considered these distinctions. When looking at Anglo-Dutch trade in the seventeenth-century Atlantic, it is not always possible to distinguish between legal, quasi-legal, and illegal trade because those individuals of both empires who engaged in occasional or partial smuggling did so not out of some innate desire to break the law, but because what had been familiar and advantageous to them had been redefined as illegal by English officials. Certainly, opportunism and greed played a role in illicit trade—especially for their governmental enablers—but colonists' use of a combination of legal and illegal tactics to maintain access to Dutch markets and goods also reflects the persistence of a collaborative and interimperial tradition that encouraged them to look for the most advantageous trade, whether it be English or Dutch.

The involvement of new groups in the *Experiment* venture was a further departure from earlier practices. Marginalized and pushed to the fringes of mercantile activity because of their religion, the Sephardic community of the British West Indies was the most important of these groups. With kinship networks extending around the Atlantic and to the Dutch Caribbean, to Amsterdam, and, after the mid-1650s, to England, Caribbean-based Sephardic traders had the right blend of contacts to be leaders in the West Indies' Dutch trade. The decision to use an English vessel, captain, and merchant for Anglo-Dutch trade was a further acknowledgment on the part of colonists, both Jewish and non-Jewish, that if they wanted to maintain their interimperial trade, they needed to adapt their practices to the patchwork mercantilist framework that Parliament and the Crown were erecting. Further indicating their willingness to work within the empire under favorable conditions, colonists paired legal, quasi-legal, and illegal trade with continued petitioning against trade laws, exploiting their political power as members of the English empire to shape metropolitan policy to fit their needs.

Read one way, colonists' sustained pursuit of Anglo-Dutch trade suggests a self-interested population eager to avoid trade laws to derive maximum personal benefit. Read another, however, this same trade embodied colonists' understanding that the complex realities of life at the periphery required begrudging adaptations to new regulations. Though it would take decades, many colonists were beginning to choose a combination of pathways for commerce, some of them offered by the English state, thereby giving their qualified consent to certain benefits of belonging in the empire.

* * *

Although it is impossible to know the precise extent of contraband trade in the English Atlantic, contemporary accounts, government officials' complaints, and direct evidence of smuggling suggest that it was constantly present. The extent of illicit activity varied over the course of the seventeenth century and between locations as different as the mid-Atlantic and the Caribbean. It is important, however, to note that most colonists did not smuggle all the time; rather, they combined illegal with legal trade to maximize profits where they could. These men (and sometimes women) understood illicit commerce as simply one of several avenues of commercial opportunity.

There is a great deal of debate about the extent and importance of illicit trade in the Atlantic world, and the British empire in particular. Scholars of late seventeenth- and early eighteenth-century Britain, for example, generally accept that the smuggling not just of luxury goods but also of tobacco, tea, and other dutied English imports was common. In 1717, one English official noted that illicit trade from France and the Netherlands equaled one-third of lawful trade from those places.[2] Many scholars who study British America, however, disagree, arguing that, beginning in the 1650s and certainly by the last quarter of the century, most illegal trade had ended and most colonists and foreign merchants obeyed trade laws.[3] In making this argument, these historians focus on trade in the most valuable commodities—sugar outward from the Caribbean to Europe, and slaves from Africa to the Americas. Where port records are sufficient to test this hypothesis by comparing colonial exports to metropolitan imports—mostly for the eighteenth century, but also for Barbados in the late seventeenth—it has been generally proved correct.[4] This record of keeping sugar exports within imperial bounds reflects the interests of London merchants, statesmen, the navy, and governors, who were also most concerned in forcing the most valuable colonial exports through metropolitan channels, simultaneously increasing the king's revenue, developing English shipping, and encouraging the domestic economy.

While devoting the greater part of their attention to the most valuable sector of colonial trade, however, officials missed other illicit activity, especially that which brought relatively low-cost supplies to the colonies and small cargoes out; the very goods that Dutch shippers had carried to English colonies for decades. This situation allowed North American colonists to move illicit goods, like foreign rum, into their ports, and

Caribbean colonists to use interisland networks to send contraband to foreign colonies. Spanish, French, Dutch, and Danish colonists also found opportunity to smuggle, with residents of St. Thomas, St. Eustatius, and Curaçao particularly profiting from delivering goods to Spanish and French colonies, much to the consternation of authorities there. In short, it appears that in a variety of empires and colonies, illegal trade was a regular feature of the seventeenth-century Caribbean. Never as important or voluminous as the Caribbean's sugar-dominated export sector, illegal, cross-national trade at Barbados and the Leeward Islands nevertheless persisted through the seventeenth century. It comprised an important proportion of merchants' cargoes and sustained particular perceptions about the proper role of merchants and imperial authorities in building empires.[5]

In the English Caribbean, the desire to smuggle varied from island to island and across time. Naturally, incentive was highest during periods of crisis that prevented English shipping, as we saw during the disturbances of the 1660s, but in times of stability colonists also had incentive as the pace of trade quickened. In these periods, smuggling often provided a profitable alternative to legal commerce. If colonists could not obtain necessary stores from English suppliers on English vessels, the relative cost of obtaining them elsewhere, at whatever price, must have been cheaper. Similarly, if English shippers could not provide enough vessels to carry colonial produce, the risks of smuggling a cargo to the Dutch were lower than allowing the produce to deteriorate at dockside. Even when English carriers offered sufficient cargo space and goods, Dutch traders encouraged illicit trade by besting English prices. As the governor of Jamaica remarked in 1682, the Dutch "sell European Goods 30 percent, cheaper than we [the English], & will paye deerer for American Goods." Similarly, Samuel Hayne noted that English merchants trading to the Caribbean had difficulty competing with those from the Netherlands because the latter avoided duties in England enabling them to save "on every voyage from *Amsterdam* or *Rotterdam*," making them able to "Sell 20 *per cent.* cheaper than the *English*." Governor Charles Wheler agreed, arguing that English merchants demanded "twice the proftt at Least, which the Dutch would [charge to] bring over our own . . . manufactures," and failed to give "Creditt, which the Dutch will for a yeare at least."[6] Because Dutch merchants could still beat English competitors on price for their manufactured goods, horses, and provisions, they continued to dock at the Leeward Islands and Barbados, where planters welcomed the cheaper imports and plentiful exports of sugar.

Compounding the incentives to smuggle that a scarcity of goods and price advantages created, the lack of authorities' consistency in enforcing trade laws further mitigated the risk of seizure and made smuggling more attractive. Dependent upon underfunded and sometimes corrupt local officers, metropolitan policy makers soon realized that they did not yet have the imperial machinery required to enforce the Navigation Acts and to close off illicit trade. As discussed earlier, a part of the administrative reforms of the 1660s, the Council of Trade made their governors responsible for enforcing the regulations, threatening them with removal if they failed. Still, they struggled to secure obedience. In 1662, the treasurer of England felt compelled to remind "the Principall Officers and Commissioners of his Majesty's Customes" to "take especiall care to see that part of the Act of Navigation, which provides that no Shipp that loades in any of the Plantations belonging to this Kingdome, doe goe into any forraigne part without touching first in England," was enforced. The order was necessary, he believed, because Sir George Downing—the English ambassador to the States-General in the Netherlands and a crafter of the Navigation Act of 1660—had told him that "divers English Shipps laden in Barbadoes . . . [commonly] arrived in Holland without touching in England."[7] A year later, the Council of State sharply rebuked Governor Francis Willoughby for allowing "divers Ships and Vessells which do come to Our islands from other Countries," to trade, depriving the Crown of duties collected on domestic craft and undermining the Navigation Acts.[8] That same year, a circular letter to all governors reminded them that if they received "any information . . . that any Ships freighted there shall, Contrary to ye Law, trade into foreign parts, His Majesty will interpret it a very great neglect in you for which he is resolved to . . . discharge" the officer from office and fine him £1,000.[9] Similar orders litter the letter books of the various committees on trade and testify to the government's frustration in its efforts to halt illegal trade.[10]

In response to these regulatory difficulties, the government constantly tinkered with trade laws, adding goods as new trades developed or adjusting mechanisms to better enforce existing laws. Starting with the separation of the administration of the Leeward Islands from Barbados and the reform of the Committee of Trade, metropolitan policy makers established a series of new rules that forced colonial governments to, in the words of John Locke, "more immediately depend on his Majesty."[11] To accomplish this, the Lords Committee of Trade and Foreign Plantations (known as the Lords of Trade and Plantations) required governors to monitor colonial shipping more closely, sent customs officials to the colonies, and ordered colonial agents to punctually and frequently report on their actions.[12] Additionally, in 1673, Parliament improved the bond system that had been first instituted in 1660. Under the 1660 laws, English subjects planning to carry enumerated goods from the colonies were required to post bond in England or Ireland to guarantee they returned there with their cargoes. Left unregulated, though, was the intercolonial shipment of enumerated goods. In 1673, Parliament closed this loophole, requiring colonial vessels to post bond as well. This innovation allowed better monitoring of ships as trade patterns became more complex, but it also introduced additional levels of administrative control that were difficult to manage. In order to make this complex bond system work and to collect customs, authorities also eventually created multiple administrative offices in each port headed by a chief collector and supported by a staff that included subcollectors, clerks, searchers, waiters, and watermen who were responsible for recording bonds and inspecting most cargoes. In theory, these multiple positions created overlapping layers of authority and provided checks against abuse; in reality, they (and the often insufficient salaries that went with them) created many opportunities for graft.[13]

This corruption constantly undermined the elaborate trade laws that administrators designed. With so many officials involved, the clever smuggler had a wide pick of likely partners within the bureaucracy. Since the bond and inspection system depended on arriving vessels being searched before they could unload their cargoes, it was with those often poorly paid and overworked officials that smugglers met with the most luck. Reporting in 1712 about Barbados's long legacy of corruption, Governor Robert Lowther noted this exact problem. He explained that he was unable to stop smuggling (in this case from Ireland) because customs officials allowed "ships to break bulk before they produce[d] their manifests, certificates, and clearance bills in the manner as the law requires. . . . [A]s long as the chief officers of the Customes, and Admiralty" were "merchants" involved in trade themselves, he continued, smuggling would persist.[14] Inattention also frustrated these efforts at reform. In October 1675, the Commissioners of the Customs in London reported that they had not received "any lists of ships or bonds from any of the Governors, except from Charles Calvert, Governor of Maryland," as the law required, a problem that persisted through that decade and the next.[15] The simple failure to file the requisite paperwork was enough to create an opening which constantly adapting colonists could exploit to drive interimperial trade.

Compounding the systematic corruption of officials on both sides of the Atlantic was that governments and customs officers in the Caribbean lacked sufficient resources to effectively monitor such a widespread area. As the English naval commissioner Captain George St. Loe pointed out, "Most of Our Islands, but especially Antegua and St. Christopher have so many bays & places where they may put on board Sugars yet it is impossible for ye Custom house Officers (tho ever so careful) to prevent" smuggling. The only remedy, he concluded, was to send "two or three Small vessels [with] good sailors to cruise up & down, [and] examine all Sloops & Boates passing to & fro."[16] Despite his optimism that a naval force would stop smuggling if given the proper resources, other governors found that even when they did get a dedicated vessel, smugglers using distant landing spots and small vessels still outmaneuvered them. After receiving intelligence about a "Hollander" trading at Stady Road in St. Christopher, for example, Captain Billop commanding the *Deptford* was unable to reach the spot before the interloper had departed.[17]

Preventing illegal trade was especially difficult when governors became complicit. Governor Willoughby of Barbados was one of the worst offenders, reportedly allowing commodities to be "exported and imported contrary to the Act of Navigation by persons most intimate with" him throughout the 1660s. Benefiting particularly from his attentions were Jewish residents of the island, whom one observer claimed Willoughby allowed to engage in trade "with their own tribe in Holland . . . to the great discouragement of English merchants."[18] Twenty years later, little had changed. In March 1685, Captain Jones of the HMS *Diamond*, "attending the service of Barbados," reported that, "foreign vessels are allowed to trade there contrary to law" and suggested that "the Governor [Richard Dutton] . . . be reminded of his duty" to stop such commerce.[19] This problem was still apparent in 1712, when Governor Robert Lowther reported that it was "not an easy matter to pursue my Instructions" to halt smuggling "because in several cases, the interest of the Queen, and that of the merchants do interfere, which happens as often as they trade illegally or make any innovations upon the Actes of Trade."[20]

Even when authorities did succeed in capturing smugglers, colonial populations were often reluctant to convict individuals of illegal trade, as Governor Richard Cony of Bermuda described in a 1685 letter. Upon hearing of the arrival of a Dutch ship which "landed 3,000l. or 4,000l. [pounds] worth of Dutch goods," Cony tried to seize the vessel and arrest the captain, "but the country [populace] forced me to set him at liberty." Then, when he ordered the Dutch goods to be marked as illegal, the sheriff refused. Complicit in the whole affair, he said, were his councilors, who refused to support his position and flouted his authority.[21] The situation in St. Christopher was similar. In 1688, Governor Sir Nathaniel Johnson pointed out he had just successfully condemned a group of smugglers who were "the first that were ever condemned here. . . . Such cases were formerly referred to tryalls at common law," he continued, where "nothing less than demonstration [absolute proof]" was "esteemed sufficient evidence for juries." It was only by removing the case from the civil court to an admiralty court that he could succeed in prosecuting the individuals. When planters united against them in such cases, governors were helpless.[22] Indeed, illicit Dutch trade was a regular feature of economic life in Barbados and the Leeward Islands. Nevertheless, these colonies' individual circumstances continued to determine the nature and frequency of the exchange. Throughout the second half of the seventeenth century, the opportunity and incentive for smuggling was probably highest for colonists in the Leeward Islands, and while the total volume of Dutch trade was probably lower than in Barbados, it was a greater share of total trade and played a more central role in these small islands' development.

Described as "very small and poor," the Leeward Islands in 1664 stood in stark contrast to Barbados, which for most Englishmen was the "fair jewell" of the Caribbean.[23] According to planters, the leading problem was that English merchants neglected them. In 1673, for example, residents of St. Christopher, Antigua, Nevis, and Montserrat reported that they had enough produce to send a hundred ships to England yearly, but that their "blooming hopes . . . [were] soon blasted . . . for wante of Shippes" from England.[24] In 1677, only eleven vessels departed London for the Leeward Islands officially—eight to Nevis, three to Antigua, and none to Montserrat or St. Christopher. That same year, forty ships traveled to Barbados and twenty-seven to Jamaica.[25] Several years later, the Council of St. Christopher observed that, "Merchants make Nevis and other islands [presumably sugar-rich Barbados and fast-developing Jamaica] their chief ports of discharge, and thus commodities reach us in a manner of second-hand, which raises the price of them twenty percent."[26] Though the Leeward Islands received more attention from English merchants after 1680, by which decade Nevis had become an important sugar producer, even in 1686 these islands received fewer arrivals from London. That year, seventy-four ships departed London for Barbados, twenty-six for Nevis, thirteen for Antigua, five for Montserrat, and three for St. Christopher. Even with the smaller size and lower populations of the Leeward Islands, the disparity in commercial interest between them and Barbados was significant.[27]

One of the major reasons for this discrepancy in shipping was that many planters in the Leewards were slow to adopt sugar. Though some had begun to experiment with it in the 1640s and it was plentiful by the 1670s, many planters continued to concentrate on tobacco, cotton, indigo, and ginger as they had in the 1640s and 1650s. There are several explanations for the persistence of these crops. First, tobacco produced in these small volcanic islands was of better quality than that produced in Barbados, enabling planters there to continue to profitably cultivate it and giving them less incentive to adopt sugar. Additionally, because tobacco could be worked on small plots, land was more widely distributed than in Barbados, where a few sugar magnates controlled large estates. Leeward Islanders' small plantations were suited to tobacco because of its low capital requirements and few economies of scale. At the same time, however, the modest profits tobacco offered prevented most planters from acquiring the capital needed to build sugar works to compete with advanced Barbadian plantations. The series of destructive wars England fought with the Dutch and French in the 1660s and 1670s also delayed planters' shift to sugar by destroying capital investment in labor and land. Even when warfare did not cause actual property loss, the fear of ruin kept many planters from investing large amounts of capital in building sugar works and acquiring labor.[28]

The net effect of the persistence of so-called "minor staples" like tobacco was that the Leeward Islands received less attention from English shippers. As the Assembly of Nevis explained in 1664, "many of the meaner sort" living on the island were still "wholly imployed in the manufacture and making [of] Tobacco," but because English merchants trading from "London & some other parts of England where Tobacco is noe Commodity" ignored this segment of the economy, tobacco planters were left lacking necessities.[29] Such an environment encouraged planters to look to Dutch buyers as they had in earlier decades. Little had changed in 1671, when Governor Charles Wheler explained that Leeward Islanders preferred Dutch trade partly as a result of "English merchants" refusing to "take the tobacco which the poor must of necessity plant." This, he concluded "makes the Planter cry out for the Kings favour, that a shipp or two onely might trade with them from Holland or from them to Holland."[30] As late as 1682, London merchant Balderson Claypole still believed Amsterdam and Rotterdam to be the best markets for Antiguan tobacco.[31] Eager to buy

European goods, unable to attract English shipping, and desirous of Dutch markets for their tobacco, colonists chose to smuggle.

The precise amount of Leeward Island produce, whether tobacco or sugar, that flowed to Dutch merchants will never be known, but several anecdotal observations indicate it was significant. For his part, St. Loe believed that though there were always several Dutch "great ships" at St. Eustatius, "two of ye least of them" could "carry a years produce of that Island," meaning all the other vessels, "which in a years time is a considerable Quantity[,] have their Loading solely from his Majesty's Plantations." Governor Lynch of Jamaica estimated that in the year 1671, "most of the produce" of Montserrat and Antigua was sent to St. Eustatius, an amount he put at 400,000 pounds, or about 170 tons. Though it is unknown how much tobacco those islands produced in 1671, if the numbers from 1677 when planters there sent 760 tons to London are any guide, Lynch's estimate of 170 tons was a considerable amount.[32]

Another facet of the Leeward Islands' perceived backwardness was that the RAC largely neglected the islands. Focused foremost on Barbados, the company refused to disembark enslaved Africans in the Leewards, forcing planters there to buy those slaves that Barbadians had rejected. Later, RAC factors established a transit hub in Nevis, but still the number of slaves sent there paled in comparison to that which Barbados received. In 1684, to take just one typical year, the RAC sent almost 4,000 slaves to Barbados and only 176 to Nevis, from which the factors were to supply the entire Leewards.[33] In 1672, Governor Sir William Stapleton reported that Antigua and Montserrat received only 300 slaves from the RAC in the previous six years.[34] Recent estimates generally validate Stapleton's claims. David Eltis finds that between 1664 and 1672, the two monopoly companies did not transport any slaves to the Leewards, relying on licensed vessels that supplied only an estimated 600 slaves to the islands between 1667 and 1672.[35]

Problems with high prices and inconsistent supply encouraged some planters in the Leeward Islands to evade the RAC monopoly and turn to others suppliers, like the Dutch. Though no Dutch trader is documented as having supplied any of the estimated 21,700 slaves landed in the English Leeward Islands between 1661 and 1688 (an annual average of 800 per year), English colonists were well aware of the Dutch ability to supply slaves from their western Atlantic depots.[36]

In a 1670 request for additional slave imports, for example, Governor William Byam of Antigua noted that if adequate supplies were not furnished, then "the Dutch would supply them" to the colonists.[37]

TABLE 4.1

Estimates of All Slaves Landed in the English Leeward Islands,
1600–1688

	Antigua	St. Kitts	Montserrat / Nevis	Total
1643–45	0	800	0	800
1661–65	0	1,000	200	1,200
1671–75	0	0	2,100	2,100
1676–80	1,200	300	5,000	6,500
1681–85	900	1,500	6,500	8,900
1686–88	600	0	2,900	3,500
Totals	2,800	3,500	16,700	22,900

SOURCE: TASTD, http://slavevoyages.org/tast/assessment/estimates.faces?yearFrom=
1600&yearTo=1688&disembarkation=309.304.30.

NOTE: Figures rounded to nearest hundred. Totals calculated by summing raw data
and then rounding to nearest hundred.

According to the RAC agents Henry Carpenter and Thomas Belcham-
ber, trade between the Leewards and the Dutch depots at Curaçao and
St. Eustatius was particularly brisk in the late seventeenth century. These
men reported that "Some of the Chiefs of our Island [Nevis] and St.
Christopher's" often "discoursed" on the "convenyence" of "supplying
themselves with negroes at an Easier rate" from "the Dutch at St. Estatia"
than from "the Royall Company."[38] The St. Christopher councilor Joseph
Crispe evidently took advantage of these Dutch supplies—sometimes at
prices 25 percent below RAC prices—and managed a "great trade to the
Dutch islands, by the Sugars sent thither by stealth and Negros slaves
brought in return in the same manner" during the 1680s.[39]

From the Dutch perspective, it is clear that the English colonists were
often insufficiently supplied with labor and thus some worked to open
English markets. In 1661, the directors of the WIC in Amsterdam ordered that "slaves shall be kept in *New Netherland*," so that they could
"be exported to the English and other Neighbours." Perhaps acting on
WIC encouragement, Paulus Heyn Ridder sailed the *Arms of Amsterdam* from the west coast of Africa to Montserrat with 101 slaves later that
year, but when a privateer intercepted his vessel, Ridder altered his course
for Virginia.[40] The Dutch also held slaves at St. Eustatius and Curaçao,
intending to sell them at surrounding Spanish, French, and English

colonies. This was precisely the fear of the RAC factor Clement Tudway, who reported in 1687 that the Dutch had plans to "establish a magazine for negroes" at St. Eustatius.[41] Another potential supplier of slaves was the Danish. In 1688, Governor Johnson warned that "a Danish Royal African Company [had recently been] established" at St. Thomas that planned to follow "the practice of our Dutch neighbours at St Eustace" in "clandestinely sending slaves to these islands . . . notwithstanding all the care and circumspection which hath been or indeed can be used."[42] Near the English Leeward Islands, these foreign colonies offered quick access to foreign slaves in a period in which the RAC struggled to meet English demand. The interimperial origins of many British West Indian slaves underscore how fully intertwined Dutch trade and English colonial development were in the seventeenth century.

Barbados's unique political economy made Anglo-Dutch trade there both less important than in the Leeward Islands and less prevalent than it had been before 1670. For one thing, British shippers and merchants played a gradually more active role in developing Barbados's economy because of the island's sugar production. By the mid-1680s, about 350 vessels a year called at Barbados, making it one of the busiest ports in English America. Of these ships, between thirty-five and seventy brought manufactures from England, between twenty-five and forty-five carried foodstuffs from Ireland, and eight vessels arrived from New England bearing horses, provisions, and lumber. Further diminishing colonists' demand for Dutch trade was a new wave of migrants that the island's bustling trade drew to Bridgetown. In 1687 alone, more than eighty new traders arrived from England. Working as partners for or tied by kinship to English traders, these migrants oriented their trade to England and pulled Barbadians along.[43] The brisk pace of trade and the involvement of more metropolitan traders in the island's economy meant that, by the 1670s, most Barbadians could satisfy their demands with English shipping.

In addition to the mercantile attention Barbados received from England, the manner in which planters sold their sugar further discouraged Anglo-Dutch trade. This arrangement, which became known as the commission system, developed in the third quarter of the seventeenth century and gradually replaced the older and less efficient merchant system, under which European traders called at English Caribbean ports to offer speculative cargoes in exchange for tropical produce. In the earliest years of settlement, it connected fledgling English West Indian planters directly to immediate sources of credit and supplies at a time before they had the ability to arrange trade for themselves. At the same time, however, because most exchanges happened in their colony where markets were small, planters often received lower prices and had limited control over their choice of partners and the timing of trade.

As they developed more and larger plantations, planters became dissatisfied with an arrangement over which they had little control. In response, they developed a commission system, under which planters bore the burden of shipping their produce to England, where it could be sold in a wider market. To make this work, planters consigned their goods to commission agents, or factors, in England who received and disbursed cargoes of sugar, paid port duties, and monitored sales. Factors also provided credit to planters by arranging return shipments of supplies and paying bills of exchange drawn on them for slaves and other goods months before the promised sugar had reached their hands. In return for their services, agents generally received 2.5 percent commission on the sale of colonial goods and the purchase of English ones. This new way of vending tropical commodities entailed greater risks for planters but also brought the potential of high profits. Overlapping with the merchant system for decades, by the end of the seventeenth century the commission system dominated in Barbados.[44]

The experience and reputation that honest and effective agents gained meant that a relatively small group of British merchants controlled most of the islands' trade. In 1686, for example, twenty-two London-based merchants controlled 40 percent of exports to the British Caribbean, and twenty-eight controlled 50 percent of imports from these colonies.[45] Dependent upon these merchants for the specialized services they provided and bound to them by growing indebtedness, the commission system restricted Barbadians' ability to seek cross-national trade by compelling them to send their goods to Britain to satisfy their creditors and keep their advantageous metropolitan contacts. This transition also distinguished Barbados from the Leeward Islands and helps explain why interimperial commerce was more pervasive in the latter colonies. A greater credit risk because of their middling status, Leeward Islanders' limited resources provoked them to seek more consistent and reliable, if lower, prices at island docks or in neighboring colonies rather than to gamble on the higher, but riskier, profits the commission system offered. With shallower connections to the metropole than Barbadians or sugar-producing Leeward Islanders who were more deeply intertwined in English credit networks, tobacco-producing planters in the Leewards could be more flexible when it came to selling colonial produce to Dutch buyers.

By the end of the seventeenth century, Barbadian planters also faced a third challenge that reduced their opportunity and need to trade sugar directly to the Dutch. In an effort to avoid the risks (and thus greater associated prices) of buying sugar from stocks smuggled out of Barbados, Dutch sugar processors increasingly bought it in London. The English mercantilist writer Sir Josiah Child explained that low interest rates of about 3 percent in the Netherlands—compared to 6 percent in England—gave Dutch merchants the cost savings they needed to bypass Barbados and buy sugar from London despite "the second freight and charges upon them between England and Holland" that buying sugar from England entailed.[46] As Dutch refiners shifted purchases of sugar to London, many colonists and their Dutch partners decided the risks of sending sugar directly to the Netherlands no longer outweighed the costs.

A fourth and final factor that connected Barbadian planters more directly to England and reduced the incentive for direct Dutch trade involved the great debts planters owed to the RAC. As the transition to sugar intensified after 1650, planters' demand for slaves climbed steadily upward as the enslaved population rose from 20,000 in 1655 to 33,184 in 1673, and 46,500 (of a total population of 66,000) in 1684.[47] An important step in making sure that demand for slaves—which was made higher by annual mortality rates of around 5 percent—could be met was Charles II's decision to award a monopoly on African trade to the RAC in 1660, an inducement that quickly paid dividends. Altogether, between 1661 and 1688, merchants carried more than 100,000 slaves to Barbados, a yearly average of almost 4,000 persons.[48]

Most Barbadians who bought slaves from the RAC could not afford them at the time of purchase, their harvests having not yet come in. Nevertheless, their creditworthiness allowed them to pay for the slaves by drawing bills of exchange on their London agents before their produce arrived in London. In order to cover these debts, planters sent their sugars to their London agents, who used the proceeds to cover the bills. Because they remained constantly in debt to the RAC, planters found that this system of credit and debit centered in London gave them no option but to send their sugar to the metropole. This was unlike those practices in the Leewards by which planters who paid for slaves with produce were free to buy imported goods from whomever they preferred. In sum, the eagerness of English merchants to do business with Barbadians, the development of the commission system, Dutch merchants' decision to buy sugar in London, and planters' indebtedness to the RAC combined to

TABLE 4.2
Estimates of All Slaves Landed in Barbados by National Carrier,
1600–1688

	Great Britain	Netherlands	British North America	France	Denmark / Baltic	Totals
1641–45	11,000	200	300	0	0	11,600
1646–50	12,900	200	400	0	700	14,200
1651–55	4,500	300	0	300	0	5,000
1656–60	10,700	500	0	0	0	11,200
1661–65	16,800	0	0	0	0	16,800
1666–70	15,700	0	0	0	0	15,800
1671–75	13,400	500	0	0	0	13,900
1676–80	15,900	0	0	0	0	15,900
1681–85	26,300	0	200	0	0	26,400
1686–88	11,300	0	0	0	0	11,200
Totals	138,400	1,700	900	300	700	142,000

SOURCE: TASTD, http://slavevoyages.org/tast/assessment/estimates.faces?yearFrom=
1600&yearTo=1688&disembarkation=302.

NOTE: Figures rounded to nearest hundred. Totals calculated by summing raw data
and then rounding to nearest hundred.

reduce Anglo-Dutch trade in Barbados.[49] Of the 100,000 slaves disembarked in Barbados between 1661 and 1688, the Dutch probably supplied about 2,000.[50]

Despite these structural factors, however, Barbadians planters still chose Dutch trade at particular times. This was especially true when sugar prices declined in the 1670s, prompting some English merchants to decide that carrying it was "scarce worth their hazard." The result was that planters could not secure sufficient "shipping to carry off one-half of their effects [produce]."[51]

Such circumstances combined with the price advantages Dutch traders still offered to influence Barbadians already in the habit of consuming Dutch goods and specialized services to pursue Anglo-Dutch trade. These norms were so ingrained that as late as 1692, Barbados governor James Kendall turned to Amsterdam to hire a master sugar

TABLE 4.3

Sugar Prices in Barbados, 1646–1694 (shillings per cwt)

Year	Price
1646	50s.
1649	37s. 5d.
1652	20s.
1653	25s.
1654	16s. 7d.
1655	25s.
1661	15s.
1673–84	12s. 6d.
1687	6s. 5d.
1694	9–10s.

SOURCE: Russell R. Menard, *Sweet Negotiations: Sugar, Slavery, and Plantation Agriculture in Early Barbados* (Charlottesville: University of Virginia Press, 2006), 69.

refiner for his plantation.[52] The thirty-five Barbadians who sent their sugar to Amsterdam through Falmouth on the *Experiment* in 1680 further testify to the continued demand for Dutch markets as do the almost 60,000 pounds of Barbadian sugar that were declared before an Amsterdam notary to have arrived in Amsterdam in 1687.[53] These few examples of Dutch trade indicate that when the opportunity to find better goods at lower prices or to avoid duties became available, Barbadians were quick to exploit advantageous interimperial trading options. For a population steeped in a cross-national heritage, it made little sense to ignore fruitful commercial opportunities. The full scope of this trade is beyond numeration, but it clearly remained a regular feature of Barbados's commercial makeup.[54]

In order to carry out interimperial trade after 1660, English West Indians had to adapt their strategies to the new Restoration regulations aimed at stopping it. Though the frequency of trade varied between Barbados and the Leeward Islands, colonists in both place used similar approaches. One of these tactics was to return to the relatively disorganized but low-risk practice of exchanging goods directly with Dutch vessels cruising the Atlantic, as they had in the merchant system. The Navigation Acts had specifically targeted such trade, but the improvisational and opportunistic nature of the practice made it difficult for authorities to stop, especially in the West Indies, where monitoring ports was so difficult. One such 400-ton cruising vessel arrived in Barbados from Amsterdam in June 1661 carrying fifty-two horses from Amsterdam. Replicating multilateral trading patterns used by earlier Caribbean ships, the master landed his cargo and quickly departed for New England, where he bought timber, salted meat, flour, and thirty more horses before returning to Barbados. The Swiss doctor Felix Christian Spoeri also signed on for a similar trip on the *St. Peter* in later years. This ship departed Amsterdam, stopped in Limerick, Ireland, to load salted meat and thirty horses before crossing the Atlantic to Barbados.[55] Late in the 1680s, another Dutch vessel followed a similar route, transporting Dutch manufactures to New London, Connecticut, exchanging some of this cargo for thirty horses and a parcel of lumber, which it then carried to Barbados along with the remaining manufactured goods.[56]

As these voyages also reveal, Dutch shippers were more willing then ever to partner with Englishmen in Caribbean ventures. Sometimes this meant merely renting space on an English ship bound for the Caribbean, but at other times it entailed Dutch merchants hiring English ships and English captains so as to pass off their ventures as English. One group even went so far as to equip the experienced Anglo-Dutch shipmaster George Armstrong with two sets of papers. One correctly identified *Het Swarten Paert* as a Dutch vessel originating in the Netherlands, and the other indicated that the vessel was the English *Black Horse*. When English authorities stopped the vessel upon arriving in Barbados in 1661, Armstrong did as instructed, throwing the papers identifying the ship as Dutch overboard and presenting the English set so as to avoid capture. That he was an Englishman with at least one English crewman only reinforced the seeming veracity of the fraudulent papers. At other times, Anglo-Dutch trade was organized by Englishmen living in Amsterdam who most likely helped unite Dutch investors with English shipowners.[57]

So many Dutch-chartered vessels called at Nevis some years that authorities felt the need to pass a law reminding colonists that "the comodities & products of this Island as—sugar, Indigo, Tobacco, Cottonwool, Ginger & the like" were not to be "shipped [in] vessels belonging to forreigners."[58] The new effort evidently had little impact for eight years later a group of metropolitan merchants living in Nevis complained that foreigners were still permitted to trade, an act they compared to allowing outsiders to "eat the bread out of [their] mouths." Claiming that colonists were eager to trade with foreigners while leaving them "unpaid and their merchandises . . . on their hands," these English traders urged Governor William Willoughby to intercede, hoping that legal maneuvers would do what their own prices and goods could not: get colonists to buy English rather than Dutch goods.[59] Such complaints failed to end illegal trade. Being informed that "there are considerable quantityes of all sorts of provisions and the most needfull goods and Commodityes carried off from his Majesty's Island by forreigners and Strangers to other places," in 1675 Governor Stapleton and his council tried another tactic, hoping that requiring all foreigners to present themselves to the "Sheriff or Provost-Marshall of this Island, to give an account what they are, from whense they come, and what their business is" within six hours of their arrival would make illegal trade more monitorable. In a further attempt to curtail trade with Dutch vessels arriving there, the law prohibited any "Inhabitants or others either in their house, or Vessels in ye roads of this Island . . . [from] Entertain[ing] any forreigner or Stranger."[60]

Mounting legislation like the 1675 act made trade more hazardous for large vessels since they required more time to load and unload. As a result, colonists improvised, switching to smaller vessels that made short trips to meet ships riding just offshore. These vessels, what one governor termed "quenou[s]" (canoes), were the perfect vehicle to bring "forbidden" goods to and from the islands because they were both difficult to spot and could make use of the many small bays and creeks that dot the Leeward Islands' coastlines.[61] Governor Stapleton noted two such places in English St. Christopher, six in Antigua, three in Montserrat, and five in Nevis.[62] A 1667 French map of St. Christopher, *Carte de l'isle de Sainct Christophle,* reveals how inviting these could be to smugglers. Denoted by anchors in the map, the island's roadsteads are clearly visible, and though one of those in the English portion of the island is in clear view of Fort Charles, the second is along the remote south-facing coast.

In an effort to stymie this mechanism for illegal trade and to better collect customs revenues, governors and their councils—sometimes of their own volition and sometimes only in response to orders from Whitehall—passed laws restricting trade to several appointed and monitorable locations, but they had little ability to enforce such laws. In Montserrat, authorities even took the relatively extreme step of decreeing that "all Owners of Boats, wherries, or Canoes, [should] every night chain or lock every one of them to some Tree or firm Post" to stop smugglers from using the watercraft. The sheer number of times that governments enacted similar laws suggests that during the seventeenth century none of these attempts was successful.[63]

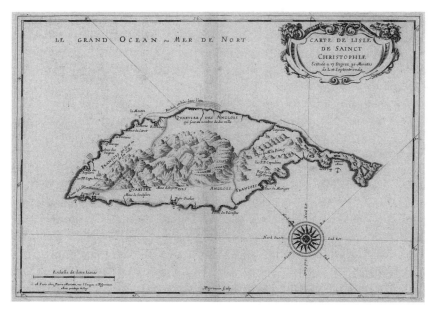

FIGURE 6. *Carte de l'isle de Sainct Christophle scituée a 17 degrez 30 Minutes de lat. septentrionale,* 1667, Paris. Courtesy of the John Carter Brown Library at Brown University.

Sometimes Dutch smugglers did not try to hide their arrival and instead exploited a loophole in English policy that sanctioned cross-national contact in times of necessity. The Treaty of Breda (1667) ending the Anglo-French War and the Second Anglo-Dutch War, included a provision which allowed "merchant ships of the contracting nations" to "enter each other's ports when, driven by storm, pirates, or other urgent need [such as water or wood], provided they do not break bulk, nor attempt to trade."[64] Of course, this was not a new idea; it had long been customary in the Atlantic to provide a safe port and aid to a fellow European vessel in distress. Over time, though, merchants abused this provision to gain access to foreign colonies in the hope of trading there. In May 1687, Captain St. Loe, investigating the "defrauding of the royal revenue in the Leeward Islands," described how smugglers executed this technique. There "are continually Several great ships lying at Statia [Dutch St. Eustatius]," he wrote, who on their way "from Holland . . . generally touch at all our Islands under ye pretext of watering." Usually staying for "7 or 8 dayes," they invite the "Planters [to] com[e] on board and agree . . . for what they have on board (they keeping particular Invoyces ready which are carried from hand to hand on purpose). . . . [H]aveing so Disposed of their Lading," the Dutch vessels then "go to Statia where they Stay till ye English Planters" send their "sugars" in smaller sloops or boats. The Dutch vessels, "having laden themselves with ye produce of his Majesty's Islands," then sail "directly to Holland."[65] Later that year, just such a Dutch vessel was trading "at Antigua under pretence of getting wood."[66]

St. Loe's description of using St. Eustatius as a base of operations for the illicit transit trade is important. Lying among the English Leeward Islands and stocked with Dutch traders, slaves, European goods, and other necessaries, St. Eustatius was a perfect base for smugglers. As the Frenchman Charles de Rochefort portrayed it, the island was "but a Mountain rising up in the midst of the Ocean, much like a Sugar-loaf," an apt description for a place through which so much sugar flowed. Made up of two craggy, extinct volcanoes, St. Eustatius has only about 1,400 acres of arable ground lying along a spine of land that connects the two peaks. The rocky island's most precious asset to seventeenth-century colonists was not this fertile plane, but the deep, protected anchorage on its west side that the Dutch called Oranje Bay. This anchorage was free of navigational hazards, straightforwardly approachable from the sea, and easily defended from the high cliffs surrounding it. A sandy beach and lines of storehouses built into the cliffs extended the length of the shoreline and provided the perfect haven for a trading entrepôt. Possessed by the Dutch not for its utility as a center for the cultivation of tropical commodities, St. Eustatius was valuable instead as a nursery of interimperial exchange.[67]

The first reports of the Dutch using St. Eustatius in this fashion to trade with English colonies comes from the 1650s, when the Montser-rat merchant Henry Waad testified that he "knowes that severall store-houses were kept in the Island [Montserrat] dureing the late Warr with ye Dutch, and that with the goods there kept a Trade was mantayned with the Dutch. . . . In order to which boats came severall tymes to the said Island from a Plantacion of ye Dutch at Stasha."[68] In the 1660s and 1670s, colonists continued to use the Dutch island as a conduit for in-terimperial trade.[69] Hoping to stop the siphoning off of so much colonial produce, the Lords of Trade ordered the island captured in 1672. Still, though, Dutch and English traders continued to employ the island to their advantage. In 1680, Governor Stapleton was forced to admit, "there was a Dutch ship at St. Eustatius, which might have traded there in defi-ance of me." Exasperated that even English occupation could not halt Dutch merchants from trading at the island, he mused that "it were to be wished that St. Eustatius, Saba, and Anguilla [the former Dutch islands] were as much under water as above it, so the people were off."[70] When St. Eustatius was restored to the Dutch in 1682, its importance for Anglo-Dutch trade only grew. The Dutch island's reputation was such that when he published the pamphlet *An Historical Account of the Rise and Growth of the West-India Collonies* in 1690, the former planter and West Indian advocate Dalby Thomas noted that a "great quantity of Commodities . . . [was] sent out of the Leeward *Caribee* Islands, and sold to the *Dutch* . . . under the name *St. Eustace* Sugar."[71]

Residents of St. Christopher could obtain Dutch trade through an even closer population of Dutch merchants—those who lived in the French portions of the island. In his depiction of the Caribbean Islands, De Rochefort reported: "The French and Dutch Merchants, who reside there constantly, are well furnish'd" with every imaginable European good "not being the growth of the Island . . . yet necessary for the better accommodation of the Inhabitants."[72] These residents' trade was of such volume that when a fire erupted in Basse-Terre, reports described the damage of 2 million livres of goods in sixty Dutch warehouses.[73] To keep these warehouses stocked and to transport planters' production, one Englishman claimed in 1662 that "hee hath seen about 12 Dutch Shipps at a time at St. Christophers, and that hee believes about 30 Dutch Shipps in a yeare are there Laden." And since, he continued, "the Commodityes growing on the French Ground and Plantations on the said Islands . . . doe, and will (as he beleiveth) lade, one yeare with . . . [only] about 12 Shipps of ordinary burthern," it was clear to this observer that English produce filled the remaining Dutch vessels.[74]

English customs collectors confirmed this hypothesis of circuitous Dutch trade when they seized the *Orange Tree*, a vessel owned by the Middelburg merchants "John Mayer Schipper and De Leaker," off Plymouth, England, for attempting to carry English tobacco from French St. Christopher to the Netherlands. The owners, the captain, and the Dutch ambassador to England protested, arguing that the vessel carried only French, not English, produce. To verify this claim, the Admiralty Court brought in experts to determine the origins of the tobacco. This was possible, they noted, because "the Rolles of Tobacco made up by the English in the English Plantation [differed] from those made up by the French, and other Inhabitants there [so much], that they are easily distinguished one from the other; the English making up theirs constantly in short Rolles, and great Twists, and without Molossus, and that the French and other Inhabitants there, doe make up theirs in small Twists, and long

Rolles with Molossus." When they then searched the vessel, the inspectors found that "at the least one third part of the said Rolles [in the vessel] were made up in a great Twist and short Rolls without Mollossus" and were thus "of the English make, and growth of the English Plantation."[75] In other words, even though the *Orange Tree* had only touched at the French portion of the island, it carried English tobacco. According to the English planter Jeaffreson, the *Orange Tree* was not unique. He claimed to know that much of the "produce of the English plantations was carried . . . into the French grounds" before being "shipped for Holland, whilst theire [Dutch] commodities were vended" to English colonists.[76] Allowed to establish warehouses in the French colony, Dutch traders then worked with English and French planters alike to send the growth of both nations' plantations to Dutch markets. In this case, intra-island trade was crucial for interimperial transatlantic commerce.

Barbadians, who lived at some distance from St. Eustatius, used Curaçao as a transfer point for their produce in the second half of the seventeenth century. Though this Dutch entrepôt was not as readily accessible as was St. Eustatius—an element that made trade their riskier—its greater size and diversity of trade gave Barbadians access to a greater range of economic opportunities there than did Leeward Islanders calling at St. Eustatius.[77] From Curaçao, Dutch traders used small-scale, relatively safe ventures to supply Barbados with foodstuffs and other plantation supplies that colonists badly needed and were difficult to obtain from England. In turn, Curaçao presented an important contact node for planters looking for a regional market for sugar and a way to step beyond the Navigation Acts.[78] The sloop the *New Yorke,* captained by Robert Darkyns, sought to capitalize on this trade when it departed Barbados with a cargo of goods "of the growh of his Majestyes dominins and carrid the same to an iseland call[ed] Carasaw" in the summer of 1676.[79]

During the 1640s, English islanders had welcomed Dutch agents who wished to reside in their ports, but after the Anglo-Dutch Wars this was more difficult to accomplish. Nonetheless, some Dutch colonists were present at English colonies as late as the 1670s and 1680s. The 1678 census of St. Christopher identifies eight Dutch male residents, three of whom had wives and children. There is little overt evidence in the census itself—such as numbers of slaves, size of landholdings, or residence in a port town—to suggest if the men were merchants, planters, or a combination of the two. Nor do any of the eight men's names match those of the merchants who were present in the 1650s.[80] However, other sources suggest that at least one of these men, Adrian van Homrkirk, was a planter.

In a 1676 letter, the St. Christopher planter Christopher Jeafferson noted that "there is one Hemskerke, a Dutchman, that lives upon the Godwin Plantations, and pays four thousand weight of sugar per annum for it and the stock."[81] Of the other men, John Monke, Peter Barrdrick, and a man called only "Limite," little else is known. Though they lived along the island's steep fertile Caribbean-facing side, none of these men is registered as having a family or large numbers of slaves, suggesting that they were there only temporarily. Perhaps, they were agents for Dutch traders like those who had lived on the island twenty years before. The other four Dutch men in the census—Jacob Trumpe, Garratt [Gerrit] Dower, John Tarridge, and Jans Timberman—appear sequentially; three of these men lived with wives and had children, but there are no hints about their occupations.

Although the census recorded only these several Dutch inhabitants, some English residents believed the number was higher. In May 1677, Jeaffreson wrote, "There are a great many French and Dutch inhabitants in the English ground" at St. Christopher and that one of them, "a Hamburger [a term often substituted for 'Dutchman'] bought part of my plantation."[82] Six years later, Governor William Stapleton supported an effort "to procure Letters of Denization for one Laurens Westerband a Dutchman," who lived in the Leewards and was the governor's acquaintance.[83] While nothing more is known about these men, it is clear that Dutch traders still remained active in the Leewards in the 1680s.

Meanwhile, those Dutch traders still interested in English trade also began to rely on English agents living in the islands or Dutchmen living there as English denizens to manage their affairs. Henry Mayer of Antigua was one such individual. When he died in February 1663, Mayer willed "John Boshman of ye city of Amsterdam, merchant, 100 acres in St. John's Division," and described himself as Boshman's "agent."[84] Now a landowner in Antigua, Boshman decided to relocate to Antigua and take up the plantation himself. Within two years after Mayer's death, Boshman and his son "Peter Boshman of Holland . . . merchant planter," along with "Peter Coene and his son Peter Coene, natives of Holland and planters," applied for status as denizens in the English empire. Their application for legal privileges—a step their countrymen seldom employed before 1650—was an acknowledgment of their optimism for continued trade in the Leewards and was consonant with steps that Dutchmen in New York City took to legitimize their presence. At the same time that it provided legal precedent for the trade, the need for denization shows that it was no longer possible for Dutch merchants to casually reside in English colonies.[85]

Most Leeward Islanders welcomed such Dutch traders and the connections they brought to their colonies, but some English competitors resented their presence. It was most likely these men who convinced the Council and Assembly of Montserrat to issue an order that forbade colonists from representing foreign traders.[86] Given the general enthusiasm of the colonists in Montserrat for Dutch trade, this law was probably forced upon the residents. Nevertheless, it must have reminded colonists and their Dutch partners alike of the ever-increasing vulnerability of their relationship.

The Sephardic Jewish community in the English West Indies made an even greater difference than did these Anglo-Dutch agent relations. Jewish colonists had an expansive international network of commercial connections that assisted commerce across imperial boundaries and proved vital in colonial development. The community was truly Atlantic. By the middle of the seventeenth century, there were Jewish traders, mostly Sephardic, in Amsterdam, Lisbon, London, the mainland English American colonies, the English, Dutch, French, Spanish and Portuguese Caribbeans, and on the Spanish Main. The historical processes that created such a broadly dispersed religious group began in the thirteenth and fourteenth centuries as Jews were banished first from England and then from France and most of Germany. Jewish persecution reached a terrible climax in the late fifteenth century, when Spain replaced its policy of forced conversion with one of outright expulsion in 1492, and then when the Portuguese, whose country had offered a haven for many Jews, reversed their policies of toleration and enacted compulsory conversion to Catholicism beginning in 1497.

As they were propelled out of western Europe, many Jews fled to the Ottoman Empire and along the eastern edge of the Mediterranean, to North Africa in the southeast, and to what is now Poland and eastern Europe to the north and east. However, not all fled. Some became Marranos (secret Jews), others became Conversos (new Christians); when the Spanish and Portuguese expanded across the Atlantic, many of these families saw better opportunities there. Not only did the dispersed nature of settlement alleviate their fears of Inquisition agents and allow more open worship, but the Americas also offered the chance for entrance into new trades. Jews, Marranos, and Conversos who had served as members of the Iberian Peninsula's mercantile elite took their significant commercial experience, contacts, and trading capital with them as they traveled around the Atlantic.[87]

Meanwhile, the revolt of the northern provinces of the Netherlands against Spain in the 1580s opened up that country to Jewish refugees and allowed Marranos already there to begin to practice their faith openly. Though life in Amsterdam was not without struggle, Jewish traders there were well positioned to help foster the economic development of the Atlantic world. The United Provinces' expansion into the Caribbean offered Jews the opportunity to cement ties between Amsterdam and their contacts in Spanish and Portuguese colonies. In other words, the very conditions of oppression and expulsion that Jews experienced in Europe left Jewish merchants and their families well situated to recognize and take advantage of colonization in the Americas. The community found Brazil to be one place of great opportunity as Portuguese New Christians already dominated the sugar trade. For more than two decades, Portuguese Jewish merchants also flourished in New Holland's main port, Recife. The community grew to nearly 5,000 before they were forced to flee once again when the Portuguese recaptured the colony. Having already established ties in the Atlantic, most returned only briefly to Amsterdam before migrating to the Dutch Caribbean possessions of Curaçao, Suriname, and Cayenne, but also to French and English colonies. It was sometime amidst the export and sugar boom of the 1650s that the first Jewish colonists arrived in Barbados, and quickly the Jewish population grew to more than 300 by the time of the island's first census in 1680.[88] Because laws prevented most Jewish colonists from owning more than two slaves and from contracting indentured servants and because of the pressure of English prejudice, they were forced into colonial ports like Bridgetown (which claimed 238 of the 303 Jews in Barbados in 1680) and Speightstown in Barbados, where many pursued commerce and established a close-knit religious and trading community.[89]

These kinship and religious networks extended around the early modern Atlantic and were instrumental in Jewish traders' success. Other groups, too, used a combination of kinship, ethnic, and religious ties to cement trade between disparate places, but the Jewish Diaspora differed from other groups both in members' "outsider" status and in the particular configuration of their networks. The Jewish Diaspora connected trading families from Dutch, English, Spanish, and Portuguese metropolitan and colonial cities and thus strengthened the possibilities for interimperial exchange. Bolstered by close cross-national networks of intermarried individuals, Jewish traders found their ability to pool capital—especially important when hoping to open new colonial markets—and to efficiently gather information about prices, the state of various markets, and news of impending wars gave them advantages over merchants without such extensive interimperial ties.[90]

The Narvarro family, based in Amsterdam, represents one such network that extended to Barbados and other English and Dutch colonies. Refugees from Portugal as young men, Arão (Aaron) Navarro and his brothers Moisés (Moseh) and Jacob arrived in Dutch Brazil from Amsterdam in the early 1630s (Jacob in the 1640s) and traded there until the 1650s, when the Portuguese reoccupation of the Dutch colony forced them to return to Amsterdam. From Amsterdam, Arão then went to Suriname and then Barbados, where he had arrived by 1658. In this English colony, he continued to rely on his previous Amsterdam contact, his eldest brother, Isaac Navarro, but also included his cousin Jacob Fundao and Fundao's brother-in-law Mordechai Senhor (Senior) in Suriname among his correspondents. While in Barbados, Arão Navarro also took advantage of new opportunities within the growing English empire, receiving cargoes from his brother Jacob through London's Luis Dias in 1666. Based in Amsterdam and linked to the Dutch and English Atlantic through migration and kinship, families such as the Navarros provided English colonial communities with ready access to numerous Dutch markets.[91]

Of these connections, it was ties between colonial Jewish traders and what their critics called "their own tribe in Holland" that were perhaps the most valuable.[92] Because Amsterdam's and Bridgetown's Jewish communities were interwoven, merchants could send large vessels to trade in the Caribbean, knowing that the odds of success were higher with local contacts than without. Sir William Davidson, an Englishman who lived in Amsterdam and who had worked with Jewish traders in 1662 and 1663, discovered that a group of Jewish merchants in Amsterdam had done exactly this in 1668. Bent on personal revenge because of an earlier experience, Davidson informed authorities that the Jewish traders had sent the fully laden *Matthew and Francis* (300 tons) and *Sarah and Mary* (270 tons) to Barbados.[93] Though word reached Barbados before the vessels had arrived, Governor Christopher Codrington refused to seize them, explaining that they had arrived legally according to English law because customs officials in England routinely allowed "shipps laden in Holland to touch & enter in some ports in England, from whence they Carry Certificates from the Custom house, upon which Lycence of trade hath always been heretofore granted." As the vessels had the appropriate documents form England, Codrington claimed he could not detain them.[94]

Codrington's evocation of the use of English outports illustrates one of the important mechanisms that allowed Jewish colonists to maintain their trade with the Netherlands legally. Traders regularly sent cargoes between English colonies and Amsterdam, or vice versa, pausing to enter them in England under the name of an English merchant or a naturalized Jew, and pay the appropriate duties before sending them to their final destination. This touching in England, while costly (in terms of time lost and duties paid), served to make Anglo-Dutch trade legal and enabled those involved to take advantage of the skills, capital, and access to markets of contacts in three different locations. Jewish traders were not unique among West Indians using this mechanism, but had an advantage over most others because the dispersed nature of their networks placed contacts in the Netherlands, England, and Barbados. In fact, it was Cromwell himself who created the opportunity for this complex configuration of trade when a group of Amsterdam Jews persuaded him to allow them to settle in London in 1656 despite London merchants' fears that the foreigners would erode their profits.[95]

Another way Jewish merchants trading between Amsterdam and the English Caribbean thwarted enforcement of trade laws was to combine quasi-legal and illegal trade in the same ventures, obscuring the legality of the whole venture as in the example of the *Experiment* which introduced this chapter. In that case, the Dutch and English colonial merchants involved sent their vessel from Barbados to Amsterdam with a stop in England to make the voyage legal. It was at that stage that they added an element of deceit by unloading and paying taxes on only a portion of their cargo. As the customs agent Samuel Hayne explained, the traders entered "some small Out-Port, and only Unloading part of the Cargo which lyes topmost, leaving the ground Tyre [tier]" in place. The maneuver enabled them to "conceal Goods of great value from the Eyes of any Officer." According to Hayne, the Jews of Barbados conspired with those of Amsterdam in this way to send considerable quantities of manufactured goods from the Netherlands to Barbados and sugars in the opposite direction. Such trade, in Hayne's view, accounted for the fact that "the *Jews* in *Barbados* Sell more *Hollands* there [in Barbados], than all the *English* merchants do."[96]

On the one hand, as Hayne and some metropolitan merchants saw it, continued interimperial commerce was damaging both to His Majesty's revenues and to English merchants who could not compete with Dutch traders, whether Jewish or Christian. Colonists, on the other hand, had a very different perspective. While surely profiting by not paying duties on the full value of their cargoes, when put into a broader context of decades of direct trade to Amsterdam, those colonists (both Jewish and Christian) who used the outport trade were not primarily motivated by a desire to cheat England. Instead their actions were attempts to maintain preexisting commercial patterns by adapting their routes and strategies to fit within recently established English mercantilist codes. In this way, West Indians' decisions to combine legal and illegal trade was an acknowledgment of the needs of both the empire and of their own communities as they reconciled local and imperial views of the empire. Altogether, legal and illegal voyages make visible the persistent cross-national commercial culture that bound the Atlantic community together.

Colonists' willingness to work within English commercial policy to secure Dutch trade when it suited them also appeared when they resumed their direct petitioning of the English government. Prompted by declining sugar prices, growing indebtedness to London merchants, high tariffs, and slowing economic growth, the planter-dominated colonial assemblies and councils of the West Indies continued to press for free trade. Accepting responsibility for helping to fund the evolving commercial and naval empire, colonists urged that metropolitan regulations be made more flexible so as to respect colonial circumstances. Having given the first signs that they were willing to compromise on free trade in the 1660s, it was during the 1670s and 1680s that they moved even more strongly in this direction. Nevertheless, Barbadians continued to draw from free trade theorists. Adapting these arguments to fit their situation, colonists maintained that the market for imports and exports should be open to international competition, provided that colonists paid customs on their production and used English shipping to carry away their goods. By deferring to those who knew local markets best to make economic decisions, they argued, the empire as a whole would benefit. Open trade would mean more efficient trade, thus making both colony and empire richer. The economic thinker Roger Coke summed up the rationale behind such claims, remarking, "Any business which is more freely managed may be greatlier managed than if it were more restrained."[97] In addition to their exhortations for free trade, colonists pressed for the ability to control the local value of coin (an important element of regulating trade and prices) and to purchase slaves from private traders.[98] These demands, too, reflect what colonists had learned during the disturbances of the 1660s: that it was they who could best manage colonial development. Such an opportunity to make their own economic choices would, according to colonists, result in added trade, more wealth, and a stronger empire.

In two letters to the newly formed and reorganized Lords of Trade and Plantations that he wrote to accompany a now missing petition from Barbados called "Grievances of Barbadoes," Governor Jonathan Atkins encapsulates both West Indians' efforts to reshape mercantile laws to fit their needs and the evolution of colonists' free trade ideology.[99] Structured in the form of answers to a standard list of questions concerning the state of the colonies that the Lords of Trade regularly asked their governors, Atkins pushed authorities to modify the Acts of Trade and Navigation to allow Barbadians to export their produce to foreign ports as others had done before, but coupled these with the guarantee that settlers would use English vessels and pay the proper duties. Atkins then appended a vigorous defense of the notion of free trade and the place of the colonies in the empire. Beginning by reminding their "Lordships" of the "Maxime that wheresoever you intend to Plant a new Collony ye must made their Ports a free Port for all People to trade wth them that will come," Atkins argued that the recent deficit of supplies had caused Barbados's economy to stagnate. Utilizing a mechanistic metaphor that described the sugar plantations as the engine driving the empire, the governor pointed out that the engine could run only if kept fueled by the machinery of the import trade. "The people upon the place who imployed [in normal circumstances] . . . will make the best use of their time," he wrote, "but when the. . . machine fayles which supplies . . . [the] people with provisions, utensils, and hands to work, the Engine must . . . stand still." Having just experienced a disruption in trade because of the coincidence of the Third Anglo-Dutch War and a severe hurricane, Atkins threatened that the colony would not be able to produce any wealth for the empire if not supplied regularly, something that current laws made difficult. "The Act for Trade and Navigation in England," he maintained, "will certainly in tyme be the ruin of all his Majesty's Forreign Plantations." Drawing upon the king's need for productive colonies and his reciprocal duties to provide for his subjects, Atkins clearly spelled out the consequences of not amending the Navigation Acts. "Who is a loser?" he asked, "His Majesty and his poore Subjects who labour for him." When the state failed the planter, in other words, its inability to supply the island also deprived the empire of its economic engine. Atkins concluded by reminding the lords that they could prevent that failure, and "the King's customs . . . [could be] considerably advanced," only if colonists were allowed to "carry their goods where they may make their best Market, . . . not making use of any but English ships," and paying proper customs in Barbados.[100]

The committee, in considering both Atkins's letter and the Barbadians' petition, decided to deliberate the suggestion that the Navigation Acts be altered and that the 4.5 percent duty they paid on sugar exports be lessened. Between November 2 and 7, 1676, the Lords invited two officials to offer their opinions on the matter. As an architect of those very policies, Sir George Downing defended the continued utility of the laws governing colonial trade. He reminded the committee of "the necessity of Maintaining the present Method of Trade for the encrease of Shipping, and Welfare of Old England" and of the possibility that the "liberty of carrying the product of our Plantations to all parts could quite destroy the Trade of England, and consequently ruyne Barbados." Disagreeing with Downing, Sir Peter Colleton, a former Barbadian planter, carefully advocated loosening the rules governing the markets to which colonists could send their produce. Colleton based his reasoning on his experiences as a planter who knew that "the State of the Plantations is very much changed Since the tyme when these Lawes [the Navigation Acts] were first enacted." Echoing the pleas of Atkins and the Barbadians, he countered that the "Sugar Trade is so much burthened and inconvenienced by being bound up to one market," and he warned that if this were not rectified, "wee must in time, necessarily be eaten out by the French." Drawing authority from his personal knowledge of the West Indies, Colleton added that it would be in the king's "interest to suspend some part of those Lawes [which] are hurt full to the English Trade." In response, Downing insisted that such a policy would be a mistake: it "would occasion a great decay of our Navigation" and decrease customs. Just as important, he added, the nation needed the colonies because it needed to export plantation goods to Europe to balance the number of goods Englishmen consumed from abroad.[101]

Ultimately, London authorities rejected both this specific request for open commerce and the theory on which it rested. In drafting their rebuke to the governor, the lords took "notice" of the proposal that "liberty of trade [w]as necessary for settling a new Plantation" and dismissed it as a "dangerous principle Contrary to the settled laws of the Kingdom" and "prejudicial to England itself."[102] The commissioners of the king's customs provided the rationale for dismissing the possibility that settlers be allowed to ship plantation commodities to foreign markets. These men explained, in response to a similar petition from New England, that if colonists were not required to transport enumerated goods to England, "Foreign parts may be made a magazine for these [goods]: and if European goods should be exported there [in return] from other places, the plantations will be thence supplied with them to the prejudice of the trade of England."[103] Although the Lords agreed with Downing that the Navigation Acts were necessary and dismissed Atkins's and the planters' concerns, the fact that this conversation took place at all indicates Barbadians' power to provoke the government to question its colonial policy. Because they were residents of the empire's wealthiest, and thus most indispensable, colony, Barbadians had faith that officials would listen to their concerns and use their power to aid them. At the same time, their repeated appeals to London coupled with the way they adapted Anglo-Dutch trade to fit mercantile policy indicates their growing realization that working within the empire could be as valuable as working outside it. This is a lesson they would remember in later years.

One immediate product of this greater acceptance of the potential of working within the empire was that the Assembly and Council of Barbados decided to coordinate and fund absentee planters in London to represent the island's interests directly to the various councils of foreign trade and colonies—something less available to poorer and less well-connected Leeward Islanders. The Gentlemen Planters' main task was to petition for a reduction in the 4.5 percent duty, which islanders had been doing since its imposition. Beyond this issue, Barbadians also instructed their representatives in London to secure additional military protection, to gain permission to establish a mint at the island, to obtain the right to purchase servants directly from Scotland, and to send their produce "to any nation in amity with England."[104] In this early incarnation of interest-group politics, the Committee of Gentlemen Planters of Barbados in London—headed by Colleton, the former president of the Barbados Council and the solicitor Ferdinando Gorges—did not have much success in altering colonial policy. But the effort itself reveals colonists' growing sophistication in shaping policy, an ability they would continue to develop into the eighteenth century.[105]

With agents—often absentee planters in London—funded by eminent planters already tied closely to England, it is unsurprising that West Indians increasingly accepted the existence of state regulation of trade even as they pressed for modifications that would enable some interimperial trade. Deciding to take their case to the coffeehouses and counting rooms of London, the Gentlemen Planters widened their audience by publishing a series of pamphlets. Perhaps the most widely read of these was *The Groans of the Plantations*, by Barbadian-born and Oxford-educated Edward Littleton. Littleton, who relocated to London in 1683 and served as Barbados's official London agent from 1691 to his death in 1702, drew on his experiences as a wealthy planter and former speaker of the Assembly of Barbados to argue that the Navigation Acts had irrevocably damaged the colonies. He wrote, "it may be truly affirmed, that the bringing of all Sugar to the *English* market, hath gone a great way in destroying that [plantation's] Trade." Recognizing the value of "confining the Plantation Trade to *English* Ships and *English* Men," he could not understand why settlers also "must fetch from *England* the Things that are produced elsewhere," since this restriction "makes the Prices Excessive" and limits productive capacities. While still maintaining that open trade for imports was advantageous, Littleton took a more moderate stance than had most British West Indians a decade earlier. Accepting the concept that English producers and shippers should benefit from the colonies, Littleton reserved his critique for the notion that support of those interests should take precedence over all other concerns, especially those interests that damaged the economic potential of the colonies and thus the wealth of the empire. What was up for debate was the precise configuration of colonists' freedoms within a mercantilist set of laws, rather than that such laws should exist at all.[106]

Littleton's middle path reflects not just the realization that colonists' arguments for free trade were not gaining ground, but his acceptance of English shipping and rules that confined tropical exports to English ports. It also indicates the changing circumstances of sugar production. Facing increased Jamaican and French production, colonists slowly began to realize that, with falling sugar prices and more competition, the guaranteed and protected markets the Navigation Acts provided for sugar outweighed the costs of selling it only in England and focused their political efforts not on pushing for open trade, but for lower taxes. An anonymous 1677 pamphlet published in London reflected this pivot. In the piece, the writer lamented the price of sugar and celebrated the benefits of the plantation trade as many had done before, but instead of calling for open markets as a remedy, the writer pleads instead for lower taxes and for punitive "Taxes on Foreign Commodities." Not a new idea, but what is different about this argument is its timing. Just one year after Barbados had made such a clear demand for free trade as a way to increase the price of sugar, this writer accepted the framework of imperial policy and called for further regulation to eliminate their French rivals as a way to prop up sugar prices.[107]

* * *

Not yet accepting regulation unconditionally by the late 1680s, some planters had begun to see how the tools of empire could stymie international competition and enrich them. With an authority derived from the sugarcane that covered "Little England," colonists had glimpsed a future in which the empire could satisfy their needs and protect their wealth. Over the course of the next several decades, Barbadians would move even more decisively in this direction. That interimperial trade was no longer as important to sugar planters as it had been a half century before (or was to less wealthy tobacco planters in the Leewards) certainly helped Barbadians make this shift more palatable. But all were not convinced. For many, the memory of earlier difficulties and the flexibility Dutch trade offered them remained an important aspect of their political economy, and when warfare again struck the Caribbean in 1689, colonists received a grim reminder of how vital interimperial trade could be.

5 /   Local Adaptations II: Anglo-Dutch Trade in New York

In the late summer of 1669, the New Yorker Aegidius Luyck received news that one of his more ambitious business ventures—a scheme which involved merchants in New York and the Dutch Republic as well as the governor of New York—was on the verge of disaster. This Dutch-born former Latin instructor and minister was in Amsterdam representing the commercial interests of a number of New York traders including the newly installed English governor, Francis Lovelace. Unfortunately, Luyck learned officials in New York City had stymied his plan to purchase and freight the *Hopewell* to trade between the Netherlands and English North America, and when the governor's investment in the undertaking came to light, Lovelace had denied all involvement, leaving Luyck to deal with the consequences. Now, trying to find another avenue for Anglo-Dutch trade, Lovelace wanted Luyck to go to England to meet with the governor's "friends" so as to learn how to carry on trade between Amsterdam and New York legally. Of particular interest to the governor were the rules regarding ship ownership, the payment of duties, and "whether the ships which pay the customs [in England] are allowed to sail from there to New York without having to break open the cargo."

Luyck's involvement in this venture began in early 1669, when he arranged for the *Hopewell*—a vessel that Luyck owned and freighted in partnership with fellow New Yorkers Willem de Maarschalck and Christoffel van Tricht, several Virginians including longtime Virginia–New York City trader Colonel Edmond Scarborough, at least three

Amsterdam merchants, and Governor Lovelace—to sail from the Netherlands to Virginia, where it was to load tobacco before returning to Amsterdam or Edam. On the way to Virginia, however, something went amiss, and the *Hopewell*'s master, Jan Janssen Bestevaer, was forced to apply for permission to stop in New York City in order to acquire fresh provisions. Explaining his mysterious arrival in New York, Bestevaer claimed that he had intended to sail directly "from Amsterdam to the West Indyes," but the vessel's passengers had prevailed upon him to stop for relief in New York after what they called a "long tedious voyage." The motives of these passengers, who identified themselves as "formerly and still belong[ing] to the City of New Yorke," are unclear. While Bestevaer did not have explicit orders to trade in New York, it appears that his passengers manufactured the ruse of needing to stop for relief—a common enough excuse in the seventeenth-century Atlantic—so as to attend to their own commercial ventures. After all, the passengers did wish not go ashore alone, but requested to "come a Shoare with their goods."

It was at this moment, however, that customs officials intervened, seizing the Dutch-owned *Hopewell* for violating the Navigation Acts. In the investigation that followed, officials learned that Besteaver carried two sets of documents, one showing that his ship was English, another that it was Dutch. More significantly, and potentially damaging to Lovelace, the investigation exposed his investment in the venture. Acting quickly to avoid scandal, the governor denied his involvement. What happened next regarding the prosecution of Besteaver and the *Hopewell* is unclear, but the vessel and its master were soon back in Amsterdam awaiting new instructions. Evidently confident that he had avoided being caught, yet worried about future endeavors, the governor dispatched a letter to his associates in Amsterdam, urging them to send Luyck to England to meet with his "friends" and to learn the nuances of the Navigation Acts so as to avoid embarrassing situations in the future.

Luyck apparently learned much for by December 1669 the *Hopewell* was again ready to sail, this time technically legally: Luyck, Van Tricht, fellow denizen Pieter Hardenbroek, and Lovelace took over official ownership of the *Hopewell*, with Amsterdam merchants investing through these New Yorkers so as to avoid being registered on the ship's papers. In addition, the vessel was also instructed to pass to New York, Virginia, and back to Amsterdam only after stopping in England to obtain the proper clearances and to pay duties.[1] The example of the *Hopewell* offers insight into the ways that New Yorkers and their Dutch contacts adapted their trade to fit (barely) within English law. Their strategies—applying for admission on pretense of a difficult journey, the use of denizens of New York to hide Amsterdam investors, and collaboration with local officials—had become common means of executing interimperial trade by the 1670s.

Taking their cue from the permissive atmosphere fostered by New York's governor, Dutch traders residing in New York City sent a flurry of vessels to and from the Dutch Republic in these years. Between the cancelation of direct trading rights in 1668 and 1674—including the war years of 1672 and 1673, during which Dutch trade in general was constrained by an English blockade—three to five large vessels per year traded between the Netherlands and New York. This number rivaled direct English shipping, which law limited to five vessels per year until 1675. Even the instability created by the Dutch recapture of New York in 1674 and its subsequent return to the English did little to interrupt the rhythm of Anglo-Dutch trade. Between 1675 and 1689, the rate of Anglo-Dutch trade remained roughly constant to the decade before. Throughout this period, around fifty New York–based traders of varying economic standings traded to the Netherlands.[2] In sum, whereas Dutch trade was an essential, though often secondary, part of most Caribbean colonists' commercial behavior, New Yorkers' legal and illegal trade to Amsterdam was a major part of their transatlantic trade for three decades following the conquest. City traders began to diversify and trade with English ports in the 1670s and 1680s, but as they laboriously developed contacts within the English empire, they held onto their former ties with the Dutch Republic, alternating among legal, quasi-legal, and illegal methods, depending on which was most advantageous at a particular moment. The involvement of Lovelace in the *Hopewell* also highlights what would be an enduring feature of New York's political economy: the ability of colonists to bring their governors into their trade so as to insulate themselves from prosecution, to earn special privileges, and to shape local law to suit their needs.

While the metropole was unable to stop persistent Anglo-Dutch trade, its increased attention nonetheless forced New Yorkers to resort to more complex and often secretive ways of maintaining Dutch trade as the *Hopewell*'s owners had in 1669 and as Caribbean traders perfected. Colonists' use of smuggling and partial legalities in both regions reflected the continued desirability of Dutch goods and the inability of metropolitan officials to change the commercial culture through legislation. What made New York's pursuit of Dutch trade distinctive, though, was both the colony's ethnic makeup and its economic situation. With an overwhelmingly Dutch population bound by family and commercial ties to the Dutch Republic, New Yorkers could more actively manage transatlantic Dutch trade than Barbadians and Leeward Islanders could, a feature that gave them more local control over it than those in the Caribbean. Spurred on by English mercantilist laws that discouraged merchants in the Dutch Republic from organizing direct Anglo-Dutch trade, New Yorkers tried all the harder to bend this trade to their needs.

At the same time that they drew on their Dutch ties to organize trade, Manhattan merchants opened up opportunities to non-Dutch immigrants. Ethnically Dutch traders found new partners who could enhance their business, especially when these individuals were well placed in government like Lovelace or provided prized entrance into English networks in the outport trade. Such collaboration also led to more fully blended cross-national ventures, with Dutch and English people in the colonies and their home ports sharing vessels, mixing cargoes, and investing in ventures. Situated in a thriving port beginning to dominate the surrounding region and with an economically and politically powerful nucleus of Dutch merchants, New Yorkers were at the center of these interimperial webs.

Though the mechanics of trade during the 1670s and 1680s were different than they had been in the 1660s, residents demanded Dutch goods for similar reasons. Because New York's leading staple—fur—was not as valuable as the tobacco and sugar West Indians produced, traders here depended on their coastal trade with New England, the Chesapeake, and the Caribbean as well as the affordable manufactured goods Dutch ships delivered. Both because of their cultural preference for Dutch goods—ranging from ceramics to textiles to building supplies—and because Dutch traders held price and selection advantages over their English rivals, colonists continued to buy them from Dutch suppliers with whom they already had commercial (and familial) relationships. In addition to the lower prices they could often offer for exports, Amsterdam merchants were willing to pay higher prices for furs until after 1700 than were buyers in London, where beaver hats had fallen out of fashion.[3] Eventually the English would be able to meet colonists' demands at competitive prices, but in the 1670s and 1680s, this was not yet the case, forcing New Yorkers to continue to rely on Anglo-Dutch trade as they had in the 1660s. Because New Yorkers trade stretched along the North American coast, Dutch goods spread to other English colonies from Manhattan.

Ignoring these commercial needs and instead believing that the root cause of Dutch competitive advantages was the Dutchmen's scurrilous infestation of English markets, English statesmen reiterated mercantilist decrees to force consumers to English markets. By the late 1660s, as we have seen, they also understood that it would require an enhanced regulatory apparatus to make these laws effective. In New York, authority fell both to the colony's proprietor as well as the Restoration government as a whole. The first years of English rule in New York had been unprofitable for the Duke of York as Governor Nicolls sought to develop a new legal framework and the Second Anglo-Dutch War sapped trade so that by the late 1660s James had become frustrated. Backed by the Restoration government, he moved to gain commercial control of the colony. First, the Board of Trade decided to revoke the royal permits that had allowed direct Dutch trade in 1668. Next, James replaced the exhausted and untrustworthy Governor Nicolls with a new administrator, Francis Lovelace.[4]

The Duke of York had great hopes that the new governor, an officer in several Stuart armies and a former employee of the Admiralty, would be able to eliminate the favorable climate for Dutch trade that Nicolls had allowed, but again he would be disappointed. James's focus on the office of governor as central to raising revenue and ending Dutch trade was consistent with most imperial administrators' view that these men—especially when connected to the government personally—were the key to better integration of the empire. But as was true throughout the empire, the conflicting roles they had to play often frustrated larger goals. In fulfilling their duties, governors had to navigate between sometimes-incompatible aims: the economic success of the empire, profit for the colonists, and individual profit. As agents of the English government they were responsible for maintaining law and order, protecting their colonies, securing revenue, implementing metropolitan policy, communicating local decisions back to London, and enforcing trade laws.[5] Lovelace, like the governors of New York immediately before and after him and his colleagues in the Caribbean, would be unable to achieve these sometimes incompatible duties, deciding instead to place his and his subjects' profits before mercantilist aims.

Almost as soon as he arrived, Lovelace moved to facilitate Dutch trade by appointing Cornelis van Ruyven, a prominent Dutch resident and the former secretary of the WIC in New Amsterdam, as the receiver-general of customs. Charged with administering commercial laws as well as collecting duties, Van Ruyven occupied a critical position from which to foster the Netherlands trade. Lovelace also supported the efforts of local merchants to trade between Amsterdam and New York City and, as we have seen, even sent his Dutch New York associate Aegidius Luyck to England in an effort to manipulate mercantilist policy. Additionally, Lovelace ingratiated himself with New York's elite Dutch mercantile community, supporting lower port duties and initiatives to funnel the colony's trade through its principal city in order to create opportunities for local merchants and to enhance their transatlantic trade. Unsurprisingly, under Van Ruyven's watch and Lovelace's stewardship, the Netherlands trade thrived.[6]

Among the most helpful actions Lovelace took in smoothing the way for the Netherlands trade was giving frequent passes to Dutch vessels. The first of these, *De Hartogh van Jorck* (The Duke of York), departed for Amsterdam shortly after Lovelace's arrival in 1668.[7] Lovelace then moved to approve other ventures, authorizing the *King Charles* to make a round-trip voyage to the Netherlands in 1669. This ship, captained by Peter Reyertsen vander Beets (probably the same man who had captained the *Nieuw Jorck* between Amsterdam and New York the previous year), carried the merchant and alderman Francis Boone, as well as the trader Christopher Hooghland to Amsterdam, where they most likely went to reassure contacts and organize future endeavors.[8] That same year, another vessel arrived, bearing "haircloth" and other things for local merchants Jacob Kip, Goossen Gerrittsz, Herman Vedder, and Hendrick Van Bal, a peltry exporter.[9] During 1670, several more vessels bearing passes from Lovelace made a similar voyage, including the *Dolphin*, which also went to Virginia; the *Fort Albany*, previously known as the *Hopewell* and owned by elite traders Cornelis Steenwyck, Jacques Cousseau, and Frederick Philipse; and the *Margaret*, which received a vague pass to go to "Europe" and traveled to the Netherlands with furs, returning with dry goods before making another round trip the following year.[10]

Even when not actively allowing Dutch vessels into port or easing their passage to surrounding colonies and the Dutch Republic, Lovelace could do little to stop New Yorkers from smuggling. With other alternatives for interimperial commerce at their disposal and with the slow decline in the fur trade that had begun in the 1670s and no comparable leading export staple, one might expect there to have been less incentive to smuggle at the port of New York. But traders here, like their colleagues in the Caribbean, evidently found the profitability of direct Dutch trade high enough to warrant the risks of capture as many accounts of ventures disrupted by the unwanted intervention of English authorities litter the records of colonial New York.[11]

One reason for the ease of smuggling in Manhattan was that, like in the Leewards, the numerous harbors and inlets along the Hudson and East rivers provided smugglers the perfect cover for secret land-ings or midnight shipside rendezvous. The *Seaflower*, for example, was instructed by one such merchant to "ride safely att Sandy hooke [New Jersey], and there land her goods and the best of her sails and rigging and then Come to Nyorke empty." Similarly, Frederick Philipse ordered his son Adolph to meet the *Charles*—which had come from Barbados with several slaves it could not sell there—"within two Miles of Rye [on Long Island]" in a small sloop, where Adolph was to receive the eight slaves and bring them to New York City along with "one bagge of Papper [,] one negro with Severall pewter Dishes, and Some Necktleth Stuff . . . [for] Cornels. Franken" of New York City. Once done, the *Charles* proceeded to Stamford, Connecticut, where it "Landed thirty odd Water Caskes, fouer Gunns, Six Musketts[,] one Sword, and one Cuttlass [and a] Great Copper kittle" to complete the Philipses' business.[12]

Lovelace did little to enforce trade laws because he had a financial stake in Anglo-Dutch trade. When the governor arrived to assume his responsibilities, he carried not only a commission from the king nam-ing him the English government's symbol of law and order, but also plans to enrich himself. To this end, he convinced his brother Thomas to accompany him and to manage his financial affairs. Together the two engaged in a variety of business schemes, including land speculation, shipbuilding, and trading between New York City and the Dutch Repub-lic. Lovelace's direct involvement with Dutch trade began in 1669, when he partnered with Luyck, who was to be a frequent Lovelace business partner, to purchase shares in the *Hopewell*.

Governor Lovelace's experience with the *Hopewell* evidently con-vinced him that interimperial trade was profitable, and during the rest of his time in New York, he pursued investment in additional Dutch or-ganized endeavors through Luyck and other Dutch New Yorkers. The latter welcomed an alliance with Lovelace because he could employ his official powers to obtain passes and other documentation to aid them. A group of merchants in the Netherlands, London, and New York used this rationale in 1670 to include Lovelace as an investor in a voyage of *The Duke of York* from the United Provinces to New York. The main organizers of the voyage seem to have been the New Yorkers Luyck (who owned one-eighth share of the cargo) and Christoffel van Tricht (who held three-sixteenths). Three London merchants, Captain James Bur-kin, Mr. John Everson (or Ibeson), and Mr. John Bus, combined to buy another one-eighth share, while Dutch merchants also invested in the endeavor through New York contacts: Jacobus van Noorthouwe bought one-sixteenth share as did Abraham de Cuyper (whose contacts helped clear the vessel through Dover, England). By investing through New York contacts, these men's partial ownership of the vessel was effectively hidden behind legal residents of the English empire. Additionally, the group took out a bottomry loan of 1,250 guilders from the Amsterdamer Anthony Maryn. Finally, Luyck purchased one-eighth share in the cargo on behalf of Lovelace. This was not Lovelace's only contribution to the voyage, however. The previous April, the governor had granted passes to twenty-seven Dutch New Yorkers, some with their wives, to travel with their goods on the *Duke of York* for Amsterdam. Among these colonists were the merchants Samuel Megapolensis, Isaac Melijn, Jacob Loockermans (the son of Govert Loockermans), and the ship's master, the Dutchman and sometime New York City resident Johannes Luyck. Lovelace's participation in granting these traders permission to transport their goods to the Netherlands suggests that the share Luyck held for the governor was payment for his services, as opposed to a direct monetary investment, and indicates the lengths to which colonial merchants would go to indirectly bribe officials.

After a brief stay in Amsterdam, where a combination of Dutch and English capital funded the refitting of the *Duke of York* and the loading of a cargo of merchandise purchased in the Netherlands and England by Amsterdam's Pieter Hardenbroeck and William Maarschalck, the vessel cleared for New York. In addition to carrying these men's cargo, the ship contained goods for at least eighteen others (many of them New Yorkers). Once safely in the English colony, Luyck managed the cargo's sale and purchased furs to return to the Dutch Republic, a service for which he received a remarkably high 10 percent commission. The involvement of English merchants and denizened New Yorkers as well as the *Duke of York*'s cursory stop in England gave the venture an appearance of legality, though the Dutch organizers' intention—to trade between the Netherlands and New York—was clearly in violation of the spirit of the Navigation Acts. Compounding this deceit, the vessel also reportedly carried false papers, which guaranteed that should the master encounter any difficulties, the ship would, as Abel de Wolff later testified, "not [be] subject to confiscation for violations of the English Navigation Act." The false papers also suggest that the organizers did not intend to obey all aspects of the Navigation Acts and had planned accordingly. That the main investors and those who stood to profit from the vessels' insurance policies were all Dutchmen investing through New York representatives shows the enduring influence Dutch capital had in funding New York City trade even as merchants in the Netherlands played a less visible role in directing that commerce.[13]

Lovelace profited from his participation in the New York–Netherlands trade, and in 1670, he, his brother Thomas, and the New Yorker Isaac Bedloe funded the construction of the "very strong and handsome . . . but costly" *Good Fame* expressly to further develop such opportunities. On July 4, 1670, Lovelace used his official capacity to ease his vessel's departure for the Netherlands, issuing a pass to allow "the Good Fame of New Yorke," and its English commander, Stephen Fryer, "together with her passengers Goods and Merchandize [to] freely and quietly . . . passe out of this Porte . . . for England and Holland and to retorne againe without any manner of . . . hinderance or molestation."[14] Previously Lovelace had been a generally passive owner of shares in such voyages, but the *Good Fame* endeavor signaled his increasingly active commitment to Dutch trade. He not only secretly helped fund the construction of the vessel and instigated its mission, but in an act of open bravado also helped its passage by issuing a letter of denization to the vessel's surgeon, John Deforest, and by giving it a pass to return directly from Amsterdam in case it had any difficulties. To fill their vessel, Lovelace and his partners attracted twenty-three freighters from New York and the Dutch Republic who put ƒ28,000 worth of beavers, deerskins, and tobacco aboard the vessel. Some of these freighters were longtime New York–Amsterdam traders based in the Republic such as Gillis van Hoornbeeck and Cornelis Jansen Moy, but indicative of the changing nature of Dutch metropolitan participation in New York's commerce, these men were only minor partners, freighting goods worth one-tenth and one-fifth of the cargo respectively. Altogether, New York–based merchants including Cornelis Darvall, Isaac de Peyster, and Nicolas Gouverneur owned the majority of the *Good Fame*'s cargo.[15] Throughout the remainder of his time in New York, Lovelace maintained similar relationships with New York merchants trading to the Netherlands, including François Hooghlandt, Nicolas Gouverneur, and Bedloe, whose 1673 will noted that he had "been intrusted with great sums of money, and considerable quantities of goods by the late Governor, Colonel Francis Lovelace, as his factor."[16] Governor Lovelace positioned himself to profit from his colonists' commerce; at the same time, city merchants understood that incorporating him in their business was essential to securing the protections they needed to trade to the Dutch Republic. This alliance of interests—personal, civic, and commercial—proved to be a model that suited future New York merchants well.

As successful as they had been in organizing Anglo-Dutch trade, the outbreak of the Third Anglo-Dutch War (1672–74) threatened New Yorkers' commerce. That spring, Dutch authorities had seized four of the city's vessels that happened to be trading in Amsterdam when the war began, including Lovelace's *Good Fame*, Steenwyck's *James*, and Frederick Philipse's *Frederick*.[17] The presence of these New York–owned vessels in Amsterdam highlights the role that prominent Dutch New Yorkers played in directing and financing the Netherlands trade, even as it reminds us of the dual vulnerability of cross-national exchange in a time of war. The war almost crippled the Dutch economy as a massive French army, led by Louis XIV, invaded the Dutch Republic and captured forty-eight fortified towns and as a combined Anglo-French fleet attacked the United Provinces' navy. Besieged at home and at sea, internal shipping and foreign trade slowed dramatically, a condition that only worsened when the States-General periodically closed Dutch ports in 1672 and 1673 to avoid further damage to their shipping. Despite Admiral Michiel de Ruyter's efforts to repulse the Anglo-French fleet, the Dutch suffered major losses, and these, coupled with the damage the land invasion did to agricultural and industrial production (the Dutch flooding Zeeland and Holland to save those provinces did not help in this regard), made it difficult for Dutch merchants to venture overseas cargoes. At the same time, Dutch privateers in the Atlantic, especially in the Caribbean, harassed English fleets, capturing hundreds of vessels.[18]

Meanwhile, in New York, the Atlantic dimension of the war threatened newly established commercial patterns when a Dutch fleet under the command of Cornelis Evertsen easily retook the city for the Dutch. Though the occupation would last just fifteen months—the city was returned to the English when the war ended in 1674—it created uncertainty for traders already suffering from the effects of war. This environment reinforced New Yorkers' growing belief that they could not rely upon outsiders willing to organize trade from Europe, and they moved to take even greater control of the New York–Netherland trade from their distracted colleagues in the besieged Dutch Republic. In this way, New Yorkers transformed their city's commerce, learning to use their new unique position within the English empire in conjunction with older Dutch ties to more fully develop a distinctive interimperial network. Combining their contacts in the Dutch Republic, new English associates, and their own wealth and status, prominent ethnically Dutch New

Yorkers such as Oloff Stevensen van Cortlandt, his son Stephanus, and their upriver relative Jeremias van Rensselaer, together with stalwarts Steenwyck and Philipse, made the twenty-two months following the end of the war an especially brisk period of Anglo-Dutch trade. At least nine, and possibly eleven or more, vessels crossed between the two ports in the nearly two years following the end of the war, ventures that had probably been planned or begun during Dutch occupation and that capitalized on pent-up demand on both sides of the Atlantic. To make this trade possible, merchants in New York City developed several new techniques. Examining the recoverable details of the roughly eleven 1674 and 1675 voyages can suggest much about the ways Anglo-Dutch trade evolved under the strains of war.[19]

Perhaps the most complicated and what would prove enduring trading strategy used in post-1674 endeavors was the use of an English intermediary port, usually Dover, Portsmouth, or Falmouth, at which traders could pay duties and clear cargoes legally for New York or Amsterdam. This technique was similar to that which Jewish Barbadians and Luyck had employed, but in the 1670s, New Yorkers perfected it. Making this trade possible was colonists' embrace of their status as denizens. As we have already seen, the Articles of Capitulation had included provisions that gave city inhabitants the ability to receive letters of denization. This status conferred to New York City merchants the privilege to send vessels to the Netherlands, provided they used an English (or colonial) vessel, employed a British crew, and stopped at an English port on each leg of the journey to pay customs and obtain the proper clearances—as would any English subject. Frederick Philipse's vessel, the *Margaret,* followed this general route with its owner aboard, stopping in London on its way to New York City from Amsterdam with a cargo of Dutch manufactured goods in 1674.[20] With their ability to trade legally as Englishmen, New Yorkers soon took over the New York–Dutch Republic trading routes that merchants in the Dutch Republic now deemed too risky. In this way, the structures of mercantilist legislation created new commercial opportunities for New Yorkers to maintain Anglo-Dutch commerce.

Not a new technique in New York City—the owners of the *Hopewell* and the *Duke of York* had used it several years before—the practice of stopping in an English port gave a gloss of legality to Dutch trade that was not always genuine. Though it is unknown if Philipse paid duties on the entirety of his 1674 cargo, there were times he did not. During a 1679 voyage of another of Philipse's vessels, the *fluytschip Charles* from Amsterdam to New York Philipse skirted the law. According to the passenger Jasper Danckaerts, the *Charles* stopped in Falmouth as the law required, but once there, "no customs-house officers came on board" to inspect the cargo as they should have. Rather, Philipse's wife, Margarita Hardenbroeck, simply ordered a small portion of the cargo unloaded to wait for another Philipse vessel—which carried the unladed goods to the "Isle of May and thence Barbados"—and then ordered the ship bearing Dutch goods on to New York.[21] Philipse, one of the richest of New York's merchants, also employed the *Charles*, the *Peter*, and the *Philip* in this manner, sending them on at least five combined round-trip journeys through Falmouth between 1679 and 1681. To smooth the vessels' path, he hired the English merchant Bryan Rogers to manage affairs in Falmouth each time just as the Jewish owners of the *Experiment* had in 1680. In 1684, the *Charles* and *Philip* were back in England, their captains entering Cowes and paying duties on tobacco and hides carried from New York City before departing for Amsterdam. Alternatively using legal and illegal trade (and sometimes combining them in the same venture), Philipse creatively manipulated the warren of English trade laws to maintain Anglo-Dutch trade.[22]

As was the case with Philipse's *Charles*, New Yorkers used the occasion of landing their cargoes at English ports not only to prosecute legal trade, but also to smuggle. Samuel Hayne, the same customs inspector who had detected the Jewish merchants of Barbados's fraudulent trade, described in detail how New Yorkers manipulated the system and avoided detection. He claimed that a "ship coming in from *Holland*, cleared at *Dover* for *New-York*" with a cargo of "*Dutch* Bricks and Grindstones," which they "pretended to be for her Ballast." Though the cargo "was Merchandize and Entred," he continued, the whole cargo was not "unloaded according to Law." Luckily for the authorities, a storm destroyed the vessel on its way out to sea, and when they recovered the ship, "behold, under her Bricks and Grindstones appeared great quantities of Guns, and other Goods both prohibited and Uncustomed, which the diligent Officers never dream'd of; but this Case is very true."[23]

As is clear from Hayne's testimony, Frederick Philipse was not alone in ordering his shipmasters to enter cargoes in England's outports under disguised conditions. The number of merchants doing this, which included some of New York's most important traders, accelerated in the 1670s as these men gained the necessary English contacts needed to execute the maneuver. In the years between the end of the Third Anglo-Dutch War and the Glorious Revolution, at least one and as many as three large vessels per year paused at an English intermediary point.

For New York merchants, Dover quickly became their entry port of choice. Dennis Maika has discovered that the most active in this trade were leading city merchants and holdovers from the Dutch period: Cornelis Steenwyck, Abraham de Peyster, Frederick Philipse, and Jacob Leisler—all New Yorkers with strong Amsterdam ties. These men worked with the English merchants Matthew Chitty, Nicholas Cullen, and Edward Lloyd, among others. In the shipments these men directed between New York City, Dover, and Amsterdam during the 1670s and 1680s, colonists continued earlier patterns of trade, remitting furs, tobacco, and occasionally lumber to Amsterdam in exchange for manufactured goods. The De Peyster family—with members deployed to Amsterdam, London, and New York City—was especially important. Abraham's father, William, established the Dover connection and worked from both Amsterdam and London to coordinate trade and attract investors in both places. At the same time, New York merchants cultivated English partners, they retained important contacts in Amsterdam to help them manage and finance their ventures, as De Peyster's experiences illustrate.[24] Likewise Steenwyck, who had traded with the Van Hoornbeecks of Amsterdam since the 1650s, maintained his relationship with the Dutch family for decades, and when he died in 1684, the Van Hoornbeecks owed Steenwyck ƒ12,000. One of New York's richest residents, Steenwyck exemplifies how New Yorkers relied upon both Dutch and English transatlantic ties to build their wealth. Steenwyck's executors inherited a tangled web of debts in many places of the English and Dutch empires when he died.[25]

This combination of New York, English, and Dutch associates interlinked financially across a number of ports of call becomes clearer in two additional voyages. On March 16, 1672, Steenwyck, Gabrielle Minvielle—also among the wealthiest of men in New York City—and the more modest trader William Darvall joined together to freight the *Justice*, "Burthen Eighty Tunns or thereabouts for a voyage from this Porte of New York to Dover in England and from thence to Amsterdame in Holland." In what was by all appearances a typical arrangement, the men instructed Captain Clayborne Hastewood to contact the English merchant Henry Ladd of New Castle when he arrived in England. Ladd in turn was then to write "Mr. Benjamin Howlin and give dispatches for Amsterdam," where "the fraightors in Holland" could then determine when the vessel should continue its voyage.[26] An even more dramatic case of the merging of English, Dutch, and New York merchants' interests was the voyage of the *Beaver* in 1686. On the Amsterdam–New

York leg of the expedition, which included a stop in Dover, Philipse and the England-based Cullen placed cargoes. But, when this same vessel returned to Amsterdam, the number of investors increased as the New Yorkers Philipse, De Peyster, and Margareta de Reimer (the widow of Cornelis Steenwyck) shared the hold with the English merchants Samuel Rawstone and Robert Story. The vessel's return from Amsterdam in 1687 was still more complex, with the New Yorkers Philipse, Stephanus van Cortlandt, Francis Rombouts, Nicholaes de Meyer, John Darvall, Andrew Teller, Margareta Schuyler, and Henricus Selyns (Margareta de Reimer's husband) all investing in a cargo of Dutch dry goods with the final quarter-share controlled by unnamed Amsterdam merchants.[27] The conjoining of New York, London, and Amsterdam merchants' skills, contacts, and capital was an opportunity most merchants in the Leeward Islands and Barbados did not have the connections to take advantage of and reminds us that local circumstances were often paramount in generating Anglo-Dutch trade.

The example of Jacob Leisler also illustrates the blending of colonial, English, and Dutch capital in Anglo-Dutch trade during the final decades of the seventeenth century. More famous for the rebellion he led in 1689, Leisler was one of the most elite Dutch traders active in New York City in the years after the conquest. Born in Frankfurt around 1640, Leisler entered into the service of the WIC before he was twenty. First working for the company in Amsterdam, he crossed to New Netherland in the early 1660s. Soon he married, left the service of the WIC, and began to trade on his own account. Initially concentrating on the Chesapeake tobacco trade as many of his colleagues did, he soon built a strong cross-national network and accumulated capital. Also well-connected through the Dutch and French reformed church community in Europe—of which his father was a prominent minister—Leisler quickly began to reexport the tobacco he was importing from the Chesapeake to The Hague and Amsterdam, often combining these cargoes with locally acquired furs. In exchange, he brought ceramics, textiles, and household goods from northern Europe and even Asia, which he vended not only in New York but in New England, the Chesapeake, and the Dutch and English Caribbean.

By the time of the English conquest, Leisler had established himself as an important trader in the city, rising to be the sixth-wealthiest property holder by 1674. Bolstered by his connections and considerable wealth, Leisler was even more active in transatlantic trade during the 1670s, employing the Amsterdam merchant Cornelis Jacobsen Moy (who also worked as an agent for Frederick Philipse) to represent his interests in the Dutch Republic, an arrangement that lasted for more than a decade. All together, Leisler was one of the more prolific of New York's outport traders between 1670 and 1688, employing contacts in the Netherlands and England to organize his trade, traveling back and forth to the Netherlands himself to oversee ventures, and acquiring a number of vessels and renting space on many others. Particularly notable in Leisler's trade was how he integrated capital and skills from around the Atlantic into the same venture. Take his experience with *The Happy Return*. Claudia Schnurmann has shown that this venture's success, which involved shipping tobacco from Maryland to Rotterdam with a stop in England and returning with building and shipbuilding materials and earthenwares to New York, rested upon Leisler's ability to call on multiple colonial shipmasters, English merchants in Penrys and Falmouth, Dutch and Scottish associates in Rotterdam, and suppliers and buyers around the Atlantic.[28]

New York merchants like Leisler gained further benefits from linking imperial subjects in far-flung places. Some, for example, sent Dutch vessels that had recently arrived from Amsterdam on to the Caribbean, where they traded with both Dutch and English colonies before returning to the Dutch Republic either through New York City or directly.[29] Frederick Philipse engaged in an even bolder scheme, parlaying his English denization and Dutch contacts into profits from the slave trade. In 1684, Philipse sent his New York–based pink *Charles* from Amsterdam to West Africa with a cargo of manufactured goods purchased in the Dutch city. There, his representatives bought 140 slaves and transported them to Barbados, where the master freely entered them, given his ship's English registration. At other times, Philipse sent Dutch goods directly to Barbados after a stop in England, or invested in Dutch slavers trading in the Dutch, French, and English Caribbean.[30] Located strategically in the mid-Atlantic, able to draw on the city's unique ethnic mix, and habituated toward cross-national trade, Leisler, Philipse, and others like them in New York enabled a remarkable degree of interimperial commercial collaboration. Making themselves wealthy, these men's goods flowed beyond New York and connected markets throughout the English and Dutch Atlantics, spreading wealth as they went.

Though traders like Philipse and Leisler utilized the outport trade for their business with the Dutch Republic, many residents did not abandon older patterns of direct trade even though it was now illicit. A representative venture in 1674 involved many of the city's wealthiest individuals, a group who also sometimes traded legally with the Netherlands through

England. The *St. Michel*, designated as being owned by "Steenwyck and Bayert [probably Nicholas Bayard]," for example, departed New York City on April 4, 1674, bound directly to Amsterdam carrying a cargo of skins on account of a wide array of New York residents including members of the Van Rensselaer family, Gabrielle Minvielle, Leisler, Oloff Stevensen van Cortlandt, and presumably the two owners of the vessel, Steenwyck and Bayard.[31] Just months later, the *De Coopman*, which had arrived at New York after a stop in Curaçao, followed the *St. Michel* to Amsterdam with more beaver pelts on the account of Van Rensselaer and Van Cortlandt.[32] These two vessels evidently avoided English authorities, but all were not so skilled, successful in bribery, or lucky. The owners of the *Beurs* (Exchange) of Amsterdam, for example, were unable to evade capture when they tried to ship "a parcel of Beavers, Peltry and tobaccoe" from New York to Amsterdam in the first months of 1675.[33] Likewise, sometime in the fall of 1675, New York City port authorities detained the ketch *Susanna*, "for Trading in the Port, contrary to [the late] Act of Parliament." This vessel was owned by "Dutchmen" in the city and had carried a Dutch cargo partly on behalf of Asser Levy.[34] On the whole, of the eleven known incidents of New York–Netherlands trade in 1674 and 1675, at least eight passed directly between the ports without a stop to make them legal.

As important as prominent merchants who had sufficient access to capital themselves or through associates in London or Amsterdam were to maintaining the colony's Dutch trade, many other New Yorkers who were not elite participated in interimperial commerce by buying shares in vessels or placing small cargoes on others' ships. An exemplary of these small-scale traders is Cornelis Clopper. Clopper arrived in New Amsterdam in the 1650s and worked as a blacksmith while also beginning to trade by renting space on various vessels. By the 1670s, he was sending grain to Barbados and Europe, tobacco and peltries to sometime New York resident Pieter Hardenbroeck in Amsterdam, and was investing in other larger ventures organized by others. In return, he purchased small lots of Dutch consumer goods for New York's market. Without access to the capital necessary to outfit his own vessel for the Netherlands trade, Clopper and other minor traders retained access to Dutch markets by investing in others' voyages, an option available to them because of the local organization of Anglo-Dutch trade.[35] Unlike in the English Caribbean, where those desiring Dutch trade largely had to depend upon nonresidents, New Yorkers could rely on local merchants with the capital and Dutch connections needed to initiate transatlantic interimperial exchange.

For their part, some Amsterdam-based merchants still *occasionally* took the lead in outfitting vessels headed to New York City in the 1670s and 1680s. One of the ships planned for use in such trade, the *Mayflower*, was hired to pass from Amsterdam to New York City in 1675 bearing a cargo of European linen and duffels; finished clothing and blankets; manufactures such as axes, mirrors, and brushes; raw materials such as bar iron, coal, and starch; and foodstuffs consisting of currants, spices, and prunes. The principal organizers of the shipment were the experienced Amsterdam traders Jan Baptiste van Rensselaer and Mattijs Ten Broeck, together with twenty-three other Amsterdam-based investors. The timing of the venture is instructive. Most likely first planned when the Dutch reclaimed New York in 1673, the endeavor was probably designed to take advantage of the return to Dutch rule. Though the trip was ultimately canceled when English authorities intervened, the rapidity with which these Amsterdam traders organized a venture to New York indicates that they and their fellow investors remained attuned to the potential profits they could still earn in New York.[36]

A few Amsterdam merchants even lobbied for Dutch retention of the colony at the end of the Third-Anglo Dutch War. When it appeared that this request would not be honored, they then urged the negotiators to include wording in the treaty that would protect unhindered trade between the Netherlands and Manhattan as New Yorkers had done in 1664. They proposed that "the inhabitants on both sides [of the Atlantic] . . . shall be at liberty, free and unmolested, to go and trade without being obliged, in the outward or homeward voyages, to touch at and pay duty in Old England." Although authorities ignored this plea as they had a similar one a decade earlier, its very proposal signaled that a few important Amsterdam merchants remained interested in the potential of direct commerce with New York City for years after the conquest.[37]

Aiming to reimpose English rule on New York again and to halt the avoidances of mercantilist restrictions that had flourished under Lovelace's leadership, the Lords of Trade installed Edmund Andros as governor in 1674. Andros was well suited for the appointment because he was both fluent in Dutch, having spent much of his youth in the Netherlands, and was a faithful servant of the Duke of York. James and his brother Charles II hoped that Andros's loyalty would lead him to put their goals of securing the colony and acquiring dependable revenue ahead of the interests of local elite merchants and his own ambitions.[38]

Though unable to immediately halt Anglo-Dutch trade, Andros was committed to ending the Dutch community's dominance of the city's trade. He took a hard stance against ethnically Dutch residents, removing many of them from prominent positions in New York's government, restoring all those who held office prior to the brief Dutch reconquest, and appointing Englishmen to his council. However, within several years he softened his position and added the ethnically Dutch merchants Frederick Philipse, William Darvall, and Stephanus van Cortland to his council.[39] All three men had established commercial ties to the Dutch Republic and would eventually wield significant influence with the governor. Their appointments indicate a transition in Andros's approach as he realized that to succeed in improving the city's economy, and thus the duke's revenue, he would need to work with elite Dutch merchants. As far as these Dutch residents and their immediate associates were concerned, their collaboration with Andros was welcome because it provided them a bulwark with which to resist English control of New York's economy. Not able to co-opt Andros by tying him to their overseas business ventures as they had Lovelace, these merchants nonetheless made Andros realize that their goals could be mutually reinforcing.

The turning point for Andros came when the Duke of York rejected Andros's idea for an assembly that could impose a revenue structure to pay for the colony's administration and contribute to the duke's coffers. As a result, Andros was forced to focus on increasing revenue from the customs duties, the major portion of provincial taxes. This situation left him with a challenging dilemma. He needed to improve the revenue collected in the colony, but could not simply raise duties or enforce their collection, as traders would surely resist. The prospects of taking revenue from Dutch trade were brighter, an idea the duke himself had suggested. Soon Andros asked for permission to suspend the Navigation Acts in order to encourage more direct commerce with the Netherlands.[40] The Duke of York's secretary, Sir John Werden, brusquely refused, writing, "'Tis certaine that whilest the Act of Navigation stands in the way, it cannot be obtained to have ships trade directly from Holland to your parts."[41] To complicate matters, the next month, the duke asked Andros (through Werden) if granting "licenses for a few ships to goe and come directly 'twixt Holland and New Yorke was heretofore ye great secret to rayse ye Customes."[42] The query came to nothing, but that they would consider the possibility at all shows that they understood the way that overbearing regulations sometimes interfered with commercial development.

Rebuffed in his request for direct trade to the Low Countries, Andros turned to other ways to encourage the city's elite ethnically Dutch merchants—several of whom sat on his council—to continue their

Amsterdam trade. Andros did not act out of a particular affection for Dutch residents; earlier he had clashed with some of them when he attempted to enforce the rules requiring Dutchmen to take an oath of allegiance to the English Crown.[43] Rather, he ingratiated himself to them because he knew only they could help him achieve his greater goals. To these ends, Andros used his power as governor to instruct the customs collector William Dyre to make sure his Dutch allies' vessels were searched cursorily, if at all. This special relationship helps to explain why, when Philipse's *Charles* entered New York in 1679, "no customs-house officers came on board" to search the ship.[44]

Andros's efforts to aid Philipse and other Dutch merchants such as Cornelis Steenwyck and the Van Cortlandt brothers appear in the historic record only anecdotally, but his favoritism toward wealthy transatlantic traders, be they Dutch or English, was part of Andros's larger strategy to transform New York City into an entrepôt that could dominate the surrounding region. Andros shared this goal with many elite New York merchants who sought to retain their hold on the province's economy. Realizing that their lack of political power within the English empire meant that pleas for continued trade to the Netherlands stood little chance of success, New Yorkers used their control of city government and their influence over the governor as council members to facilitate their Dutch trade and reinforced these efforts by working to control the regional economy; both of these strategies, in turn, insulated them from distant English control. Unlike in the Leeward Islands, where a fragmented plantation-based elite sitting in small individual assemblies did not have the political power to shape governor's trade policies, New Yorkers had an institutionalized legacy that gave them such influence.

To accomplish their intertwined goals of developing the port and collecting revenues, colonists and the governor almost immediately launched a plan to improve the city's infrastructure. First, Andros ordered that the canal running through the city be paved over to create a wide commercial street, the so-called Broad Street (or Broadway) to aid transportation. In 1675, the governor then unveiled a plan to build a new wharf off the city's southeast shore, and the council readily agreed to the proposal. When finished, the so-called "Great Dock" consisted of two stone and timber breakwaters forming a half moon that encircled a new pier and provided a deep, protected harbor on the East River. With its ability to accommodate larger vessels, the dock was designed to benefit city merchants, yet required the inhabitants of all towns in the colony to contribute to its construction. (The dock is just visible behind the vessel in figure 1). The steep special assessment that funded construction was easily absorbed by the eminent traders who were Andros's leading advisors, but because it came in a period of stagnant trade, the tax was a significant burden on rising traders, twenty-five of whom threatened to abandon the city instead of paying. For the Van Cortlandt brothers and Frederick Philispe, who all bought land in the heart of Manhattan's new commercial district and near the new shipping facilities during Andros's administration, however, these improvements were richly rewarding.[45]

To further secure the city's position as the province's connection to the rest of the Atlantic, the council and Andros revived measures first imposed by the WIC to bring the profitable Albany trade under the purview of city merchants. In 1678, Andros, working with the council, restricted trade along the Hudson to those who obtained permission from him and ordered that all ships trading to Albany must pass through New York City.[46] City traders garnered another victory when the council and Andros prohibited transatlantic trade originating in other ports.[47] These restrictions seemingly helped all city traders, but Andros, remembering the duke's charge to increase revenues, paired them with a higher duty on beaver pelts and more rigorous customs collection. Because eminent traders who controlled the fur trade, such as Philipse and Stephanus van Cortlandt, could afford the extra expense—at least in the short run—they and Andros reaped the benefits of economic regulation, unlike the small and middling traders, who were also part of the colony's mercantile community.[48]

Two years later, Andros and his council again attempted to strengthen city commerce at the expense of surrounding regions; this time, middling city merchants, too, shared the benefits. In January 1680, the council passed a resolution that granted New York City millers and merchants a monopoly on the milling and export of flour. This law was designed to funnel grain exports through the city and to help foster the West Indies grain trade as a way of strengthening the city's economy while weakening competing ports in eastern New Jersey and Long Island. Though the chief benefactors of this measure were eminent Dutch merchants such as the Philipses, the Van Cortlandts, and Steenwyck, who had diversified their business practices by bringing the West Indian flour markets into their commercial orbits, middling traders who could venture small vessels to the Caribbean also gained.[49] Additional restrictions on liquor distilling and leather tanning reserved additional guaranteed markets for rum imported from the West Indies and hides from surrounding areas for Manhattan merchants. These laws not only increased the duke's revenue directly by creating new income streams and enhancing Andros's ability to collect duties, but they also fostered an expansive trade for the city.[50]

As incidents of Andros's favoritism to the elite core of ethnically Dutch merchants mounted, English New Yorkers who traded to London, including John Robinson, William Pinhorn, Robert Woolley, and Thomas Griffeth, convinced the Duke of York to investigate Andros. Motivated by their inability to compete with Dutch traders, some of these Englishmen were the same merchants who had joined middling traders in threatening to abandon the city in opposition to the construction of the new dockyards.[51] Among other improprieties, Andros was accused of "favoring Dutchmen before English in trade, or making by Laws hurtfull to ye English in generall, or detayneing ships undully for private reasons, or admitting Dutch ships immediately to trade wth you [Andros], or trading . . . [himself] in ye names of others."[52] Earlier, Andros had beaten back the charges of the Englishmen George Heathcote and John Robinson that he allowed Dutch trade in Albany, but this time the weight of the evidence required him to return to London to defend himself. The results of the investigation were not surprising, given that the man picked to run it, John Lewen, was a close associate of at least one of the men who had launched the complaint—Robert Woolley.[53] Lewen particularly directed his ire at Andros's favoritism of Frederick Philipse and Stephanus van Cortlandt, whom Andros, in Lewen's account, conspired with to allow "goods to be brought in contrary to the Act of Navigacôn & Trade." Though Lewen's report emphasized the power of Dutch residents as a group, Philipse and Van Cortlandt became symbols to middling and noncity traders of the commercial advantages that Andros secured for elites in general. The governor was eventually cleared of the charges, but they clearly demonstrated that a relatively small group of elite merchants, Philipse and Van Cortlandt most directly, had combined with their governor to bend the local economy to meet their larger, often Anglo-Dutch trading needs.[54]

Andros's replacement, Colonel Thomas Dongan, the younger son of a Catholic Stuart family, arrived with a familiar charge: quickly end Dutch trade, halt other forms of smuggling, and regain administrative control of the city.[55] Almost as soon as he landed in New York, however, Dongan learned that because of the scope of the problems awaiting him, his task would be virtually impossible. Not only did he face a crippled government, but the acting governor was also an active participant in Dutch trade. As an interim governor without strong allies, Captain Anthony

Brockholls had been unable to muster the authority needed to collect duties or enforce trade laws, though as a participant there is little to indicate that he was inclined to anyway. Together with the merchant Jacob Milbourne, Brockholls owned the *Susan*, a vessel that in 1687 traveled from New York to Virginia and then to Rotterdam carrying rum, tobacco, and other colonial goods. In addition to the *Susan*, he held an interest in at least one other vessel, the *Happy Return*, which itself was seized for trading in violation of the Navigation Acts.[56]

Determined to gain control of the chaotic situation, Dongan took a particularly active role in prosecuting illegal trade. On August 8, 1685, for example, he reaffirmed the Navigation Acts and called for individuals to inform on their neighbors. "It is hereby ordered," Dongan wrote, "that if any Person or Persons hereafter have any Information to give in Affidavitts to make Against any Vessel for Acting or trading contrary to the Acts of Navigation . . . [they] must inform the Governor or other official."[57] In April 1686, the governor escalated his attempts to curb smuggling by dispatching John Harlow and a detail of soldiers to the smugglers' den of Long Island to hunt for interlopers.[58] Even those in the circle of the influential and powerful Frederick Philipse were not beyond Dongan's reach; Dongan's agents seized Philipse's *Charles* in 1685 for violating the Navigation Acts.[59]

Though committed to ending illegal trade, Dongan was not always successful. Like governors in other mainland North American colonies and in the Caribbean, he could not always depend upon the loyalty and honesty of those he charged with enforcing regulations. Dongan's chief problem was with his customs collector, Lucas Santen. Also a member of the council, Santen was accused of a variety of offenses including allowing vessels to enter port without registering or paying duties; making incomplete reports; and defrauding the king of about £3,000 in customs revenues. Santen was eventually cleared of these charges, but the number of accusations suggests his complicity in illegal trade.[60] With allies like Santen, unruly residents and corrupt officials continued to frustrate the new governor's best attempts at enforcing mercantile policy at the periphery.

Another obstacle blocking Dongan's reform efforts was that his administration overlapped with the influx of new groups of migrants that soon joined elite ethnically Dutch traders in Anglo-Dutch trade. Rather than Anglicizing New York's trade, these new arrivals enhanced Dutch commerce. Before Dongan's arrival in 1682, many London merchants had been unwilling to send their representatives to New York or to migrate themselves because they believed Andros's favoritism toward ethnically Dutch inhabitants restricted opportunity for them. With Andros in London, though, increased numbers of British merchants migrated to the city. As New York City prospered—by 1685, it boasted 3,500 residents (up from 1,500 in 1664)—these arrivals brought new wealth and new connections.[61] Increased English immigration meant a quickening of trade with English ports, particularly London, but it also resulted in new entrants into Dutch trade. In many cases, newcomers gained access to interimperial commerce by integrating themselves into Dutch familial networks; others brought important English connections desirable to those ethnically Dutch residents hoping to use English outports. One of the early English arrivals to assimilate himself into Dutch networks was William Darvall, who with his father had brought the *Margaret* to New York in 1675. Ethnically English, Darvall's father, Cornelis, had married into the family of a Leiden trader, a decision that gave his son important Dutch links. With the aid of his father and father-in-law, the English merchant Thomas Delavalle, William Darvall had the connections necessary to prosper from the New York City to Dover to Amsterdam trade, sometimes using the *Susanna,* of which his father owned one-third. Darvall also helped direct his father's vessels once they arrived in the colonies, receiving cargoes they had obtained in the Caribbean and dispatching them back to the Dutch Republic again with goods from New York. In New York City, Darvall also benefited from his distant relations to the Van Rensselaers and Van Cortlandts—his brother John was the brother-in-law of Jacobus van Cortlandt and Jeremais van Renselaer, and the son-in-law of Oloff Stevensen van Cortlandt. Eventually Darvall achieved sufficient status to be named an alderman of the city.[62]

English merchants were not the only new arrivals eager to participate in Dutch trade. Robert R. Livingston became a salient example of newcomers outside England. Livingston was born in Scotland but spent his youth in Rotterdam, where he acquired a merchant's education. Eventually, after short stays in Scotland, Boston, and on the English fur-trading frontier, he made his way to Albany, where, in 1675, the twenty-one-year-old Livingston entered the ranks of the interior port's middling merchants. Livingston possessed Dutch language skills, knowledge of Dutch commerce, and distant Rotterdam connections, but he lacked capital. Like many young merchants, he rectified this deficit with a fortuitous marriage. Though he was courting another woman when the newly widowed Alida Schuyler—the sister-in-law of Stephanus van Cortlandt—drew his attention, Livingston seized the chance to marry a well-connected

Dutch woman and skilled trader in her own right. As his friend Thomas Delavalle wrote to him after the marriage, "now . . . [you have married] into ye Ranke of honest men." His marriage connected Livingston to the Schuyler and Van Cortlandt families, and the young aspiring trader quickly capitalized on these new links. By 1680, he regularly ventured goods with Stephanus van Cortlandt to Amsterdam and Barbados and several years later had established the necessary ties and capital to trade directly to these places on his own account. Concurrently, Livingston exploited English connections to establish a fifteen-year business relationship with the London merchant John Harwood.[63] That Livingston, a new arrival in 1675, identified enough promise in trading to the Dutch Republic to structure his career around those prospects testifies to Dutch trade's persistent attractiveness. Livingston was part of a larger migration of Scottish, French, and German traders into the British mainland colonies, and his biography indicates the creative paths that could sustain Dutch trade. In the Caribbean, there were many fewer connections to the Low Countries after 1660; instead, colonists there relied on Dutch merchants at adjacent islands.

Also expanding their Dutch trade after 1664 was New York's relatively small, yet commercially active, Jewish population. New York's Jewish community got its start with the 1654 arrival of twenty-five individuals—some from Amsterdam and some from Brazil—and it slowly grew during the Dutch occupation, achieving first the right to remain in the colony and eventually to trade freely.[64] In the next several decades, the small community flourished as Jewish merchants took advantage of their ties to the Dutch Republic and the Dutch Caribbean, particularly Curaçao. Part of a larger trade in which many New Yorkers carried locally produced flour, cheese, butter, and dried meat, together with imported goods such as wine, cloth, and other dry goods to Caribbean plantation colonies in exchange for rum, molasses, ginger, and other tropical products, New York's Jewish community was particularly well placed to trade to the Dutch island.[65] By the last decades of the seventeenth century, many of the chief commercial figures in Curaçao were Jewish merchants, some of whom had family connections among New York City's Jewish population. These Jewish merchants worked with the WIC to encourage trade with Manhattan, probably helping the New Yorker Jacob Lucena to receive a pass "to bring comestibles to Curaçao in exchange for slaves." New York Jewish traders (who were not among the city's wealthiest inhabitants) also snatched the opportunity to venture vessels to the Caribbean because this trade required less capital to enter than did transatlantic exchange. By 1715/6, just over 32 percent of the yearly departures of Jewish vessels from New York City carried flour and other goods bound for Curaçao.[66] As in Barbados, Jewish traders in New York did not limit themselves to American routes but continued to trade in Amsterdam's beneficial markets and act as commercial agents for merchants in Amsterdam. Asser Levy, who arrived from Amsterdam in 1654, served as the agent of Amsterdam's Abraham Cohen and was charged with collecting Cohen's debts and relaying furs to him in Amsterdam.[67] The changing imperial situation did not sever Levy's ties to the Netherlands, for he continued to do business with Jewish and Christian merchants there through the 1670s and 1680s. In Amsterdam, Levy worked with the merchant Elias de Pommares, who in turn hired the New York attorney William Darvall to collect debts Levy owed him. Levy and one of his partners, New York's Valentijn Valack, also appointed Elias Salomon of Amsterdam to represent the two New Yorkers in the Dutch city.[68] In December 1680, Joshua Sarfati, another New York Jewish trader tied to an eminent Amsterdam family, issued a bill of exchange drawn on George de Spinosa of Amsterdam "to pay to Samiel Wilsen [of New York] on order the sum of one thousand and seventy-five guilders . . . for goods received" at New York. The bill eventually reached the notary J. H. Outgers, who demanded its payment on behalf of Wilsen (var. Wilson) in April 1681.[69] In remitting such a large sum for what were presumably European manufactures sent from Amsterdam, Sarfati's interimperial trade was clearly significant.

Levy left an estate valued at more than £550 upon his sudden death in 1682, a sum that placed Levy in the middle rank of the city's traders. Reflective of New York's relative toleration for Jews, among those listed as his debtors were some of the city's most prominent traders, including Stephanus van Cortlandt, Jacob Kip, and Nicholas Bayard.[70] It is clear that Levy was able to extend his commercial sphere beyond Jewish associates, but at the same time his important religious-based connections to Amsterdam enabled him to participate in the most eminent of economic sectors and perhaps enabled him to connect others to Amsterdam's networks. On the one hand, the connections between New York and Amsterdam's Jewish communities were less valuable for New York City's economy, which had an established Dutch mercantile community, than they were in Barbados, where there were usually few, if any, resident Dutch traders to manage exchange with the Dutch Republic. On the other hand, though, New York's Jews enjoyed vital cross-national networks that extended around the Atlantic world and enabled their community to survive and prosper even as the city became increasingly English.

Because of the variety of secretive methods Manhattan merchants employed, it is unclear exactly how many ships passed between New York and Amsterdam between the return of English rule in 1674 and Leisler's Rebellion in 1689.[71] On the whole, the fragmentary evidence indicates that at least two and as many as five vessels a year traveled between Dutch ports and Manhattan either directly or indirectly, but the true number is probably higher. If Governor Andros's report of between ten and fifteen arrivals at the port in 1678 is accurate, and evidence suggests it is, then the Dutch trade accounted for between one-fifth and one-third of all transatlantic trade at the port.[72] Even as English officials fostered the "Anglicization" of New York, ethnically Dutch merchants—increasingly joined by English and Jewish individuals—successfully negotiated the changing climate to trade in familiar ways, rerouting their trading patterns through England, attracting new capital and partners, and exploiting new markets in the process. No longer trading to the Low Countries simply because they had few alternatives but rather because they believed Anglo-Dutch trade to be their most profitable option, Manhattan merchants' interimperial commerce continued to fuel New York City's expanding economy. By 1687, the city boasted "about nine or ten three mast vessels of about 80 to 100 tons burthen[,] two or three ketches & Barks of about 40 tun: and about twenty sloops of about twenty or five & twenty Tunn . . . All of which trade for England Holland[,] & the West Indies except six or seven sloops that use the river trade to Albany."[73]

The city's development was undoubtedly linked to merchants' creative manipulation of trade laws and commercial opportunities. Rarely did city merchants have to argue vociferously for the privilege of trading outside the British empire; rather, they simply pursued it. Further, since ethnic Dutchmen still dominated the city's governing structure through the 1680s, these men were cultural and political outsiders within the English state, and thus they saw little efficacy in direct lobbying. Able to rest their demands only on their status as denizens, rather than as true-born Englishmen, New Yorkers did not yet have as authoritative a claim to enjoy the rights of Englishmen. As we have seen, Barbadians more actively pursued legal permissions to trade outside the empire.

New Yorkers' economic interests also diverged from those in the English West Indies. Even though there were advantages to exporting peltry to Amsterdam over London, this trade was in decline in the 1660s, leaving New York without a staple commodity resembling tobacco and sugar in the Caribbean. Therefore, New Yorkers found it harder over time to argue that free trade would enable them to send their commodities to the best European markets. Additionally, there was far less demand for grain and flour, a secondary commodity produced in the New York region, in European markets. Instead, city traders decided to turn their efforts inward, collaborating with their governors and using their local political power to ensure Manhattan's dominance over the interior where they could control trade with regulations.[74] Unlike those of Caribbean ports, New York City's economic circumstances were tied to a large continental landmass with a developing agricultural hinterland that was beginning to shape urban development and the character of the city's exports. As such, the city functioned both as a periphery and a (colonial) center with its own agricultural periphery. Eventually, as flour exports replaced fur as the leading sector of New York's trade, and as warfare discouraged transatlantic trade, New Yorkers shifted their commercial perspectives again. These transformations, which were only beginning to unfold in the 1680s, compelled New Yorkers—elite and middling, Dutch and English—to reconsider their position on regulated trade.

* * *

Anglo-Dutch trade was an important feature of colonial life in the four decades following the Restoration. Though their local situations determined the precise mechanics of interimperial trade, colonists living in New York and the English West Indies shared a persistent quest for Dutch trade that was rooted in two factors: a commercial culture that prized interimperial exchange and an English administration that could not effectively staunch Dutch trading with English laws. Nevertheless, more effective, coercive, and coherent—if still inconsistent—Restoration policies forced colonists to develop new legal and illegal techniques to maintain their interimperial trade, including more direct English colonial control over trade. Learning to use small craft to hazard goods to Dutch vessels or islands, bribing officials, collaborating with English governors and port officials, and organizing the outport trade, colonists themselves managed more Anglo-Dutch trade by the end of the 1680s than they had in earlier decades. In time, this local control of interimperial trade blended with colonists' realization that the English state was becoming more robust. Most clearly seen in Barbadians' willingness to accept the payment of duties in exchange for partial free trade, and in Caribbean planters and New York merchants' embracing state power to regulate trade when it benefited them, metropolitan officials had begun to convince some influential colonists that a powerful empire could benefit all.

It was then that European events interceded again. The almost twenty years of international warfare that William III, Prince of Orange, touched off when he seized control of the English crown in 1688 created turmoil throughout the Atlantic and provoked colonists to grasp tightly to the interimperial connections that had sustained them in other crises. Though, with Catholic France replacing the Dutch Republic as Britain's rival, with a Dutchman on the English throne, and with drastically more developed colonies, settlers' interimperial trade would look very different than it had in earlier decades.

PART THREE

MATURITY, 1689–1713

6 / "A Conspiracy in People of All Ranks": The Evolution of Intracolonial Networks

Working in the Caribbean during the first decade of the eighteenth century, the English mariner Samuel Brise was well placed to monitor the ship traffic that made these waters among the busiest in the Western Hemisphere. Based in Curaçao between 1704 and 1708, Brise later recalled to the Council of Trade and Plantations the names, shipmasters, cargoes, and destinations of numerous British colonial vessels that called at the Dutch colony. Even though he claimed that he "could [have] give[n] a far Larger account of . . . this Clandestine Trade" if he had not "Lost Many of . . . [his] Papers," Brise nonetheless offered the council an impressive catalogue of illicit commerce. For example, take those vessels he encountered in June 1704. In that typical month, Brise was in Curaçao when a sloop owned by a Mr. Dewden arrived from Barbados "Loaden with Sugar and Provisions." After exchanging his cargo for "dry goods," the captain "sailed to Rhode Island and [from] there to Barbados with Provisions." Soon thereafter, a Captain Sloe arrived on a similar venture with "Sugar and Provisions" from Barbados that he traded for dry goods at Curaçao. The pattern set forth by these vessels had changed little three years later, when Brise, still in Curaçao, witnessed the arrival of "three sloopes" from Barbados "Laden with Rum, sugar, Beefe and Butter." Owned by a merchant of Rhode Island and two traders from Barbados, these sloops "Carried back Dutch goods" to the English colonies.[1]

From Brise's perspective, interimperial trade was as persistent in the first decade of the eighteenth century as it had been before despite significant advances in British enforcement of trade laws and in the ability of British merchants to meet colonists' needs. What was different about Brise's description of cross-national exchange in this period from that which dominated the seventeenth century, however, was the increased role of colonial shipmasters and merchants in driving trade. Reminiscent of the cruising patterns of Dutch vessels and the intra-Caribbean sloop trade that distinguished earlier years, the vessels Brise observed calling at many ports of various empires were nonetheless distinctive because of the enhanced role colonists played in owning and operating them, the wider variety of cargoes the vessels carried, and the more multilateral routes they sailed.

While Brise's description of Anglo-Dutch trade is unusually detailed and sweeping, what is missing from his testimony is the larger context that framed colonists' choices to hold tightly to cross-national ties. Most notably, Brise failed to mention the Atlantic dimension of two major European wars that profoundly shaped the lives of British West Indians in these years. The War of the League of Augsburg (1689–97) and the War of the Spanish Succession (1702–13) were complex conflicts involving many of the rising states of western Europe, but what dominated their Atlantic phase was warfare between the English and French. These conflicts disrupted shipping, doubled the cost of what shipping remained, distracted planters, occupied naval fleets, and resulted in the destruction of plantations throughout the Atlantic, particularly in the British West Indies, which, because of their small size and proximity to foreign islands, remained especially vulnerable.[2]

In response to this turbulence, islanders chose to maintain patterns of commerce familiar to them, seeking out interimperial markets for their sugar and tobacco when metropolitan ties failed to meet their expectations as they had done in the century before. Grasping tightly to older habits when wars closed in on them, colonists reversed the momentum that English policies and economic conditions had gathered during the 1670s and 1680s in pushing them away from Anglo-Dutch trade. Capitalizing on the economic evolution and growth of their colonies, British West Indians, as Brise witnessed, also developed new markets and connections, exporting provisions and plantation supplies themselves, buying slaves from foreign islands, and building economically diverse and profitable cross-national intra-Caribbean exchange networks that revolved around the Dutch islands of St. Eustatius and Curaçao and Danish St. Thomas. Whereas in earlier decades colonists had largely traded tropical staples for desperately needed manufactured goods and provisions from Dutch traders who arrived at their colonies, later years saw colonists exchange a broader range of goods through increasingly complex networks that bound settlers from many nations around the Atlantic together and in which British colonists took the initiative. Perhaps most notably, colonists' increasingly active role in the slave trade at the end of the seventeenth century indicates the growing sophistication of cross-national trade and the way slavery continued to bind together the Atlantic. British colonists had started their transition to greater control over interimperial commerce with the outport trade and with creative use of loopholes in imperial arrangements to smuggle more in the 1660s and 1670s; warfare enhanced these conditions further and placed British colonists in the forefront of Anglo-Dutch trade by the end of the century.

Colonists living in New York City did not experience fighting as directly during the Anglo-French wars as those in the Caribbean, but the two decades of warfare nevertheless disrupted their shipping, destroyed New Yorkers' vessels, and forced merchants to adapt to depressed market conditions. Never completely abandoning exchange with the Dutch Republic, New Yorkers, like those in the Caribbean, turned more than ever to intercolonial commerce to weather wartime conditions and exploit the new opportunities that wars helped create. Capitalizing on agricultural expansion in New York City's hinterlands, colonists developed new markets for grain, flour, and timber that were in high demand in the British and foreign West Indies. Among the most important of these places was Curaçao, an island becoming ever more important to the Dutch Republic's trade with the Spanish Main, and a place with which New Yorkers had long traded. With the fur trade in decline, Caribbean trade evolved into the central component of New Yorkers' economic activity, and although their most important connections shifted to the British West Indies, New Yorkers continued to visit foreign islands regularly.

In both the Caribbean and along the mainland of North America, therefore, colonists responded to the imperial warfare of the late seventeenth and early eighteenth centuries by creatively modifying older interimperial networks and trading techniques to match new circumstances. The trajectory of economic relations between Britain and its colonies in the early eighteenth century was toward a more integrated British Atlantic empire, but underlying imperial developments were colonists' new colonially managed interimperial linkages, arrangements that not only enabled survival but also generated capital that could be invested in local economies.

* * *

Though the European wars that embroiled England beginning in 1689 led to periodic economic disturbances—such as the currency crisis of 1695–96 and the depression in the cloth market during 1696–97—they caused no long-term deep dislocations to what was by then a fast-developing mercantile economy. In England, many observers connected rising wealth among merchants with a stronger state and the improved government regulation of colonial trade. As Josiah Child wrote, the country would not own "one half of the shipping, nor trade, nor employ . . . one half of the seamen which we do at present" without the Navigation Acts.[3] While assorted trade laws encouraged England's commerce, the statutes themselves were not primarily behind economic expansion. More important was the expansion in the internal economy that rebounding woolen exports created. Previously these "old draperies" had dominated England's overseas trade, and it had been their failure that had decimated the English export trade in the early 1600s. As exports rose, English traders freed themselves from dependence on Dutch markets and gained greater control over trade in the North Sea/Baltic area and over reexports to Europe, developments that drew capital into London where it could be used to fund commercial ventures, especially those in the Atlantic. All of these changes were facilitated by Parliament's efforts to eliminate the privileged trade companies; most notably this included an attack on the Merchant Adventurers' monopoly of the woolens trade, a decision that invigorated rising merchants.

Central to growing trade and manufacturing during the last quarter of the seventeenth century was a stronger commercial and financial infrastructure (largely borrowed from the United Provinces) that could support shipbuilding, new commercial services, and a strong navy to protect overseas trade. Largely a product of wartime innovations to meet the demands of war, the heart of England's interlocked revenue and credit system was the Bank of England (founded in 1694), an institution characterized by a partnership between private entrepreneurs and the state, with the former providing initial capital and management and the latter guaranteeing loans with tax revenues. Acting as both the banker of the government and as a private corporation, the Bank of England lubricated trade and underwrote military expenditure. While it may not have "furnish[ed] Stock enough to drive the Trade of the whole Commercial World," as William Petty predicted in 1682, the bank nonetheless staved off financial crises and established a foundation for both commercial and state expansion.[4]

The growing English Atlantic colonies—the total population of the English Caribbean increased from 59,000 to 135,000 between 1630 and 1690 and had reached perhaps 155,000 by 1713—were also instrumental in creating demand for British commerce and manufactures of woolens, copper and iron products, silks, hats, linens, and other handicraft goods. Indicative of this larger export market, the number of ships transporting English goods from London to the West Indies rose from 45 in 1664 to 133 in 1686. This trade, of course, was not one-way. Perhaps the most important stimulus to the English economy was the great increase in imported plantation goods, rising from a value of £421,000 in 1663/1669 to £1,107,000 in 1699/1701. By 1700, tobacco, sugar, and calicoes flooded into England and accounted for 80 percent of the value of the country's imports and two-thirds of its reexports to Europe. It was these reexports, particularly, which enabled England to overcome its own balance of payment weaknesses. As a further inducement to the English economy, accelerated sugar production meant accelerated demand for slaves in islands such as Barbados. Enhanced trade created additional demand for shipbuilding, insurance, and other shipping services. As a whole, English trade increased about sixfold over the course of the seventeenth century.[5]

Though matters were more complicated than Child revealed, observers were right in noting that a central goal of the Navigation Acts had been largely achieved by the early eighteenth century: British carriers had replaced Dutch in much of the British empire's trade.[6] In the Caribbean, the better codification of trade laws and a greater naval presence had allowed authorities to be generally successful in stamping out direct foreign trade (or at least raising its costs); by the late 1670s and 1680s, few Dutchmen dared trade directly and openly at British Atlantic ports. What officials struggled to do was to stop trade between West Indians and those at nearby foreign colonies. This interisland trade, usually carried out on plantation- and Dutch-owned vessels of between 15 and 40 tons, provided an important means for settlers of both empires to retain access to each other's markets. The chief entrepôt for the sloop trade was Dutch St. Eustatius as it had been before. Though the English held the island in the 1670s, the Dutch reclaimed it in 1682 and expanded illegal trade based there so that, by 1688, St. Eustatius had again developed into such a hazard for English trade that authorities decided interimperial commerce could not "be destroyed, unless by the destruction of the settlements of our Dutch and Danish Neighbours."[7]

When the French captured the island at the start of the War of the

TABLE 6.1
Muscovado and White Sugars Imported to Great Britain,
1697–1719 (cwt)

Year	From Barbados	From the English Leeward Islands
1697	241,021	93,340
1698	271,585	127,970
1699	202,944	164,697
1700	268,489	160,251
1701	200,577	163,257
1702	68,690	151,824
1703	160,835	162,765
1704	100,455	126,634
1705	260,352	199,091
1706	217,375	51,242
1707	141,943	147,238
1708	180,293	89,792
1709	185,388	107,959
1710	167,652	225,332
1711	186,548	90,258
1712	140,834	142,399
1713	121,250	260,961
1714	226,363	191,519
1715	288,782	204,924
1716	235,409	327,482
1717	279,861	278,458
1718	252,904	94,390
1719	127,222	300,010

SOURCE: John J. McCusker, *Rum and the American Revolution: The Rum Trade and the Balance of Payments of the Thirteen Continental Colonies* (New York: Garland, 1989), appendix D10–D13, D15.

NOTE: These are the most accurate export numbers to include Barbados and the Leeward Islands. McCusker has adjusted for wastage in shipping to better reflect export totals.

League of Augsburg, the English again had an excuse to invade, expelling the French in 1690. Hoping to put an end to the island's role as a smuggling haven, English officials ignored an Anglo-Dutch alliance and ordered the first Governor Codrington to destroy the island's port infrastructure. Knowing how valuable the Dutch trading base was to his colonies, however, Codrington ignored the order and "invited the former Dutch settlers to reoccupy it." Living in what was still technically an English possession (until 1693), returning Dutch inhabitants soon dominated the island's trade.[8] In 1696, the Dutch WIC received formal commercial control of the island and set about enhancing its role as an entrepôt by allowing foreign vessels to trade there after paying a 5 percent duty and by using the company's trading power to keep it stocked with European manufactured goods and, later, slaves. For the remainder of the long eighteenth century, St. Eustatius remained the Caribbean's central node for interimperial trade among British, Dutch, and French colonies.[9]

Similar to St. Eustatius in its accessibility to British West Indians was Dutch Curaçao. Founded originally as a Caribbean transfer point for the Dutch WIC, by the end of the seventeenth century it had blossomed into a critical interimperial entrepôt. And while most of this island's trade was with the Spanish Main, British colonists called here as well. None other than one of the Leeward Islands' richest planters and the islands' political leader, Governor Christopher Codrington, owned five ships "by which he se[nt] a fine store of sugar," "Cotton, Woll, & indico" to the island in exchange for "Goods and Commodities being of the manufacture of Europe."[10] At other times, the governor even allegedly used British naval vessels attached to his command to carry sugars to Curaçao and slaves in return. While these complaints against Codrington were motivated by political differences and thus may be exaggerated, Codrington's earlier efforts to trade with Dutch islands confirm at least part of their accuracy.[11] Codrington was not alone in this endeavor, though most of his colonists lacked the resources he commanded and focused their trade on nearby St. Eustatius.[12] In 1701, the surveyor general of customs, Edward Randolph, captured the extent of the island sloop trade, complaining that colonists secreted "Great Quantities of Sugar" out of Nevis, Antigua, and St. Christopher to St. Eustatius and Curaçao, where, according to the commissioners of the customs, "her Majesty's Subjects receive in Exchange from the Dutch Commodities of the growth of Europe."[13]

Randolph's revelation that the main commodity Leeward Islanders were secreting to Dutch colonies by 1700 was sugar is an important one.

Forty years before, one of the major motivations for colonists to trade at Dutch islands had been to dispose of their tobacco, but by 1700, some Leeward Islanders had begun to prefer London markets, where tobacco prices were now higher.[14] Meanwhile, Leeward Islanders had begun to plant much less of the leaf in favor of sugar. Soon West Indian planters found themselves prospering as lower production costs, fresh land, and a wartime spike in sugar prices produced a sugar-led export boom.[15] In 1686, tobacco accounted for only about 5 percent of the value of the products the Leeward Islands sent to London, and in 1703, Antigua was the only Leeward Island still exporting significant amounts of tobacco to London.[16] In Barbados, the transition to sugar and the greater need of capital, commission merchants, and the Royal African Company that sugar cultivation produced led colonists to forge closer ties with the metropole during that island's sugar boom. But in the Leewards, ongoing warfare delayed the intensification of metropolitan trade until after 1713, leaving colonists to rely upon older habits.

As English freight rates rose steeply during the Anglo-French wars—prompting planters in the Caribbean to intervene with legislation to cap them—supplies from the metropole dwindled and prices for imports rose.[17] With Dutch traders—whose shipping was affected disproportionately less by the wars—still able to offer British planters "European Goods" from their islands at "much lower Rates" in exchange for colonial produce bought at rates "much higher" than colonists could obtain in Britain, Anglo-Dutch trade remained brisk.[18] Exacerbating warfare's effect on shipping was the direct damage it caused to colonies. French raids against St. Christopher in 1689 and 1690, Nevis in 1706, and Montserrat between 1710 and 1712 destroyed thousands of pounds' worth of plantation infrastructure and increased demand for already scarce goods. The situation was so bad in 1690 that newly arrived Governor Kendall claimed that, "with the high price of freight, and the scarcity of provisions, caused by a long drought and by the war," there was risk of starvation in Barbados.[19] In response, colonists looked to interimperial trade for relief. Those in St. Christopher, for example, petitioned the queen for the freedom to trade with foreigners as they had done in the 1660s and 1670s.[20] Meanwhile, Jamaica's governor argued the colonists' case, observing that a lack of goods coming from England made "all goods excessive[ly] dear" and lamenting the strict laws that prevented colonists from trading with "the Dutch our neighbours where we could have what we wanted at easy rates." Unlike this governor, many desperate colonists were undeterred by the laws, calling upon their long experience with interimperial experience to find relief wherever it lay regardless of imperial boundaries and trade laws.[21]

Even as war strained resources, a deficit of goods meant that merchants who had the ability to secure interimperial trade stood to prosper. With its small cargoes, low capital requirements, and quick turn-around times, the sloop trade proved attractive to modest island-based merchants—referred to as "mean persons" by one official—to earn great sums, perhaps as much as "1000lb a man." At other times, it was the factors of English merchants living in the Leeward Islands who used their employers' "effect[s], to Carry on this Trade and pretend in their letters, that they have trusted the Planter and cant get in their Debts."[22]

As is the case for the rest of the seventeenth century, a precise accounting of the levels of shuttle sloop trade between the English Leeward Islands and foreign colonies is impossible. Records kept by the WIC in St. Eustatius for later years indicate that hundreds of vessels yearly engaged in intra-Caribbean exchange with foreign colonies, but no similar accounts remain for the period before 1729.[23] Similarly, Dutch notarial records sometimes include details about sugar shipments that originated in English colonies, though not in a systematic manner.[24] As far as British records are concerned, the Naval Officer Shipping Lists provide a glimpse of the sloop trade in the Leeward Islands and Barbados, but because they exist for only selected years between 1689 and 1713, they are unreliable for measuring interimperial trade.[25] The most complete series of naval lists in these years for Barbados covers seventy of the seventy-five months between December 29, 1694, and March 24, 1701, and ninety of the 102 months spanning March 25, 1701, and September 24, 1709. In the first of these periods, about 350 vessels called at Barbados. Of these, a recorded ten vessels entered from or cleared to Curaçao, and another thirty arrived from or departed for the Dutch colony of Suriname. In the second of these periods, ten vessels arrived from or departed to Curaçao, and twenty-nine came or went from or to Suriname. The most complete port records for the Leeward Islands between 1689 and 1713 are for the years 1704 to 1708, a period of sixty months. In this time, various lists of arrivals and departures for St. Christopher cover thirty-three months, Nevis forty-four, Antigua twenty-eight, and Montserrat eleven. No vessels arriving or departing to Dutch colonies are listed in these returns for St. Christopher, Nevis, and Montserrat, and they indicate that only two vessels left Antigua for Curaçao and one for Danish St. Thomas. That such limited statistical data are incompatible with anecdotal evidence suggests these records missed much of the cross-national intra-Caribbean trade.[26]

According to the second Governor Christopher Codrington, smuggling remained a regular feature of Leeward Island commerce, estimating that colonists secreted "many millions of sugars to St. Eustatius, Curaçao and Danish St. Thomas."[27] As he noted in 1701, "there is so much ignorance, laziness or Corruption in Naval and Customhouse officers, and so general a Conspiracy in people of all ranks and qualitys here to elude ye Acts of Trade, that I have ye Mortification of Knowing a hundred things are done every day, (which I cannot possibly prevent), prejudicial to ye trade and interest of England."[28] Resistance to trade laws was so strong in the Leewards that when Codrington's successor, Daniel Parke, refused bribes of £1,000 per year to allow illegal trade upon taking office, he perhaps touched off the conflict that would result in his murder.[29] Another indication of corruption is the numerous vessels that customs officers recorded as having left port without a cargo, such as the brig *Mary*, a vessel of 50 tons captained by Henry Hooper and registered in Antigua that left that island for Curaçao on November 27, 1707, with "nothing on board." At other times, ships entered "with no cargo" but left fully laden.[30] Colonial trade statistics also understate the legal sloop trade because officials routinely omitted trade "in boates and sloopes transported daily from island to Island for their mutuall maintenance" from their lists because it was "so very intricate and troublesome" to record them all.[31]

Even when naval officers and customs inspectors were honest and tried to halt illegal trade, colonists' half century of experience at smuggling easily thwarted authorities' efforts to suppress it. Perhaps the most important late seventeenth-century innovation in smuggling involved the growing boat trade between Bermuda and St. Eustatius. As Michael Jarvis has shown, Bermudians responded to increased Caribbean-wide demand for small sloops designed for interisland exchange by developing shallow-draft and inexpensive vessels that were perfect for smuggling. By the end of the seventeenth century, Dutch merchants in St. Eustatius were among the chief consumers of these sloops, buying not only the vessel, but often its British registration as well, which enabled masters to pass off themselves, their ships, and their cargoes as British when trading at British colonies. An increased number of small vessels from mainland North America trading in a multilateral pattern throughout the Caribbean complicated tracking these ships, and many appear to be missing from shipping records.[32]

Subjective and incomplete as narrative descriptions of trade are, such accounts are valuable for the extraordinary amount of detail they offer in lieu of adequate quantifiable information. Take, for example, a report submitted to the Council of Trade by Peter Holt, a West Indian mariner possibly based in Barbados with twelve years of local experience. Holt, who worked on a variety of ships trading among English, Dutch, Danish, and French colonies, provided a vivid description of the volume and makeup of the legal and illegal trade between British and Dutch colonies during the War of the Spanish Succession. Whereas many earlier accounts of interimperial trade concentrated on English colonists avoiding duties or securing cheaper manufactured goods by smuggling tropical staples to Dutch vessels calling speculatively at English islands or waiting just off the coast, Holt placed Leeward Islanders and Barbadians at the center of complex trading networks spanning the Atlantic. Still sending sugar, tobacco, and indigo to Dutch islands in exchange for dry goods, Holt, like his contemporary Samuel Brise, observed that island merchants, owner-operators, and shipmasters also reexported butter, beef, pork, and flour brought from Philadelphia, New York, and New England to St. Thomas and Curaçao, exchanging these foodstuffs for French wine, cocoa, and textiles. Others, he wrote, carried "Rumm, beef and Sugar" from Montserrat and Barbados to Curaçao, trading them for "Dutch goods" that they transported to North America. Another option for shipowners was to rent their vessels to foreign merchants at Curaçao, who, since the vessels carried British registrations and crews, undoubtedly used them to enter British colonies with foreign goods. So prevalent was the sloop trade to Curçaco that numerous Barbados-based vessels were named the *Curaçao Merchant*. Meantime, British West Indians were able by the late seventeenth century to secure sufficient foodstuffs and other supplies from British colonies in North America, and to exchange some North American provisions and lumber for European textiles from Dutch and Danish colonists. On the whole, Holt estimated that if Curaçao "was sunk under water, it wou[l]d be beter for England by 5 or £600,000 in one year" and that "thear is not a marcht. [merchant] in England that trades to ye West Indies but what is, has been[,] and will be the worse for that Island."[33]

Benefiting from strong interimperial family ties, Sephardic Jewish merchants provided British West Indians with their smoothest link to neighboring islands, especially Curaçao. First glimpsed in the wake of the 1655 seizure of Dutch vessels in Barbados, this trade was reinforced after the relocation of refugees from Dutch Brazil to the Dutch and English West Indies in subsequent decades. From Curaçao, Jewish traders used small-scale, relatively safe ventures to supply Barbados with the foodstuffs and other plantation supplies which colonists badly needed and which were difficult to obtain from England. In turn, Curaçao presented an important contact node for Jewish colonists in English islands looking for a regional supply of manufactured goods and a way to step beyond the Navigation Acts. Emmanuel Levy, a shopkeeper in Barbados, for example, evidently obtained wares for his shop from his brother Gabriel Levy of Curaçao.[34]

Another of those who linked Barbados to Curaçao was Philipe Henriquez, alias Jacob Senior, who traded between Curaçao and both British and Spanish colonies. Probably born in Amsterdam in 1660, Henriquez/Senior seems to have plied the Caribbean Sea, stopping at various ports in the intra-Caribbean transit trade over a period of twenty years.[35] In Nevis, the Navarro family connected Leeward Islanders to Curaçao. Born in Madrid but raised in Amsterdam, Isaac Pinheiro probably arrived in Nevis via New York City in the closing decades of the seventeenth century. Once established, he rose quickly as a merchant and plantation owner all the while remaining commercially tied to his father Abraham in Amsterdam, his sister and her husband in Curaçao, and Jacob Sattur and his wife, Mary, in South Carolina. Pinheiro also traded with the brothers Joseph Bueno de Mesquita of New York City and Abraham Bueno de Mesquita of Nevis, who had in turn migrated from Barbados. When Pinheiro died in 1710, his wife, Esther, continued the business, eventually working with Jewish and non-Jewish merchants from Nevis, Curaçao, New York City, and Boston. Though the cargoes of the numerous vessels Isaac and Esther Pinero owned and dispatched around the Atlantic are unknown, their intracolonial patterns suggest that they resembled other British West Indians in carrying a wide variety of manufactured goods and foodstuffs that the Pinheiros then resold in Nevis.[36]

The perception that Jewish merchants dominated the retail sector sparked the outrage of a group of Barbadians, who petitioned Governor William Willoughby, claiming that Jewish traders' control of local food markets was "extremely prejudicial to the poor of our own nation, who might be comfortably supported thereby."[37] In the Leeward Islands, too, Jews' frequent specialization in retailing foodstuffs and other wares provoked a backlash. Singling out the Jewish community as the cause of great suffering in Nevis due to their "buying . . . & engrossing al[l] manner of Goods brought thither to be sold," a 1694 law banned Jewish retailing. The passage of this discriminatory law underscores islanders' fears of their own vulnerability; dependent on imports for their survival, colonists were preoccupied with guaranteeing that necessaries were affordable and accessible. And because of their prominent position as the importers of foodstuffs, their willingness to sell to free and unfree alike, and the ease with which they were identifiable, Jewish traders often bore the burden of excessive regulation and discrimination. In Barbados, they paid between 20 and 50 percent more than in taxes than non-Jews during the seventeenth and eighteenth centuries.[38]

Opposition to Jewish merchants was not universal. When faced with the Navigation Act of 1660, planters in Barbados explicitly supported the admission of Jews to the island, citing their commercial connections as an advantage for the island. Their governor, too, welcomed Jewish residents, modifying local law so as to allow Jewish colonists to testify in court, ostensibly because this step would enable them to collect debts and dispute contracts.[39] At other times, governors prevented or overturned discriminatory measures that had the potential to destabilize the economy. Lieutenant Governor Stede of Barbados, for example, believed that Jewish merchants were all that kept the island supplied with necessaries during difficult periods. Similarly, the Leeward Islands Assembly reversed course and repealed their anti-Jewish law under pressure from their governor in 1701.[40]

Just as colonists' trade with Curaçao expanded at the end of the seventeenth century, commerce with Suriname attracted British West Indian trade as well. This colony, founded by the English in the 1650s and transferred to the Dutch at the Peace of Breda (1667), struggled for much of its early history but began to expand when the WIC bought it in 1682 and turned it over to the Sociëteit van Surinamee (Suriname Corporation), a concern run jointly by the WIC Amsterdam chamber, the City of Amsterdam, and the Van Aerssen van Sommelsdijck family. At first the directors of the corporation—which gave the WIC a monopoly over the slave trade but allowed private investment, plantation ownership, and licensed trade—forbid foreign trade at the island. As the number of acres in cultivation rose and as demand for horses, lumber, and foodstuffs increased, desperate residents sought out foreign trade anyway. Then, in 1704, the directors shifted direction. Recognizing the reality of interimperial trade, they decided to try to benefit from it, deciding to officially allow British vessels to trade there. Soon close to half of all vessels calling at Suriname had come from colonial North America (especially New York) or the British Caribbean.[41]

Vessels calling at Suriname, ranging in size from 15 to 100 tons, carried a variety of supplies including lumber, staves, heading (the tops of casks), foodstuffs, and horses (which Dutch officials required accompany every shipment). New England and New York merchants who regularly traded to Suriname and Curaçao also called at Barbados, importing provisions and lumber from North America that had not sold in Suriname and wine and dry goods from Europe that they had purchased in the Dutch colony. In return, some carried Barbadian sugar back to Suriname from whence it was reexported to the Dutch Republic.[42] Some Barbadians reshipped tobacco for North American traders who carried it from New York and Philadelphia to Dutch colonies, where they transferred it to island-based shipmasters who smuggled it duty-free into Britain past customs officers who did "not expect tobacco on board Barbados ships." The result, according to one official, was that "the saving of the duty makes it [tobacco] a far better trade than any commodity they can carry from Barbados."[43]

These multilateral patterns of exchange and the wide variety of goods traded indicate the evolution of cross-national trade. Still an important feature of colonial commerce, interimperial trade was now characterized less by the speculative stopping of one or another empire's vessels at one or another nation's ports, but rather by the truer blending of resources within the Western Hemisphere as colonial traders shared vessels, markets, and credit. In short, the Caribbean sloop trade produced sophisticated, if fleeting, interimperial networks that provided numerous economic opportunities for colonists who increasingly found economic success as middlemen selling locally produced or (more often) imported goods from Europe, New England, and New York to surrounding islands.

In addition to the general outline of trade Holt related in his account, he also described the variety of mechanisms used to avoid detection when trading illegally. Some captains achieved this deception by declaring alternate destinations and alternate cargoes when leaving port. Take the example of an unnamed sloop Holt sailed on in the spring of 1704. According to Holt, this Antigua-based vessel "went down . . . to Curaçao laden with Sugar[,] Tobacco[,] Rumm[,] and bottle Liquors," but when it left Antigua, it "was enter'd [in the Naval Officer register] for Anguilla [a nearby English island] and the tobacco . . . was entered for [as] bottle beer and the Sugar for flower and the Rumm for Tarr." It was only on the way back to Antigua with a cargo of cocoa, linen, and horses that the sloop stopped in Anguilla, to sell the linen. Stopping here on his departure and return enabled the master to enter his cargo as having come from this British island when he arrived in Antigua and made his exchange appear legal. Though Holt did not name the vessel in his example, perhaps it was the 35-ton *Lark* that entered Antigua from Anguilla with a cargo of "Cocoa Nuts" on May 20, 1706, an official cargo listing that probably obscured the full range of its trade.[44] One reason this duplicity was possible, Holt noted, was that customshouse officers such as Mr. William Gerrish in Montserrat and several in Antigua participated in interimperial trade themselves.[45] Merchants from different empires also collaborated by sharing information about the vigilance of various officials, with one trader warning in 1706, for example, to avoid Jamaica since "a great deal of Dutch goods had been seized" there.[46]

Of the new smuggling routes Holt detailed, the most significant was the increased use of St. Thomas. While the Anglo-French wars drew the major Atlantic powers into conflict, the small neutral colony of St. Thomas became an attractive trading center. This colony, governed first by the Dutch and then by the Danes, was inhabited by merchants from all over northern Europe and was controlled by a multinational trading firm financed mostly by Dutch merchants excluded from the WIC. The Brandenburgisch-Africaisch-Americanische Compagnie (BAAC) was never a financial success, collapsing in 1697, but it did bring a large Dutch population to St. Thomas's main port, Charlotte Amalia, during the first decades of the eighteenth century. Soon these Dutch merchants dominated the island's commerce.[47] With Denmark remaining neutral in the Anglo-French wars, Dutch and Danish merchants made St. Thomas into a haven for interimperial commerce, and the island quickly attracted the attention of British officials.[48]

Writing in 1697, the first Governor Christopher Codrington was able to quantify the advantages merchants gained by trading at St. Thomas. The Danish colony offered "great temptation to our [Leeward Island] merchants," he wrote, "for they [merchants from St. Thomas] will give a third more" for sugar than British traders and "pay for it ready money, or rather negroes, Dutch linen and dry goods, which they sell fifty per cent cheaper than is afforded among us. To make such profits men will run great hazards."[49] By 1703, the Council of Trade had noticed the rising power of St. Thomas and urged the queen to instruct officials to be vigilant in inspecting goods traveling between the island and British colonies, as St. Thomas–based traders had been discovered landing goods in Nevis and English traders found coming from the colony.[50] St. Thomas also attracted ships from North America "laden with bread, beer, flower and bacon," whose masters chose St. Thomas over English colonies because it offered a "better market than any . . . [of the] English Plantations."[51] Lieutenant Governor Johnson in Antigua noted another

problem with St. Thomas: it attracted "the common people and artifi-
cers, whose fortunes are easily remov'd with them," and who, Johnson
feared, would "turne privateers during the wars and pyrates ever after."[52]

The fear that British colonists would migrate to St. Thomas and organize illegal trade from there was not unfounded. In 1700, the English
colonist Manuel Manasses Gilligan relocated to St. Thomas and swore
"loyalty to ye Danish Majesty before ye then Governor," receiving in
return a pass to trade at "neighbouring Islands." Evidently fearing impending war between Britain and France, Gilligan decided to declare his
loyalty to a neutral government, an action that enabled him to trade as
a Dane and thereby protected his ability to enter British, Dutch, French,
and Spanish ports during wartime without fear of attack by privateers or
seizure for carrying contraband goods. All went well for Gilligan until
1703, when a British naval vessel encountered Gilligan's sloop, *Charles II,*
off the coast of the Spanish Main. Declaring that the sloop was "unlaw-
fully Tradeing . . . Contraband Goods[,] provisions[,] and ammunitions"
to "the Spaniard," the naval officers captured what they considered an
English vessel and carried it into Carlisle Bay, Barbados, as a prize.
There, Gilligan, the captain, and several crew members protested, claiming that the cargo was from neutral St. Thomas and consisted of only dry
goods to be traded for cacao. As a naturalized Dane, Gilligan also insisted that he had violated no English laws. The Vice-Admiralty Court of
Barbados disagreed. Considering Gilligan still English, they condemned
the vessel.[53] Allowing English colonists like Gilligan to take residence
at St. Thomas was dangerous, the governor of Barbados explained, because St. Thomas had the potential "in time of war" of becoming the
"Staple for all sort of indirect and illegal trade."[54] Eventually, though,
Gilligan appealed his case in England and won a reversal of the decision, Attorney-General Sir Edward Northey ruling that as a resident of
St. Thomas, he was free to trade with foreigners unless trading "stores of
war."[55] Gilligan's creative decision to settle in the Danish colony reflects
the importance of interimperial trade to colonists, some of whom saw
opportunity for profit even if it required relocation and naturalization.
At the same time, British authorities, too, realized they could profit from
the experience of merchants like Gilligan, eventually charging him with
establishing a trade in slaves to the Spanish Main and sending him to
help negotiate the Asiento Treaty in Madrid in 1713.[56]

As detailed as Holt's account of intra-Caribbean trade was, he ignored at least one other important late seventeenth-century innovation.
During the Anglo-French wars, colonists, especially Leeward Islanders,

increasingly called at Dutch islands for desperately needed slaves. While reports of the importation of slaves from Dutch islands for most of the seventeenth century are exaggerated, there is better evidence, both circumstantial and anecdotal, to suggest this trade was more important in a narrow window of time at the end of the century. As we have seen, during the 1670s and 1680s, some English officials believed Leeward Island planters bought slaves from St. Eustatius; this trade increased markedly when the almost constant warfare between 1689 and 1713 convinced many British slave traders not to venture African cargoes. On the eve of the War of the League of Augsburg in 1689, British merchants sent almost 7,000 slaves to the British Caribbean; in 1690, these shipments fell 65 percent to 2,500. During the War of the Spanish Succession, slave exports fell even more dramatically from more than 21,000 in 1701 and 17,000 in 1702 to fewer than 7,000 in 1703. Leeward Islanders, never the first to receive shipments, particularly felt this deficit, while always better-supplied Barbados suffered less. Whereas estimates indicate they had regularly received almost 4,000 slaves each year on British vessels between 1700 and 1702, in the ten war years of 1703 to 1712, Leeward Islanders probably received fewer than 2,000 slaves annually, a figure that fell to a low of 580 in 1707. Adding to wartime difficulties, the dissolution of the RAC in 1698 forced a structural change in the English transatlantic slave trade, and while independent traders soon replaced RAC slavers, planters in the Leeward Islands who were trying to expand their plantations struggled to obtain sufficient slaves at affordable prices in the interim.[57]

These were the years when Dutch traders expanded their supply of slaves to the Americas. While most of these slaves were bound for Spanish colonies, some traders left small quantities at Curaçao, St. Eustatius, and Danish St. Thomas, where Dutch, British, and French colonists called to purchase them. Moreover, with their foothold in St. Thomas, traders from Brandenburg also increased their trade in slaves to the Caribbean. According to the most recent data, all traders landed 2,430 slaves at St. Eustatius and 16,514 at St. Thomas between 1688 and 1713.[58]

Even though the slave trade from Dutch to English islands is not quantifiable, evidence of intra-Caribbean networks, disruptions to regular trade, the associated steep decline in British slave imports, and reports that slaves could be and were bought more cheaply in foreign islands like St. Eustatius and St. Thomas suggest that, in the period between 1689 and 1713, planters in the Leeward Islands turned to foreign sources for slaves to supplement British trade. This pattern continued in the later

TABLE 6.2

Estimates of All Slaves Landed in the British Caribbean by British Traders, 1689–1713

Year	English Leeward Islands	Barbados	Total British Caribbean
1689	1,800	2,500	7,500
1690	300	900	3,000
1691	0	3,300	8,000
1692	0	4,000	10,000
1693	300	3,100	8,600
1694	400	4,000	9,400
1695	800	3,700	6,700
1696	700	4,900	8,000
1697	300	8,600	9,400
1698	800	4,500	7,200
1699	1,700	5,100	13,900
1700	4,000	6,500	22,300
1701	3,800	8,400	25,100
1702	4,700	11,200	20,700
1703	1,600	3,600	8,300
1704	1,900	4,400	12,800
1705	1,600	3,200	11,300
1706	1,700	4,400	11,100
1707	600	1,200	6,100
1708	1,400	1,900	14,600
1709	1,400	1,100	7,100
1710	1,500	1,500	11,200
1711	1,300	1,800	13,100
1712	1,400	3,500	10,900
1713	3,300	4,200	13,300
Totals	37,600	101,400	279,400

SOURCE: TASTD, http://slavevoyages.org/tast/assessment/estimates.faces?yearFrom=1689&yearTo=1713&disembarkation=309.311.305.304.302.307.310.306.301.303.308.

NOTE: Figures rounded to nearest hundred. Totals calculated by summing raw data and then rounding to nearest hundred.

eighteenth century at St. Eustatius after the Dutch established an open slave market. While British wartime purchases of slaves from the Dutch did not constitute a structural change in increasing British dominance of their own slave trade, it does indicate another way that the habit of interimperial trade allowed colonists to adapt to exogenous crises and to maintain colonial development when regular channels of exchange were disrupted.[59]

Though angered and frustrated by the reports they received of continued Dutch trade in the colonies, British officials focused more attention between 1689 and 1713 on reports that their colonists had been supplying French colonies with provisions despite the empires being at war with each other. As was the case in the British Caribbean, the Anglo-French wars limited French shipping and created opportunities for Dutch, Danish, and British merchants based in the Caribbean to relieve French planters' needs. That desperate French governors authorized foreign trade during the War of the League of Augsburg only further encouraged British West Indians' trade. Because of their increasing economic sophistication and their strengthened ties to North America, British West Indians were able to exploit the resulting deficit of goods in the French sugar colonies of St. Christopher, Martinique, and Guadeloupe, selling flour, beef, and other supplies to the French in exchange for raw sugar (French planters reserved clayed sugar for French markets), which the Englishmen repackaged in new casks and exported to Britain as locally produced sugar. With British (raw) sugar prices ranging anywhere from one-third to one-quarter higher than those in France, and with French demand unable to match production, this intraisland exchange benefited both French planters, who found a market for their produce, and British colonists, who prospered by exploiting the price differential between their protected home market and the world price of sugar. British colonists even co-opted official lines of communication between British and French colonies to effect this exchange, using flags of truce—vessels used for the exchange of prisoners—to carry goods. While the higher food prices and increased competition that resulted were a threat to long-term British interests, their main short-term fear before 1713 was that these provisions helped outfit French privateers, a practice some governors and the Council of Trade and Plantations tried vigorously to end.[60]

British officials' concentration on Anglo-French rather than Anglo-Dutch trade is indicative of the changing axis of competition in the Atlantic. Though the Council of Trade and Plantations thought that two brigantines of ten or twelve guns should patrol the waters surrounding Curaçao and St. Thomas to prevent interimperial trade, the fear of Dutch commercial dominance in the British Caribbean that had dominated the 1670s and 1680s had largely disappeared.[61] Politically and culturally, England was forging a new political alliance between the United Provinces and England, itself a product of the Glorious Revolution; along with this, English public opinion was shifting away from an anti-Dutch stance and toward an anti-French (and anti-Catholic) one as French competition increased during the last years of the century.[62] Undoubtedly, these changes affected merchants' commercial choices in the Caribbean, more so by the opening of the eighteenth century. But a deeper shift involved the diminishing ability of Dutch carriers to satisfy British islanders' demands for European good and provisions, or to take away islanders' tropical goods.

The War of the League of Augsburg marked a turning point for the Dutch empire. After this long, expensive, and disruptive war, Dutch trade failed to rebound as it had after previous conflicts. Not only did trade to the eastern Mediterranean collapse, but the Dutch also began to lose control of the important carrying trades through the Baltic to the British. Adding to these pressures, the Spanish Netherlands, a region whose economy had long been dominated by the Dutch and which was vital to the Dutch reexport trades because it provided access to Spanish and French markets, began to resist Dutch economic control. Low tariffs in this region had previously allowed cheap imports from the United Provinces to dominate the provinces' economy, a policy the Spanish rulers had long accepted as the price for Dutch help in resisting French ambitions in the area. With Spanish influence fading in the late 1690s, however, and their economy suffering, people in the southern provinces (especially Flemish textile manufacturers) attacked Dutch economic power by drastically increasing tariffs to discourage imports of Dutch manufactures and agricultural goods.[63] When the United Provinces responded with retaliatory duties and embargoes of their own, they achieved little except to further stifle commerce. Together declining trade and economic disruptions were already seriously hampering the Netherlands' economy when the War of the Spanish Succession broke out in 1702. This eleven-year conflict drove up the republic's debt and forced Dutch merchants to reduce their international commitments; Dutch slave trading declined during the early 1700s as well. Eventually it became impossible for the Dutch Republic to maintain its commercial influence in the Atlantic.[64]

Moreover, as the English and French empires developed their own (protected) carrying and mercantile infrastructures—as William Temple had predicted—Dutch merchants began to look elsewhere for profits. In doing so, many merchants turned away from the Atlantic, choosing to focus on other regions as well as on agricultural trade with their European neighbors.[65] This transfer of resources away from the Atlantic was possible largely because of the nature of Dutch settlement there. Without many plantation-based colonies, it was relatively easy and logical for Dutch traders to decrease their investment in the Atlantic in favor of places such as the East Indies where trade was more profitable. This shift in emphasis was neither total nor immediate—the entrepôts of St. Eustatius and Curaçao and the plantation colony of Suriname remained important through the eighteenth century—but by the beginning of the eighteenth century, it was clear the Atlantic had become less attractive to most Dutch investors. Although the Dutch never pulled out fully, it was now more often British colonists than Dutch merchants who initiated trade.[66]

Holt's and Brises's depictions of commercial patterns in the early eighteenth-century Caribbean, therefore, were a result of both continued economic development and population growth in the British West Indies and the simultaneous restructuring of worldwide Dutch trade. Even as British planters became more intertwined with British traders as they wove elaborate networks of credit and exchange in order to build sugar fortunes, they maintained parallel intra-Caribbean commercial networks that allowed them to withstand wartime disturbances and enabled new commercial opportunities. Now in the forefront of this cross-national trade and no longer reliant on Dutch traders, British West Indians were able to guide their own prosperity more than ever. When peace came to the Caribbean in 1713, West Indians had not only survived, but through the networks they had built were ready to take advantage of the postwar boom in trade.

* * *

The changing balance of power and the expansion of avenues for profit within the British empire were apparent in New York City by 1700. While the Anglo-French wars slowed trade, the steps that New Yorkers took to adjust to new economic conditions created the foundation for the future economic expansion of the city. Plagued by the same wartime difficulties that reduced transatlantic trade in the West Indies, direct trade between New York City and Europe became more expensive and risky as well. Simultaneously, problems unique to New York such as falling fur prices, specie shortages, declining Dutch investment, and increased competition from New England endangered economic development. Moreover, Leisler's Rebellion, the brief local uprising associated with the Glorious Revolution, brought religious, ethnic, and status unrest to the surface in the city's mercantile community, forcing merchants to choose sides and creating political factionalism that would color much of the city's and province's early eighteenth-century history. Through all of these crises, however, New York City traders persevered, many even finding new sources of profitable trade like those bold few who carried grain to West Africa, Madagascar (supplying South Seas pirates), and Lisbon during the French wars. More significantly, New Yorkers of diverse ethnic and economic backgrounds expanded their trade to the West Indies. Drawing upon an expanding hinterland, increased demand from developing colonies less able to trade with Europe, and their ties to multiple empires, New Yorkers increasingly transported flour, lumber, beef, pork, beer, staves, wax, and similar goods to Dutch, Danish, Spanish, and British colonies. As in the Caribbean, it would be colonial merchants in New York who exploited these new opportunities by building on their newfound control over transatlantic Anglo-Dutch trade to gain the same management over interimperial exchange within the Western Hemisphere.[67]

After 1689, the vessels that still cleared New York for the Dutch Republic were increasingly English ships financed by newly arriving British merchants often in combination with ethnically Dutch New York families. This transition to colonial control of Anglo-Dutch trade was symptomatic of broader changes in Manhattan's mercantile community. As New York City grew in the 1680s, London firms became eager to exploit growing markets and sent more agents there. As the English population rose, so did the importance of English merchants, who were quickly becoming the richest residents of Manhattan. By 1703, only about half of the city's roughly 5,000 inhabitants and just one-third of its merchants were Dutch. Though the richest individuals were still of Dutch descent, English residents now controlled most of the city's wealth.[68]

The rising English population and increased attention from London merchants enjoying recent prosperity produced new opportunities for profitable alliances between Dutch New Yorkers and English traders. After 1690, it was evident to many elite New York merchants from Dutch families that their economic future depended on gaining access to English networks and the new sources of capital they controlled. One way these traders gained such connections was through marriage. Two Philipse children, for example, married into New York's expanding English community in these years. Experience in English ports was another path to success. Jacobus van Cortlandt, Stephanus's brother, who had gone to Boston as a young man to learn English and to trade, gained English associates and connections by working as the family's agent in that city and in the West Indies before returning to New York. By the end of the seventeenth century, he was shipping more cargoes to London than to Amsterdam, fifteen to the former and just one to the latter between 1699 and 1702. Another member of the interwoven Philipse–Van Cortlandt family, Adolph Philipse, traveled to London to build relationships and also helped connect Jacobus van Cortlandt with the London merchant John Blackall. Van Cortlandt also used ties to the New Yorkers Oloff van Sweeten and Rip van Dam to do business with London merchants Thomas Bond and Robert Hackshaw. Similarly, in the 1690s, the Albany-born Van Dam took advantage of the connections in England of his English son-in-law, Walter Thong, and became the New York attorney for the London merchant Michael Kinkaid, allowing him to secure access to London capital. Abraham de Peyster, who had been sent to Amsterdam to learn the business as a young man, took another path, associating himself with Governor Lord Bellomont when he arrived in 1698 and employing an alliance with the governor to develop English contacts.[69]

As important as links with London had become by 1700, some New York wholesalers continued to trade to the United Provinces, though now more often as a complement to their trade to England. In general, this trade advanced along lines that had been laid out in the two decades since the English conquest, with traders using a combination of legal trade through British outports and the illegal landing of cargoes in New York and its surrounding bays and inlets to carry North American products to Europe in exchange for manufactures and luxuries. Because Amsterdam remained the best market for furs, Jacobs van Cordtlandt, Abraham de Peyster, and both Frederick and Adolph Philipse continued to send pelts there. In return, these men received textiles, brandy, firearms, dry goods, and spices. Some new arrivals to New York like the Bostonian Benjamin Faneuil and the Huguenot Stephen De Lancey saw enough promise in the Netherlands trade to enter it during the 1690s, using the same methods that Dutch New Yorkers did to access the London trade. In that decade, De Lancey married into the Van Cortlandt family and partnered with the Van Cortlandts, the Philipses, and De Peyster in loading furs for Amsterdam and returning assorted merchandise to New York. As they had in earlier decades, those vessels trading between Manhattan and Amsterdam carried goods for many city merchants. For example, when the ship *Margaret's Galley* departed New York City bound to "Engld & Holld" in March 1707, Benjamin Faneuil, Stephen De Lancey, Jacobus van Cortlandt, and Abraham de Peyster all paid duties on their portion of the cargo of peltry they exported. When it returned to Manhattan in July 1708, the vessel carried goods for more than fifteen different New York traders, a number that was typical of such voyages.[70]

As they had in previous decades, New Yorkers still smuggled if it could help them avoid port duties or expensive stops at English ports. By some accounts, this behavior increased during the 1690s because higher wartime freight and insurance costs eroded merchants' profits. New Yorkers also continued to feel confident in conspiring to land Dutch goods and to send enumerated goods to foreign ports because of the complicity of a range of government officials from governors to customs collectors and their underlings. Most notably, Governor Benjamin Fletcher, who also allowed pirates to operate freely from New York, and his appointee as customs collector and receiver general, Childey Brooke, were corrupt, routinely profiting by disregarding the landing of Dutch and East Indian goods. Brooke, who took office in January 1693, quickly adapted to the opportunities corruption offered, allowing *King David,* a 350-ton Dutch *fluytschip* into port in the summer of 1693 and letting it remain through December while the crew was busy selling "Holland and other linen cloth" to New Yorkers in exchange for provisions.[71]

Similarly, Governor Robert Treat of Connecticut allowed at least one Dutch vessel to land its cargo in New Haven "under pretence of Wanting Wood and water." Once there, the vessel "[u]nliverd great parts of her loading, which was carryd to New Yorke, & having taken horses aboard, Saild with the Remainder of the Goods to Barbados."[72] When Governor Bellomont arrived in 1698, he reported that "the carelessness and corruption of the officers of the revenue and customes have been so great for some years past that although the Trade of this place hath been four times as much as formerly and the City greatly enlarged, and inriched, yet His Majesty's revenue arising from the Customes, hath decreased the one half."[73] As was the case in earlier decades, even when Bellomont and his successor, Lord Cornbury, worked to stop the contraband trade, colonists; corrupt officials such as Sheriff Isaac de Riemer, a De Peyster associate; and the customs collector Thomas Byerly frustrated their efforts.[74]

Some elite New Yorkers also found new opportunities for illegal trade when their involvement with the slave trade in West Africa helped them discover the riches they could earn trading with pirates based in Madagascar. Among the most active traders in this regard were Frederick and Adolphe Philipse. These men supplied guns and ammunition to the infamous Red Sea pirates, exchanging these pirate necessities along with foodstuffs for slaves and East India goods that they sent to New York City, the Dutch Republic, and Germany. In order to execute this trade, they engaged in a complex maneuver in which they intercepted one of their own vessels returning from Madagascar in Delaware Bay and transferred its cargo of calicoes and other East Indian goods to another Philipse-owned vessel. This other ship was then sailed directly to Hamburg and Amsterdam before returning to New York via an English outport. Meanwhile, the Madagascar ship took its remaining cargo (usually slaves) to New York City. Although they were not alone in trading to Madagascar, the Philipses were the most successful.[75] These examples of illegal trade, paired with the two to four vessels that continued to journey between Manhattan and Amsterdam legally, indicate that the pace of the Dutch trade remained constant between the late 1670s and the first decade of the eighteenth century. But, with a growing port and more vessels clearing and entering the province than in previous years, this level represented a proportional decline in both the number of total ships clearing New York and the value of goods passing through the port. As a whole, by the first decade of the eighteenth century, it was clear to most New Yorkers that the greatest avenues of opportunity lay in building new commercial linkages, not solely in reviving older ties.[76]

One destination that offered great promise in the 1690s was the West Indies. Relying on their ethnic connections to residents in foreign colonies as well as capitalizing on expanding markets in the British Caribbean that were themselves a result of larger slave populations and more widespread sugar planting, New Yorkers increased their trade to the Caribbean so that, by the end of the 1680s, they were exporting 60,000 barrels each of grain and flour to the islands.[77] The Anglo-French wars made transatlantic trade more risky and costly, encouraging New Yorkers to look elsewhere for opportunity. With developing islands and wartime shortages, the Caribbean became an increasingly attractive market. When peace came in 1698, New Yorkers rushed to further develop this trade, making Lord Bellomont exclaim in 1701 that New York was the "growingest town in America." By 1705, a group of almost fifty New York merchants, both elite and middling, announced that "the principal staple of the trade of this Province is the manufactory of wheat" and its export to "the West Indies." In New York merchants' ventures to the Caribbean, their commercial patterns resembled those of British West Indians, trading indiscriminately at British islands like Jamaica, Barbados, and the Leeward Islands as well as the foreign colonies of Curaçao, Suriname, and St. Thomas.[78]

As is the case for the Leeward Islands, there are no complete sets of port records for New York City that would give a full picture of city merchants' trade to the West Indies, particularly when they went to foreign colonies. However, there are some fragmentary records. In September 1698, Edward Randolph, who had been sent to the colonies to investigate the defrauding of the king's revenues, forwarded a list of fifteen vessels that cleared New York for Curaçao between March 25 and August 17, 1698.[79] If representative of other years and if adjusted for seasonal patterns, this rate would mean that perhaps as many as twenty vessels a year cleared New York for Curaçao. A more complete view of the trade to the West Indies can be found in New York City's customs records, which are extant for most months between 1701 and 1709.[80] Because they list vessel names, sizes, masters, the merchants freighting goods on them, and the port they had come from, these registers offer a wealth of information. However, like the Naval Officer lists, these documents have limitations. Collectors recorded only vessels carrying dutied goods— imports of dry goods, wine, and rum, and exports of fur—and the quantity of the duty rather than the volume of goods carried. This means that the customs records do not list vessels without dutied goods, leaving out much of New York's outgoing West Indies trade.

An alternative to relying on the customs ledger alone for 1701 to 1709 is to combine it with lists of ship clearances for New York printed in the *Boston Newsletter*. The weekly reports probably did not announce every vessel leaving New York, and many vessels had several destinations, but these lists do give us an indication of larger commercial patterns. Taking care not to double-count those vessels listed in both, these sources reveal that each year from 1701 to 1713, between fifty and eighty vessels entered New York City and between 110 and 170 departed the city. Of these, an average of at least forty entered from the Caribbean with about seventy clearing for the islands. The most popular stated destinations of these vessels were the British islands of Barbados and Jamaica, which each received as many as twenty or more arrivals from New York. The Leeward Islands were also common destinations, with between four and ten vessels a year clearing to each of these colonies. Almost as important as trade to the British West Indies was trade to the Dutch Caribbean. About fifteen vessels cleared for Curaçao each year, with trade to Suriname and St. Thomas lagging behind but still significant. Again, these numbers should not be considered complete, but they do show roughly the minimum number of vessels New Yorkers sent to the foreign Caribbean.[81]

Of New York City's mercantile community, one of the more active Curaçao traders during the late seventeenth and early eighteenth centuries was Jacobus van Cortlandt, and his business helps one understand the cargoes that New Yorkers sent to the Caribbean in this period. He consigned shipments on twenty vessels—usually smaller (one-masted) sloops but also some (two-masted) brigantines—from New York to Curaçao between August 12, 1699, and June 20, 1702, a route that accounted for almost one-quarter of his business. His contacts there varied, but most commonly he sent an assortment of provisions including butter, flour, and meats to two widows, Neeltien Vessers and Sara Abondana (var. Abendana). While we know little about Vessers, Abondana was a member of one of Amsterdam's and Curaçao's most prominent Portuguese Jewish families, and it is possible Van Cortlandt became connected to her either through Manhattan's rising Jewish community or through Amsterdam's traders. Van Cortlandt also traded similar cargoes to English islands, including Jamaica, Nevis, Barbados, and Antigua, bringing returns of logwood (a dyestuff), rum, sugar, indigo, cotton, cocoa, slaves, bills of exchange, and specie back to New York.[82] Jacobus's brother Stephanus and nephew Philip van Cortlandt exported "flower for Suraname, Curacao and St. Thomas" in return for cocoa, logwood, and other goods that they in turn sent to Amsterdam and London to cover imports of "Holland linen" and other dry goods to New York City.[83] Other elite traders who ventured foodstuffs and merchandise to Dutch and English colonies were many of those who had been regular New York–Amsterdam traders in the 1660s and 1670s, including Abraham de Peyster, Stephen De Lancey, Frederick Philipse, Nicholas Bayard, Richard Willet, Joseph Bueono, and Rip van Dam. Mirroring those in the Caribbean, New Yorkers also cultivated trade with St. Thomas. Perhaps the most active trader to this colony was De Peyster, who sent the brig *Suzannah*, a vessel in which he owned a three-eighths share, and *Betty*, a vessel he owned outright, to the island several times a year. On the whole, New York merchants did not concentrate on just one island, but rather freighted vessels as individuals or partners to British, Dutch, Danish, and French colonies. This combination of imperial and interimperial trade allowed New

Yorkers to diversify their routes and cargoes as flexibly as markets and credit arrangements allowed.[84]

Among the most significant imports that New Yorkers brought from the West Indies was specie. Curaçao was particularly important for its trade with the Spanish Main for Spanish pieces of eight, which New Yorkers eagerly accepted in return for their outbound cargoes of provisions and lumber. Once returned to New York, merchants like Van Cortlandt forwarded the coin to London or Amsterdam to fund the importation of dry goods from wholesalers there. Mired in a general transatlantic trading slump and with the fur trade in decline, New Yorkers ran large trading deficits with Britain. Desperate for specie to cover their debts, trade with Curaçao (and other islands where specie was plentiful) allowed New Yorkers to maintain their importation of European goods. In this way, interimperial trade was important for wholesalers wishing to please consumers clamoring for goods from London and for covering imperial trade imbalances.[85]

In addition to supplying provisions and lumber to the Caribbean, some New Yorkers served as middlemen for Chesapeake planters, sending tobacco to Dutch colonies along with their flour. As enumerated goods, trade of these commodities was illegal, and New Yorkers developed elaborate mechanisms to avoid detection. According to Robert Quary, vice admiralty judge for Pennsylvania and the Jersies, this trade involved legally loading and registering a small amount of tobacco in the Chesapeake and declaring for New York. Once under way, the master paused to load a larger quantity of tobacco, which lay "ready for him at some convenient place in the [Chesapeake] Bay." Then, just before arriving in New York, the vessel stopped again, putting "ashore all the tobacco except what he hath a cocquet for, at a small Dutch village [on Long Island]. . . . [I]f it happens that any vessels are ready to sail for Surinamee, Curesaw or Newfoundland," Quary continued, "they touch in and take in the tobacco." If there were no vessels available, "then the wood-boats take in the tobacco under their wood and carry it up to [New] York." Once there, the "boats lie at a convenient place" until nightfall, when it is "landed and repacked for the next opportunity of shipping it off" to foreign colonies.[86] Alternatively, some colonists worked with corrupt officials, like Collector of Customs Thomas Byerly, who allowed "two hund, weight of cocoa to be put on Board the sloop of one Claas Evertsen, one Zybersten Commander which was bound to Suriname."[87]

Bilateral trade was not the only aspect to the burgeoning interimperial Caribbean trade. Many merchants—Van Cortlandt, De Peyster, De

Lancey, and Philipse among them—used these islands as a way to trade with the Dutch Republic. In 1699, for example, Jacobus van Cortlandt combined British and Dutch connections to ship a cargo of New York goods to Nevis, where he exchanged them for sugar that was subsequently sent on to Bristol, England. Once the cargo arrived, his London correspondent John Blackall had the sugar sold and remitted the returns to Van Cortlandt's creditors in Amsterdam. At other times, Van Cortlandt combined with his nephew Philip van Cortlandt, Frederick Philipse, and De Peyster to make "returns for Holland by way of Curaçao & Surinamee."[88] Some New Yorkers also used French colonies for the same purpose, sending "Flower, Bacon, & some Horses" to Martinique and Guadeloupe, "in Return for which they export[ed] great Quantitys of Sugar & Cocoa, & Ship[ed] it directly to Holland."[89] This trade also worked in reverse, with New York merchants buying Dutch manufactured goods in Dutch colonies. In order to avoid detection, these vessels sometimes landed at Sandy Hook—a common place for smuggling located off the northeast tip of New Jersey at the entrance to Manhattan's shipping lanes. There the smugglers unloaded the illegal Dutch goods and had them transported to New York in small boats.[90] Other merchants purchased wine at Madeira and sent it either to Amsterdam or to New York with the returns they garnered from the Caribbean trade.[91]

The presence of at least one Dutch factor in New York during the second decade of the eighteenth century provided another important link to the United Provinces and to Dutch colonies. As Cathy Matson has shown, this merchant received dry goods from the Amsterdam merchant Albert Hodshon (with whom Jacobus van Cortlandt and Olof van Sweeten traded as well). The factor then sold these dry goods to New York merchants, who either carried them to the West Indies, returning with cacao, molasses, slaves, and bills of exchange, or sold them locally for cargoes of flour for the Caribbean. Eventually the factor then forwarded bills of exchange from the sale of Caribbean goods to Hodshon in Amsterdam to cover the cost of the dry good shipments.[92]

At other times, Dutch vessels from Curaçao called at New York themselves so as to bypass reshipment on New York vessels. The *Rebecca,* for example, brought "2 packs, 2 Cases[,] four Barrels, European dry goods with Nine bolts Hollands [a coarsely woven linen]" from Curaçao to New York in November 1694, two years after the *Zelandia,* bearing "wine, Duffles, Holland & c to the Value of £5000 & Upwards" had tried to trade there as well. Then, in March 1707, the Jewish Curaçaoan Moses Mears employed Englishman Peter Rowland to carry a vessel with Dutch goods from Curaçao to Jamaica, St. Thomas, and New York, pretending that the vessel and its contents were owned by Rowland, who was then to return to Curaçao with a cargo of flour and other provisions.[93]

The example of Hodshon together with the large number of New Yorkers who traded with the Dutch West Indies suggests that trade with the Dutch still had broad appeal to a wide range of New Yorkers. Ethnicity was not a qualification for trade to Dutch colonies as Hugenot traders like Benjamin Faneuil and Stephen De Lancey, Englishmen like Matthew Ling and Richard Willet, and Dutch elites like Van Cortlandt and De Peyster all prospered in these trades. Neither was wealth determinative. The proximity of the West Indies, which were between three to six weeks away, together with merchants' ability to use small vessels, meant even those with limited capital could relatively easily enter Caribbean trade. Shorter trips and smaller ships meant traders also had to assume less risk, something that middling merchants enjoyed. Moreover, many traders collaborated in sending vessels to and from the West Indies; often between five and twenty individuals invested in a single voyage, enabling them to pool capital and further limit uncertainty.[94]

As an economic catalyst, the expanding West Indian trade, both British and foreign, was vital to New York City's prosperity. At the same time, however, in linking the countryside to the Caribbean, it forced New Yorkers to reconfigure their expectations about what role their city would play within the colony as a whole. New York City's hinterland (which had roughly 13,000 of the province's 18,000 residents in 1698) provided the grain needed to exploit West Indian markets, but as it did so, it exacerbated divisions between city merchants and grain producers. The flashpoint for these tensions was the city's monopoly over the bolting of flour. A debate over this issue had arisen first in the 1670s, but it reached a critical point after 1690, when the economic and social forces unleashed during Leisler's Rebellion gave it new resonance. Encouraged by small farmers and merchants from the countryside, the Leislerian government removed the city's monopoly on flour bolting and carriage in 1690. This change benefited country producers and small shippers, who now gained more control over the export of grain. These moves, however, created anger among city merchants who traditionally controlled the colony's trade. Significantly, opponents to the repeal of the Bolting Act came not only from the ranks of elite city merchants, but also from middling merchants, the very men who had begun to find success in exporting wheat to the West Indies and who had supported Leisler. Although they advanced a combination of arguments relying upon public interest, customary Dutch corporate rights and privileges, as well as a new argument based on the importance of New York City to the empire, merchants were unable to restore the monopoly.[95]

Manhattan traders' arguments are most clear in a series of petitions the Common Council submitted to British officials between 1692 and 1698. Each of these pleas begins by stressing the importance that "Trafique and Comerce" played as the "foundation of Riches" for New York and reminds their audience that Manhattan's "Natural Scitutaion is Convenient for trade & Navigation." In recognition of the importance of the city's trade, Dutch and English authorities had long allowed those who settled the city to enjoy "many Priviliedges & Franchises," especially those which gave them control of the grain trade. These privileges, they stressed, had been essential to economic development in the past since it was eminent merchants who could best regulate grain exports, simultaneously maintaining their quality, ensuring a ready supply of wheat for local residents, and exporting enough to foster development in the interior. In this way, giving city residents control over grain bolting and exports had provided for the "publick and Common good, of the whole Province as well as for the Advancement and Interest of the Crown."[96] Without a city monopoly on bolting, though, the Common Council pointed out that "Every Planters hutt throughout this Province is now become a Markett for wheat for wheate Flower and Bisket." Such a situation, they argued, not only "Reduced [trade] to Confusion," but also made it impossible for the city to "procure Corne Enough in Store to Supply itts Inhabitants with their dayly Nessessities of bread." Finally, they claimed that a lack of regulation eroded the quality of wheat inhabitants exported to neighboring colonies, reducing the price and reputation of New York's key export and damaging the province's future.[97]

In calling for the restoration of the bolting monopoly and tying it to the general interest of the colony as a whole, city residents called upon their "Former Rights and Priviledges," privileges they had secured in recognition of the vital role merchants played in the economic health of cities. Under the Dutch government, these customary rights were central to the city's political economy, and English rule had preserved them for three decades. In the 1690s, though, merchants added a new element to these claims. Paralleling arguments that colonists in the Caribbean had been making for years, New Yorkers now also began to stress how important their control of the bolting trade was not only to local economic success and the king's revenue, but also to the British empire as a whole. Writing to the king in 1697, the city government announced that "not only [will] Your Majestys Subjects within this Citty . . . Suffer and loose [*sic*] their Improvements" without a bolting monopoly, "but likewise the lives of Your Majesty's subjects in the West Indies are thereby much Endangered."[98] Where New Yorkers continued to differ from West Indians was in their embrace of monopoly. Whereas Caribbean planters continued calling for more freedom in trade, merchants in New York, driven by their colony's divergent economic makeup, wanted regulation.

As these petitioners maintained, New York's burgeoning West Indian trade formed the foundation of the larger region's economy. With farmers in a growing hinterland clamoring for desperately needed export markets by 1700, the sugar plantations of the Caribbean had come to play a more important role in the economic development of New York (as they were for New England, the Chesapeake, and Pennsylvania). Likewise, slave trading and the demands of provisioning enslaved workers created a larger dependency of the islands on North America. These linkages between mainland North America and the Caribbean were those that Dutch WIC and writers such as Adriaen van der Donck had envisioned more than a half century before. As New Netherland became New York and as British colonial markets expanded, local residents developed a Caribbean trade that utilized ethnic and familial ties to maintain older connections to Dutch places while simultaneously capitalizing on the opportunities that being an English colony provided.

* * *

Though English authorities had made strides in reducing Anglo-Dutch trade in the 1680s, the warfare of the Anglo-French wars interrupted these efforts and created new opportunities for cross-national exchange. But with Dutch merchants less able and willing to organize this trade, it fell to colonists to take the lead. In both the Caribbean and New York, British colonists developed new colonial trades, especially in foodstuffs, timber, rum, molasses, other lesser staples, and slaves, that sustained them and advanced their colonies. As they cruised the Caribbean, met with colonists of many states, and navigated the interstices of empire, these individuals understood their colonies not only as cogs in a larger British Atlantic, but also as pieces of an integrated cross-national and interdependent Atlantic community. In the process, they built the foundations of a more multilateral, sophisticated, and sometimes still interimperial economy that would become such an important feature of the rest of the eighteenth-century Atlantic world. Though it was not clear in 1713, this shift toward increased colonial control of cross-national trade would lay the groundwork for the diminishing importance of Anglo-Dutch trade in the next decades. Once in greater control of this vital piece of their commerce, the shift away from Dutch markets became more acceptable to colonists, especially since it was now in the hands of locals rather metropolitan policy makers. And as war ended, as the market need for interimperial trade faded, as the cross-national culture of their colonies dimmed, many British colonists made the choice to abandon interimperial trade and instead to choose an exclusive British empire. But as this transition unfolded during the eighteenth century, local interests continued—as they had in the seventeenth century—to interact with imperial ones to shape Atlantic-wide conditions.

Epilogue. Diverging Interests: Anglo-Dutch Trade and the Molasses Act

In the two decades that followed the end of the War of the Spanish Succession in 1713, British West Indians' and British North Americans' interests diverged. The Anglo-French wars were costly for colonists, but they failed to disrupt the trajectory of colonial development, and over time the British West Indies and British North America developed ever-more distinctive economies, the first dominated by production of one leading staple, the second by a diverse blend of economic activity. Though interdependent, the regions' growing economic divergence caused colonists' perspectives on interimperial trade to pull further apart. Trade between British and foreign colonies in the Caribbean would remain a regular feature of life for the remainder of the century (after all, there would always be incentive to escape duties or relieve wartime shortages), but never again would it achieve the prominence it had in earlier years nor that it retained in New York. Whereas the governor of the Leeward Islands, John Hart, described a pattern of interimperial trade in 1724 that closely resembled that of earlier years, with British West Indians buying mules from Curaçao and from the Spanish, secreting in slaves from St. Eustatius, and deceiving customs officials in the process, by 1727 he reported that the importation of slaves from St. Eustatius (and thus the export of sugar to the same island) had virtually stopped because of a dramatic increase in supplies from British slavers. Even in 1724, the most significant trade of tropical produce to Dutch merchants came not from the Leeward Islands but from small islands in what are now the British

Virgin Islands—Anguilla, Spanish Town, and Tortola—where quantities were limited. As long as British shipping remained sufficient, Hart maintained, Anglo-Dutch trade would no longer be a threat to the empire's interests.[1]

It is clear from Hart's reports that regulations alone were not responsible for the decline in interimperial trade, but rather it was improved attention from British traders that limited cross-national trade. Also important was the continued expansion of sugar cultivation in the Leeward Islands, a development that made planters there resemble Barbadians even more closely. Discouraged from planting tobacco because of a general slump in prices during the first three decades of the eighteenth century, and drawn to sugar because of the swell in demand that came with the peace of 1713, planters in the Leeward Islands accelerated the shift from the lesser staples to sugar that had been gradually under way since the 1660s. In all, British West Indian sugar production rose steadily from the end of the war until the 1730s. This rise was most dramatic in the Leeward Islands, which exported more sugar than Barbados in the five years between 1716 and 1720.[2] In his 1724 report, Hart did not even list tobacco among the list of products exported from the Leewards, concentrating on sugar and its by-products and noting only small quantities of cotton, ginger, and indigo.[3]

As sugar came to dominate the Leeward Islands, a new generation of planters owning ever-larger plantations arrived and combined with the most prosperous of residents to solidify elite planters' control over the islands' economy and political structure. This process, which began in the 1680s, intensified after 1700 so that, by 1715, islands such as Antigua had received significant numbers of new migrants from Britain (including many from Scotland after the Act of Union in 1707) who bought large plantations. Other new plantation owners were lawyers and agents of planters who used the returns from the sale of British goods to buy land and consolidate smaller plantations into larger concerns. In St. Christopher, a similar evolution occurred where a relatively few wealthy St. Christopher planters and merchant syndicates based in London gained control of the newly ceded French lands. With sufficient capital, ties to Britain, and a lack of knowledge about the important legacy of Dutch trade in the Caribbean, new island inhabitants had less incentive to pursue interimperial trade than had their predecessors.

Likewise, elite planters already living in the Leeward Islands exploited the additional disruptions and hardships war created for already struggling planters to increase their land and slave holdings. In the process,

TABLE 7.1

Sugar Imported into England and Wales, 1711–1730
(annual averages in hundreds cwt)

	Total	From Barbados	From Leeward Islands
1711–15	484.3	173.7	171.7
1716–20	652.9	202.5	251.9
1721–25	671.4	165.8	286.4
1726–30	866.8	197.8	386.9

SOURCE: Richard Sheridan, *Sugar and Slavery: An Economic History of the British West Indies, 1623–1775* (Barbados: Caribbean University Press, 1974), table 18.1, 418.

they pushed out the modest and less well-connected planters—especially those still producing tobacco on small plots—who had the most incentive to pursue Dutch trade. For example, in St. Mary's Parish, Antigua—the one Antiguan parish for which tax records are extant—the proportion of taxed individuals owning slaves rose from 30 percent in 1688 to almost 85 percent in 1706. In that same period, the number of colonists owning more than a hundred slaves rose from zero to four, and those owning more than twenty increased from six to sixteen. The postwar economic boom also intensified Leeward Islanders' demand for capital to rebuild, forcing them to look to outsiders to help fund agricultural expansion. This bound Leeward Islanders firmly to the English commission merchants to whom planters turned for credit and thereby restricted their future commercial flexibility. Meanwhile, in Barbados, lower sugar prices reversed the trend that saw island merchants gaining greater control of transatlantic trade between 1689 and 1713 and sent planters back to London commission merchants, who now received the bulk of the island's produce directly in return for British goods. It was these large planters, some of whom were now absentees, who combined with new migrants to bend West Indian policy toward their need for the protected sugar markets and constant supply of slaves that only the British empire could guarantee by 1713. As their economic and social makeup changed, West Indians began to consider interimperial trade to be a detriment to their interests.[4]

Larger Atlantic forces were also at work reshaping West Indians' commercial perspectives. The market conditions that encouraged British colonists to reroute French sugar through British colonies during the last

TABLE 7.2

Annual Produce of the British Leeward Islands, 1724

	Sugar (hhds)	Rum (hhds)	Molasses (hhds)	Cotton (lbs)	Ginger (lbs)	Indigo (lbs)
Antigua	12,000	4,000	850	200,000	200,000	
St. Christopher	8,000	300	2,000	40,000		
Nevis	5,000	150	1,500	20,000		
Montserrat	2,500	50	800	25,000		10,000
Total	27,500	4,500	5,150	285,000	200,000	10,000

SOURCE: July 12, 1724, Governor John Hart to the Board of Trade, CO 152/14, fol. 329v, TNA-PRO.

decades of the seventeenth century intensified after 1713. Despite losses during the wars, French sugar production accelerated rapidly between about 1710 and 1729. For example, Martinique, which had about 280 sugar works in 1713, had 437 in 1730. Colonists in Guadeloupe and Saint-Domingue witnessed similar growth, doubling their number of sugar works in the same period. Benefiting from fresh soil, French laws that allowed planters to produce semi-refined sugars, new injections of capital, and low prices that stimulated demand in France, French sugar production soon began to rival (and eventually surpass) British production; by the beginning of the American Revolutionary War, Saint-Domingue produced more sugar than all the British West Indies combined.[5] New French competition initially benefited some in the British West Indies who continued to route French sugar to Britain through British islands as they had been doing since the beginning of the century. Soon, however, the comparatively low price of French sugar in Europe became a problem for British planters and metropolitan merchants alike who, now unable to compete with French planters, saw their reexports to continental Europe decline from nearly 40 percent of total imports in 1698–1700 to just over 4 percent in 1733–37.[6]

By 1730, it was clear to many eminent British planters that although laws that confined British sugar to Britain were burdensome, without the protected markets they created planters would be unable to compete with French production. Desperate to secure markets in Britain and its colonies and seeking to injure French interests, sugar planters began to blame North Americans for their difficulties, claiming that they enabled

French strength and drove British West Indians' costs upward. Indeed, British North Americans had benefited handsomely from French development during the wars of the late seventeenth century and after. Already in the West Indies trading with British islands, New England and New York merchants found ready markets for "Boards, Shingle, Joist, Plank, Hogshead-Staves, Hoops, Horses, Bread, Flower, Gammons, Salt Fish, and many other [goods of] the like" in French colonies.[7]

As New Yorkers and New Englanders incorporated the French colonies into their intercolonial transit trade, French sugar, molasses, and rum joined that already coming from Dutch islands. When these foreign sugar products flowed into the hands of British North American consumers, they competed with that produced in British islands. Soon British sugar planters began to complain about the danger that New England and New York imports of foreign sugar products posed to their interests; not only did this trade push sugar, rum, and molasses prices downward but demand from foreign colonial markets also drove the prices for provisions higher. Though they could do little on their own to stop North Americans' trade with French and Dutch colonies, island governments, beginning with Barbados and Antigua in 1715 and 1716, enacted legislation to prevent the importation of foreign sugar products to their colonies by applying duties to imported goods or, as happened in Antigua, legislating an outright ban on the importation of outside sugars. Though the Crown quickly disallowed some of these laws, islanders tried again in 1721. These sustained attempts to control local trade with foreign colonies reveal a shift in the economic and political balance of power within Caribbean colonies. Whereas, in the 1670 and 1680s, most West Indian colonists had agreed that interimperial trade was critical to their colonies' success, by the 1720s, many planters believed that their greatest interest lay in stopping interimperial trade so as to preserve the empire's protected sugar markets. In Antigua, this was most clear. There Charles Dunbar, the surveyor general of customs for Barbados and the Leeward Islands, observed the debate and noted that it was the planters who supported them and interisland Caribbean traders who opposed the duties on intra-Caribbean trade.[8]

The effectiveness of eminent planters' regulatory efforts was limited, however, because unlike in New York City, where local merchants could act to restrain their hinterland, the councils and assemblies of Barbados and the Leeward Islands could not legislate for the North Americans who kept French colonies stocked. Instead they had to turn to the metropole for relief. Working through absentee planters in England, allying themselves with metropolitan merchants who traded to the West Indies, and calling upon their extensive local experience, planters worked to convince Parliament to intercede on their behalf. Though still demanding lower duties, after 1713, British West Indians' main complaint was no longer that their trade was restricted but rather that traders from the *"Northern* Colonies" had too much commercial freedom. These merchants, planters argued, undercut their business by supplying "the Colonies of *Martinico, Guadaope, St. Thomas, and St. John's* . . . *St Eustace, Curasoa, Surname, Esacape* [Essequibo], and the other *French* and *Dutch* Sugar Settlements in the *West-Indies"* with "those very Supplies, without which they could not enlarge their Plantations, as they daily do." Moreover, by consuming foreign "Sugar, Rum, and Molasses," North Americans' interimperial trade eroded West Indians options for profit. "EVERY Country," one pamphleteer argued, echoing economic theorists like Josiah Child and William Petty, "requires a profitable Vend for its Commodities; such a Vend will encourage more People; more People will beget a greater Produce; a greater Produce will begat more Riches; and all these will establish a greater Power, which will of course overcome a less."[9] In other words, from the planters' perspective, sugar remained the "engine" that would drive the British empire to European prominence, pulling shipping, refining, and manufacturing in its wake and as such the "Sugar Plantations should have suitable Supports and Aids from the Government."[10] The sugar complex was too big to fail.

In comparison to the sugar colonies, which were a "Fountain of Treasure," planters described the northern colonies as a "Rival and Supplantress of its Mother Country" that competed with British shipping interests and thus had the potential to destroy the empire. Underlying this point, one writer compared the North American colonies to "the Cuckow [that] sucks the Eggs, and destroys the offspring of that very Bird which hatch'd it first into life."[11] The only remedy to save the empire, another argued, was to return the mainland provinces to their secondary position, as supportive of the sugar islands. Quoting the mercantilist thinker Charles Davenant, Robert Robertson pointed out that "such is the Interest of our Nation in her Sugar Colonies, that . . . the Preservation of them in the *best*, or *only* Thing that all her *Northern* Colonies are good for."[12]

At the same time that they worked to control the actions of North Americans, West Indians also targeted what one governor called the "mean sort" of traders who drove cross-national, intra-island commerce. With the planter class firmly in place, not only in Barbados but also in the Leewards, with planters' ties to Britain cemented by credit and debt, and with island stability regained, local independent merchants were increasingly seen as a detriment to island interests. According to planters, these men's trade of manufactured goods to foreign islands simultaneously raised the price of plantation supplies and, because they brought their returns in sugar, pushed sugar prices lower on the British market.[13] As growing French and Dutch demand for foodstuffs and a shrinking North American market for molasses and rum increased planters' costs, British interests united to call for regulation of what they termed a "pernicious Trade."[14] Arguing that any "Encrease to Foreigners is a proportionable Diminution of our own Sugar Colonies, and consequently a Disadvantage to *Great Britain*" and appealing to the "great Goodness" of the king and Parliament, they urged the British government to "abolish a Trade so destructive to our own Colonies, and at the same time conductive to the Advancement of the Power and Wealth of *France*." Beginning in the 1720s as local efforts led by planter-dominated assemblies, planters' attempts to regulate local traders moved in the 1730s to London, where they were combined with attacks on North Americans' interimperial trade.[15]

West Indian planters' about-face from the pursuit of free trade to the search for protectionism was made possible by larger Atlantic economic and strategic changes as well as by the growing Western Hemispheric control of interimperial trade that resulted from the Anglo-French wars. This transformation is most evident in planters' ability to target middling traders. In the century before, a wide spectrum of colonists had benefited from the trade these cross-nationally connected traders brought, but this changed after 1713 as prosperity and stability lowered demand for cross-national exchange. And, since Anglo-Dutch trade was now in local hands, it was possible for planters to target it more precisely than if it had been driven by Dutch merchants as had been true in the mid-1600s. Receiving the local cooperation for which they had long been desperate, imperial authorities soon found that they could more effectively end smuggling. In other words, interlopers and smugglers were defeated by what imperial mandates had never been able to change: market conditions that reduced demand for cross-national trade and cooperative colonists who desired imperial protection.

In continental North America, colonists reacted to changing economic conditions differently. Nowhere was this more true than in New York City. There, New Yorkers used to maintaining their control over the interior fiercely defended the benefits of free trade in exports as they had for a century. Still desirous of protecting their diminished Amsterdam trade, but now more concerned with the attempts by the West Indian lobby to convince Parliament to legislate against their commerce with French and Dutch colonies, New Yorkers entered imperial discussions. Employing their own lobbyists and pamphleteers and petitioning the king, Parliament, and their governors, they attacked West Indian calls for restrictions on foreign trade. While New Yorkers could appreciate the opportunities the Navigation Acts had afforded them by damaging Dutch participation in the Atlantic carrying trade—opening new avenues of profit by allowing them control over Amsterdam trade and increasing their role in the Caribbean—they could not accept limitations on interimperial trade. For New Yorkers (as well as their neighbors in New England), a law forbidding or discouraging trade with the foreign West Indies would compel them to "pay whatever they [British planters] please" for sugar and molasses. Such a situation, they concluded, would necessarily reduce consumption and thus would ultimately hurt sugar planters, the very group the law was designed to help.[16] Beyond its effects on prices, North Americans also argued that without the right to import French and Dutch molasses, rum, cocoa, specie, and bills of exchange they would not longer have the ability to import a "vast Quantity of *British* Manufactures." With an annual trade deficit to Britain of roughly £25,000 and little specie on hand, New Yorkers needed to export flour to Dutch, French, and Spanish colonies in order to "make even with England." And it was this market for British goods that made the mid-Atlantic settlements of "great Importance . . . to this Kingdom [more even] than the Sugar-Islands."[17] Extending this claim, one pamphleteer explained that New England and the mid-Atlantic colonies' commerce with the foreign West Indies was at the center of Atlantic trade because it enabled North American colonists not only to balance their accounts with British traders, but also to supply rum to the "Fisheries," to "carry on a profitable Trade with the *Indians*," and to foster a vibrant ship-building industry.[18] All of these activities made protecting of the colonies' trade with the Dutch and French West Indies of the "highest Importance to this Kingdom."[19] The real reason that West Indians had lost the European sugar market, these writers concluded, was not that northern colonists failed to supply planters' needs (they claimed that they could meet "*ten* Times the Demand"), but that the "*British* Planters" charged "an unreasonable Price" for their sugars far "beyond what the market can bear."[20] They accused British West Indians of being reluctant to lower prices because they had fallen "into an excess of Luxury beyond compare." If they simply followed the model of their northern "industrious" brethren, who "earn[ed] their bread with the sweat of their brows" and lived with "Frugality," the West Indies would be "more profitable" and would not need protective legislation.[21]

Central to the claims of mainland colonists and their supporters was an understanding that artificially driving up the price of molasses and rum for northerners by restricting their trade to the British Caribbean would ultimately destroy advantageous commerce for the empire as a whole. Since British North Americans supplied French planters with needed goods and carried their rum, molasses, and sugar away, New Yorkers maintained that their foreign West Indian trade enabled the British empire to capture some of the profits that otherwise would have remained in France. In the words of Captain Fayer Hall, the mainland colonies played the role of "the *Dutch*" to "the British" in earlier years. "Have not we (over and above what is sufficient for our own Trade in the *West-Indies*)," Hall asked, "sent to the *French* Islands, at least one third Part of the whole *Shipping*, for the produce of the *French* Islands? Would it not be a real Damage to us should the *Dutch* or any other People serve us so? And," he continued, "should not we plainly perceive the *Advantage* and *Gain* they would thereby make? Whence then this Compassion for the *French*? But I would still hope that our islanders do not beg thus for the Sakes of the *French*, tho' in Effect *they alone* would be the Gainers." If the Parliament supported the Molasses Act, Hall concluded, then "the *French* will *increase*" their shipping, "just in proportion to our *Decrease*; the *French* will have ten Ships to one of ours, as the *Dutch* had formerly."[22] New Yorkers paid close attention to Hall's arguments, reprinting his testimony to Parliament in the *New-York Gazette*. After all, with a century-long legacy of interimperial relationships and an economic foundation that rested on Dutch New Netherlanders' trade with New England and Virginia, New Yorkers had long believed in the benefits of open trade.[23] Embracing the advantageous West Indian markets that being a part of the British empire offered, New Yorkers would never agree that a fully integrated and exclusive British empire was best because it would never fit their economic interests. While not eschewing the benefits the empire created, New Yorkers welcomed them only to the extent that they enhanced their opportunities for profitable trade.

Willing to deploy their political power to stifle free trade in their own province's hinterland, New York's leading traders and politicians vigorously opposed West Indians' efforts to do the same. But with political power firmly in the hands of West Indians by 1730, it would be sugar planters who triumphed when Parliament passed the Molasses Act in

1733. This law, which had come close to approval in 1731 and 1732, placed an import duty of five shillings per hundredweight on foreign sugar, nine pence per gallon on rum, and six pence per gallon on molasses.[24] Then, in 1739, planters further succeeded in finally winning the permission for which they had been pleading since 1650: the right to export sugar directly to foreign ports. In 1739, however, few took advantage of the opportunity. It was too late. With protected British prices higher than those in the rest of Europe and the French selling their sugar by as much as 40 percent cheaper, British planters chose buyers within the empire.[25] After almost a century, British West Indians had come to realize that their new economic situation made protected trade a net benefit, not a cost. Unable to pass laws to stop what they saw as a detrimental, planters seamlessly adjusted their view on free trade and embraced metropolitan regulation. Hidden behind this political reorientation was colonists' understanding of interimperial trade. As they gained control of these networks and blended British and Dutch resources together to find economic success, colonists created the environment that allowed them to react to the post-1713 economic boom in the ways they did. It was this colonial ideological pivot, as much as it was the commercial regulations passing from the metropole to periphery, that produced the exclusive and powerful commercial empire that would dominate the Atlantic for the remainder of the eighteenth century.

* * *

The creation of the British Atlantic was a negotiated effort that relied both upon English colonists and Dutch merchants working across imperial boundaries and upon English authorities' attempts to give shape to the constantly shifting process of colonial development. It is important to recognize that it was the first of these elements, the interimperial community, that was in place before the second, the state, could bring struggling communities into a coherent empire. Emphasizing the order of these events highlights the interimperial foundations of the British empire and indicates that the radical innovation in the middle of the seventeenth century was not colonists' refusal to accept an exclusive empire, but rather was state builders' attempts to impose this structure on a preexisting colonial culture that prized cross-national exchange.

Throughout the seventeenth century, Anglo-Dutch trade allowed immature English settlements to survive exogenous and endogenous crises and spurred their internal economic development through the supply of needed goods and services. Driven by local market conditions and Dutch commercial strength, colonists were able to continue trading beyond the official bounds of empire, even as mercantile policies multiplied. Because commercial regulations were not applied uniformly throughout the English Atlantic, older informal relations endured alongside of, and in competition with, increasing institutional cohesiveness. Bound to their Dutch trading partners by productive and essential trade, English colonists were unwilling simply to reorient their trade when the English government deemed it illegal. Rather, it was only when economic conditions changed that colonists adjusted their perspective. Ultimately, individuals, seeking out the best opportunities for themselves and their colonies, helped drive the growth of English colonial economies in the seventeenth and early eighteenth centuries. In the process, they made the British Atlantic empire.

It is tempting to read the collaboration between English and Dutch peoples in the Atlantic across the tableau of Anglo-Dutch conflict of the seventeenth century. With anti-Dutch rhetoric swirling through the coffeehouses and theaters of Restoration England, and with the two empire's navies clashing at sea, it is easy see Anglo-Dutch trade not merely as destructive to English efforts to build a stable empire, but also as traitorous. One of the central arguments of this book, however, has been that Anglo-Dutch trade, as profitable as it was for some, was motivated by neither greed nor disloyalty alone, but instead by a colonial-centric view of empire which maintained that before there could be a successful empire, there must be successful colonies. As such, colonists came to believe that they should pursue viable trade regardless of imperial boundaries.

The foregoing account had been ultimately one of declension. In the 1630s and 1640s, Anglo-Dutch trade constituted a far greater percentage of total colonial trade in the English colonies than it did during the 1660s or between 1710 and 1720. Importantly, though, this decline in cross-national exchange was not uniform. Some periods—such as the warfare of the late seventeenth and early eighteenth centuries—witnessed an increase in interimperial exchange, indicating how profound a part of colonial culture it was and how important local economic conditions were in producing the desire for Anglo-Dutch trade. Nevertheless, the trajectory was generally away from cross-national trade and toward an exclusive English empire over the course of the seventeenth century. If looked at from the perspective of the eighteenth century, this view suggests that Anglo-Dutch trade had no lasting legacy; once eliminated by the organs of empire, it was forgotten. But, as I have argued, this macrolevel view neglects not only the real contribution interimperial trade made to daily colonial life and to the economic development of the British Atlantic, but also ignores the actual process of imperial formation. It was only by eliminating this interimperial culture, something impossible to do without the cooperation of colonists, that Britain could reshape the Atlantic empire to meet its eighteenth-century needs.

Another way to judge the importance of Anglo-Dutch trade is to consider the counterfactual: What would have happened if the Dutch had been unable or unwilling to supply the goods and services that English colonists needed? If the Dutch had not been able to provide goods and services for English colonists and to help them rebuild from natural and man-made disasters, it is likely that the development of the British Atlantic would have been delayed. Certainly the English would have produced tobacco in the Leeward Islands and sugar in Barbados in the 1650s and 1660s; however, without the ability to attract Dutch goods, buyers, and credit (especially in the tobacco-reliant Leeward Islands), it is clear they would not have developed as rapidly. While it may at first seem that the low profitability of tobacco would have led planters in the Leeward Islands to switch to sugar, as they did in Barbados, constant warfare and the lack of sufficient capital would have most likely made this very difficult, if not impossible, in the short run. With French competition in the region, it might not have been worth the financial and personal risk for English colonists to remain at these vulnerable colonies. At the same time, without Dutch traders willing to provide livestock and other supplies to Barbadians, that island's development would have been more difficult. It would have been possible for Barbadians to produce sugar since they had sufficient capital from England and supplies from New England, but their demand for Dutch goods indicates these were neither always sufficient, nor always preferable. Therefore, without a Dutch presence, this island, too, would have developed differently. In New York, the legacy of interimperial commerce is more clear. In the two decades following the conquest, those ethnically Dutch merchants who dominated the colony's commercial and political sectors drove its transatlantic economy. More indirect, however, is the way that a long tradition of cross-national trade undergirded the commercial orientation of residents there for a century and helped make possible the colony's position as a regional entrepôt.

A lack of English demand for Dutch trade also would have altered the ideological development of these British colonies. Without the experience of interacting with Dutch traders at the periphery, English colonists would have understood colonial development differently. Just as their interaction with Africans and Native Americans changed colonists' ideological understandings of Englishness, access to Dutch goods affected their economic ideologies. These settlers' experience with Dutch trade helped engender the development of a particular colonial understanding of how best to structure colonial economies. As these ideas clashed with metropolitan ones, authorities and colonists alike had to negotiate between the two poles of understanding. Without exposure to cross-national trade, colonists may never have developed these ideas.

* * *

The Dutch influence on the development of the British Atlantic cannot be measured by hogsheads of sugar, rolls of tobacco, or pieces of duffles. Instead, its profound influence appears in the commercial culture of colonists who understood the benefits of a collaborative and multiethnic community because it had sustained them through the early decades of building colonies. The attention that English officials paid to eliminating this earlier culture and the difficulty they had in doing so for seventy years reveal the powerful legacy of Anglo-Dutch trade in shaping the British Atlantic. British authorities could not simply call upon their common Englishness to create an exclusive empire; instead, colonists had to accept those terms before there could be a truly integrated British empire. This process was so slow, uneven, and difficult because for it to be completed colonists had to replace an ingrained interimperial culture with a new imperial culture. Early modern British efforts to build empire, then, were not solely about collecting disparate and wayward communities of colonists together into a more cohesive whole, but required actually transforming them, a process that was not complete until colonists wanted to change. By the second decade of the eighteenth century, colonial and metropolitan interests had converged enough for this to happen. Economic development and self-interest had done what the Navigation Acts had attempted to mandate as colonists themselves eagerly sought a place in the growing empire and hoped its prosperity would enrich them as well. Just as colonists' desires and needs had provided the impetus for Anglo-Dutch trade one hundred years before, it was colonists' new interests that led to its decline. Interimperial trade did not disappear, but more than ever before British colonists now belonged to a powerful, expanding, and integrated empire, a set of developments made possible by the foundation that Anglo-Dutch trade afforded both colonists and this new British empire as a whole.

Notes

Abbreviations Used in the Notes

AJA-NA	Amsterdam Notarial Deeds, 1659–1681, Municipal Archives Amsterdam, trans. Simon Hart, deposited at JRM-AJA.
Andros	*The Andros Papers: Files of the Provincial Secretary of New York during the Administration of Governor Sir Edmund Andros, 1674–1680.* Edited by Peter R. Christoph and Florence A. Christoph. Syracuse, N.Y.: Syracuse University Press, 1989.
APCC	*Acts of the Privy Council: Colonial Series.* Edited by W. L. Grant and James Munro. 6 vols. London: H. M. Stationery Office, 1908–12.
BL	British Library, London.
Calendar	*Calendar of Historical Manuscripts in the Office of the Secretary of State.* Edited by E. B. O'Callaghan. 2 vols. Albany, N.Y.: Weed, Parsons, & Co., 1865–66.
Correspondence, 1647–1653	*Correspondence, 1647–1653. New Netherlands Documents.* Edited by Charles T. Gehring. Vol. 11. Syracuse, N.Y.: Syracuse University Press, 2000.
Correspondence, 1654–1658	*Correspondence, 1654–1658. New Netherlands Documents.* Edited by Charles T. Gehring. Vol. 12. Syracuse, N.Y.: Syracuse University Press, 2003.
CSPC	*Calendar of State Papers: Colonial Series, America and the West Indies, 1574–1738.* Edited by W. Noel Sainsbury, J. W. Fortescue, and Cecil Headlam. 44 vols. London: H. M. Stationery Office, 1860–1969.
Danckaerts	*Journal of Jasper Danckaerts.* Edited by Bartlett Burleigh James and J. Franklin Jameson. New York: Scribner's Sons, 1913.

De Peyster Papers	Abraham de Peyster Papers, 1690–1709. Some Mss translations by Dingham Versteeg. Microfilm.
Dongan	*The Dongan Papers: Admiralty Court and Other Records of the Administration of New York Governor Thomas Dongan.* Edited by Peter R. Christoph. 2 vols. *New York Historical Manuscript Series.* Syracuse, N.Y.: Syracuse University Press, 1993.
DRCHNY	*Documents Relative to the Colonial History of the State of New York.* Edited and transcribed by E.B. O'Callaghan and Berthold Fernow. 15 vols. Albany, N.Y.: Weed, Parsons, & Co., 1853–87.
GAA:NA	Notarieel Archief, Gemeentearchief Amsterdam, Netherlands
GAR:OND	Oud Notarieel Archief, Gemeentearchief Rotterdam, Netherlands. All Rotterdam notarial records accessed via www.gemeentearchief.rotterdam.nl/.
General Entries	*New York Historical Manuscripts English: Books of General Entries of the Colony of New York, 1664–1688.* Edited by Peter R. Christoph and Florence A. Christoph. 2 vols. Baltimore: Genealogical Publishing, 1982.
HHV GAA:NA	"English Translations of Notarial Documents in the Gemeentearchief Amsterdam Pertaining to North America." Historic Hudson Valley, Tarrytown, N. Y.
HMR	Julius M. Bloch et al. eds. *An Account of Her Majesty's revenue in the province of New York, 1701–09. The customs records of early colonial New York.* Ridgewood, N.J.: Gregg Press, 1967.
JBMHS	*Journal of the Barbados Museum and Historical Society.*
JDRL	John D. Rockefeller Library, Williamsburg, Va.
JRM:AJA	Jacob Rader Marcus Center of the American Jewish Archives, Cincinnati Campus, Hebrew Union College-Jewish Institute of Religion, Cincinnati, Ohio.
JVC Letter Book	Jacobus van Cortlandt, Letter Book, 1698–1701.
JVC Shipping Book	Jacobus van Cortlandt, Shipping Book, 1699–1702.
JVRC	*Correspondence of Jeremias van Rensselaer, 1651–1674.* Edited by A. J. F van Laer. Albany: University of the State of New York, 1932.
Lachaire	*New York Historical Manuscripts: Dutch. The Register of Soloman Lachaire, Notary Public of New Amsterdam, 1661–2.* Edited by Kenneth Scott and Kenneth Stryker-Rodda. Baltimore: Genealogical Publishing, 1978.
LOC:BL Trans.	British Library Transcripts, Library of Congress, Washington, D.C.
MMC	*New York Historical Manuscripts: Minutes of the Mayor's Court of New York, 1674–5.* Edited by Kenneth Scott. Baltimore: Genealogical Publishing, 1983.
Nicolls and Lovelace	*New York Historical Manuscripts English: Administrative Papers of Governors Richard Nicolls and Francis Lovelace, 1664–1673.* Edited by Peter R. Christoph. Vol. 22. Baltimore: Genealogical Publishing, 1980.

NYCCMCM	Mayor's Court Minutes, County Clerk's Office, Division of Old Records, New York City.
NYHMDPD	*Delaware Papers (Dutch Period): A Collection of Documents Pertaining to the Regulation of Affairs on the South River of New Netherland, 1648–1664.* Edited by Charles T. Gehring. 1981. Reprint, Baltimore: Genealogical Publishing, 2000.
NYHS	New-York Historical Society
NYHSC	*New-York Historical Society Collections*
PVC Letter Book	Philip van Cortlandt Letter Book, 1713–22.
Randolph Papers	*Edward Randolph; including his letters and official papers from the New England, middle, and southern colonies in America, with other documents relating chiefly to the vacating of the royal charter of the colony of Massachusetts Bay, 1676–1703.* Edited by R. N. Toppan and A. T. S. Goodrick. *Publications of the Prince Society.* Vols. 24–28, 30–31. 1909. Reprint, New York: Burt Franklin, 1967.
Riches from Atlantic Commerce	*Riches from Atlantic Commerce Dutch Transatlantic Trade and Shipping, 1585–1817.* Edited by Johannes Postma and Victor Enthoven. Leiden: Brill, 2003.
RNA	*The Records of New Amsterdam from 1653 to 1674.* Edited by Berthold Fernow. 7 vols. New York: Knickerbocker Press, 1897.
TASTD	Voyages: The Trans-Atlantic Slave Trade Database.
TNA:PRO	The National Archives–Public Records Office, Kew, England.
TSP	*A Collection of the State Papers of John Thurloe.* Edited by Thomas Birch. 7 vols. London, 1742.
WMQ	*William and Mary Quarterly.*
Young Squire	"A Young Squire of the Seventeenth Century." From the Papers of Christopher Jeaffreson, of Dullingham House, Cambridgeshire. Edited by John C. Jeaffreson. 2 vols. London: Hurst and Blackett Publishers, 1878.

Notes to the Introduction

1. Though this image originally commemorated the reconquest of New York by the Dutch in 1673, it was copied by English engravers and was often used to celebrate English New York in prints and on maps, as in this ca. 1700 example. Typical of these prints, the artist has left Dutch flags on the vessels.

2. The best synthesizing of work before 1985 is found in Ralph Davis, *The Rise of the Atlantic Economies* (Ithaca, N.Y.: Cornell University Press, 1973); and John J. McCusker and Russell R. Menard, *The Economy of British America, 1607–1789, With Supplementary Bibliography* (Chapel Hill: University of North Carolina Press, 1985, 1991). David Hancock, "Rethinking *The Economy of British America*," in *The Economy of Early America: Historical Perspectives and New Directions*, ed. Cathy Matson (University Park: Pennsylvania State University Press, 2006), covers directions since 1985.

3. The origins of Atlantic history are varied, but it began to coalesce as a distinct approach to understanding European expansion in the Americas at the end of the 1980s. Ian K. Steele, *The English Atlantic, 1675–1740: An Exploration of Communication and Community* (New York: Oxford University Press, 1986); James Tracy, ed., *The*

Rise of Merchant Empires, Long-Distance Trade in the Early Modern World, 1350–1750 (Cambridge: Cambridge University Press, 1990); Alan L. Karras, "The Atlantic World as a Unit of Study," in *Atlantic American Societies: From Columbus through Abolition, 1492–1888*, ed. Alan K. Karras and J. R. McNeil (New York: Routledge, 1992), 1–15. The breadth and pace of work in this field resist characterization, but to begin, see, most recently, Bernard Bailyn, "Introduction: Reflections on Some Major Themes," in *Soundings in Atlantic History: Latent Structures and Intellectual Currents, 1500–1830*, ed. Bailyn and Patricia L. Denault (Cambridge: Harvard University Press, 2009), 1–43; Philip D. Morgan and Jack P. Greene, "Introduction: The Present State of Atlantic History," in *Atlantic History: A Critical Appraisal*, ed. Greene and Morgan (New York: Oxford University Press, 2009), 3–33; Carole Shammas, introduction to *The Creation of the British Atlantic World*, ed. Elizabeth Mancke and Shammas (Baltimore: Johns Hopkins University Press, 2005), 1–16; and Alison Games, "Atlantic History: Definitions, Challenges, and Opportunities," *American Historical Review* 111, no. 3 (2006): 741–57. Also consider the critiques of the Atlantic approach found in Peter A. Coclanis, "*Drang nach Osten*: Bernard Bailyn, the World-Island, and the Idea of Atlantic History," *Journal of World History* 13 (2002): 169–82; and Pierre Gervais, "Neither Imperial nor Atlantic: A Merchant Perspective on International Trade in the Eighteenth Century," *History of European Ideas* 34 (2008): 465–66, 472–73.

4. Shammas, introduction to *The Creation of the British Atlantic World*, ed. Mancke and Shammas, 3–4; April Lee Hatfield, *Atlantic Virginia: Intercolonial Relations in the Seventeenth Century* (Philadelphia: University of Pennsylvania Press, 2004), 1–3; Games, "Atlantic History: Definitions, Challenges, and Opportunities," 744–47, 749. See also David Hancock, "'A World of Business to Do': William Freeman and the Foundations of England's Commercial Empire, 1645–1707," *WMQ*, 3rd ser., 57 (2000): 3–34, esp. 3–4. This is also a major theme of Hancock's commodity study of Madeira wine (David Hancock, *Oceans of Wine: Madeira and the Emergence of American Trade and Taste* [New Haven: Yale University Press, 2009]).

Much of the work on Virginia surrounding the four-hundredth anniversary of its founding has situated Virginia in a wider Atlantic and has stressed cultural and, to a lesser extent, commercial ties to other colonies and empires. Robert Appelbaum and John Wood Sweet, eds., *Envisioning an English Empire: Jamestown and the Making of the North Atlantic World* (Philadelphia: University of Pennsylvania Press, 2005); J. H. Elliott, *Empires of the Atlantic World: Britain and Spain in America, 1492–1830* (New Haven: Yale University Press, 2006); Karen Ordahl Kupperman, *The Jamestown Project* (Cambridge: Belknap Press of Harvard University Press, 2007); Peter Mancall, ed., *The Atlantic World and Virginia, 1550–1624* (Chapel Hill: University of North Carolina Press, 2007).

5. For those working on the connections between the English empire and others in the seventeenth-century Atlantic, see April Lee Hatfield, "Dutch New Netherland Merchants in the Seventeenth-Century English Chesapeake," in *The Atlantic Economy during the Seventeenth and Eighteenth Centuries: Organization, Operation, Practice, and Personnel*, ed. Peter Coclanis (Columbia: University of South Carolina Press. 2005), 205–28; Hatfield, "Mariners, Merchants, and Colonists in Seventeenth-Century English America," in *The Creation of the British Atlantic World*, ed. Mancke and Shammas, 139–59; Claudia Schnurmann, *Atlantische Welten. Engländer und Niederländer im amerikanisch-atlantischen Raum, 1648–1713*, Wirtschafts- und Sozialhistorische

Studien, no. 9 (Cologne, 1998); Claudia Schnurmann, "Atlantic Trade and American Identities: The Correlations of Supranational Commerce, Political Opposition, and Colonial Regionalism," in *The Atlantic Economy*, ed. Coclanis, 186–204; Claudia Schnurmann, "Representative Atlantic Entrepreneur: Jacob Leisler, 1640–1691," in *Riches from Atlantic Commerce*, 259–83; Cynthia J. van Zandt, *Brothers among Nations: The Pursuit of Intercultural Alliances in Early America, 1580–1660* (New York: Oxford University Press, 2008); Eliga H. Gould, "AHR Forum: Entangled Histories, Entangled Worlds: The English-Speaking Atlantic as a Spanish Periphery," *American Historical Review* 112 (2007): 764–86, and the discussion that ensued; Gould, "Entangled Atlantic Histories: A Response from the Anglo-American Periphery," *American Historical Review* 112, no. 5 (2007): 1415–22; and Jorge Cañizares-Esguerra, "The Core and Peripheries of Our National Narratives: A Response from IH-35," *American Historical Review* 112, no. 5 (2007): 1423–31.

Recent work on interimperial trade in the Atlantic has tended to focus on the role of "supranational" entrepreneurs as individuals and has neglected their influence on empires. Exceptions include Nuala Zahedieh, "Trade, Plunder, and Economic Development in Early English Jamaica, 1655–89," *Economic History Review*, 2nd ser., 39 (1986): 205–22; and Nuala Zahedieh, "Merchants of Port Royal, Jamaica, and the Spanish Contraband Trade, 1655–1692," *WMQ*, 3rd ser., 43 (1986): 570–93. Wim Klooster suggests that interimperial trade was more important to economic development than previously believed, though the scope of his essay means his findings are only provisional (Wim Klooster, "Inter-Imperial Smuggling in the Americas, 1600–1800," in *Soundings in Atlantic History*, ed. Bernard Bailyn and Patricia L. Denault, 141–80).

Scholars working on the Jewish Diaspora are also attuned to interimperial commerce, but they usually study it in reference to the building and maintenance of the Jewish community, not imperial development. For the Caribbean, see Daniel M Swetschinski, "Conflict and Opportunity in 'Europe's Other Sea': The Adventure of Caribbean Jewish Settlement," *American Jewish Historical Quarterly* 72 (1982): 212–40; Stephen A. Fortune, *Merchants and Jews: The Struggle for British West Indian Commerce, 1650–1715* (Gainesville: University of Florida, 1984); and Paolo Bernardini and Norman Fiering, eds., *The Jews and the Expansion of Europe to the West, 1450–1800* (New York: Berghahn Books, 2001).

Those studying the Dutch Atlantic have done a better job integrating border crossing with economic development (see Wim Klooster, *Illicit Riches: Dutch Trade in the Caribbean, 1648–1795* [Leiden: KITLV Press, 1998]; Wim Klooster, "Anglo-Dutch Trade in the Seventeenth Century: An Atlantic Partnership?" in *Shaping the Stuart World, 1603–1714: The Atlantic Connection*, ed. Allan I. Macinnes and Arthur H. Williamson [Boston: Brill, 2006], 61–82; Linda M. Rupert, "Contraband Trade and the Shaping of Colonial Societies in Curaçao and Tierra Firma," *Itinerario* 30, no. 3 [2006]: 35–54; and the essays in *Riches from Atlantic Commerce*, ed. Postma and Enthoven).

6. On the fiscal-military state, see H. V. Bowen, *Elites, Enterprise and the Making of the British Overseas Empire, 1688–1775* (New York: St. Martin's Press, 1996); Henry G. Roseveare, *The Financial Revolution, 1660–1760* (New York: St. Martin's Press, 1991); P. K. O'Brien and P. A. Hunt, "The Rise of a Fiscal State in England, 1485–1815," *Historical Research* 66 (1993): 129–76; Daniel A. Baugh, "Maritime Strength and Atlantic Commerce: The Uses of 'a Grand Marine Empire,'" in *An Imperial State at War: Britain from 1689 to 1815*, ed. Lawrence Stone (New York: Routledge, 1994), 185–90;

Michael J. Braddick, *The Nerves of State: Taxation and the Financing of the English State, 1558–1714* (New York: Manchester University Press, 1996); David Ormrod, *The Rise of Commercial Empires: England and the Netherlands in the Age of Mercantilism, 1650–1770* (New York: Cambridge University Press, 2003); and Jonathan Scott, *England's Troubles: Seventeenth-Century English Political Instability in European Context* (New York: Cambridge University Press, 2000).

7. Many early scholars of the English Caribbean discussed Dutch trade but did not make it central to their work: C. S. S. Higham, *The Development of the Leeward Islands under the Restoration, 1660–1688* (Cambridge: Cambridge University Press, 1921); Vincent T. Harlow, *A History of Barbados, 1625–1685* (Oxford: Clarendon Press, 1926), James A. Williamson, *The Caribbee Islands under the Proprietary Patents* (Oxford: Oxford University Press, 1926). See also Richard Dunn, *Sugar and Slaves: The Rise of the Planter Class in the English West Indies, 1624–1713* (Chapel Hill: University of North Carolina Press, 1972); Carl and Roberta Bridenbaugh, *No Peace beyond the Line: The English in the Caribbean, 1624–1690* (New York: Oxford University Press, 1972); Richard Pares, *Merchants and Planters. Economic History Review,* Supplement no. 4. (Cambridge: Published for the *Economic History Review* at Cambridge University Press, 1960); Richard Sheridan, *Sugar and Slavery: An Economic History of the British West Indies, 1623–1775* (Barbados: Caribbean University Press, 1974). More recently, Russell Menard has challenged these historians' most significant claim: that the Dutch introduced sugar to the English Caribbean (Russell R. Menard, *Sweet Negotiations: Sugar, Slavery, and Plantation Agriculture in Early Barbados* [Charlottesville: University of Virginia Press, 2006]).

Historians of New Netherland/New York have studied the type and quality of ties that remained between colonial merchants and the Dutch empire after the 1664 English conquest. However, most of these historians' otherwise thoughtful analysis focuses on political, cultural, and social persistence, not economic (see Thomas J. Archdeacon, *New York City, 1664–1710: Conquest and Change* [Ithaca, N.Y.: Cornell University Press, 1976]; Robert Ritchie, *The Duke's Province: A Study of New York Politics and Society, 1654–1691* [Chapel Hill: University of North Carolina Press, 1977]; Joyce Goodfriend, *Before the Melting Pot: Society and Culture in Colonial New York City, 1664–1730* [Princeton, N.J.: Princeton University Press, 1992]; Albert E. McKinley, "The Transition from Dutch to English Rule in New York: A Study in Political Imitation," *American Historical Review* 6 [1901]: 693–724; Donna Merwick, *Possessing Albany, 1630–1710: The Dutch and English Experiences* [Cambridge: Cambridge University Press, 1990]; and Donna Merwick, *Death of a Notary: Conquest and Change in Colonial New York* [Ithaca, N.Y.: Cornell University Press, 1999]). Those studying economic development have looked at enduring commercial connections but have looked at the period between 1664 and 1713 as either a prelude or a coda, rather than as a transformative moment in and of itself (Oliver A. Rink, *Holland on the Hudson: An Economic and Social History of Dutch New York* [Ithaca, N.Y.: Cornell University Press, 1986]; Cathy Matson, *Merchants and Empire: Trading in Colonial New York* [Baltimore: Johns Hopkins University Press, 1998]; Dennis J. Maika, "Commerce and Community: Manhattan Merchants in the Seventeenth Century" [Ph.D. diss., New York University, 1995]).

8. The first volume of the five-volume *Oxford History of the British Empire* stresses the decentralized origins of the empire before 1660, but this work still treats this as

an aberrant, and short, phase of development (see particularly John C. Appleby, "War, Politics, and Colonization, 1558–1625"; N. A. M. Rodger, "Guns and Sails in the First Phases on English Colonization, 1500–1650"; Hilary McD. Beckles, "The 'Hub of Empire': The Caribbean and Britain in the Seventeenth Century"; Michael J. Braddick, "The English Government, War, Trade, and Settlement, 1625–1688"; all in *The Origins of Empire*, ed. Nicholas Canny, vol. 1, *The Oxford History of the British Empire,* ed. Wm Roger Lewis [Oxford: Oxford University Press, 1998]).

9. Central to this project is scholarship examining the negotiated nature of Atlantic empires. Collectively, this work has shown that colonial understandings of empire heavily influenced and shaped early modern empires (Christine Daniels and Michael V. Kennedy, eds. *Negotiated Empires: Centers and Peripheries in the Americas, 1500–1820* [New York: Routledge, 2002], esp. Jack P. Greene, "Transatlantic Colonization and the Redefinition of Empire in the Early Modern Era: The British-American Experience," 268–70, 272–73; and Elizabeth Mancke, "Negotiating an Empire: Britain and Its Overseas Peripheries, c. 1550–1780," 236–37, 248–49). See also David Lambert and Alan Lester, "Introduction: Imperial Spaces, imperial subjects," in *Colonial Lives across the British Empire: Imperial Careering in the Long Nineteenth Century,* ed. David Lambert and Alan Lester (New York: Cambridge University Press, 2006), 6–13; and Greene, "Negotiated Authorities: The Problem of Governance in the Extended Polities of the Early Modern Atlantic World," in *Negotiated Authorities: Essays in Colonial Political and Constitutional History,* Greene (Charlottesville: University of Virginia Press, 1994), 1–24. David Armitage has reinforced the idea of the negotiated nature of the English empire, arguing that colonists had a hand in shaping its meaning (Armitage, *Ideological Origins of the British Empire* [Cambridge: Cambridge University Press, 2000]). Hancock, "A World of Business to Do," 5; Andrew Fitzmaurice, "The Commercial ideology of Colonization in Jacobean England: Robert Johnson, Giovanni Botero, and the Pursuit of Greatness," *WMQ,* 3rd ser., 64, no. 4 (2007): 817; Carla Gardiner Pestana, *The English Atlantic in an Age of Revolution, 1640–1661* (Cambridge: Harvard University Press, 2004). Lauren Benton has shown the local, ad hoc, and fragmented origins of the empire in oceanic law (Lauren Benton, "Legal Space of Empire: Piracy and the Origins of Ocean Regionalism," *Comparative Studies in Society and History* 47, no. 4 [2005]: 700–706; Benton, "Spatial Histories of Empire," *Itinerario* 30, no. 3 [2006]: 20–22, 27). Kathleen Wilson, meanwhile, has critiqued the use of the center-periphery model, questioning not the mutual exchange and negotiation between colony and metropole, but instead the usefulness of such labels in a period of unstable and flexible power and influence throughout the empire (Wilson, "Introduction: Histories, Empire, Modernities," in *A New Imperial History: Culture, Identity and Modernity in Britain and the Empire, 1660–1840,* ed. Wilson [New York: Cambridge University Press, 2004], 17).

10. Tony Claydon, *Europe and the Making of England, 1660–1760* (New York: Cambridge University Press, 2007), 11–12; and, in a more explicitly Atlantic context, Alison Games, *The Web of Empire: English Cosmopolitans in an Age of Expansion, 1560–1660* (New York: Oxford University Press, 2008); and Kupperman, *The Jamestown Project.*

11. Thomas Mun, *England's Treasure by Foreign Trade, or, the Balance of our Foreign Trade is the Rule of our Treasure* (London, 1664), 204–5.

12. Adam Smith, *An Inquiry into the Nature and Causes of the Wealth of Nations,* ed. R. H. Campbell and A. S. Skinner (1776; repr., Indianapolis: Liberty Classics, 1976),

898; Joshua M. Smith, *Borderland Smuggling: Patriots, Loyalists, and Illicit Trade in the Northeast, 1783–1820* (Gainesville: University Press of Florida, 2006), 10–12.

Notes to Chapter 1

1. During the seventeenth century, the English still used the older Julian calendar, and the Dutch had switched to the Gregorian calendar, meaning the English calendar was ten days behind the Dutch. Additionally the English did not begin the new year until March 21. Therefore, the date March 1, 1661, was rendered March 1, 1660/61. I will include the date that each document carries. While I have preserved the original syntax in most quotations, when necessary for clarity I have eliminated double letters and expanded abbreviations.

2. Referred to as St. Kitts beginning in the eighteenth century, most seventeenth-century Europeans referred to the island as St. Christopher.

3. David Pietersz. de Vries, *Voyages from Holland to America: 1632–1644*, trans. Henry C. Murphy (New York, 1853), 28–30.

4. Simon Schama, *The Embarrassment of Riches: An Interpretation of Dutch Culture in the Golden Age* (New York: Knopf, 1987), esp. chaps. 5–6.

5. Israel, *Dutch Primacy in World Trade, 1585–1740* (New York: Oxford University Press, 1989), esp. chaps. 3–4, quotation 85; Boxer, *The Dutch Seaborne Empire: 1600–1800* (New York: Knopf, 1965), chaps. 1–4; De Vries, *The Dutch Rural Economy in the Golden Age, 1500–1700* (New Haven: Yale University Press, 1974), chap. 4.

6. For this and the paragraph above, see Violet Barbour, "Dutch and English Merchant Shipping in the Seventeenth Century," *Economic History Review*, 2nd ser., 2 (1930): 261–90; Barbour, *Capitalism in Amsterdam in the Seventeenth Century*, Johns Hopkins University Studies in Historical and Political Science, ser. 67, no. 1 (Baltimore: John Hopkins University Press, 1950); Israel, *Dutch Primacy in World Trade*, chaps. 1–5; Davis, *The Rise of Atlantic Economies*, chap. 11; J. A. van Houtte, *An Economic History of the Low Countries, 800–1800* (New York: St. Martin's Press, 1977), pt. 3; Immanuel Wallerstein, *Mercantilism and the Consolidation of the European World-Economy, 1600–1750, Studies in Social Discontinuity*, vol. 2, *The Modern World System* (New York: Academic Press, 1980), chap. 2; Niels Steensgaard, "The Growth and Composition of the Long-Distance Trade of England and the Dutch Republic before 1750," in *The Rise of Merchant Empires*, ed. Tracy, 102–45; Jan de Vries and Ad van der Woude, *The First Modern Economy: Success, Failure and Perseverance of the Dutch Economy, 1500–1815* (New York: Cambridge University Press, 1997), chap. 4; W. Fritschy, " A 'Financial Revolution' Reconsidered: Public Finance in Holland during the Dutch Revolt, 1568–1648," *Economic History Review*, 2nd ser., 56 (2003): 57–89; John J. McCusker, "The Demise of Distance: The Business Press and the Origins of the Information Revolution in the Early Modern Atlantic World," *American Historical Review* (April 2005), www.historycooperative.org/journals/ahr/110.2/mccusker.html, pars 25–26; and, as a contrast, Ormord, *The Rise of Commercial Empires*. First two quotations, John Evelyn, *De Vita Propria Pars Prima*, in *The Diary of John Evelyn*, ed. E. S. de Beer (Oxford: Clarendon Press, 1955), 1:33, 34. Final quotation, Lewes Roberts, *The Marchants Mapp of Commerce* (London, 1638), 110.

7. Cornelis Charles Goslinga, *The Dutch in the Caribbean and on the Wild Coast, 1580–1680* (Gainesville: University of Florida Press, 1971), chaps. 1–3, 116–38; Christopher Ebert, "Dutch Trade with Brazil before the Dutch West India Company,

1587–1621," in *Riches from Atlantic Commerce*, 49–75; Emmer, "The West India Company, 1621–1791: Dutch or Atlantic?" in *Companies and Trade: Essays on Overseas Trading Companies during the Ancien Regime*, ed. Leonard Blussé and Femme Gaastra (Leiden: Leiden University Press, 1981), 76–80.

8. Van Cleaf Bachman, *Peltries or Plantations: The Economic Policies of the Dutch West Indies Company in New Netherland, 1623–1639* (Baltimore: Johns Hopkins University Press, 1969), chaps. 2–3; Goslinga, *The Dutch in the Caribbean and on the Wild Coast*, chap. 7; Emmer and Wim Klooster, "The Dutch Atlantic, 1600–1800: Expansion Without Empire," *Itinerario* 23 (1999): 48–69; Victor Enthoven, "Early Dutch Expansion in the Atlantic Region, 1585–1621," 18–47, Ebert, "Dutch Trade with Brazil before the Dutch West India Company, 1587–1621," 49–75; and Henk Den Heijer, "The Dutch West India Company, 1621–1791," 77–114, all in *Riches from Atlantic Commerce*. On Brazil, see Stuart B. Schwartz, "A Commonwealth within Itself: The Early Brazilian Sugar Industry, 1550–1670," in *Tropical Babylons: Sugar and the Making of the Atlantic World, 1450–1680*, ed. Schwartz (Chapel Hill: University of North Carolina Press, 2004), 158–200.

9. Johannes Postma, *The Dutch in the Atlantic Slave Trade, 1600–1815* (New York: Cambridge University Press, 1990), chaps. 1, 3, 5; and his recent update of those statistics (Johannes Postma, "A Reassessment of the Dutch Slave Trade," in *Riches from Atlantic Commerce*, 115–38).

10. Israel, *Dutch Primacy in World Trade*, chaps. 5–6.

11. De Vries, *Voyages from Holland*, 25–26. See also note 8 above.

12. Merrill Gordon, *The Historical Geography of St. Kitts and Nevis, The West Indies* (Mexico City: Instituto Panamericano de Geographia e Historia, 1958), 18–25; Lydia Mihelio Pulsipher, "The Cultural Landscape of Montserrat, West Indies, in the Seventeenth Century: Early Environmental Consequences of British Colonial Development" (Ph.D. diss. Southern Illinois University, 1977), chaps. 1–2; David Watts, *West Indies, Patterns of Development, Culture, and Environmental Change since 1492* (New York: Cambridge University Press, 1987), 3–34.

13. Andrews, *Trade, Plunder and Settlement: Maritime Enterprise and the Genesis of the British Empire, 1480–1630* (New York: Cambridge University Press, 1984), 2–14, 56–63, 116–28; David Beers Quinn, *England and the Discovery of America, 1481–1620* (New York: Knopf, 1974), pt. 3; Elliott, *Empires of the Atlantic World*, 8–28. On the English economy, see Keith Wrightson, *Earthly Necessities: Economic Lives in Early Modern Britain* (New Haven: Yale University Press, 2000), chaps. 5–6; and Wilson, *England's Apprenticeship, 1603–1763* (New York: St. Martin's Press, 1965), 40–53.

14. Andrews, *Trade, Plunder and Settlement*, introduction, chaps. 1–3; David Beers Quinn and A. N. Ryan, *England's Sea Empire, 1550–1642* (London: Allen and Unwin, 1983), esp. chaps. 3–5; Kupperman, *The Jamestown Project*, 28–38; Robert Brenner, *Merchants and Revolution: Commercial Change, Political Conflict, and London's Overseas Traders, 1550–1653* (Princeton: Princeton University Press, 1993), chaps. 1–2. This, of course, is well-covered ground, but for a good summary, see John C. Appleby, "War, Politics, and Colonization, 1558–1625," in *The Origins of Empire*, ed. Canny, 55–78.

15. Karen Ordahl Kupperman, *Providence Island, 1630–1641: The Other Puritan Colony* (New York: Cambridge University Press, 1993), 214–15.

16. Kenneth R. Andrews, *The Spanish Caribbean: Trade and Plunder 1530–1630* (New Haven: Yale University Press, 1978), chap. 9; Joyce Lorimer, "The English

Contraband Tobacco Trade in Trinidad and Guiana, 1590–1617," in *The Westward Enterprise: English Activities in Ireland, the Atlantic, and America 1480–1650*, ed. K. R. Andrews, N. P. Canny, P. E. H. Hair (Detroit: Wayne State University Press, 1979), 124–34; Vincent T. Harlow, ed., *Colonising Expeditions to the West Indies and Guiana, 1623–1667*, Hakluyt Society, ser. 2, vol. 56 (London, 1924), pt. 5. For specific English private initiatives, see Karen Ordahl Kupperman, *Roanoke: The Abandoned Colony* (New York: Rowman and Allanheld, 1984); Kupperman, *The Jamestown Project*, esp., 183–240; Peter E. Pope, *Fish into Wine: The Newfoundland Plantation in the Seventeenth Century* (Chapel Hill: University of North Carolina Press, 2004), esp. 45–65; and the works on the English Caribbean cited in this chapter.

17. For this paragraph and the next, see Harlow, "Introduction," xv–xxviii, and "Relation of the First Settlement of St. Christophers and Nevis, by John Hilton, Storekeeper and Chief Gunner of Nevis," 1675 in *Colonising Expeditions*, ed. Harlow, 4–17; Brenner, *Merchants and Revolution*, 125–27; Bridenbaugh and Bridenbaugh, *No Peace beyond the Line*, 29–34; Dunn, *Sugar and Slaves*, 118–20; Higham, *The Development of the Leeward Islands*, 1–27; Williamson, *The Caribbee Islands*, 74–81; and Michael A. LaCombe, "Warner, Sir Thomas (c. 1580–1649)," *Oxford Dictionary of National Biography* (Oxford University Press, 2004), www.oxforddnb.com/view/article/28768. For 20,000 pounds of tobacco, see *APCC* 1:122.

18. "Relation of the First Settlement of St. Christophers and Nevis," in *Colonising Expeditions*, ed. Harlow, 4–17 (quotation 11). There are only scattered population estimates for the English Leeward Islands before the census of 1678. Richard Sheridan estimated Antigua's population at between 1,000 and 2,000 in 1655, while St. Christopher had 20,000 residents (free and unfree) in 1643 (up from 3,000 in 1629). A correspondent of William Blathwayt put the population of Antigua in 1669 at 1,700 whites (300 of these were women) and 700 slaves. He also estimated the population of Nevis at 2,000 whites; in 1672, the number of men who could bear arms was recorded as 1,411. There were 1,739 slaves that same year, but no other data were given for the remainder of the island's population. The same correspondent estimated Montserrat's population at 1,400 whites and 300 blacks. In 1672, the total white population of the Leeward Islands was 10,408. These whites owned 8,449 slaves (May 12, 1669, "An Account of the Carybee Islands," Blathwayt Papers, 1656/7–1716, Collections of the Henry E. Huntington Library and Art Gallery, microfilm, roll 1, unpaginated [hereafter Blath.-Hunt.]; Sheridan, *Sugar and Slavery*, 151, 162, 185). For the 1678 census, see TNA:PRO CO 1/42, fol. 334v–381v; and Dunn, *Sugar and Slaves*, 118–21, 127.

19. Lisa Jardine, *Going Dutch: How England Plundered Holland's Glory* (New York: HarperCollins, 2008), 47.

20. Joan Thirsk, *Economic Policy and Projects: The Development of a Consumer Society in Early Modern England* (1978; repr., Oxford: Clarendon Press, 1988), 43–47, 80–85, 93–98, 106–7; R. A. Holderness, "The Reception and Distribution of the New Draperies in England," in *The New Draperies in the Low Countries and England, 1300–1800*, ed. N. B. Harte (New York: Oxford University Press, 1997), 217–20, 232–33. On the 1635 travelers, see Alison Games, *Migration and the Origins of the English Atlantic World* (Cambridge: Harvard University Press, 1999), 21, 31–34. On the influence of Dutch finance and accounting, see Jonathan Scott, "'Good Night Amsterdam': Sir George Downing and Anglo-Dutch Statebuilding," *English Historical Review* 108, no. 47 (2003): 334–56; Jacob Sell, "Accounting for Government: Holland and the Rise of

Political Economy in Seventeenth-Century Europe," *Journal of Interdisciplinary History* 40, no. 2 (Autumn 2009): 229–31.

21. Jardine, *Going Dutch*, 69–72.

22. Lucas Janszoon Waghenaer, *The Mariners Mirrour.* . . . (London, 1588).

23. Kees Zandvliet, *Mapping for Money: Maps, Plans and Topographic Paintings and Their Role in Dutch Overseas Expansion during the 16th and 17th Centuries* (Amsterdam: Batavian Lion International), 37–49, 164–86; G. R. Crone, *Maps and Their Makers: An Introduction to the History of Cartography*, 5th ed. (Hamden, Conn.: Archon Books, 1978), 68–70; J. B. Harley and Kees Zandvliet, "Art, Science, and Power in Sixteenth-Century Dutch Cartography," *Cartographica* 29 (1992): 11–12, 15; Helen M. Wallis, "Geographie Is Better than Divinite: Maps, Globes, and Geography in the Days of Samuel Pepys," in *The Compleat Plattmaker: Essays on Chart, Map, an Globe Making in England in the Seventeenth and Eighteenth Centuries*, ed. Norman J. W. Thrower (Berkeley and Los Angeles: University of California Press, 1978), 4–19, 31–32.

24. Zandvliet, *Mapping for Money*, 34–37; Crone, *Maps and Their Makers*, 63–66; Eric H. Ash, *Power, Knowledge, and Expertise in Elizabethan England* (Baltimore: Johns Hopkins University Press, 2004), 93–94.

25. Otis P. Starkey, *The Economic Geography of Barbados: A Study of the Relationships between Environmental Variations and Economic Development* (1939; repr., Westport, Conn.: Negro Universities Press, 1971), 3–5 (quotation, 4); Dunn, *Sugar and Slaves*, 4–5, 26–30.

26. "A Brief Collection of the Depositions of Witnesses and Pleadings of Commissioners at Law in a difference depending between the merchants and inhabitants of Barbados on the one part, and the Earl of Carlisle, Lord Willoughby, &c., on the other part," and "The Description of Guyana," in *Colonizing Expeditions*, ed. Harlow, 25–42, 140; George Edmundson, "The Dutch in Western Guiana," *Economic History Review* 16 (1901): 658–60; Sheridan, *Sugar and Slavery*, 81–82; Larry Gragg, *Englishmen Transplanted: The English Colonization of Barbados, 1627–1660* (Oxford: Oxford University Press, 2003), 19, 29–32.

27. For this paragraph and the one that follows, see Harlow, *History of Barbados*, chap. 1; Dunn, *Sugar and Slaves*, 49–50; and Gragg, *Englishmen Transplanted*, chap. 1.

28. Gragg, *Englishmen Transplanted*, 35–40.

29. Dunn, working from John Camden Hotten, ed., *The Original Lists of Persons of Quality . . . and Others Who Went from Great Britain to the American Plantations, 1600–1700* (London, 1874), 33–145, tabulated these figures for 1635 (Dunn, *Sugar and Slaves*, 51–55). On Barbados's social instability, see Colt, "The Voyage of Sir Henrye Colt Knight to ye Ilands of ye Antilleas,"ca. 1631, in *Colonising Expeditions*, ed. Harlow, 65–69). Recent work has tempered Colt's description (Gragg, *Englishmen Transplanted*, chap. 8).

30. Colt, "The Voyage of Sir Henrye Colt," in *Colonising Expeditions*, ed. Harlow, 94; Klooster, "Anglo-Dutch Trade in the Seventeenth Century," in *Shaping the Stuart World*, ed. Macinnes and Williamson, 264. Examples of interactions abound: *CSPC, 1574–1660*, 146, 162, 194; October 20–December 26, 1644, "Ledger of the accounts of the ship het Wapen van Rensselaerswyck," in *New York State Library: Van Rensselaer Bowier Manuscripts: Being the Letters of Kiliaen van Rensselawer, 1630–1643, and other Documents Relating to the Colony of Rensselaerswyck*, ed. J. F. van Laer (Albany: University of the State of New York, 1908), 719–20; *NYHMDPD*, 362; John Smith, *The True*

Travels, Adventures and Observations of Captain John Smith into Europe, Asia, Africa, and America from Ann. Dom. 1593 to 1629 (London, 1630; repr., 1704), 406–7.

31. William Duke, *Memoirs of the First Settlement of the Island of Barbados, and other the Carribbee Islands* (London, 1743), 18.

32. September 5, 1627, *APCC*, 1:119.

33. Gragg, *Englishmen Transplanted*, 29–34, 88, 89–90, 95; F. C. Innes, "The Pre-Sugar Era of European Settlement in Barbados," *Journal of Caribbean History* 1 (1970): 14–15; Pares, *Merchants and Planters*, 20–21; Sheridan, *Sugar and Slavery*, 394; Alison Games, "Opportunity and Mobility in Early Barbados," in *The Lesser Antilles in the Age of European Expansion*, ed. Stanley L. Engerman and Robert L. Paquette (Gainesville: University of Florida Press, 1996), 165–81; Russell R. Menard, "Plantation Empire: How Sugar and Tobacco Planters Built Their Industries and Raised an Empire," *Agricultural History* 81, no. 3 (2007): 319–21; Menard, "The Tobacco Industry in the Chesapeake Colonies, 1617–1730: An Interpretation," *Research in Economic History* 5 (1980): 109–77. For taxes, see depositions of William Roper, Thomas Horne, and James Barrey, in N. Darnell Davis, ed., "Papers Relating to the Early History of Barbados and St. Kitts," *Timehri* 6 (1892): 333–37.

34. Colt, "The Voyage of Sir Henrye Colt" in *Colonising Expeditions*, ed. Harlow, 101. For other English West Indians selling tobacco in the Dutch Republic, see Robert South and Maurice Thomson V. ___ King, February 21, 1632/3, Deposition of Thomas Murthwaithe in *English Adventurers and Emigrants, 1630–1660: Abstracts of Examinations in the High Court of Admiralty with Reference to Colonial America*, ed. Peter Wilson Coldham (Baltimore: Genealogical Publishing Company, 1984), 39; Mary Limbre v. __ Willson, January 8, 1639/40, Deposition of Richard Cooper. TNA:PRO HCA 13/55, fol. 439; Smith, *The True Travels*, 406–7.

35. Brenner, *Merchants and Revolution*, 128–32, 184–95.

36. Barbour, *Capitalism in Amsterdam*, 62–63, 93 n. 33; De Vries and Van der Woude, *The First Modern Economy*, 324–26; Israel, *Dutch Primacy in World Trade*, 265–66, 356, 363; Jacob M. Price, "The Economic Growth of the Chesapeake and the European Market, 1697–1775," *Journal of Economic History* 24 (1964): 499–501.

37. K. G. Davies, "The Origins of the Commission System in the West India Trade," *Transactions of the Royal Historical Society*, 5th ser., 1–2 (1952): 90–94; Pares, *Merchants and Planters*, 33–34; Sheridan, *Sugar and Slavery*, chap. 12; Davis, *The Rise of the English Shipping Industry: In the Seventeenth and Eighteenth Centuries* (Newton Abbot, England: David and Charles, 1962), 270–71.

38. November 7, 1634, GAR:ONA, 142: 46/78; November 21, 1634, GAA:NA 1225/ fol. 49v, not. Isaacz Henricxsen v. Gierteren; November 21, 1635, GAA:NA 671/355, not. J. Warnaertsz; December 12, 1635, GAA:NA 1043/p. 188, not. Joost van de Ven; October 21, 1644, GAA:NA 1861/462–3; *CSPC, 1574–1660*, 151. On the Dutch cruising trade, see Klooster, "Anglo-Dutch Trade in the Seventeenth Century: An Atlantic Partnership?" in *Shaping the Stuart World*, ed. Macinnes and Williamson, 267, 269–70. On delftware and England, see A. Moor, "The Evidence for Artistic Contact between Norfolk and the Netherlands 1500–1800," in *The North Sea and Culture (1550–1800): Proceedings of the International Conference Held at Leiden 21–22 April 1995*, ed. Juliette Roding and Lex Heerma van Voss (Hilversum, the Netherlands: Verloren, 1996), 362–68; De Vries and Van der Woude, *The First Modern Economy*, 303–9; and Michael Archer, *Delftware: The Tin-Glazed Earthenware of the British Isles: A Catalogue of the*

Collection in the Victoria and Albert Museum (London: Victoria and Albert Museum, 1997), 32–34.

39. May 21, 1635, *Winthrop's Journal, "History of New England," 1630–1649,* Original Narratives of Early American History, ed. James Kendall Hosmer (New York: Charles Scribner's Sons, 1906), 151; Klooster, "Anglo-Dutch Trade in the Seventeenth Century," in *Shaping the Stuart World,* ed. Macinnes and Williamson, 267 n. 23.

40. Dunn, *Sugar and Slaves,* 53–54.

41. November 8, 1636, GAA:NA 1045/359, not. J.v.d. Ven; March 25, 1637, GAA:NA 919/120; P. F. Campbell, "The Merchants and Traders of Barbados, Part 1," *JBMHS* 34 (1972): 85–86; Dunn, *Sugar and Slaves,* 52–53; Gragg, *Englishmen Transplanted,* 38–39, 91–98.

42. Andrews, *Ships, Money, and Politics,* 84–104.

43. *APCC,* 1:174–76, 176–77; Brenner, *Merchants and Revolution,* 129–34.

44. "Sir John Pennington's Journal," in "Lord Muncaster's MSS," *Historical Commission,* Tenth Report, pt. 4, 285–86.

45. The King to the feoffes of Jas. late Earl of Carlisle, April 1637, TNA:PRO CO 1/9, fol. 124r. Authorities faced a similar problem in Virginia: *APCC,* 1:187; H. Roper, "Charles I, Virginia, and the Idea of Atlantic History," *Itinerario* 30, no. 2 (2006): 36. French authorities, too, wrestled with the problem (see Stewart L. Mims, *Colbert's West India Policy* [New Haven: Yale University Press, 1912], 53–55).

46. Alfred Rive, "A Brief History of the Regulation and Taxation of Tobacco in England," *WMQ,* 2nd ser., 9 (1929); 1–12, 73–87; Michael J. Braddick, "The English Government, War, Trade, and Settlement, 1625–1688," in *The Origins of Empire,* ed. Canny, 290–95.

47. De Vries, *Voyages from Holland,* 30–57. There are several other descriptions of New Netherland, though few date from before 1633: Nicolaes Van Wassenaer, "The Historiisch Verhael," and "Letter of Isaack de Rasieres to Samuel Blommaert, 1628," both in *Narratives of New Netherland, 1609–1664,* ed. J. Franklin Jameson, vol. 19, *Original Narratives of Early American History* (New York, 1909), 88–89, 102–5.

48. Bachman, *Peltries or Plantations,* chaps. 5–6; Rink, *Holland on the Hudson,* chap. 4.

49. Bachman, *Peltries or Plantations,* chap. 7; Matson, *Merchants and Empire,* chap. 1; Rink, *Holland on the Hudson,* chap. 5; Ritchie, *The Duke's Province,* chaps. 1–2; Simon Middleton, *From Privileges to Rights: Work and Politics in Colonial New York City* (Philadelphia: University of Pennsylvania Press, 2006), 13–49. The most important general studies of New Amsterdam are Thomas J. Condon, *New York Beginnings: The Commercial Origins of New Netherland* (New York: New York University Press, 1968); Goodfriend, *Before the Melting Pot;* Jaap Jacobs, *New Netherland: A Dutch Colony in Seventeenth-Century America* (Boston: Brill, 2005). For work on upriver Dutch settlement, see Merwick, *Possessing Albany;* Janny Venema, *Beverwijck: A Dutch Village on the American Frontier, 1652–1664* (Albany: State University of New York Press, 2003). For the Dutch on the Delaware, see C. A. Weslager, *Dutch Explorers, Traders, and Settlers in the Delaware Valley, 1609–1644* (Philadelphia: University of Pennsylvania Press, 1961). Numbers of vessels from Henk Den Heijer, "The Dutch West India Company, 1621–1791," in *Riches from Atlantic Commerce,* 94.

50. "Proposed Articles for the Colonization and Trade of New Netherland," August 30, 1638, *DRCHNY* 1:112 (quotation); Condon, *New York Beginnings,* chaps. 4–6; Rink,

Holland on the Hudson, chaps. 3–5; Matson, *Merchants and Empire*, 13–25; Charlotte Wilcoxen, "Dutch Trade with New England," in *"A Beautiful and Fruitful Place": Selected Rensselaerswijk Seminar Papers,* ed. Nancy Anne McClure Zeller (Albany, N.Y.: New Netherland Publications, 1991), 235–41.

51. Isaack de Rasière to Bradford, March 9, 1627, quoted in *Bradford's History of Plymouth Plantation, 1606–1646, Original Narratives of Early American History,* ed. William T. Davis (New York: Scribner's Sons, 1920), 224–25, 234–35; Van Zandt, "Isaac Allerton and the Dynamics of English Cultural Anxiety in the *Gouden Eeuw,*" in *Connecting Cultures: The Netherlands in Five Centuries of Transatlantic Exchange,* ed. Rosemarijn Hoefte and Johanna C. Kardux (Amsterdam: VU University Press, 1994), 68–70; Wilcoxen, "Dutch Trade with New England," 236–37.

52. *Bradford's History of Plymouth Plantations,* ed. Davis, 226–27, 234–35.

53. Entry for August 2, 1634, in *Winthrop's Journal,* 76, 102, 109, 130–31 (quotation), 151, 152.

54. Lynn Ceci, "The First Fiscal Crisis in New York," *Economic Development and Cultural Change* 28 (1980): 839–44.

55. *Calendar* 5, 12, 15, 18, 46; Cynthia J. Van Zandt, "The Dutch Connection: Isaac Allerton and the Dynamics of English Cultural Anxiety in the *Gouden Eeuw,*" 52–55, 67–68, 76; Van Zandt, *Brothers among Nations,* 103–8, 215 n. 59.

56. *DRCHNY* 1:190–91.

57. De Vries, *Voyages from Holland,* 107–12; *Van Rensselaer-Bowier Manuscripts: Being the Letters of Kiliaen van Rensselaer, 1630–1643, and other Documents Relating to the Colony of Rensselaerswyck,* ed. A. J. F. van Laer (Albany: University of the State of New York, 1908), 557, 565; Records of the General Court of Virginia, MSS copy by Conway Robinson, Misc. MSS, Box 1, #11, NYHS; May 12, 1640, HHV GAA:NA 1525/pp. 251–52, not. Jan Volkaertsz. Oli. Among the most important of the Virginia factors were Arent and Dirck Corssen Stam, who were supercargoes for Van Rensselaer (December 28, 1639, HHV GAA NA 1499/pp. 179–80, not. Jan Volckaertsz. Oli; July 30, 1640, HHV GAA:NA 1555/pg. 113, not. Jan Volckaertsz. Oli; November 26, 1642, HHV GAA:NA 1501/p. 165, not. Jan Volkaertsz. Oli). See also John R. Pagan, "Dutch Maritime and Commercial Activity in Mid-Seventeenth-Century Virginia," *Virginia Magazine of History and Biography* 90 (1982): 486–87; Hatfield, *Atlantic Virginia,* 63–69; and Brenner, *Merchants and Revolution,* 129–34.

58. *DRCHNY* 1:259–61, 269, 271–318.

Notes to Chapter 2

1. Charles H. Wilson, *Profit and Power: A Study of England and the Dutch Wars* (New York: Longmans and Green, 1957), 49–77; Brenner, *Merchants and Revolution,* 628–32; Ormrod, *The Rise of Commercial Empires,* 33, 37; contrast with J. R. Jones, *The Anglo-Dutch Wars of the Seventeenth Century* (New York: Longman, 1996), 8–14.

2. The Dutch traders included Jacob Clause and "Messrs Van-gagell-dounce and Van-dekenderth of Amsterdam," in Montserrat, Garrett and Jacob Derrick (probably Derrickson) in Antigua, and Alex Jacobsen, Garratt Enes, and Anthony Cornelius in St. Christopher ("Mountserrat and Antigua accoumpts, 1654 to 1656," Egerton MSS. 2395, fols. 54–59, BL; "Nevis and St. Christopher's Accounts," Egerton MSS. 2395, fols. 69–77, BL). Unfortunately, the accounts for Nevis and St. Christopher do not name all those who did business with the Dutch. Of all these Dutch traders, the most is

known about Jacob Derrickson, who was also active in French St. Christopher and in Maryland's tobacco trade, supplying Dutch manufactured goods and buying tobacco (John Metcalf v. Jacob Dirrickson, April 22, 1652, in *Judicial and Testamentary Business of the Provincial Court, 1649/50–1657*, ed. William Hand Browne, vol. 10, *Archives of Maryland* [Baltimore: Historical Society of Maryland, 1891], 162). A Dutchman named Derrick Derrickson bought land in York County, Virginia, where he, too, was involved in tobacco production and distribution (Pagan, "Dutch Maritime and Commercial Activity," 487–88 n. 9). About these seizures, see Dunn, *Sugar and Slaves*, 122–23; and Pulsipher, "The Cultural Landscape of Montserrat, West Indies, in the Seventeenth Century," 36–44. Dutch merchants also lived in French St. Christopher (Charles de Rochefort, *The history of the Caribby-Islands. . . .*, trans. John Davies [London, 1666], 23).

3. Menard, "Plantation Empire," 317–21; Robert Carlyle Batie, "Why Sugar? Economic Cycles and the Changing of Staples on the English and French Antilles," *Journal of Caribbean History* 8 (1976): 3–4, 6–10, 16–17, 31–32 n. 8; Gragg, *Englishmen Transplanted*, 92; Innes, "The Pre-Sugar Era of European Settlement in Barbados," 17; Price, "The Economic Growth of the Chesapeake," 497–99. While there are no tobacco price series for Amsterdam until 1674, because of the reexport market they most likely mirrored London's (Nicholaas W. Posthumas, *Inquiry into the History of Prices in Holland*, vol 1. [Leiden: E. J. Brill, 1946], 85–86).

4. With no price series for the English Caribbean, we must use the farm price (the price planters received at their plantations) series that Russell Menard constructed for the Chesapeake. Since these prices are not always comparable, they should be used only to grasp price trends rather than for specific prices (Russell R. Menard, "A Note on Chesapeake Tobacco Prices, 1618–1660," *Virginia Magazine of History and Biography* 84 [1976]: 402–8; Paul G. E. Clemens, *The Atlantic Economy and Colonial Maryland's Eastern Shore: From Tobacco to Grain* [Ithaca, N.Y.: Cornell University Press, 1980], 33; Menard, *Sweet Negotiations*, 19–23). Richard Ligon claimed that Barbados tobacco was "so earthy and worthless, as it could give them little or no return from *England*, or else-where; so that for a while they lingered on in a lamentable condition." *A True & Exact History of the Island of Barbados. . . .*, 2nd ed. (London, 1673), 24; J. H. Bennett, "The English Caribbees in the Period of the Civil War, 1642–1646," *WMQ*, 3rd ser., 24 (1967): 359–66; Dunn, *Sugar and Slaves*, 120; Sheridan, *Sugar and Slavery*, 152.

5. *Caribbeana: Being Miscellaneous Papers Relating to the History, Genealogy, Topography, and Antiquities of the British West Indies*, ed. Vere Langford Oliver (London, 1909–19), 3:197–200.

6. HCA 24/100, no. 214, TNA:PRO, quoted in John C. Appleby, "English Settlement during War and Peace, 1603–1660," in *The Lesser Antilles*, ed. Engerman and Paquette, 95. On the effects of the Civil War on Atlantic shipping and trade, see Brenner, *Merchants and Revolution*, 581, 585–87; and Gragg, *Englishmen Transplanted*, 42–48. For the Civil War in the colonies, see Pestana, *The English Atlantic in the Age of Revolution*.

7. Verbrugge and Son to Loockermans, December 17, 1649, Misc. MSS, Stuyvesant Family, NYHS; Matson, *Merchants and Empire*, 337 n. 9; David M. Riker, "Govert Loockermans: Free Merchant of New Amsterdam," *de Halve Maen* 54 (1981): 4–10; Oliver Rink, *Holland on the Hudson*, 177–80. For Stuyvesant, see "Extract of a counter protest of Vice-Director van Dincklage against the Director and Council," February 28, 1651, *DRCHNY* 1:455–56 (quotations); see also *Correspondence, 1647–1653*, 63, 67, 123.

8. "Letters of Samuel Winthrop," *Collections of the Massachusetts Historical Society*, 5th ser., 8 (1882): 234–65; Bridenbaugh and Bridenbaugh, *No Peace beyond the Line*, 67–68.

9. Though becoming less common, the cruising trade nevertheless persisted. See November 18, 1645, GAR:ONA, 153: 323/459, not. Adriaan Kieboom; January 31, 1648, GAR:ONA, 96: 144/232, not. Jan van Aller Az.; July 20, 1649, GAR:ONA, 172: 5/07, not. Nicolaas Vogel Adriaansz; Oliver, ed. *Caribbeana*, 2:9. See also Klooster "Anglo-Dutch Trade in the Seventeenth Century," 267–68.

10. Bridenbaugh and Bridenbaugh, *No Peace beyond the Line*, 65–68. For similar behavior in Virginia, see Hatfield, *Atlantic Virginia*, 97–100; and Pagan, "Dutch Maritime and Commercial Activity in Mid-Seventeenth-Century Virginia," 488–90.

11. Johnson to Trustees, March 10, 1642, Hay MSS, BL, cited in Bennet, "The English Caribbees in the Period of the Civil War," 364–65; May 12, 1677, Christopher Jeaffreson to Colonel George Gamiell, *Young Squire*, 1:214–17; Pulsipher, "The Cultural Landscape of Montserrat," 38–43; Sheridan, *Sugar and Slavery*, 269–74.

12. Deposition of Richard Waad, May 1, 1654, in Aubrey Gwynn, ed., "Documents Relating to the Irish in the West Indies," *Analecta Hibernica* 4 (1932): 226; October 6, 1649, GAR:ONA, 96: 201/325, not. Jan van Aller Az.

13. For the practice in the eighteenth-century Chesapeake, see Price, "The Economic Growth of the Chesapeake," 509.

14. "Tobaccoes entred in the porte of London in Fower yeeres from Lady day 1637," Add. Mss. 35865, fol. 248-8v, BL. For anecdotal evidence supporting this, see "A Proposition that Shipps may bee Sett-out," ca. 1650, Egerton Mss. 2395, fol. 105r, BL.

15. Ligon, *A True & Exact History*, 22; Menard, *Sweet Negotiations*, chap. 1; Gragg, *Englishmen Transplanted*, 92–93; Innes, "The Pre-Sugar Era of European Settlement in Barbados," 18–20.

16. Colt, "The Voyage of Sir Henrye Colt," in *Colonising Expeditions*, ed. Harlow, 69; Starkey, *The Economic Geography of Barbados*, 55; Gragg, *Englishmen Transplanted*, 94–97.

17. Nicholas Foster, *A Brief Relation of the Late Horrid Rebellion Acted in he Island Barbadas, In the West-Indies* (London, 1650), 2 (quotation); "Thomas Verney's Account of Barbadoes. Addressed to his father Edmund," February 10, 1638; Sir Edmund Verney to Thomas Verney, 1639, in *Letters and Papers of the Verney Family Down to the End of the Year 1639*, ed. John Bruce (London, 1852), 192, 266–67. On cotton production and textile diversification in England, see Lewes Roberts, *The Treasure of Trafficke* (London 1641); Wilson, *England's Apprenticeship*, 192–95; and Wrightson, *Earthly Necessities*, 237–39.

18. Pares, *Merchants and Planters*, 75 n. 30.

19. March 21, 1646, GAA:NA 1646a/77, not. J. van der Hoeven.

20. Ligon, *True & Exact History*, 40.

21. March 25, 1646, GAA:NA 849/98, not. Joseph Steyns; Menard, *Sweet Negotiations*, 24–25.

22. Ligon, *A True & Exact History*, 30, 37; "A Letter from Barbados by ye way of Holland Concerning ye condition of Honest Men There," August 9, 1651, in *The English Civil War in Barbados, 1650–1652: Eyewitness Accounts*, ed. Edward Hutson (Barbados: Barbados National Trust, 2001), 71–72. It is most likely that the author of this letter was Giles Sylvester (December 1646, GAA:NA 1846/fol. 48, not. Nicolaes Kruys; July 7, 1651, GAA:NA 1097/288, not. J.v.d. Ven; "The State of ye Differences as

it is presssed between ye Merchants and ye Planters in relations to free Trade att ye Charibee Islands," ca. 1655–58, Add. Mss. 11411, original fols. 3r–4v [LOC: BL Trans., pp. 7–8], LOC). See also "An Account of the English Sugar Plantations," ca. time of Charles II, Egerton MSS 2395, fols. 629–35, BL; Bennett, "The English Caribbees in the Period of the Civil War," 362–64; and Harlow, *History of Barbados*, 93–94.

23. On Dutch Brazil, see Israel, *Dutch Primacy in World Trade*, 167–69; and Schwartz, "A Commonwealth within Itself," in *Tropical Babylons*, 166–72. For sugar and tobacco prices, see Batie, "Why Sugar?" 2–16; and Noel Deerr, *The History of Sugar*, 2 vols. (London: Chapman and Hall, 1949–50), 2:528–32.

24. Menard, *Sweet Negotiations*, chaps. 1–3; Pares, *Merchants and Planters*, passim; B. W. Higman, "The Sugar Revolution," *Economic History Review*, 2nd ser., 53 (2000): 213–36; Gragg, *Englishmen Transplanted*, 99–100, 141. On London merchants' increased investment in Barbados, see Brenner, *Merchants and Revolution*, 162–66; S. D. Smith, *Slavery, Family, and Gentry Capitalism in the British Atlantic: The World of the Lascellas, 1648–1834* (Cambridge: Cambridge University Press, 2006), 23, 43–44. From the Dutch perspective, see Klooster, "Anglo-Dutch Trade in the Seventeenth Century," in *Riches from Atlantic Commerce*, 271–74; P. C. Emmer, "Jesus Was Good, but Trade Was Better": An Overview of the Transit Trade of the Dutch Antilles, 1634–1795," in *The Lesser Antilles*, ed. Engerman and Paquette, esp. 209–12; and Matthew Edel, "The Brazilian Sugar Cycle of the Seventeenth Century and the Rise of West Indian Competition," *Caribbean Studies* 9 (1969): 35–41.

25. December 12, 1643, GAA:NA 1570/439, not. Pieter Capoen; April 4, 1647, GAA:NA 849/110, not. Joseph Steijns; August 7, 1651, GAA:NA 1819/681, not. Albert Eggericx; September 20, 1651, GAA:NA 1098/8v, 85, not. J.v.d. Ven; December 28, 1644, GAR, ONA, 86: 336/637, not. Jan van Aller Az; March 12, 1646, GAR:ONA 334: 38/97, not. Arent van der Graeff; May 2, 1646, GAR:ONA 334: 135/341, not. Arent van der Graeff; Will of John Arnett, June 4, 1659, in *Barbados Records, Wills and Administrations, 1639–1680*, ed. Joanne Mcree Sanders (Marceline, Mo.: Sanders Historical Publications, 1979), 8; March 17, 1646, GAR:ONA 334: 46/114, not. Arent van der Graeff; January 16, 1644, GAR:ONA 248: 103/198, not. Jacob Duyfhuysen; October 16, 1647, GAA:NA 1082/235v–36v. Compare with Claudia Schnurmann, "Atlantic Trade and American Identities," in *The Atlantic Economy during the Seventeenth and Eighteenth Centuries*, ed. Coclanis, 186–204.

26. Well-connected London merchants such as Maurice Thomson invested in St. Christopher, but in general Barbadians attracted more capital (Appleby, "English Settlement during War and Peace, 1600–1660," 96, 98; Bridenbaugh and Bridenbaugh, *No Peace beyond the Line*, 32, 34; Menard, *Sweet Negotiations*, 52–60). On Dutch capital, see Klooster, "Anglo-Dutch Trade in the Seventeenth Century," 272; and Emmer, "Jesus Christ Was Good," 212.

27. Estimate primarily drawn from GAA:NA and GAR:OND; British state paper series CO, HCA and T at TNA:PRO; *CSPC*; and all other sources used in this work. For turnaround times, see March 25, 1646, GAA:NA 849/99, not. Joseph Steijns.

28. For slave statistics, see TASTD, http://slavevoyages.org/tast/database/search. faces?yearFrom=1600&yearTo=1688&mjslptimp=34200; http://slavevoyages.org/tast/assessment/estimates.faces?yearFrom=1600&yearTo=1688&disembarkation=302. Compare with William A. Green, "Supply versus Demand in the Barbadian Sugar Revolution," *Journal of Interdisciplinary History* 18 (1988): 403–18.

29. For the *Casteel van Sluys,* see December 28, 1644, GAR, ONA 86: 336/637, not. Jan van Aller Az. A musketoon is a short musket with a large bore. The WIC's *Princess* was also at Barbados in 1646 (*Correspondence, 1647–1653,* 63, 123).

30. There is a large literature on the policies of the Interregnum related to foreign affairs and colonization. Most useful for this study were Pestana, *The English Atlantic in an Age of Revolution,* esp. chaps. 2–3; Brenner, *Merchants and Revolution,* esp. chap. 12; Barry Coward, *The Cromwellian Protectorate* (Manchester: Manchester University Press, 2002); Steven C. A. Pincus, *Protestantism and Patriotism: Ideologies and the Making of English Foreign Policy, 1650–1668* (Cambridge: Cambridge University Press, 1996); Ormrod, *The Rise of Commercial Empires,* 33–43, and, though overly Anglo-centric, Timothy Venning, *Cromwellian Foreign Policy* (New York: St. Martin's, 1995), esp. chaps. 1, 5, 11. The classic account of the Civil War in Barbados is N. Darnell Davis, *Cavaliers and Roundheads, 1650–2* (George Town, British Guiana: Argosy Press, 1887).

31. For this paragraph and the next, see Lawrence A. Harper, *The English Navigation Laws: A Seventeenth-Century Experiment in Social Engineering* (1939; repr., New York: Octagon Books 1964), 39–49; Charles Wilson, *Profit and Power,* 48–77; Sheridan, *Sugar and Slavery,* 39–44; Brenner, *Merchants and Revolution,* 592–97, 625–32; McCusker and Menard, *The Economy of British America,* 46–50; Michael J. Braddick, "The English Government, War, Trade, and Settlement, 1625–1688," in *The Origins of Empire,* ed. Nicolas Canny, 292–96; and Daniel A. Baugh, "Maritime Strength and Atlantic Commerce: The Uses of 'a Grand Marine Empire,'" in *An Imperial State at War,* ed. Stone, 185–223.

32. John Paige to Gowen Paynter and William Clerke, March 13, 1652, in *The Letters of John Paige, London Merchant, 1648–1658,* ed. George F. Steckley, vol. 21 (London: London Record Society, 1984), #58a, 67; "Mich Pack to Right Honourble ye Lord president of ye right Honourable Counsell of States," February 18, 1651/2, CO 1/11. fol. 121r, TNA:PRO; The Board of Admiralty in Zeeland to the States-General, February 4/14, 1652, in *Letters and Papers Relating to the First Dutch War, 1652–1654,* ed. Samuel Rawson Gardiner (London: Navy Record Society, 1899–1930), 1:75–77; *Correspondence, 1647–1653,* 146. Some Dutch vessels received permission to trade in Barbados in 1651 (*Calendar of State Papers, Domestic Series, 1651* ed. Mary Anne Everett Green [London: Her Majesty's Printing Office, 1877], 53; *Mercurius Politicius* [May 8–15, 1651], 49:794).

33. Estimate primarily drawn from GAA:NA and GAR:OND; British state paper series CO, HCA and T at TNA:PRO; *CSPC*; and all other sources used in this work.

34. This account is based on letters from John Paige to William Clerke between September 20, 1650, and September 28, 1651 (*Letters of John Paige,* ed. Steckley, 26–54 [quotations 26–7, 47]). The *Meda* was also accompanied by another unnamed vessel.

35. Gov. Searle to Council of State, June 3, 1652, CO 1/11, fol. 139v (first quotation), TNA:PRO; "Letter from Barbados to ye Commissioners of ye Admiralty of ye Commonwealth of England, Endorsed: Thomas Modyford, John Roberts, Ri. Saundards, and John Yeamans," August 9, 1655, Add. Mss, 18986, fols. 205–6 (second quotation), BL; October 7, 1652, *Acts and Statutes of the island of Barbados. . . .* (London, 1654), 30. Searle was not always consistent in his laxity. Sometimes he seized Dutch vessels such as the "[t]hree Hollanders, merchant ships . . . [and] the *Mary,* of Amsterdam,

laden with French wine and brandy," trying to trade at Barbados in 1652 (Gov. Searle to Council of State, June 3, 1652, *CSPC, 1574–1660,* 380).

36. *The Narrative of General Venables: With an Appendix of Papers Relating to the Expedition to the West Indies and the Conquest of Jamaica, 1654–1655,* ed. C. H. Firth (New York: Longmans, Green,, 1900), 8 (quotation), 10. Other accounts of the incident include I. S., *A brief and perfect Journal of the late Proceedings and Successe of the English Army in the West-Indies* (London, 1655), 9–10; "Henry Whistler's Journal: Admiral Penn's Voyage to the West Indies," Sloane MSS 3926, fols. 7–8, BL; John F. Battick, ed., "Richard Rooth's Seas Journal of the Western Design, 1654–1655," *Jamaica Journal* 5 (1971): 3–22; Admiral Penn to Privy Council, September 12, 1655, *TSP* 4:28–30; Captain George Butler to the Protector, February 7, 1654[5], *TSP* 1:142; and February 17, 1654[/5], Mr. J. Berkenhead to Thurloe, *TSP*, 3:157–59. An unnamed correspondent's version appeared in two weekly London papers: *A perfect diurnall of some passages and proceedings of, and in relation to, the armies in England and Ireland* 283 (May 7–May 14, 1655): 4344–45; *The weekly intelligencer of the Common-wealth* 93 (May 8–May 15, 1655): 2–3.

37. For the records of the seizures, see CO 1/66, fols. 21r-51v, TNA:PRO; for depositions by crews, see CO 1/66, fols. 64r-82v, TNA:PRO; for the valuations, see CO 1/66, f. 83r, TNA:PRO. See also Captain Gregory Butler to the Protector (1655), *TSP* 3:754–55.

38. Examination of Garret Johnson, February 13, 1655, CO 1/66, fol. 23r, TNA:PRO.

39. The vessel carrying slaves was the *Peace* (or *Vrede*) (Examination of Herman Barrentson, February 1655, CO 1/66, fol. 33, TNA:PRO).

40. Examinations of Jacob Hendrickson, master of the *Brownfish*; John Buys, "sterman"; and Lawrence Johnson, boatswain, February 13, 1655, CO 1/66, fols. 21r- 22v, TNA:PRO.

41. "Henry Whistler's Journal," Sloane MSS, 3926, fol. 10, BL; "Petition of Anthony Rouse to Council of State," November 18, 1656, in "Documents and Letters in the Brotherton Collection Relating to Barbados," *JBHMS* 24 (1956/7): 185 (quotations); Ligon, *True & Exact History,* 56, 87; *CSPC, 1574–1660,* 343; Dunn, *Sugar and Slaves,* 96, 192–93; Bridenbaugh and Bridenbaugh, *No Peace beyond the Line,* 97. On New England, see James E. McWilliams, "New England's First Depression: Beyond an Export-Led Interpretation," *Journal of Interdisciplinary History* 33 (2002): 5–6.

42. Examinations of Jacob Hendrickson, master of the *Brownfish*; John Buys, "sterman"; and Lawrence Johnson, boatswain, February 13, 1655, CO 1/66, fols., 21–2, TNA:PRO; Examination of Joris Petersen of Horne, June 9, 1655, HCA 13/70, fol. 372, TNA:PRO.

43. The vessels were the *Young Elizabeth, King David* of Amsterdam, *Armes of Farnamburke,* and *King David* of Rotterdam (Examinations of Hans Gotchy, Nicholas Florinson, Dow Dirickson, February 23, 25, 1655, CO 1/66, fols. 41r, 47r, 43r, 25r, TNA:PRO; Deposition of Cornelius Abrahamson, June 7, 1655, HCA 13/70, fols. 370v-371r, TNA:PRO).

44. Examination of Symon Peterson, February 14, 1655, CO 1/66, fol. 29r, TNA:PRO; Deposition of Tousine Le Sage, February 17, 1655, CO 1/66, fol. 35, TNA:PRO.

45. Jacob Hendrickson reported that he had received payment for the *Brownfish*'s European cargo part in "300 gild [guilders] . . . [a]nd part in Sugar which is yet ashore . . . except 4000 lbs weight which hee sent [to the Netherlands] in a Flemish ship," and was also scheduled to load "sugar [as] the price of his said [twenty-four]

horses [from Curaçao] (being about 40000 lbs weight)." He intended to convey both cargoes to Holland before Penn's fleet arrived (Examinations of Jacob Hendrickson; John Buys, "sterman"; and Lawrence Johnson, boatswain, February 3, 1655, CO 1/66, fols. 21r–22r, TNA:PRO). Likewise, the masters of the *King David* of Rotterdam, the *King David* of Amsterdam, the *Hare*, the *Armes of France*, and the *Strong Rowland* were to load unspecified quantities of sugar, or in the case of the *Hare*, "one Caske of Sugar [and] 45 Rolls of tobacco"), for the Netherlands (CO 1/66, fols. 25, 37r, 39r, 45r, 47r, TNA:PRO; Depositions of Derrick Cornelisson, June 9, 1655, HCA 13/70 fol. 409, TNA:PRO). A French ship, arriving in the spring of 1654, also evidently carried away a full load of sugar in return for its lading of brandy (Jerome S. Handler, ed., "Father Antione Biet's Visit to Barbados in 1654," *JBMHS* 32 [1965–66]: 63). Compare to Schnurmann, "Atlantic Trade and American Identities," in *The Atlantic Economy during the Seventeenth and Eighteenth Centuries*, ed. Coclanis, 189.

46. Export estimates from John J. McCusker, *Rum and the American Revolution: The Rum Trade and the Balance of Payments of the Thirteen Continental Colonies* (New York: Garland, 1989), 199, 208–9, 215.

47. Those traveling from the Netherlands to Martinique to Barbados were the *French Arms, Strong Rowland*, and *King David* of Rotterdam. Only the *French Arms* sold cargo there (CO 1/66, fols. 37r, 39r, 45r, TNA:PRO; Deposition of Derrick Cornelisson, June 9, 1655, HCA 13/70, fol. 409, TNA:PRO). The *Armes of Farnamburke* cleared Texel on the January 15, 1654, and delivered a portion of its cargo at both Guadeloupe and St. Christopher (Deposition of Dow Dirickson, February 25, 1655/6, CO 1/66, fol. 43r, TNA:PRO).

48. The vessels that shared this direct route were the *Greenfoot, Hare, Black Lyon, King David* of Amsterdam, and *Love* (CO 1/66, fols. 23r, 25, 35, 47, TNA:PRO). For the *Love*, see *CSPC, 1574–1660*, 437; and *CSPC, 1675–76, Add., 1574–1674*, 517. Additionally, the Danish *Golden Star* traveled directly from Copenhagen to Barbados (Examination of Bartlett Fock, February 14, 1655, CO 1/66, fol. 26, TNA:PRO). Richard Rooth's account claims that *King David* of Amsterdam had come from Curaçao (Battick, ed., "Richard Rooth's Sea Journal," 6).

49. Examination of Symon Peterson, February 14, 1655, CO 1/66, fol. 29r, TNA:PRO.

50. Examination of Albert Albertson, March 3, 1655, CO 1/66, fol. 49 (quotation), TNA:PRO.

51. Examination of Garret Johnson, skipper of the *Greenfoot*, February 13, 1655, CO 1/66, fol. 23r (quotation), TNA:PRO. For the other vessels, respectively, see CO 1/66 fols. 32, 35, 45r, 47r, TNA:PRO; and for the *Peace,* Deposition of Garret Gillison, June 9, 1655, HCA 13/70, fol. 410v, TNA:PRO. Henry Cornelison, master of the 40-ton *Hare*, was sent to Barbados, but did have the option of going to "Matincico, St. Christopher, & Eustatius, or other of ye Leeward Islands" if there was a better market there (Deposition of Henry Cornelison, February 14, 1655, CO 1/66, fol. 25, TNA:PRO).

52. Examination of Herman Barrentson, February 1655, CO 1/66, fol. 33, TNA:PRO.

53. Examination of John Leonards, February 25, 1655, CO 1/66, fol. 45r, TNA:PRO; Deposition of Cornelius Abrahamson of Flushing, June 7, 1655, HCA 13/70, fols. 370v–371r, TNA:PRO; Deposition of Albert Albertson, March 3, 1655, CO 1/66, fol. 49, TNA:PRO.

54. Examination of John Peterson, February 19, 1655, CO 1/66, fol. 37r, TNA:PRO.

55. "Sir Edward Turner reports from the Committee to whom the Bill for

Naturalizing is referred, Amendments to the said Bill: Which were, upon the Question, agreed unto," August 24, 1660, "House of Commons Journal Volume 8: 24 August 1660," Journal of the House of Commons: volume 8: 1660–1667 (1802), pp. 133–35, www.british-history.ac.uk/report.asp?compid=26275&strquery=Vane. On his trade, see January 1, 1640, GAR:ONA 169: 65/102, not. Nocolaas Vogel Adriaansz.; December 13, 1640, GAR: OND 262: 330/534, not., Arnout Hofflant; January 31, 1641, GAR:ONA 95: 62/98, not. Jan va Aller Az. Giles Silvester died in Amsterdam in 1652, and his "widow and heirs" applied to the Commonwealth government for permission "that they not be looked upon as Dutch but as English" (November 19, 1652, *CSPC, 1574–1660*, 393).

56. March 15, 1641, GAA:NA 489/98, not. Evert Cocq.; April 9 1643, and August 31, 1643, GAA:NA 1570/120 and 292, not. Pieter Capoen. Giles Silvester later sued Constant because he did not follow his father's wishes and seems to have taken the plantation for himself (August 22, 1647, GAA:NA 849/123, not. Joseph Steijns). Ligon mentions Constant's presence in Barbados as a sugar planter (Ligon, *True & Exact History*, 45). Constant's Silvester's will, dated April 7, 1671, is abstracted in *Barbados Records, Wills and Administrations, 1639–1680*, ed. Sanders, 324. See also *CSPC, 1675–76, Add., 1574–1674*, 139. Silvester has been a confusing figure for historians because of his mixed English and Dutch connections (see Dunn, *Sugar and Slaves*, 78; Henry B. Hoff, "The Sylvester Family of Shelter Island," *New York Genealogical and Biographical Record* 125 [1994]: 13–18, 88–93; and Frederick H. Smith, "Disturbing the Peace in Barbados: Constant Silvester of Constant Plantation in the Seventeenth Century," *JBMHS* 44 [1998]: 40).

57. "A Letter from Barbados by ye way of Holland Concerning ye condition of Honest Men There," August 9, 1651, in *The English Civil War in Barbados*, ed. Hutson, 72. With a bottomary loan, the merchant used his vessel, or its bottom, as the collateral to borrow capital to fund a venture (Rink, *Holland on the Hudson*, 265).

58. Smith, "Disturbing the Peace in Barbados," 42.

59. Richard Vines to John Winthrop, April 29, 1648, *The Winthrop Papers, 1498–1654*, ed. Worthington C. Ford et al. (Boston: Massachusetts Historical Society, 1929–92), 5:219–20. Estimate of 100 traders in Pedro L.V. Welch, *Slave Society in the City, Bridgetown, Barbados 1680–1834* (Kingston: Ian Randle, 2003), 72.

60. Barbados Council Minutes, Lucas Transcripts, November 8, 1654, quoted in Pestana, *The English Atlantic*, 129. On Van de Loo, see July 7, 1651, GAA:NA 1097/288, not. J.v.d. Ven. For other Dutchmen living in Barbados temporarily, see December 22, 1644, GAA:NA 1920/121, not. Joris de Wijee; June 7, 1645, GAA:NA 1077, fol. 13v, not. J.v.d. Ven; October 25, 1647, GAA:NA 1574/p. 633, not. Pieter Capoen; and October 25, 1649, GAA:NA 1092/69v, not. J.v.d. Ven.

61. Examination of Hans Gotchy, February 23, 1655, CO 1/66, fol. 41r, TNA:PRO.

62. McCusker and Menard, "The Sugar Industry in the Seventeenth Century," 316–17 n. 20; Israel, *Empires and Entrepots: The Dutch, The Spanish Monarchy and the Jews, 1585–1713* (London: Hambledon Press, 1990), 436–37.

63. Alexander Gunkel and Jerome S. Handler, eds., "A German Indentured Servant in Barbados in 1652: The Account of Heinrich Von Ucheritz," *JBMHS* 33 (1970): 94–95.

64. Petition of Frederick Osten, shipmaster of Hoorn in Holland to Lord Protector, CO 1/32, fol. 147, TNA:PRO. Giles Silvester provides further evidence of Osten's presence in Barbados, commenting to his father in August 1651 that he had sent letters

"by Symon Allirsen, Jan Clinten & Frederick Asten" ("A Letter from Barbados by ye way of Holland Concerning ye condition of Honest Men There," August 9, 1651, in *The English Civil War in Barbados*, ed. Hutson, 69).

65. November 11, 1647, GAA:NA 1574/p. 643, not. Pieter Capoen; Examinations of Thomas Barrett, James Mountjoy, Mathew Benham, Richard Galey, Richard Stockdale, Nicholas Salmon, George Lyne, and Peter Janson before the Provincial Court of Maryland, May 31, June 1, June 2, June 3, 1659, *Proceedings of the Provincial Court, 1658–1662*, ed. Bernard Christian Steiner, vol. 41 of *Archives of Maryland* (Baltimore: Maryland Historical Society, 1922), 306–10.

66. April 2, 1647, GAA:NA 849/116, not. Joseph Steijns; "List of the Names of the Inhabitants of Barbados, in the Year 1638 who then possess'd more than ten Acres of Land," in P. F. Campbell, *Some Early Barbados History* (St. Michael, Barbados: Caribbean Graphics and Letchworth, 1993), 232–38. In 1651, the planter Thomas Blundell died while in Amsterdam (January 31, 1651 GAA:NA 849/191, not. Joseph Steijns).

67. Mr. Ed. Winslow to Secretary Thurloe, March 16, 1654[5], *TSP*, 3:249–51 (first quotation). For "great extortioners," see Captain George Butler to the Protector, February 7, 1654[5], *TSP*, 1:142. An unknown member of the Commonwealth's fleet whose description of these events appeared in an English weekly paper shared Winslow's view of the locals' preference for Dutch trade, commenting that colonists "love to trade with the Dutch" (*A perfect diurnall of some passages and proceedings of, and in relation to, the armies in England and Ireland*, May 7–May 14, 1655, 283, 434–35). On the trial in general, see Harlow, *History of Barbados,* 85–87. For the continued pattern of Barbadians questioning and defying the legality and authority of the Commissioners of the Admiralty in Barbados, see "Letter from Barbados to ye Commissioners of ye Admiralty of ye Commonwealth of England, Endorsed: Thomas Modyford, John Roberts, Ri. Saundards, and John Yeamans," August 9, 1655, Add Mss, 18986, fols. 205–6, BL; "The State of ye Differences as it is presssed between ye Merchants and ye Planters in relations to free Trade att ye Charibee Islands," ca. 1655–58, Add. Mss. 11411, original fol. 5, (LOC: BL Trans., pp. 8–10), LOC. On legal confusion about which courts—common law or Admiralty—had authority over prosecuting violations of the Navigation Acts, see Helen J. Crump, *Colonial Admiralty Jurisdiction in the Seventeenth Century* (New York: Longmans, Green, 1931), 52–54; Joanne Mathiesen, "Some Problems of Admiralty Jurisdiction in the 17th Century," *American Journal of Legal History* 2 (1958): esp. 219–22; David R. Owen and Michael C. Tolley, *Courts of Admiralty in Colonial America: The Maryland Experience, 1634–1776* (Durham, N.C.: Carolina Academic Press, 1995), 27–28, 105–8, 117; Benton, "Legal Space of Empire," 717–18. A contemporary view is *Plantation Justice. . . .* (London, 1701), esp. 7–9.

68. Colonel Kaynell to the Committee for Trade and Navigation, April 1656, CO 1/12, fols. 152v–53r (quotations), TNA:PRO; The Committee of Trade & Navigation, May 2, 1656, CO 1/12 fols. 154v–55r, 156v, TNA:PRO; "Petition of merchants, planters and others concerned in the good government of St. Christopher's to the Council of State," January 25, 1659, CO 1/15, fol. 151r, TNA:PRO; *CSPC, 1575–1660*, 440.

69. "Petition of certain Dutch merchants to the States General," November 1651, *DRCHNY* 1:436–37.

70. "William Nieuport to the Gressier Ruysch," 1655, *TSP*, 3:749–50; *DRCHNY* 1: 437. These efforts had begun in June 1651. "Draft Treaty Between the United Provinces and England proposed by the Commissioners of the State-General," June 14, 1651,

MS. Dep. C. 171, fol. 234v, Bodleian Library, Oxford, reproduced in Virginia Colonial Records Project, Survey Report no. (x) 167, JDRL, microfilm.

71. Edward Winslow to Secretary Thurloe, March 17, 1654/5, *TSP*, 3:251. On the *Peerboom*, see July 30, 1655, GAA:NA 2199/fols. 124–25, not. Adr. Lock; September 20, 1655, GAA:NA 2116/382, not. Joacjim Thielman; April 27, 1657, GAA:NA 1899/205, not. F. Uyttenbogaert. For a slightly different interpretation, see Charles T. Gehring, "Introduction," in *Correspondence, 1654–1658*, xv; Harlow, *History of Barbados*, 88–89. It appears that these three vessels were not part of the group that was seized by Penn and Venables as many scholars have assumed. Stuyvesant's fleet was allowed to leave the island on April 15 with their cargoes intact (*TSP*, 1:142). Whether this eight made up a portion of the sixteen valued beginning the next day is unclear, but it is certain that Stuyvesant's vessel, *De Peerboom*, was not one of those seized and brought to trial (see CO 1/66, fol. 83r, TNA:PRO; *CSPC, 1685–8*, 627–29). For the documents relating to Stuyvesant's arrival from the Dutch perspective, see *Correspondence, 1654–1658*, 53, 71, 75. Stuyvesant had sent vessels from New Netherland to Barbados before (*NYH-MDPD*, 29–30).

72. On Dutch efforts to secure free trade with Virginia, see below. During the same years, English colonists at St. Christopher also made a free trade agreement with Swedish mariners calling there and bound for the Swedish settlement in what today is Delaware (Gov. Johan Risingh, *Journal, 1654–1655*, in *The Rise and Fall of New Sweden: Governor Johan Risingh's Journal, 1654–1655 In Its Historical Context*, ed. Stellan Dahlgren and Hans Norman, trans. Marie Clark Nelson [Uppsala: Almquist and Wiksell, 1988], 143–45; Pesanta, *The English Atlantic in an Age of Revolution*, 173–74).

73. On the half-century ties between the House of Orange and the Stuarts, see Jardine, *Going Dutch*, 53–80.

74. "Articles agreed on the 11th day of January 1651 by and between the Lord Willoughby of Parham on the one part, and Sr. George Ayscue, Knt. Daniell Sealre Esqu^r, and Capt Michaell Packe on the other parte for the rendicon of the Island of Barbados &c," January 11, 1652, Add MSS. 11411, orig. fols. 95r–97r (LOC: BL Trans., pp. 291–98, quotation 293), LOC.

75. "Extraordinary session held in the residence of the honorable vice-director M. Beck," February 21, 1656, *Curaçao Papers*, 87–88. On the Jewish community of Curaçao, see Herbert B. Cone, "The Jews in Curaçao," *Publications of the American Jewish Historical Society* 10 (1902): 141–57; and Isaac S. and Suzanne A. Emmanuel, *History of the Jews of the Netherlands Antilles*, 2 vols. (Cincinnati: American Jewish Archives, 1970), 1:68.

76. *Curaçao Papers*, 91.

77. It is unlikely that Stuyvesant made the precise arrangements since Beck was surprised by the *Constant Anna*'s arrival, meaning Stuyvesant probably did not know of the trip. Beck almost refused De Fonseca's offer (*Curaçao Papers*, 91). Nonetheless, it is possible Stuyvesant had planted the seed for such an arrangement in conversations with Searle as he had already tried to do in Virginia and Maryland (see Hatfield, *Atlantic Virginia*, 49–50, and below).

78. Yosef Hayim Yerushalmi makes a similar argument about Jewish merchants acting as intermediaries between Christian and Muslim traders in the fifteenth and sixteenth centuries (Yerushalmi, "Between Amsterdam and New Amsterdam: The Place of Curaçao and the Caribbean in Early Modern Jewish History," *American*

Jewish Historical Quarterly 72 [1982/3]: 181–82). See also Holly Snyder, "A Sense of Place: Jews, Identity and Social Status in Colonial British America" (Ph.D. diss., Brandeis University, 2000). For "Hebrew nation," see "An [Barbados] act appointing how the Testimony of People of the Hebrew Nation, shall be admitted in all courts and causes," February 19, 1674, in N. Darnell Davis, "Notes on the History of the Jews in Barbados," *Publications of the American Jewish Historical Society* 18 (1909): 133. On De Fonseca's ties to Amsterdam, see July 8, 1664, GAA:NA 3684/617, not. Fr. Tixerandet.

79. Jonathan I. Israel, "Menasseh ben Israel and the Dutch Sephardic Colonization Movement of the Mid-Seventeenth Century (1645–1657)," in *Menasseh Ben Israel and His World*, ed. Yosef Kaplan, Henry Méchoulan and Richard H. Popkin (New York: Brill, 1989), 150; September 13, 1657 HHV GAA NA: 1539/p. 81, not. Jan Volkaertsz Oli. For the *Invention of Newcastle*, January 30, 1658, GAA:NA 1539/p. 263, not. Jan Volkaertsz Oli. For the *Pauw*, October 10, 1656, GAA:NA 1119/32, not. J.v.d. Ven. *De Drie Oijevaars*, July 30, 1658, GA: NA 2205/173, not. A. Lock.

80. "Report of Commissioners of the Admiralty," July 31, 1658, CO 1/13, fol. 300r, TNA:PRO; Col. Edw. D'Oyley, Col. Fras. Barrington, and Capt. Christ. Mings to Peter Pugh, February, 26, 1658, CO 1/33, fol. 103v, TNA:PRO; Capt. Christopher Myng [Mings] to Commissioners of the Admiralty, January 30, 1659, CO 1/33, fol. 130, TNA:PRO.

81. TASTD, http://slavevoyages.org/tast/database/search.faces?yearFrom=1600& yearTo=1688&mjslptimp=34200&natinimp=8, voyage #'s 44209 and 44210. In 1674, two WIC vessels landed slaves at Barbados, the *Maria* carrying 110 slaves and the *Asia* with 394. Both of these vessels were captured by English authorities, but tellingly only after delivering their cargoes (TASTD, http://slavevoyages.org/tast/database/search. faces?yearFrom=1600&yearTo=1688&mjslptimp=34200&natinimp=8 [voyage nos. 11575 and 44194]).

82. Depositions of Thomas Barrett, James Maountioy, Mathew Benham, Richard Galey, Richard Stockdale, Nicholas Salmon, George Lyne, and Peter Janson in front of Provincial Court of Maryland, May 31, June 1, June 2, June 3, 1659, in *Proceedings of the Provincial Court, 1658–1662*, ed. Steiner, 306–10.

83. January 30, 1659, GAA NA, 1539/263, not. J. Volkaertsz. For the eleven in 1660, see GAA:NA.

84. There are no port records for Barbados until the 1660s, but several visitors noted shipping levels between 100 and 200 a year (Foster, *A Brief Relation*, 3; Ligon, *True & Exact History*, 40; "Whistler's Journal: Admiral Penn's Voyage to the West Indies in 1654/5," Sloane MSS, 3926, fol. 10, BL; Jerome S. Handler, ed., "Father Antoine Biet's Visit to Barbados in 1654," 66). Estimates of Dutch vessels drawn from GAA:NA and GAR:OND; British state paper series CO, HCA and T at TNA:PRO; *CSPC*; and all other sources used in this work. Yda Schreuder, "Evidence from the Notarial Protocols in the Amsterdam Municipal Archives about Trade Relationships between Amsterdam and Barbados in the Seventeenth Century," *JBHMS* 52 (December 2006): 54–82, finds similar numbers of Dutch vessels. In the years after 1651, Barbadian merchants also increasingly traded with Dutch merchants in Curaçao (*Curaçao Papers*, 123).

85. "John Bayes to His right honorable The Committee for Foreign Affairs," February 4/14 1652/3, CO 1/12 fol. 7v ("well furnished"), TNA:PRO; "The State of ye Differences as it is presssed between ye Merchants and ye Planters in relations to free Trade

att ye Charibee Islands," ca. 1655–58, Add. Mss. 11411, original fol. 3 (LOC:BL Trans. pp. 7–8) ("forraigners" and "not of necessary"), LOC.

86. Council and Assembly of Barbados, *A Declaration Set forth. . . .* (The Hague, 1651), 2–3, emphasis in the original.

87. De Vries, *Voyages from Holland to America*, 112, 118; Hatfield, "Dutch and New Netherland Merchants in the Seventeenth-Century English Chesapeake," 205–28; and Schnurmann, "Atlantic Trade and American Identities," 187–89, both in *The Atlantic Economy during the Seventeenth and Eighteenth Centuries*, ed. Coclanis; Pagan, "Dutch Maritime and Commercial Activity in Mid-Seventeenth-Century Virginia," 485–87; Susie M. Ames, *Studies of the Virginia Eastern Shore in the Seventeenth Century* (1940; New York: Russell and Russell, 1973), chap. 3, esp. 45. On Dutch trade to New England that expanded in this period, see *Correspondence, 1647–1653*, 91; Charlotte Wilcoxen, "Dutch Trade with New England," 237–39; Bernard Bailyn, *The New England Merchants in the Seventeenth Century* (1955; New York: Harper and Row, 1964), 93–94. Between 1641 and 1656, the Verbrugges sent fourteen ships directly from Amsterdam to Virginia (Rink, *Holland on the Hudson*, 178–80).

88. For the *Goude Leeu*, October 18, 1652, HVV GAA:NA 1511/p. 20, not. Jan Volkaertsen Oli; WIC Directors to Stuyvesant, June 14, 1656, *Correspondence, 1654–1658*, 92–93 (quotation).

89. Rink, *Holland on the Hudson*, 179 (quotation); Verbrugge and Son to Loockermans, December 17, 1649, Misc. MSS, Stuyvesant Family, NYHS; Edmund B. O'Callaghan, "Powers of Attorney, Acknowledgments, Indentures of Apprentices, Inventories, etc.," *Year Book of the Holland Society of New York* (1900), 154. For others following the Verbrugges' lead, see O'Callagan, "Powers of Attorney," 181; June 18, 1653, HVV GAA:NA 2434/pp. 1680–81, not. Johannes Cross.

90. "Petition for the Committee of the Commonality of New Netherland," October 13, 1649, *DRCHNY* 1:259–61 (quotation). For follow-up petitions including the "Remonstrance of New Netherland," see *DRCHNY* 1:269, 271–318. On the Nine Men, see Middleton, *From Privileges to Rights*, 31–35, 37–52; and Jacobs, *New Netherland*, 142–52, 168–78.

91. WIC Directors to Stuyvesant, April 26, 1651, *DRCHNY*, 14:138–39.

92. Stuyvesant to John Winthrop (copy), March 6, 1653, NYC, Misc. MSS, Box 1, #1, NYHS (quotations). For the role of the WIC, see *Correspondence, 1654–1658*, 3, 9, 31, 92–93, 104–5. For the text of the agreement with Virginia, see "Articles of amitie and commerce " (1660), in *European Treaties Bearing on the History of the United States and Its Dependencies*, ed. Frances Gardiner Davenport (Washington, D.C.: Carnegie Institution of Washington, 1929), 2:55–56.

93. "Ordinance Regulating the Inspection of Tobacco," March 20 1657, in *Laws of Writs of Appeal, 1647–1663*, ed. Charles T. Gehring (Syracuse, N.Y.: Syracuse University Press, 1991), 49–50, 81–83 (quotation 82). For complaints from Amsterdam, *Correspondence, 1654–1658*, 104–5, 154–55.

94. "Resolution of the Director General and Council of New Netherland," August 24, 1655, in *Voyages of the Slavers St. John and Arms of Amsterdam, 1659, 1663; Together with Additional papers illustrative of the Slave Trade under the Dutch. New York Colonial Tracts*, ed. Edmund O'Callaghan, (Albany, N.Y.: J. Munsell, 1867), 111.

95. *Lachaire*, 196–97, 213–16. On cruising techniques in the Chesapeake, see Hatfield, *Atlantic Virginia*, 57–63.

96. Verbrugge and Son to Loockermans, December 17, 1649, Misc. MSS, Stuyvesant Family, NYHS; *Lachaire*, 90–91, 159–60; O'Callaghan, "Powers of Attorney," 177.

97. *Lachaire*, 131, 133–34.

98. For Steenwyck and Mills's complex relationship, see a 1662 debt case between the men (*Lachaire*, 27, 126–28, 182–84, 205–6; and Maika, "Commerce and Community," 120–23). The ties between James Mills and New Amsterdam extend back until at least 1654, when he bought the frigate *St. Charel* from Captain Symon Velle (November 7, 1654, "Powers of Attorney," ed. O'Callaghan, 176). Steenwyck's connection to Gillis and Tobias Van Hoornbeeck endured into the 1680s (Cornelis Steenwyck, Two notes to Gillis and Tobias Van Hoernbeck, 1682, Misc. MSS., NYC Churches, Box #30, NYHS, photostat). On Nicholas Varlet, see Edwin R. Purple, "Contributions to the History of the Ancient Families of New York," *New York Genealogical and Biographical Record* 9 (1878): 56–57.

99. "Minutes of Council of secret Trade with the Dutch," August 25 and December 7, 1662, DRCHNY 3:44, 47

100. July 1 1661, *Proceedings of the Council of Maryland, 1636–1660*, ed. Browne, 427–28.

101. *Records of the Colony of Rhode Island and Providence Plantations in New England, 1636–1663*, ed. John Russell Bartlett (1856; repr., New York: AMS Press, 1968), 126 (quotation). On New Netherland's trade with New England, see *Correspondence, 1647–1653*, 54; Wilcoxen, "Dutch Trade with New England," 237–40; and Van Zandt, *Brothers among Nations*, 109–11.

102. On Herrman's early trading career, see June 29, 1644, Receipt, Augustyn Herrmans and Luweris Cornelissen, agents of Peter Gabry and sons and Conrast Coymans, NY Coll Mss, v. 2, p. 112b, photostat in Burton Notebooks, vol. 4, MS 437, Maryland Historical Society; *NYHMDPD*, 20, 34; DRCHNY 1:430; DRCHNY 12:70–71; *Calendar*, 46, 129; and RNA, 2:119. See also Thomas Capek, *Augustine Herrman of Bohemia Manor* (Praha, Czechoslovakia: State Printing Office, 1930), 9–11; Paul G. Burton, "The Age of Augustine Herrman," *New York General Biographical Record* 78 (1947): 130–31; Earle L. W. Heck, *Augustine Herrman, Beginner of the Virginia Tobacco Trade, Merchant of New Netherland, and First Lord of Bohemia Manor in Maryland* (Englewood, Ohio: self-published, 1941), 14–19; and Hatfield, "Dutch and New Netherland Merchants," in *The Atlantic Economy during the Seventeenth and Eighteenth Centuries*, ed. Coclanis, 211–17, 213–16, 224–26.

103. *Proceedings of the Council of Maryland, 1636–1667*, ed. Browne, 398–9; *NYHMDPD*, 217.

104. RNA, 3:558–9; 6:120; 7:12–13; Heck, *Augustine Herrman*, 20–3; Ames, *Studies of the Virginia Eastern Shore*, 66–67.

105. Wim Klooster, "Curaçao and the Caribbean Transit Trade," in *Riches from Atlantic Commerce*, 203–6 (quotation 204); Han Jordaan, "The Curacao Slave Market: From *Asiento* Trade to Free Trade, 1700–1730," in *Riches from Atlantic Commerce*, 219–58; Israel, *Dutch Primacy in World Trade*, 240–44.

106. For repeated claims in 1643 that New Netherland was not supplying needed "flour and pottage," see *Curaçao Papers*, 18, 20, 23, 25, 26, 28, 29.

107. Gehring, introduction to *Curacao Papers*, xv–xvi.

108. *Curacao Papers*, 115–16, 168–69, 218. For more about this trade, including the efforts of the company to advance it by offering salt and horses at low rates, see Matson, *Merchants and Empire*, 26–28.

109. January 13, 1651, HHV:GAA:NA: 1837/14 not. Nicolas Kruys.

110. See the various documents relating to the *Nieuw Amstel*, May 2, 1659, and May 16, 1659, in *Curacao Papers*, 135–39.

111. See accounts of the *De Vergulde Vos* in *Curacao Papers*, 181–83.

112. Matthias Beck to Stuyvesant, May 16, 1659, *Curacao Papers*, 122–24.

113. Adriaen Van der Donck, *A Description of New Netherland*, trans. Jeremias Johnson, ed. Thomas O'Donnell (Syracuse, N.Y.: Syracuse University Press, 1968), 131–33.

Notes to Chapter 3

1. "Petition of Governor Russell and the Assembly of Nevis," November 27, 1668, CO 1/23, fols. 174v–75r, TNA:PRO. The origin of all of these vessels is unclear. While Russell refers to them as "Hamburghers," perhaps to ameliorate his actions, Governor William Willoughby calls them "Dutch" in his defense of Russell's decision (Gov. Willoughby to Lord Arlington, September 28, 1668, CO 1/23, fol. 108r, TNA:PRO).

2. Population estimates from McCusker and Menard, *The Economy of British America*, 153; slave imports and sugar production figures from Menard, *Sweet Negotiations*, 46–47, 68, 72–77; Alfred D. Chandler, "The Expansion of Barbados," JBMHS 8 (1945/6): 106–36; and Sheridan, *Sugar and Slavery*, 128–38.

3. C. G. A. Clay, *Economic Expansion and Social Change*, vol. 2: *Industry, Trade and Government* (New York: Cambridge University Press, 1984), chaps. 8–9; Menard, *Sweet Negotiations*, chaps. 3–4.

4. "Instructions for the Council of Trade" [draft] (1660), Egerton MSS 2395, fol. 268, BL (first quotation); Sir William Temple, *Observations upon the United Provinces of the Netherlands* (London, 1673), 186–87 (second quotation); Diary of Samuel Pepys, February 2, 1663/4, in *The Diary of Samuel Pepys*, ed. Henry B. Wheatley (New York: Groscup and Sterling, 1894), 4:29 (third quotation); Baugh, "Maritime Strength and Atlantic Commerce" in *An Imperial State at War*, ed. Stone, 186–93; Ormrod, *The Rise of Commercial Empires*, 32–33. "Communities of interest" is a phrase used by Michael Braddick, "State Formation and Social Change in Early Modern England: A Problem Stated and Approaches Suggested," *Social History* 16 (1991): 5.

5. Braddick, "The English Government, War, Trade, and Settlement," 302–8; Harper, *The English Navigation Laws*, 59–60; Robert M. Bliss, *Revolution and Empire: English Politics and the American Colonies in the Seventeenth Century* (Manchester : Manchester University Press, 1990), 103–60; Perry Gauci, *The Politics of Trade: The Overseas Merchant in State and Society, 1660–1720* (New York: Oxford University Press, 2003), 10–12, 177–79, 272.

6. Wood, *The Great advantages of our Colonies and Plantations in Great Britain* (1728), in *Select Dissertations on colonies and plantations. By those celebrated authors, Sir Josiah Child, Charles D'Avenant, LL.D and Mr. William Wood. . . .*, ed. Charles Whitworth (London, 1775), 89. For other contemporary views, see Charles Davenant, *An essay upon the probable methods of making a people gainers in the balance of trade. . . .* (London, 1699), 89. The notion that plantation trade needed regulation was also supported by those who thought all commerce was best when directed to profitable channels (Mun, *England's Treasure by Foreign Trade*).

7. Downing to Lord Clarendon, February 12, 1663/4, in T. H. Lister, *Life and Administration of Edward, Earl of Clarendon* (London: Longman, Orne, Brown, Green, and Longmans, 1838) 3:277.

8. K. G. Davies, *The Royal African Company* (1957; New York: Longmans, Green, 1970), 57–62; Philip D. Curtin, *The Atlantic Slave Trade, A Census* (Madison: University of Wisconsin Press, 1969), 121–26; Eltis, "The British Transatlantic Slave Trade before 1714: Annual Estimates of Value and Direction," in *The Lesser Antilles*, ed. Paquette and Engerman, 182–95.

9. Alison Gilbert Olson, *Anglo-American Politics 1660–1775: The Relationship between Parties in England and Colonial America* (New York: Oxford University Press, 1973), 24–38.

10. A. P. Thornton, *West-India Policy under the Restoration* (Oxford: Clarendon Press, 1956), chap. 2; Pestana, *The English Atlantic in an Age of Revolution*, 220–23.

11. "Letters to ye Severall Govs of his Majesty's Plantations in America," June 24, 1663, CO 5/903, fols. 11–5, TNA:PRO; "Circular letter for the King to [the Governors of all his Majesty's Plantations]," August 25, 1663, CO 1/17, fol. 181, TNA:PRO; "An order concerning shipping," September 13, 1664, O'Callaghan transcripts, NYHS.

12. Thurloe, rec., March 28, 1661, BL Add. Mss. 4200, fol. 113, quoted in C. H. Firth, "Secretary Thurloe on the Relations of England and Holland," *English Historical Review* 21 (1906): 325. On the origins of these wars, see Wilson, *Profit and Power*, esp. 111–21; Israel, *Dutch Primacy in World Trade*, 271–79. See also the cultural interpretations of Pincus, "Popery, Trade and Universal Monarchy: The Ideological Context of the Outbreak of the Second-Anglo-Dutch War," *English Historical Review* 107 (1992): 1–29; and of Claydon, *Europe and the Making of England*, 131–45; the court interpretation of Jones, *The Anglo-Dutch Wars of the Seventeenth Century*; and the political and mercantilist interpretation of Gijs Rommelse, *The Second Anglo-Dutch War (1665–1667): Raison d'état, Mercantilism and Maritime Strife* (Hilversum: Verloren, 2006), esp. 101–5, 108–11, 198–99. On the war's effects on commerce, see Rommelse, "Prizes and Profits: Dutch Maritime Trade during the Second Anglo-Dutch War," *International Journal of Maritime History* 19 (2007): 139–58.

13. Council and Assembly of Barbados, *A Declaration Set forth*, 2–3 (emphasis in original); Bliss, *Revolution and Empire*, 62–66; Pestana, *The English Atlantic in an Age of Revolution*, 102–3. For the use of "political" arguments in analyzing economic ideologies, see Tim Keirn, "Monopoly, Economic Thought, and the Royal African Company," in *Early Modern Conceptions of Property*, ed. John Brewer and Susan Staves (New York: Routledge, 1995), 428–30. Compare to Schnurmann, "Atlantic Trade and American Identities," in *The Atlantic Economy during the Seventeenth and Eighteenth Centuries*, ed. Coclanis, 190–91, 198–99.

14. Searle to the Council of State, October 8, 1652, CO 1/11, fol. 188r, TNA:PRO; "The State of ye Differences as it is presssed between ye Merchants and ye Planters in relations to free Trade att ye Charibee Islands," ca. 1655–58, Add. Mss. 11411, original fol. 3r (LOC: BL Trans., p. 6), LOC. Colonists on Somers Island (Bermuda) made the same point (*CSPC, 1574–1660*, 370).

15. Council and Assembly of Barbados, *A Declaration Set forth*, 3 (mispaginated), emphasis in original.

16. Pestana, *The English Atlantic in an Age of Revolution*, esp. 158–70 (quotation 164). Though Pestana describes the free trade arguments Barbadians articulated, she sees them as being rooted in arguments over political authority, as opposed to economic theory. See also Gary A. Puckrein, *Little England: Plantation Society and Anglo-*

Barbadian Politics, 1627–1700 (New York: New York University Press, 1984), chaps. 7–8; and Bliss, *Revolution and Empire*, 28–32, chaps. 2–3.

17. Council and Assembly of Barbados, *A Declaration Set forth*, 4 (mispaginated), emphasis in original.

18. "Petition of the President, Council and Assembly of Barbados to His Majesty's Commissioners for Foreign Plantations," May 11, 1661, *CSPC, 1661–8*, 30. Colonists in the Leeward Islands, too, greeted the Navigation Acts with objections and counterproposals (*CSPC, 1661–8*, 204–5, 229–30, 234–35).

19. "An Account of the English Sugar Plantations," ca. time of Charles II, Egerton MSS 2395, fols. 629–35, BL.

20. George Martin to Colonel Henry Martin, March 19, 1652, "Documents and Letters in the Brotherton Collection," 182. For the profit estimate of "three for one," see Tanner MSS, Bodleian Library, Oxford, England, cited in Harlow, *History of Barbados*, 38–39 n. 3.

21. "The State of ye Differences as it is presssed between ye Merchants and ye Planters in relations to free Trade att ye Charibee Islands," ca. 1655–58, Add. Mss. 11411, original fol. 3r (LOC: BL Trans. pg 6), LOC. For sugar prices, see chap 4.

22. Thornton, *West-India Policy*, 3 (quotation); Davis, *The Rise of the English Shipping Industry*, 13–14.

23. Thornton, *West-India Policy*, 3; Harlow, *History of Barbados*, 169–71.

24. The President and Council of Barbadoes to [Sec. Nicholas], July 10, 1661, CO 1/15, fol. 133r, TNA:PRO.

25. Ligon, *A True & Exact History*, 40 (quotation). See also Thomas Verney's Account of Barbadoes, February 10, 1638, in *Letters and Papers of the Verney Family*, ed. Bruce, 197; Lease of Three Houses Plantation, St. Philip [Parish], August 10, 1658, "The Lucas Manuscript Volumes in the Barbados Public Library," *Journal of the Barbados Museum and Historical Society* 22 (1954/5), 110–18; Jeaffreson to William Poyntz, July 23, 1678, in *Young Squire*, 1:233–36.

26. *CSPC, 1661–8*, 328; Sheridan, *Sugar and Slavery*, 148–49.

27. Gov. Willoughby to the King, May 12, 1666, CO 1/20, fols. 148–50 (quotation fol. 149r), TNA:PRO. On De Ruyter's invasion see Harlow, *History of Barbados*, 153–7; Goslinga, *The Dutch in the Caribbean and on the Wild Coast*, 385–86.

28. Gov. Willoughby to the King, July 15, 1666, CO 1/20, fol. 206r, TNA:PRO.

29. *CSPC, 1661–68*, 432, 435–36.

30. "L. Willoughbie, proposalls concerning the West Indies," April 8, 1672, Egerton MSS 2395, fol. 477, BL.

31. Gov. Stapleton to the Council for Trade and Foreign Plantations, July 17, 1672, *CSPC, 1669–74*, 393; Sheridan, *Sugar and Slavery*, 148–49.

32. Owen Felltham, *A Brief Character of the Low Countries* (London, 1627), cited in Schama, *The Embarrassment of Riches*, 238.

33. Rommelse, "Prizes and Profits: Dutch Maritime Trade during the Second Anglo-Dutch War," 154–56; Pincus, *Protestantism and Patriotism*, 247.

34. Samuel Winthrop to John Winthrop, Jr., April 1667, "Letters of Samuel Winthrop," 255–58.

35. Jeaffreson to Colonel Geroge Gamiell, May 12, 1677, in *Young Squire*, 1:215.

36. Gov. Russell to Wm. Lord Willoughby, July 10, 1667, *CSPC, 1661–8*, 478–79.

37. John Bushel, *A true and perfect narrative of the late dreadful fire which happened at Bridge-Town in the Barbadoes.* . . . (London, 1668), 1–2, 5. For other reports of the fire, see *CSPC, 1661–8*, 561, 563, 601; A. Berenberg's Widow & Heirs to Charles Marescoe, November 12, 1669, in *Markets and merchants of the Late Seventeenth Century, the Marescoe–David Letters, 1668–1680, Records of Social and Economic History*, new ser. 12, ed. Henry Roseveare (Oxford: Oxford University Press, 1987), 302; and Handler, "Father Antoine Biet's Visit to Barbados in 1654," 65.

38. Petition of John Harris to his Majesty, June 26, 1668, 1/22, fol. 210, TNA:PRO.

39. *CSPC, 1661–8*, 635–36; *CSPC, 1669–1674*, 2; Christopher Codrington, Deputy Gov. to [Sec. Lord Arlington], April 21, 1669, CO 1/24, 77r (quotation), TNA:PRO. Codrington pledged to bring the *Matthew and Francis* to a new trial. Wilfred S. Samuel, "Sir William Davidson, Royalist, (1616–1689) and the Jews," *Transactions of the Jewish Historical Society of England* 14 (1940): 39–79.

40. "Petition of Martin Noell, William Chamberlain, Col. Braxe, Col. Hooper, Peter Leere, Capt. Manyford, and Mr. Basten, merchants, planters and traders to Barbados to the Lord Protector and Council," November 18, 1656, *CSPC, 1574–1660*, 451 (quotation). For reports of hurricanes and their effects, see *CSPC, 1681–5*, 140, 338; *Young Squire*, 1:274–80; Petition from the Council and Assembly of Nevis, 1687, CO 155/1, fol. 90, TNA:PRO. On hurricanes in the early modern Caribbean, see Matthew Mulcahy, *Hurricanes and Society in the British Greater Caribbean, 1624–1783* (Baltimore: Johns Hopkins University Press, 2006), 16–17.

41. Gov. Atkins to Sec. Williamson, October 3/13, 1675, CO 1/35, 210r, TNA:PRO.

42. A. Berenberg's Widow & Heirs to Charles Marescoe, November 12, 1669; J. A. Fock to Jacob David, December 14, 1675, both in *Merchants and Markets*, ed. Roseveare, 54, 173–74, 302, 396.

43. J. Handler, "Slave Revolts and Conspiracies in Seventeenth-Century Barbados," *New West Indian Guide* 56 (1982): 9–12.

44. Gov. Atkins to Sec. Williamson, October 3/13, 1675, CO 1/35, 210r, TNA:PRO.

45. Petition of the Representatives from Barbados to the King, September 5, 1667, CO 1/20, fol. 207r, TNA:PRO.

46. Joyce Oldham Appleby, *Economic Thought and Ideology in Seventeenth-Century England* (Princeton: Princeton University Press, 1978), chaps. 2–5; Matson, *Merchants and Empire*, introduction, chap. 1; Andrea Finkelstein, *Harmony and the Balance: An Intellectual History of Seventeenth-Century English Economic Thought* (Ann Arbor: University of Michigan Press, 2000).

47. Pieter de la Court, *The True Interests and Political Maxims of the Republick of Holland and West Friesland* (1662; repr., London, 1702); Gerald Malynes, *The Maintenance of Free Trade* (London, 1620); William Petty, *A Treatise of Taxes* (London, 1662); *A Discourse, consisting of Motives for the Enlargement of Freedom of Trade*. On the circulatory model in economics, see Edward Misseldon, *The Circle of Commerce* (London, 1623); Josiah Child, *A Treatise Concerning the East India Trade* (London, 1681); Child, *A new Discourse of Trade*. . . ., 4th ed. (1693; repr., London, 1740); William Petty, *Political arithmetick* (London, 1690); Appleby, *Economic Thought and Ideology*, chaps. 4, 8; and Matson, *Merchants and Empire*, 39–45.

48. Appleby, *Economic Thought and Ideology*, 77–78, 106–14; Matson, *Merchants and Empire*, 37–49.

49. *A discourse consisting of motives for the enlargement and freedom of trade* (London, 1645); Appleby, *Economic Thought and Ideology,* 109–10.

50. Edward Littleton, *Groans of the Plantations....* (London, 1689), 5–7 (quotations); "An Account of the English Sugar Plantations," ca. time of Charles II, Egerton MSS 2395, fols. 629–35, BL; Dalby Thomas, *An Historical Account of the Rise and Growth of the West-India Collonies....* (London, 1690), 43–44.

51. Roger Coke, *A discourse of trade* (London, 1670), quoted in Appleby, *Economic Thought and Ideology,* 120; Tryon, *The Merchant, Citizen and Country man's Instructor* (London, 1701), 194–221; Matson, *Merchants and Empire,* 40–41, 344–45 nn. 7–8.

52. Petty, *Political arithmetick,* 90. On Petty, see Finkelstein, *Harmony and the Balance,* chap. 7.

53. Petition of the Representatives for Barbados to the King, September 5, 1667, CO 1/21, fol. 207r (first quotation) TNA:PRO; "Petition of the President, Council and Assembly of Barbados to His Majesty's Commissioners for Foreign Plantations," May 11, 1661, *CSPC, 1661–8,* 30 (second quotation). There are many similar petitions from Barbados and the Leewards ("Proposition of the President and Council of Barbados to the Assembly," July 4, 1661, CO 31/1, pp. 53–56, TNA:PRO; *CSPC, 1661–8,* 45–47, 282–83; 412–13).

54. The petitions of assemblies and councils of Antigua, Montserrat, and St. Christopher were forwarded to the king in a letter from Willoughby (September 20, 1664, CO 1/18, fols. 245r–48v, TNA:PRO; Gov. Willoughby to Sec. Lord Arlington, August 25, 1664, CO 1/18, fol. 226v [quotation], TNA:PRO).

55. "Answers sent to the several clauses of the letter from the Council for Foreign Plantations to Lord Willoughby," May 1661, *CSPC, 1661–8,* 29.

56. Gov. Willoughby to the King, September 10, 1663, CO 1/17, fols. 195–96, TNA:PRO; Gov. Willoughby to the King, November 4, 1663, CO 1/17, fols. 220–21, TNA:PRO.

57. The President and Council of Barbadoes to [Sec. Nicholas], July 10, 1661, CO 1/15, fol. 133r, TNA:PRO; *CSPC, 1661–8,* 30.

58. Gov. Willoughby to the King, September 20, 1664, CO 1/18, fols. 245r–48v, TNA:PRO.

59. Gov. Willoughby to the King, May 12, 1666, CO 1/20, fols. 148–50 (quotation fol. 149r), TNA:PRO.

60. For a similar argument, see Harlow, *History of Barbados,* 172–73.

61. *Poor Robins character of a Dutch-man* (London, 1672), 2, cited in Pincus, "From Butterboxes to Wooden Shoes: The Shift in English Popular Sentiment from Anti-Duch to Anti-French in the 1670s," *Historical Journal* 38 (1995): 337; John Dryden, *Amboyna: a tragedy as it is acted at the Theatre-Royal* (London, 1672); Pincus, "Popery, Trade and Universal Monarchy," 1–29.

62. *A Familiar discourse, between George, a true-hearted English gentleman: and Hans, a Dutch merchant* (London, 1672), 4.

63. Petition of the Representatives for Barbados to the King, September 5, 1667, CO 1/21, fol. 207r, TNA:PRO.

64. "Minute of the Council for Foreign Plantations, upon complaint of the Farmers of the Customs of an illicit trade between the Dutch and English Plantations in America, &c.," December 7, 1663, *DRCHNY* 3:47 ("great quantities"); Several letters from Samuel Mavericke to the Earl of Clarendon, ca.1661 in *The Clarendon Papers,*

Collections of the New-York Historical Society, 2 (1869), 1–43, ("tenn thousand") 20, ("Commodious,") 38; George Downing to Lord Clarendon, May 6, 1664, in Lister, *Life and Administration of Edward, Earl of Clarendon*, 3:320 ("all the world"). See also *DRCHNY* 1: 43–44; 3:43. For York's patent, see *DRCHNY*, 2:295–98. For Nicolls's commission, see *General Entries*, 1:5–6. On the conquest, see Ritchie, *The Duke's Province*, 9–18; and Feiling, *British Foreign Policy*, 123–25.

65. *DRCHNY*, 2:366. Population estimate from Ritchie, *The Duke's Province*, 27.

66. Colonel Winthrop to Gov. Winthrop, August 22, 1664, *General Entries* 1:28.

67. Accounts of the invasion are many; see, particularly, Kammen, *Colonial New York*, 70–72; Ritchie, *The Duke's Province*, chap. 1; and Rink, *Holland on the Hudson*, 260–63. The negotiations between Nicolls and Stuyvesant are in *General Entries*, 1:25–37. The negotiations between the burghers of New Netherland and Stuyvesant are in *DRCHNY* 2:444–45; 13:393–94. For Stuyvesant's perspective, see *DRCHNY*, 2:365–410, 427–47.

68. "Articles of Surrender Consented to By Colonel Nicolls, his delegates, and Director General Stuyvesant's Delegates," August 27, 1664, *General Entries*, 1:35–37.

69. "Warrant of Thomas Delavall to Oversee Payment of Export Duties," October 26, 1664, *General Entries*, 1:57. Nicolls's instructions had ordered "kindnesse and encouragement" to the Dutch residents ("Private Instructions to Coll. R. Nicolls &c.," April 23, 1664, *DRCHNY* 3:57–61).

70. Rink, *Holland on the Hudson*, 188–213.

71. Records relating to the voyage are in *General Entries*, 1:104, 204–5, 208–14.

72. Beck to Stuyvesant, April 16, 1665, *Curaçao Papers*, 208–14.

73. "The Condemnation of the Vessell or Galliott Called the Hope," September 22, 1666, in "Abstracts of Wills on File in the Surrogate's Office, City of New York, vol. 1, 1665–1707," *NYHSC* 25 (1892): 71–72 (quotations). See also *Nicolls and Lovelace*, 2.

74. *General Entries*, 1:397–98.

75. Nicolls to the Secretary of State, October 1664, *DRCHNY*, 3:69.

76. Nicolls to the Secretary of State, July 31, 1665, *DRCHNY*, 3:103.

77. Nicolls to the Duke of York, November 1665, *DRCHNY*, 3:104.

78. Nicolls to Clarendon, April 7, 1666, in *Clarendon Papers*, 118.

79. Cathy Matson, "Commerce after the Conquest: I, Dutch Traders and Goods in New York City, 1664–1764," *De Halve Maen* 59 (1987): 8–10; Ritchie, *The Duke's Province*, 53–59.

80. *General Entries*, 1:57. Scheduled to leave in October, the vessel left on December 14, 1664 (*JVRC*, 361, 367–67, 370–71, 374).

81. "Permit to Cornelis Steewick to Trade to Holland," December 13, 1664; "Liberty granted to Mr. Steewick and Jaques Cousseau, to send the Shipp Hopewell to Holland," January 30, 1664/5; "Ship's pass for David Jochems, Master of the *Hopewell*," March 31, 1665; "Liberty Granted for the *Crost Heart* to come into this Port," February 12, 1664/5; "Liberty given to the same [the *Crost Heart*] of importing goods from Holland within one year," April 21, 1665, all in *General Entries*, 1:68, 75, 82–83, 105, 106; Oloff Stevensen van Cortlandt to Jeremias Van Rensselaer, January 1665, *JVRC*, 371; *JVRC*, 378 n. 778.

82. On the *Eendracht*, see Maika, "Commerce and Community," 136–37; *Calendar*, 3. On the *Hopewell*, April 1, 1666, HHV GAA:NA 277/pp. 9–10, not. Pieter van Buijtene; February 13, 1668, HHV GAA:NA 3193/pp. 128, 128v., not. Hendrik Outgers; *JVRC*, 387–91.

83. There is some confusion over the specifics of this voyage. Nicolls granted a pass for the ship to travel to Hamburg in June 1667 (*General Entries* 1:150). Jeremias van Rensselaer reported the departure of the vessel from Rensselaerswyck (*JVRC*, 390; Maika, "Commerce and Community," 137–38). For slightly different timing, see Rink, *Holland on the Hudson*, 188–90.

84. Nicolls to Lord Arlington, April 9, 1666, *DRCHNY*, 3:114.

85. Petition of the Common Council of New-York to the Duke of York, 1669, *DRCHNY*, 3:187; *General Entries*, 1:36.

86. Middleton, *From Privileges to Rights*, 31–77, 55–63; Ritchie, *The Duke's Province*, 22–23, 56–59; John M. Murrin, "English Rights as Ethnic Aggression: The English Conquest, the Charter of Liberties of 1683, and Leisler's Rebellion in New York," in *Authority and Resistance in Early New York*, ed. William Penack and Conrad Edick Wright (New York: New-York Historical Society, 1988), 65.

87. "Petition of Petrus Stuyvesant to the King and Privy Council," October 23, 1667, *DRCHNY*, 3:164–65 (first quotation); "Proposals to his Royal Highness, the Duke of York, by Peter Stuyvesant," October 1667, *DRCHNY*, 3:163–64 (subsequent quotations). Despite signing a treaty in September 1664 which proclaimed: "the Indian princes above named [on the treaty] and their subjects, shall have such wares and commodities from the English for the future, as heretofore they had from the Dutch," the English were ultimately never able to carry through in this pledge ("Articles between Col. Cartwright and the New York Indians," September 25, 1665, *DRCHNY*, 3:67).

88. Nicolls to Lord Arlington, April 9, 1666, *DRCHNY*, 3:114 (quotation); The Director General and Council of New Netherland to the Chamber of the WIC at Amsterdam, February 28, 1664, *DRCHNY*, 2:230–34. Samuel Maverick reported the penetration of New England traders into Virginia (Samuel Maverick to Nicolls, July 5, 1669, *DRCHNY*, 3:182–83). Hatfield, *Atlantic Virginia*, 245 n. 52; Matson, *Merchants and Empire*, 18, 53; Pagan, "Dutch Maritime and Commercial Activity," 499–501.

89. *DRCHNY*, 3:166–67. A subcommittee of the King's Council recommended that the council approve the trade because they understood the "necessity of a present trade in those parts which cannot at this time bee supplied from hence [London]" ("Report of the Committee of the Council on the proceeding petition [from Stuyvesant]," October 17, 1667, *DRCHNY*, 3:165–66).

90. February 27, 1668, HHV GAA:NA 2784/pp. 447–50, not. Pieter van Buijtene. Steenwyck and Stuyvesant received ƒ1,200 as compensation for acquiring the permits (Rink, *Holland on the Hudson*, 203–5; Maika, "Commerce and Community," 140–41).

91. *JVRC*, 403–4, 410–12.

92. "Order in Council prohibiting Dutch Ships to trade to New York," November 18, 1668, *DRCHNY*, 3:177–78.

93. The Board of Trade to the king, 1668, *DRCHNY*, 3:175–76; "Order in Council Prohibiting Dutch Ships to trade to New-York," November 18, 1668, *DRCHNY*, 3:177–78.

94. August 20, 1669, HHV GAA:NA 2790/pp. 663–64, not. Pieter van Buijtene; Rink, *Holland on the Hudson*, 203–4.

95. "Petition of the Common Council of New York to the Duke of York," 1668, *DRCHNY*, 3:187.

96. *DRCHNY*, 3:178–79; *JVRC*, 404–8, 410–12; Merwick, *Death of a Notary*, 136–37.

97. The estimates of ship numbers are from the sources cited in this chapter and are

closely mirrored by those of other scholars (see Matson, "Commerce after the Conquest, I," 10–11; table 4.5 "Shipping between the Dutch Republic and New Netherland, 1620–1674", Henk Den Heijer, "The Dutch West India Company, 1621–1791," in *Riches from Atlantic Commerce*, 94. For the England–New York shipping, see Ritchie, *The Duke's Province*, 57, 253 n. 41.

Notes to Chapter 4

1. Samuel Hayne, *An abstract of all the statutes made concerning aliens* (London, 1685), 15–38; "Treasury reference to the Customs Commissioners of the petition of Sam. Haine," July 6, 1681, "Entry Book: July 1681, 4–9," Calendar of Treasury Books, Volume 7: 1681–1685 (1916), 204–17, www.british-history.ac.uk/report.aspx?compid=83812. While Hayne's claims of bribery are not verifiable, customs officers did record the *Experiment* in the Falmouth Port Books as entering from Barbados. The ship was assessed and paid duties on at least 10 butts of tobacco, 49 butts of sugar, one-half ton of molasses and 167 bags and a parcel of ginger on October 1, 1680 (October 6, 1680, TNA:PRO E 190/1044/18). It left Falmouth bound for Amsterdam on November 4, 1680 (TNA:PRO E 190/1044/12). For the Amsterdam organizers, see October 20, 1683, GAA:NA 4108/p. 212, not. Dork van de Groe. On Dias and Lousada in Barbados, see November 19, 1699, GAA:NA 5873/77, not. Joan Hoekebak; Wilfred S. Samuel, "A Review of the Jewish Colonists in Barbados in the Year 1680," *Transactions of the Jewish Historical Society of England* 13 (1936): 16–17; and Welch, *Slave Society in the City*, 123. David Raphael Mercado lived in Barbados and had sent sugar to his brother in Amsterdam previously. October 3, 1672, GAA:NA 4075/240, not. Dirck van der Groe; October 22 1675, GAA:NA 4081, not. Dirk van der Groe. In May 1681, Emmanuel Rodrigo and Sutton collaborated again, sending the *Philip* from Amsterdam to Barbados and New York (with Frederick Philipse) through Falmouth (TNA:PRO E 190/1045/26; Hayne, *An abstract of all the statutes*, 13–14).

2. On the smuggling of tea, see Hoh-Cheung and Lorna H. Mui, "Smuggling and the British Tea Trade before 1784," *American Historical Review* 74 (1968): 44–73; W. A. Cole, "Trends in Eighteenth-Century Smuggling," in *The Growth of English Overseas Trade in the Seventeenth and Eighteenth Centuries,* ed. W. E. Minchinton (London: Methuen, 1969), 121–43, esp. 138–42; Hoh-Cheung and Lorna H. Mui, "'Trends in Eighteenth-Century Smuggling' Reconsidered," *Economic History Review*, 2nd ser., 28 (1975): 28–43; W. A. Cole, "The Arithmetic of Eighteenth-Century Smuggling: Rejoinder," *Economic History Review*, 2nd ser., 28 (1975): 44–49. G. D. Ramsey was among the first to identify smuggling as being responsible for distorting official British statistics (G. D. Ramsay, "The Smugglers' Trade: A Neglected Aspect of English Commercial Development," *Transactions of the Royal Historical Society*, 5th ser. 11 [1952]: 131–57). For the estimate of one-third, see Ormrod, *The Rise of Commercial Empires*, 69. On coastal smuggling, see Cal Winslow, "Sussex Smugglers," in *Albion's Fatal Tree: Crime and Society in Eighteenth-Century England*, ed. Douglas Hay et al. (London: Allen Lane, 1975), 148–49; Paul Monod, "Dangerous Merchandise: Smuggling, Jacobitism, and Commercial Culture in Southeast England, 1690–1760," *Journal of British Studies* 30 (1991): 150–82. And on tobacco, see Robert Nash, "The English and Scottish Tobacco Trade in the Seventeenth and Eighteenth Centuries: Legal and Illegal Trade," *Economic History Review*, 2nd ser., 35 (1982): 355.

3. Most notably, Lawrence Harper argued that while "the lurid accounts of frauds contained in administrative reports and court records make interesting reading, they must not be allowed to confuse to the extent of illegal activities" (Harper, *The English Navigation Laws*, 246–74 [quotation 263]). More recently, see McCusker, "British Mercantilist Policies and the American Colonies," in *The Cambridge Economic History of the United States*, vol. 1, *The Colonial Era*, ed. Stanley L. Engerman and Robert E. Gallman (Cambridge: Cambridge University Press, 1996), 349–56.

4. For Barbados, see David Eltis, "The Total Product of Barbados, 1664–1701," *Journal of Economic History* 55 (1995): 321–38; David Eltis, "New Estimates of Exports from Barbados and Jamaica, 1665–1701," *WMQ*, 3rd ser., 52 (1995): 636–38.

5. On colonial coastal and interisland smuggling, see Harper, *The English Navigation Laws*, 263–64; McCusker, *Rum and the American Revolution*, 61; Richard Pares, *War and Trade in the West Indies, 1739–1763* (1939; repr., London: Cass, 1963), 113–23; Sheridan, *Sugar and Slavery*, esp. 45, 435; Zahedieh, "The Merchants of Port Royal, Jamaica," 572–79, 591–93; David Hancock, introduction to *The letters of William Freeman, London merchant, 1678–1685*, ed. Hancock, xxvii–xxix. For New Yorkers as intermediaries, see Matson, *Merchants and Empire*, 83–86, 203–14, 298–99; Thomas M. Truxes, *Defying Empire: Trading with the Enemy in Colonial New York* (New Haven: Yale University Press, 2008), 55–64, 77–86, 89–94. For the Dutch Caribbean, see Klooster, *Illicit Riches;* and Linda M. Rupert, "Contraband Trade and the Shaping of Colonial Societies in Curaçao and Tierra Firma," 35–54. For the French Caribbean, see James Pritchard, *In Search of Empire: The French in the Americas, 1670–1730* (New York: Cambridge University Press, 2004), 204–9; and Kenneth Banks, "Official Duplicity: The Illicit Slave Trade of Martinique, 1713–1763," in *The Atlantic Economy during the Seventeenth and Eighteenth Centuries*, ed. Coclanis, 229–51.

6. Sir Thomas Lynch to Lords of Trade and Plantations, August 29, 1682, CO 1/49, fol. 33v, TNA:PRO; Hayne, *An abstract of all the statutes*, 10–14; Answer of Gov. Charles Wheler to the inquiries of the Council of Foreign Plantations, December 9, 1671, CO 1/27, fol. 152v, TNA:PRO.

7. August 15, 1662, *APCC*, 1:334–35.

8. Instructions for Gov. Willoughby, June 12, 1663, *APCC*, 1:355–61.

9. "Letters to ye Severall Govs of his Majesty's Plantations in America," June 24, 1663, CO 5/903, 11–5, TNA:PRO. See also *CSPC, 1661–8*, 156.

10. For a full listing of these circulars, see Leonard Woods Labaree, ed., *Royal Government in America: A Study of the British Colonial System before 1783*, Yale Historical Publications, Studies, vol. 6 (New Haven, Conn., 1930) 2, 752–74. For complaints about smuggling, see *CSPC, 1574–1660*, 473; *CSPC, 1661–8*, 630; *CSPC, 1685–8, Add., 1652–87*, 25–6, 74–5, 380, 553; *APCC*, 3: 81–2; and Gov. Willoughby to Board of Trade, July 9, 1668, Egerton MSS 2395, #102, fols. 569–70, BL.

11. Locke to Secretary Lord Arlington, January 6, 1674, CO 1/31, fol. 33r, TNA:PRO. In 1675, the duties of the Council of Trade and Foreign Plantations were handed over to a committee of the Privy Council itself; this body was called the Lords Committee of Trade (Olson, *Anglo-American Politics*, 57–58; Ralph Paul Bieber, "The British Plantation Councils of 1670–4," *English Historical Review* 40 [1925]: 93–106).

12. For instructions to West Indian governors in the mid-1670s, see *CSPC, 1675–76*, 235, 287, 371; and *CSPC, 1677–80*, 204.

13. Beer, *The Old Colonial System, 1660–1754*, pt. 1, *The Establishment of the System,*

1660–1688 (New York: Macmillan, 1912), 75–98, 224–315; Thornton, *West-India Policy*, 164–65.

14. Gov. Lowther to the Council of Trade and Plantations, April 9, 1712, *CSPC, 1711–12*, 260–61.

15. "Report of the Commissioners of the Customs to the Committee for Plantations," October 11, 1675, *CSPC, 1675–76*, 296–97. This problem was widespread and persistent (see *CSPC, 1675–76*, 319; *CSPC, 1681–5*, 112–13, 549).

16. "Report of Captain George St. Loe," May 1687, CO 1/62, 224–225r, TNA:PRO. The next year the situation was the same (Gov. Sir Nathaniel Johnson to Lords of Trade and Plantations, June 2, 1688, CO 1/64, fol. 333v, TNA:PRO).

17. "Log of the *Deptford*, 1678–1682," November 29, 1679, ADM 51/289, pts. 8–10, TNA:PRO. See also Atkins to Blathwayt, June 3/13, 1678, Blath. Papers, vol. 29, fol. 1, JDRL; and John Witham to Blathwayt, October 4, 1680, Blath. Papers, vol. 37, fol. 1, JDRL.

18. "Petition of Thomas Newton, gent., in his own and fellow subjects' behalf to the King and Council," May 15, 1665, *CSPC, 1661–8*, 295–96.

19. "Representation of the Commissioners of the Customs concerning foreign ships trading to the Plantations," March 30, 1685, Add. MSS. 38714, fol. 87, BL.

20. Gov. Lowther to the Council of Trade and Plantations, April 9, 1712, *CSPC, 1711–12*, 260–61.

21. Gov. Cony to the Earl of Sunderland, June 4, 1685, *CSPC, 1685–8, Add., 1653–87*, 49–51.

22. Gov. Johnson to Lords of Trade and Plantations, June 2, 1688, CO 1/64, fol. 333r, TNA:PRO; David Barry Gaspar, *Bondsmen & Rebels: A Study of Master-Slave Relations in Antigua with Implications for Colonial British America* (Baltimore: Johns Hopkins University Press, 1985), 69–70.

23. Gov. Willoughby to Secretary Lord Arlington, August 8, 1664, *CSPC, 1661–8*, 229–30 (first quotation); Gov. Willoughby to the King, May 12, 1666, CO 1/20, fol. 148v, TNA:PRO (second quotation).

24. "The Humble Petition of the Representatives of his Ma'ties Islands St Christophers, Nevis, Moutserrat & Antigua" (1673), in *The History of the Island of Antigua, One of the Leeward Caribbees in the West Indies, From the First Settlement in 1635 to the Present Time,* ed. Vere Langford Oliver (London, 1894–99) 1:xlix.

25. "An Account of the Number of Ships with their Burthens, Entered Outwards at ye port of London in ye year ending Michaelmas 1677," April 22, 1678, CO 1/42, fols. 116–118, TNA:PRO. For a first-person observation of the lack of shipping in the Caribbean, see the letters of Christopher Jeaffreson. For example, Correspondence of Jeaffreson to Colonel George Gamiell, May 12, 1677, May 31, 1678, and to William Poyntz, January 3, 1678/9, in *Young Squire*, 1:216–17, 229, 243–44.

26. The Council of St. Christopher to the Lords of Trade and Plantations, June 12, 1680, *CSPC, 1677–80*, 571–74 (quotation 572).

27. Zahedieh, "London and the Colonial Consumer in the Late Seventeenth Century," 249; Higham, *The Development of the Leeward Islands*, 207–10.

28. "Answer of Gov. Charles Wheler to the inquiries of the Council of Foreign Plantations," December 9, 1671, CO 1/27, 149r, TNA:PRO; *CSPC, 1677–80*, 574–75. On these developments, see Sheridan, *Sugar and Slavery*, 148–54, 161–64, 170–72, 184–91; Donald Harman Akenson, *If the Irish Ran the World: Montserrat, 1630–1730*

(Montreal: McGill-Queen's University Press, 1997), chap. 3; Dunn, *Sugar and Slaves*, 117–48; Higham, *The Development of the Leeward Islands*, chap. 8; Pares, *Merchants and Planters*, 27–28; and Pulsipher, "The Cultural Landscape of Montserrat," 34–46.

29. "Petition of the Council and Assembly of Nevis to Francis Lord Willoughby," April 29, 1664, CO 1/18, fol. 127r, TNA-PRO. See also *CSPC, 1669–74*, 205–6; *CSPC, 1677–80*, 574–75.

30. "Answer of Gov. Charles Wheler to the inquiries of the Council of Foreign Plantations," December 9, 1671, CO 1/27, fol. 152v, TNA:PRO.

31. Correspondence of William Claypole to Daniel Lodge & Company, and Robert Rogers, May 25, June 5 and June 19, 1682, in *James Claypole's Letter Book: London and Philadelphia, 1681–1684*, ed. Marion Balderson (San Marino, Calif.: Huntington Library, 1967), 137, 141, 144.

32. Gov. Sir Thomas Lynch to Secretary Arlington, June 15, 1671, CO 1/26, fol. 188, TNA:PRO; "An Account of the Number of Ships with their Burthens, Entered Inwards at ye port of London in ye year ending Michaelmas 1677," CO 1/42, fols. 116–18, TNA:PRO.

33. TASTD, http://slavevoyages.org/tast/database/search.faces?yearFrom=1670&yearTo=1688&mjslptimp=33400.33500.33600.33700.34200; TNA:PRO, CO 1/34, fols. 108r, 109r. It was not until 1686 that the RAC placed factors at Antigua and Montserrat (Akenson, *If the Irish Ran the World*, 74; Higham, *The Development of the Leeward Islands*, 161; Stephanie E. Smallwood, *Saltwater Slavery: A Middle Passage from Africa to American Diaspora* [Cambridge: Harvard University Press, 2007], 173–74).

34. *CSPC, 1669–74*, 392–93.

35. Eltis, "British Transatlantic Slave Trade," 186.

36. TASTD, http://slavevoyages.org/tast/assessment/estimates.faces?yearFrom=1600&yearTo=1688&disembarkation=309.304.303. The unnamed St. Christopher vessel arrived in 1644 with 263 slaves. Voyage # 33684, TASTD, http://slavevoyages.org/tast/database/search.faces?yearFrom=1600&yearTo=1688&mjslptimp=33400.33500.33600.33700.

37. William Byam to Gov. Willoughby, 1670, *CSPC, 1669–74*, 205–6.

38. The Agents [Henry Carpenter and Thomas Belchamber] of the Royal African Company to the Company, July 9, 1686, CO 1/59, fol. 396r, TNA:PRO; Petition of the Royal African Company to the King, October 18, 1686, CO 324/4, pp. 117–20, TNA:PRO.

39. Gov. Sir Nathaniel Johnson to Lords of Trade and Plantations, June 2, 1688, CO 1/64, fol. 331r, TNA:PRO. For the estimate of 25 percent below market price, see Bennett, "Cary Helyar, Merchant and Planter of Seventeenth-Century Jamaica," 63.

40. *Voyage of the Slavers St. John and Arms of Amsterdam*, ed. O'Callaghan, 89.

41. Ibid., xxv; Charter of the ship Eyckenboom, 1659, in *Documents Illustrative of the History of the Slave Trade to America*, ed. Elizabeth Donnan, (Washington, D.C., 1930–35) 3:417–19; Clement Tudway to RAC, January 7, 1687, T 70/12, fol. 78, TNA:PRO.

42. Gov. Sir Nathaniel Johnson to Lords of Trade and Plantations, June 2, 1688, CO 1/64, fol. 332, TNA:PRO.

43. Naval Officer Shipping Lists for Barbados, June 1681–June 1685, CO 33/13–14, TNA:PRO. See also "An Account of Barbados and its Government, map included. Abstract of Trade for Barbados," ca. 1684, Sloane MSS, 2411, BL. On new migrants and

the changing mercantile community, see Campbell, "The Merchants and Traders of Barbados, Part I," 88–89; and Smith, *Slavery, Family and Gentry Capitalism in the British Atlantic*, 19-20, 44–49, 56–59.

44. Davies, "The Origins of the Commission System in the West India Trade," 90–102; Pares, *Merchants and Planters*, 33–34; Sheridan, *Sugar and Slavery*, chap. 12; Jacob M. Price, "Credit in the Slave Trade and Plantations Economies," in *Slavery and the Rise of the Atlantic System*, ed. Barbara L. Solow (New York: Cambridge University Press, 2001), 300–302; Hancock, "A World of Business to Do," 6–7, 17–19, 23–32.

45. Nuala Zahedieh, "Credit, Risk and Reputation in Late Seventeenth-Century Colonial Trade," in *Merchant Organization and Maritime Trade in the North Atlantic, 1660-1815*, ed. Olaf Uwe Janzed (St. John's, Newfoundland: International Maritime Economic History Association, 1998), 62–67.

46. Child, *A New Discourse of Trade*, 24–25.

47. Table 4, "Barbados Population Estimates 1655–1715," in Dunn, *Sugar and Slaves*, 87. On mortality rates, see Sheridan, *Sugar and Slavery*, 246–47; Curtin, *The Atlantic Slave Trade*, 52–61; and Puckrein, *Little England*, 159–62.

48. For estimated arrivals, see TASTD, http://slavevoyages.org/tast/assessment/estimates.faces?yearFrom=1600&yearTo=1688&disembarkation=302. For actual recorded voyages, see TASTD, http://slavevoyages.org/tast/database/search.faces?yearFrom=1600&yearTo=1688&mjslptimp=34200.

49. Davies, 'The Origins of the Commission System," 95, 99–100. Even though holding bills from many planters the RAC had a notoriously difficult time in collecting these obligations (*CSPC, 1669–1674*, 363–64).

50. See note 48 above.

51. Gov. Atkins to Secretary Sir Joseph Williamson, April 20, 1675, *CSPC, 1675–76, Add., 1574–1674*, 210. The letters of the London merchant James Claypole testify to growing worry about the decline in the price of sugar. See correspondence of March 21, 1681, July 29, 1681, April 23, 1682, June 6, 1682, and July 5, 1682. During this time, Claypole reported the London price of clayed Barbadian sugar fell from 24s. per cwt to 18s (*James Claypole's Letter Book*, ed. Balderson, 33, 62–63, 111, 124, 140, 146–47).

52. "Will of William Kirton of the parish of Christ Church, Barbados," November 11, 1669, *Caribbeana*, ed. Oliver, 1:65–67; April 23, 1692, GAA:NA 5843 not. Joan Hoekeback.

53. September 9, 1687, GAA:NA 1430.

54. There is direct evidence of Dutch vessels trading in Barbados for most years between 1660 and 1688, with as many as six vessels recorded in any one year. The indirect nature of Anglo-Dutch trade and the increasingly complex illegal techniques traders used, however, mean these numbers do not accurately reflect the scope of the trade.

55. Alexander Gunkle and Jerome S. Handler, eds., "A Swiss Medical Doctor's Description of Barbados in 1661: The Account of Felix Christian Spoeri," *JBMHS* 33 (1969): 3, 10–11. *Den Dolphin* and *Het Witte Postpaert* took a similar path through Ireland for Barbados (November 29, 1660, GAA:NA 905/739, not. Jacob van Zwieten; August 23, 1660, GAA:NA 1540/pag. 213, not. Jan Volkaertsz Oli). For two cruising vessels that stopped in Virginia before continuing on to Barbados, see October 21, 1660, HHV GAA NA: 2554/pp. 499–500, not. Reynier Loenius; November 3, 1671, HHV GA: NA 3209/p. 157, not. Hendrik Outgers.

56. *Randolph Papers*, 5:41.

57. On renting space, see June 24, 1664, GAA:NA 2157/154, not. Johannes d'Amour; December 10, 1697 GAA NA 5863/651, not. Joan Hoekeback. On Armstrong, see September 29, 1662, GAA:NA 2156/p. 361, not. Johannes d'Amour. On Englishmen in Amsterdam, see June 24, 1664, GAA:NA 2157/p. 157, not. Johannes d'Amour.

58. "Act prohibiting foreigners to trade," December 27, 1660, CO 154/1 fol. 11, TNA:PRO.

59. "First petition of the merchants of Nevis to Gov. Willoughby," January 10, 1668, *CSPC, 1661-8*, 538–39, 548–49.

60. "Act against Carrying of Commodityes and entertaining foreigners," May 26, 1675, CO 154/2, fols. 138–39, TNA:PRO.

61. Gov. Stapleton to the Lords of Trade and Plantations, July 27, 1681, CO 1/47, 88v (quotations), TNA:PRO. See also "Act Concerning going on board Shipps and other Vessells," May 26, 1675, CO 154/2, fol. 123, TNA:PRO; *CSPC, 1685-8, Add., 1653-87*, 49–51.

62. "Answers to inquiries sent to Colonel Stapleton by command of the Lords of Trade and Plantations," November 22, 1676, CO 1/38 fols. 306v–7r, TNA:PRO.

63. Different islands passed such laws at different times. Consider these statutes as representative. Montserrat: "An Act for Restricting trade of this island into three towns," September 29, 1670, CO 154/1, fol. 82, TNA:PRO (quotation); "An Act for preventing Abuses that arise by Persons going on board Vessels before the Master hath made his Appearance to the Gov. and for the better ordering Boats and Wherries" (1693), in *Montserrat Code of Laws: From 1668, to 1788* (London, 1788). Nevis: "Order ascertaining the Ports and places for shipping of commerce," n.d., CO 154/1, fol. 107, TNA:PRO. Antigua: *CSPC, 1669-74*, 597.

64. "Extract from an article of the Treaty of Breda," June 18, 1687, *CSPC, 1685-8, Add., 1653-87*, 383.

65. "Report of Captain George St. Loe," May 1687, TNA:PRO CO 1/62, 224, 225r.

66. Commissioners of Customs to Lords of Treasury, June 2, 1687, *CSPC, 1685-8, Add., 1653-87*, 380.

67. De Rochefort, *The history of the Caribby-Islands*, 25; Norman F. Barka, "Citizens of St. Eustatius, 1781, A Historical and Archaeological Study," in *The Lesser Antilles*, ed. Paquette and Engerman, 223–29; Edwin Dethlefsen, "The Historical Archaeology of St. Eustatius," *Journal of New World Archaeology* 5 (1982): 73–80; Klooster, "Curaçao and the Caribbean Transit Trade," in *Riches from Atlantic Commerce*, 203–18.

68. Gwynn, ed., "Documents Relating to the Irish in the West Indies," 226.

69. Gov. Willoughby, "An account of Statia, Sabea & Tortula," July 9, 1668, Egerton MSS, 2395, #102, fols. 569–70, BL; Gov. Sir Thomas Lynch to Secretary Arlington, June 15, 1671, CO 1/26, fol. 188r, TNA:PRO.

70. Gov. Stapleton to the Lords of Trade and Plantations, May 18, 1680, *CSPC, 1677-80*, 526–27.

71. Thomas, *An Historical Account*, 44; Gov. Nathaniel Johnson to the Lords of Trade and Plantations, June 2, 1688, CO 1/64, fol. 333v, TNA:PRO.

72. De Rochefort, *The history of the Caribby-Islands*, 23.

73. Higham, *The Development of the Leeward Islands*, 37–38.

74. October 15, 1662, *APCC*, 1:338–39.

75. Ibid. The documents relating to this case can be found in *APCC*, 1:337–43.

76. Jeaffreson to Colonel George Gamiell, May 12, 1677, in *Young Squire*, 1:216–17.

77. Klooster, "Curaçao and the Caribbean Transit Trade," in *Riches from Atlantic Commerce*, 203–18.

78. *CSPC, 1574–1660*, 451; Fortune, *Merchants and Jews*, chaps. 3–4.

79. August 31, 1676, NYCCMCM (1675–1677), unpaginated.

80. Census of St. Christopher, 1678, CO 1/42, #98, 1, fols. 334–436, TNA:PRO.

81. Jeaffreson to John Jeafferson, November 11, 1676, in *Young Squire*, 1:202.

82. Jeaffreson to Colonel George Gamiell, May 12, 1677, in *Young Squire*, 1:216–17.

83. Gov. Stapleton to William Blathwayt and Patrick Trant, July 16, 1683, Blath. Papers, vol. 37, fol. 5, JDRL.

84. Will of Henry Mayer, February 15, 1663, in *History of Antigua*, ed. Oliver, 2:263.

85. Applications for Denization, March 1665, *CSPC, 1675–6, Add., 1574–1674*, 144. Neither of these men is listed in the census of 1678.

86. Pulsipher, "The Cultural Landscape of Montserrat," 43.

87. For this and the preceding paragraph, see Israel, *European Jewry in the Age of Mercantilism, 1550–1750*, 3rd ed. (London: Littman Library of Jewish Civilization, 1998), chaps. 5–6.

88. Fortune, *Merchants and Jews*, 71–77; Gordon Merrill, "The Role of the Sephardic Jews in the British Caribbean Area during the Seventeenth Century," *Caribbean Studies Journal* 4 (1964): 33–39; Swetschinski, "Conflict and Opportunity in 'Europe's Other Sea,'" 212–32; Yerushalmi, "Between Amsterdam and New Amsterdam," 172–92; Samuel, "A Review of the Jewish Colonists in Barbados," 1–111; Gragg, *Englishmen Transplanted*, 74–76; Harlow, *History of Barbados*, 263–64; and Israel, "The Republic of the United Netherlands until about 1750: Demography and Economic Activity," in *The History of the Jews in the Netherlands*, ed. Blom, Fuks-Manfield, and Schöffer, 93–95.

89. Samuel, "A Review of the Jewish Colonists in Barbados," 6–7, 110–11; Michelle M. Terrell, *The Jewish Community of Early Colonial Nevis: A Historical Archaeological Study* (Gainesville: University Press of Florida, 2005), esp. chap. 9; Welch, *Slave Society in the City*, 121–24.

90. The classic works on commercial networks and the ways in which they could lower transactions costs are Bernard Bailyn, "Communications and Trade: The Atlantic in the Seventeenth Century," *Journal of Economic History* 13 (1953): 378–87; and Price, *Capital and Credit in British Overseas Trade*. More recently, see Hancock, *Citizens of the World: London Merchants and the Integration of the British Atlantic Community, 1735–1785* (New York: Cambridge University Press, 1995); and Peter Mathias, "Risk, Credit and Kinship in Early Modern Enterprise," in *Modern Atlantic Economy*, ed. McCusker and Morgan, 15–35. On Jewish networks specifically, see Yerushalmi, "Between Amsterdam and New Amsterdam," 172–92; Swetschinski, "Conflict and Opportunity in 'Europe's Other Sea,'" 212–40; and Fortune, *Merchants and Jews*.

91. Wim Klooster, "Networks of Colonial Entrepreneurs: The Founders of the Jewish Settlements in Dutch America, 1650s and 1660s," in *Atlantic Diasporas: Jews, Conversos, and Crypto-Jews in the Age of Mercantilism, 1500–1800*, ed. Richard L. Kagan and Philip D. Morgan (Baltimore: Johns Hopkins University Press, 2009), 35, 37; Will, Aaron Navarro, Barbados, July 4, 1685, proved October 29, 1685, Samuel, "A Review of the Jewish Colonists in Barbados," 72–74, 110–11. Luis Dias, who died in London at the end of 1704 or the beginning of 1705, maintained investments in the Dutch WIC. It is unclear if Luis Dias was the same man as Lewis Diaz, who lived in Barbados, as

the Christian aliases Jewish traders used often overlapped. But it is possible that Dias lived a time in both Barbados and London (Samuel, "A Review of the Jewish Colonists in Barbados," 16–17, 78–79).

92. "Petition of Thomas Newton to the King and Council," May 15, 1665, *CSPC, 1661–8*, 295–96.

93. *CSPC, 1661–8*, 635–36; *CSPC, 1669–1674*, 2; Samuel, "Sir William Davidson, Royalist," 58. Davidson did not turn the men in because of loyalty, but rather commercial rivalry, and in fact he sometimes traded directly from Amsterdam to English colonies (August 19 and 20, 1671, HHV GAA NA: 3208/pp. 156–57, not., Hendrik Outgers).

94. Codrington to [Sec. Lord Arlington], April 21, 1669, CO 1/24, fol. 76v, TNA:PRO.

95. Israel, "The Republic of the United Netherlands," 93–95; Swetschinski, *Reluctant Cosmopolitans*, 123–42.

96. Hayne, *An abstract of all the statutes*, 10–14.

97. Coke, *A discourse of trade*, quoted in Appleby, *Economic Thought and Ideology*, 116.

98. For these petitions, see *CSPC, 1669–74*, 30, 132–34; *CSPC, 1681–5*, 691. On English debates about the money supply, see A. V. [A. Vickaries], *An Essay for Regulating of the Coyn: wherein also is set forth. . . .* (London, 1696); Child, *A new Discourse of Trade*, 31–56; Andrew Yarranton, *England's Improvement by Sea and Land to Out-do the Dutch without Fighting. . . .* (London, 1677); and Appleby, *Economic Thought and Ideology*, chap. 8.

99. The Journal of the Lords of Trade of October 16, 1676, mentions "a paper lying before the Committee, called 'Grievances of Barbadoes,' presented by petition to his Majesty in Council 24th November 1675." The document does not seem to have survived (*CSPC, 1675–6, Add., 1574–1674*, 475).

100. Gov. Atkins to the Lords of Trade and Plantations, July 4/14, 1676, CO 1/37, fols. 54v–55r, TNA:PRO). See also Gov. Atkins to Secretary Sir Joseph Williamson, April 3/13, 1676, CO 1/36, 70, TNA:PRO; and Gov. Atkins to Secretary Sir Joseph Williamson, January 22, 1677, CO 1/39, fols. 18–19, TNA:PRO.

101. Journal of the Lords of Trade and Plantations, November 2–7, 1676, CO 390/1, fols. 239–41, TNA:PRO. The most complete discussions of these proceedings are Thornton, *West-India Policy under the Restoration*, 187–90; and Bliss, *Revolution and Empire*, 179–81.

102. Journal of the Lords of Trade and Plantations, November 2–7, 1676, CO 390/1, fols. 239–41, TNA:PRO.

103. "Report of the Commissioners of the Customs to the Council for Foreign Plantations on the execution of the Navigation Acts in New England," May 12, 1675, *CSPC, 1675–6*, 231.

104. "The Assembly of Barbados to Sir Peter Colleton and ten other Gentlemen Planters in London," April 20, 1671, *CSPC, 1669–74*, 200. For the group's lobbying in the 1670s, see *CSPC, 1669–74*, 229, 284, 369, 371–73.

105. Lilian M. Penson, *The Colonial Agents of the British West Indies: A Study in Colonial Administration, Mainly in the Eighteenth Century* (London: University of London Press, 1924), chap. 3; Alison Gilbert Olson, *Making the Empire Work London and American Interest Groups, 1690–1790* (Cambridge: Harvard University Press, 1992), 27–36.

106. Littleton, *Groans of the Plantations,* 5, emphasis in original; Larry Gragg, "Littleton, Edward (*bap.* 1625, *d.* 1702)," in H. G. C. Matthew and Brian Harrison, eds., *Oxford Dictionary of National Biography* (New York: Oxford University Press, 2004). Just a year later, Dalby Thomas, a former London-based West Indies merchant, echoed Littleton's arguments in opposing the same sugar duty (Thomas, *An Historical Account,* 30–31).

107. *The Case of His Majesties Sugar Plantations* (London, 1677). For a similar position, see "Inhabitants and Planters of Barbados to the King," March 7, 1687, Sloane MSS. fols. 214–20, BL.

Notes to Chapter 5

1. The account in this and the preceding paragraphs is drawn from "Liberty graunted to the Passengers of the Ship Hopewell to come Ashoare," *General Entries* 1:285–86 ("long tedious" "formerly belonging" and "a shore"); April 30, 1669, HHV GAA:NA 2789/pp. 137–39, not. Pieter van Buijtene; August 1, 1669, HHV GAA:NA 3493 V/45, not. Gerrit van Breugel ("friends"); February 27, 1670, HHV GAA:NA 3496 II/32, not. Gerrit van Breugel; June 9, 1670, HHV GAA:NA 2557/pp. 471–74, not. Reynier Loenius; Maika, "Commerce and Community," 144–47.

2. For Anglo-Dutch trade in New York between 1669 and 1673, see April 30, 1669, HHV GAA:NA 2789/pp. 137–39, not. Pieter van Buijtene; August 1, 1669, HHV GAA:NA 3493 V/45, not. Gerrit van Breugel; February 27, 1670, HHV GAA:NA 3496 II/32, not. Gerrit van Breugel; and June 9, 1670, HHV GAA:NA 2557/pp. 471–74, not. Reynier Loenius; September 25, 1670, HHV GAA:NA 3204/462, not. Hendrik Outgers; October 2, 1670, HHV GAA:NA 3496 II/105, not. Gerrit van Breugel; March 8, 1669, HHV GAA:NA 2788/337, not. Pieter van Buijteme; June 19, 1669, HHV GAA:NA 3503 V/28, not. Gerrit van Breugel; December 17, 1670, HHV GAA:NA 3769/209–11, not. Adiaen van Santen; December 15, 1670, HHV GAA:NA 3501 VI/72, not. Gerrit van Breugel; January 14, 1671, HHV GAA:NA 3206/pp. 49–49v., not. Hendrik Outgerts; April 11, 1671, HHV GAA:NA 3207/pp. 49–49v, not. Hendrik Outgers; January 4, 1674, HHV GAA:NA 2447 I/p. 4, not. Jan Molengraeff; November 15, 1669, HHV GAA:NA 3215/pp. 66–66v, not. Hendrik Outgers; *General Entries,* 1: 236–37, 254–55, 285–96, 330, 375, 397–98, 486; *JVRC,* 419, 422, 426, 435–36, 437–38, 444–45, 446, 448–49, 460; *Albany Court,* 486–87.

For Anglo-Dutch trade in New York between 1674 and 1689, see *General Entries,* 2:74, 321; *Andros* 1:10, 16–17; *MCC,* 30, 55–74; *SCMCM,* 565; *DRCHNY* 3:233; *JVRC,* 455, 464, 466, 470; *Correspondence of Maria van Rensselaer, 1669–1689,* ed. A. J. F. Van Laer (Albany: University of the State of New York, 1935), 82; *CSPC, 1675–76, Add., 1574–1674,* 277–78; TNA:PRO E 190/664/2; TNA:PRO E 190/1044/12; TNA:PRO E 190/1045/26; TNA:PRO E 190/833–1, 2; July 14, 1675, HHV GAA:NA 3778/pp. 711–17; July 4, 1678, HHV GAA:NA 3786/pp. 1199–200, not. Adriaen van Santen; August 4, 1679, HHV GAA:NA 2312/pp. 233–34, not. Jacob de Winter; March 28, 1682, HHV GAA:NA 2794/pp. 109–10, not. Pieter van Buijtene; May 5, 1684, HHV GAA:NA 3818/pp. 1126–27, not. Adriaen van Santen; May 22, 1677, September 19, 1677, October 19, 1677, September 4, 1699, NYCCMCM; *Danckaerts,* 5–62; Hayne, 13–14, 15; *Dongan* 1:79, 171–72, 231–32, 234, 239, 243, 270–72, 345; *Dongan* 2:225, 239, 242–44; *New York City Court Records, 1684–1760: genealogical data from the Court of Quarter Sessions,* no. 50, Special Publications of the National Genealogical Society, ed. Kenneth Scott (Washington, D.C.: National Genealogical Society, 1982), 178; Schnurmann,

"Representative Atlantic Entrepreneur: Jacob Leisler, 1640–1691," in *Riches from Atlantic Commerce*, 275–76, 278, 281–82; Maika, "Commerce and Community,"149–51, 389, 390 n. 6, 391, 392 n. 8, 399–400, 474–75; Rink, *Holland on the Hudson*, 204–5; Matson, *Merchants and Empire*, 55; Henk Den Heijer, "The Dutch West India Company, 1621–1791," in *Riches from Atlantic Commerce*, 94. The nature of the evidentiary basis, however, makes these numbers a rough guide. For English shipping statistics, see Ritchie, *The Duke's Province*, 109, 115.

3. Curtis Nettles, *The Money Supply of the American Colonies Before 1720* (1934; repr., Clifton, N.J.: Augustus M. Kelley, 1973), 78 n. 27; Matson, "Commerce after the Conquest, I," 10–11.

4. Ritchie, *The Duke's Province*, 58–59.

5. For sample instructions to governors, see Labaree, ed., *Royal Instructions to British Colonial Governors*.

6. Kupp, "Aspects of New York-Dutch Trade under the English, 1670–1674," *New York Historical Society Quarterly* 58 (1974): 142–42; Matson, *Merchants and Empire*, 52–53; Paul David Nelson, "Lovelace, Francis (c. 1621–1675)," *Oxford Dictionary of National Biography* (Oxford, 2004), www.oxforddnb.com/view/article/17053.

7. *JVRC*, 398–400.

8. *General Entries*, 1:254–55.

9. "Extraordinary session of the Court of Albany, Rensselaerswyck and Schenectady," August 4, 1669, in *Minutes of the Court of Albany, Rensselaerswyck, and Schenectady, 1668–1673*, ed. A. J. F. Van Laer (Albany: University of the State of New York, 1926), 1:91–93.

10. On the *Dolphin*, see September 25, 1670, HHV GAA:NA 3204/462, not. Hendrik Outgers; and October 2, 1670, HHV GAA:NA 3496 II/105, not. Gerrit van Breugel. On the *Fort Albanie*, see March 8, 1669, HHV GAA:NA 2788/337, not. Pieter van Buijteme; June 19, 1669, HHV GAA:NA 3503 V/28, not. Gerrit van Breugel; December 17, 1670, HHV GAA:NA 3769/209–11, not. Adiaen van Santen; *General Entries*, 1:330. On the *Margaret*, see *General Entries*, 1:375; *JVR, Correspondence*, 419, 426, 430, 435–36, 446–49.

11. Evidence of the smugglers whom authorities captured can be found throughout New York City's early records, especially NYCCMCM; *General Entries*; and *Dongan*. Other scholars have discussed the volume of illegal trade in New York along similar lines. See those cited in this chapter, especially Matson, *Merchants and Empire*, 83–86, 126–27, 203–14, 270–71; and, for the later eighteenth century, Truxes, *Defying Empire*.

12. "Plea of George Lockhart and English Smith in defense of the ship *Seaflower*" 1684; and "A Deposition by Charles Barham and John Wilson," 1685, both in *Dongan*, 1:91, 270–72.

13. April 12, 1670, HHV GAA:NA 3504 V/30, not. Gerrit van Breugel; May 3, 1670, HVV GAA:NA 3502 VI/22, not. Gerrit van Breugel; June 6, 1670, HHV GAA:NA 3494 I/44, not. Gerrit van Breugel; June 11, 1670, HHV GAA:NA 3504 I/40, not. Gerrit van Breugel; August 5, 1670, HHV GAA:NA 3501 VI/45, not. Gerrit van Breugel; August 20, 1671, HHV GAA:NA 2301/pp. 73–74, not. Jacob de Winter; *General Entries*, 1:235–38; Kupp, "Aspects of Dutch-New York Trade," 141–46. De Wolff quotation from Oliver Rink, "Unraveling a Secret Colonialism: I," *de Halve Maen* 59 (1987): 16.

14. "A Passe for the Governors Ship the Good Fame of New York to Engl[and] and Holland," July 4, 1670, *General Entries*, 1:358.

15. "Certificate of denization for John Deforest," July 6, 1670, NYC Misc., MSS, Box 3, #7, NYHS; November 20, 1670, HHV GAA:NA: 3205/pp. 311–13, not. Hendrik Outgers; December 15, 1670, HHV GAA:NA 3501 VI/72, not. Gerrit van Breugel; January 14, 1671, HHV GAA:NA 3206/pp. 49–49v, not. Hendrik Outgers; April 11, 1671, HHV GAA:NA 3207/pp. 49–49v, not. Hendrik Outgers; January 4, 1674, HHV GAA:NA 2447 I/p. 4, not. Jan Molengraeff; DRCHNY, 3:185; JVRC, 423–25; Rink, Holland on the Hudson, 204–5. A vessel named Good Fame, now captained by Jacob Maurits and owned by a group of denizened New Yorkers, sailed to New York in April 1671 and returned to Amsterdam in September. It is unclear if this was the same vessel (April 27, 1671, HHV GAA:NA 3207/pp. 93–93v, not. Hendrik Outgers; January 4, 1674, HHV GAA:NA 2447 I/p. 4, not. Jan Molengraeff).

16. Will of Isaac Bedloe, February 1672/3, in "Abstracts of Wills on File in the Surrogate's Office, City of New York, Volume 1, 1665–1707," 30.

17. General, 1:486–87; March 27, 1670, HHV GAA:NA 3107/91–91v, not. Hendrick Rosa.

18. Israel, Dutch Primacy in World Trade, 293–99; Jones, The Anglo-Dutch Wars, 216–20; C. R. Boxer, "Some Second Thoughts on the Third Anglo-Dutch War, 1672–1674," Transactions of the Royal Historical Society, 5th ser., 19 (1969): 81–82.

19. For the eleven voyages, see NYCCMCM; DRCHNY 3:233; General Entries 2:74; Andros 1:10, 16–17, 55–74, 3:233; SCMCM, 565; MMC, 30, 55; CSPC, 1675–76, Add,, 1574–1674, 277–78; JVRC, 455, 464, 466, 470; Maika, "Commerce and Community" 150–51, 389, 391 n. 6; and Rink, Holland on the Hudson, 204–5.

20. Ritchie, The Duke's Province, 86; Maika, "Commerce and Community," 150–51.

21. Danckaerts, 25–32.

22. The Charles entered Falmouth from Amsterdam on May 1, 1680. It was back in Falmouth on October 7, 1680, left November 8, 1680, for Amsterdam, and stopped again in Falmouth on the way to New York on June 1, 1681 (TNA:PRO E 190/1044/18; E 190/1044/12; E 190/1045/26). Governor Dongan seized this vessel for illegal trade in 1684 (Dongan 1:171–72, 270–72). The Peter of London stopped in Falmouth on a passage from Amsterdam to New York in May 1680 (TNA:PRO E 190/1044/18; E 190/1044/12). The Philip passed through Falmouth in May 1680 (TNA:PRO E 190/1045/26). In 1684, the Charles entered Cowes on April 21, and the Phillip on May 31 (TNA:PRO E 190/833–1, 190/833–2).

23. Hayne, An abstract of all the statutes made concerning aliens, 15.

24. Maika, "Commerce and Community," 389–98; Ritchie, The Duke's Province, 109; Schnurman, "Atlantic Trade and American Identities," in The Atlantic Economy during the Seventeenth and Eighteenth Centuries, ed. Coclanis, 192–96. For the De Peysters' enduring connections to Amersterdam, see G. Bancker at Amsterdam to A. de Peyster at New York City, March 17, 1699, De Peyster Papers, manuscript translations by Digman Versteeg, NYHS, microfilm.

25. Cornelis Steenwyck, "Two notes to Gillis and Tobias Van Hoernbeck" (1682), Misc. MSS., NYC Churches, Box 30, NYHS, photostat; March 13, 1688, HHV GAA:NA 2331/pp. 299–318, not. Jacob de Winter.

26. May 22, 1677, NYCCMCM (1675–77), unpaginated. Darvall continued to work with Minvielle ("Suit of Wm Swan Boatswaine George Saye boatswaine mate John Johnson Carpenter & Robert Howard Gunner & alsoe the Rest of the Company of Saylors of the Shipp Friends Adventure, plt" against "James Sattman Master & William

Darvall & Gabriel Minviel merchants & parte Owners of the Shipp friends Advantue, deft," June 27, 1682, NYCCMCM [1677–1682], fols. 234b-4).

27. The suits and countersuits between these individuals reveal the details of the exchange in *Dongan*, 1:234–43.

28. Schnurmann, "Representative Atlantic Entrepreneur: Jacob Leisler, 1640–1691," in *Riches from Atlantic Commerce*, 259–83; D. W. Voorhees, "The Fervent Zeal of Jacob Leisler," *WMQ*, 3rd ser., 51 (1994): 447–72. On Moy's role as a representative of Philipse, see August 12, 1683, HHV GAA:NA: 3266/141, not. Hendrick Outgers.

29. June 18, 1680, and August 16, 1680, GAA:NA: 4958/494, 548, not. P. de Wit; February 18, 1684, GAA:NA 2323, fols. 177–80.

30. *Dongan*, 1:171–72, 270–71; *Danckaerts*, 28.

31. JVR to Oloff Stevensen van Cortlandt, March 27, 1674, and JVR to Richard van Rensselaer, July 3, 1674, *JVR, Correspondence*, 255, 266; Schnurmann, "Representative Atlantic Entrepreneur," 275. Bayard traded with David Coirtrio among others in Amsterdam (August 3, 1677, NYCCMCM [1675–77], unpaginated).

32. *JVR, Correspondence*, 264–66, 470.

33. Among the investors, owning one-third of the cargo was the Englishman William Radney (March 16 and August 17, 1675, *MMC*, 22, 30, 55).

34. "A Certificate about the Sale of the Ketch *Susannah*, now called the *Mary*," October 1, 1675, *General* 2:74 (quotations); John Hollovtt, plt., Asser Levy, deft., November 22, 1681, NYCCMCM, (1677–1682), fols. 307–8.

35. Cornelis Clopper Ledger, Misc. Mss., NYHS; Maika, "Commerce and Community," 420–27; Matson, *Merchants and Empire*, 54–55.

36. July 14, 1675, HHV GAA:NA, 3778/pp. 711–17, not. Adriaen van Santen. A decade later, Cornelies Jansen Moy and the Gilles van Hoornbeek were both occasionally still organizing trade for New York in the 1680s. April 3, 1685, HHV GAA:NA 3276/pp. 151–51v, not. Hendrik Outgers; June 4, 1685, HHV GAA:NA 2325/pp. 537–43, not. Jacob de Winter.

37. "Merchants trading to New Netherland to the Admiralty at Amsterdam" (1674), *DRCHNY*, 2:541–42.

38. *DRCHNY*, 3:216–19; Mary Lou Lustig, *The Imperial Executive in America: 1637–1717* (Madison: University of Wisconsin Press, 2002), 25, 38; Ritchie, *The Duke's Province*, 93–94, 100–101; Stephen Saunders Webb, "The Trials of Sir Edmund Andros," in *The Human Dimensions of Nation Making*, ed. James Kirby Martin (Madison: University Wisconsin Press, 1976), 23–53.

39. *Calendar of Council Minutes, 1668–1788*, ed. Berthold Fernow and A. J. F. van Laer, (Harrison, N.Y.: Harbor Hill Books, 1987), 7. Before 1677, twelve of the twenty-three magistrates for the city were English, at a time when three-quarters of the population was Dutch (Ritchie, *The Duke's Province*, 98–99).

40. Werden apparently received three letters from Andros, dated February 15, 1675, February 16, 1675, and April 20, 1675, but these did not survive (*DRCHNY*, 3:232).

41. Werden to Gov. Andros, January 28, 1675/6, *DRCHNY*, 3:236.

42. Werden to Gov. Andros, February 13, 1674/5, *DRCHNY*, 3:228–29.

43. *DRCHNY*, 3:232–34, 236–37.

44. *Danckaerts*, 5, 25–26, 36 (quotation), 167; *DRCHNY*, 3:233; *Andros*, 3:xx–xxi.

45. For the canal, see *General Entries*, 2:98–99; *Calendar of Council Minutes*, ed. Fernow and Van Laer, 42. On the dock, see *Minutes of the Common Council of the*

City of New York, 1675–1776, ed. Herbert L. Osgood et al. (New York: Dodd, Mead, 1905), 1:25–26, 27–37; *DRCHNY,* 3:303; James D. Kornwolf and Georgiana W. Kornwolf, *Architecture and Town Planning in Colonial North America: Creating the North American Landscape* (Baltimore: Johns Hopkins University Press, 2002), 391; and Middleton, *From Privileges to Rights,* 73, 80.

46. *DRCHNY,* 13:531–32.

47. *Calendar of Council Minutes,* ed. Fernow and Van Laer, 42; Ritchie, *The Duke's Province,* 114.

48. Matson, *Merchants and Empire,* 79, 94–95.

49. *Minutes of the Common Council,* ed. Osgood et al., 1:80; Matson, *Merchants and Empire,* 75–80, 94–104.

50. *DRCHNY,* 3:268; *Danckaerts,* 244–49.

51. For their petition, see *DRCHNY,* 3:283; Murrin, "English Rights as Ethnic Aggression," in *Authority and Resistance in Early New York,* ed. Penack and Wright, 66–69.

52. Werden to Gov. Andros, May 24, 1680, *DRCHNY,* 3:283–84.

53. On Lewen, see *DRCHNY,* 3:279–82; and Ritchie, *The Duke's Province,* 117–23.

54. "Report of Sir John Lewen to the Duke of York," November 2, 1681, *DRCHNY,* 3:302–8; "Answer of Sir Edmund Andros to Mr. Lewin's report," December 31, 1682, *DRCHNY,* 3:308–13.

55. For Dongan's instructions, see *DRCHNY,* 3:369–75, 382–84.

56. On Brockholls, see *DRCHNY,* 3:287–89, 292, 318–19; and *Dongan,* 1:224–29, 236–38; 2:226–74. For the customs dispute, see Ritchie, *The Duke's Province,* 155–57.

57. "Order regularizing the reporting of ships violating the Navigation laws," August 6, 1685, *General,* 2:344.

58. *General,* 2:373–74.

59. *Dongan,* 1:270–72.

60. For the charges against Santen and his response, see *DRCHNY,* 3:389–90, 399, 401–8, 421–28, 493–95, 495–500; and 1687, Governor's Report on the State of the Province of *The Documentary History of the State of New York,* ed. Edmund B. O'Callaghan (Albany, N.Y.: Weed, Parsons, and Comp., 1850–51), 1:176–78, 182–85.

61. Ritchie, *The Duke's Province,* 127–39; Archdeacon, *New York City,* 40–41; Matson, *Merchants and Empire,* 55. Population from Goodriend, *Before the Melting Pot,* 61.

62. Maika, "Commerce and Community," 394–95; Ritchie, *The Duke's Province,* 98–99; Van Laer, *Correspondence of Maria van Rensselaer,* index. On the *Susanna,* November 5, 1678, HHV GAA:NA 3236/pp. 921–921v, not. Hendrik Outgers. For other trade with his father, see June 18, 1680, GAA:NA 4958/494, not. P. de Wit; August 2 1680, GAA:NA 4780/381, not. Godert van Hille.

63. Lawrence Leder and Vincent P. Carosso, "Robert Livingston (1654–1728): Businessman of Colonial New York," *Business History Review* 30 (1956): 18–20, 24–27 (quotation, 25); Cynthia A. Kierner, *Traders and Gentlefolk: The Livingstons of New York, 1675–1790* (Ithaca, N.Y.: Cornell University Press, 1992), chap. 2.

64. On the arrival of the Jews in New Amsterdam, see Leo Hershkowitz, "By Chance or Choice: Jews in New Amsterdam, 1654," *de Halve Maen* 77 (2004): 23, which revises earlier scholarship.

65. For example, October 10, 1676, and August 31, 1676, NYCCMCM (1675–77), unpaginated.

66. Hershkowitz, "Some Aspects of the New York Jewish Merchant and Community, 1654–1820," *American Jewish Historical Quarterly* 6 (1767/7): 25–26.

67. January 27, 1659, AJA-NA, #2443/479–80, not. Jan Molengraff; Asser Levy, pltf., vs. Cornelis Pluyvier (Plavier), deft, May 22, 1662, *RNA*, 4:173.

68. Valack's wife, Rachel, hired Saloman in Amsterdam (Power of Attorney, Elias de Pommares, May 25, 1678, AJA-NA, #4087/pp.177–78, not. Dirk van der Groe; Power of Attorney, July 23, 1680, Rachel Valentijn, AJA-NA, #2315/pp.77–78, not. Jacob de Winterf). See also Leon Hühner, "Asser Levy, A Noted Jewish Burgher of New Amsterdam," *Publications of the Jewish Historical Society* 8 (1900): 9–23; Leo Hershkowitz, "Asser Levy and the Inventories of Early New York Jews," *American Jewish Historical Quarterly* 80 (1990/91): 21–55.

69. April 17, 1681, AJA-NA, #3252/239, not. J. H. Outgers.

70. In 1678, Andros noted that "a merchant worth 100 pounds or 500 pounds is accompted a good substantiall merchant" ("Answers of Gov. Andros to Enquiries About New York," April 16, 1678, *DRCHNY*, 3:260–62). See also Matson, *Merchants and Empire*, 340 n. 40, 348 n. 39.

71. See note 2 above.

72. For Andros's estimate, see *DRCHNY*, 3:260–62.

73. "Gov. Dongan's Report to the Committee of Trade on the Province of New-York," February 22, 1687, *The Documentary History of the State of New York*, ed. O'Callaghan, 1:160.

74. Cathy Matson, "'Damned Scoundrels' and 'Libertisme of Trade': Freedom and Regulation in Colonial New York's Fur and Grain Trades," *WMQ*, 3rd ser., 51 (1994): 389–418, esp. 400–405, 408–9.

Notes to Chapter 6

1. Samuel Brise to the Council of Trade and Plantations, received January 19, 1710, CO 388/12, fol. 267, TNA-PRO.

2. For the effects of the wars in the Caribbean, see *CSPC, 1689–92*, 504–6; *CSPC, 1693–6*, 557; *CSPC, 1696–7*, 305, 391; Richard Pares, "Barbados History from the Records of the Prize Courts, 2. The *Six Friends* of London, 1693," *JBMHS* 5(1938/9): 12–15; William Thomas Morgan, "The British West Indies during King William's War (1689–97)," *Journal of Modern History* 2 (1930): 378–409; and Davis, *The Rise of the English Shipping Industry in the Seventeenth and Eighteenth Centuries*, 316–19, 324, 327–28, 334.

3. Child, *A New Discourse* (1692), 91; M. G. Hall, "The House of Lords, Edward Randolph, and the Navigation Act of 1696," *WMQ*, 3rd ser., 14 (1957): 501–4; I. K. Steele, *Politics of Colonial Policy: The Board of Trade in Colonial Administration, 1696–1720* (Oxford: Clarendon Press, 1968), 44–53.

4. For this and the paragraph above, see Sir William Petty, *Quantulumcunque Concerning Money* (1682; repr., London, 1695), 165; Ralph Davis, "English Foreign Trade, 1660–1700," in *The Growth of English Overseas Trade in the Seventeenth and Eighteenth Centuries*, ed. Minchinton, 80–84, 95–96; Ormrod, *The Rise of Commercial Empires*, 35–59, 62–66, 278–87, 341–45; Jonathan Scott, "'Good Night Amsterdam,'" 337–39, 348–56; O'Brien and Hunt, "The Rise of a Fiscal State in England," 129–76; and Baugh, "Maritime Strength and Atlantic Commerce," in *An Imperial State at War*, ed. Stone, 185–90.

5. Nuala Zahedieh, "London and the Colonial Consumer in the Late Seventeenth Century," *Economic History Review*, 2nd ser., 47 (1994): 239–61; Ormord, *The Rise of Commercial Empires*, chap. 6; Sheridan, *Sugar and Slavery*, 155–57, 181–83, 192–97, 415–26; Eltis, "The Total Product of Barbados," 321–38. For population estimates, see Milary McD. Beckles, "A 'Riotous and Unruly Lot': Irish Indentured Servants and Freemen in the English West Indies, 1644–1713," *WMQ*, 3rd ser., 47 (1990): 505; McCusker and Menard, *Economy of British America*, 154.

6. Davis, *The Rise of the English Shipping Industry*, esp. 22–43.

7. Gov. Johnson to Lords of Trade and Plantations, June 2, 1688, CO 1/64, fol. 333v, TNA:PRO.

8. "Extract of a letter from Gov. Codrington," February 12, 1690, *CSPC, 1689–92*, 388; Morgan, "The British West Indies during King William's War," 386.

9. Cornelis Ch. Goslinga, *The Dutch in the Caribbean and in the Guianas, 1680–1791* (Dover, N.H.: Van Gorcum, 1985), 189–98.

10. "Copy of a letter to Admiral Nevill [from J. Johns Sonn]," May 4, 1697, *CSPC, 1696-7*, 476–77 (first quotation); "Deposition of Sr Timothy Thornhill," June 27, 1691, and "Deposition of Joseph Crisp," July 2, 1691, CO 28/37, fols. 145–46 (second quotation), TNA-PRO.

11. "Memorial of the Leeward Islands being complaints against the Governor & was sent to ye Board in a Penny post without date or name," March 4, 1697/8, CO 152/2, fols. 182r–85r, TNA-PRO; *CSPC, 1697-8*, 192–203; *CSPC, 1689–92*, 481–82; Vincent T. Harlow, *Christopher Codrington, 1668–1710* (1928; repr., London: St. Martin's Press, 1990), 32–34.

12. Gov. Parke to the Lords of Trade and Plantations, October 1, 1708, CO 153/10, fols. 292–93, TNA:PRO; *CSPC, 1710-1*, 94–95; Pittman, *The Development of the British West Indies*, 204–5.

13. Randolph to the Council of Trade and Plantations, March 17, 1701, *Randolph Papers*, 5: 226–27, 257–60 (first quotation 258); "Extract of a Report of Commissioners of the Customs," October 29, 1703, CO 323/5, fol. 109 (second quotation), TNA:PRO.

14. James Claypole to Robert Rogers, June 19, 1682 in *James Claypole's Letter* Book, ed. Balderson, 144.

15. Sheridan, *Sugar and Slavery*, 398–410, 496.

16. Only tobacco import statistics for London survive. For 1686, see Zahedieh, "London and the Colonial Consumer," 246. For 1703, see "An Account of the Imports and Exports of Sugar & Tobacco from Christmas 1702 to Christmas 1722, Rec'd from Mr. Oxenford," June 10, 1724, CO 390/5, TNA:PRO. For other fragmentary quantities and estimates, see "Account of exports and imports to and from St Christopher to London, Christmas 1698 to Christmas 1699," CO 390/6, fol. 103, TNA:PRO; and Higham, *Development of the Leeward Islands*, 207.

17. Gov. Codrington to Lords of Trade and Plantations, June 4, 1690, *CSPC, 1689–92*, 278. For efforts to control freight rates, see *CSPC, 1689–92*, 373, 405–6; Edward Singleton on behalf of the Assembly to King, March 2, 1693, CO 28/2, fols. 140–41, TNA:PRO. For the law, see CO 28/2, fol. 83, TNA:PRO.

18. This claim was made by Gov. Parke in response to colonists' complaints about his administration. "Articles of Complaint Exhibited against Daniel Parke, Esq. with his ANSWERS respectively to each ARTICLE," September 9, 1709, in George French,

The History of Col. Park's Administration Whilst he was Captain-General and Chief Governor of the Leeward Islands. . . . (London, 1717), 198.

19. Gov. Kendall to Lords of Trade and Plantations, August 22, 1690, *CSPC, 1689–93*, 311.

20. See, for example, *CSPC, 1706–8*, 137–38.

21. "Extract from a letter of Sir William Beeston to William Blathwayt," March 18, 1697, *CSPC, 1696–7*, 403–4.

22. William Popple to John Sansom, January 22, 1701/2, CO 153/7, pp. 387–89 (first quotation 388), TNA-PRO; Gov. Parke to the Lords of Trade and Plantations, October 1, 1708, CO 153/10, pp. 288–300, (second quotation 292), TNA:PRO; S. D. Smith, "The Account Book of Richard Poor, Quaker Merchant of Barbados," *WMQ*, 3rd. ser., 66 (2009): 607.

23. By the 1730s, the trade from St. Eustatius to foreign Caribbean islands involved nearly one hundred ships a year (Goslinga, *The Dutch in the Caribbean and in the Guianas*, 81–95, 189–200).

24. July 12 1692, GAA:NA 4773, not. Stephen Pelgrom; November 6, 1696, GAA:NA 5859/175, not. Joan Hoekebak.

25. On the limitations of these returns, see Zahedieh, "The Merchants of Port Royal, Jamaica, and the Spanish Contraband Trade," 576, 578; Menard and McCusker, *The Economy of British America*, 76–77; and Eltis, "New Estimated of Exports from Barbados and Jamaica," 632–34.

26. The lists for Barbados can be found at CO 33/13–5, TNA:PRO; and for the Leeward Islands at CO 157/1, TNA:PRO. Total numbers of vessels entering and exiting: Antigua, 201, 315; St. Christopher, 71, 38; Montserrat, 65, 71; Nevis, 191, 137. See also Enthoven, "An Assessment of Dutch Transatlantic Commerce, 1585–1817," in *Riches from Atlantic Commerce*, table 14.5, 413.

27. Gov. Codrington to the Council of Trade and Plantations, June 30, 1701, *CSPC, 1701*, 327–28. See also *Randolph Papers*, 5:226–27; "Memorial of Mr. Holt relating to ye Trade carried on between Curacoa & St. Thomas and the British Plantations, received December 15, 1709," CO 388/12, fol. 251v, TNA:PRO; and "Articles of Complaint Exhibited against Daniel Parke, Esq., with his ANSWERS respectively to each ARTICLE," in French, *The History of Col. Park's Administration*, 197–98.

28. Gov. Codrington to Lords of Trade and Plantations, May 5, 1701, CO 152/4, fols. 56r–59v, TNA:PRO. For just several examples of continued corruption and the inability to stop illegal trade, see Gov. Codrington to the Lords of Trade, January 12, 1701, CO 152/4, fols. 29r–31r, TNA:PRO; *CSPC, 1697–8*, 122; *CSPC, 1700*, 436–37; *CSPC, 1702–3*, 686–87; *CSPC, 1711–1*, 91–92, 94–95, 177.

29. Gov. Parke to Lords of Trade and Plantations, October 1, 1708, CO 153/10, pp.. 288–300, TNA:PRO; General Assembly to Lt. Gov. and Council, January 26, 1710/11, in "Minutes of the Assembly of Antigua, January 26, 1710/11 to July 19, 1711," CO 9/2, unpaginated, TNA:PRO. Parke noted the attempt to bribe him when responding to complaints against his administration. French, *The History of Col. Park's Administration*, 198–99; Natalie Zacek, "A Death in the Morning: The Murder of Daniel Parke," in *Cultures and Identities in Colonial British America*, ed. Robert Olwell and Alan Tully (Baltimore: Johns Hopkins University Press, 2006), 223–43, esp. 235.

30. On the *Mary*, see "Antigua shipping returns September 25, 1707 to December 25, 1707," TNA:PRO CO 157/1, fol. 7.

31. Lt. Gov. Johnson [Nevis] to the Council of Trade and Plantations, May 24, 1705, *CSPC, 1704–5*, 521.

32. Michael J. Jarvis, *'In the Eye of All Trade': Bermuda, Bermudians, and the Maritime Atlantic World, 1680–1783* (Chapel Hill: University of North Carolina Press, 2010), 171–73.

33. "Memorial of Mr. Holt," CO 388/12, fols. 251r–255r, 257r–261r (quotation 253v), TNA:PRO; Samuel Brise to the Council of Trade and Plantations, received January 19, 1710, 388/12, fol. 267, TNA-CO; "Peter Holt to Capt. William Billton enclosed in Nov 4, 1709, Mr. Burchett to Mr. Popple," *CSPC, 1708–9*, 505–6 (final quotation). For *Curaçao Merchant*, see CO 33/15, fols. 28–31, 32–34v, 35–37v, TNA-PRO.

34. Will of Eleazer Valverde, Barbados, May 14, 1725, Korn Papers, Box 2, fol. 11, JRM-AJA; Fortune, *Merchants and Jews*, 142; Swetschinski, "Conflict and Opportunity," 232–34.

35. On Senior/Henriquez, see Emmanuel and Emmanuel, *History of the Jews of the Netherlands Antilles*, 1:73, 76–78; 2:739; Samuel Oppenheim, "An Early Jewish Colony in Western Guiana, 1658–1666: And Its Relation to the Jews in Suriname, Cayenne and Tobago," *Publications of the American Jewish Historical Society* 16 (1907): 95–186, 106; Arnold Wiznitzer, "The Members of the Brazilian Jewish Community (1648–1653)," *Publications of the American Jewish Historical Society* 42 (1952): 395.

36. Pinheiro died in New York City in 1710 (Will of Isaac Pinheiro, Nevis, November 12, 1708, in Lee M. Friedman, ed. "Wills of Early Jewish Settlers in New York," *Publications of the American Jewish Historical Society* 23 [1915]: 147–61, 157–58; Malcolm H. Stern, "Some Notes on the Jews of Nevis," n.d., manuscript at JRM-AJA; Eli Faber, *Jews, Slaves, and the Slave Trade: Setting the Record Straight* (New York: New York University Press, 1998), 102; Terrell, *The Jewish Community of Early Colonial Nevis*, 51, 99–100, 160 n. 1.

37. "Presentment and requests of the Grand Jury to Gov. Willoughby," October 23, 1668, *CSPC, 1661–8*, 620.

38. "An Act against Jews ingrossing Commodities imported in the Leeward Islands," August 31, 1694, CO 8/1, fols. 64–65, TNA:PRO. The act was eventually repealed December 10, 1701, CO 8/1, fols. 148–49, TNA:PRO. For earlier complaints about Jewish traders, see *CSPC, 1661–8*, 49, 295–96, 530, 620; *CSPC, 1677–80*, 446. On taxes, see Welch, *Slave Society in the City*, 122.

39. For support of Jewish traders, see *CSPC, 1661–1668*, 49; *CSPC, 1669–74*, 464–65; *CSPC, 1681–85*, 81, 99; *APCC*, 1:534–35.

40. Lt. Gov. Stede to the Lords of Trade and Plantations, September 19, 1687, *CSPC, 1685–8*, 444; "An act of repeal a certain Act against the Jewes," December 10, 1701, CO 8/1, fols. 148–9, TNA-PRO.

41. Postma, "Suriname and its Atlantic Connections, 1667–1795," in *Riches from Atlantic Commerce*, 289–90, 294–95, 297, 300–305.

42. William Gordon to Board of Trade, August 17, 1720, CO 5/867, fols. 344–345r, TNA:PRO. For trade to Suriname via Barbados, see the cargoes listed in CO 33/13–15, TNA:PRO, and November 6, 1696, GAA; NA 5859/175, not. Joan Hoekebak.

43. Robert Quay to the Commisioners of Customs, March 6, 1700, *CSPC, 1700*, 107–8.

44. "Memorial of Mr. Holt," CO 388/12, fol. 251r, TNA:PRO. The shipping list for May 25 to September 25, 1704, does not indicate a vessel making such a journey,

though there are no records for the months before May 1704. For the arrival of the *Lark,* see CO 157/1, fol. 6r, TNA:PRO.

45. "Memorial of Mr. Holt," CO 388/12, fols. 251r, 253r, TNA:PRO. For other similar reports, see *CSPC, 1704–5,* 616; *CSPC, 1710–1,* 97.

46. "Memorial of Mr. Holt," CO 388/12, fol. 252r, TNA:PRO.

47. Eberhard Schmitt, "The Brandenburg Overseas Trading Companies in the 17th Century," in *Companies and Trade,* ed. Blussé and Gaastra, 163–70; Neville A. T. Hall, *Slave Society in the Danish West Indies: St. Thomas, St. John, and St. Croix,* ed. B. W. Higman (Baltimore: Johns Hopkins University Press, 1992), 3–9; Isaac Dookhan, *A History of the Virgin Islands of the United States* (Jamaica: Canoe Press, 1994), 61, 94. Contemporaries claimed the Dutch dominated St. Thomas as well (*The Memoirs of Père Labat, 1693–1705,* ed. John Eaden [1931; repr., London: Frank Cass, 1970], 200–201; "Minutes of the Common Council of Antigua, June 8, 1709 to November 21, 1709," November 4, 1709, CO 9/1, 57–59 TNA:PRO; *CSPC, 1699, Add., 1621–98,* 503).

48. Minutes of Nevis Council, July 22, 1695, CO 157/1, fol. 162, TNA:PRO; *CSPC, 1701,* 697; *CSPC, 1702–3,* 843; *CSPC, 1704–5,* 369; Gov. Parke to Captain George Ramsey, Commander of Her Majesty's Ship *Diamond,* January 1, 1709/10, CO 9/1, p. 10, TNA:PRO; January 19, 1709/10, Phillip Meadows, J[?] Gullenet, Robt Montalon, Stamford to Gov. Crowe, CO 29/12, pp. 76–78, TNA:PRO.

49. Gov. Codrington to the Council of Trade and Plantations, September 27, 1697, *CSPC, 1696–7,* 621–22

50. "Extract of a Report of Commissioners of the Customs to the Excellent Honorable The Lord High Treasurer of England," October 29, 1703, CO 323/5, fol. 109, TNA:PRO.

51. Lt. Gov. Bennett to the Council of Trade and Plantations, October 19, 1703, *CSPC, 1702–3,* 750.

52. Lt. Gov. Johnson to Mr. Secretary Hedges, May 28, 1706, *CSPC, 1706–8,* 137.

53. "The State of the Case Manasses Gilligan as drawn up by ye Judge of the Admiralty, the Attorney & Solicitor General of Barbados," October 29, 1703, CO 28/7, fols. 549–50 (first quotation), 560 (nonconsecutive pagination), TNA:PRO; Minutes of the Council of Barbados, September 1, 1703, *CSPC, 1702–3,* 662–3 (second quotation). On the value of St. Thomas because of its neutrality, see Gov. Granville to the Board of Trade, September 3, 1703, CO 28/6, fols. 424v–25r, TNA:PRO. The best accounts of Gillian are in Pares, "Barbados History from the Records of the Prize Courts, 3, A Trader with the Enemy, 1702: Manuel M. Gilligan," *Journal of the Barbados Museum* 6, no. 2 (1939): 59–66; and Pittman, *The Development of the British West Indies,* 195.

54. Gov. Granville to Board of Trade, October 3, 1703, CO 28/7, fol. 511, TNA:PRO. For more on the use of St. Thomas as a base to trade to the Leeward Islands, see Hart to Board of Trade, July 12, 1724, CO 152/14, fols. 325r–40v, TNA:PRO.

55. Attorney General to the Council of Trade and Plantations, March 22, 1704, *CSPC, 1704–5,* 82–3 (quotation). See also the Queen to Gov. Sir B. Grenville, July 29, 1705, *CSPC, 1704–5,* 600.

56. Sunderland to Board of Trade, September 14, 1708, CO 28/11 fol. 131r, TNA:PRO.

57. The tallies of slaves for 1701 and 1702 may be slightly inflated due to continued efforts by planters to make up for those they could not buy during the War of the League of Augsburg (TASTD, http://slavevoyages.org/tast/database/search.faces?yearFrom=1689 &yearTo=1713&natinimp=7&mjslptimp=33400.33500.33600.33700.34200.35100.35500;

and http://slavevoyages.org/tast/assessment/estimates.faces?yearFrom=1689&yearTo
=1713&disembarkation=309.311.305.304.302.307.310.306.301.303.308; Pettigrew, "Free
to Enslave: Politics and the Escalation of Britain's Transatlantic Slave Trade, 1688–
1714," 5 n 2).

58. Data for St. Eustatius include recorded deliveries only and include slaves from
the Netherlands (946) and those from Brandenburg (1,484). "Trans-Atlantic Slave
Trade Database," http://slavevoyages.org/tast/database/search.faces?yearFrom=1688
&yearTo=1713&mjslptimp=32150. Data for St. Thomas only include recorded deliveries from Great Britain (97), the Netherlands (1,080) and Danish and Baltic carriers
(15,337), TASTD, http://slavevoyages.org/tast/database/search.faces?yearFrom=1688&
yearTo=1713&mjslptimp=37020. See also Johannes Postma, "A Reassemsment of the
Dutch Atlantic Slave Trade," in *Riches from Atlantic Commerce*, 134, 137; Johannes
Postma, "The Dispersal of African Slaves in the West by Dutch Slave Traders, 1630–
1803," in *The Atlantic Slave Trade: Effects on Economics, Societies, and Peoples in Africa, the Americas and Europe*, ed. Joseph E. Inikori and Staley L. Engerman (Durham,
N.C.: Duke University Press, 1992), 293–97.

59. Reports of the sale of slaves from these islands to English colonies are numerous
in the decades before and after 1700 (*CSPC, 1696–7*, 476–77, 621–22; *CSPC, 1697–8*,
333–35; *CSPC, 1716–7*, 301–2; *Documents Illustrative of the History of the Slave Trade*,
ed. Donnan, 2:241–42; *The Importance of the British Plantations in America To This
Kingdom* (London, 1731), 32–34. See also Gaspar, *Bondsmen & Rebels*, 69–75; Welch,
"Intra-American and Caribbean Destinations and Transit Points for the Slave Trade,"
Journal of Caribbean History 42, no. 1 (2008): 51–52; and Seymore Drescher, "Jews and
New Christians in the Atlantic Slave Trade," in *The Jews and the Expansion of Europe
to the West*, ed. Bernardini and Fiering, 150.

60. Pittman, *The Development of the British West Indies*, 196; Pares, *War and Trade
in the West Indies*, 419–20; Harlow, *Christopher Codrington*, 115, 127; Richard B. Sheridan, "The Molasses Act and the Market Strategy of the British Sugar Planters," *Journal
of Economic History* 17 (1957): 62–64; Andrew Jackson O'Shaughnessy, *An Empire Divided: The American Revolution and the British Caribbean* (Philadelphia: University
of Pennsylvania Press, 2000), 60–61; Pritchard, *In Search of Empire*, 175–78, 201–7,
213–16, 377–79. For flags of truce, see *CSPC, 1702–3*, 179–80, 577–78, 596; General Assembly of Antigua to the Council of Antigua, "Minutes of the Council and Assembly
of Antigua, September 23, 1710 to January 26, 1710/11," December 5, 1710, CO 9/2, pp.
33–34, TNA:PRO; Deposition of John Broll, June 18, 1709, "Minutes of the Council
of Antigua, June 8 1709 to November 21 1709," CO 9/2, pp. 17–18, TNA:PRO; "Gov.
Parke to Capt George Ramsey Commander of Her Majesty's Ship Diamond," January 1, 1709/10, "Minutes of the Council of Antigua, January 4, 1709/10 to March 14
1709/10," CO 9/1, p. 10, TNA:PRO; *CSPC, 1710–1*, 59, 61; French, *Parke Defense*, 154,
209; "An Act to prevent the Supplying of her Majesty's Enemy with Provisions and
warlike Stores," March 17, 1710, "Antigua, Minutes of Council in Assembly, February
22, 1710/1 to March 15, 1711," TNA:PRO, CO 9/2, pp. 15–16.

61. For the order to place two brigantines in the Caribbean, see Mr. Popple to Mr.
Carkesse, February 3, 1710, *CSPC, 1710–1*, 40.

62. Israel, "The Dutch Role in the Glorious Revolution," in *The Anglo-Dutch Moment: Essays on the Glorious Revolution and Its World Impact*, ed. Israel (New York:
Cambridge University Press, 1991), 114–20; Patrick K. O'Brien, "Mercantilism and

Imperialism in the Rise and Decline of the Dutch and British Economies, 1585–1815," *De Economist* 148 (2000): 469–501; Pincus, "From Butterboxes to Wooden Shoes," 333–61.

63. Israel, *Dutch Primacy in World Trade*, 359–62.

64. E. H. Kossman, "The Dutch Republic in the Eighteenth Century," in *The Dutch Republic in the Eighteenth Century: Decline, Enlightenment, and Revolution*, ed. Margaret C. Jacob and Wijnand W. Mijnhardt (Ithaca, N.Y.: Cornell University Press, 1992), 30.

65. Kossman, "The Dutch Republic in the Eighteenth Century," in *The Dutch Republic in the Eighteenth Century*, ed. Jacob and Minjnhardt, 20.

66. Israel, *Dutch Primacy in World Trade*, chaps. 8–9. As important as the Dutch shift away from the Atlantic was, recent scholarship has shown that for some individual Dutch merchants, the Atlantic remained a place of opportunity. This is the general theme of Klooster, *Illicit Riches*; more particularly, see Klooster, "An Overview of Dutch Trade with the Americas," 376–82; and Enthoven, "An Assessment of Dutch Transatlantic Commerce," 410–15, 440–44, both in *The Riches from Atlantic Commerce*.

67. Matson, *Merchants and Empire*, 58–72, 106–9; Kammen, *Colonial New York*, 152–53, 161–73; Jacob Judd, "Frederick Philipse and the Madagascar Trade," *New-York Historical Society Quarterly* 55 (1971): 354–74; Curtis Nettles, "British Policy and Colonial Money Supply," *Economic History Review* 3 (October 1931): 220, 238–40.

68. Archdeacon, *New York City*, 40–41, 50–51, 57; Ritchie, *The Duke's Province*, 126; Matson, *Merchants and Empire*, 50.

69. JVC Shipping Book and JVC Letter Book, both in NYHS; Gov. Bellomont to De Peyster, October 30, 1699, De Peyster Papers, NYHS; Archdeacon, *New York City*, 73–75; *The Revolutionary War Memoir and Selected Correspondence of Philip Van Cortlandt*, vol. 1, *The Van Cortlandt Family Papers*, ed. Jacob Judd (Tarrytown, N.Y.: Sleepy Hollow Press, 1976), 19–24; Matson, *Merchants and Empire*, 54–56, 72, 208–9.

70. May 28, 1702, JVC Shipping Book, NYHS; JVC to John Blackall, May 2 1698, JVC Letter Book, fol. 4, NYHS; G. Bancker to A. De Peyster, March 17, 1699; Wendell to De Peyster, June 1, 1699; A. Wendell to De Peyster, June 5, 1699; A. Wendell to De Peyster, June 26, 1699, all in De Peyster Papers, fols. 30, 33–34, 36–37, 49, 50, 51, NYHS; Stephanus van Cortlandt to Mr. Joseph Redman, May 10, 1719, PVC Letter Book, fol. 195, NYHS. For Philipse, see HCA 13/82, fol. 312, TNA:PRO; *HMR*, 5, 161, 233 (*Margaret's Galley*) 239, 263–67 (*Margaret's Galley*), 271.

71. Lord Bellomont to the Council of Trade and Plantations, November 7, 1698, *DRCHNY* 4:419. On Brooke, see *HMR*, xii–xiv. On smuggling during this period, see Archdeacon, *New York City*, 69–70, 130–31; and Matson, *Merchants and Empire*, 83–87.

72. "Memorial of Edward Randolph to the Commissioners of his Majesty's Customs," November 10, 1696, *Randolph Papers*, 5:158. See also *Randolph Papers*, 7:404–6.

73. Bellomont to the Lords of Trade, May 8, 1698, *DRCHNY* 4:302–6 (quotation 303).

74. *Randolph Papers*, 5:192; *Randolph Papers*, 7:546–47; Bellomont to De Peyster, August 21, 1699, De Peyster Papers, NYHS; Lord Cornbury to Blathwayt, July 11, 1705, Blath. Hunt., unpaginated, microfilm at JDRL.

75. For the operation of the Philipses' Madagascar trade, see *CSPC, 1697–8*, 413–14; *DRCHNY*, 4: 300–302, 320–26, 542–44, 792–93. The best work on the connections

between New York and the Red Sea pirates is Robert C. Ritchie, *Captain Kidd and the War against the Pirates* (Cambridge: Harvard University Press, 1986).

76. There are no tonnage statistics for New York City until 1714, but the number of vessels arriving and clearing increased as did trade to Britain over the course of the 1690s and early 1700s (Matson, *Merchants and Empire*, 320–33, 398 n. 84).

77. *CSPC, 1697–8*, 587–88; Matson, *Merchants and Empire*, 100.

78. Gov. Bellomont to the Lords of Trade, January 2, 1700/1, *DRCHNY* 4: 820–27 (first quotation 826); "Petition of the Merchants of the City of New-York relating to Foreign Coin," February 19, 1694/5, *DRCHNY* 4:1133 (second quotation); Nettles, *The Money Supply of the American Colonies Before 1720*, 114–16; Matson, *Merchants and Empire*, 183–96.

79. "List of Vessels trading to Madagascar and Curawa [Curaçao] from New York," September 6, 1698, Blathwayt Papers, vol. 8, folder 8, Blathwayt Papers, JDRL, microfilm.

80. These records are collated and reprinted in *HMR*.

81. I have included Suriname as a West Indian destination. One reason for the discrepancy between entrances and clearances is that only vessels carrying duties goods (wine, rum, and dry goods) were recorded (*HMR*; *Boston-News Letter*).

82. JVC, Shipping Book, and JVC, Letterbook, NYHS. On Sara Abondana, see Pool, *Portraits*, 140. On logwood, see Nettles, *The Colonial Money Supply*, 85–86.

83. Stephanus Van Cortlandt, Ledger, 1695–1701, NYHS, microfilm; Philip van Cortlandt to Joseph Redman, May 10 and 20, 1719, PVC Letter Book, fols. 195 (quotation), 196b–97, NYHS.

84. For the *Suzannah*, see A Wendell to A. de Peyster, June 1, 1699, De Peyster Papers, NYHS. For the *Betty*, see Deposition of Humphrey Perkins, October 6, 1698, CO 5/1041, fol. 567r, TNA:PRO. Traders, destinations, and cargoes derived from *HMR*; *DRCHNY* 4:1133; *CSPC, 1702–3*, 617, 771; "Master Josurum Cordosse ver. William Lamont," May 23, 1704, NYCCMCM (1682–95), fol. 440; and "Robert Allison ver. David Collings," September 26, 1704, NYCCMCM (1704–10), fols. 3–7. And for the most complete discussion of trade to the region, see Matson, *Merchants and Empire*, 77–79, 134–35, 184.

85. "Bill of Lading for the *Welcome*," November 11, 1699, JVC Shipping Book, NYHS; Deposition of Humphrey Perkins, October 6, 1698, CO 5/1041, fol. 567r, TNA:PRO; *DRCHNY* 5:685–86; Nettles, *The Money Supply of the American Colonies*, 86–87; Pittman, *The Development of the British West Indies*, 212.

86. March 6, 1700, Robert Quary to the Commissioners of Customs, *CSPC, 1700*, 107–8. For similar reports, see *CSPC, 1702–3*, 16; *CSPC, 1704–5*, 145–46.

87. On Evertsen, Gov. Cornbury to the Commissioners for Trade and Plantations, June 13, 1705, *DRCHNY* 4:1143 (quotation); Wendell to De Peyster, July 1699, De Peyster Papers, fols. 53–54, NYHS.

88. Van Cortlandt to John Blackall, May 2, 1698 and July 18, 1698, JVC Letter Book, fols. 4, 13–14, NYHS; Van Cortlandt to Miles and Risbell, April 22, 1700, JVC Letter Book, fol. 25, NYHS; G. Bancker to A. De Peyster, March 17, 1699, De Peyster Papers, fols. 25–26, NYHS; Philip van Cortlandt to [?], May 29, 1719, PVC Letter Book, NYHS, fols. 196b–97 (quotation), NYHS.

89. William Gordon to Board of Trade, August 17, 1720, CO 5/867, fol. 344v, TNA:PRO.

90. "Report of Ducie Hungerford, Surveyor of Customs in New York," 1698, NYC Misc. Mss., Box 3, #17, NYHS; Deposition of Gustava Kingsland, June 8, 1689, New Netherland's Oldest New York and Colonial Government, Historical Letters & Manuscripts, fol. 33, NYHS; *CSPC, 1704-5*, 145-46.

91. *HMR*; JVC Shipping Book, NYHS.

92. Matson, *Merchants and Empire*, 185. For Van Cortlandt's and Van Sweeten's connections to Hodshon, see bills of lading for June 4 and June 9, 1701, JVC Shipping Book, NYHS.

93. Samuel [Childey?] Brooke to William Blathwayt, November 24, 1694, CO 5/1038, fols. 421-22r, TNA:PRO; "Report of Ducie Hungerford," 1698, NYC Misc. Mss, Box 3, #17, NYHS; Lords of Trade to Gov. Hunter, Jan 19, 1710, CO 5/1122, fols. 151-54, TNA:PRO; *Randolph Papers*, 7:404-6.

94. *HMR*.

95. Though often overlooked, Leisler's Rebellion brought major changes in political economy to New York (Matson, *Merchants and Empire*, esp. 80-82, 105-10; Middleton, *From Rights to Privileges*, 77-80, 88-94).

96. "The Humble Address & petition of the Mayor Recorder Aldermen and Commonaliy of this their Majesties Citty of New York Covened in Common Council To his Excellency Benjamin Fletcher," February 9, 1682/3, *MCCNY*, 1:311-13.

97. New York City Common Council to the King, May 29, 1697, *MCCNY*, 2:7-9 (first quotation); Mayor, Recorder, Aldermen and Assistant of the City in Common Council to Lord Bellomont, June 29, 1698, *MCCNY*, 2:32-3 (second quotation).

98. New York City Common Council to the King, May 29, 1697, *MCCNY*, 2:7-9.

Notes to Epilogue

1. Gov. John Hart to Horatio Walpole, April 4, 1722, "Volume 239: January 11–June 27, 1722," Calendar of Treasury Papers, Volume 6: 1720-1728 (1889), 116-42, www.british-history.ac.uk/report.aspx?compid=85094; Gov. John Hart to the Board of Trade, July 12, 1724, CO 152/14, fols. 325r-340v, TNA-PRO; Gov. John Hart to the Board of Trade, February 1727, CO 152/15, fols. 323r-324v, TNA-PRO.

2. Smith, *Slavery, Family, and Gentry Capitalism*, 170.

3. Gov. John Hart to the Board of Trade, July 12, 1724, CO 152/14, fol. 329v, TNA-PRO.

4. For this and the preceding paragraph, see R. B. Sheridan, "The Rise of a Colonial Gentry: A Case Study of Antigua, 1730-1775," *Economic History Review*, 2nd ser., 13, no. 2 (1961): 342-57; and Sheridan, *Sugar and Slavery*, 155-58, 172-76, 194-200. St. Mary's parish data are from Dunn, *Sugar and Slaves*, 141-48. For closer ties between Leeward Island planters (or their agents) and their London commission agents, see the letters reproduced in *The Letters of William Freeman*, ed. Hancock; and Edwin F. Gay, "Letters from a Sugar Plantation in Nevis, 1723-1732," *Journal of Economic and Business History* 1 (November 1928), 149-73. See also Davies, "The Origins of the Commission System in the West India Trade," 89-107; Hancock, "A World of Business to Do," 22-23; Nuala Zahedieh, "Credit, Risk and Reputation in Late Seventeenth-Century Colonial Trade," in *Merchant Organization and Maritime Trade*, ed. Janzed, 62-66. This transition had happened earlier in Barbados, but the Peace of Utrecht also marked an influx of British investment and new traders here (Smith, *Slavery, Family, and Gentry Capitalism*, esp. 35-38, 43-48, 55-59).

5. Pritchard, *In Search of Empire*, 173–86; Robert Stein, "The French Sugar Business in the Eighteenth Century: A Quantitative Study," *Business History* 22 (1980): 3–4, 6, 8; Sheridan, "The Molasses Act and the Market Strategy of the British Sugar Planters," 63–64; O'Shaughnessy, *An Empire Divided*, 60–62.

6. Sheridan, "The Molasses Act and the Market Strategy of the British Sugar Planters," 64; O'Shaughnessy, *An Empire Divided*, 61–42.

7. Robert Robertson, *A Detection of the State and Situation of the present Sugar Planters of Barbadoes and the Leeward Islands* (London, 1732), 58–59.

8. Pittman, *The Development of the British West Indies*, 198–210, 229–30; Sheridan, "The Molasses Act," 68–69.

9. Robertson, *A Detection of the State and Situation of the present Sugar Planters*, 58–59; *The Present State of the British Sugar Colonies Consider'd* (London, 1731), 11, 19.

10. Thomas Tryon, *The Merchant, Citizen and Country man's Instructor: Or, a Necessary Companion for all People* (London, 1701), 221.

11. *A Comparison Between the British Sugar Colonies and New England As they relate to the Interest of Great Britain* (London, 1732), 26 ("Fountain," 5; "Rival," 7; "Cuckow," 9–12).

12. Robertson, *A Supplement to the Detection of the State and Situation of the Present Sugar Planters* (London, 1732), 27.

13. Sheridan, "The Molasses Act," 65–67.

14. *The Present State*, 7.

15. Ibid., 9; *A Comparison Between the British Sugar Colonies and New England*, 17, 26.

16. Fayer Hall, *Considerations on the Bill now depending in Parliament, concerning the British sugar-colonies in America. . . .* (London, 1713), 4. See also Matson, *Merchants and Empire*, 193–96, 204–5.

17. *A True State of the Case Between the British Northern-Colonies and the Sugar Islands in America, Impartially Considered*, (London, 1732), 34 ("vast quantity" and "great Important"); June 25, 1723, Mr. Colden's Account of the Trade of New York, *DRCHNY* 5:685–86 ("make even"). See also *DRCHNY*, 5:555–56, 601.

18. *A Short Answer to an Elaborate Pamphlet, Entitled: "The Importance of the Sugar Plantations &c."* (London, 1731), 11–13 (quotation 13).

19. Hall, *Considerations on the Bill*, 3 (quotation); June 25, 1723, Mr. Colden's Account of the Trade of New York, *DRCHNY* 5:687–89.

20. Hall, *Considerations on the Bill*, 8 ("ten times"); *A True State*, 5–6 ("British Planters").

21. *A Short Answer*, 21, 23; *A True State*, 6 ("Frugality").

22. Hall, *Considerations on the Bill*, 11–12, 22.

23. *New-York Gazette*, July 24, July 31, August 14, August 21, 1732.

24. O'Shaughnessy, *An Empire Divided*, 63–64.

25. Sheridan, "The Molasses Act," 73–75.

Index

ABOUT THE AUTHOR

Christian J. Koot is an assistant professor of history at Towson University in Towson, Maryland.

.

NEWNES POWER ENGINEERING SERIES

Power Electronic Control in Electrical Systems

NEWNES POWER ENGINEERING SERIES

Series editors
Professor TJE Miller, University of Glasgow, UK
Associate Professor Duane Hanselman, University of Maine, USA
Professor Thomas M Jahns, University of Wisconsin-Madison, USA
Professor Jim McDonald, University of Strathclyde, UK

Newnes Power Engineering Series is a new series of advanced reference texts covering the core areas of modern electrical power engineering, encompassing transmission and distribution, machines and drives, power electronics, and related areas of electricity generation, distribution and utilization. The series is designed for a wide audience of engineers, academics, and postgraduate students, and its focus is international, which is reflected in the editorial team. The titles in the series offer concise but rigorous coverage of essential topics within power engineering, with a special focus on areas undergoing rapid development.

The series complements the long-established range of Newnes titles in power engineering, which includes the *Electrical Engineer's Reference Book*, first published by Newnes in 1945, and the classic *J&P Transformer Book*, as well as a wide selection of recent titles for professionals, students and engineers at all levels.

Further information on the **Newnes Power Engineering Series** is available from
bhmarketing@repp.co.uk
www.newnespress.com

Please send book proposals to Matthew Deans, Newnes Publisher
matthew.deans@repp.co.uk

Other titles in the Newnes Power Engineering Series
Miller   Electronic Control of Switched Reluctance Machines   0-7506-5073-7
Agrawal   Industrial Power Engineering and Applications Handbook   0-7506-7351-6

NEWNES POWER ENGINEERING SERIES

Power Electronic Control in Electrical Systems

E. Acha
V.G. Agelidis
O. Anaya-Lara
T.J.E. Miller

Newnes

OXFORD • AUCKLAND • BOSTON • JOHANNESBURG • MELBOURNE • NEW DELHI

Newnes
An imprint of Butterworth-Heinemann
Linacre House, Jordan Hill, Oxford OX2 8DP
225 Wildwood Avenue, Woburn, MA 01801-2041
A division of Reed Educational and Professional Publishing Ltd

 A member of the Reed Elsevier plc group

First published 2002

British Library Cataloguing in Publication Data
A catalogue record for this book is available from the British Library

ISBN 0 7506 5126 1

Typeset in India by Integra Software Services Pvt Ltd,
Pondicherry, India 605005; www.integra-india.com
Printed and bound in Great Britain by MPG Books Ltd, Bodmin, Cornwall

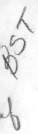

Contents

Preface

Although the basic concepts of reactive power control in power systems remain unchanged, state-of-the-art developments associated with power electronics equipment are dictating new ways in which such control may be achieved not only in high-voltage transmission systems but also in low-voltage distribution systems. The book addresses, therefore, not only the fundamental concepts associated with the topic of reactive power control but also presents the latest equipment and devices together with new application areas and associated computer-assisted studies.

The book offers a solid theoretical foundation for the electronic control of active and reactive power. The material gives an overview of the composition of electrical power networks; a basic description of the most popular power systems studies and indicates, within the context of the power system, where the Flexible Alternating Current Transmission Systems (FACTS) and Custom Power equipment belong.

FACTS relies on state-of-the-art power electronic devices and methods applied on the high-voltage side of the power network to make it electronically controllable. From the operational point of view, it is concerned with the ability to control the path of power flows throughout the network in an adaptive fashion. This equipment has the ability to control the line impedance and the nodal voltage magnitudes and angles at both the sending and receiving ends of key transmission corridors while enhancing the security of the system.

Custom Power focuses on low-voltage distribution systems. This technology is a response to reports of poor power quality and reliability of supply to factories, offices and homes. Today's automated equipment and production lines require reliable and high quality power, and cannot tolerate voltage sags, swells, harmonic distortions, impulses or interruptions.

Chapter 1 gives an overview of electrical power networks. The main plant components of the power network are described, together with the new generation of power network controllers, which use state-of-the-art power electronics technology to give the power network utmost operational flexibility and an almost instantaneous speed of response. The chapter also describes the main computer assisted studies used by power systems engineers in the planning, management and operation of the network.

Chapter 2 provides a broad review of the basic theoretical principles of power engineering, with relevant examples of AC circuit analysis, per-unit systems, three-phase systems, transformer connections, power measurement and other topics. It covers the basic precepts of power and frequency control, voltage control and load balancing, and provides a basic understanding of the reactive compensation of loads.

Chapter 3 reviews the principles of transmission system compensation including shunt and series compensation and the behaviour of long transmission lines and cables.

Chapter 4 addresses the mathematical modelling of the electrical power network suitable for steady state analysis. Emphasis is placed on the modelling of plant components used to control active and reactive power flows, voltage magnitude and network impedance in high-voltage transmission. The model of the power network is the classical non-linear model, based on voltage-dependent nodal power equations and solved by iteration using the Newton–Raphson method. The basic method is then expanded to encompass the models of the new generation of power systems controllers. The new models are simple and yet comprehensive.

Chapter 5 introduces the power semiconductor devices and their characteristics as part of a power electronic system. It discusses the desired characteristics to be found in an ideal switch and provides information on components, power semiconductor device protection, hardware issues of converters and future trends.

Chapter 6 covers in detail the thyristor-based power electronic equipment used in power systems for reactive power control. It provides essential background theory to understand its principle of operation and basic analytical expression for assessing its switching behaviour. It then presents basic power electronic equipment built with voltage-source converters. These include single-phase and three-phase circuits along with square wave and pulse-width modulation control. It discusses the basic concepts of multilevel converters, which are used in high power electronic equipment. Energy storage systems based on superconducting material and uninterruptible power supplies are also presented. Towards the end of the chapter, conventional HVDC systems along with VSC-based HVDC and active filtering equipment are also presented.

Chapter 7 deals with the all-important topic of power systems harmonics. To a greater or lesser extent all power electronic controllers generate harmonic currents, but from the operator's perspective, and the end-user, these are parasitic or nuisance effects. The book addresses the issue of power systems harmonics with emphasis on electronic compensation.

Chapter 8 provides basic information on how the industry standard software package PSCAD/EMTDC can be used to simulate and study not only the periodic steady state response of power electronic equipment but also their transient response. Specifically, detailed simulation examples are presented of the Static Var compensator, thyristor controlled series compensator, STATCOM, solid-state transfer switch, DVR and shunt-connected active filters based on the VSC concept.

Dr Acha would like to acknowledge assistance received from Dr Claudio R. Fuerte-Esquivel and Dr Hugo Ambriz-Perez in Chapter 4. Dr Agelidis wishes to acknowledge the editorial assistance of Ms B.G. Weppler received for Chapters 5 and 6. Mr Anaya-Lara would like to express his gratitude to Mr Manual Madrigal for his assistance in the preparation of thyristor-controlled series compensator simulations and analysis in Chapter 8.

Enrique Acha
Vassilios G. Agelidis
Olimpo Anaya-Lara
Tim Miller

1

Electrical power systems – an overview

1.1 Introduction

The main elements of an electrical power system are generators, transformers, transmission lines, loads and protection and control equipment. These elements are interconnected so as to enable the generation of electricity in the most suitable locations and in sufficient quantity to satisfy the customers' demand, to transmit it to the load centres and to deliver good-quality electric energy at competitive prices.

The quality of the electricity supply may be measured in terms of:

- constant voltage magnitude, e.g. no voltage sags
- constant frequency
- constant power factor
- balanced phases
- sinusoidal waveforms, e.g. no harmonic content
- lack of interruptions
- ability to withstand faults and to recover quickly.

1.2 Background

The last quarter of the nineteenth century saw the development of the electricity supply industry as a new, promising and fast-growing activity. Since that time electrical power networks have undergone immense transformations (Hingorani and Gyugyi, 2000; Kundur, 1994). Owing to the relative 'safety' and 'cleanliness' of electricity, it quickly became established as a means of delivering light, heat and motive power. Nowadays it is closely linked to primary activities such as industrial production, transport, communications and agriculture. Population growth, technological innovations and higher capital gains are just a few of the factors that have maintained the momentum of the power industry.

Clearly it has not been easy for the power industry to reach its present status. Throughout its development innumerable technical and economic problems have been overcome, enabling the supply industry to meet the ever increasing demand for energy with electricity at competitive prices. The generator, the incandescent lamp and the industrial motor were the basis for the success of the earliest schemes. Soon the transformer provided a means for improved efficiency of distribution so that generation and transmission of alternating current over considerable distances provided a major source of power in industry and also in domestic applications.

For many decades the trend in electric power production has been towards an interconnected network of transmission lines linking generators and loads into large integrated systems, some of which span entire continents. The main motivation has been to take advantage of load diversity, enabling a better utilization of primary energy resources. It may be argued that interconnection provides an alternative to a limited amount of generation thus enhancing the security of supply (Anderson and Fouad, 1977).

Interconnection was further enhanced, in no small measure, by early breakthroughs in high-current, high-power semiconductor valve technology. Thyristor-based high voltage direct current (HVDC) converter installations provided a means for interconnecting power systems with different operating frequencies, e.g. 50/60 Hz, for interconnecting power systems separated by the sea, e.g. the cross-Channel link between England and France, and for interconnecting weak and strong power systems (Hingorani, 1996). The rectifier and inverter may be housed within the same converter station (back-to-back) or they may be located several hundred kilometres apart, for bulk-power, extra-long-distance transmission. The most recent development in HVDC technology is the HVDC system based on solid state voltage source converters (VSCs), which enables independent, fast control of active and reactive powers (McMurray, 1987). This equipment uses insulated gate bipolar transistors (IGBTs) or gate turn-off thyristors (GTOs) 'valves' and pulse width modulation (PWM) control techniques (Mohan et al., 1995). It should be pointed out that this technology was first developed for applications in industrial drive systems for improved motor speed control. In power transmission applications this technology has been termed HVDC Light (Asplund et al., 1998) to differentiate it from the well-established HVDC links based on thyristors and phase control (Arrillaga, 1999). Throughout this book, the terms HVDC Light and HVDC based on VSCs are used interchangeably.

Based on current and projected installations, a pattern is emerging as to where this equipment will find widespread application: deregulated market applications in primary distribution networks, e.g. the 138 kV link at Eagle Pass, interconnecting the Mexican and Texas networks (Asplund, 2000). The 180 MVA Directlink in Australia, interconnecting the Queensland and New South Wales networks, is another example.

Power electronics technology has affected every aspect of electrical power networks; not just HVDC transmission but also generation, AC transmission, distribution and utilization. At the generation level, thyristor-based automatic voltage regulators (AVRs) have been introduced to enable large synchronous generators to respond quickly and accurately to the demands of interconnected environments. Power system stabilizers (PSSs) have been introduced to prevent power oscillations from building up as a result of sympathetic interactions between generators. For instance, several of the large generators in Scotland are fitted with

PSSs to ensure trouble-free operation between the Scottish power system and its larger neighbour, the English power system (Fairnley et al., 1982). Deregulated markets are imposing further demands on generating plant, increasing their wear and tear and the likelihood of generator instabilities of various kinds, e.g. transient, dynamic, sub-synchronous resonance (SSR) and sub-synchronous torsional interactions (SSTI). New power electronic controllers are being developed to help generators operate reliably in the new market place. The thyristor-controlled series compensator (TCSC) is being used to mitigate SSR, SSTI and to damp power systems' oscillations (Larsen et al., 1992). Examples of where TCSCs have been used to mitigate SSR are the TCSCs installed in the 500 kV Boneville Power Administration's Slatt substation and in the 400 kV Swedish power network. However, it should be noted that the primary function of the TCSC, like that of its mechanically controlled counterpart, the series capacitor bank, is to reduce the electrical length of the compensated transmission line. The aim is still to increase power transfers significantly, but with increased transient stability margins.

A welcome result of deregulation of the electricity supply industry and open access markets for electricity worldwide, is the opportunity for incorporating all forms of renewable generation into the electrical power network. The signatories of the Kyoto agreement in 1997 set themselves a target to lower emission levels by 20% by 2010. As a result of this, legislation has been enacted and, in many cases, tax incentives have been provided to enable the connection of micro-hydro, wind, photovoltaic, wave, tidal, biomass and fuel cell generators. The power generated by some of these sources of electricity is suitable for direct input, via a step-up transformer, into the AC distribution system. This is the case with micro-hydro and biomass generators. Other sources generate electricity in DC form or in AC form but with large, random variations which prevent direct connection to the grid; for example fuel cells and asynchronous wind generators. In both cases, power electronic converters such as VSCs provide a suitable means for connection to the grid.

In theory, the thyristor-based static var compensator (SVC) (Miller, 1982) could be used to perform the functions of the PSS, while providing fast-acting voltage support at the generating substation. In practice, owing to the effectiveness of the PSS and its relative low cost, this has not happened. Instead, the high speed of response of the SVC and its low maintenance cost have made it the preferred choice to provide reactive power support at key points of the transmission system, far away from the generators. For most practical purposes they have made the rotating synchronous compensator redundant, except where an increase in the short-circuit level is required along with fast-acting reactive power support. Even this niche application of rotating synchronous compensators may soon disappear since a thyristor-controlled series reactor (TCSR) could perform the role of providing adaptive short-circuit compensation and, alongside, an SVC could provide the necessary reactive power support. Another possibility is the displacement of not just the rotating synchronous compensator but also the SVC by a new breed of static compensators (STATCOMs) based on the use of VSCs. The STATCOM provides all the functions that the SVC can provide but at a higher speed and, when the technology reaches full maturity, its cost will be lower. It is more compact and requires only a fraction of the land required by an SVC installation. The VSC is the basic building block of the new generation of power controllers emerging from flexible alternating current transmission systems (FACTS) and Custom Power research (Hingorani and Gyugyi, 2000). In high-voltage transmission, the most promising equipment is: the STATCOM, the unified power flow controller (UPFC) and the HVDC Light. At the low-voltage distribution level, the VSC provides the basis for the distribution STATCOM (D-STATCOM), the dynamic voltage restorer (DVR), the power factor corrector (PFC) and active filters.

1.3   General composition of the power network

For most practical purposes, the electrical power network may be divided into four parts, namely generation, transmission, distribution and utilization. The four parts are illustrated in Figure 1.1.

This figure gives the one-line diagram of a power network where two transmission levels are observed, namely 400 kV and 132 kV. An expanded view of one of the generators feeding into the high-voltage transmission network is used to indicate that the generating plant consists of three-phase synchronous generators driven by either hydro or steam turbines. Similarly, an expanded view of one of the load points is used to indicate the composition of the distribution system, where voltage levels are shown, i.e. 33 kV, 11 kV, 415 V and 240 V. Within the context of this illustration, industrial consumers would be supplied with three-phase electricity at 11 kV and domestic users with single-phase electricity at 240 V.

Figure 1.1 also gives examples of power electronics-based plant components and where they might be installed in the electrical power network. In high-voltage transmission systems, a TCSC may be used to reduce the electrical length of long transmission lines, increasing power transfers and stability margins. An HVDC link may be used for the purpose of long distance, bulk power transmission. An SVC or a STATCOM may be used to provide reactive power support at a network location far away from synchronous generators. At the distribution level, e.g. 33 kV and 11 kV, a D-STATCOM may be used to provide voltage magnitude support, power factor improvement and harmonic cancellation. The interfacing of embedded DC generators, such as fuel cells, with the AC distribution system would require a thyristor-based converter or a VSC.

Also, a distinction should be drawn between conventional, large generators, e.g. hydro, nuclear and coal, feeding directly into the high-voltage transmission, and the small size generators, e.g. wind, biomass, micro-gas, micro-hydro, fuel cells and photovoltaics, embedded into the distribution system. In general, embedded generation is seen as an environmentally sound way of generating electricity, with some generators using free, renewable energy from nature as a primary energy resource, e.g. wind, solar, micro-hydro and wave. Other embedded generators use non-renewable resources, but still environmentally benign, primary energy such as oxygen and gas. Diesel generators are an example of non-renewable, non-environmentally friendly embedded generation.

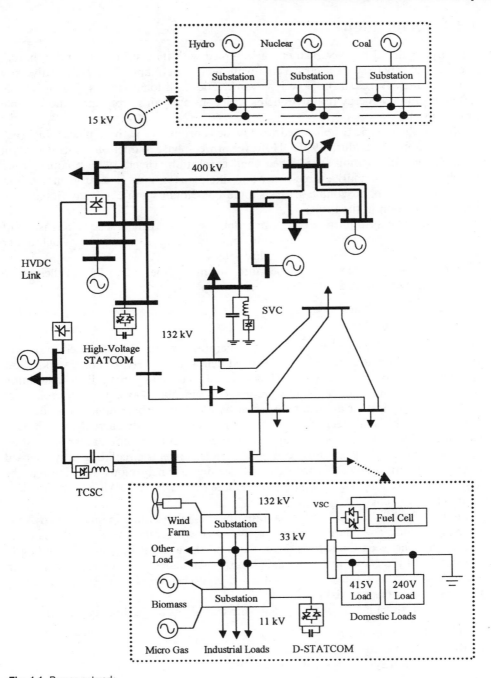

Fig. 1.1 Power network.

1.3.1 Generation

The large demand for electrical energy coupled with its continuous varying nature and our inability to store electrical energy in significant quantities calls for a diversity of generating sources in the power network. The traditional view is that the use of different primary energy resources helps with continuity of supply and a more stable pricing mechanism.

Most of the electricity consumed worldwide is produced by three-phase synchronous generators (Kundur, 1994). However, three-phase induction generators will increase their production share when wind generation (Heier, 1998) becomes more widely available. Similarly, three-phase and single-phase static generators in the form of fuel cells and photovoltaic arrays should contribute significantly to global electricity production in the future.

For system analysis purposes the synchronous machine can be seen as consisting of a stationary part, i.e. armature or stator, and a moving part, the rotor, which under steady state conditions rotates at synchronous speed.

Synchronous machines are grouped into two main types, according to their rotor structure (Fitzgerald et al., 1983):

1. salient pole machines
2. round rotor machines.

Steam turbine driven generators (turbo-generators) work at high speed and have round rotors. The rotor carries a DC excited field winding. Hydro units work at low speed and have salient pole rotors. They normally have damper windings in addition to the field winding. Damper windings consist of bars placed in slots on the pole faces and connected together at both ends. In general, steam turbines contain no damper windings but the solid steel of the rotor offers a path for eddy currents, which have similar damping effects. For simulation purposes, the currents circulating in the solid steel or in the damping windings can be treated as currents circulating in two closed circuits (Kundur, 1994). Accordingly, a three-phase synchronous machine may be assumed to have three stator windings and three rotor windings. All six windings will be magnetically coupled.

Figure 1.2 shows the schematic diagram of the machine while Figure 1.3 shows the coupled circuits. The relative position of the rotor with respect to the stator is given by the angle between the rotor's direct axis and the axis of the phase A winding in the stator. In the rotor, the direct axis (d-axis) is magnetically centred in the north pole. A second axis located 90 electrical degrees behind the direct axis is called the quadrature axis (q-axis).

In general, three main control systems directly affect the turbine-generator set:

1. the boiler's firing control
2. the governor control
3. the excitation system control.

Figure 1.4 shows the interaction of these controls and the turbine-generator set.

The excitation system control consists of an exciter and the AVR. The latter regulates the generator terminal voltage by controlling the amount of current supplied to the field winding by the exciter. The measured terminal voltage and the

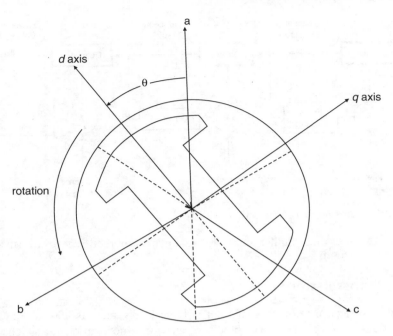

Fig. 1.2 Schematic diagram of a synchronous machine.

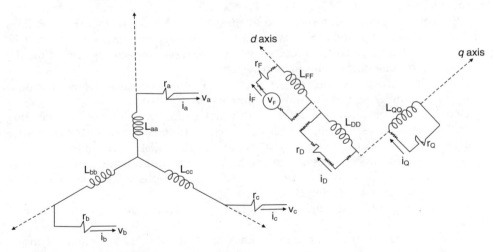

Fig. 1.3 Coupled windings of a synchronous machine.

desired reference voltage are compared to produce a voltage error which is used to alter the exciter output. Generally speaking, exciters can be of two types: (1) rotating; or (2) static. Nowadays, static exciters are the preferred choice owing to their higher

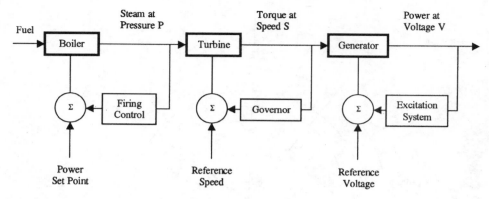

Fig. 1.4 Main controls of a generating unit.

speed of response and smaller size. They use thyristor rectifiers to adjust the field current (Aree, 2000).

1.3.2 Transmission

Transmission networks operate at high voltage levels such as 400 kV and 275 kV, because the transmission of large blocks of energy is more efficient at high voltages (Weedy, 1987). Step-up transformers in generating substations are responsible for increasing the voltage up to transmission levels and step-down transformers located in distribution substations are responsible for decreasing the voltage to more manageable levels such as 66 kV or 11 kV.

High-voltage transmission is carried by means of AC overhead transmission lines and DC overhead transmission lines and cables. Ancillary equipment such as switchgear, protective equipment and reactive power support equipment is needed for the correct functioning of the transmission system.

High-voltage transmission networks are usually 'meshed' to provide redundant paths for reliability. Figure 1.5 shows a simple power network.

Under certain operating conditions, redundant paths may give rise to circulating power and extra losses. Flexible alternating current transmission systems controllers are able to prevent circulating currents in meshed networks (IEEE/CIGRE, 1995).

Overhead transmission lines are used in high-voltage transmission and in distribution applications. They are built in double circuit, three-phase configuration in the same tower, as shown in Figure 1.6.

They are also built in single circuit, three-phase configurations, as shown in Figure 1.7.

Single and double circuit transmission lines may form busy transmission corridors. In some cases as many as six three-phase circuits may be carried on just one tower.

In high-voltage transmission lines, each phase consists of two or four conductors per phase, depending on their rated voltage, in order to reduce the total series impedance of the line and to increase transmission capacity. One or two sky wires are used for protection purposes against lightning strikes.

Underground cables are used in populated areas where overhead transmission lines are impractical. Cables are manufactured in a variety of forms to serve different

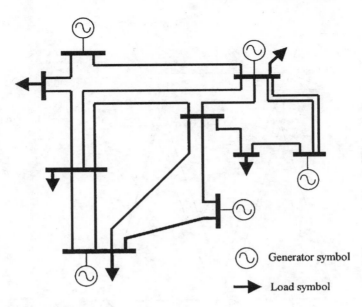

Fig. 1.5 Meshed transmission network.

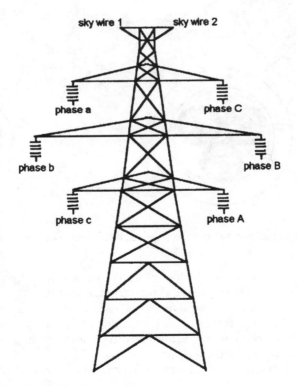

Fig. 1.6 Double circuit transmission line.

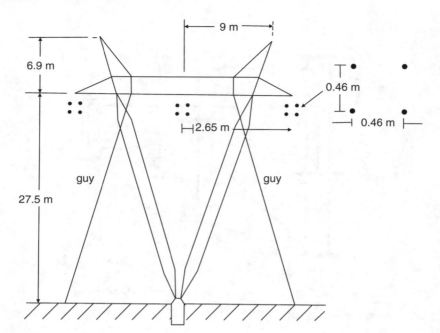

Fig. 1.7 Single circuit transmission line.

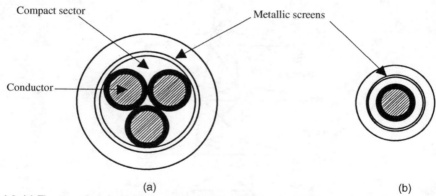

Fig. 1.8 (a) Three-conductor, shielded, compact sector; and (b) one-conductor, shielded.

applications. Figure 1.8 shows shielded, three-phase and single-phase cables; both have a metallic screen to help confine the electromagnetic fields.

Belted cables are generally used for three-phase, low-voltage operation up to approximately 5 kV, whilst three-conductor, shielded, compact sector cables are most commonly used in three-phase applications at the 5–46 kV voltage range. At higher voltages either gas or oil filled cables are used.

Power transformers are used in many different ways. Some of the most obvious applications are:

- as step-up transformers to increase the operating voltage from generating levels to transmission levels;
- as step-down transformers to decrease the operating voltage from transmission levels to utilization levels;
- as control devices to redirect power flows and to modulate voltage magnitude at a specific point of the network;
- as 'interfaces' between power electronics equipment and the transmission network.

For most practical purposes, power transformers may be seen as consisting of one or more iron cores and two or three copper windings per phase. The three-phase windings may be connected in a number of ways, e.g. star–star, star–delta and delta–delta.

Modern three-phase power transformers use one of the following magnetic core types: three single-phase units, a three-phase unit with three legs or a three-phase unit with five legs.

Reactive power equipment is an essential component of the transmission system (Miller, 1982). It is used for voltage regulation, stability enhancement and for increasing power transfers. These functions are normally carried out with mechanically controlled shunt and series banks of capacitors and non-linear reactors. However, when there is an economic and technical justification, the reactive power support is provided by electronic means as opposed to mechanical means, enabling near instantaneous control of reactive power, voltage magnitude and transmission line impedance at the point of compensation.

The well-established SVC and the STATCOM, a more recent development, is the equipment used to provide reactive power compensation (Hingorani and Gyugyi, 2000). Figure 1.9 shows a three-phase, delta connected, thyristor-controlled reactor (TCR) connected to the secondary side of a two-winding, three-legged transformer. Figure 1.10 shows a similar arrangement but for a three-phase STATCOM using GTO switches. In lower power applications, IGBT switches may be used instead.

Although the end function of series capacitors is to provide reactive power to the compensated transmission line, its role in power system compensation is better understood as that of a series reactance compensator, which reduces the electrical length of the line. Figure 1.11(a) illustrates one phase of a mechanically controlled, series bank of capacitors whereas Figure 1.11(b) illustrates its electronically controlled counterpart (Kinney et al., 1994). It should be pointed out that the latter has the ability to exert instantaneous active power flow control.

Several other power electronic controllers have been built to provide adaptive control to key parameters of the power system besides voltage magnitude, reactive power and transmission line impedance. For instance, the electronic phase shifter is used to enable instantaneous active power flow control. Nowadays, a single piece of equipment is capable of controlling voltage magnitude and active and reactive power. This is the UPFC, the most sophisticated power controller ever built (Gyugyi, 1992). In its simplest form, the UPFC comprises two back-to-back VSCs, sharing a DC capacitor. As illustrated in Figure 1.12, one VSC of the UPFC is connected in shunt and the second VSC is connected in series with the power network.

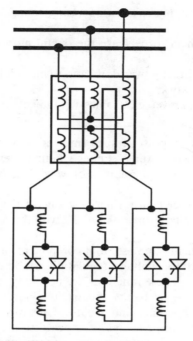

Fig. 1.9 Three-phase thyristor-controlled reactor connected in delta.

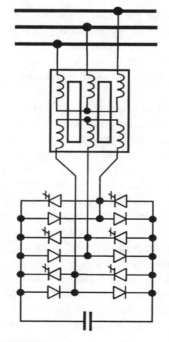

Fig. 1.10 Three-phase GTO-based STATCOM.

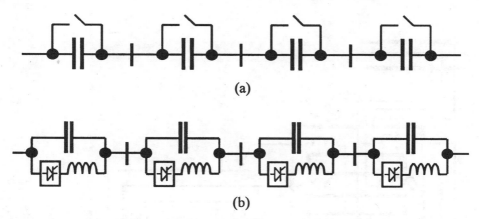

Fig. 1.11 One phase of a series capacitor. (a) mechanically controlled; and (b) electronically controlled.

HVDC Light is a very recent development in electric power transmission. It has many technical and economical characteristics, which make it an ideal candidate for a variety of transmission applications where conventional HVDC is unable to compete. For instance, it can be used to supply passive loads, to provide reactive power support and to improve the quality of supply in AC networks. The installation contributes no short-circuit current and may be operated with no transformers. It is said that it has brought down the economical power range of HVDC transmission to only a few megawatts (Asplund et al., 1998). The HVDC Light at Hellsjön is reputed to be the world's first installation and is rated at 3 MW and ±10 kV DC. At present, the technology enables power ratings of up to 200 MW. In its simplest form, it comprises two STATCOMs linked by a DC cable, as illustrated in Figure 1.13.

1.3.3 Distribution

Distribution networks may be classified as either meshed or radial. However, it is customary to operate meshed networks in radial fashion with the help of mechanically operated switches (Gönen, 1986). It is well understood that radial networks are less reliable than interconnected networks but distribution engineers have preferred them because they use simple, inexpensive protection schemes, e.g. over-current protection. Distribution engineers have traditionally argued that in meshed distribution networks operated in radial fashion, most consumers are brought back on supply a short time after the occurrence of a fault by moving the network's open points. Open-point movements are carried out by reswitching operations.

Traditional construction and operation practices served the electricity distribution industry well for nearly a century. However, the last decade has seen a marked increase in loads that are sensitive to poor quality electricity supply. Some large industrial users are critically dependent on uninterrupted electricity supply and suffer large financial losses as a result of even minor lapses in the quality of electricity supply (Hingorani, 1995).

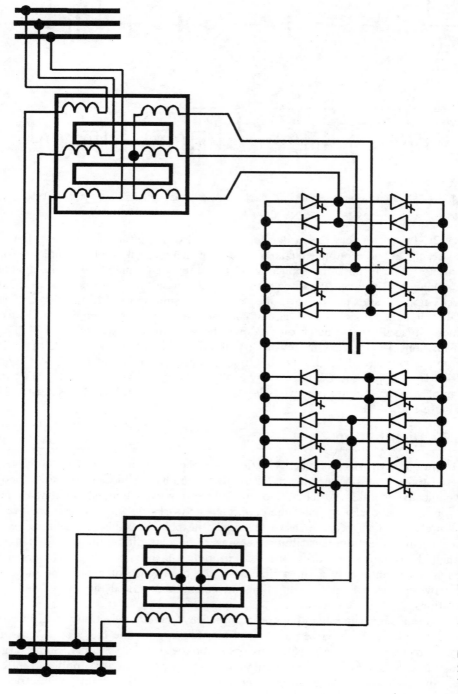

Fig. 1.12 Three-phase unified power flow controller.

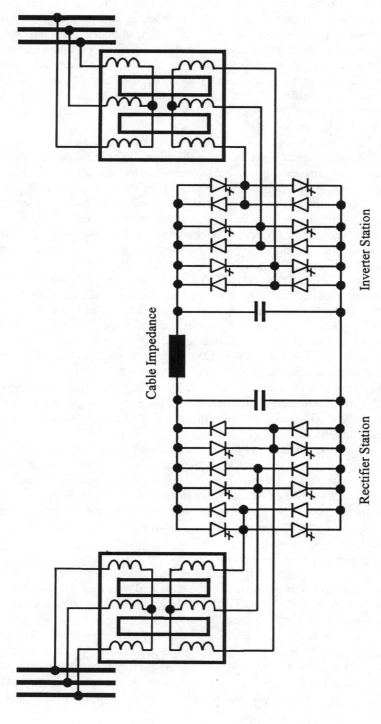

Fig. 1.13 HVDC Light systems using VSCs.

These factors coupled with the ongoing deregulation and open access electricity markets, where large consumers may shop around for competitively priced, high-quality electricity, have propelled the distribution industry into unprecedented change. On the technical front, one major development is the incorporation of power electronics controllers in the distribution system to supply electricity with high quality to selected customers. The generic, systematic solution being considered by the utility to counter the problem of interruptions and low power quality at the end-user level is known as Custom Power. This is the low voltage counterpart of the more widely known FACTS technology.

Although FACTS and custom power initiatives share the same technological base, they have different technical and economic objectives (Hingorani and Gyugyi, 2000). Flexible alternating current transmission systems controllers are aimed at the transmission level whereas Custom Power controllers are aimed at the distribution level, in particular, at the point of connection of the electricity distribution company with clients with sensitive loads and independent generators. Custom Power focuses primarily on the reliability and quality of power flows. However, voltage regulation, voltage balancing and harmonic cancellation may also benefit from this technology.

The STATCOM, the DVR and the solid state switch (SSS) are the best known Custom Power equipment. The STATCOM and the DVR both use VSCs, but the former is a shunt connected device which may include the functions of voltage control, active filtering and reactive power control. The latter is a series connected device which precisely compensates for waveform distortion and disturbances in the neighbourhood of one or more sensitive loads. Figure 1.10 shows the schematic representation of a three-phase STATCOM. Figure 1.14 shows that of a DVR and Figure 1.15 shows one phase of a three-phase thyristor-based SSS.

The STATCOM used in Custom Power applications uses PWM switching control as opposed to the fundamental frequency switching strategy preferred in FACTS applications. PWM switching is practical in Custom Power because this is a relatively low power application.

On the sustainable development front, environmentally aware consumers and government organizations are providing electricity distribution companies with a good business opportunity to supply electricity from renewable sources at a premium. The problem yet to be resolved in an interconnected system with a generation mix is how to comply with the end-user's desire for electricity from a renewable source. Clearly, a market for renewable generation has yet to be realized.

1.3.4   Utilization

The customers of electricity vendors may be classified as industrial, commercial and domestic (Weedy, 1987). In industrialized societies, the first group may account for as much as two fifths of total demand. Traditionally, induction motors have formed the dominant component in the vast array of electric equipment found in industry, both in terms of energy consumption and operational complexity. However, computer-assisted controllers and power electronics-based equipment, essential features in modern manufacturing processes, present the current challenge in terms of ensuring their trouble-free operation. This equipment requires to be supplied with high quality electricity.

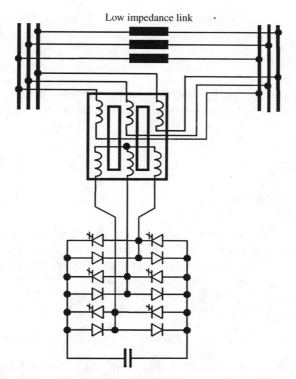

Fig. 1.14 Three-phase dynamic voltage restorer.

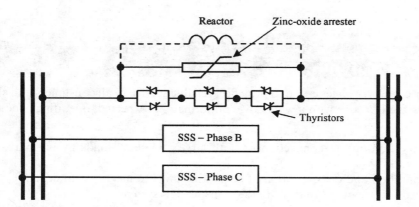

Fig. 1.15 Thyristor-based solid state switch.

Some loads draw constant current from the power system and their operation may be affected by supply voltage and frequency variations. Examples of these loads are:

- induction motors
- synchronous motors
- DC motors.

Other types of loads are less· susceptible to voltage and frequency variations and exhibit a constant resistance characteristic:

- incandescent lighting
- heating.

Large clusters of end user loads based on power electronics technology are capable of injecting significant harmonic currents back into the network. Examples of these are:

- colour TV sets
- microwave ovens
- energy saving lamps
- computer equipment
- industrial variable speed motor drives
- battery recharging stations.

Electric energy storage is an area of great research activity, which over the last decade has experienced some very significant breakthroughs, particularly with the use of superconductivity and hydrogen related technologies. Nevertheless, for the purpose of industrial applications it is reasonable to say that, apart from pumped hydro storage, there is very little energy storage in the system. Thus, at any time the following basic relation must be met:

$$Generation = Demand + Transmission\ Losses$$

Power engineers have no direct control over the electricity demand. Load shedding may be used as a last resort but this is not applicable to normal system control. It is normally carried out only under extreme pressure when serious faults or overloads persist.

1.4   An overview of the dynamic response of electrical power networks

Electrical power systems aim to provide a reliable service to all consumers and should be designed to cope with a wide range of normal, i.e. expected, operating conditions, such as:

- connection and disconnection of both large and small loads in any part of the network
- connection and disconnection of generating units to meet system demand
- scheduled topology changes in the transmission system.

They must also cope with a range of abnormal operating conditions resulting from faulty connections in the network, such as sudden loss of generation, phase conductors falling to the ground and phase conductors coming into direct contact with each other.

The ensuing transient phenomena that follow both planned and unplanned events bring the network into dynamic operation. In practice, the system load and the generation are changing continuously and the electrical network is never in a truly steady state condition, but in a perpetual dynamic state. The dynamic performance of the network exhibits a very different behaviour within different time frames because of the diversity of its components (de Mello, 1975):

- rotating machinery
- transmission lines and cables
- power transformers
- power electronics based controllers
- protective equipment
- special controls.

The various plant components respond differently to the same stimulus. Accordingly, it is necessary to simplify, as much as is practicable, the representation of the plant components which are not relevant to the phenomena under study and to represent in sufficient detail the plant components which are essential to the study being taken. A general formulation and analysis of the electrical power network is complex because electrical, mechanical and thermal effects are interrelated.

For dynamic analysis purposes the power network has traditionally been sub-divided as follows (Anderson and Fouad, 1977):

- synchronous generator and excitation system
- turbine-governor and automatic generation control
- boiler control
- transmission network
- loads.

The importance of the study, the time scales for which the study is intended and the time constants of the plant components are some of the factors which influence model selection (de Mello, 1975). Figure 1.16 gives a classification of power systems' dynamic phenomena.

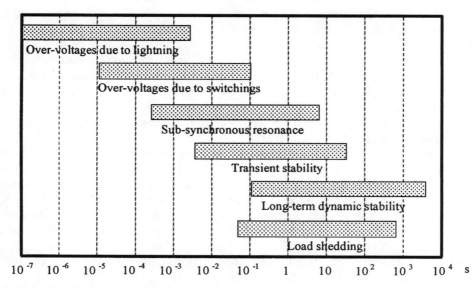

Fig. 1.16 Classification of power systems' dynamic studies.

Studies involving over-voltages due to lightning and switching operations require a detailed representation of the transmission system and the electrical properties of the generators, with particular attention paid to the capacitive effects of transmission lines, cables, generators and transformers. Over very short time scales the mechanical parameters of the generators and most controls can be ignored because they have no time to react to these very fast events, which take place in the time scale $10^{-7}\,\text{s} \leq t \leq 10^{-2}\,\text{s}$.

On the other hand, the long term dynamics associated with load frequency control and load shedding involve the dynamic response of the boiler and turbine-governor set and do not require a detailed representation of the transmission system because at the time scales $10^{-1}\,\text{s} \leq t \leq 10^{3}\,\text{s}$, the electrical transient has already died out. However, a thorough representation of the turbine governor and boiler controls is essential if meaningful conclusions are to be obtained. The mechanical behaviour of the generators has to be represented in some detail because mechanical transients take much longer to die out than electrical transients.

1.4.1   Transient stability

Sub-synchronous resonance and transient stability studies are used to assess power systems' dynamic phenomena that lie somewhere in the middle, between electromagnetic transients due to switching operations and long-term dynamics associated with load frequency control. In power systems transient stability, the boiler controls and the electrical transients of the transmission network are neglected but a detailed representation is needed for the AVR and the mechanical and electrical circuits of the generator. The controls of the turbine governor are represented in some detail. In sub-synchronous resonance studies, a detailed representation of the train shaft system is mandatory (Bremner, 1996).

Arguably, transient stability studies are the most popular dynamic studies. Their main objective is to determine the synchronous generator's ability to remain stable after the occurrence of a fault or following a major change in the network such as the loss of an important generator or a large load (Stagg and El-Abiad, 1968).

Faults need to be cleared as soon as practicable. Transient stability studies provide valuable information about the critical clearance times before one or more synchronous generators in the network become unstable. The internal angles of the generator give reasonably good information about critical clearance times.

Figure 1.17 shows a five-node power system, containing two generators, seven transmission lines and four load points.

A three-phase to ground fault occurs at the terminals of Generator two, located at node two, and the transient stability study shows that both generators are stable with a fault lasting 0.1 s, whilst Generator two is unstable with a fault lasting 0.2 s. Figure 1.18 shows the internal voltage angles of the two generators and their ratio of actual to rated speed. Figures 1.18(a) and (b) show the results of the fault lasting 0.1 s and (c) and (d) the results of the fault lasting 0.2 s (Stagg and El-Abiad, 1968).

Transient stability studies are time-based studies and involve solving the differential equations of the generators and their controls, together with the algebraic equations representing the transmission power network. The differential equations are discretized using the trapezoidal rule of integration and then combined with the network's equations using nodal analysis. The solution procedure is carried out step-by-step (Arrillaga and Watson, 2001).

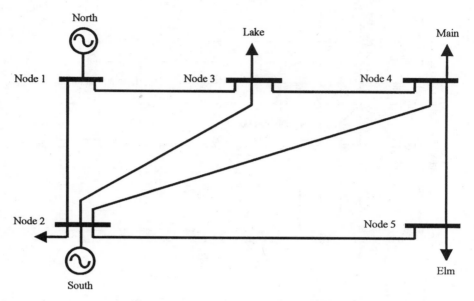

Fig. 1.17 A five-node power network with two generators, seven transmission lines and four loads.

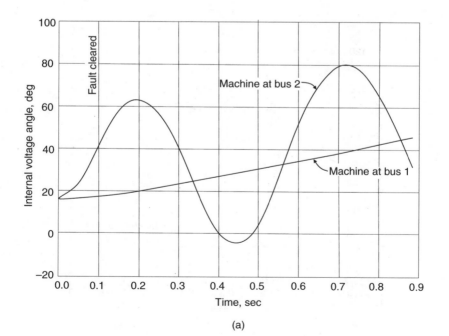

(a)

Fig 1.18 (*continued*)

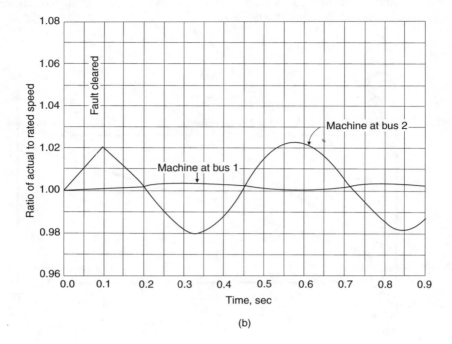

(b)

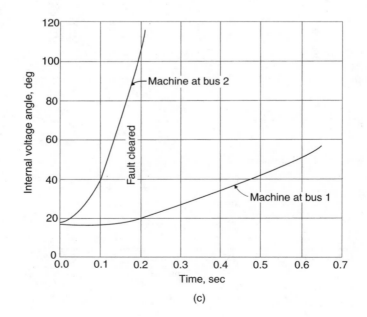

(c)

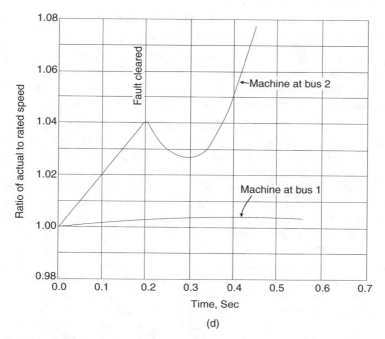

Fig. 1.18 Internal voltage angles of the generators in a five-node system with two generators: (i) fault duration of 0.1 s: (a) internal voltage angles in degrees; (b) ratio of actual to rated speed; (ii) fault duration of 0.2 s: (c) internal voltage angles in degrees; and (d) ratio of actual to rated speed (1) (© 1968 McGraw-Hill).

Flexible alternating current transmission systems equipment responds with little delay to most power systems' disturbances occurring in their vicinity. They modify one or more key network parameters and their control objectives are: (i) to aid the system to remain stable following the occurrence of a fault by damping power oscillations; (ii) to prevent voltage collapse following a steep change in load; and (iii) to damp torsional vibration modes of turbine generator units (IEEE/CIGRE, 1995). Power system transient stability packages have been upgraded or are in the process of being upgraded to include suitable representation of FACTS controllers (Edris, 2000).

1.5 Snapshot-like power network studies

1.5.1 Power flow studies

Although in reality the power network is in a continuous dynamic state, it is useful to assume that at one point the transient produced by the last switching operation or topology change has died out and that the network has reached a state of equilibrium, i.e. steady state. This is the limiting case of long-term dynamics and the time frame of such steady state operation would be located at the far right-hand side of Figure 1.16. The analysis tool used to assess the steady state operation of the power system is known as Load Flow or Power Flow (Arrillaga and Watson, 2001), and in its most basic form has the following objectives:

- to determine the nodal voltage magnitudes and angles throughout the network;
- to determine the active and reactive power flows in all branches of the network;
- to determine the active and reactive power contributed by each generator;
- to determine active and reactive power losses in each component of the network.

In steady state operation, the plant components of the network are described by their impedances and loads are normally recorded in MW and MVAr. Ohm's law and Kirchhoff's laws are used to model the power network as a single entity where the nodal voltage magnitude and angle are the state variables. The power flow is a non-linear problem because, at a given node, the power injection is related to the load impedance by the square of the nodal voltage, which itself is not known at the beginning of the study. Thus, the solution has to be reached by iteration. The solution of the non-linear set of algebraic equations representing the power flow problem is achieved efficiently using the Newton–Raphson method. The generators are represented as nodal power injections because in the steady state the prime mover is assumed to drive the generator at a constant speed and the AVR is assumed to keep the nodal voltage magnitude at a specified value.

Flexible alternating current transmission systems equipment provides adaptive regulation of one or more network parameters at key locations. In general, these controllers are able to regulate either nodal voltage magnitude or active power within their design limits. The most advanced controller, i.e. the UPFC, is able to exert simultaneous control of nodal voltage magnitude, active power and reactive power. Comprehensive models of FACTS controllers suitable for efficient, large-scale power flow solutions have been developed recently (Fuerte-Esquivel, 1997).

1.5.2   Optimal power flow studies

An optimal power flow is an advanced form of power flow algorithm. Optimal power flow studies are also used to determine the steady state operating conditions of power networks but they incorporate an objective function which is optimized without violating system operational constraints. The choice of the objective function depends on the operating philosophy of each utility company. However, active power generation cost is a widely used objective function. Traditionally, the constraint equations include the network equations, active and reactive power consumed at the load points, limits on active and reactive power generation, stability and thermal limits on transmission lines and transformers. Optimal power flow studies provide an effective tool for reactive power management and for assessing the effectiveness of FACTS equipment from the point of view of steady state operation. Comprehensive models of FACTS controllers suitable for efficient, large-scale optimal power flow solutions have been developed recently (Ambriz-Perez, 1998).

1.5.3   Fault studies

If it is assumed that the power network is operating in steady state and that a sudden change takes place due to a faulty condition, then the network will enter a dynamic state. Faults have a variable impact over time, with the highest values of current

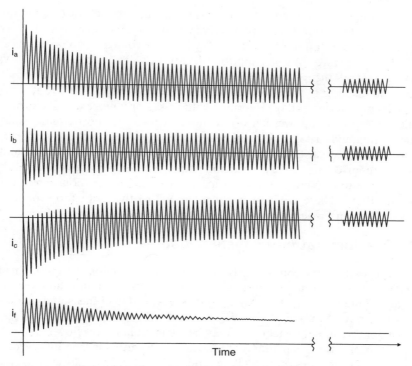

Fig. 1.19 Short-circuit currents of a synchronous generator (© 1995 IEEE).

being present during the first few cycles after the disturbance has occurred. This can be appreciated from Figure 1.19, where a three-phase, short-circuit at the terminals of a synchronous generator give rise to currents that clearly show the transient and steady (sustained) states. The figure shows the currents in phases a, b and c, as well as the field current. The source of this oscillogram is (Kimbark, 1995).

Faults are unpredictable events that may occur anywhere in the power network. Given that faults are unforeseen events, strategies for dealing with them must be decided well in advance (Anderson, 1973). Faults can be divided into those involving a single (nodal) point in the network, i.e. shunt faults, and those involving two points in one or more phases in a given plant component, i.e. series faults. Simultaneous faults involve any combination of the above two kinds of faults in one or more locations in the network. The following are examples of shunt faults:

- three-phase-to-ground short-circuit
- one-phase-to-ground short-circuit
- two-phase short-circuit
- two-phase-to-ground short-circuit.

The following are examples of series faults:

- one-phase conductor open
- two-phase conductors open
- three-phase conductors open.

In addition to the large currents flowing from the generators to the point in fault following the occurrence of a three-phase short-circuit, the voltage drops to extremely low values for the duration of the fault. The greatest voltage drop takes place at the point in fault, i.e. zero, but neighbouring locations will also be affected to varying degrees. In general, the reduction in root mean square (rms) voltage is determined by the electrical distance to the short-circuit, the type of short-circuit and its duration.

The reduction in rms voltage is termed voltage sag or voltage dip. Incidents of this are quite widespread in power networks and are caused by short-circuit faults, large motors starting and fast circuit breaker reclosures. Voltage sags are responsible for spurious tripping of variable speed motor drives, process control systems and computers. It is reported that large production plants have been brought to a halt by sags of 100 ms duration or less, leading to losses of hundreds of thousands of pounds (McHattie, 1998). These kinds of problems provided the motivation for the development of Custom Power equipment (Hingorani, 1995).

1.5.4 Random nature of system load

The system load varies continuously with time in a random fashion. Significant changes occur from hour to hour, day to day, month to month and year to year (Gross and Galiana, 1987). Figure 1.20 shows a typical load measured in a distribution substation for a period of four days.

The random nature of system load may be included in power flow studies and this finds useful applications in planning studies and in the growing 'energy stock market'. Some possible approaches for modelling random loads within a power flow study are:

- modelling the load as a distribution function, e.g. normal distribution;
- future load is forecast by means of time series analysis based on historic values, then normal power flow studies are performed for each forecast point;
- the same procedure as in two but load forecasting is achieved using Neural Networks.

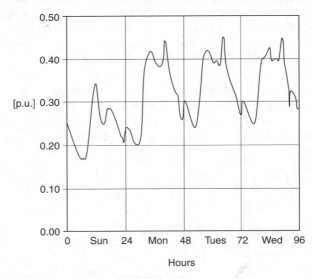

Fig. 1.20 A typical load measured at a distribution substation.

1.5.5 Non-linear loads

Many power plant components have the ability to draw non-sinusoidal currents and, under certain conditions, they distort the sinusoidal voltage waveform in the power network. In general, if a plant component is excited with sinusoidal input and produces non-sinusoidal output, then such a component is termed non-linear, otherwise, it is termed linear (Acha and Madrigal, 2001). Among the non-linear power plant components we have:

- power electronics equipment
- electric arc furnaces
- large concentration of energy saving lamps
- saturated transformers
- rotating machinery.

Some of the more common adverse effects caused by non-linear equipment are:

- the breakdown of sensitive industrial processes
- permanent damage to utility and consumer equipment
- additional expenditure in compensating and filtering equipment
- loss of utility revenue
- additional losses in the network
- overheating of rotating machinery
- electromagnetic compatibility problems in consumer installations
- interference in neighbouring communication circuits
- spurious tripping of protective devices.

1.6 The role of computers in the monitoring, control and planning of power networks

Computers play a key role in the operation, management and planning of electrical power networks. Their use is on the increase due to the complexity of today's interconnected electrical networks operating under free market principles.

1.6.1 Energy control centres

Energy control centres have the objective to monitor and control the electrical network in real-time so that secure and economic operation is achieved round the clock, with a minimum of operator intervention. They include:

- 'smart' monitoring equipment
- fast communications
- power systems application software
- an efficient database
- mainframe computers.

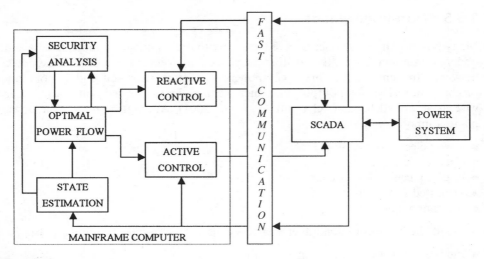

Fig. 1.21 Real-time environment.

The main power systems software used for the real-time control of the network is (Wood and Wollenberg, 1984):

- state estimation
- security analysis
- optimal power flows.

These applications provide the real-time means of controlling and operating power systems securely. In order to achieve such an objective they execute sequentially. Firstly, they validate the condition of the power system using the state estimator and then they develop control actions, which may be based on economic considerations while avoiding actual or potential security violations.

Figure 1.21 shows the real-time environment where the supervisory control and data acquisition (SCADA) and the active and reactive controls interact with the real-time application programmes.

1.6.2   Distribution networks

Most distribution networks do not have real-time control owing to its expense and specialized nature, but SCADA systems are used to gather load data information. Data is a valuable resource that allows better planning and, in general, better management of the distribution network (Gönen, 1986). The sources of data typically found in UK distribution systems are illustrated in Figure 1.22. These range from half hourly telemetered measurements of voltage, current and power flow at the grid supply point down to the pole mounted transformer supplying residential loads, where the only information available is the transformer rating. Most distribution substations have the instrumentation needed to measure and store current information every half hour, and some of them also have provision to measure and store voltage information. Large industrial customers may have SCADA systems of their

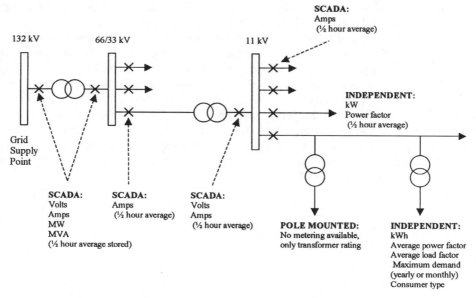

Fig. 1.22 Distribution system data sources.

own and are able to measure electricity consumption, power factor and average load factor.

1.6.3 Planning

At the planning level, increasingly powerful computer resources are dedicated to hosting the extensive power systems analysis tools already available (Stoll, 1989). At present, the emphasis is on corporate databases, geographic information systems and interactive graphics to develop efficient interfaces which blend seamlessly with legacy power systems software. The current trend is towards web applications and e-business which should help companies to cope with the very severe demands imposed on them by market forces.

1.7 Conclusion

This chapter has presented an overview of the composition of electrical power networks and the computer assisted studies that are used for their planning, operation and management.

The main plant components used in modern power networks are described, and the growing ascendancy of power electronics-based equipment in power network control is emphasized. This equipment is classified into equipment used in high voltage transmission and equipment used in low voltage distribution. The former belongs to the family of plant components known as FACTS equipment and the latter belongs to the family of Custom Power equipment. A generic power system network has been used to give examples of FACTS and Custom Power plant equipment and in which locations of the network they may be deployed.

The random nature of the power system load, the ability of a certain class of loads to generate harmonic distortion, and our limited capacity to store electrical energy in significant quantities are issues used to exemplify some of the challenges involved in the planning and operation of electrical power networks. This is in addition to the fact that power networks span entire continents and they are never in a steady state condition but rather in a perpetual dynamic state. This is part of the complex background which since the late 1950s has continuously called for the use of state-of-the-art computers and advanced algorithms to enable their reliable and economic operation. The main computer-based studies used in today's power systems are outlined in this introductory chapter.

2

Power systems engineering – fundamental concepts

2.1 Reactive power control

In an ideal AC power system the voltage and frequency at every supply point would be constant and free from harmonics, and the power factor would be unity. In particular these parameters would be independent of the size and characteristics of consumers' loads. In an ideal system, each load could be designed for optimum performance at the given supply voltage, rather than for merely adequate performance over an unpredictable range of voltage. Moreover, there could be no interference between different loads as a result of variations in the current taken by each one (Miller, 1982).

In three-phase systems, the phase currents and voltages must also be balanced.[1] The *stability* of the system against oscillations and faults must also be assured. All these criteria add up to a notion of *power quality*. A single numerical definition of power quality does not exist, but it is helpful to use quantities such as the maximum fluctuation in rms supply voltage averaged over a stated period of time, or the total harmonic distortion (THD), or the 'availability' (i.e. the percentage of time, averaged over a period of, say, a year, for which the supply is uninterrupted).

The maintenance of constant frequency requires an exact balance between the overall power supplied by generators and the overall power absorbed by loads, irrespective of the voltage. However, the voltage plays an important role in maintaining the stability of power transmission, as we shall see. Voltage levels are very sensitive to the flow of reactive power and therefore the control of reactive power is

---

[1] Unbalance causes negative-sequence current which produces a backward-rotating field in rotating AC machines, causing torque fluctuations and power loss with potential overheating.

important. This is the subject of *reactive compensation*. Where the focus is on individual loads, we speak of *load compensation*, and this is the main subject of this chapter along with several related fundamental topics of power systems engineering. Chapter 3 deals with reactive power control on long-distance high-voltage transmission systems, that is, *transmission system compensation*.

Load compensation is the management of reactive power to improve the quality of supply at a particular load or group of loads. Compensating equipment – such as power-factor correction equipment – is usually installed on or near to the consumer's premises. In load compensation there are three main objectives:

1. power-factor correction
2. improvement of voltage regulation[2]
3. load balancing.

Power-factor correction and *load balancing* are desirable even when the supply voltage is 'stiff': that is, even when there is no requirement to improve the voltage regulation. Ideally the reactive power requirements of a load should be provided locally, rather than drawing the reactive component of current from a remote power station. Most industrial loads have lagging power factors; that is, they absorb reactive power. The load current therefore tends to be larger than is required to supply the real power alone. Only the real power is ultimately useful in energy conversion and the excess load current represents a waste to the consumer, who has to pay not only for the excess cable capacity to carry it, but also for the excess Joule loss in the supply cables. When load power factors are low, generators and distribution networks cannot be used at full efficiency or full capacity, and the control of voltage throughout the network can become more difficult. Supply tariffs to industrial customers usually penalize low power-factor loads, encouraging the use of power-factor correction equipment.

In *voltage regulation* the supply utilities are usually bound by statute to maintain the voltage within defined limits, typically of the order of ±5% at low voltage, averaged over a period of a few minutes or hours. Much more stringent constraints are imposed where large, rapidly varying loads could cause voltage dips hazardous to the operation of protective equipment, or flicker annoying to the eye.

The most obvious way to improve voltage regulation would be to 'strengthen' the power system by increasing the size and number of generating units and by making the network more densely interconnected. This approach is costly and severely constrained by environmental planning factors. It also raises the fault level and the required switchgear ratings. It is better to size the transmission and distribution system according to the maximum demand for *real* power and basic security of supply, and to manage the reactive power by means of compensators and other equipment which can be deployed more flexibly than generating units, without increasing the fault level.

Similar considerations apply in *load balancing*. Most AC power systems are three-phase, and are designed for balanced operation. Unbalanced operation gives rise to components of current in the wrong phase-sequence (i.e. negative- and zero-sequence

---

[2] 'Regulation' is an old-fashioned term used to denote the variation of voltage when current is drawn from the system.

components). Such components can have undesirable effects, including additional losses in motors and generating units, oscillating torque in AC machines, increased ripple in rectifiers, malfunction of several types of equipment, saturation of transformers, and excessive triplen harmonics and neutral currents.[3]

The harmonic content in the voltage supply waveform is another important measure in the quality of supply. Harmonics above the fundamental power frequency are usually eliminated by filters. Nevertheless, harmonic problems often arise together with compensation problems and some types of compensator even generate harmonics which must be suppressed internally or filtered.

The ideal compensator would

(a) supply the exact reactive power requirement of the load;
(b) present a constant-voltage characteristic at its terminals; and
(c) be capable of operating independently in the three phases.

In practice, one of the most important factors in the choice of compensating equipment is the underlying rate of change in the load current, power factor, or impedance. For example, with an induction motor running 24 hours/day driving a constant mechanical load (such as a pump), it will often suffice to have a fixed power-factor correction capacitor. On the other hand, a drive such as a mine hoist has an intermittent load which will vary according to the burden and direction of the car, but will remain constant for periods of one or two minutes during the travel. In such a case, power-factor correction capacitors could be switched in and out as required. An example of a load with extremely rapid variation is an electric arc furnace, where the reactive power requirement varies even within one cycle and, for a short time at the beginning of the melt, it is erratic and unbalanced. In this case a dynamic compensator is required, such as a TCR or a saturated-reactor compensator, to provide sufficiently rapid dynamic response.

Steady-state power-factor correction equipment should be deployed according to economic factors including the supply tariff, the size of the load, and its uncompensated power factor. For loads which cause fluctuations in the supply voltage, the degree of variation is assessed at the 'point of common coupling' (PCC), which is usually the point in the network where the customer's and the supplier's areas of responsibility meet: this might be, for example, the high-voltage side of the distribution transformer supplying a particular factory.

Loads that require compensation include arc furnaces, induction furnaces, arc welders, induction welders, steel rolling mills, mine winders, large motors (particularly those which start and stop frequently), excavators, chip mills, and several others. Non-linear loads such as rectifiers also generate harmonics and may require harmonic filters, most commonly for the 5th and 7th but sometimes for higher orders as well. Triplen harmonics are usually not filtered but eliminated by balancing the load and by trapping them in delta-connected transformer windings.

The power-factor and the voltage regulation can both be improved if some of the drives in a plant are synchronous motors instead of induction motors, because the synchronous motor can be controlled to supply (or absorb) an adjustable amount of reactive power and therefore it can be used as a compensator. Voltage dips caused by

---

[3] *Triplen* (literally *triple-n*) means harmonics of order $3n$, where n is an integer. See §2.12.

Table 2.1 Typical voltage fluctuation standards

Load	Limits of voltage fluctuation
Large motor starts	1–3% depending on frequency
Mine winders, excavators, large motor drives	1–3% at distribution voltage level
	$\frac{1}{2}$–$1\frac{1}{2}$% at transmission voltage level
Welding plant	$\frac{1}{4}$–2% depending on frequency
Induction furnaces	Up to 1%
Arc furnaces	$<\frac{1}{2}$%

Table 2.2 Factors to consider in specifying compensating equipment

1. Continuous and short-time reactive power requirements.
2. Rated voltage and limits of voltage variation.
3. Accuracy of voltage regulation required.
4. Response time of the compensator for a specified disturbance.
5. Maximum harmonic distortion with compensator in service.
6. Performance with unbalanced supply voltages and/or with unbalanced load.
7. Environmental factors: noise level; indoor/outdoor installation; temperature, humidity, pollution, wind and seismic factors; leakage from transformers, capacitors, cooling systems.
8. Cabling requirements and layout; access, enclosure, grounding; provision for future expansion; redundancy and maintenance provisions.
9. Protection arrangements for the compensator and coordination with other protection systems, including reactive power limits if necessary.
10. Energization procedure and precautions.

motor starts can also be avoided by using a 'soft starter', that is, a phase-controlled thyristor switch in series with the motor, which gradually ramps the motor voltage from a reduced level instead of connecting suddenly at full voltage.

Standards for the quality of supply. One very noticeable effect of supply voltage variations is flicker especially in tungsten filament lamps. Slow variations of up to 3% may be tolerable, but rapid variations within the range of maximal visual sensitivity (between 1 and 25 Hz) must be limited to 0.25% or less. A serious consequence of undervoltage is the overcurrent that results from the fact that AC motors run at a speed which is essentially determined by the frequency, and if the voltage is low the current must increase in order to maintain the power. On the other hand, overvoltage is damaging to insulation systems.

Table 2.1 gives an idea of the appropriate standards which might be applied in different circumstances, but local statutes and conditions should be studied in each individual case.

Specification of a load compensator. Some of the factors which need to be considered when specifying a load compensator are summarized in Table 2.2.

2.2   Conventions used in power engineering

In power engineering it is helpful to have a set of conventions for symbols. Unfortunately many people disregard conventions, and this causes confusion. There is no universal standard, but the simple conventions given in Table 2.3 are widely used, practical, and consistent with most classic textbooks.

Table 2.3 Font and symbol conventions

Type	What is meant	Examples
Lower-case italic	*instantaneous* values	v, i
Upper-case italic	RMS values or DC values	V, I
	Resistance, reactance, and impedance magnitude	R, X Z
	Inductance and capacitance	L, C
Upper-case boldface roman	Phasors	**V**, **I**
	Impedance	**Z**

In handwritten work, you can't really use boldface, so use a bar or arrow or tilde – preferably *over* the symbol, e.g. $\vec{V}$, $\overline{V}$, $\tilde{V}$.

Subscripts can be roman or italic; it is a matter of style

In three-phase systems, various conventions are used for the subscripts used to denote the three phases. In Europe (particularly Germany): U, V, W. In the UK: R, Y, B (for red, yellow, blue), or a, b, c. In the United States: a, b, c or A, B, C. You will also see 1, 2, 3 used: this seems an obvious choice, but if you are working with symmetrical components these subscripts can be confused with the positive, negative, and zero-sequence subscripts 1, 2, 0 (sometimes +, −, 0). The best advice is to be very careful! Never confuse **phasor** values with *scalar* values!

Examples	
Typeset	Comment
$V = RI$	RMS AC; or DC
$\mathbf{V} = jX\mathbf{I}$	**V** and **I** are phasors
	X is a scalar (reactance)
	jX is an impedance (complex)
$\mathbf{Z} = R + jX$	**Z** is complex (impedance)
	R is scalar (resistance)
	X is scalar (reactance)
$v = V_{\mathrm{m}} \cos \omega t$	v is an instantaneous value
	V_{m} is a fixed scalar value

2.3 Basic source/load relationships

2.3.1 Fault level and circuit-breaker ratings

The *fault level* (sometimes called *short-circuit level*) is a term used to describe the 'strength' of a power supply: that is, its ability to provide *both* current and voltage. It is defined as:

$$\text{Fault level} = \text{Open-circuit voltage} \times \text{Short-circuit current [VA/phase]}$$

The fault level provides a single number that can be used to select the size of circuit-breaker needed at a particular point in a power system. Circuit-breakers must interrupt fault currents (i.e. the current that flows if there is a short-circuit fault). When the contacts of the circuit-breaker are separating, there is an arc which must be extinguished (for example, by a blast of compressed air). The difficulty of extinguishing the arc depends on both the current and the system voltage. So it is convenient to take the product of these as a measure of the size or 'power' of the circuit-breaker that is needed. The fault level is used for this. The rating of a circuit-breaker should

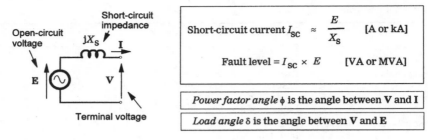

Fig. 2.1 Thévenin equivalent circuit of one phase of a supply system (neglecting resistance).

always exceed the fault level at the point where the circuit-breaker is connected – otherwise the circuit-breaker might not be capable of interrupting the fault current. This would be very dangerous: high-voltage circuit-breakers are often the final means of protection, and if they fail to isolate faults the damage can be extreme – *it would be like having a lightning strike that did not switch itself off.*

2.3.2   Thévenin equivalent circuit model of a power system

At any point where a load is connected to a power system, the power system can be represented by a Thévenin equivalent circuit[4] having an open-circuit voltage **E** and an internal impedance $Z_s = R_s + jX_s$ (see Figure 2.1). Usually X_s is much bigger than R_s and Z_s is approximately equal to jX_s (as in the diagrams). The short-circuit current is $I_{sc} \approx E/X_s$ and the short-circuit level is $EI_{sc} = E^2/X_s$ in each phase. The short-circuit level is measured in volt-amperes, VA (or kVA or MVA), because **E** and I_{sc} are almost in phase quadrature.

2.3.3   Loads and phasor diagrams

A *resistive load R* on an AC power system draws power and produces a phase angle shift δ between the terminal voltage **V** and the open-circuit voltage **E**. δ is called the *load angle* (see Figure 2.2). The voltage drop across the Thévenin equivalent

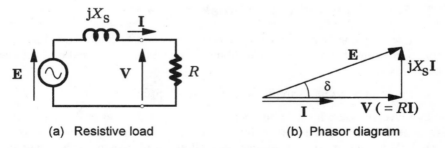

(a) Resistive load   (b) Phasor diagram

Fig. 2.2 Resistive load. (a) circuit diagram; and (b) phasor diagram.

---

[4] The Thévenin equivalent circuit is a series equivalent circuit, in which the source is a voltage source and it is in series with the internal impedance. In the *Norton* equivalent circuit, the source is a current source in parallel with the internal impedance.

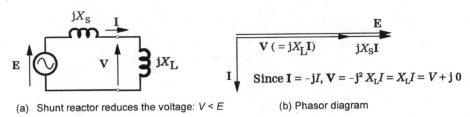

(a) Shunt reactor reduces the voltage: $V < E$ (b) Phasor diagram

Fig. 2.3 Purely inductive load. (a) circuit diagram; and (b) phasor diagram.

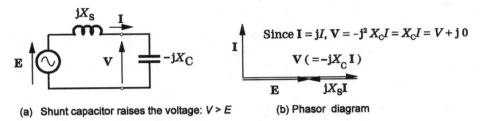

(a) Shunt capacitor raises the voltage: $V > E$ (b) Phasor diagram

Fig. 2.4 Purely capacitive load. (a) circuit diagram; and (b) phasor diagram.

impedance is $jX_s\mathbf{I}$, which is orthogonal to the terminal voltage $\mathbf{V}(= R\mathbf{I})$. Because of the orthogonality, V does not fall very much below E, even though $X_s I$ might be a sizeable fraction of E. Note that the *power factor angle* ϕ is zero for resistive loads; ϕ is the angle between $\mathbf{V}$ and $\mathbf{I}$.[5]

A *purely inductive load* draws no power and produces no phase-angle shift between $\mathbf{V}$ and $\mathbf{E}$: i.e. $\delta = 0$ (see Figure 2.3). The terminal voltage V is quite sensitive to the inductive load current because the volt-drop $jX_s\mathbf{I}$ is directly in phase with both $\mathbf{E}$ and $\mathbf{V}$. You might ask, 'what is the use of a load that draws no power?' One example is that *shunt reactors* are often used to limit the voltage on transmission and distribution systems, especially in locations remote from tap-changing transformers or generating stations. Because of the shunt capacitance of the line, the voltage tends to rise when the load is light (e.g. at night). By connecting an inductive load (shunt reactor), the voltage can be brought down to its correct value. Since the reactor is not drawing any real power (but only reactive power), there is no energy cost apart from a small amount due to losses in the windings and core.

A *purely capacitive load* also draws no power and produces no phase-angle shift between $\mathbf{V}$ and $\mathbf{E}$: i.e. $\delta = 0$. The system volt-drop $jX_s\mathbf{I}$ is directly in *anti-phase* with $\mathbf{E}$ and $\mathbf{V}$, and this causes the terminal voltage V to *rise* above E. Again you might ask 'what is the use of a load that draws no power?' An example is that *shunt capacitors* are often used to raise the voltage on transmission and distribution systems, especially in locations remote from tap-changing transformers or generating stations. Because of the series inductance of the line, the voltage tends to fall when the load is heavy (e.g. mid-morning), and this is when shunt capacitors would be connected.

---

[5] It is assumed that the AC voltage and current are sinewaves at fundamental frequency, so ϕ is the phase angle at this frequency.

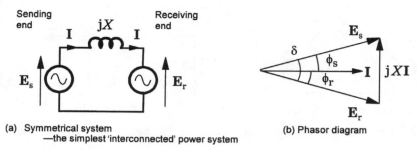

(a) Symmetrical system
—the simplest 'interconnected' power system

(b) Phasor diagram

Fig. 2.5 Symmetrical system.

Shunt reactors and capacitors are sometimes thyristor-controlled, to provide rapid response. This is sometimes necessary near rapidly-changing loads such as electric arc furnaces or mine hoists. Of course the use of thyristors causes the current to contain harmonics, and these must usually be filtered.

2.3.4 The symmetrical system

The *symmetrical system* is an important example – indeed the simplest example – of an interconnected power system, Figure 2.5. It comprises two synchronous machines coupled by a transmission line. It might be used, for example, as a simple model of a power system in which the main generating stations are at two locations, separated by a transmission line that is modelled by a simple inductive impedance jX. The loads (induction motors, lighting and heating systems, etc., are connected in parallel with the generators, but in the simplest model they are not even shown, because the power transmission system engineer is mostly concerned with the power flow along the line, and this is controlled by the prime-movers at the generating stations (i.e. the steam turbines, water turbines, gas turbines, wind turbines etc.).

Although the circuit diagram of a symmetrical system just looks like two generators connected by an inductive impedance, power can flow in *either direction*. The symmetrical system can be used to derive the *power flow equation*, which is one of the most important basic equations in power system operation; see §2.8. If E_s and E_r are the open-circuit voltages at the two generators, then

$$P = \frac{E_s E_r}{X} \sin \delta \tag{2.1}$$

where δ is the phase angle between the phasors $\mathbf{E}_s$ and $\mathbf{E}_r$. Note that in Figure 2.5 there are two power factor angles: ϕ_s between $\mathbf{E}_s$ and $\mathbf{I}$ at the sending end, and ϕ_r between $\mathbf{E}_r$ and $\mathbf{I}$ at the receiving end.

2.4 Complex power, apparent power, real and reactive power

Consider a simple load $R + jX$ with a current $\mathbf{I}$ and voltage $\mathbf{V}$, Figure 2.6. The *complex power* $\mathbf{S}$ is defined as

$$\mathbf{S} = \mathbf{V}\mathbf{I}^* = P + jQ \tag{2.2}$$

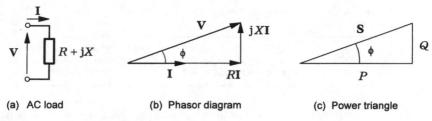

(a) AC load   (b) Phasor diagram   (c) Power triangle

Fig. 2.6 Development of the complex power triangle.

S can be expressed graphically as the complex number $P + jQ$, as shown in Figure 2.6, where

P is the real power in W, kW or MW, averaged over one cycle
Q is the reactive power in VAr, kVAr, or MVAr, also averaged over one cycle[6]
$S = |\mathbf{S}|$ is the apparent power or 'volt–amperes', in VA, kVA or MVA[7]

Let $\mathbf{V}$ be the reference phasor, and suppose that the load is inductive. Then

$$\mathbf{I} = Ie^{-j\phi} = I\cos\phi - jI\sin\phi \tag{2.3}$$

where $\phi = \tan^{-1}(X/R) = \tan^{-1}(Q/P)$. The negative phase rotation $-j\phi$ means that the current lags behind the voltage. When we take the conjugate $\mathbf{I}^*$ and multiply by $\mathbf{V}$ we get

$$P = VI\cos\phi \quad \text{and} \quad Q = VI\sin\phi \tag{2.4}$$

Evidently P is positive and so is Q. A load that has positive reactive power is said to 'absorb' VArs. Inductive loads absorb VArs. Conversely, a capacitive load would have

$$\mathbf{I} = Ie^{+j\phi} = I\cos\phi + jI\sin\phi \tag{2.5}$$

In this case the current leads the voltage. P is still positive, but when we take the conjugate $\mathbf{I}^*$ we get negative Q. We say that a capacitive load *generates* or *supplies* VArs.

There is a distinction between the receiving end and the sending end. The expression '$VI\cos\phi$' is correctly interpreted as *power absorbed by the load* at the receiving end. But at the sending end the generated power P is supplied *to* the system, not absorbed *from* it. The distinction is that the sending end is a source of power, while the receiving end is a sink. In Figure 2.5, for example, both $P_s = E_sI\cos\phi_s$ and

---

[6] VAr = 'volt–amperes, reactive'
[7] Although $\mathbf{S}$ is a complex number, it is not a phasor quantity. The power triangle merely represents the relationship between P, Q, ϕ, and the apparent power S. Note that P, Q, and S are all *average* quantities (averaged over one cycle); they are not rms quantities. On the other hand V and I are rms quantities.

Table 2.4 Generating and absorbing reactive power: sink and source conventions

	Lagging PF (**I** lags **V**)	Leading PF (**I** leads **V**)
Load (sink)	$Q_r > 0$ Absorbing VArs	$Q_r < 0$ Generating VArs
Generator (source)	$Q_s > 0$ Generating VArs	$Q_s < 0$ Absorbing VArs

$P_r = E_r I \cos \phi_r$ are positive, supplied *to* the system at the sending end and taken *from* it at the receiving end.[8]

A similar distinction arises with reactive power. The receiving end in Figure 2.5 evidently has a lagging power factor and is absorbing VArs. The sending end has a leading power factor and is *absorbing* VArs. In Figure 2.9, the power factor is lagging at both the generator and the load, but the load is absorbing VArs while the generator is generating VARs. These conventions and interpretations are summarized in Table 2.4.

Note that

$$\tan \phi = \frac{Q}{P} \quad \text{and} \quad \cos \phi = \frac{P}{\sqrt{P^2 + Q^2}} \tag{2.6}$$

where $\cos \phi$ is the power factor.

Remember that phasors apply only when the voltage and currents are purely sinusoidal, and this expression for power factor is meaningless if either the voltage or current waveform is non-sinusoidal. A more general expression for power factor with non-sinusoidal current and waveforms is

$$PF = \frac{\text{Average Power}}{\text{RMS volts} \times \text{RMS amps}} \tag{2.7}$$

2.5 Leading and lagging loads

Figure 2.7 shows a circuit with a supply system whose open-circuit voltage is **E** and short-circuit impedance is $Z_s = 0 + jX_s$, where $X_s = 0.1\,\Omega$. The load impedance is

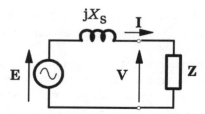

Fig. 2.7 AC supply and load circuit.

---

[8] For a source, the arrows representing positive voltage and current are in the same direction. For a sink, they are in opposite directions. This convention is not universal: for example, in German literature the opposite convention is used.

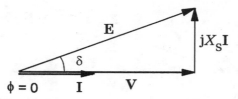

Fig. 2.8 Phasor diagram, resistive load.

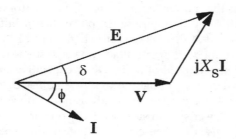

Fig. 2.9 Phasor diagram, inductive load.

$Z = 1\,\Omega$ but the power factor can be unity, 0.8 lagging, or 0.8 leading. For each of these three cases, the supply voltage E can be adjusted to keep the terminal voltage $V = 100$ V. For each case we will determine the value of E, the power-factor angle ϕ, the load angle δ, the power P, the reactive power Q, and the volt–amperes S.

Unity power factor. In Figure 2.8, we have $E\cos\delta = V = 100$ and $E\sin\delta = X_s I$ $= 0.1 \times 100/1 = 10$ V. Therefore $\mathbf{E} = 100 + \mathrm{j}10 = 100.5\mathrm{e}^{\mathrm{j}5.71°}$ V. The power-factor angle is $\phi = \cos^{-1}(1) = 0$, $\delta = 5.71°$, and $\mathbf{S} = P + \mathrm{j}Q = \mathbf{VI}^* = 100 \times 100\mathrm{e}^{\mathrm{j}0} = 10\,\mathrm{kVA}$, with $P = 10\,\mathrm{kW}$ and $Q = 0$.

Lagging power factor. In Figure 2.9, the current is rotated negatively (i.e. clockwise) to a phase angle of $\phi = \cos^{-1}(0.8) = -36.87°$. Although $I = 100$ A and $X_s I$ is still 10 V, its new orientation 'stretches' the phasor $\mathbf{E}$ to a larger magnitude: $\mathbf{E} = \mathbf{V} + \mathrm{j}X_s\mathbf{I} = (100 + \mathrm{j}0) + \mathrm{j}0.1 \times 100\mathrm{e}^{-\mathrm{j}36.87°} = 106.3\mathrm{e}^{\mathrm{j}4.32°}$ V. When the power-factor is lagging a higher supply voltage E is needed for the same load voltage. The load angle is $\delta = 4.32°$ and $\mathbf{S} = \mathbf{VI}^* = 100 \times 100\mathrm{e}^{+\mathrm{j}36.87} = 8000 + \mathrm{j}6000$ VA. Thus $S = 10\,\mathrm{kVA}$, $P = 8\,\mathrm{kW}$ and $Q = +6\,\mathrm{kVAr}$ (absorbed).

Leading power factor. The leading power factor angle causes a reduction in the value of E required to keep V constant: $\mathbf{E} = 100 + \mathrm{j}0.1 \times 100\mathrm{e}^{+\mathrm{j}36.87°} = 94.3\mathrm{e}^{\mathrm{j}4.86°}$ V. The load angle is $\delta = 4.86°$, and $\mathbf{S} = 10000\mathrm{e}^{-\mathrm{j}36.87°} = 8000 - \mathrm{j}6000$; i.e. $P = 8\,\mathrm{kW}$ and $Q = 6\,\mathrm{kVAr}$ (generated).

We have seen that when the load power and current are kept the same, the inductive load with its lagging power factor requires a higher source voltage E, and the capacitive load with its leading power factor requires a lower source voltage. Conversely, if the source voltage E were kept constant, then the inductive load would have a lower terminal voltage V and the capacitive load would have a higher terminal voltage. As an exercise, repeat the calculations for $E = 100$ V and determine V in each case, assuming that $Z = 1\,\Omega$ with each of the three different power factors.

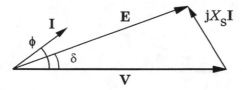

Fig. 2.10 Phasor diagram, capacitive load.

We can see from this that power-factor correction capacitors (connected in parallel with an inductive load) will not only raise the power factor but will also increase the voltage. On the other hand, if the voltage is too high, it can be reduced by connecting inductors in parallel. In modern high-voltage power systems it is possible to control the voltage by varying the amount of inductive or capacitive current drawn from the system at the point where the voltage needs to be adjusted. This is called *reactive compensation* or *static VAR control*. In small, isolated power systems (such as an automotive or aircraft power system supplied from one or two generators) this is not generally necessary because the open-circuit voltage of the generator E can be varied by field control, using a *voltage regulator*.

2.6   Power factor correction

The load in Figure 2.7 can be expressed as an admittance $\mathbf{Y} = G + jB$ supplied from a voltage $\mathbf{V}$, where $\mathbf{Y} = 1/\mathbf{Z}$. G is the *conductance*, i.e. the real part of the admittance $\mathbf{Y}$, and B is the *susceptance*, i.e. the reactive or imaginary part of the admittance $\mathbf{Y}$. The load current is $\mathbf{I}$ and for an inductive load the reactive component is negative (equation (2.3)) so we can write

$$\mathbf{I} = I_R - jI_X = \mathbf{V}(G - jB) = VG - jVB \tag{2.8}$$

Both $\mathbf{V}$ and $\mathbf{I}$ are phasors, and equation (2.8) is represented in the phasor diagram (Figure 2.11) in which $\mathbf{V}$ is the reference phasor. The voltage $\mathbf{V}$ and current $\mathbf{I}$ are in common with Figure 2.9, but Figure 2.11 shows the components of the current $\mathbf{I}$ and omits $\mathbf{E}$ and the voltage drop across the supply impedance. The load current has a 'resistive' or 'real' component I_R in phase with $\mathbf{V}$, and a 'reactive' or 'imaginary' component, $I_X = VB$ in quadrature with $\mathbf{V}$. The angle between $\mathbf{V}$ and $\mathbf{I}$ is ϕ, the power-factor angle. The apparent power supplied to the load is given by equation (2.2) with $P = V^2 G$ and $Q = V^2 B$. For a capacitive load I_X is positive and $Q = V^2 B$, which is negative.

The real power P is usefully converted into heat, mechanical work, light, or other forms of energy. The reactive volt–amperes Q cannot be converted into useful forms of energy but is nevertheless an inherent requirement of the load. For example, in AC induction motors it is associated with production of flux and is often called the 'magnetizing reactive power'.

The supply current exceeds the real component by the factor $1/\cos\phi$, where $\cos\phi$ is the power factor: that is, the ratio between the real power P and the apparent power S. The power factor is that fraction of the apparent power which can be

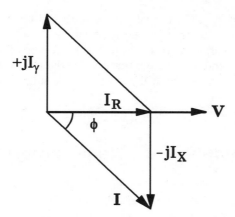

Fig. 2.11 Phasor diagram for power factor correction.

usefully converted into other forms of energy. The Joule losses in the supply cables are increased by the factor $1/\cos^2 \phi$. Cable ratings must be increased accordingly, and the losses must be paid for by the consumer.

The principle of power-factor correction is to compensate for the reactive power; that is, to provide it locally by connecting in parallel with the load a compensator having a purely reactive admittance of opposite sign to that of the reactive component of the load admittance. An inductive load is compensated by a capacitive admittance $+jB_\gamma$ and a capacitive load by an inductive admittance $-jB_\gamma$. If the compensating admittance is equal to the reactive part of the load admittance, then for an inductive load the supply current becomes

$$\mathbf{I}_s = \mathbf{I} + \mathbf{I}_\gamma = \mathbf{V}(G - jB) + \mathbf{V}(jB) = VG = I_R \qquad (2.9)$$

which is in phase with $\mathbf{V}$, making the *overall* power-factor unity. Figure 2.11 shows the phasor diagram.

With 100% compensation the supply current $\mathbf{I}_s$ now has the smallest value capable of supplying full power P at the voltage V, and all the reactive power required by the load is supplied locally by the compensator. The reactive power rating of the compensator is related to the rated *power* P of the load by $Q_\gamma = P \tan \phi$. The compensator current Q_γ/V equals the reactive current of the load at rated voltage. Relieved of the reactive requirements of the load, the supply now has excess capacity which is available for supplying other loads. The load may also be partially compensated (i.e. $|Q_\gamma| < |Q|$).

A fixed-admittance compensator cannot follow variations in the reactive power requirement of the load. In practice a compensator such as a bank of capacitors can be divided into parallel sections, each switched separately, so that discrete changes in the compensating reactive power may be made, according to the requirements of the load. More sophisticated compensators (e.g. synchronous condensers or static compensators) are capable of continuous variation of their reactive power.

The foregoing analysis has taken no account of the effect of supply voltage variations on the effectiveness of the compensator in maintaining an overall power factor of unity. In general the reactive power of a fixed-reactance compensator will not vary in sympathy with that of the load as the supply voltage varies, and a compensation 'error' will arise. In Section 2.7 the effects of voltage variations are examined, and we will find out what extra features the ideal compensator must have to perform satisfactorily when both the load and the supply system parameters can vary.

2.7 Compensation and voltage control

Figure 2.12 shows a one-line diagram of an AC power system, which could represent either a single-phase system, or one phase of a three-phase system. Figure 2.13 shows the phasor diagram for an inductive load.

When the load draws current from the supply, the terminal voltage V falls below the open-circuit value E. The relationship between V and the load current I is called the *system load line*, Figure 2.14.

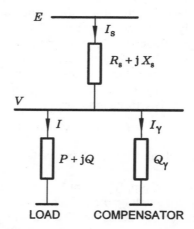

Fig. 2.12 Equivalent circuit of supply and load.

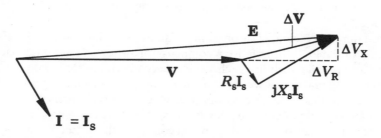

Fig. 2.13 Phasor diagram (uncompensated).

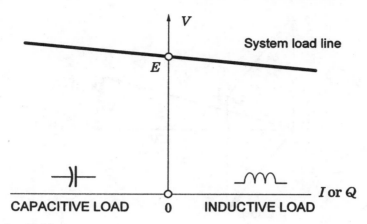

Fig. 2.14 System load line.

The 'load' can be measured by its current I, but in power systems parlance it is the reactive volt-amperes Q of the load that is held chiefly responsible for the voltage drop. From Figures 2.12 and 2.13,

$$\Delta \mathbf{V} = \mathbf{E} - \mathbf{V} = \mathbf{Z_s I} \qquad (2.10)$$

where $\mathbf{I}$ is the load current. The complex power of the load (per phase) is defined by equation (2.2), so

$$\mathbf{I} = \frac{P - jQ}{\mathbf{V}} \qquad (2.11)$$

and if $\mathbf{V} = V + j0$ is taken as the reference phasor we can write

$$\Delta \mathbf{V} = (R_s + jX_s)\left(\frac{P - jQ}{V}\right) = \frac{R_s P + X_s Q}{V} + j\frac{X_s P - R_s Q}{V} = \Delta V_R + j\Delta V_X \qquad (2.12)$$

The voltage drop $\Delta \mathbf{V}$ has a component ΔV_R in phase with $\mathbf{V}$ and a component ΔV_X in quadrature with $\mathbf{V}$; Figure 2.13. Both the magnitude and phase of $\mathbf{V}$, relative to the open-circuit voltage E, are functions of the magnitude and phase of the load current, and of the supply impedance $R_s + jX_s$. Thus $\Delta \mathbf{V}$ depends on both the real and reactive power of the load.

By adding a compensating impedance or 'compensator' in parallel with the load, it is possible to maintain $|\mathbf{V}| = |\mathbf{E}|$. In Figure 2.15 this is accomplished with a purely reactive compensator. The load reactive power is replaced by the sum $Q_s = Q + Q_\gamma$, and Q_γ (the compensator reactive power) is adjusted in such a way as to rotate the phasor $\Delta \mathbf{V}$ until $|\mathbf{V}| = |\mathbf{E}|$. From equations (2.10) and (2.12),

$$|\mathbf{E}|^2 = \left[V + \frac{R_s P + X_s Q_s}{V}\right]^2 + \left[\frac{X_s P - R_s Q_s}{V}\right]^2 \qquad (2.13)$$

The value of Q_γ required to achieve this 'constant voltage' condition is found by solving equation (2.13) for Q_s with $V = |\mathbf{E}|$; then $Q_\gamma = Q_s - Q$. In practice the value can be determined automatically by a closed-loop control that maintains constant

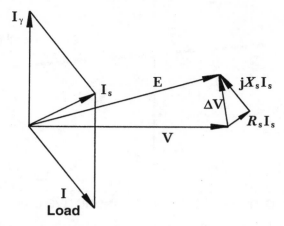

Fig. 2.15 Phasor diagram, compensated for constant voltage.

voltage V. Equation (2.13) always has a solution for Q_s, implying that: *A purely reactive compensator can eliminate voltage variations caused by changes in both the real and the reactive power of the load.*

Provided that the reactive power of the compensator Q_γ can be controlled smoothly over a sufficiently wide range (both lagging and leading), and at an adequate rate, the compensator can perform as an *ideal voltage regulator.*

We have seen that a compensator can be used for power-factor correction. For example, if the power factor is corrected to unity, $Q_s = 0$ and $Q_\gamma = Q$. Then

$$\Delta\mathbf{V} = (R_s + jX_s)\frac{P}{V} \tag{2.14}$$

which is independent of Q and therefore not under the control of the compensator. Thus: *A purely reactive compensator cannot maintain both constant voltage and unity power factor at the same time.*

The only exception is when $P = 0$, but this is not of practical interest.

2.7.1 System load line

In high-voltage power systems R_s is often much smaller than X_s and is ignored. Instead of using the system *impedance*, it is more usual to talk about the system *short-circuit level* $S = E^2/X_s$. Moreover, when voltage-drop is being considered, ΔV_X is ignored because it tends to produce only a phase change between $\mathbf{V}$ and $\mathbf{E}$. Then

$$\Delta\mathbf{V} = \Delta V_R \quad \text{and} \quad \frac{\Delta V}{V} = \frac{X_s Q}{V^2} \approx \frac{Q}{S} \tag{2.15}$$

and

$$V \approx E\left(1 - \frac{Q}{S}\right) \tag{2.16}$$

This relationship is a straight line, as shown in Figure 2.14. It is called the *system load line.*

2.8 Control of power and frequency

In power systems it is essential to keep the *frequency* and the *voltage* close to their rated values. The frequency is controlled by controlling the balance between the power supplied to the system and the power taken from it. Figure 2.16 shows a transmission system with a prime mover driving a generator, and a motor driving a mechanical load. Table 2.5 gives examples of prime movers and loads.

The power P_{in} supplied *to* the system is determined by the prime mover(s). In a steam-turbine generator, the steam valves are the main means of control. Of course, if the valves are opened wide, the boiler must be able to provide sufficient steam (at the correct pressure and temperature) to develop the required power. This means that the boiler control must be coordinated with the steam valves. Similarly, in a wind turbine the power transmitted to the generator is determined by the wind speed and the blade pitch, which can be varied to control the power to the required level.

The power P_{out} taken *from* the system is determined by the mechanical and electrical loads. For example, consider a direct-connected induction motor driving a pump. The motor rotates at a speed determined by the intersection of its torque/speed characteristic with the pump's torque/speed characteristic. Since the motor torque/speed characteristic is very steep near synchronous speed, the motor tends to run near synchronous speed and the torque is then determined by the requirements of the pump (depending on the pressure head and the flow rate). So the power is jointly determined by the pump and the motor. With passive electrical loads (such as lighting and heating), the power supplied to the load depends on the voltage and the load impedance.

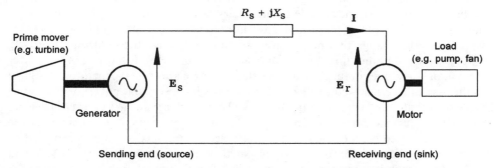

Fig. 2.16 Transmission system with prime mover, generator, motor and load. The voltages at both ends of the transmission system are assumed to be controlled, so the symbol **E** is used instead of **V**. At the sending end, the voltage is E_s; at the receiving end, E_r.

Table 2.5 Examples of prime movers and mechanical loads

Examples of prime movers	Examples of mechanical loads
Steam turbine-generator (coil, oil, gas, nuclear, etc. – i.e. 'thermal')	Pumps (water, sewage, process fluids, foods, etc.)
Hydro-electric turbine generator	Fans and blowers (air-moving)
Wind turbine generator	Compressors
Diesel engine	Machinery, hoists, conveyors, elevators

It is evident that P_{in} and P_{out} are determined quite independently. Yet in the steady state they must be essentially equal, otherwise energy would be accumulating somewhere in the transmission system.[9] The power system operator can control P_{in} but s/he has no control over P_{out}, since customers can connect and disconnect loads at will. The power system operator does not even have any practical means of measuring P_{out} for the entire system, and in any case, even if this parameter was available, there may be several generating stations in the system, so it appears to be somewhat arbitrary as to what contributions should be supplied by the individual generating stations at any instant.

In the short term (i.e. over a period of a fraction of a second), it is the *frequency control* that ensures that $P_{in} = P_{out}$, and this control is effected by maintaining the speed of the generators extremely close to the nominal value. Suppose the power system is in a steady state and $P_{in} = P_{out}$. Suppose that the load increases so that more power is taken from the system, tending to make $P_{out} > P_{in}$. The prime mover and the generator will tend to slow down. Therefore the prime mover has a *governor* (i.e. a valve controller) that increases P_{in} when the frequency is below the rated value, and decreases P_{in} when the frequency is above the rated value.

In an isolated power system with only one generator, the governor has a relatively simple job to do, to maintain the speed of the generator at the correct synchronous speed to hold the frequency constant. But what happens in a power system with multiple generators? In this case usually there is a mixture of power stations. The large ones which produce the most economical power are usually best operated at constant power for long periods, without varying their contribution to P_{in}. Apart from the economics, one reason for this is that if the power is varied, the temperature distribution in the turbine, boiler, and generator will be affected, and 'thermal cycling' is considered undesirable in these very large machines. So these generators have a relatively steep or insensitive governor characteristic, such that the frequency would have to change by quite a large amount to change the contribution to P_{in} ('Quite a large amount' might mean only a fraction of 1 Hz). Elsewhere in the power system, or sometimes in the same power station, there are special generators assigned to the task of frequency control. These generators have very flat governor characteristics such that a tiny change in frequency will cause a large swing in power. They are usually gas turbine powered, up to 20 MW or so, but very large rapid-response generators are sometimes built into hydro-electric pumped-storage schemes. For example, the Dinorwic power station in North Wales has a rating of 1800 MW and can change from zero to maximum power in a few tens of seconds.

The rapid-response generators in a large interconnected power system (such as the United Kingdom system) are used for frequency control in the short term (over a few minutes or hours). They provide a time buffer to allow the larger power stations to vary their contribution. As the total system load changes during the day, the frequency is maintained almost constant, within 0.1 Hz. Averaged over 24 hours, the frequency is kept virtually dead accurate .

---

[9] Losses in the transmission system are assumed to be negligible for the purposes of this discussion.

[10] In fossil-fuel power stations two-pole generators predominate, and the speed is 3000 rev/min in a 50-Hz system or 3600 rev/min in a 60-Hz system. In nuclear power stations, four-pole generators are more common, running at 1500 rev/min (1800 rev/min at 60 Hz). In hydro plants, the generators have larger numbers of poles with speeds in the range 100–1000 rev/min.

Some of the generators in a large system may be operated at light load in a state of readiness or 'spinning reserve', in case the system load increases suddenly by a large amount. This can happen, for example, at the end of television transmissions when the number of viewers is exceptionally high.

2.8.1 Relationships between power, reactive power, voltage levels and load angle

The phasor diagram for the system in Figure 2.16 is shown in Figure 2.17, assuming that the load has a lagging power factor angle ϕ. The line or cable is represented by its impedance $R_s + jX_s$, and R_s is again neglected (being usually much smaller than X_s). The voltage drop across the transmission line is jX_sI, which leads the phasor $\mathbf{I}$ by 90°. The angle between $\mathbf{E}_s$ and $\mathbf{E}_r$ is the *load angle*, δ and

$$E_s \cos \delta = E_r + X_sI \sin \phi \quad \text{and} \quad E_s \sin \delta = X_sI \cos \phi \qquad (2.17)$$

Also

$$P + jQ = \mathbf{E}_r\mathbf{I}^* = E_rI \cos \phi + jE_rI \sin \phi \qquad (2.18)$$

From this we get the power flow equation

$$P = \frac{E_sE_r}{X_s} \sin \delta \qquad (2.19)$$

and the reactive power equation for the receiving end

$$Q_r = E_r \frac{E_s \cos \delta - E_r}{X_s} \qquad (2.20)$$

Evidently $P = P_s = P_r$ as long as the transmission losses are negligible. At the sending end,

$$P_s + jQ_s = E_sI \cos(\phi + \delta) + jE_sI \sin(\phi + \delta) \qquad (2.21)$$

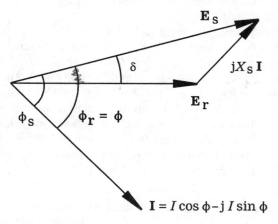

Fig. 2.17 Phasor diagram for Figure 2.16.

from which it can be shown that

$$Q_s = E_s I(\sin \delta \cos \phi + \cos \delta \sin \phi)$$

$$= E_s \sin \delta \frac{E_s \sin \delta}{X_s} + E_s \cos \delta \frac{E_s \cos \delta - E_r}{X_s} \qquad (2.22)$$

$$= E_s \frac{E_s - E_r \cos \delta}{X_s}$$

Note the symmetry between this expression and the one for Q_r in equation (2.20).

Example 1

Suppose $E_s = E_r = 1.0$ p.u. and $P = 1.0$ p.u.[11] The transmission system has $X_s = 0.1$ p.u. and R_s is negligible. We have $\sin \delta = PX_s/E_s E_r = 1 \times 0.1/1 \times 1 = 0.1$ so $\delta = 5.739°$ and $\cos \delta = 0.995$. Then $Q_s = 1.0 \ (1.0 - 1.0 \times 0.995)/0.1 = +0.050$ p.u. and $Q_r = 1.0 \ (1.0 \times 0.995 - 1.0)/0.1 = -0.050$ p.u. Thus the receiving end is generating reactive power and so is the sending end. The power factor is lagging at the sending end and leading at the receiving end. The phasor diagram is shown in Figure 2.5b (not to scale).

Example 2

Suppose $E_s = 1.0$ p.u. while the receiving-end voltage is reduced to $E_r = 0.95$ p.u., with $P = 1.0$ p.u. and $X_s = 0.1$ p.u. Now $\sin \delta = 1.0 \times 0.1/1.0 \times 0.95 = 0.105$ and $\delta = 6.042°$, slightly larger than in example 1 because E_r is reduced by 5%. Also $Q_s = 1.0 \ (1.0 - 0.95 \cos 6.042°)/0.1 = 0.553$ p.u. and $Q_r = 0.95 \ (1.0 \cos 6.042° - 1.0)/0.1 = 0.422$ p.u. Since Q_s is positive, the sending-end generator is generating VArs. Q_r is also positive, meaning that the receiving-end load is absorbing VArs. The phasor diagram is similar to that shown in Figure 2.17 (but not to the same scale).

Notice that a 5% reduction in voltage at one end of the line causes a *massive* change in the reactive power flow. Conversely, a change in the power factor at either end tends to cause a change in the voltage. A 5% voltage swing is, of course, a very large one. Changes in the *power* tend to produce much smaller changes in voltage; instead, the load angle δ changes almost in proportion to the power as long as δ is fairly small (then $\sin \delta \approx \delta$).

The transmission system has an inductive impedance and therefore we would expect it to absorb VArs. If we regard jX_s as another impedance in series with the load impedance, we can treat it the same way. The current is obtained from $I \sin \phi = (E_s \cos \delta - E_r)/X_s = 0.444$ p.u., and $I \cos \phi = E_s \sin \delta/X_s = 1.053$ p.u. Therefore $\mathbf{I} = 0.444 + j1.053$ p.u. $= 1.143 e^{j22.891°}$ p.u. (with $\mathbf{E}_r$ as reference phasor). The voltage drop across X_s is $jX_s \mathbf{I}$ and the reactive power is $I^2 X_s = 1.143^2 \times 0.1 = 0.131$ p.u. Note that this equals the difference between Q_s and Q_r.

We could have made a similar calculation in example 1, where $I^2 X_s = 0.1$. Again this is $Q_s - Q_r$. In Example 1 also $|Q_s| = |Q_r|$, which means that each end of the line is supplying half the reactive VArs absorbed in X_s.

---

[11] The per-unit system is explained in Section 2.13. If you aren't familiar with it, try to read these examples as practice in the use of normalized (per-unit) values. In effect, they make it possible to forget about the units of volts, amps, etc.

2.9 Three-phase systems

Most power systems (from 415 V upwards) are three-phase systems. When the phases are balanced, the phasor diagrams and equations of one phase represent all three phases.

Why three-phase? The main reasons for having more than one phase are as follows:

(a) better utilization of materials such as copper, iron, and insulation in lines, cables, transformers, generators and motors
(b) constant power flow
(c) diversity and security of supply and
(d) 'natural rotation', permitting the widespread use of AC induction motors.

2.9.1 Development of three-phase systems

To achieve 'diversity' – that is, the ability to supply different loads from different circuits so that a failure in one circuit would not affect the others – we can use separate circuits or 'phases' as shown in Figure 2.18.

The power in each phase is $V_{ph}I_{ph} \cos \phi$ where V_{ph} and I_{ph} are the RMS voltage and current as shown in Figure 2.18. The total power is $3 V_{ph}I_{ph} \cos \phi$. Assuming that the cable works at a certain current-density determined by its allowable temperature rise, the total cross-section area of conductor is $6A$.

Suppose that the three phase currents are shifted in time phase by 120° from one another as shown in Figure 2.19. The RMS currents are unchanged, as is the power in each phase and the total power. The sum of the three currents is zero, and we can express this in terms of instantaneous or phasor values

$$i_a + i_b + i_c = 0 \quad \text{and} \quad \mathbf{I}_a + \mathbf{I}_b + \mathbf{I}_c = 0 \tag{2.23}$$

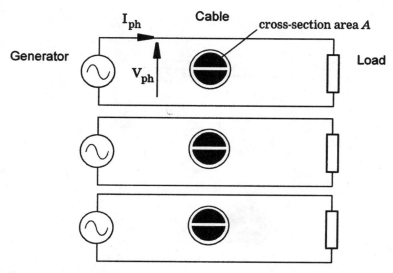

Fig. 2.18 Three single-phase cables.

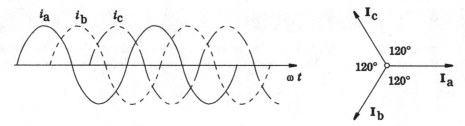

Fig. 2.19 Three-phase instantaneous and phasor currents.

This suggests that the circuit could be equally well served by the *three-phase* connection shown in Figure 2.20, which has only half the number of conductors compared with Figure 2.18. Figure 2.20 also shows the cross-section of a three-phase cable capable of carrying the required current. The total cross-section of conductor is 3 A, that is a saving of 50%.

In the voltage phasor diagram in Figure 20, the voltage across each phase of the load remains the same as in Figure 2.20, but the voltage between lines is increased: evidently from the geometry of the triangles

$$\mathbf{V}_{ab} = \mathbf{V}_a - \mathbf{V}_b = \sqrt{3}V e^{j30°}$$
$$\mathbf{V}_{bc} = \mathbf{V}_b - \mathbf{V}_c = \sqrt{3}V e^{-j90°} \qquad (2.24)$$
$$\mathbf{V}_{ca} = \mathbf{V}_c - \mathbf{V}_a = \sqrt{3}V e^{j150°}$$

where $\mathbf{V}$ is the reference phase voltage taken as $\mathbf{V}_a$, measured between line A and the 'star point' of the load or the 'neutral point' of the supply. Likewise the phase voltage $\mathbf{V}_b$ is measured between line B and the star-point of the load, and $\mathbf{V}_c$ between line C and the star point. The line–line voltages are $\sqrt{3}$ times the phase voltages. In Figure 2.20 both the load and the generator are 'wye connected' and in terms of the RMS values only, we have

$$V_{LL} = \sqrt{3}V_{ph} \quad \text{and} \quad I_L = I_{ph} \qquad (2.25)$$

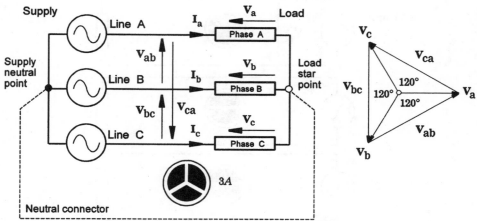

Fig. 2.20 Three-phase connection with wye-connected load and phasor diagram.

where I_L is the line current and I_{ph} is the phase current. With wye connection they are one and the same current. The dotted line in Figure 2.20 shows the possibility of a connection between the neutral point of the supply and the star point of the load. This connection may be used to stabilize the potential of the star point where there is an excess of triplen harmonics in the current or voltage waveforms of the load.

The current and voltage in Figures 2.19 and 2.20 are displaced in phase by the power factor angle ϕ. Figure 2.21 shows a complete phasor diagram for a balanced wye-connected load with a lagging power factor.

An alternative connection of the three phases is the delta connection shown in Figure 2.22 together with the construction of the phasor diagram under balanced conditions with a lagging power factor.

For the delta connection,

$$V_{LL} = V_{ph} \quad \text{and} \quad I_L = \sqrt{3}I_{ph} \tag{2.26}$$

The delta connection is used to provide a path for triplen harmonic currents. For example, when transformers operate at higher than normal voltage the magnetizing

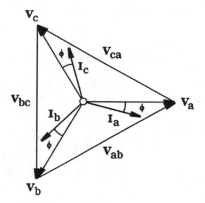

Fig. 2.21 Phasor diagram for balanced wye-connected load.

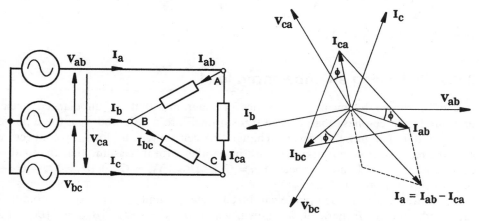

Fig. 2.22 Three-phase connection with delta-connected load and phasor diagram.

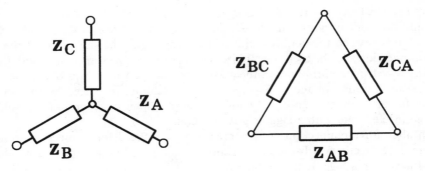

Fig. 2.23 Wye–delta transformation.

current in each phase tends to become distorted, and the triplen harmonics are allowed to flow locally in a delta-connected winding without entering the external circuit. In electric motors a delta winding permits the use of a larger number of turns of smaller-gauge wire, because the phase voltage is increased while the phase current is decreased, compared with the wye connection.

2.9.2   The wye–delta transformation

A wye-connected load can be represented by a virtual load connected in delta, and vice-versa, Figure 2.23. To transform the delta connection into a wye connection,

$$\mathbf{Z_A} = \frac{\mathbf{Z_{AB}Z_{CA}}}{\mathbf{Z_\Delta}}; \quad \mathbf{Z_B} = \frac{\mathbf{Z_{BC}Z_{AB}}}{\mathbf{Z_\Delta}}; \quad \mathbf{Z_C} = \frac{\mathbf{Z_{CA}Z_{BC}}}{\mathbf{Z_\Delta}} \tag{2.27}$$

where $\mathbf{Z_\Delta} = \mathbf{Z_{AB}} + \mathbf{Z_{BC}} + \mathbf{Z_{CA}}$. To transform the wye connection into a delta connection,

$$\mathbf{Y_{AB}} = \frac{\mathbf{Y_A Y_B}}{\mathbf{Y_Y}}; \quad \mathbf{Y_{BC}} = \frac{\mathbf{Y_B Y_C}}{\mathbf{Y_Y}}; \quad \mathbf{Y_{CA}} = \frac{\mathbf{Y_C Y_A}}{\mathbf{Y_Y}} \tag{2.28}$$

where $\mathbf{Y_Y} = \mathbf{Y_A} + \mathbf{Y_B} + \mathbf{Y_C}$

2.9.3   Balancing an unbalanced load

It can be shown by means of a series of diagrams, that an unbalanced linear ungrounded three-phase load can be transformed into a balanced, real three-phase load without changing the power exchange between source and load, by connecting an ideal reactive compensating network in parallel with it. Assume that the load is delta-connected with admittances $\mathbf{Y_{ab}} = G_{ab} + jB_{ab}$, $\mathbf{Y_{bc}} = G_{bc} + jB_{bc}$, $\mathbf{Y_{ca}} = G_{ca} + jB_{ca}$, as shown in Figure 2.24.

The power factor of each phase can be corrected to unity by connecting compensating admittances in parallel, as shown, where $jB_{\gamma ab} = -jB_{ab}$, $jB_{\gamma bc} = -jB_{bc}$, and $jB_{\gamma ca} = -jB_{ca}$. The resulting network is real, Figure 2.25.

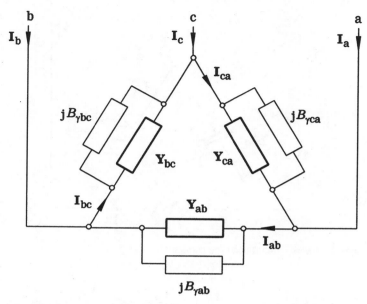

Fig. 2.24 Unbalanced delta-connected load with power-factor correction admittances.

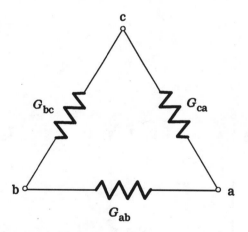

Fig. 2.25 Unbalanced load corrected with unity power factor in each phase.

If we now take one of the resistive admittances, G_{ab}, we can connect this in a so-called Steinmetz network with an inductor and a capacitor to produce balanced line currents as shown in Figure 2.26. The phasor diagram in Figure 2.27 shows how the balanced line currents are achieved, and the resulting equivalent circuit in Figure 2.28 is real, balanced, and wye-connected.

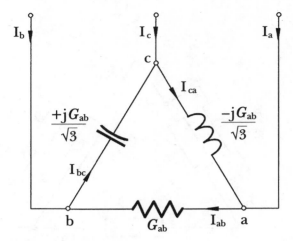

Fig. 2.26 Steinmetz network with balanced line currents.

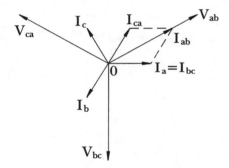

Fig. 2.27 Phasor diagram for Steinmetz network.

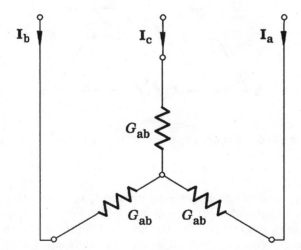

Fig. 2.28 Balanced network resulting from compensation of G_{ab} with the Steinmetz network.

The resulting compensating admittances are given in equation (2.29).

$$jB_{\gamma ab} = -jB_{ab} + j(G_{ca} - G_{bc})/\sqrt{3}$$
$$jB_{\gamma bc} = -jB_{bc} + j(G_{ab} - G_{ca})/\sqrt{3} \qquad (2.29)$$
$$jB_{\gamma ca} = -jB_{ca} + j(G_{bc} - G_{ab})/\sqrt{3}$$

2.10 Power flow and measurement

2.10.1 Single-phase

Suppose we have a single-phase load as in Figure 2.7 supplied with a sinusoidal voltage whose instantaneous value is $v = V_m \cos \omega t$. The RMS value is $V = V_m/\sqrt{2}$ and the phasor value is **V**. If the load is linear (i.e. its impedance is constant and does not depend on the current or voltage), the current will be sinusoidal too. It leads or lags the voltage by a phase angle ϕ, depending on whether the load is capacitive or inductive. With a lagging (inductive) load, $i = I_m \cos(\omega t - \phi)$; see Figure 2.29. The instantaneous power is given by $p = vi$, so

$$p = V_m I_m \cos \omega t \cos(\omega t - \phi) = \frac{V_m I_m}{2}[\cos \phi + \cos(2\omega t - \phi)] \qquad (2.30)$$

This expression has a constant term and a second term that oscillates at double frequency. The constant term represents the *average* power P: we can write this as

$$P = \frac{V_m}{\sqrt{2}} \times \frac{I_m}{\sqrt{2}} \cos \phi = VI \cos \phi \qquad (2.31)$$

P is equal to the product of the rms voltage $V = V_m/\sqrt{2}$, the RMS current $I = I_m/\sqrt{2}$, and the power factor $\cos \phi$. The amplitude of the oscillatory term is fixed: i.e. it does not depend on the power factor. It shows that the instantaneous power p varies from 0 to $V_m I_m$ to $-V_m I_m$ and back to 0 twice every cycle. Since the

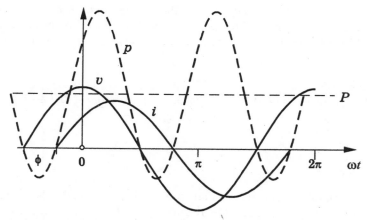

Fig. 2.29 Instantaneous current, voltage and power in a single-phase AC circuit.

average power is $V_m I_m/2$, this represents a peak–peak fluctuation 200% of the mean power, at double frequency. The oscillation of power in single-phase circuits contributes to lamp flicker and causes vibration in motors and transformers, producing undesirable acoustic noise.

2.10.2   Two-phase

Suppose we have a two-phase load with phases a and b, with $v_a = V_m \cos \omega t$, $i_a = I_m \cos (\omega t - \phi)$ and $v_b = V_m \sin \omega t$, $i_b = I_m \sin (\omega t - \phi)$. This system is said to be *balanced*, because the voltages and currents have the same RMS (and peak) values in both phases, *and* their phase angles are orthogonal. The total instantaneous power is now given by

$$
\begin{aligned}
p &= v_a i_a + v_b i_b \\
&= V_m I_m [\cos(\omega t) \cos(\omega t - \phi) + \sin(\omega t) \sin(\omega t - \phi)] \\
&= V_m I_m \cos \phi \\
&= 2VI \cos \phi
\end{aligned}
\tag{2.32}
$$

The oscillatory term has vanished altogether, which means that the power flow is constant, with no fluctuation, and the average power P is therefore equal to the instantaneous power p. Note that if the phases become unbalanced, an oscillatory term reappears.

2.10.3   Three-phase

Suppose we have a three-phase load as in Figures 2.20 and 2.22, with phases a, b and c, with

$$
\begin{aligned}
v_a &= V_m \cos \omega t & i_a &= I_m \cos(\omega t - \phi) \\
v_b &= V_m \cos(\omega t - 2\pi/3) & i_b &= I_m \cos(\omega t - 2\pi/3 - \phi) \\
v_c &= V_m \cos(\omega t + 2\pi/3) & i_c &= I_m \cos(\omega t + 2\pi/3 - \phi)
\end{aligned}
\tag{2.33}
$$

This system is said to be *balanced*, because the voltages and currents have the same RMS (and peak) values in all three phases, and their phase angles are equi-spaced (i.e. with a 120° symmetrical phase displacement). The total instantaneous power is now given by

$$
\begin{aligned}
p &= v_a i_a + v_b i_b + v_c i_c \\
&= V_m I_m [\cos(\omega t) \cos(\omega t - \phi) + \cos(\omega t - 2\pi/3) \cos(\omega t - 2\pi/3 - \phi) \\
&\quad + \cos(\omega t + 2\pi/3) \cos(\omega t + 2\pi/3 - \phi)] \\
&= \frac{3}{2} V_m I_m \cos \phi \\
&= 3VI \cos \phi
\end{aligned}
\tag{2.34}
$$

As in the two-phase system, the oscillatory term has vanished. The power flow is constant, with no fluctuation, and the average power P is equal to the instantaneous power p. If the phases become unbalanced, an oscillatory term reappears.

The voltages and currents in equation (2.34) are *phase* quantities. In terms of *line* quantities, for a wye connection we have $V_L = \sqrt{3} V_{ph}$ and $I_L = I_{ph}$, whereas for a delta connection we have $I_L = \sqrt{3} I_{ph}$ and $V_{LL} = V_{ph}$. In both cases, therefore,

$$P = \sqrt{3} V_{LL} I_L \cos \phi \qquad (2.35)$$

where ϕ is the angle between the phasors $\mathbf{V}_{ph}$ and $\mathbf{I}_{ph}$.

2.10.4 Power measurement

Classical electro-dynamometer wattmeter or 'Wattmeter'

The classical wattmeter circuit symbol (Figure 2.30) is derived from the classical wattmeter (Figure 2.31), which is still widely used. Accuracy is typically 0.5% in calibrated instruments. The readings of these instruments are usually reliable if the voltage and current waveforms are sinusoidal with fairly high power factor. They are generally not suitable with distorted waveforms, but special versions have been manufactured for use at low power factor.

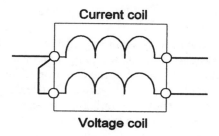

Fig. 2.30 Wattmeter symbol.

Fig. 2.31 Classical electro-dynamometer wattmeter.

Electronic wattmeter

These instruments multiply the instantaneous voltage and current together and take the average. Both digital and analog models are available. They are designed to be used with CTs and VTs, (current transformers and voltage transformers) and they come in single-phase and three-phase versions. Single-phase instruments have band-widths up to several hundred kHz, so they give effective readings with distorted waveforms such as are caused by rectifiers and inverters, provided the harmonic content is not too great. See Figure 2.32.

Processing of sampled waveforms

The most exacting power measurements are in circuits with high-frequency switching (as in power electronics with PWM [pulse-width modulation]), especially if the power factor is low. In these cases the technique is to sample the voltage and current at high frequency and then digitally compute the power from the voltage and current samples: $\upsilon\,[1, 2, \ldots k \ldots N]$ and $i\,[1, 2, \ldots k \ldots N]$. The *average* power over time T is computed from:

$$P_{avg} = \frac{1}{T}\sum_{k=1}^{N} p[k]\Delta t = \frac{1}{T}\sum_{k=1}^{N} \upsilon[k]i[k]\,\Delta t, \quad \text{where} \quad T = (N-1)\Delta t \qquad (2.36)$$

Some digital processing oscilloscopes can perform this function, but there are specialist data acquisition systems with fast sampling and analog/digital conversion, and they may include software for processing the equation (2.36).

The sampling process is illustrated in Figure 2.33. The double samples at the steep edges in the voltage waveform show the ambiguity (uncertainty) that arises when the sampling rate is too low relative to the frequency content of the sampled waveform. This is a particular problem in power electronics, where the voltage may switch from 0–100% in the order of 1 µs. If we use a sampling frequency of 10 MHz to give 10 samples on each voltage switching, then if the fundamental frequency is 50 Hz we will need $1/50 \times 10^{7} = 200\,000$ samples for just one cycle. This illustrates the tradeoff between sample length and sampling frequency. The tradeoff is more difficult if a high resolution is required (for example, 12-bit A/D conversion, a resolution of 1 part in 4096).

Wattmeter connections

Figure 2.34 shows the connection of three wattmeters to measure the total power in three phases. The voltage coils of the wattmeters are returned to a common point which effectively forms a false neutral point 0. This is convenient because the star point of the load may not be available for connection (particularly if the load is an induction motor). The instantaneous power is

$$p = \upsilon_{as}i_a + \upsilon_{bs}i_b + \upsilon_{cs}i_c \qquad (2.37)$$

where i_a is the instantaneous current in phase A and υ_{as} is the instantaneous voltage across phase A, etc. In a three-wire connection, however,

$$i_a + i_b + i_c = 0 \qquad (2.38)$$

and if we use this to eliminate i_c from equation (2.37) we get

$$\begin{aligned} p &= (\upsilon_{as} - \upsilon_{cs})i_a + (\upsilon_{bs} - \upsilon_{cs})i_b \\ &= \upsilon_{ac}i_a + \upsilon_{bc}i_b \end{aligned} \qquad (2.39)$$

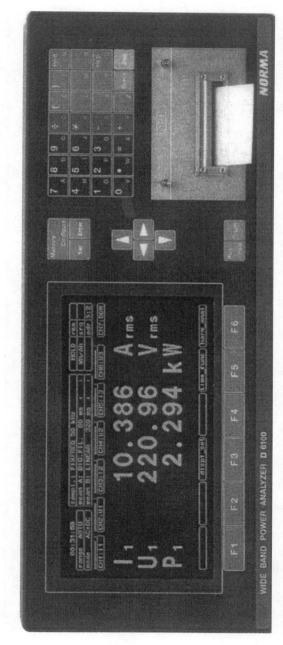

Fig. 2.32 Electronic wattmeter (Norma).

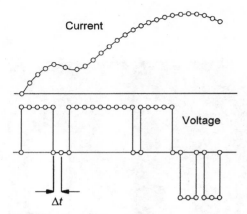

Fig. 2.33 Sampled voltage and current waveforms.

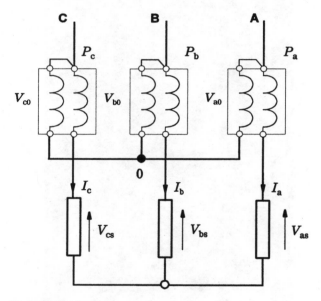

Fig. 2.34 Three-wattmeter connection.

which indicates that only two wattmeters are required, connected as shown in Figure 2.35. Since this is valid for instantaneous power, it is also valid for average power. It is valid irrespective of the waveforms of voltage and current, requiring only that the connection is three-wire.

Under sinusoidal AC conditions the two-wattmeter connection can be described by the equations

$$
\begin{aligned}
P_1 &= \langle v_{ac} i_a \rangle = \mathrm{Re}\{\mathbf{V}_{ac}\mathbf{I}_a^*\} = V_{ac} I_a \cos \phi_1 \\
P_2 &= \langle v_{bc} i_b \rangle = \mathrm{Re}\{\mathbf{V}_{bc}\mathbf{I}_b^*\} = V_{bc} I_b \cos \phi_2
\end{aligned}
\tag{2.40}
$$

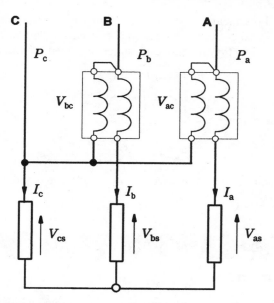

Fig. 2.35 Two-wattmeter connection.

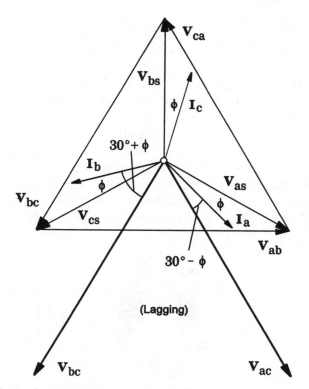

Fig. 2.36 Phasor diagram for two-wattmeter connection.

where the $\langle\ \rangle$ symbols mean 'time average' over one cycle, ϕ_1 is the phase angle between $\mathbf{V}_{ac}$ and $\mathbf{I}_a$, and ϕ_2 is the phase angle between $\mathbf{V}_{bc}$ and $\mathbf{I}_b$. These relationships are further illustrated in Figure 2.36, and under balanced conditions

$$P_1 = V_{LL}I_L \cos(30° - \phi)$$
$$P_2 = V_{LL}I_L \cos(30° + \phi)$$

(2.41)

from which it follows that

$$\tan\phi = \sqrt{3}\frac{P_1 - P_2}{P_1 + P_2}$$

(2.42)

The wattmeter readings can be used in this equation to determine the power factor.

2.11 Polyphase transformers

2.11.1 Definition

A transformer is a set of 1, 2 or more magnetically coupled windings, usually wound on a common laminated magnetic iron core, Figure 2.37.

In an ideal transformer the voltages and currents on the primary and secondary sides are related by

$$\frac{\mathbf{V}_1}{\mathbf{V}_2} = \frac{N_1}{N_2} \quad \text{and} \quad \frac{\mathbf{I}_1}{\mathbf{I}_2} = \frac{N_2}{N_1}$$

(2.43)

where N_1/N_2 is the primary/secondary turns ratio. Equation (2.43) is valid not only for phasor values but also for instantaneous values. It follows from equation (2.43) that

$$\mathbf{V}_1\mathbf{I}_1^* = \mathbf{V}_2\mathbf{I}_2^*$$

(2.44)

so that the real and reactive power are both transmitted unaltered through an ideal transformer. The same is true for the instantaneous power. The ideal transformer has no losses and no reactive power requirement of its own. Of course, real transformers depart from the ideal, in that they have resistance, imperfect coupling, magnetizing

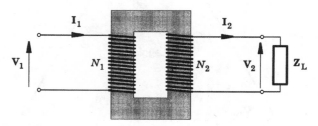

Fig. 2.37 Basic transformer.

current, and core losses; but these can be neglected when considering many of the main functions of transformers.[12]

The impedance 'looking into' the transformer at the primary terminals is the ratio $\mathbf{V}_1/\mathbf{I}_1$, and from equation (2.43) this is equal to $(N_1/N_2)^2\mathbf{Z}_L$, where $\mathbf{Z}_L$ is the load impedance connected on the secondary side. This is called the 'referred' impedance, $\mathbf{Z}'_L$. If the primary side has a higher voltage than the secondary side, i.e. $N_1/N_2 > 1$, then $\mathbf{Z}'_L$ will be larger than $\mathbf{Z}_L$. For example, in an $11\,\text{kV}/415\,\text{V}$ transformer the impedance ratio is $(11\,000/415)^2 = 702.5$.

2.11.2 Functions

Transformers have several functions in power transmission and distribution, for example:

(a) transform voltage level for optimum transmission
(b) isolate coupled circuits
(c) impedance matching
(d) introduce series impedance (to limit fault current)
(e) create a neutral point (e.g. ground connection remote from power station)
(f) suppress harmonics (especially triplen harmonics)
(g) provide tappings for loads along a tranmission line
(h) produce phase shift or multiple phases (e.g. for multiple-pulse converters)
(i) frequency-multiplication (saturated core)
(j) constant-voltage reactive compensation (saturated core).

Three-phase transformers are often wound on common cores such as the one shown in Figure 2.38. The windings on both sides may be connected in wye or delta, giving

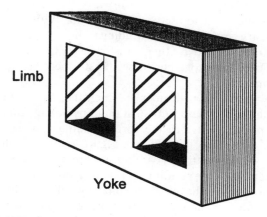

Fig. 2.38 Unwound 3-limb transformer core.

---

[12] These 'imperfections' can usually be included in calculations by means of additional parasitic impedances added to the equivalent circuit of Figure 2.37. One of the most important of these impedances is the leakage reactance which represents the imperfect magnetic coupling between the primary and secondary windings and appears as a series reactance either in the primary or secondary circuit, or shared between them.

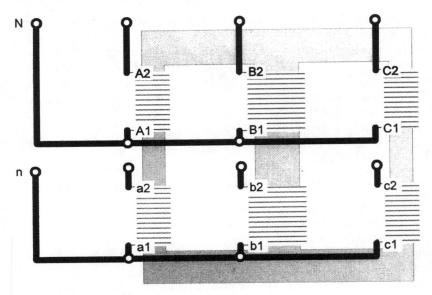

Fig. 2.39 Electrical connections of a Yyo transformer.

rise to a range of useful operational features. The simplest case is that of a Yy0 transformer shown in Figure 2.39. in which both sets of windings are wye-connected, and corresponding voltages are in phase. The windings are labelled A, B, C on the high-voltage side and a, b, c on the low-voltage side, with terminal two at higher potential than terminal one. The polarities are such that current flowing into terminal A2 would produce flux in the same direction as current flowing into terminal a2. From these considerations it is a straightforward matter to construct the voltage phasor diagram, as shown at top left in Figure 2.40. With no phase shift between corresponding primary and secondary windings, the Yy transformer is designated Yy0. In Figure 2.40 there are two other transformer connections with this property, the Dd0 and the Dz0,[13] and together these transformers are collectively known as 'Group 1' transformers.[14]

Figure 2.41 shows a Yd1 transformer in which the low-voltage winding is delta-connected, producing a 30° phase shift such that any voltage on the low-voltage side is retarded 30° in phase relative to the corresponding voltage on the high-voltage side: for example V_{AB} leads V_{ab} by 30° (see Figure 2.40). The phase shift of −30° is denoted by a '1' in the designation Yd1, and it refers to the clock position of a low-voltage phasor, when the corresponding high-voltage phasor is at 12 o'clock. In some cases the connection does not have a high-voltage winding with a voltage that sits at 12 o'clock without rotating the phasor diagram, so to preserve the orientation and symmetry in Figure 2.40 it is usual in these cases to construct an imaginary neutral which provides the required phasor: an example is the Dy1 transformer in Group III.

---

[13] 'Z' stands for 'zig-zag' which is a composite winding in which half the turns of each phase are on different limbs and their voltages are phase-shifted by 120°.
[14] These conventions are consistent with B.S. 171 or IEC 76/I.

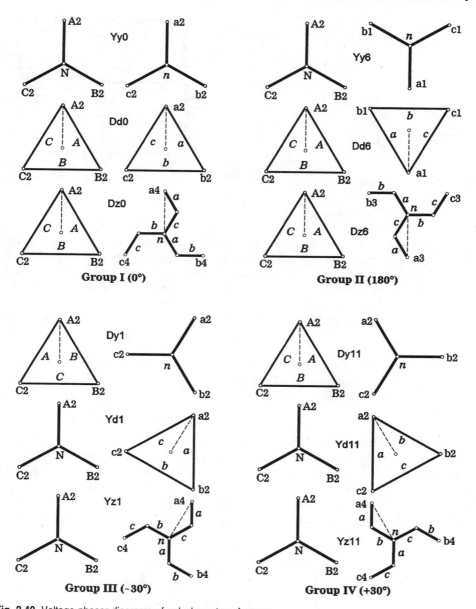

Fig. 2.40 Voltage phasor diagrams of polyphase transformers.

Note that the voltage and current ratios are affected by the connection. For example in a Yd1 transformer with N_1 turns per phase on the high-voltage winding and N_2 turns per phase on the low-voltage winding, the ratio between phase voltages is N_1/N_2, but the ratio between line–line voltages is $\sqrt{3} \times N_1/N_2$, while the ratio between line currents is $(N_1/N_2)/\sqrt{3}$. The impedance referral ratio is therefore $3(N_1/N_2)^2$.

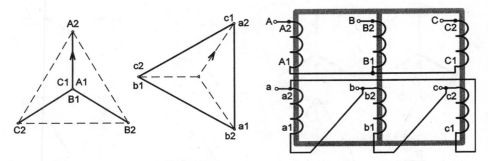

Fig. 2.41 Yd1 transformer.

2.11.3 Parallel operation

For connection in parallel, transformers must be designed for the same frequency and the same primary and secondary voltages, and they must be connected with the correct polarities. (That's why the labelling of transformer terminals is so important.)

The way in which parallel transformers share the load is important. To introduce the analysis it might be helpful to consider the simpler case of two DC batteries supplying a common load, Figure 2.42. By virtue of the parallel connection we have

$$V = E_1 - R_1 I_1 = E_2 - R_2 I_2 \qquad (2.45)$$

Suppose we require battery one to supply a fraction x of the load current, and battery two to supply fraction $(1 - x)$. Then $I_1 = xI$ and $I_2 = (1 - x)I$. Substituting in equation (45) and rearranging, we get

$$E_1 - E_2 = [xR_1 - (1 - x)R_2]I \qquad (2.46)$$

For this to be true for all values of the load current $I = I_1 + I_2$, we require the coefficient of I to be zero, which implies at least that $E_1 = E_2$. It further implies that the load is shared according to the values of R_1 and R_2, since $x = R_2/(R_1 + R_2)$ and $(1 - x) = R_1/(R_1 + R_2)$. Only when $R_1 = R_2$ is the load shared equally ($x = 0.5$). From this it is clear that the internal impedance of a supply is important in determining its contribution to the load when it is connected in parallel with other supplies.

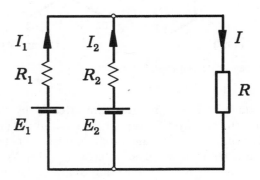

Fig. 2.42 Parallel batteries supplying a DC load.

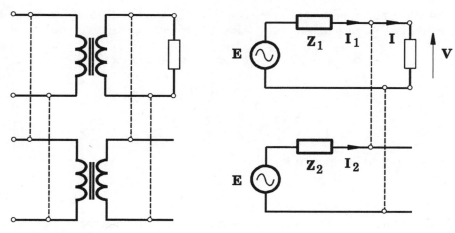

Fig. 2.43 Parallel transformers.

This theory can be extended to the parallel operation of transformers by representing them by their Thévenin equivalent circuits, in which the series impedance is approximately the leakage reactance. In general they are not required to share the load equally, but in proportion to their ratings. For this we shall see that their per-unit impedances must be equal, when evaluated on their own respective MVA bases and a common voltage base.

Working with Figure 2.43, the load current is

$$\mathbf{I} = \mathbf{I}_1 + \mathbf{I}_2 = \frac{\mathbf{E} - \mathbf{V}}{\mathbf{Z}_1} + \frac{\mathbf{E} - \mathbf{V}}{\mathbf{Z}_2} = (\mathbf{E} - \mathbf{V})\left[\frac{1}{\mathbf{Z}_1} + \frac{1}{\mathbf{Z}_2}\right] \tag{2.47}$$

and the respective transformer contributions are

$$\mathbf{I}_1 = \frac{1/\mathbf{Z}_1}{1/\mathbf{Z}_1 + 1/\mathbf{Z}_2}\mathbf{I} = \frac{\mathbf{Y}_1}{\mathbf{Y}_1 + \mathbf{Y}_2}\mathbf{I} = \frac{\mathbf{Z}_2}{\mathbf{Z}_1 + \mathbf{Z}_2}\mathbf{I} \tag{2.48}$$

and

$$\mathbf{I}_2 = \frac{1/\mathbf{Z}_2}{1/\mathbf{Z}_1 + 1/\mathbf{Z}_2}\mathbf{I} = \frac{\mathbf{Y}_2}{\mathbf{Y}_1 + \mathbf{Y}_2}\mathbf{I} = \frac{\mathbf{Z}_1}{\mathbf{Z}_1 + \mathbf{Z}_2}\mathbf{I} \tag{2.49}$$

Taking the ratio of equations (2.48) and (2.49),

$$\frac{\mathbf{I}_1}{\mathbf{I}_2} = \frac{\mathbf{Y}_1}{\mathbf{Y}_2} = \frac{\mathbf{Z}_2}{\mathbf{Z}_1} \tag{2.50}$$

i.e. the currents are in inverse proportion to the ohmic impedances.

Now calculate the complex powers through the two transformers, as fractions of the total complex power $\mathbf{S} = \mathbf{VI}^*$:

$$\mathbf{S}_1 = \mathbf{VI}_1^* = \left[\frac{\mathbf{Y}_1}{\mathbf{Y}_1 + \mathbf{Y}_2}\right]^* \mathbf{S} \quad \text{and} \quad \mathbf{S}_2 = \mathbf{VI}_2^* = \left[\frac{\mathbf{Y}_2}{\mathbf{Y}_1 + \mathbf{Y}_2}\right]^* \mathbf{S} \tag{2.51}$$

Dividing these two equations,

$$\frac{\mathbf{S}_1}{\mathbf{S}_2} = \frac{\mathbf{Y}_1^*}{\mathbf{Y}_2^*} = \frac{\mathbf{Z}_2^*}{\mathbf{Z}_1^*} \tag{2.52}$$

Now define the per-unit complex powers $s_1 = S_1/S_{1b}$ and $s_2 = S_2/S_{2b}$ where 'b' means the 'base' MVA for each transformer.[15] Also, the per-unit impedances are defined as

$$\mathbf{z}_1 = \frac{\mathbf{Z}_1}{Z_{1b}} = \mathbf{Z}_1 \times \frac{S_{1b}}{V_{1b}^2} \quad \text{and} \quad \mathbf{z}_2 = \frac{\mathbf{Z}_2}{Z_{2b}} = \mathbf{Z}_2 \times \frac{S_{2b}}{V_{2b}^2} \tag{2.53}$$

so that

$$\frac{\mathbf{s}_1}{\mathbf{s}_2} = \frac{S_1/S_{1b}}{S_2/S_{2b}} = \frac{\mathbf{Z}_2^*}{\mathbf{Z}_1^*} \times \frac{S_{2b}}{S_{1b}} = \frac{\mathbf{z}_2^*}{\mathbf{z}_1^*} \times \frac{V_{2b}^2}{V_{1b}^2} \tag{2.54}$$

If V_{1b} is chosen to be equal to V_{2b}, then

$$\frac{\mathbf{s}_1}{\mathbf{s}_2} = \frac{\mathbf{z}_2^*}{\mathbf{z}_1^*} \tag{2.55}$$

If the transformers are to be loaded in proportion to their ratings, then $\mathbf{s}_1 = \mathbf{s}_2$, which requires that $\mathbf{z}_1 = \mathbf{z}_2$. That is, the per-unit impedances of the transformers must be equal, when evaluated on their own respective MVA bases and a common voltage base.

When three-phase transformers are connected in parallel, the requirement for 'correct polarity' is slightly more complicated. The phase shift between corresponding primary and secondary voltages must be the same in both transformers. This means that both transformers must belong to the same *group*. For example, a Yy0 transformer can be paralleled with a Dd0 transformer, because the phase shift is zero through both of them. But a Yd1 cannot be paralleled with a Yy0, because the Yd1 has a phase shift of $-30°$.

2.11.4 Zero-sequence effects in three-phase transformers

In normal operation of a three-phase system, the voltages and currents are balanced and

$$\mathbf{I}_a + \mathbf{I}_b + \mathbf{I}_c = 0 \tag{2.56}$$

This equation is satisfied not only by the line currents, but also by the line-neutral voltages and the line–line voltages in balanced operation.

In a transformer core the voltages establish fluxes in the core. If each phase winding has the same number of turns on each limb of the core, then the limb fluxes will also be balanced: i.e.,

$$\mathbf{\Phi}_a + \mathbf{\Phi}_b + \mathbf{\Phi}_c = 0 \tag{2.57}$$

In balanced operation, the flux through any limb at any instant is returning through the other two limbs, so there is no tendency for flux to leak outside the three limbs. (Figure 2.44).

If the operation is unbalanced there may be a 'residual' current, $\mathbf{I}_0 = \mathbf{I}_a + \mathbf{I}_b + \mathbf{I}_c$, and/or a residual voltage $\mathbf{V}_0 = \mathbf{V}_a + \mathbf{V}_b + \mathbf{V}_c$, and a residual flux $\mathbf{\Phi}_0 = \mathbf{\Phi}_a + \mathbf{\Phi}_b + \mathbf{\Phi}_c$. These residual quantities are also called 'zero-sequence' quantities.[16] Zero-sequence components are all in phase with each other. Unlike positive/negative-sequence

---

[15] See §2.13.

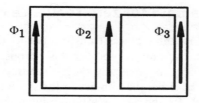

Fig. 2.44 Fluxes in 3-limb core.

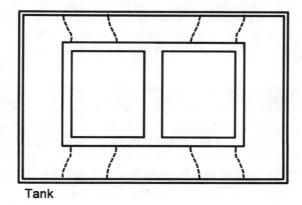

Tank

Fig. 2.45 Residual fluxes in 3-limb core and tank.

quantities, they do not sum to zero. The residual flux Φ_0 can be visualized as flux that is flowing in all three limbs at the same time. It must find a return path *outside the three main limbs*. In Figure 2.45 the return path is through the space surrounding the core and into the tank. Since the tank is not laminated it is liable to carry induced eddy-currents which can cause it to overheat. The flux path for the residual flux has a high reluctance and therefore a low inductance, because the flux must travel a long way through the gap between the core and the tank. Consequently the zero-sequence inductance is low, and the zero-sequence currents (which flow in the neutral wire) can be large. If there is no neutral, the potential of the neutral point will oscillate (see Figure 2.48).

In a five-limb core the return path is provided through two extra unwound limbs at the ends of the transformer core. The reluctance of the zero-sequence or residual flux-path is now low, so the zero-sequence inductance is high. This tends to limit the zero-sequence current in the neutral connection to a low value. The residual flux does not leak outside the core and there is therefore no risk of overheating the tank by eddy-currents.

---

[16] The term 'zero-sequence' comes from the theory of *symmetrical components*, which is the mathematical basis for analysis of unbalanced three-phase systems.

2.11.5   Providing a path for zero-sequence currents

It is generally essential in three-phase transformers to provide a path for zero-sequence current. A delta winding is used for this purpose. Zero-sequence currents can flow in the delta without magnetically short-circuiting the entire core.

The delta winding can be either the primary or the secondary, or it can be a *tertiary* winding provided specially for the purpose of mopping up residual current (especially when the primary and secondary are wye-connected). Tertiary windings have other uses: for example, they may be used to connect local loads, power factor correction capacitors, or static compensators. The tertiary winding must be designed for the full fault level at that point in the transmission system, but its continuous thermal rating is usually less than those of the primary and secondary.

2.12   Harmonics

Ideally the voltage and current in an AC power system are purely sinusoidal. When the waveform is distorted, it can be analysed (by Fourier's theorem) into components at the fundamental frequency and multiples thereof. Frequency components other than the fundamental are called *harmonics*. The main origins of harmonics are as follows:

(a) non-linear magnetic elements, such as saturated transformer cores
(b) non-sinusoidal airgap flux distribution in rotating AC machines and
(c) switched circuit elements, such as rectifiers, triacs, and other power-electronic converters.

The main undesirable effects can be summarized as follows:

(i)   additional heating of cables, transformers, motors etc.
(ii)   interference to communications and other electrical/electronic circuits
(iii) electrical resonance, resulting in potentially dangerous voltages and currents and
(iv)   electromechanical resonance, producing vibration, noise, and fatigue failure of mechanical components.

Fourier's theorem provides the mathematical tool for resolving a periodic waveform of virtually any shape into a sum of harmonic components: thus an arbitrary periodic voltage waveform $v(t)$ is written

$$v(t) = v_0 + \sum_{m=1}^{\infty} \sqrt{2} V_m \cos(m\omega t + \phi_m)$$

$$= v_0 + \sum_{m=1}^{\infty} [a_m \cos(m\omega t) + b_m \sin(m\omega t)] \tag{2.58}$$

where v_0 is the average (DC) component. The first form expresses each harmonic in terms of its RMS value V_m and its phase ϕ_m. Each harmonic is itself sinusoidal and can be considered as a phasor, except that it rotates at m times the fundamental frequency. The second form expresses each harmonic in terms of cosine and sine coefficients a_m and b_m respectively. The main limitation is that the waveform $v(t)$ must be periodic, that is, it must repeat after a time $T = 1/f = 2\pi/\omega$, where f is the fundamental frequency in Hz and $\omega = 2\pi f$. According to Fourier the coefficients a_m and b_m can be determined from the original waveform by the integrations

$$a_m = \frac{2}{2\pi} \int_0^{2\pi} \upsilon(\omega t) \cos(m\omega t)\, d(\omega t)$$

$$b_m = \frac{2}{2\pi} \int_0^{2\pi} \upsilon(\omega t) \sin(m\omega t)\, d(\omega t)$$

(2.59)

and the DC value from the integral

$$\upsilon_0 = \frac{1}{2\pi} \int_0^{2\pi} \upsilon(\omega t)\, d(\omega t)$$

(2.60)

2.12.1 Harmonic power

In general $p = \upsilon i$ so

$$
\begin{aligned}
P_{avg} &= \frac{1}{2\pi} \int_0^{2\pi} p(\omega t)\, d(\omega t) \\
&= \frac{1}{2\pi} \int_0^{2\pi} \sum_{\substack{m=0 \\ n=0}}^{\infty} \sqrt{2} V_m \cos(m\omega t) \cdot \sqrt{2} I_n \cos(n\omega t + \phi_n)\, d(\omega t) \\
&= \sum_{\substack{m=0 \\ n=0}}^{\infty} \frac{1}{2\pi} \int_0^{2\pi} V_m I_n \{\cos[(m+n)\omega t + \phi_n] + \cos[(m-n)\omega t - \phi_n]\} \\
&= \sum_{m=0}^{\infty} V_m I_m \cos\phi_m \\
&= V_0 I_0 + V_1 I_1 \cos\phi_1 + V_2 I_2 \cos\phi_2 + \ldots
\end{aligned}
$$

(2.61)

Products of the mth voltage harmonic and the nth current harmonic integrate to zero over one period, if $m \neq n$, leaving only the products of harmonics of the same order. The power associated with each harmonic can be determined individually with an equation of the form $VI \cos\phi$, where V and I are the rms voltage and current of that harmonic and ϕ is the phase angle between them.

2.12.2 RMS values in the presence of harmonics

If the current flows through a resistor R, $V_m = RI_m$ and the average power dissipation is

$$P_{avg} = \sum_{m=0}^{\infty} I_m^2 R = I^2 R \quad \text{where} \quad I = \sqrt{\sum_{m=0}^{\infty} I_m^2}$$

(2.62)

I is the rms current and equation (2.62) is consistent with the definition of rms current

$$I_{rms} = \sqrt{\frac{1}{T} \int_0^T i^2(t)\, dt}$$

(2.63)

Similar considerations apply to the voltage, such that

$$V_{rms} = \sqrt{\sum_{m=0}^{\infty} V_m^2} \tag{2.64}$$

2.12.3 Phase sequence of harmonics in balanced three-phase systems

The three phase voltages can be expanded in terms of their harmonic components

$$
\begin{aligned}
v_{an} &= V_1 \cos(\omega t) + V_3 \cos(3\omega t) + V_5 \cos(5\omega t) + \ldots \\
v_{bn} &= V_1 \cos(\omega t - 2\pi/3) + V_3 \cos 3(\omega t - 2\pi/3) + V_5 \cos 5(\omega t - 2\pi/3) + \ldots \quad (2.65) \\
v_{cn} &= V_1 \cos(\omega t + 2\pi/3) + V_3 \cos 3(\omega t + 2\pi/3) + V_5 \cos 5(\omega t + 2\pi/3) + \ldots
\end{aligned}
$$

that is

$$
\begin{aligned}
v_{an} &= V_1 \cos(\omega t) + V_3 \cos(3\omega t) + V_5 \cos(5\omega t) + \ldots \\
v_{bn} &= V_1 \cos(\omega t - 2\pi/3) + V_3 \cos(3\omega t) + V_5 \cos(5\omega t + 2\pi/3) + \ldots \quad (2.66) \\
v_{cn} &= V_1 \cos(\omega t + 2\pi/3) + V_3 \cos(3\omega t) + V_5 \cos(5\omega t - 2\pi/3) + \ldots
\end{aligned}
$$

The three fundamental components form a balanced three-phase set of phasors rotating at the fundamental electrical angular velocity ω rad/s with *positive sequence abc*. Likewise the fifth harmonic phasors form a balanced set rotating at 5ω rad/s, but with *negative sequence acb*. The third harmonic components rotate at 3ω radians/s but they are all in phase with one another and are said to have *zero phase sequence*. They do not form a balanced set. The phasors are illustrated in Figure 2.46.

Positive sequence harmonics include those of orders 1, 7, 13, 19, 25, 31, 37, ...; negative sequence those of orders 5, 11, 17, 23, 29, 35, ...; and zero-sequence harmonics all the triplen harmonic orders 3, 9, 15, 21, 27. Note that $\mathbf{V}_{a1} + \mathbf{V}_{b1} + \mathbf{V}_{c1} = 0$, $\mathbf{V}_{a3} + \mathbf{V}_{b3} + \mathbf{V}_{c3} = 3\mathbf{V}_{a3} \neq 0$, and $\mathbf{V}_{a5} + \mathbf{V}_{b5} + \mathbf{V}_{c5} = 0$.

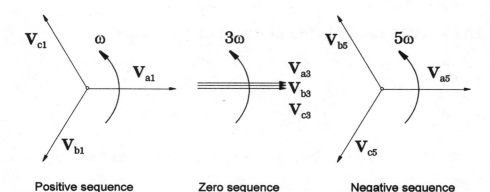

Positive sequence Zero sequence Negative sequence

Fig. 2.46 Harmonic phasors.

2.12.4 Harmonics in balanced networks

In a wye connection we can observe that the actual instantaneous line–line voltage obeys the equation $v_{ab} = v_{an} - v_{bn}$, and so does its fundamental component: $v_{ab1} = v_{an1} - v_{bn1}$. However, the third harmonic component is $v_{ab3} = v_{an3} - v_{bn3} = 0$, which means that no triplen harmonic voltage can appear between two lines in a balanced system.

If there is no neutral, $i_a + i_b + i_c = 0$. Since $i_{a3} = i_{b3} = i_{c3}$, they must all be zero. In a three-wire balanced system, no triplen harmonic currents can flow in the lines. This is true for wye-connected and delta-connected loads. However, triplen harmonic currents can circulate around a delta without appearing in the lines. This property is used to provide the third-harmonic component of magnetizing current in saturated transformers. If the neutral (4th wire) is connected, the neutral current is

$$i_N = i_a + i_b + i_c = +3(i_3 + i_9 + \ldots) \tag{2.67}$$

The neutral connection helps to prevent oscillation of the neutral voltage.

A non-linear load can draw non-sinusoidal currents in each phase, including 3rd harmonics. If such a load is connected in delta, the triplen harmonics can flow in the delta without appearing in the lines. The equivalent circuit of such a load must include a fictitious voltage source for each triplen harmonic, in series with the non-linear load impedance. In a delta connection, the sum of the triplen source voltage and the triplen harmonic voltage drop across the non-linear load impedance will be zero, so that no triplen harmonic voltage component appears between the lines. This is illustrated in Figure 2.47, with

$$\mathbf{E}_3 + \mathbf{Z}_3 \mathbf{I}_3 = 0 \tag{2.68}$$

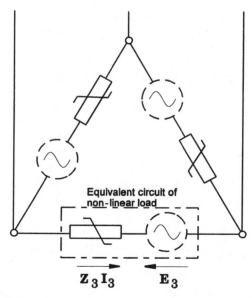

Equivalent circuit of non-linear load

$$\mathbf{Z}_3 \mathbf{I}_3 \qquad \mathbf{E}_3$$

Fig. 2.47 Equivalent circuit of non-linear load.

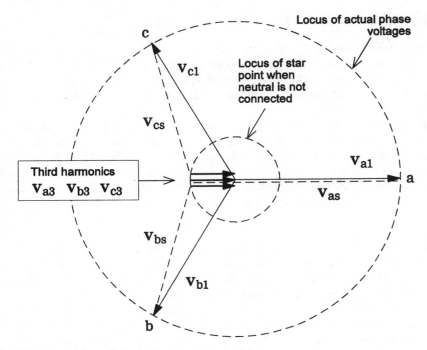

Fig. 2.48 Third-harmonic oscillation of the star-point potential.

in each phase. If the same load is reconnected in wye, the equivalent circuit does not change, but with a three-wire connection the zero-sequence triplen-harmonic currents are prevented from flowing, and therefore the load cannot operate normally. On the other hand, the triplen-harmonic voltage sources may still be active, and in this case, in order to eliminate the triplen-harmonic voltage components from the line–line voltages, the potential of the start point will oscillate, as shown in Figure 2.48.

2.12.5   AC line harmonics of three-phase rectifier

As an example of a harmonic-generating load, Figure 2.49 shows the circuit of a three-phase rectifier supplying a DC load. If the DC current has negligible ripple (i.e. the DC load has enough inductance to keep the current essentially constant through a 120° period), and if the commutation is perfect (i.e. the current passes from one SCR to the next at the instant when the voltage on the incoming phase exceeds the voltage on the outgoing phase), then the AC line current waveform is a 120° squarewave, Figure 2.50. By Fourier's theorem, using 1/4-cycle symmetry,

$$I_h = \frac{2}{2\pi} \times 4 \int_0^{\pi/2} I \cos(h\theta) d\theta = \frac{4}{h\pi} \sin\left(\frac{h\pi}{3}\right) \qquad (2.69)$$

If $h = 1, \sin \pi/3 = \sqrt{3}/2$ and $I_1/I = 4\sqrt{3}/2\pi = 2\sqrt{3}/\pi = 1.103$. If $h = 3, \sin 3\pi/3 = 0$ and $I_3/I = 0$. If $h = 5, \sin 5\pi/3 = -\sqrt{3}/2$ and $|I_5| = I_1/5$. If $h = 7, \sin 7\pi/3 = -\sqrt{3}/2$

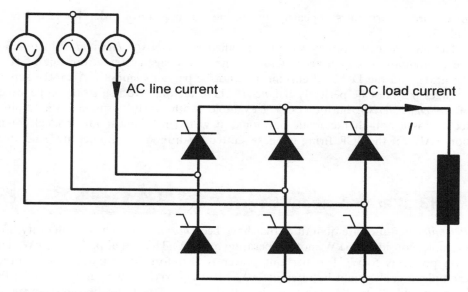

Fig. 2.49 Three-phase rectifier circuit.

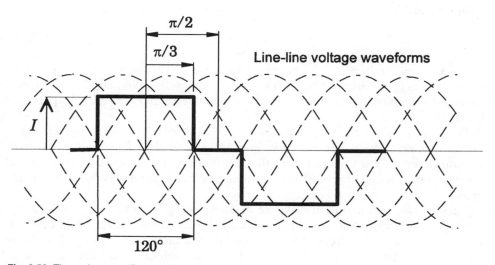

Fig. 2.50 Three-phase rectifier waveforms.

and $|I_7| = I_1/7$. Thus in general if h is an odd non-triplen integer, $|I_h| = I_1/h$. The harmonic orders present in the ideal three-phase rectifier are $h = kq \pm 1$, where k is any positive integer and q is the pulse number of the rectifier circuit. The circuit shown in Figure 2.49 is a six-pulse rectifier. Higher pulse numbers (e.g. 12, 24) are obtained by supplying two parallel rectifiers from phase-shifted secondaries of a three-phase transformer. For example, a 12-pulse rectifier uses one wye-connected secondary and one delta-connected secondary. The 30° phase shift between these secondaries eliminates harmonics of orders 5 and 7, so that the lowest-order harmonics appearing in the line current are of order $1 \times 12 \pm 1 = 11$ and 13.

The harmonics of orders $kq \pm 1$ are called *characteristic harmonics*. In practice the commutation is imperfect (it takes time to transfer current from one SCR to the next), and the DC load current may not be perfectly smooth. Also, the supply voltages may not be perfectly balanced. These factors give rise to the appearance of *non-characteristic* harmonics. For example, a 5th or 7th harmonic in a 12-pulse rectifier is a non-characteristic harmonic: it would not appear under ideal conditions. Also, if the SCR firing is phase-shifted, additional harmonics are generated.

2.13   Per-unit quantities

Per-unit quantities are quantities that have been *normalized* to a *base* quantity. For example, consider a 5 kW motor operating at 3 kW. The actual power is 3 kW. The base power is 5 kW. The per-unit power is therefore $3/5 = 0.6$ p.u. As another example, a cable might be rated at 150 A. If it is carrying 89 A, and if we take the base current to be the same as the rated current, then the per-unit current is $89/150 = 0.593$ p.u.

In general,[17]

$$\mathbf{x} = \frac{X}{X_b} \text{ p.u.} \tag{2.70}$$

where $\mathbf{x}$ is a per-unit value, X is an actual value, and X_b is the base value. X and X_b are expressed in ordinary units, such as volts, amps, watts, Nm, etc. Per-unit quantities have no dimensions but it is normal practice to express them 'in p.u.', for example, 1.05 p.u.

Per-unit quantities express *relative* values – that is, relative to the base value. The choice of base value is important. In the simple example quoted above, the most natural choice of base was the rated value, which is the value associated with 'normal full-load operation'. However, base values may be freely chosen, as the next example shows.

Imagine two motors in parallel, one of 5 kW rating, the other of 50 kW rating, connected to a supply that is rated at 150 A. Suppose that the smaller motor draws its rated current of 7.5 A from the supply, while the larger one draws 75 A. If we consider each motor individually we could say that each one is working at 1 p.u. or 100% of its own rating. But if we choose 150 A as the common base current, then the first motor is drawing $7.5/150 = 0.05$ p.u. while the second one draws $75/150 = 0.5$ p.u. The total current is 0.55 p.u., or 82.5 A. This clearly expresses the fact that the smaller motor is taking 5% of the supply current while the larger one is taking 50%. The supply is working at only 55% of its capacity. Evidently we could add motors and almost double the load.

Per-unit systems are especially useful when we have a more complicated network with transformers, in which there may be several different voltage and current levels.

---

[17] Boldface lowercase letters denote per-unit values. Italic letters denote values in ordinary units.

When quantities are expressed in per-unit, most voltages are close to one under normal operation; higher values indicate overvoltage and lower values may indicate overload. This helps the engineer in scanning the results of a load-flow analysis or fault study, because abnormal conditions are immediately recognizable: for example, currents outside the 0–1 range, or voltages that deviate more than a few per cent from one. Under transient conditions, larger voltage and current swings may be encountered.

Engineering formulas often contain 'funny' coefficients such as $2\pi/\sqrt{2}$ or even constants such as 1.358, and it is often far from obvious where these came from.[18] In a well-chosen per-unit system, factors that are common to both the actual and the base values cancel out, and this gets rid of many of the spurious coefficients. Per-unit expressions are therefore less cluttered and express the essential physical nature of the system economically.

An example of this is the normalization of power in a three-phase system: in ordinary units

$$P = \sqrt{3} V_{LL} I_L \cos \phi \quad [\text{W}] \tag{2.71}$$

The bases P_b, V_b and I_b must be related by the same equation: thus

$$P_b = \sqrt{3} V_b I_b (\cos \phi)_b \quad [\text{W}] \tag{2.72}$$

Normalizing means dividing equation (2.71) by equation (2.72). Taking the base value of the power factor to be $(\cos \phi)_b = 1$, we get

$$\mathbf{p} = \mathbf{vi} \cos \phi \tag{2.73}$$

The factor $\sqrt{3}$ cancels out: this not only simplifies computation, but also expresses the power equation in a fundamental general form that is independent of the number of phases or whether the load is connected in wye or delta.

2.13.1   Standard formulas for three-phase systems

A three-phase system is rated according to its MVA capacity, S. Let the base value for volt-amperes be S_b MVA. If the base line–line voltage is V_b and the base line current is I_b, then

$$S_b = \sqrt{3} V_b I_b \tag{2.74}$$

Usually, V_b is expressed in kV and I_b is in kA. By convention the base impedance Z_b is the line-neutral impedance

$$Z_b = \frac{V_b/\sqrt{3}}{I_b} \ \Omega \tag{2.75}$$

---

[18] They usually arise in the theoretical derivation of the formula but they may arise because of the particular units used for parameters in the equation. A simple example is the equation $y = 25.4x$ to represent a length y in mm that is equal to another length x in inches. The equation expresses the essential equality of the dimensions y and x, but the 25.4 factor appears in the equation because of the difference in measurement units and makes y and x look as though they are unequal!

Combining equations (2.74) and (2.75), we get

$$Z_b = \frac{V_b^2}{S_b} \ \Omega \qquad (2.76)$$

If V_b is expressed in kV and S_b in MVA, we can express equation (2.76) in the form that is widely used by power engineers

$$Z_b = \frac{(kV_{base})^2}{MVA_{base}} \ \Omega \qquad (2.77)$$

2.13.2   Changing base

Sometimes the parameters for two elements in the same circuit are quoted in per-unit on different bases. For example, we might have a cable whose series impedance is quoted as $0.1 + j0.3$ p.u. on a base of 100 MVA and 33 kV. Suppose this cable is connected to a load whose impedance is given as $1.0 + j0.2$ p.u. on a base of 150 MVA and 22 kV. What is the combined series impedance? To proceed we must choose a single set of base quantities and convert all per-unit impedances to that set. Let us choose the cable's base values as the common base values: 100 MVA and 33 kV. We can convert the load impedance to this base set by ratioing, using equation (2.77)

$$Z_{new} = Z_{old} \times \frac{(kV_{b\ old})^2}{(kV_{b\ new})^2} \times \frac{MVA_{b\ new}}{MVA_{b\ old}} \qquad (2.78)$$

The per-unit load impedance on the new (cable) base is therefore

$$(1.0 + j0.2) \times \frac{22^2}{33^2} \times \frac{100}{150} = 0.2963 + j0.0593 \ \text{p.u.} \qquad (2.79)$$

With both impedances on the same base, we can now add them together to get $0.3963 + j0.3593$ p.u. (on a base of 100 MVA and 33 kV).

It is clear that 'p.u.' is not an absolute unit, since the same impedance can have different values, depending on the base. *A per-unit value is incomplete unless the base is stated.*

Per-unit quantities are used widely in power engineering. They are useful for expressing characteristics that are common to different devices. For example, in power stations the series impedance of most large 'unit transformers' (the ones that step up the generator voltage to 400 kV) is almost always about 0.10–0.15 p.u. The ohmic values differ widely according to the ratings and the actual voltages. Similarly, the magnetizing current of small induction motors is typically in the range 0.2–0.5 p.u. The ampere values vary over a wide range, depending on the ratings and the voltages, and therefore they obscure the essential uniformity of this design characteristic. Often a per-unit calculation can give insight that is not apparent when working in ordinary units.

2.13.3   Transformers in per-unit systems

One of the most useful simplifications of working in per-unit is in dealing with transformers. The ratio of base voltages between the primary and secondary can logically be taken to be the turns ratio, n. Then the ratio of base currents must be the inverse of the turns ratio, $1/n$. Therefore the ratio of base impedances must be the square of the turns ratio, n^2. But this is precisely the ratio by which an impedance is referred from the secondary to the primary. Therefore, if we normalize an impedance to the base on one side of the transformer, and then refer this per-unit impedance to the other side, the per-unit value comes out exactly the same. This means that in a consistent per-unit system, ideal transformers simply disappear. Mathematically, this can be expressed as follows

$$Z_{b1} = n^2 Z_{b2} \qquad (2.80)$$

On the secondary base, a load impedance Z (ohms) on the secondary side has the per-unit value

$$z = \frac{Z}{Z_{b2}} \, \text{p.u.} \qquad (2.81)$$

If we refer Z to the primary it becomes $Z' = n^2 Z$. The per-unit value of this on the primary base, is

$$z' = \frac{Z'}{Z_{b1}} = \frac{n^2 Z}{n^2 Z_{b2}} = z \qquad (2.82)$$

This says that the per-unit value of an impedance is the same on both sides of the transformer. In other words, in per-unit the turns ratio of the transformer is unity and it can be removed from the circuit. This is only true if the primary and secondary base impedances are in the ratio n^2.

These comments apply to ideal transformers only. But real transformers can be modelled by an ideal transformer together with parasitic impedances (resistances, leakage reactances etc.) that can be lumped together with the other circuit impedances on either side. The equivalent circuit of a transformer in per-unit is just a series impedance equal to $\mathbf{r} + \mathbf{jx}$, where $\mathbf{r}$ is the sum of the per-unit primary and secondary resistances and $\mathbf{x}$ is the sum of the per-unit primary and secondary leakage reactances. The magnetizing branch appears as a shunt impedance. Wye/delta transformers have a more complex representation but still the ideal transformer disappears from the equivalent circuit. Similarly, tap-changing transformers can be represented by a simple network.

2.14 Conclusion

This chapter has laid the basic technical foundation for the study of reactive power control in power systems, with most of the analytical theory required for calculation of simple AC circuits including three-phase circuits and circuits with reactive compensators. Power-factor correction and the adjustment of voltage by means of reactive power control have been explained using phasor diagrams and associated circuit equations. The basic theory of transformers, harmonics, and per-unit systems has also been covered.

In the next chapter the simple analytical theory of reactive power control is extended to transmission systems which are long enough to be considered as distributed-parameter circuits.

3

Transmission system compensation

3.1 Introduction

It has always been desirable to transmit as much power as possible through transmission lines and cables, consistent with the requirements of stability and security of supply. Power transmission is limited mainly by thermal factors in cables, short transmission lines, transformers and generators; but in long lines and cables the variation of voltage and the maintenance of stability also constrain the power transmission. The voltage 'profile' and the stability of a transmission line or cable can be improved using 'reactive compensation'. In the early days reactive compensation took the form of fixed-value reactors and capacitors, usually controlled by mechanical switchgear. Synchronous condensers and large generators were used in cases where it was necessary to vary the reactive power continuously. Since the 1970s power-electronic equipment has been developed and applied to extend the range of control, with a variety of methods and products.

Bulk AC transmission of electrical power has two fundamental requirements:

1. *Synchronism*. The basis of AC transmission is a network of synchronous machines connected by transmission links. The voltage and frequency are defined by this network, even before any loads are contemplated. All the synchronous machines must remain constantly in synchronism: i.e. they must all rotate at exactly the same speed, and even the phase angles between them must not vary appreciably. By definition, the *stability* of the system is its tendency to recover from disturbances such as faults or changes of load.

The power transmitted between two synchronous machines can be slowly increased only up to a certain level called the *steady-state stability limit*. Beyond this level the synchronous machines fall out of step, i.e. lose synchronism. The steady-state stability limit can be considerably modified by the excitation level of the synchronous machines (and therefore the line voltage); by the number and connections of transmission lines; and by the pattern of real and reactive power flows in the system, which can be modulated by reactive compensation equipment.

A transmission system cannot be operated too close to the steady-state stability limit, because there must be a margin to allow for disturbances. In determining an appropriate margin, the concepts of *transient* and *dynamic stability* are useful. Dynamic stability is concerned with the ability to recover normal operation following a specified *minor* disturbance. Transient stability is concerned with the ability to recover normal operation following a specified *major* disturbance.

2. *Voltage profile*. It is obvious that the correct voltage level must be maintained within narrow limits at all levels in the network. Undervoltage degrades the performance of loads and causes overcurrent. Overvoltage is dangerous because of the risks of flashover, insulation breakdown, and saturation of transformers. Most voltage variations are caused by load changes, and particularly by the reactive components of current flowing in the reactive components of the network impedances. If generators are close by, excitation levels can be used to keep the voltage constant; but over long links the voltage variations are harder to control and may require reactive compensation equipment.

Different techniques are used for controlling the voltage according to the underlying rate of change of voltage. Cyclic, diurnal load variation is gradual enough to be compensated by excitation control or the timely switching in and out of capacitors and reactors. But sudden overvoltages – such as those resulting from disconnection of loads, line switching operations, faults, and lightning – require immediate suppression by means of surge arrestors or spark gaps. Between these extremes there are many possibilities for controlled reactive compensation equipment operating over time scales ranging from a few milliseconds to a few hours.

Table 3.1 is a matrix of methods for stability and voltage control, including a range of reactive power compensators. Some of the compensator devices can serve several functions, which makes the subject somewhat complicated. Table 3.2 lists some of the main advantages and disadvantages of the different compensators.

3.2 Uncompensated lines

3.2.1 Voltage and current equations of a long, lossless transmission line

Figure 3.1 shows one phase of a transmission line or cable with distributed inductance l H/m and capacitance c F/m. The voltage and current phasors $\mathbf{V}(x)$ and $\mathbf{I}(x)$ both obey the transmission line equation

$$\frac{d^2\mathbf{V}}{dx^2} = \Gamma^2\mathbf{V} \quad \text{where} \quad \Gamma = \sqrt{(r + j\omega l)(g + j\omega c)} \tag{3.1}$$

and x is distance along the line. r is the resistance per unit length [ohm/m] in series with l and g is the 'shunt' conductance per unit length [S/m] in parallel with c. ω is the radian frequency $2\pi f$. If r and g are both small, then $\Gamma = j\beta$ where $\beta = \omega\sqrt{(lc)}$ is the *wavenumber*. The propagation velocity $u = 1/\sqrt{(lc)}$ is rather lower than the speed of light $(3 \times 10^5 \text{ km/s})$ and $\beta = 2\pi f/u = 2\pi/\lambda$ where $\lambda = u/f$ is the wavelength. For example, at 50 Hz $\lambda = 3 \times 10^5/50 = 6000$ km and $\beta = 1.047 \times 10^{-3}$ rad/km $= 6.0°/100$ km.

Table 3.1 Methods for stability and voltage control

		Increase transmission voltage	Increase no. of lines in parallel	Transformer Tapchanging	Slow AVR control	Fast AVR control	Fast turbine valving	Rapid line-switching operations, Reclosing of circuit-breakers	Braking resistors	Shunt reactor (Switched/unswitched, linear/non-linear)	Shunt capacitor	Series reactor	Series capacitor	Synchronous condenser	Polyphase saturated reactor	Thyristor controlled reactor	Thyristor switched capacitor	Short-circuit limiting coupling (or fault current limiter)
1. Maintain synchronism	Improve steady-state stability	•	•		•	•				•	•		•	•	•	•	•	
	Improve dynamic stability					•								•		•	•	
	Improve transient stability	•				•	•	•	•		•		•	•	•	•	•	
2. Maintain voltage profile	Limit rapid voltage change					•		•			•			•	•	•	•	
	Limit slow voltage change			•	•						•			•	•	•	•	
	Limit overvoltages due to lightning, switching etc.									•				•	•	•		
Other requirements	Reactive power support at DC converter terminals													•	•	•	•	
	Increase short-circuit level												•	•				
	Decrease short-circuit level											•						•

Table 3.2 Advantages and disadvantages of different types of compensating equipment for transmission systems

Compensating equipment	Advantages	Disadvantages
Switched shunt reactor	Simple	Fixed value
Switched shunt capacitor	Simple	Fixed value
		Switching transients
Series capacitor	Simple	Requires over-voltage protection and subharmonic filters
		Limited overload capability
Synchronous condenser	Has useful overload capability	High maintenance requirement
	Fully controllable	Slow response
	Low harmonics	Heavy
Polyphase-saturated reactor (TCR)	Rugged construction	Fixed value
	Large overload capability	Noisy
	Low harmonics	
Thyristor-controlled reactor (TCR)	Fast response	Requires shunt capacitors/filters
	Fully controllable	Generates harmonics
	No effect on fault level	
Thyristor-switched capacitor (TSC)	No harmonics	No inherent absorbing capability to limit over-voltages
		Complex buswork
		Low frequency resonances with system

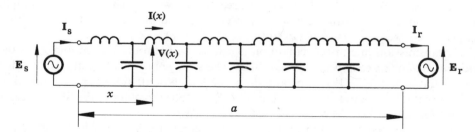

Fig. 3.1 Transmission line with distributed series inductance and shunt capacitance.

If a is the length of the line, $\theta = \beta a$ is the *electrical length*; for example, if $a = 100\,\text{km}$, $\theta = 6.0°$.

The solution to equation (3.1) for a lossless line is

$$\mathbf{V}(x) = \mathbf{V}_r \cos \beta(a - x) + \mathrm{j}Z_0 \mathbf{I}_r \sin \beta(a - x)$$

$$\mathbf{I}(x) = \mathrm{j}\frac{\mathbf{V}_r}{Z_0}\sin \beta(a - x) + \mathbf{I}_r \cos \beta(a - x) \tag{3.2}$$

where $Z_0 = \sqrt{(l/c)}$ is the *surge impedance* [ohm]. A typical value of Z_0 for a high-voltage line is $250\,\Omega$, but cables have lower values because of their higher capacitance. Note that if $x_L = \omega l$ is the series inductive reactance [ohm/m] and $x_C = 1/\omega c$ is the shunt capacitive reactance [also ohm/m] then we can write $Z_0 = \sqrt{(x_L x_C)}$ and $\beta = \sqrt{(x_L/x_C)}$.

3.2.2 Surge impedance and natural loading of a transmission line

The surge impedance is the driving-point impedance of an infinitely long line, or a line which is terminated in a load impedance Z_0 such that $\mathbf{V_r} = Z_0\mathbf{I_r}$. In either case, at a point x along the line, the ratio between the voltage $\mathbf{V}(x)$ and the current $\mathbf{I}(x)$ is given by equations (3.2) as

$$Z(x) = \frac{\mathbf{V}(x)}{\mathbf{I}(x)} = \frac{Z_0\mathbf{I_r}[\cos\ \beta(a-x)+j\sin\ \beta(a-x)]}{\mathbf{I_r}[\cos\ \beta(a-x)+j\sin\ \beta(a-x)]} = Z_0 \qquad (3.3)$$

which is not only independent of x but is real and equal to Z_0. This means that $\mathbf{V}$ and $\mathbf{I}$ are in phase at all points along the line. However, the phase angles of both phasors vary linearly along the line since

$$\mathbf{V}(x) = \mathbf{V_r}e^{j\beta(a-x)} \quad \text{and} \quad \mathbf{I}(x) = \mathbf{I_r}e^{j\beta(a-x)} \qquad (3.4)$$

The phasor diagram of a line terminated in Z_0 is shown in Figure 3.2. The power transmitted along such a line is

$$P_0 = \frac{V^2}{Z_0} \qquad (3.5)$$

If V is the line-neutral voltage this is the power per phase. If V is the line–line voltage it is the total power. The reactive power is zero at both ends of the line, since $\mathbf{V}$ and $\mathbf{I}$ are in phase at all points. If we equate the reactive power absorbed per unit length in the series inductance with the reactive power generated per unit length in the shunt capacitance, we get $V^2\omega c = I^2\omega l$, so that $V/I = \sqrt{(l/c)} = Z_0$.

A transmission line in this condition is said to be naturally loaded and P_0 is the *natural load* or *surge impedance load* (SIL). The voltage profile of a naturally loaded line is flat, since $|\mathbf{V}| = V$ is constant along the line. Note that P_0 is proportional to V^2, so that if we upgrade a 275 kV line with $Z_0 = 250\,\Omega$ to 400 kV, the SIL increases from $275^2/250 = 302.5$ MW to $400^2/250 = 640$ MW.

The surge impedance load is not a limit: it is merely the load at which the voltage profile is flat and the line requires no reactive power. Lines can be operated above or below the SIL. If the actual load is less than the SIL, the voltage tends to rise along the line; and if the load is less than the SIL, it tends to fall: see Figure 3.3. The SIL is

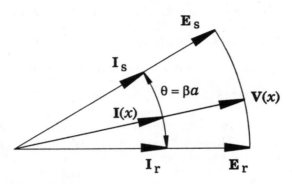

Fig. 3.2 Phasor diagram of line terminated in Z_0.

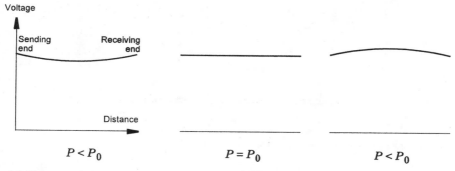

$$P < P_0 \qquad\qquad P = P_0 \qquad\qquad P < P_0$$

Fig. 3.3 Voltage profiles along a long, lossless symmetrical transmission line.

important with very long lines when there are no intermediate substations at which the voltage level can be controlled. Evidently it is desirable to operate such lines as close as possible to the SIL, to maintain a flat voltage profile. Shorter lines (typically those less than 50–100 km) do not have such a problem with the variation of the voltage profile with load, and the power transmission through them is more likely to be limited by other factors, such as the fault level or the current-carrying capacity of the conductors (which is thermally limited).

3.2.3 The uncompensated line on open-circuit

A lossless line that is energized by generators at the sending end and is open-circuited at the receiving end is described by equation (3.2) with $I_r = 0$, so that

$$V(x) = V_r \cos \beta(a - x) \tag{3.6}$$

and

$$I(x) = j\left[\frac{V_r}{Z_0}\right] \sin \beta(a - x) \tag{3.7}$$

The voltage and current at the sending end are given by these equations with $x = 0$.

$$E_s = V_r \cos \theta \tag{3.8}$$

$$I_s = j\left[\frac{V_r}{Z_0}\right] \sin \theta = j\left[\frac{E_s}{Z_0}\right] \tan \theta \tag{3.9}$$

E_s and V_r are in phase, which is consistent with the fact that there is no power transfer. The phasor diagram is shown in Figure 3.4.

The voltage and current profiles in equations (3.6) and (3.7) are more conveniently expressed in terms of E_s:

$$V(x) = E_s \frac{\cos \beta(a - x)}{\cos \theta} \tag{3.10}$$

$$I(x) = j\frac{E_s}{Z_0} \frac{\sin \beta(a - x)}{\cos \theta} \tag{3.11}$$

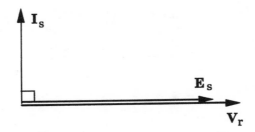

Fig. 3.4 Phasor diagram of uncompensated line on open-circuit.

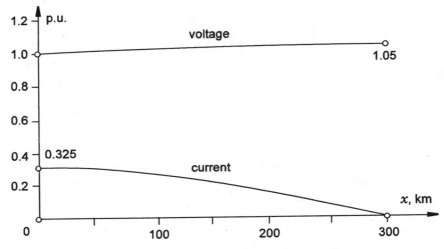

Fig. 3.5 Voltage and current profiles for a 300-km line at no load (open-circuit).

The general forms of these profiles are shown in Figure 3.5. For a line 300 km in length at 50 Hz, $\beta = 360° \times f/3 \times 10^5 = 6°$ per 100 km, so $\theta = 6 \times 3 = 18°$. Then $V_r = E_s/\cos\theta = 1.05E_s$ and $I_s = (E_s/Z_0)\tan\theta = 0.329$ p.u. based on the SIL. The voltage rise on open-circuit is called the *Ferranti effect*.

Although the voltage rise of 5% seems small, the 'charging' current is appreciable and in such a line it must all be supplied by the generator, which is forced to run at leading power factor, for which it must be underexcited.[1] Note that a line for which $\theta = \beta a = \pi/2$ has a length of $\lambda/4$ (one quarter-wavelength, i.e. 1500 km at 50 Hz), producing an infinite voltage rise. Operation of any line approaching this length is completely impractical without some means of compensation.

In practice the open-circuit voltage rise will be greater than is indicated by equation (3.10), which assumes that the sending-end voltage is fixed. Following a

---

[1] The extent to which generators can absorb reactive power is limited by stability and core-end heating. Operation of generators in the absorbing mode, with a leading power factor, is called 'under-excited' because the field current and open-circuit emf are reduced below their normal rated-load values.

sudden open-circuiting of the line at the receiving end, the sending-end voltage tends to rise immediately to the *open-circuit voltage* of the sending-end generators, which exceeds the terminal voltage by approximately the voltage drop due to the prior current flowing in their short-circuit reactances.

3.3 Uncompensated lines under load

3.3.1 Radial line with fixed sending-end voltage

A load $P + jQ$ at the receiving end of a transmission line or cable (Figure 3.6) draws the current

$$\mathbf{I}_r = \frac{P - jQ}{\mathbf{V}_r^*} \tag{3.12}$$

The sending- and receiving-end voltages are related by

$$\mathbf{E}_s = \mathbf{V}_r \cos\theta + jZ_0 \frac{P - jQ}{\mathbf{V}_r^*} \sin\theta \tag{3.13}$$

If $\mathbf{E}_s$ is fixed, this quadratic equation can be solved for $\mathbf{V}_r$. The solution shows how $\mathbf{V}_r$ varies with the load and its power factor, and with the line length. A typical result is shown in Figure 3.7.

For each load power factor there is a maximum transmissible power, P_{max}, the *steady-state stability limit*. For any value of $P < P_{max}$, there are two possible solutions for $\mathbf{V}_r$, since equation (3.13) is quadratic. Normal operation is always at the upper value, within narrow limits around 1.0 p.u. Note that when $P = P_0$ and $Q = 0$, $V_r = E_s$.

The load power factor has a strong influence on the receiving-end voltage. Loads with lagging power factor tend to reduce V_r, while loads with leading power factor tend to increase it.

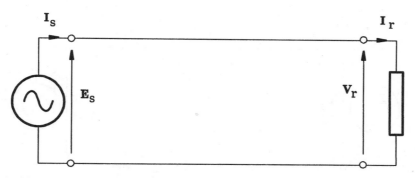

Fig. 3.6 Radial line or cable with load $P + jQ$.

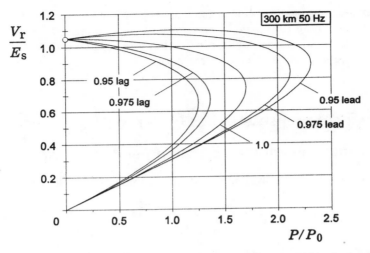

Fig. 3.7 Receiving-end voltage magnitude $|\mathbf{V_r}|$ as a function of load P/P_0 for a 300-km lossless radial line, at different power factors.

3.3.2   Uncompensated symmetrical line: variation of voltage and reactive power with load

The symmetrical line in Figure 3.8 has equal voltages at the sending and receiving ends, and the mid-point voltage and current are $\mathbf{V_m}$ and $\mathbf{I_m}$ respectively. The phasor diagram is shown in Figure 3.9. The equations for the sending-end half of the line are

$$\mathbf{E_s} = \mathbf{V_m} \cos\frac{\theta}{2} + j Z_0 \mathbf{I_m} \sin\frac{\theta}{2}$$

$$\mathbf{I_s} = j\frac{\mathbf{V_m}}{Z_0} \sin\frac{\theta}{2} + \mathbf{I_m} \cos\frac{\theta}{2}$$

(3.14)

At the mid-point,

$$P_m + jQ_m = \mathbf{V_m}\mathbf{I_m^*} = P$$

(3.15)

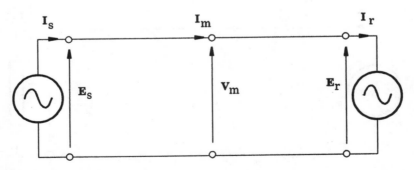

Fig. 3.8 Symmetrical line.

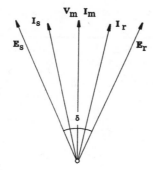

Fig. 3.9 Phasor diagram of symmetrical line.

where P is the transmitted power. Note that $Q_m = 0$, that is, no reactive power flows past the mid-point. The real and reactive power at the sending end are

$$P_s + jQ_s = \mathbf{E}_s \mathbf{I}_s^* \tag{3.16}$$

Substituting for $\mathbf{E}_s$ and $\mathbf{I}_s$ from equation (3.14) and treating $\mathbf{V}_m$ as reference phasor, $P_m = V_m I_m$ and

$$P_s + jQ_s = P + j\left[Z_0 I_m^2 - \frac{V_m^2}{Z_0}\right]\frac{\sin \theta}{2} \tag{3.17}$$

Since the line is assumed lossless, the result $P = P_s = P_r$ is expected. The expression for Q_s can be arranged as follows, making use of the relations $P_0 = V_0^2/Z_0$ and $P_m = V_m I_m$: thus

$$Q_s = P_0\left[\frac{P^2}{P_0^2}\frac{V_0^2}{V_m^2} - \frac{V_m^2}{V_0^2}\right]\frac{\sin \theta}{2} \tag{3.18}$$

This equation shows how the reactive power requirements of the symmetrical line are related to the mid-point voltage. By symmetry, equation (3.18) applies to both ends of the line, and each end supplies half the total reactive power. Because of the sign convention for $\mathbf{I}_s$ and $\mathbf{I}_r$ in Figure 3.8, this is written $Q_s = -Q_r$.

When $P = P_0$ (the natural load), if $V_m = 1.0$ then $Q_s = Q_r = 0$, and $E_s = E_r = V_m = V_0 = 1.0$ p.u. On the other hand, at no-load $P = 0$, and if the voltages are adjusted so that $E_s = E_r = V_0 = 1.0$ p.u., then $I_m = 0$ and

$$Q_s = -P_0 \tan\frac{\theta}{2} = -Q_r \tag{3.19}$$

i.e. each end supplies the line-charging reactive power for half the line. If the terminal voltages are adjusted so that the mid-point voltage V_m is equal to 1.0 p.u. at all levels of power transmission, then from equation (3.18)

$$Q_s = P_0\left[\frac{P^2}{P_0^2} - 1\right]\frac{\sin \theta}{2} = -Q_r \tag{3.20}$$

Table 3.3 Effect of power transmitted on voltage profile and reactive power requirements

$P < P_0$	$V_m > E_s$, E_r. There is an excess of line-charging reactive power, which is absorbed at the ends: $Q_s < 0$ and $Q_r > 0$.
$P > P_0$	$V_m < E_s$, E_r. There is a deficit of line-charging reactive power, which is supplied at the ends: $Q_s > 0$ and $Q_r < 0$.
$P = P_0$	$V_m = V_0 = E_s = E_r$. The voltage profile is flat. The line requires no reactive power and $Q_s = Q_r = 0$.

Moreover, from equations (3.12) and (3.13) it can be shown that if $V_m = V_0$,

$$E_s = E_r = V_0 \sqrt{1 - \left[1 - \frac{P^2}{P_0^2}\right] \sin^2 \frac{\theta}{2}} \tag{3.21}$$

Equations (3.20) and (3.21) illustrate the general behaviour of the symmetrical line. Note that the reactive power requirement is determined by the *square* of the transmitted power. According to equation (3.20) the line can be said to have a deficit or an excess of reactive power, depending on the ratio P/P_0, as summarized in Table 3.3.

Example: consider a line or cable with $\theta = 18°$ operating with $P = 1.5P_0$. Then $\sin \theta = 0.309$. From equation (3.20), $Q_s = -Q_r = 0.193P_0$. For every megawatt of power transmitted, a total reactive power of $2 \times 0.193/1.5 = 0.258$ MVAr has to be supplied from the ends. This represents a power factor of 0.968 at each end.

3.3.3   Maximum power and steady-state stability

Equation (3.13) is valid for synchronous and non-synchronous loads alike. If we consider the receiving end to be an equivalent synchronous machine, E_r is written instead of V_r and if this is taken as reference phasor, E_s can be written as

$$\mathbf{E_s} = E_s e^{j\delta} = E_s(\cos \delta + j \sin \delta) \tag{3.22}$$

where δ is the phase angle between $\mathbf{E_s}$ and $\mathbf{V_r}$ (Figure 3.9). δ is called the *load angle* or *transmission angle*. Equating the real and imaginary parts of equations (3.13) and (3.22)

$$E_s \cos \delta = E_r \cos \theta + Z_0 \frac{Q}{E_r} \sin \theta$$

$$E_s \sin \delta = Z_0 \frac{P}{E_r} \sin \theta \tag{3.23}$$

The second of these equations can be rearranged as

$$P = \frac{E_s E_r}{Z_0 \sin \theta} \sin \delta \tag{3.24}$$

A more familiar form of this equation is obtained for short lines, for which $\sin \theta \simeq \theta = \beta a = \omega a \sqrt{(lc)}$. Then $Z_0 \theta = \omega a \sqrt{(lc)} \times \sqrt{(l/c)} = \omega al = X_L$, the series inductive reactance of the line. So

$$P = \frac{E_s E_r}{X_L} \sin \delta \qquad (3.25)$$

This equation is important because of its simplicity and wide-ranging validity. If E_s and E_r are held constant (as is normally the case), the power transmission is a function of only one variable, δ. As noted earlier, there is a maximum transmissible power,

$$P_{max} = \frac{E_s E_r}{X_L} = \frac{P_0}{\sin \theta} \qquad (3.26)$$

This is shown in Figure 3.10, which is usually plotted with δ as the independent variable; but in fact P is generally the independent variable and the power transmission has to be controlled to keep δ within safe limits below P_{max}. Typically δ is kept below $30°$, giving a safety margin of 100% since $\sin 30° = 0.5$.

The reactive power required at the ends of the line can also be determined from equation (3.23): thus

$$Q_r = \frac{E_r(E_s \cos \delta - E_r \cos \theta)}{Z_0 \sin \theta}$$

$$Q_s = -\frac{E_s(E_r \cos \delta - E_s \cos \theta)}{Z_0 \sin \theta} \qquad (3.27)$$

If $E_s = E_r$ then

$$Q_s = -\frac{E_s^2(\cos \delta - \cos \theta)}{Z_0 \sin \theta} = -Q_r \qquad (3.28)$$

If $P < P_0$ and $E_s = 1.0$ p.u., then $\delta < \theta$, $\cos \delta > \cos \theta$, and $Q_s < 0$ and $Q_r > 0$. This means that there is an excess of line charging current and reactive power is being absorbed at both ends of the line. If $P > P_0$, reactive power is generated at both ends. If $P = 0$, $\cos \delta = 1$ and equation (3.28) reduces to equation (3.19).

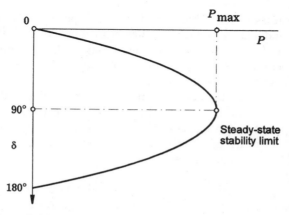

Fig. 3.10 Power vs. transmission angle.

For an electrically short line, $\cos \theta \to 1$ and $Z_0 \sin \theta \to X_L$, so that with $E_s = E_r$ equation (3.28) reduces to

$$Q_s = \frac{E_s^2(1 - \cos \delta)}{X_L} = -Q_r \qquad (3.29)$$

3.4 Compensated transmission lines

Reactive compensation means the application of reactive devices

(a) to produce a substantially flat voltage profile at all levels of power transmission;
(b) to improve stability by increasing the maximum transmissible power; and/or
(c) to supply the reactive power requirements in the most economical way.

Ideally the compensation would modify the surge impedance by modifying the capacitive and/or inductive reactances of the line, so as to produce a virtual surge-impedance loading P_0' that was always equal to the actual power being transmitted. According to equation (3.4), this would ensure a flat voltage profile at all power levels. However, this is not sufficient by itself to ensure the *stability* of transmission, which depends also on the electrical line length θ; see equation (3.26). The electrical length can itself be modified by compensation to have a virtual value θ' shorter than the uncompensated value, resulting in an increase in the steady-state stability limit P_{max}.

These considerations suggest two broad classifications of compensation scheme, *surge-impedance compensation* and *line-length compensation*. Line-length compensation in particular is associated with series capacitors used in long-distance transmission. A third classification is *compensation by sectioning*, which is achieved by connecting constant-voltage compensators at intervals along the line. The maximum transmissible power is that of the weakest section, but since this is necessarily shorter than the whole line, an increase in maximum power and, therefore, in stability can be expected.

3.4.1 Passive and active compensators

Passive compensators include shunt reactors and capacitors and series capacitors. They modify the inductance and capacitance of the line. Apart from switching, they are uncontrolled and incapable of continuous variation. For example, shunt reactors are used to compensate the line capacitance to limit voltage rise at light load. They increase the virtual surge impedance and reduce the virtual natural load P_0'. Shunt capacitors may be used to augment the capacitance of the line under heavy loading. They generate reactive power which tends to boost the voltage. They reduce the virtual surge impedance and increase P_0'. Series capacitors are used for line-length compensation. A measure of surge-impedance compensation may be necessary in conjunction with series capacitors, and this may be provided by shunt reactors or by a dynamic compensator.

Active compensators are usually shunt-connected devices which have the property of tending to maintain a substantially constant voltage at their terminals. They do this by generating or absorbing precisely the required amount of corrective reactive

Table 3.4 Classification of compensators by function and type

Function	Passive	Active
Surge-impedance compensation	Shunt reactors (linear or non-linear)	Synchronous machines
	Shunt capacitors	Synchronous condensers Saturated-reactor compensators Thyristor-switched capacitors Thyristor-controlled reactors
Line-length compensation	Series capacitors	—
Compensation by sectioning	—	Synchronous condensers Saturated-reactor compensators Thyristor-switched capacitors Thyristor-controlled reactors

power in response to any small variation of voltage at their point of connection. They are usually capable of continuous (i.e. stepless) variation and rapid response. Control may be inherent, as in the saturated-reactor compensator; or by means of a control system, as in the synchronous condenser and thyristor-controlled compensators.

Active compensators may be applied either for surge-impedance compensation or for compensation by sectioning. In Z_0-compensation they are capable of all the functions performed by fixed shunt reactors and capacitors and have the additional advantage of continuous variability with rapid response. Compensation by sectioning is fundamentally different in that it is possible *only* with active compensators, which must be capable of virtually immediate response to the smallest variation in power transmission or voltage. Table 3.4 summarizes the classification of the main types of compensator according to their usual functions.

The automatic voltage regulators used to control the excitation of synchronous machines also have an important compensating effect in a power system. By dynamically maintaining constant voltage at the generator terminals they remove the Thévenin equivalent source impedance of the generator (i.e. the synchronous reactance) from the equivalent circuit of the transmission system.[2]

Compensating equipment is often an economical way to meet the reactive power requirements for transmission. An obvious example is where the power can be safely increased without the need for an additional line or cable. But compensators bring other benefits such as management of reactive power flows; damping of power oscillations; and the provision of reactive power at conventional HVDC converter terminals. Both passive and active compensators are in growing use, as are all the compensation strategies: virtual surge-impedance, line-length compensation and compensation by sectioning.

3.5 Static shunt compensation

Shunt reactors are used to limit the voltage rise at light load. On long lines they may be distributed at intermediate substations as shown in Figure 3.11, typically at intervals of the order of 50–100 km.

---

[2] During transients, however, the source impedance reappears with a value approaching the transient reactance x_d'.

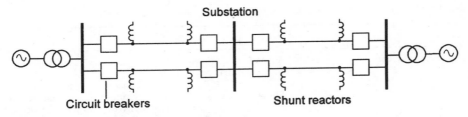

Fig. 3.11 Shunt reactors distributed along a high-voltage AC line.

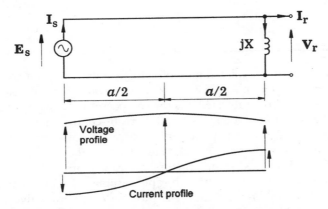

Fig. 3.12 Voltage and current profiles of a shunt-compensated system at no-load.

Consider the simple circuit in Figure 3.12, which has a single shunt reactor of reactance X at the receiving end and a pure voltage source $\mathbf{E}_s$ at the sending end. The receiving-end voltage is given by

$$\mathbf{V}_r = jX\mathbf{I}_r \tag{3.30}$$

From equation (3.2), $\mathbf{E}_s(x = 0)$ is given by

$$\mathbf{E}_s = \mathbf{V}_r \cos \beta a + jZ_0\mathbf{I}_r \sin \beta a = \mathbf{V}_r \left[\cos \theta + \frac{Z_0}{X} \sin \theta \right] \tag{3.31}$$

which shows that $\mathbf{E}_s$ and $\mathbf{V}_r$ are in phase, in keeping with the fact that the real power is zero. For the receiving-end voltage to be equal to the sending-end voltage, $V_r = E_s$, X must be given by

$$X = Z_0 \frac{\sin \theta}{1 - \cos \theta} \tag{3.32}$$

The sending-end current is given by equation (3.2) as

$$\mathbf{I}_s = j\frac{\mathbf{E}_s}{Z_0} \sin \theta + \mathbf{I}_r \cos \theta \tag{3.33}$$

Making use of equations (3.30–3.32), this can be arranged to give

$$\mathbf{I}_s = j\frac{\mathbf{E}_s}{Z_0} \frac{1 - \cos \theta}{\sin \theta} = j\frac{\mathbf{E}_s}{X} = -\mathbf{I}_r \tag{3.34}$$

since $\mathbf{E}_s = \mathbf{V}_r$. This means that the generator at the sending end behaves exactly like the shunt reactor at the receiving end in that both absorb the same amount of reactive power:

$$Q_s = -Q_r = \frac{E_s^2}{X} = \frac{E_s^2}{Z_0}\left[\frac{1-\cos\theta}{\sin\theta}\right] \tag{3.35}$$

The charging current divides equally between the two halves of the line. The voltage profile is symmetrical about the mid-point, and is shown in Figure 3.12 together with the line-current profile. In the left half of the line the charging current is negative; at the mid-point it is zero; and in the right half it is positive. The maximum voltage occurs at the mid-point and is given by equation (3.2) with $x = a/2$

$$\mathbf{V}_m = \mathbf{V}_r\left[\cos\frac{\theta}{2} + \frac{Z_0}{X}\sin\frac{\theta}{2}\right] = \frac{\mathbf{E}_s}{\cos(\theta/2)} \tag{3.36}$$

Note that $\mathbf{V}_m$ is in phase with $\mathbf{E}_s$ and $\mathbf{V}_r$, as is the voltage at all points along the line. For a 300 km line at 50 Hz, $\theta = 18°$ and with $E_s = V_0 = 1.0$ p.u., the mid-point voltage is 1.0125 p.u. and the reactive power absorbed at each end is 0.158 P_0. These values should be compared with the receiving-end voltage of 1.05 p.u. and the sending-end reactive-power absorption of $Q_s = 0.329\, P_0$ in the absence of the reactor. For continuous duty at no-load with a line–line voltage of 500 kV, the rating of the shunt reactor would be 53 MVAr per phase, if $Z_0 = 250\,\Omega$.

Equation (3.36) shows that at no-load the line behaves like a symmetrical line as though it were two separate open-circuited lines connected back-to-back and joined at the mid-point. The open-circuit voltage rise on each half is given by equation (3.36) which is consistent with equation (3.21) when $P = 0$.

3.5.1 Multiple shunt reactors along a long line

The analysis of Figure 3.12 can be generalized to deal with a line divided into n sections by $n - 1$ shunt reactors spaced at equal intervals, with a shunt reactor at each end. The voltage and current profiles in Figure 3.12 could be reproduced in every section if it were of length a and the terminal conditions were the same. The terminal voltages at the ends of the section shown in Figure 3.12 are equal in magnitude and phase. The currents are equal but opposite in phase. The correct conditions could, therefore, be achieved by connecting shunt reactors of half the reactance given by equation (3.32) at every junction between two sections, as shown in Figure 3.13. The shunt reactors at the ends of the line are each of twice the reactance of the intermediate ones. If a is the total length of the composite line, replacing a by a/n in equation (3.32) gives the required reactance of each intermediate reactor

$$X = \frac{Z_0}{2}\left[\frac{\sin(\theta/n)}{1-\cos(\theta/n)}\right] \tag{3.37}$$

In Figure 3.13, the sending-end generator supplies no reactive current. In practice it would supply, to a first approximation, only the losses. If the sending-end reactor was removed, the generator would have to absorb the reactive current from the nearest half of the leftmost section. Each intermediate reactor absorbs the line-charging

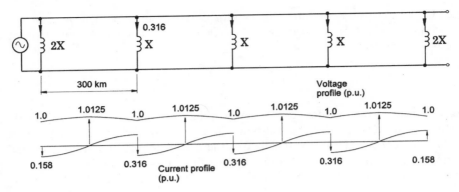

Fig. 3.13 Multiple shunt reactors along a long line.

current and reactive power from two half-sections of line, each of length $a/2n$ on either side of it, whereas the reactors at each end absorb the reactive power from the half-section on one side only. This again explains why the intermediate reactors have half the reactance.

3.5.2 Voltage control by means of switched shunt compensation

Figure 3.14 shows the principle of voltage control by means of switched shunt reactors. Voltage curves are shown for a line such as the one in Figure 3.12. Curve L applies when the shunt reactor is connected, and curve C applies when the shunt capacitor is connected. The receiving-end voltage can be kept within a narrow band as the load varies, by switching the reactor and the capacitor in and out.

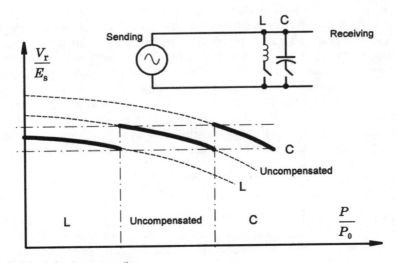

Fig. 3.14 Switched shunt compensation.

3.5.3 The mid-point shunt compensator

Figure 3.15 shows a symmetrical line with a mid-point shunt compensator of admittance jB_γ. Each half of the line is represented by a π-equivalent circuit. The synchronous machines at the ends are assumed to supply or absorb the reactive power for the leftmost and rightmost half-sections, leaving the compensator to supply or absorb only the reactive power for the central half of the line.

If the compensator can vary its admittance continuously in such a way as to maintain $V_m = E$, then in the steady state the line is sectioned into two independent halves with a power transmission characteristic given by

$$P = \frac{2E^2}{X_L}\sin\frac{\delta}{2} \tag{3.38}$$

The maximum transmissible power is $2E^2/X_L$, twice the steady-state limit of the uncompensated line. It is reached when $\delta/2 = \pi/2$, that is, with a transmission angle δ of 90° across each half of the line, and a total transmission angle of 180° across the whole line, Figure 3.16.

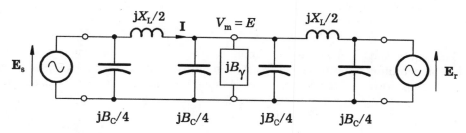

Fig. 3.15 Mid-point shunt compensator.

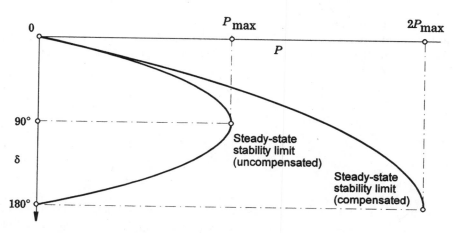

Fig. 3.16 Power transmission characteristic with dynamic shunt compensation.

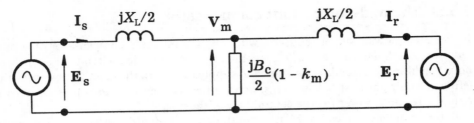

Fig. 3.17 Mid-point shunt compensator.

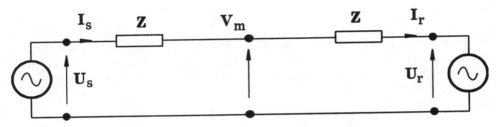

Fig. 3.18 Thévenin equivalent circuit of line with mid-point shunt compensation.

The equivalent circuit can be simplified to the one shown in Figure 3.17. The compensating admittance is expressed in terms of the 'degree of compensation' k_{m}, which is positive if the compensator is inductive and negative if it is capacitive

$$jB_\gamma = -k_{\mathrm{m}} \times \frac{jB_{\mathrm{c}}}{2} \tag{3.39}$$

The total shunt admittance in the centre is equal to

$$2 \times \frac{jB_{\mathrm{c}}}{4} + jB_\gamma = 2 \times \frac{jB_{\mathrm{c}}}{4} - k_{\mathrm{m}} \times \frac{jB_{\mathrm{c}}}{2} = \frac{jB_{\mathrm{c}}}{2} \times (1 - k_{\mathrm{m}}) \tag{3.40}$$

The equivalent circuit can be simplified still further by splitting the central admittance into two equal parallel admittances and then reducing each half to its Thévenin equivalent, as in Figure 3.18. The Thévenin equivalent voltage at the sending end is

$$U_{\mathrm{s}} = \frac{\frac{1}{jB_{\mathrm{c}}(1-k_{\mathrm{m}})/4}}{\frac{1}{jB_{\mathrm{c}}(1-k_{\mathrm{m}})/4} + \frac{jX_{\mathrm{L}}}{2}} E_{\mathrm{s}} = \frac{E_{\mathrm{s}}}{1-s} \quad \text{where} \quad s = \frac{X_{\mathrm{L}}}{2}\frac{B_{\mathrm{c}}}{4}(1 - k_{\mathrm{m}}) \tag{3.41}$$

and

$$\mathbf{Z} = \frac{1}{jB_{\mathrm{c}}(1 - k_{\mathrm{m}})/4 + \frac{1}{jX_{\mathrm{L}}/2}} = \frac{jX_{\mathrm{L}}/2}{1-s} \tag{3.42}$$

The parameter s is a potentiometer ratio determined by the relative values of X_{L}, B_{c} and k_{m}. If we assume that $E_{\mathrm{s}} = E_{\mathrm{r}} = E$, the phasor diagram is as shown in Figure 3.19 and the mid-point voltage is given by

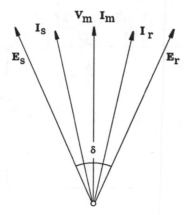

Fig. 3.19 Phasor diagram of symmetrical line.

$$V_m = \frac{E \cos (\delta/2)}{1 - s} \tag{3.43}$$

If we now substitute for s in equation (3.43) we can determine the value of compensating susceptance B_γ required to maintain a given ratio V_m/E: thus

$$B_\gamma = -\frac{4}{X_L} \left[1 - \frac{E}{V_m} \cos \frac{\delta}{2} \right] + \frac{B_c}{2} \tag{3.44}$$

This equation tells how B_γ must vary with the transmission angle δ in order to maintain a given value of mid-point voltage V_m. Naturally, through δ, B_γ varies with the power being transmitted. From Figure 3.19, using the analogy with the symmetrical line in Figure 3.8 and equation (3.25), the power transmission can be deduced to be controlled by the equation

$$P = \frac{E^2}{(1 - s)X_L} \sin \delta = \frac{E_m E}{X_L \cos (\delta/2)} \sin \delta = 2 \frac{E_m E}{X_L} \sin \frac{\delta}{2} \tag{3.45}$$

This establishes equation (3.38) which was earlier written down by inspection of Figure 3.15.

3.6   Series compensation

A series capacitor can be used to cancel part of the reactance of the line. This increases the maximum power, reduces the transmission angle at a given level of power transfer, and increases the virtual natural load. Since the effective line reactance is reduced, it absorbs less of the line-charging reactive power, so shunt reactors may be needed as shown in Figure 3.20. Series capacitors are most often used in very long distance transmission, but they can also be used to adjust the power sharing between parallel lines. A line with 100% series compensation would have a resonant frequency equal to the power frequency, and since the damping in power systems is

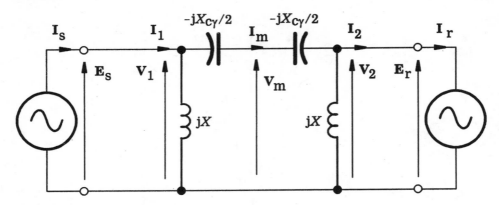

Fig. 3.20 Series compensated transmission line.

very low, such a system would be hypersensitive to small changes. For this reason the degree of series compensation is limited in practice to about 80%.

It is not practicable to distribute the capacitance in small units along the line, so in practice lumped capacitors are installed at a small number of locations (typically one or two) along the line. This makes for an uneven voltage profile.

The line in Figure 3.20 is assumed to be a lossless, symmetrical line with a mid-point series capacitor with equal shunt reactors connected on either side. To permit the line to be analysed in two halves, the capacitor is split into two equal series parts.

3.6.1 Power-transfer characteristics and maximum transmissible power

The general phasor diagram is shown in Figure 3.21. Note that $\mathbf{V}_2$ leads $\mathbf{V}_1$ in phase as a result of the voltage $\mathbf{V}_{C\gamma}$ inserted by the capacitor. Considering the sending-end half, the conditions at its two ends are related by equation (3.2)

$$\mathbf{E}_s = \mathbf{V}_1 \cos\frac{\theta}{2} + \mathrm{j}Z_0\mathbf{I}_1 \sin\frac{\theta}{2}$$

$$\mathbf{I}_s = \mathrm{j}\frac{\mathbf{V}_1}{Z_0}\sin\frac{\theta}{2} = \mathbf{I}_1 \cos\frac{\theta}{2} \tag{3.46}$$

The receiving-end half behaves similarly. The capacitor reactance is $X_{C\gamma} = 1/\omega C_\gamma$ and the voltage across the capacitor is given by

$$\mathbf{V}_{C\gamma} = \mathbf{V}_1 - \mathbf{V}_2 = -\mathrm{j}\mathbf{I}_m X_{C\gamma} \tag{3.47}$$

By symmetry, $P = V_m I_m$, $E = E_r$, and

$$\mathbf{V}_m = \mathbf{V}_1 - \tfrac{1}{2}\mathbf{V}_{C\gamma} = \mathbf{V}_2 + \tfrac{1}{2}\mathbf{V}_{C\gamma} \tag{3.48}$$

The currents $\mathbf{I}_1$ and $\mathbf{I}_2$ are given by

$$\mathbf{I}_m = \mathbf{I}_1 + \frac{\mathrm{j}\mathbf{V}_1}{X} = \mathbf{I}_2 - \mathrm{j}\frac{\mathbf{V}_2}{X} \tag{3.49}$$

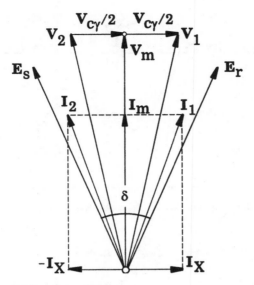

Fig. 3.21 Series compensated line: phasor diagram.

Using these relationships, and taking $\mathbf{V}_m$ as reference phasor, it is possible to derive the basic power-transfer characteristic as

$$P = \frac{E_s V_m}{Z_0 \sin \theta/2 - \frac{X_{C\gamma}}{2}\left[\cos\frac{\theta}{2} + \frac{Z_0}{X}\sin\frac{\theta}{2}\right]} \sin\frac{\delta}{2} \tag{3.50}$$

with

$$E_s \cos\frac{\delta}{2} = V_m\left[\cos\frac{\theta}{2} + \frac{Z_0}{X}\sin\frac{\theta}{2}\right] = E_r \cos\frac{\delta}{2} \tag{3.51}$$

If V_m is substituted from equation (3.51) into equation (3.50), the following result is obtained for the symmetrical line, if $E_s = E_r$:

$$P = \frac{E_s E_r}{\left[Z_0 \sin\theta - \frac{X_{C\gamma}}{2}(1 + \cos\theta)\mu\right]\mu} \sin\delta \tag{3.52}$$

where

$$\mu = 1 + \frac{Z_0}{X}\frac{\sin\theta}{1 + \cos\theta} = 1 + \frac{Z_0}{X}\tan\frac{\theta}{2} \tag{3.53}$$

With no shunt reactors, $\mu = 1$. With fixed terminal voltages, $E_s = E_r = E$, the transmission angle δ can be determined from equation (3.52) for any level of power transmission below the maximum. Once δ is known, V_m can be determined from equation (3.50). Then $\mathbf{V}_1$, $\mathbf{V}_2$, $\mathbf{V}_{C\gamma}$ and other quantities follow.

One simplification is to ignore the shunt capacitance of the line and remove the shunt reactors. Then $Z_0 \sin\theta$ is replaced by X_L and $\mu = 1$, so that with $E_s = E_r = E$,

$$P = \frac{E^2}{X_L - X_{C\gamma}} \sin\delta \tag{3.54}$$

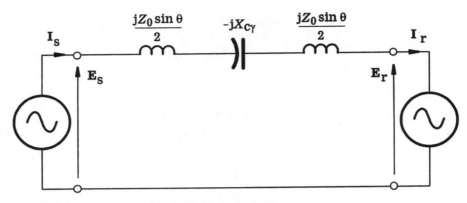

Fig. 3.22 Simplified equivalent circuit of series compensated line.

If the degree of series compensation k_{se} is defined by

$$k_{se} = \frac{X_{C\gamma}}{X_L} = \frac{X_{C\gamma}}{\omega a l} \qquad (3.55)$$

then

$$P = \frac{E^2}{X_L(1 - k_{se})}\sin \delta \qquad (3.56)$$

Another important special case arises when the shunt reactors are chosen to compensate the line capacitance perfectly as discussed in Section 3.4. Their reactances are then each

$$X = Z_0 \frac{\sin(\theta/2)}{1 - \cos(\theta/2)} \qquad (3.57)$$

From equation (3.53) the shunt reactance factor μ reduces to $\sec(\theta/2)$ and the power-transfer characteristic becomes (with $E_s = E_r = E$)

$$P = \frac{E^2}{2Z_0 \sin \theta/2 - X_{C\gamma}}\sin \delta \qquad (3.58)$$

Shunt compensation of the capacitance of each half of the line leaves only the series reactance in the equivalent circuit, Figure 3.22. This equivalent circuit does not take into account the fact that because the shunt-inductive compensation is concentrated, the line voltage profile is not perfectly flat, even at no-load.

3.7 Conclusion

This chapter has examined the behaviour of long-distance, high-voltage transmission lines with distributed parameters, in which the voltage and current tend to vary along the line. The same behaviour is obtained with cables of only moderate length (upwards of 50 km). The theory covers the operation at all load levels and considers the reactive power requirements, the voltage profile, and the stability. Compensation methods are identified for improving the performance with respect to all three of these aspects, including both shunt and series compensating elements, and both passive (fixed-value) and active compensators.

4

Power flows in compensation and control studies

4.1 Introduction

The main objective of a power flow study is to determine the steady state operating condition of the electrical power network. The steady state may be determined by finding out the flow of active and reactive power throughout the network and the voltage magnitudes and phase angles at all nodes of the network.

The planning and daily operation of modern power systems call for numerous power flow studies. Such information is used to carry out security assessment analysis, where the nodal voltage magnitudes and active and reactive power flows in transmission lines and transformers are carefully observed to assess whether or not they are within prescribed operating limits. If the power flow study indicates that there are voltage magnitudes outside bounds at certain points in the network, then appropriate control actions become necessary in order to regulate the voltage magnitude. Similarly, if the study predicts that the power flow in a given transmission line is beyond the power carrying capacity of the line then control action will be taken.

Voltage magnitude regulation is achieved by controlling the amount of reactive power generated/absorbed at key points of the network as well as by controlling the flow of reactive power throughout the network (Miller, 1982). Voltage regulation is carried out locally and, traditionally, the following devices have been used for such a purpose:

1. Automatic voltage regulators, which control the generator's field excitation in order to maintain a specified voltage magnitude at the generator terminal.
2. Sources and sinks of reactive power, such as shunt capacitors, shunt reactors, rotating synchronous condensers and SVCs. Shunt capacitors and reactors are

only capable of providing passive compensation since their generation/absorption of reactive power depends on their rating, and the voltage level at the connection point. On the other hand, the reactive power generated/absorbed by synchronous condensers and SVCs is automatically adjusted in order to maintain fixed voltage magnitude at the connection points.

3. Load-tap changing transformers (LTCs), which are used to regulate voltage magnitude at the LTC terminals by adjusting its transformation ratio.

If no control action is taken, active and reactive power flows in AC transmission networks are determined by the topology of the network, the nodal voltage magnitudes and phase angles and the impedances of the various plant components making up the network. However, stable operation of the power network under a wide range of operating conditions requires good control of power flows network-wide. For instance, reactive power flows are minimized as much as possible in order to reduce network transmission losses and to maintain a uniform voltage profile. Reactive power flow control may be achieved by generating/absorbing reactive power at suitable locations in the network using one or more of the plant components mentioned above. On the other hand, the options for controlling the path of active power flows in AC transmission networks have been very limited, with on-load phase shifting transformers having provided the only practical option. These transformers are fitted with a tap changing mechanism, the purpose of which is to control the voltage phase angle difference across its terminals and, hence, to regulate the amount of active power that flows through the transformer.

4.2 FACTS equipment representation in power flows

Until very recently, with the exception of the SVC, all plant components used in high-voltage transmission to provide voltage and power flow control were equipment based on electro-mechanical technology, which severely impaired the effectiveness of the intended control actions, particularly during fast changing operating conditions (Ledu et al., 1992). This situation has begun to change; building on the operational experience afforded by the many SVC installations and breakthroughs in power electronics valves and their control, a vast array of new power electronics-based controllers has been developed. Controllers used in high-voltage transmission are grouped under the heading of FACTS (Hingorani, 1993) and those used in low-voltage distribution under the heading of Custom Power (Hingorani, 1995). The most prominent equipment and their main steady state characteristics relevant for power flow modelling are discussed below.

4.2.1 The SVC

From the operational point of view, the SVC behaves like a shunt-connected variable reactance, which either generates or absorbs reactive power in order to regulate the voltage magnitude at the point of connection to the AC network (Miller, 1982). In its simplest form, the SVC consists of a TCR in parallel with a bank of capacitors. The thyristor's firing angle control enables the SVC to have an almost instantaneous

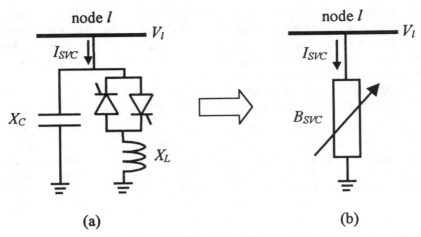

Fig. 4.1 SVC. (a) structure formed by fixed capacitor and TCR; and (b) variable susceptance representation.

speed of response. It is used extensively to provide fast reactive power and voltage regulation support. It is also known to increase system stability margin and to damp power system oscillations (Kundur, 1994).

In power flow studies the SVC is normally modelled as a synchronous generator with zero active power generation; upper and lower limits are given for reactive power generation. The generator representation of the SVC is changed to a constant admittance if the SVC reaches one of its limits (IEEE Special Stability Controls Working Group, 1995).

A more flexible and realistic SVC power flow model is presented in this chapter. It is based on the concept of a non-linear shunt reactance, which is adjusted using Newton's algorithm to satisfy a specified voltage magnitude at the terminal of the SVC (Ambriz-Perez et al., 2000). The schematic representation of the SVC and its equivalent circuit are shown in Figure 4.1, where a TCR is connected in parallel with a fixed bank of capacitors. A more detailed schematic representation of the TCR is shown in Figure 1.9.

An ideal variable shunt compensator is assumed to contain no resistive components, i.e. $G_{SVC} = 0$. Accordingly, it draws no active power from the network. On the other hand, its reactive power is a function of nodal voltage magnitude at the connection point, say node l, and the SVC equivalent susceptance, B_{SVC}

$$P_l = 0$$
$$Q_l = -|V_l|^2 B_{SVC}$$

(4.1)

4.2.2 The TCSC

The TCSC varies the electrical length of the compensated transmission line with little delay. Owing to this characteristic, it may be used to provide fast active power flow regulation. It also increases the stability margin of the system and has proved very effective in damping SSR and power oscillations (Larsen et al., 1992).

The TCSC power flow model presented in this chapter is based on the concept of a non-linear series reactance, which is adjusted using Newton's algorithm to satisfy a specified active power flow across the variable reactance representing the TCSC (Fuerte-Esquivel and Acha, 1997). The schematic representation of the TCSC and its equivalent circuit are shown in Figure 4.2. This schematic representation is a lumped equivalent of the TCSC shown in Figure 1.11(b).

The active power transfer P_{lm} across an impedance connected between nodes l and m is determined by the voltage magnitudes $|V_l|$ and $|V_m|$, the difference in voltage phase angles θ_l and θ_m and the transmission line resistance R_{lm} and reactance X_{lm}. In high-voltage transmission lines, the reactance is much larger than the resistance and the following approximate equation may be used to calculate the active power transfer P_{lm}

$$P_{lm} = \frac{|V_l||V_m|}{X_{lm}} \cdot \sin(\theta_l - \theta_m) \tag{4.2}$$

If the electrical branch is a TCSC controller as opposed to a transmission line then P_{lm} is calculated using the following expression

$$P_{lm}^{reg} = \frac{|V_l||V_m|}{X_{TCSC}} \cdot \sin(\theta_l - \theta_m) \tag{4.3}$$

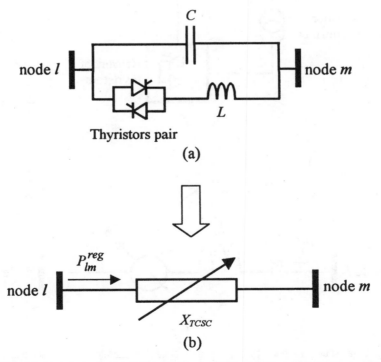

Fig. 4.2 TCSC. (a) structure formed by fixed capacitor and TCR; and (b) variable reactance representation.

where X_{TCSC} is the equivalent reactance of the TCSC controller which may be adjusted to regulate the transfer of active power across the TCSC, hence, P_{lm} becomes $P_{\text{lm}}^{\text{reg}}$.

4.2.3 The static phase shifter

The static phase shifter (SPS) varies the phase angles of the line end voltages with little delay. This is achieved by injecting a voltage in quadrature with the line end voltage at the sending end. This equipment may also be used to provide fast active power flow regulation (Hingorani and Gyugyi, 2000).

The power flow model of the static phase shifter presented in this chapter is based on the concept of a lossless transformer with complex taps. The control variable is a phase angle, which is adjusted using Newton's algorithm to satisfy a specified active power flow across the lossless transformer representing the static phase shifter (Fuerte-Esquivel and Acha, 1997). The schematic representation of the SPS and its equivalent circuit are shown in Figure 4.3.

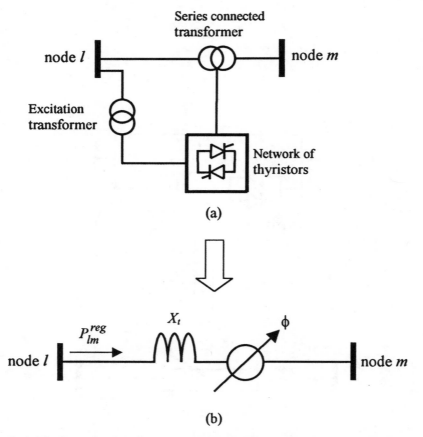

(a)

(b)

Fig. 4.3 SPS. (a) structure formed by a series transformer, an excitation transformer and a network of thyristors; and (b) variable phase angle representation.

A phase shifting controller with the complex phase angle relationships: $T_V = \cos\phi + j\sin\phi$ and $T_I = \cos\phi - j\sin\phi$ has the following transfer admittance matrix

$$\begin{bmatrix} I_l \\ I_m \end{bmatrix} = \frac{1}{X_t} \begin{bmatrix} 1 & -(\cos\phi + j\sin\phi) \\ -(\cos\phi - j\sin\phi) & 1 \end{bmatrix} \begin{bmatrix} V_l \\ V_m \end{bmatrix} \tag{4.4}$$

where X_t is the leakage reactance of the series transformer and T_V and T_I are complex tap changing variables related to each other by the conjugate operation. Their magnitude is 1 and their phase angle is ϕ.

The active power transfer across the phase shifter P_{lm} is calculated using the following expression

$$P_{lm}^{\text{reg}} = \frac{|V_l||V_m|}{X_t} \cdot \sin(\theta_l - \theta_m - \phi) \tag{4.5}$$

Suitable adjustment of the phase angle ϕ enables regulation of active power P_{lm}^{reg} across the phase shifter. It should be remarked that the phase shifter achieves phase angle regulation at the expense of consuming reactive power from the network.

4.2.4 The STATCOM

The STATCOM is the static counterpart of the rotating synchronous condenser but it generates/absorbs reactive power at a faster rate because no moving parts are involved. In principle, it performs the same voltage regulation function as the SVC but in a more robust manner because unlike the SVC, its operation is not impaired by the presence of low voltages (IEEE/CIGRE, 1995). It goes on well with advanced energy storage facilities, which opens the door for a number of new applications, such as energy markets and network security (Dewinkel and Lamoree, 1993).

The schematic representation of the STATCOM and its equivalent circuit are shown in Figure 4.4. A fuller representation of the STATCOM is shown in Figure 1.10.

The STATCOM has the ability to either generate or absorb reactive power by suitable control of the inverted voltage $|V_{vR}|\angle\theta_{vR}$ with respect to the AC voltage on the high-voltage side of the STATCOM transformer, say node l, $|V_l|\angle\theta_l$.

In an ideal STATCOM, with no active power loss involved, the following reactive power equation yields useful insight into how the reactive power exchange with the AC system is achieved

$$Q_{vR} = \frac{|V_l|^2}{X_{vR}} - \frac{|V_l||V_{vR}|}{X_{vR}} \cdot \cos(\theta_l - \theta_{vR}) = \frac{|V_l|^2 - |V_l||V_{vR}|}{X_{vR}} \tag{4.6}$$

where $\theta_{vR} = \theta_l$ for the case of a lossless STATCOM.

If $|V_l| > |V_{vR}|$ then Q_{vR} becomes positive and the STATCOM absorbs reactive power. On the other hand, Q_{vR} becomes negative if $|V_l| < |V_{vR}|$ and the STATCOM generates reactive power.

In power flow studies the STATCOM may be represented in the same way as a synchronous condenser (IEEE/CIGRE, 1995), which in most cases is the model

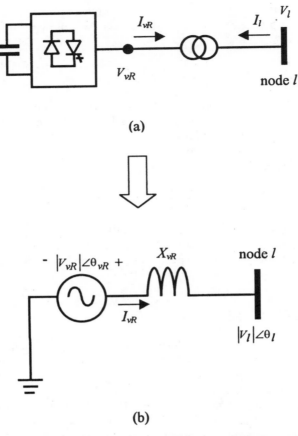

(a)

(b)

Fig. 4.4 STATCOM. (a) VSC connected to the AC network via a shunt transformer; and (b) shunt connected variable solid-state voltage source.

of a synchronous generator with zero active power generation. A more flexible STATCOM power flow model is presented in this chapter. It adjusts the voltage source magnitude and phase angle using Newton's algorithm to satisfy a specified voltage magnitude at the point of connection with the AC network

$$V_{vR} = |V_{vR}|(\cos\theta_{vR} + j\sin\theta_{vR}) \tag{4.7}$$

It should be pointed out that maximum and minimum limits will exist for $|V_{vR}|$ which are a function of the STATCOM capacitor rating. On the other hand, θ_{vR} can take any value between 0 and 2π radians but in practice it will keep close to θ_l.

4.2.5 The DVR

The DVR is a series connected VSC. The strength of this device is in low-voltage distribution applications where it is used to alleviate a range of dynamic power quality problems such as voltage sags and swells (Hingorani, 1995).

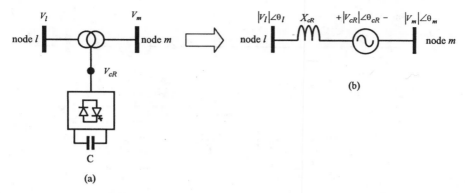

Fig. 4.5 DVR. (a) VSC connected to the AC network via a series transformer; and (b) series connected variable solid state voltage source.

For the purpose of steady state operation, the DVR performs a similar function to the SPS; it injects voltage in quadrature with one of the line end voltages in order to regulate active power flow. However, the DVR is a far more versatile controller because it does not draw reactive power from the AC system; it has its own reactive power provisions in the form of a DC capacitor. This characteristic makes the DVR capable of regulating both active and reactive power flow within the limits imposed by its rating. It may perform the role of a phase shifter and a variable series impedance compensator. The schematic representation of the DVR and its equivalent circuit are shown in Figure 4.5.

The DVR power flow model presented in this chapter is based on the concept of a series connected voltage source

$$V_{cR} = |V_{cR}|(\cos \theta_{cR} + j \sin \theta_{cR}) \tag{4.8}$$

The magnitude and phase angle of the DVR model are adjusted using Newton's algorithm to satisfy a specified active and reactive power flow across the DVR. Similarly to the STATCOM, maximum and minimum limits will exist for the voltage magnitude $|V_{cR}|$, which are a function of the DVR capacitor rating. On the other hand, the voltage phase angle θ_{cR} can take any value between 0 and 2π radians.

4.2.6 The UPFC

The UPFC may be seen to consist of one STATCOM and one DVR sharing a common capacitor on their DC side and a unified control system. The UPFC allows simultaneous control of active power flow, reactive power flow and voltage magnitude at the UPFC terminals. Alternatively, the controller may be set to control one or more of these parameters in any combination or to control none of them. A simpler schematic representation of the UPFC shown in Figure 1.12 is given in Figure 4.6 together with its equivalent circuit (Fuerte-Esquivel et al., 2000).

The active power demanded by the series converter is drawn by the shunt converter from the AC network and supplied via the DC link. The inverted voltage of the series converter is added to the nodal voltage, at say node l, to boost the nodal voltage at node m. The voltage magnitude of the inverted voltage $|V_{cR}|$ provides voltage

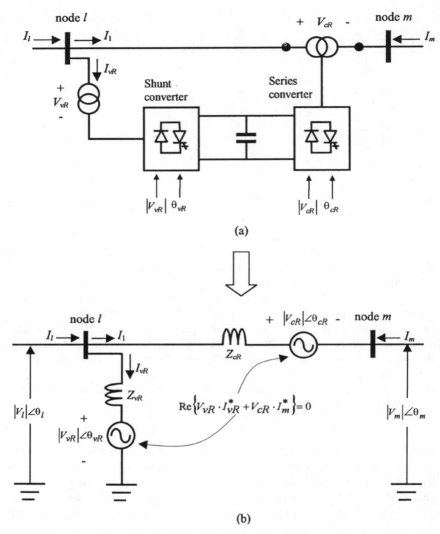

Fig. 4.6 UPFC. (a) back-to-back VSCs with one VSC connected to the AC network via a shunt transformer and a second VSC connected to the AC network via a series transformer; and (b) equivalent circuit based on solid-state voltage sources.

regulation and the phase angle θ_{cR} determines the mode of power flow control (Hingorani and Gyugyi, 2000):

1. If θ_{cR} is in phase with the voltage phase angle θ_l, it regulates no active power flow.
2. If θ_{cR} is in quadrature with the voltage phase angle θ_l, it controls active power flow performing as a phase shifter but drawing no reactive power from the AC network.

3. If θ_{cR} is in quadrature with the current angle then it controls active power flow performing as a variable series impedance compensator.
4. At any other value of θ_{cR}, it performs as a combination of a phase shifter and a variable series impedance compensator. This is in addition to being a voltage regulator by suitable control of $|V_{cR}|$.

In addition to providing a supporting role in the active power exchange that takes place between the series converter and the AC system, the shunt converter may also generate or absorb reactive power in order to provide independent voltage magnitude regulation at its point of connection with the AC system.

The UPFC power flow model presented in this chapter uses the equivalent circuit shown in Figure 4.6(b), which consists of a shunt connected voltage source, a series connected voltage source and an active power constraint equation which links the two voltage sources

$$V_{vR} = |V_{vR}|(\cos\theta_{vR} + j\sin\theta_{vR}) \tag{4.9}$$

$$V_{cR} = |V_{cR}|(\cos\theta_{cR} + j\sin\theta_{cR}) \tag{4.10}$$

$$\text{Re}\{-V_{vR}I_{vR}^* + V_{cR}I_m^*\} = 0 \tag{4.11}$$

These equations are adjusted in a coordinated fashion using Newton's algorithm to satisfy the specified control requirements. Similarly to the shunt and series voltage sources used to represent the STATCOM and the DVR, respectively, the voltage sources used in the UPFC application would also have limits. For the shunt converter the voltage magnitude and phase angle limits are: $V_{vR\min} \leq V_{vR} \leq V_{vR\max}$ and $0 \leq \theta_{vR} \leq 2\pi$. The corresponding limits for the series converter are: $V_{cR\min} \leq V_{cR} \leq V_{cR\max}$ and $0 \leq \theta_{cR} \leq 2\pi$.

4.2.7 The HVDC-Light

The HVDC-Light comprises two VSCs, one operating as a rectifier and the other as an inverter. The two converters are connected either back-to-back or joined together by a DC cable, depending on the application. Its main function is to transmit constant DC power from the rectifier to the inverter station, with high controllability. The schematic representation of the HVDC light and its equivalent circuit are shown in Figure 4.7. A fuller schematic representation is shown in Figure 1.13.

One VSC controls DC voltage and the other the transmission of active power through the DC link. Assuming lossless converters, the active power flow entering the DC system must equal the active power reaching the AC system at the inverter end minus the transmission losses in the DC cable. During normal operation, both converters have independent reactive power control.

The power flow model for the back-to-back HVDC light may be based on the use of one voltage source for the rectifier and one voltage source for the inverter linked together by a constrained power equation

$$V_{vR1} = |V_{vR1}|(\cos\theta_{vR1} + j\sin\theta_{vR1}) \tag{4.12}$$

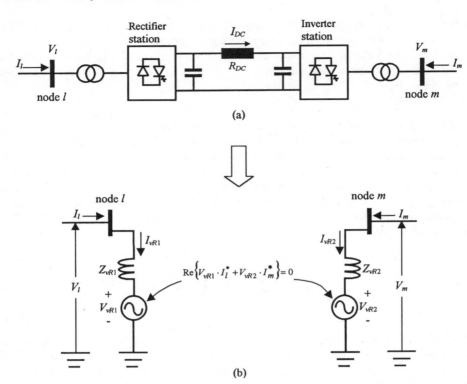

Fig. 4.7 HVDC Light. (a) the VSC at the sending end performs the role of rectifier and the VSC at the receiving end performs the role of inverter; and (b) equivalent circuit.

$$V_{vR2} = |V_{vR2}|(\cos\theta_{vR2} + j\sin\theta_{vR2}) \tag{4.13}$$

$$\mathrm{Re}\{-V_{vR1}I^* + V_{vR2}I_m^*\} = 0 \tag{4.14}$$

In this application the two shunt voltage sources used to represent the two converters have the following voltage magnitudes and phase angles limits: $V_{vR\min1} \leq V_{vR1} \leq V_{vR\max1}; 0 \leq \theta_{vR1} \leq 2\pi; V_{vR\min2} \leq V_{vR2} \leq V_{vR\max2}$ and $0 \leq \theta_{vR2} \leq 2\pi$.

4.3 Fundamental network equations

4.3.1 Nodal admittances

Nodal analysis is a tool of fundamental importance in power systems calculations. The nodal matrix equation of an AC electrical circuit may be determined by combining Ohm's law and Kirchhoff's current law.

The following relationships exist in an electrical branch of impedance Z_k connected between nodes l and m

$$V_l - V_m = Z_k I_k \qquad \Rightarrow \qquad I_k = \frac{V_l - V_m}{Z_k} = Y_k \Delta V \tag{4.15}$$

where $\Delta V = V_l - V_m$ and $Y_k = \frac{1}{Z_k}$.

The injected nodal current at node i may be expressed as a function of the currents entering and leaving the node through the q branches connected to the node

$$I_i = \sum_{k=1}^{q} I_k \qquad (4.16)$$

where I_i is the nodal current at node i and branch k is connected to node i. Also, I_k is the current in branch k.

Combining equations (4.15) and (4.16) leads to the key equation used in nodal analysis

$$I_i = \sum_{k=1}^{q} Y_k(V_l - V_m) \qquad (4.17)$$

which can also be expressed in matrix form for the case of n nodes

$$\begin{bmatrix} I_1 \\ I_2 \\ I_3 \\ \vdots \\ I_n \end{bmatrix} = \begin{bmatrix} Y_{11} & Y_{12} & Y_{13} & \cdots & Y_{1n} \\ Y_{21} & Y_{22} & Y_{23} & \cdots & Y_{2n} \\ Y_{31} & Y_{32} & Y_{33} & \cdots & Y_{3n} \\ \vdots & \vdots & \vdots & \ddots & \vdots \\ Y_{n1} & Y_{n2} & Y_{n3} & \cdots & Y_{nn} \end{bmatrix} \begin{bmatrix} V_1 \\ V_2 \\ V_3 \\ \vdots \\ V_n \end{bmatrix} \qquad (4.18)$$

where $i = 1, 2, 3, \cdots n$.

4.3.2 Numerical example 1

The theory presented above is used to determine the nodal matrix equation for the circuit in Figure 4.8. This circuit consists of six branches and four nodes. The branches are numbered 1 to 6 and the nodes are a, b, c and d. All branches have admittance values Y, with the values of the diagonal elements being negative.

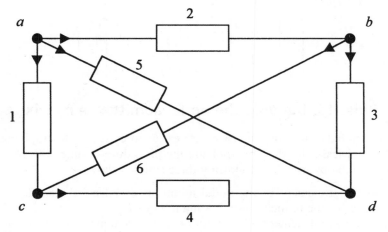

Fig. 4.8 Lattice circuit.

The arrows show the directions of the currents assumed for this example. It should be remarked that these currents serve the purpose of the nodal analysis and may not correspond to physical currents.

The following conventions are used in nodal analysis:

- currents leaving the node are taken to be positive
- currents entering the node are taken to be negative.

Using Ohm's law

$$\begin{aligned}
I_1 &= Y(V_a - V_c) \\
I_2 &= Y(V_a - V_b) \\
I_3 &= Y(V_b - V_d) \\
I_4 &= Y(V_c - V_d) \\
I_5 &= -Y(V_a - V_d) \\
I_6 &= -Y(V_b - V_c)
\end{aligned} \tag{4.19}$$

and from Kirchhoff's current law

$$\begin{aligned}
+I_2 + I_1 + I_5 &= I_a \\
-I_2 + I_6 + I_3 &= I_b \\
-I_1 - I_6 + I_4 &= I_c \\
-I_5 - I_3 - I_4 &= I_d
\end{aligned} \tag{4.20}$$

Substituting equations (4.19) into equations (4.20) gives

$$\begin{aligned}
+YV_a - YV_b - YV_c + YV_d &= I_a \\
-YV_a + YV_b + YV_c - YV_d &= I_b \\
-YV_a + YV_b + YV_c - YV_d &= I_c \\
+YV_a - YV_b - YV_c + YV_d &= I_d
\end{aligned} \tag{4.21}$$

or, in matrix form

$$\begin{bmatrix} I_a \\ I_b \\ I_c \\ I_d \end{bmatrix} = \begin{bmatrix} Y & -Y & -Y & Y \\ -Y & Y & Y & -Y \\ -Y & Y & Y & -Y \\ Y & -Y & -Y & Y \end{bmatrix} \begin{bmatrix} V_a \\ V_b \\ V_c \\ V_d \end{bmatrix} \tag{4.22}$$

4.3.3 Rules for building the nodal admittance matrix

In practice, nodal admittance matrices are easier to construct by applying a set of available empirical rules than by applying the procedure outlined above. The same result is obtained by using the following three simple rules:

1. Each diagonal element in the nodal admittance matrix, Y_{ii}, is the sum of the admittances of the branches terminating in node i.
2. Each off-diagonal element of the nodal admittance matrix, Y_{ij}, is the negative of the branch admittance connected between nodes i and j.

3. If no direct connection exists between nodes i and j then the corresponding off-diagonal element in the nodal admittance matrix will have a zero entry.

Applying this set of rules to form the nodal admittance matrix of the circuit of Figure 4.8 produces the following nodal admittance matrix

$$\mathbf{Y} = \begin{bmatrix} (Y+Y-Y) & -Y & -Y & Y \\ -Y & (Y+Y-Y) & Y & -Y \\ -Y & Y & (Y+Y-Y) & -Y \\ Y & -Y & -Y & (Y+Y-Y) \end{bmatrix} = \begin{bmatrix} Y & -Y & -Y & Y \\ -Y & Y & Y & -Y \\ -Y & Y & Y & -Y \\ Y & -Y & -Y & Y \end{bmatrix}$$

$$(4.23)$$

which is identical to the result generated in Example 1.

This result illustrates the simplicity and efficiency with which nodal admittance matrices can be generated. This is particularly useful in the study of large-scale systems.

It should be pointed out that the inverse of nodal admittance matrix equation (4.23) does not exist, i.e. the matrix is singular. The reason is that no reference node has been selected in the electrical circuit of Figure 4.8. In most practical cases a reference node exists and the nodal admittance matrix can be inverted. In electrical power networks, the reference node is the ground, which in power systems analysis is taken to be at zero potential.

4.3.4 Nodal impedances

If the nodal admittance matrix of the network can be inverted then the resulting matrix is known as the nodal impedance matrix. In an n-node network, the nodal impedance matrix equation takes the following form

$$\begin{bmatrix} V_1 \\ V_2 \\ V_3 \\ \vdots \\ V_n \end{bmatrix} = \begin{bmatrix} Z_{11} & Z_{12} & Z_{13} & \cdots & Z_{1n} \\ Z_{21} & Z_{22} & Z_{23} & \cdots & Z_{2n} \\ Z_{31} & Z_{32} & Z_{33} & \cdots & Z_{3n} \\ \vdots & \vdots & \vdots & \ddots & \vdots \\ Z_{n1} & Z_{n2} & Z_{n3} & \cdots & Z_{nn} \end{bmatrix} \begin{bmatrix} I_1 \\ I_2 \\ I_3 \\ \vdots \\ I_n \end{bmatrix}$$

$$(4.24)$$

There are several well-established ways to determine the nodal impedance matrix, some of which are mentioned below:

- By inverting the nodal admittance matrix (Shipley, 1976), i.e.

$$\begin{bmatrix} Y_{11} & Y_{12} & Y_{13} & \cdots & Y_{1n} \\ Y_{21} & Y_{22} & Y_{23} & \cdots & Y_{2n} \\ Y_{31} & Y_{32} & Y_{33} & \cdots & Y_{3n} \\ \vdots & \vdots & \vdots & \ddots & \vdots \\ Y_{n1} & Y_{n2} & Y_{n3} & \cdots & Y_{nn} \end{bmatrix}^{-1} = \begin{bmatrix} Z_{11} & Z_{12} & Z_{13} & \cdots & Z_{1n} \\ Z_{21} & Z_{22} & Z_{23} & \cdots & Z_{2n} \\ Z_{31} & Z_{32} & Z_{33} & \cdots & Z_{3n} \\ \vdots & \vdots & \vdots & \ddots & \vdots \\ Z_{n1} & Z_{n2} & Z_{n3} & \cdots & Z_{nn} \end{bmatrix}$$

$$(4.25)$$

In most practical situations, the resulting impedance matrix contains no zero elements regardless of the degree of sparsity of the admittance matrix, i.e. ratio of zero to non-zero elements. Therefore, this approach is only useful for small networks or large networks which are fully interconnected and therefore have a low degree of sparsity. In such cases there is no advantage gained by using sparsity techniques.

- By factorizing the nodal admittance matrix using sparsity techniques (Zollenkopf, 1970). In this case, the nodal admittance matrix is not inverted explicitly and the resulting vector factors will contain almost the same degree of sparsity as the original matrix. Sparsity techniques allow the solution of very large-scale networks with minimum computational effort.
- By directly building up the impedance matrix (Brown, 1975). A set of rules exists to form the nodal impedance matrix but they are not as simple as the rules used to form the nodal admittance matrix. It outperforms the method of explicit inversion in terms of calculation speed but the resulting impedance matrix is also full. This approach is not competitive with respect to sparse factorization techniques.

4.3.5　Numerical example 2

The network impedance shown in Figure 4.9 is energized at node one with a current source of 1 p.u. The branch admittances all have values of 1 p.u. Let us determine the nodal voltages in the network.

The nodal admittance matrix for this circuit is formed using the empirical rules given above.

$$
\begin{bmatrix} I_1 \\ I_2 \\ I_3 \\ I_0 \end{bmatrix} = \begin{bmatrix} (1+1) & -1 & 0 & -1 \\ -1 & (1+1+1) & -1 & -1 \\ 0 & -1 & (1+1) & -1 \\ -1 & -1 & -1 & (1+1+1) \end{bmatrix} \begin{bmatrix} V_1 \\ V_2 \\ V_3 \\ V_0 \end{bmatrix} = \begin{bmatrix} 2 & -1 & 0 & -1 \\ -1 & 3 & -1 & -1 \\ 0 & -1 & 2 & -1 \\ -1 & -1 & -1 & 3 \end{bmatrix} \begin{bmatrix} V_1 \\ V_2 \\ V_3 \\ V_0 \end{bmatrix}
$$

$$(4.26)$$

The nodal admittance matrix is singular and, hence, the nodal impedance matrix does not exist. However, the singularity can be removed by choosing a reference node. In power systems analysis the ground node (node 0) is normally selected as the reference node because the voltage at this node has a value of zero. The row and column corresponding to node 0 are removed from the nodal matrix equation and in this example the solution for the nodal voltages is carried out via a matrix inversion operation.

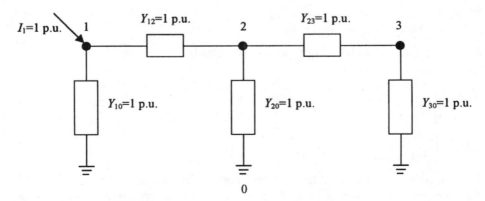

Fig. 4.9 Network of admittances.

$$\begin{bmatrix} V_1 \\ V_2 \\ V_3 \end{bmatrix} = \begin{bmatrix} 2 & -1 & 0 \\ -1 & 3 & -1 \\ 0 & -1 & 2 \end{bmatrix}^{-1} \begin{bmatrix} 1 \\ 0 \\ 0 \end{bmatrix} = \frac{1}{8} \begin{bmatrix} 5 & 2 & 1 \\ 2 & 4 & 2 \\ 1 & 2 & 5 \end{bmatrix} \begin{bmatrix} 1 \\ 0 \\ 0 \end{bmatrix} = \frac{1}{8} \begin{bmatrix} 5 \\ 2 \\ 1 \end{bmatrix} \qquad (4.27)$$

4.4 The power flow theory

4.4.1 Basic concepts

From the mathematical modelling point of view, the power flow exercise consists in solving the set of non-linear, algebraic equations which describe the power network under steady state conditions. Over the years, several approaches have been put forward for the solution of the power flow equations (Freris and Sasson, 1968; Stott, 1974). Early approaches were based on numerical techniques of the Gauss–Seidel type, which exhibit poor convergence characteristic when applied to the solution of networks of realistic size. They have been superseded by numerical techniques of the Newton–Raphson type, owing to their very strong convergence characteristic.

In conventional power flow studies, nodes can be of three different types:

1. *Voltage controlled node.* If sufficient reactive power is available at the node, the nodal voltage magnitude may be regulated and the node will be of the voltage controlled type. Synchronous generators and SVCs may be used to provide voltage regulation. In the case of generators the amount of active power which the generator has been scheduled to meet is specified whereas in the case of SVCs the active power is specified to be zero. The unknown variables are the nodal voltage phase angle and the net reactive power. These nodes are also known as PV type, where P relates to active power and V relates to voltage magnitude.
2. *Load node.* If no generation facilities exist at the node, this will be of the load type. For these kinds of nodes the net active and reactive powers are specified and the nodal voltage magnitude and phase angle are unknown variables. These nodes are also known as PQ type. In this case P and Q relate to active and reactive power, respectively. If neither generation nor demand exist in a particular node, it will be treated as a PQ type node with zero power injection. Practical design considerations impose limits in the amount of reactive power that a generator can either supply or absorb. If such limits are violated, the generator will be unable to regulate the nodal voltage magnitude. To represent this practical operational condition in the power flow algorithm, the node will change from PV to PQ type.
3. *Slack node.* The third kind of node in a power flow study is the Slack node. In conventional power flow studies one node is specified to be the Slack node. The need for a Slack node arises from the fact that both the active and reactive losses in the power network are not known prior to the power flow solution. The generator connected to the Slack node will generate enough power to meet the transmission losses and to pick up any demand surplus which the other generators in the network might not have been able to meet. To a certain extent the specification of the Slack node is arbitrary, as long as there is sufficient generation available in that node, or as long as such a node is a grid supply point. In this kind

of node the voltage magnitude and phase angle are known variables, whilst the active and reactive powers are the unknown variables.

4.4.2 Conventional power plant representation

Alternating current power transmission networks are designed and operated in a three-phase manner. However, for the purpose of conventional power flow studies, a perfect geometric balance between all three phases of the power network is assumed to exist. In most cases this is a reasonable assumption, and allows the analysis to be carried out on a per-phase basis, using only the positive sequence parameters of the power plant components. More realistic, though more time consuming solutions may be achieved by means of three-phase power flow studies.

The plant components of the electrical power network normally represented in power flow studies are generators, transformers, transmission lines, loads and passive shunt and series compensation. Substation busbars are represented as buses, i.e. nodal points in the power network. Nodal transfer admittance representations are used for transmission lines and transformers whereas generators and loads are represented by sources/sinks of active and reactive power.

A generic node, say node l, including generation, load, transmission lines and active and reactive power flows is shown in Figure 4.10. In this figure, the generator injects active and reactive powers into node l whereas the load draws active and reactive powers from the node. The figure also indicates that active and reactive powers flow from node l to node k, active and reactive powers flow from node n to node l, active power flows from node l to node m and reactive power flows from node m to node l.

The nominal π-circuit shown in Figure 4.11 is used to derive the transfer admittance matrix of the transmission line model used in fundamental frequency studies.

$$
\begin{bmatrix} I_l \\ I_m \end{bmatrix} = \begin{bmatrix} \frac{1}{R+jX_l} + \frac{jB_c}{2} & -\frac{1}{R+jX_l} \\ -\frac{1}{R+jX_l} & \frac{1}{R+jX_l} + \frac{jB_c}{2} \end{bmatrix} \begin{bmatrix} V_l \\ V_m \end{bmatrix} \tag{4.28}
$$

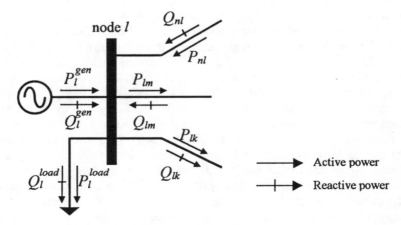

Fig. 4.10 Generic node of the electrical power network.

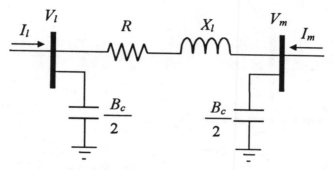

Fig. 4.11 Nominal π representation of the transmission line.

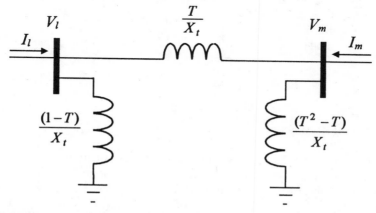

Fig. 4.12 Circuit representation of tap-changing transformer.

In power flow studies, the transformer is normally represented only by its leakage reactance X_t, i.e. the resistance is neglected. The π-circuit shown in Figure 4.12 is used to derive the transfer admittance of a transformer with off-nominal tap setting T:1.

$$\begin{bmatrix} I_l \\ I_m \end{bmatrix} = \begin{bmatrix} \frac{1}{jX_t} & -\frac{T}{jX_t} \\ -\frac{T}{jX_t} & \frac{T^2}{jX_t} \end{bmatrix} \begin{bmatrix} V_l \\ V_m \end{bmatrix} \tag{4.29}$$

Series compensation is represented by a capacitive reactance X_c connected between nodes l and m, as shown in Figure 4.13. The transfer admittance of the series capacitor is,

$$\begin{bmatrix} I_l \\ I_m \end{bmatrix} = \begin{bmatrix} -\frac{1}{jX_c} & \frac{1}{jX_c} \\ \frac{1}{jX_c} & -\frac{1}{jX_c} \end{bmatrix} \begin{bmatrix} V_l \\ V_m \end{bmatrix} \tag{4.30}$$

By way of example, the nodal admittance matrix of the three-node network shown in Figure 4.14 is given as

$$\begin{bmatrix} I_1 \\ I_2 \\ I_3 \end{bmatrix} = \begin{bmatrix} \frac{1}{jX_t} & -\frac{T}{jX_t} & 0 \\ -\frac{T}{jX_t} & \frac{T^2}{jX_t} + \frac{1}{R+jX_l} + \frac{jB_c}{2} & -\frac{1}{R+jX_l} \\ 0 & -\frac{1}{R+jX_l} & \frac{1}{R+jX_l} + \frac{jB_c}{2} - \frac{1}{jX_c} \end{bmatrix} \begin{bmatrix} V_1 \\ V_2 \\ V_3 \end{bmatrix} \tag{4.31}$$

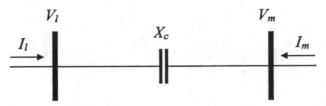

Fig. 4.13 Representation of series capacitor.

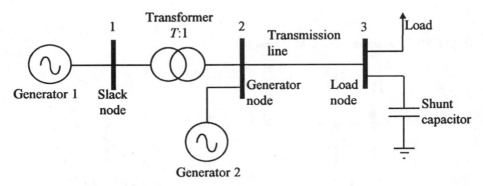

Fig. 4.14 A three-node test system.

It should be mentioned that in power flow studies the contribution of generators and loads is made through the vector of nodal currents as opposed to the nodal admittance matrix. In this example, the admittance elements in equation (4.29) were placed in locations $(1, 1)$, $(1, 2)$, $(2, 1)$ and $(2, 2)$ of the matrix in equation (4.31) since the transformer is connected between nodes one and two of the network. Similarly, the admittances in equation (4.28) were placed in locations $(2, 2)$, $(2, 3)$, $(3, 2)$ and $(3, 3)$ since the transmission line is connected between nodes 2 and 3. The contribution of the shunt capacitor is only in location $(3, 3)$. It should be noted that zero entries exist in locations $(1, 3)$ and $(3, 1)$ since there is no transmission element directly linking nodes one and three in this network.

4.4.3 Nodal impedance based power flow method

Power flow solutions may be achieved quite simply by using equation (4.18), which is the nodal admittance matrix equation of the network. The simplest case corresponds to a power network where only one generator exists in the system. By definition, this would be the Slack generator and the voltage magnitude and phase angle become known at its point of connection, say node one,

$$
\begin{bmatrix} I_1 \\ I_2 \\ I_3 \\ \vdots \\ I_n \end{bmatrix} = \begin{bmatrix} Y_{11} & Y_{12} & Y_{13} & \cdots & Y_{1n} \\ Y_{21} & Y_{22} & Y_{23} & \cdots & Y_{2n} \\ Y_{31} & Y_{32} & Y_{33} & \cdots & Y_{3n} \\ \vdots & \vdots & \vdots & \ddots & \vdots \\ Y_{n1} & Y_{n2} & Y_{n3} & \cdots & Y_{nn} \end{bmatrix} \begin{bmatrix} V_1 \\ V_2 \\ V_3 \\ \vdots \\ V_n \end{bmatrix} \tag{4.32}
$$

This equation may be partitioned as follows

$$[I_1] = [Y_{11}][V_1] + [Y_{12} \ Y_{13} \cdots Y_{1n}] \begin{bmatrix} V_2 \\ V_3 \\ \vdots \\ V_n \end{bmatrix} \tag{4.33}$$

$$\begin{bmatrix} I_2 \\ I_3 \\ \vdots \\ I_n \end{bmatrix} = \begin{bmatrix} Y_{21} \\ Y_{31} \\ \vdots \\ Y_{n1} \end{bmatrix} [V_1] + \begin{bmatrix} Y_{22} & Y_{23} & \cdots & Y_{2n} \\ Y_{32} & Y_{33} & \cdots & Y_{3n} \\ \vdots & \vdots & \ddots & \vdots \\ Y_{n2} & Y_{n3} & \cdots & Y_{nn} \end{bmatrix} \begin{bmatrix} V_2 \\ V_3 \\ \vdots \\ V_n \end{bmatrix} \tag{4.34}$$

Equation (4.34), in rearranged form, is used to find the solution for the unknown $n - 1$ nodal complex voltages by iteration

$$\begin{bmatrix} V_2 \\ V_3 \\ \vdots \\ V_n \end{bmatrix}^{(r+1)} = \begin{bmatrix} Z_{22} & Z_{23} & \cdots & Z_{2n} \\ Z_{32} & Z_{33} & \cdots & Z_{3n} \\ \vdots & \vdots & \ddots & \vdots \\ Z_{n2} & Z_{n3} & \cdots & Z_{nn} \end{bmatrix} \left\{ \begin{bmatrix} I_2 \\ I_3 \\ \vdots \\ I_n \end{bmatrix}^{(r)} - \begin{bmatrix} Y_{21} \\ Y_{31} \\ \vdots \\ Y_{n1} \end{bmatrix} [V_1] \right\} \tag{4.35}$$

where (r) is an iteration counter and V_1 is the complex voltage at the Slack node. The voltage phase angle at this node is normally specified to be 0 and provides a reference for the remaining $n - 1$ voltage phase angles in the network. The voltage magnitude is also specified at this node.

The vector of complex current injections is obtained from the active and reactive powers consumed by the $n - 1$ loads and voltage information calculated at the previous iteration

$$\begin{bmatrix} I_2 \\ I_3 \\ \vdots \\ I_n \end{bmatrix}^{(r)} = \begin{bmatrix} -(P_2^{\text{load}} - jQ_2^{\text{load}})/V_2^{*(r)} \\ -(P_3^{\text{load}} - jQ_3^{\text{load}})/V_3^{*(r)} \\ \vdots \\ -(P_n^{\text{load}} - jQ_n^{\text{load}})/V_n^{*(r)} \end{bmatrix} \tag{4.36}$$

The voltages $V_2, \ldots V_n$ are not known at the beginning and initial estimates are given to these nodes to start the iterative process. It should be noted that the current expressions in equation (4.36) are derived from the complex power equation, i.e. $S = VI^*$, and that the negative sign outside the parentheses is due to the fact that the loads consume power. The symbol $*$ is used to denote the conjugate complex operation.

The convergence characteristic of equation (4.35) is reasonably good for small and medium size systems. Although limited to networks containing only one generator, the method has found application in industrial systems where the Slack node is the electricity company's infeed point to the plant. Equation (4.35) may also be modified to include voltage-controlled nodes (Stagg and El-Abiad, 1968) but it has been found that its convergence characteristic deteriorates rapidly with the number of voltage-controlled nodes in the network. In spite of its simplicity and intuitive appeal, this has prevented its use in most practical applications. To overcome this limitation, the Newton–Raphson algorithm and derived formulations have been used instead (Tinney and Hart, 1967; Peterson and Scott-Meyer, 1971).

The issue of convergence has become even more critical today, with the wide range of power systems controllers that need inclusion in power flow computer algorithms (Fuerte-Esquivel, 1997; Ambriz-Perez, 1998). As outlined in Section 4.2, the new controllers regulate not just voltage magnitude but also voltage phase angle, imped-ance magnitude and active and reactive power flow. It is unlikely that the nodal impedance based method would be able to cope with the very severe demands imposed by the models of the new controllers on the power flow algorithms. Inten-sive research work has shown the Newton–Raphson algorithm to be the most reliable vehicle for solving FACTS upgraded networks (Acha et al., 2000; Ambriz-Perez et al., 2000; Fuerte-Esquivel et al., 2000), with other formulations derived from the Newton–Raphson method becoming viable but less desirable alternatives (Acha, 1993; Noroozian and Andersson, 1993).

4.4.4 Newton–Raphson power flow method

The equation describing the complex power injection at node l is the starting point for deriving nodal active and reactive power flow equations suitable for the Newton–Raphson power flow Algorithm (Tinney and Hart, 1967)

$$S_l = P_l + jQ_l = V_l I_l^* \tag{4.37}$$

where S_l is the complex power injection at node l,
  P_l is the active power injection at node l,
  Q_l is the reactive power injection at node l,
  V_l is the complex voltage at node l and
  I_l is the complex current injection at node l.
  The injected current I_l may be expressed as a function of the currents flowing in the n branches connected to node l,

$$I_l = \sum_{m=1}^{n} Y_{lm} V_m \tag{4.38}$$

where $Y_{lm} = G_{lm} + jB_{lm}$ and Y_{lm}, G_{lm} and B_{lm} are the admittance, conductance and susceptance of branch l–m, respectively.

Substitution of equation (4.38) into equation (4.37) gives the following inter-mediate result

$$P_l + jQ_l = V_l \sum_{m=1}^{n} Y_{lm}^* V_m^* \tag{4.39}$$

Expressions for the active and reactive powers are obtained by representing the complex voltages in polar form, $V_l = |V_l|e^{j\theta_l}$ and $V_m = |V_m|e^{j\theta_m}$

$$P_l + jQ_l = |V_l| \sum_{m=1}^{n} |V_m|(G_{lm} - jB_{lm})e^{j(\theta_l - \theta_m)} \tag{4.40}$$

$$P_l + jQ_l = |V_l| \sum_{m=1}^{n} |V_m|(G_{lm} - jB_{lm})\{\cos(\theta_l - \theta_m) + j\sin(\theta_l - \theta_m)\} \tag{4.41}$$

$$P_l = |V_l| \sum_{m=1}^{n} |V_m| \{G_{lm} \cos(\theta_l - \theta_m) + B_{lm} \sin(\theta_l - \theta_m) \qquad (4.42)$$

$$Q_l = |V_l| \sum_{m=1}^{n} |V_m| \{G_{lm} \sin(\theta_l - \theta_m) - B_{lm} \cos(\theta_l - \theta_m) \qquad (4.43)$$

where $|V_l|$ and $|V_m|$ are the nodal voltage magnitudes at nodes l and m and θ_l and θ_m are the nodal voltage phase angles at nodes l and m.

These equations provide a convenient device for assessing the steady state behaviour of the power network. The equations are non-linear and their solution is reached by iteration. Two of the variables are specified while the remaining two variables are determined by calculation to a specified accuracy. In PQ type nodes two equations are required since the voltage magnitude and phase angle $|V_l|$ and θ_l are not known. The active and reactive powers P_l and Q_l are specified. In PV type nodes one equation is required since only the voltage phase angle θ_l is unknown. The active power P_l and voltage magnitude $|V_l|$ are specified. For the case of the Slack node both the voltage magnitude and phase angle $|V_l|$ and θ_l are specified, as opposed to being determined by iteration. Accordingly, no equations are required for this node during the iterative step.

Equations (4.42) and (4.43) can be solved efficiently using the Newton–Raphson method. It requires a set of linearized equations to be formed expressing the relationship between changes in active and reactive powers and changes in nodal voltage magnitudes and phase angles. Under the assumption that node one is the Slack node, the linearized relationship takes the following form for an n-node network

$$
\begin{bmatrix} \Delta P_2 \\ \Delta P_3 \\ \vdots \\ \Delta P_n \\ \hline \Delta Q_2 \\ \Delta Q_3 \\ \vdots \\ \Delta Q_n \end{bmatrix}^{(r)}
=
\begin{bmatrix}
\frac{\partial P_2}{\partial \theta_2} & \frac{\partial P_2}{\partial \theta_3} & \cdots & \frac{\partial P_2}{\partial \theta_n} & \frac{\partial P_2}{\partial |V_2|} & \frac{\partial P_2}{\partial |V_3|} & \cdots & \frac{\partial P_2}{\partial |V_n|} \\
\frac{\partial P_3}{\partial \theta_2} & \frac{\partial P_3}{\partial \theta_3} & \cdots & \frac{\partial P_3}{\partial \theta_n} & \frac{\partial P_3}{\partial |V_2|} & \frac{\partial P_3}{\partial |V_3|} & \cdots & \frac{\partial P_3}{\partial |V_n|} \\
\vdots & \vdots & \ddots & \vdots & \vdots & \vdots & \ddots & \vdots \\
\frac{\partial P_n}{\partial \theta_2} & \frac{\partial P_n}{\partial \theta_3} & \cdots & \frac{\partial P_n}{\partial \theta_n} & \frac{\partial P_n}{\partial |V_2|} & \frac{\partial P_n}{\partial |V_3|} & \cdots & \frac{\partial P_n}{\partial |V_n|} \\
\hline
\frac{\partial Q_2}{\partial \theta_2} & \frac{\partial Q_2}{\partial \theta_3} & \cdots & \frac{\partial Q_2}{\partial \theta_n} & \frac{\partial Q_2}{\partial |V_2|} & \frac{\partial Q_2}{\partial |V_3|} & \cdots & \frac{\partial Q_2}{\partial |V_n|} \\
\frac{\partial Q_3}{\partial \theta_2} & \frac{\partial Q_3}{\partial \theta_3} & \cdots & \frac{\partial Q_3}{\partial \theta_n} & \frac{\partial Q_3}{\partial |V_2|} & \frac{\partial Q_3}{\partial |V_3|} & \cdots & \frac{\partial Q_3}{\partial |V_n|} \\
\vdots & \vdots & \ddots & \vdots & \vdots & \vdots & \ddots & \vdots \\
\frac{\partial Q_n}{\partial \theta_2} & \frac{\partial Q_n}{\partial \theta_3} & \cdots & \frac{\partial Q_n}{\partial \theta_n} & \frac{\partial Q_n}{\partial |V_2|} & \frac{\partial Q_n}{\partial |V_3|} & \cdots & \frac{\partial Q_n}{\partial |V_n|}
\end{bmatrix}^{(r)}
\begin{bmatrix} \Delta\theta_2 \\ \Delta\theta_3 \\ \vdots \\ \Delta\theta_n \\ \hline \Delta|V_2| \\ \Delta|V_3| \\ \vdots \\ \Delta|V_n| \end{bmatrix}^{(r)} \qquad (4.44)
$$

where
$\Delta P_l = P_l^{\text{net}} - P_l^{\text{calc}}$ is the active power mismatch at node l,
$\Delta Q_l = Q_l^{\text{net}} - Q_l^{\text{calc}}$ is the reactive power mismatch at node l,
P_l^{calc} and Q_l^{calc} are the calculated active and reactive powers at node l,
$P_l^{\text{net}} = P_l^{\text{gen}} - P_l^{\text{load}}$ is the net scheduled active powers at node l,
$Q_l^{\text{net}} = Q_l^{\text{gen}} - Q_l^{\text{load}}$ is the net scheduled reactive powers at node l,
P_l^{gen} and Q_l^{gen} are the active and reactive powers generated at node l,
P_l^{load} and Q_l^{load} are the active and reactive powers consumed by the load at node l,

$\Delta\theta_l$ and $\Delta|V_l|$ are the incremental changes in nodal voltage magnitude and phase angle at node l,

(r) represents the r-th iterative step and $l = 2, 3, 4, \ldots n$.

The elements of the Jacobian matrix can be found by differentiating equations (4.42) and (4.43) with respect to θ_l, θ_m, $|V_l|$ and $|V_m|$.

For the case when $l = m$:

$$\frac{\partial P_l}{\partial \theta_l} = |V_l| \sum_{m=l}^{n} |V_m|\{-G_{lm}\sin(\theta_l - \theta_m) + B_{lm}\cos(\theta_l - \theta_m)\} - |V_l|^2 B_{ll} = -Q_l - |V_l|^2 B_{ll}$$

(4.45)

$$\frac{\partial P_l}{\partial |V_l|} = \sum_{m=1}^{n} |V_m|\{G_{lm}\cos(\theta_l - \theta_m) + B_{lm}\sin(\theta_l - \theta_m)\} + |V_l|G_{ll} = \frac{P_l}{|V_l|} + |V_l|G_{ll} \quad (4.46)$$

$$\frac{\partial Q_l}{\partial \theta_l} = |V_l| \sum_{m=l}^{n} |V_m|\{G_{lm}\cos(\theta_l - \theta_m) + B_{lm}\sin(\theta_l - \theta_m)\} - |V_l|^2 G_{ll} = P_l - |V_l|^2 G_{ll}$$

(4.47)

$$\frac{\partial Q_l}{\partial |V_l|} = \sum_{m=l}^{n} |V_m|\{G_{lm}\sin(\theta_l - \theta_m) - B_{lm}\cos(\theta_l - \theta_m)\} - |V_l|B_{ll} = \frac{Q_l}{|V_l|} - |V_l|B_{ll}$$

(4.48)

For the case when $l \neq m$

$$\frac{\partial P_l}{\partial \theta_m} = |V_l||V_m|\{G_{lm}\sin(\theta_l - \theta_m) - B_{lm}\cos(\theta_l - \theta_m)\} \quad (4.49)$$

$$\frac{\partial P_l}{\partial |V_m|} = |V_l|\{G_{lm}\cos(\theta_l - \theta_m) + B_{lm}\sin(\theta_l - \theta_m)\} = -\frac{1}{|V_m|}\frac{\partial Q_l}{\partial \theta_m} \quad (4.50)$$

$$\frac{\partial Q_l}{\partial \theta_m} = -|V_l||V_m|\{G_{lm}\cos(\theta_l - \theta_m) + B_{lm}\sin(\theta_l - \theta_m)\} \quad (4.51)$$

$$\frac{\partial Q_l}{\partial |V_m|} = |V_l|\{G_{lm}\sin(\theta_l - \theta_m) - B_{lm}\cos(\theta_l - \theta_m)\} = \frac{1}{|V_m|}\frac{\partial P_l}{\partial \theta_m} \quad (4.52)$$

To start the iterative solution, initial estimates of the nodal voltage magnitudes and phase angles at all the PQ nodes and voltage phase angles at all the PV nodes are given to calculate the active and reactive power injections using equations (4.42–4.43). Since it is unlikely that the initial estimated voltages will agree with the voltages at the solution point, the calculated power injections will not agree with the known specified powers.

The mismatch power vectors may be defined as

$$\Delta \mathbf{P}^{(r)} = (\mathbf{P}^{\text{gen}} - \mathbf{P}^{\text{load}}) - \mathbf{P}^{\text{calc},(r)} = \mathbf{P}^{\text{net}} - \mathbf{P}^{\text{calc},(r)} \quad (4.53)$$

$$\Delta \mathbf{Q}^{(r)} = (\mathbf{Q}^{\text{gen}} - \mathbf{Q}^{\text{load}}) - \mathbf{Q}^{\text{calc},(r)} = \mathbf{Q}^{\text{net}} - \mathbf{Q}^{\text{calc},(r)} \quad (4.54)$$

The Jacobian elements are then calculated and the linearized equation (4.44) is solved to obtain the vectors of voltage updates

$$\boldsymbol{\theta}^{(r+1)} = \boldsymbol{\theta}^{(r)} + \Delta\boldsymbol{\theta}^{(r)} \quad (4.55)$$

$$|\mathbf{V}|^{(r+1)} = |\mathbf{V}|^{(r)} + \Delta|\mathbf{V}|^{(r)} \quad (4.56)$$

The evaluation of equations (4.42)–(4.44) and (4.53)–(4.56) are repeated in sequence until the desired change in power injection (power mismatch) ΔP and ΔQ are within a small tolerance, e.g. $\varepsilon = 10^{-12}$

As the process approaches the solution, the linearized equation (4.44) becomes more and more accurate and convergence is very rapid. Figure 4.15 gives the overall flow diagram for the power flow Newton–Raphson method.

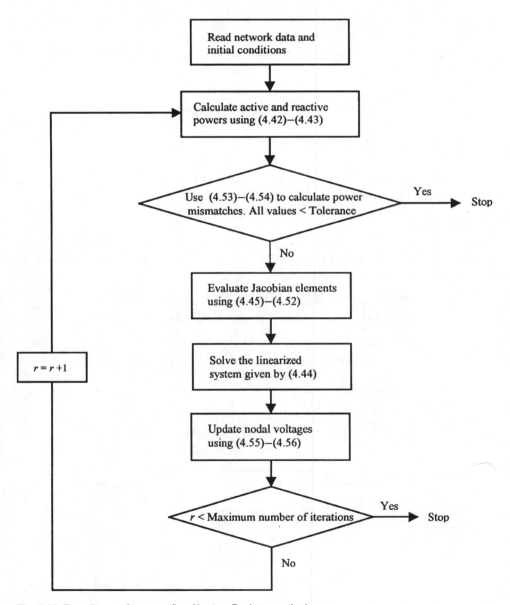

Fig. 4.15 Flow diagram for power flow Newton–Raphson method.

4.4.5 Numerical example 3

The power transmission circuit shown in Figure 4.16 consists of two nodes, one generator, one transmission line and one load. The load has a value of $1 + j0.5$ p.u. and the reactance of the transmission line is 0.1 p.u. The voltage magnitude and phase angle at the generator point (Slack node) are kept at 1 p.u. and 0 radians, respectively.

Using the Newton–Raphson power flow method, the nodal voltage magnitude and phase angle at node two will be determined using 1 p.u. voltage magnitude and zero phase angle at the load point as the initial condition.

Applying the theory presented in Section 4.3, the nodal admittance matrix is formed for this system

$$\mathbf{Y} = \mathbf{G} + j\mathbf{B} = \begin{bmatrix} -j10 & j10 \\ j10 & -j10 \end{bmatrix} \text{p.u.}$$

The net active and reactive powers are calculated

$$\mathbf{P}^{net} = \mathbf{P}^{gen} - \mathbf{P}^{load} = \begin{bmatrix} ? \\ -1 \end{bmatrix} \text{p.u.} \qquad \mathbf{Q}^{net} = \mathbf{Q}^{gen} - \mathbf{Q}^{load} = \begin{bmatrix} ? \\ -0.5 \end{bmatrix} \text{p.u.}$$

First iteration

Using the initial voltage values $|V_1| = |V_2| = 1$, $\theta_1 = \theta_2 = 0$ and the values in the nodal admittance matrix in equations (4.42) and (4.43), the following powers are calculated

$$
\begin{aligned}
P_2^{calc} &= |V_2||V_1|\{G_{21} \cos(\theta_2 - \theta_1) + B_{21} \sin(\theta_2 - \theta_1)\} \\
&\quad + |V_2||V_2|\{G_{22} \cos(\theta_2 - \theta_2) + B_{22} \sin(\theta_2 - \theta_2)\} = 0 \\
Q_2^{calc} &= |V_2||V_1|\{G_{21} \sin(\theta_2 - \theta_1) - B_{21} \cos(\theta_2 - \theta_1)\} \\
&\quad + |V_2||V_2|\{G_{22} \sin(\theta_2 - \theta_2) - B_{22} \cos(\theta_2 - \theta_2)\} = 0
\end{aligned}
\tag{4.57}
$$

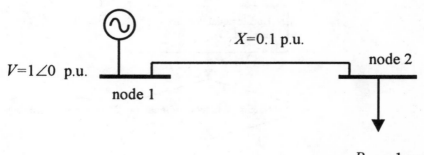

$V=1\angle 0$ p.u.

node 1

$X=0.1$ p.u.

node 2

$P_{load}=1$ p.u.
$Q_{load}=0.5$ p.u.

Fig. 4.16 A two-node system.

According to equations (4.53) and (4.54), the mismatch power equations are

$$\begin{bmatrix} \Delta P_1 \\ \Delta P_2 \end{bmatrix}^{(1)} = \begin{bmatrix} P_1^{net} \\ P_2^{net} \end{bmatrix} - \begin{bmatrix} P_1^{calc} \\ P_2^{calc} \end{bmatrix} = \begin{bmatrix} ? \\ -1 \end{bmatrix} \text{p.u.}$$

$$\begin{bmatrix} \Delta Q_1 \\ \Delta Q_2 \end{bmatrix}^{(1)} = \begin{bmatrix} Q_1^{net} \\ Q_2^{net} \end{bmatrix} - \begin{bmatrix} Q_1^{calc} \\ Q_2^{calc} \end{bmatrix} = \begin{bmatrix} ? \\ -0.5 \end{bmatrix} \text{p.u.}$$

(4.58)

The Slack node plays no role during the iterative solution. Using equations (4.45)–(4.52), and the numeric values $P_2^{calc} = 0$ and $Q_2^{calc} = 0$ calculated above, the Jacobian elements for node two are

$$\frac{\partial P_2}{\partial \theta_2} = 10 \qquad \frac{\partial P_2}{\partial |V_2|} = 0 \qquad \frac{\partial Q_2}{\partial \theta_2} = 0 \qquad \frac{\partial Q_2}{\partial |V_2|} = 10$$

The solution of the linearized system of equations is

$$\begin{bmatrix} \Delta P_2 \\ \Delta Q_2 \end{bmatrix}^{(1)} = \begin{bmatrix} 10 & 0 \\ 0 & 10 \end{bmatrix} \begin{bmatrix} \Delta \theta_2 \\ \Delta |V_2| \end{bmatrix}^{(1)} \Rightarrow \begin{bmatrix} \Delta \theta_2 \\ \Delta |V_2| \end{bmatrix}^{(1)} = \begin{bmatrix} 0.1 & 0 \\ 0 & 0.1 \end{bmatrix} \begin{bmatrix} -1 \\ -0.5 \end{bmatrix} = \begin{bmatrix} -0.1 \\ -0.05 \end{bmatrix} \quad (4.59)$$

Using equations (4.55) and (4.56) the voltage magnitude and phase angle at the end of the first iteration are

$$\begin{bmatrix} \theta_2 \\ |V_2| \end{bmatrix}^{(1)} = \begin{bmatrix} 0 \\ 1 \end{bmatrix}^{(0)} + \begin{bmatrix} -0.1 \\ -0.05 \end{bmatrix}^{(1)} = \begin{bmatrix} -0.1 \\ 0.95 \end{bmatrix} \text{p.u.} \qquad (4.60)$$

It should be noted that the voltage magnitude is in p.u. and the phase angle is in radians.

Second iteration
Using updated voltage information, i.e. $|V_1| = 1$, $|V_2| = 0.95$, $\theta_1 = 0$ and $\theta_2 = -0.1$, in equations (4.42) and (4.43), new active and reactive powers are calculated, giving the following result

$$P_2^{calc} = -0.94841 \text{ p.u.}$$

$$Q_2^{calc} = -0.4275 \text{ p.u.}$$

The mismatch power equations are

$$\begin{bmatrix} \Delta P_1 \\ \Delta P_2 \end{bmatrix}^{(2)} = \begin{bmatrix} P_1^{net} \\ P_2^{net} \end{bmatrix} - \begin{bmatrix} P_1^{calc} \\ P_2^{calc} \end{bmatrix} = \begin{bmatrix} ? \\ -1 \end{bmatrix} - \begin{bmatrix} ? \\ -0.948417 \end{bmatrix} = \begin{bmatrix} ? \\ -0.051583 \end{bmatrix} \text{p.u.}$$

$$\begin{bmatrix} \Delta Q_1 \\ \Delta Q_2 \end{bmatrix}^{(2)} = \begin{bmatrix} Q_1^{net} \\ Q_2^{net} \end{bmatrix} - \begin{bmatrix} Q_1^{calc} \\ Q_2^{calc} \end{bmatrix} = \begin{bmatrix} ? \\ -0.5 \end{bmatrix} - \begin{bmatrix} ? \\ -0.42754 \end{bmatrix} = \begin{bmatrix} ? \\ -0.07246 \end{bmatrix} \text{p.u.}$$

(4.61)

It should be noted that the power mismatches have decreased by almost one order of magnitude compared to the mismatch values obtained during the first iteration.

The Jacobian elements for node two are:

$$\frac{\partial P_2}{\partial \theta_2} = 9.45254 \qquad \frac{\partial P_2}{\partial |V_2|} = -0.998334 \qquad \frac{\partial Q_2}{\partial \theta_2} = -0.948417 \qquad \frac{\partial Q_2}{\partial |V_2|} = 8.574958$$

The solution of the linearized system of equations is

$$\begin{bmatrix} \Delta P_2 \\ \Delta Q_2 \end{bmatrix}^{(2)} = \begin{bmatrix} 9.45254 & -0.998334 \\ -0.948417 & 8.574958 \end{bmatrix} \begin{bmatrix} \Delta \theta_2 \\ \Delta |V_2| \end{bmatrix}^{(2)}$$

$$\begin{bmatrix} \Delta \theta_2 \\ \Delta |V_2| \end{bmatrix}^{(2)} = \begin{bmatrix} 0.107042 & 0.012462 \\ 0.011839 & 0.117996 \end{bmatrix} \begin{bmatrix} -0.051583 \\ -0.07246 \end{bmatrix} = \begin{bmatrix} -0.006425 \\ -0.009161 \end{bmatrix} \qquad (4.62)$$

The voltage magnitude and phase angle at node two at the end of the second iteration are

$$\begin{bmatrix} \theta_2 \\ |V_2| \end{bmatrix}^{(2)} = \begin{bmatrix} -0.1 \\ 0.95 \end{bmatrix}^{(1)} + \begin{bmatrix} -0.006425 \\ -0.009161 \end{bmatrix}^{(2)} = \begin{bmatrix} -0.106425 \\ 0.940839 \end{bmatrix} \qquad (4.63)$$

At this stage, the complex voltages at nodes one and two are

$$\begin{bmatrix} V_1 \\ V_2 \end{bmatrix}^{(2)} = \begin{bmatrix} 1 \angle 0 \\ 0.940839 \angle -0.106425 \end{bmatrix} \text{p.u.} \qquad (4.64)$$

These voltages are quite close to the actual solution. If the procedure is repeated for two more iterations then ΔP_2 and ΔQ_2 become smaller than 10^{-6}.

4.4.6 Numerical example 4

The test system shown in Figure 4.17 is used in this example (Stagg and El-Abiad, 1968). The original figure has been redrawn to accommodate the power flow results. In subsequent examples in this chapter, the system is used in modified form, to illustrate how the various FACTS controllers perform in network-wide applications.

The original test system is solved using a power flow computer program written in C + + using object-oriented programming (OOP) techniques (Fuerte-Esquivel, 1997). The power flow results are shown on Figure 4.17 and the nodal voltage magnitudes and phase angles are given in Table 4.1. The network parameters required for the power flow study are given in Tables 4.2–4.4. This power flow solution will be used as the base case against which all other solutions will be compared.

In conventional power flow calculations, generators are set to generate a pre-specified amount of active power, except the Slack generator which is left free, since it has to generate sufficient active power to meet any shortfall in system generation. It will also generate or absorb any reactive power excess in the system. In this example, the generator connected at the North node is selected to be the Slack generator, generating 131.12 MW and 90.81 MVAr. The voltage magnitude was kept at 1.06 p.u and the voltage phase angle at 0°. The generator connected at the South node was set to generate 40 MW and the power flow solution indicates that it absorbs 61.59 MVAr to keep the nodal voltage magnitude at the specified value of 1 p.u. The remaining three nodes contain no equipment to provide local reactive support and their nodal

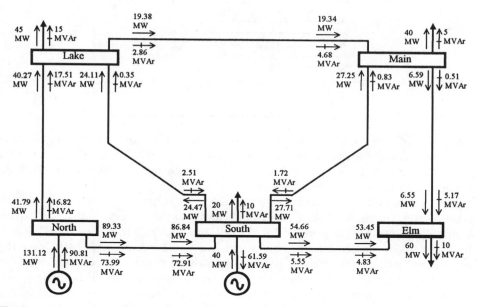

Fig. 4.17 Test network and power flow results for base case.

Table 4.1 Nodal complex voltages of original network

Voltage information	System nodes				
	North	South	Lake	Main	Elm
$\lvert V \rvert$ (p.u.)	1.06	1	0.987	0.984	0.972
θ (degrees)	0	−2.06	−4.64	−4.96	−5.77

Table 4.2 Network connectivity and transmission line parameters

Sending node	Receiving node	R (p.u.)	X (p.u.)	B (p.u.)
North	South	0.02	0.06	0.06
North	Lake	0.08	0.24	0.05
South	Lake	0.06	0.18	0.04
South	Main	0.06	0.18	0.04
South	Elm	0.04	0.12	0.03
Lake	Main	0.01	0.03	0.02
Main	Elm	0.08	0.24	0.05

Table 4.3 Generator parameters

Node	P_G(MW)	Q_{min}(MVAr)	Q_{max}(MVAr)	$\lvert V \rvert$(p.u.)
South	40	−300	300	1

Table 4.4 Load parameters

Node	P_{load}(MW)	Q_{load}(MVAr)
South	20	10
Lake	45	15
Main	40	5
Elm	60	10

voltage magnitudes drop below 1 p.u. However, they keep above 0.95 p.u., which is the minimum accepted value by most electricity companies. So, the power network does not seem to be in risk of undergoing voltage collapse at any point if an incremental load increase were to occur.

It should be noted that the maximum phase angle difference between any pair of adjacent nodes is smaller than 5°, which indicates that the power network is not over-stretched in terms of active power flows. The largest active power flow takes place in the transmission line connecting the North and South nodes: 89.33 MW leave the sending end of the transmission line and 86.84 MW reach the receiving end. The largest transmission active power loss also takes place in this transmission line, 2.49 MW. From the planning and operational point of view, this may be considered a good result. However, it should be pointed out that no attempt was made to optimize the performance of the operation. If an optimized solution is required, where generator fuel cost and transmission power loss are minimized then an optimal power flow algorithm (Ambriz-Perez, 1998) would be used as opposed to a conventional power flow algorithm (Fuerte-Esquivel, 1997).

4.5   Reactive power control

4.5.1   General aspects

In electric power systems, nodal voltages are significantly affected by load variations and by changes in transmission network topology. When the network is operating under heavy loading the voltage may drop considerably and even collapse. This will cause operation of under-voltage relays and other voltage sensitive controls, leading to extensive disconnection of loads, adversely affecting customers. On the other hand, when the level of load in the system is low, over-voltages may arise due to Ferranti effect in unloaded lines, leading to capacitive over-compensation and over-excitation of synchronous machines. Over-voltages cause equipment failures due to insulation breakdown and produce magnetic saturation in transformers, resulting in undesirable harmonic generation. Accordingly, voltage magnitudes throughout the network cannot deviate significantly from their nominal values if an efficient and reliable operation of the power system is to be achieved.

Traditionally, iron-cored inductors have been used to absorb reactive power, resulting in a reduction of the voltage level at the point of connection. Conversely, banks of capacitors have been used to supply reactive power resulting in a voltage level increase at the point of connection. When adaptive voltage regulation was required, synchronous condensers were employed. They generate and absorb reactive power from the network depending on whether they are operated in an over-excited or in an under-excited mode, in a not dissimilar manner as synchronous generators do, except that they do not produce active power. Advances in power electronics together with sophisticated electronic control methods made possible the development of fast SVC equipment in the early 1970s, leading to a near displacement of the synchronous condenser (Miller, 1982). The most recent development in the area of electronically controlled shunt compensation is the STATCOM (Hingorani and Gyugyi, 2000). It is based on the VSC and combines the operational advantages of the rotating synchronous condenser and the SVC. For most practical purposes, it is expected to replace the SVC once the technology becomes more widely understood among practising engineers and prices drop.

4.5.2 SVC power flow modelling

There are several SVC models available in the open literature for power flow studies. In particular, the models recommended by Conférence Internationale des Grands Reseaux Électriques (CIGRE) (Erinmez, 1986; IEEE Special Stability Controls Working Group, 1995) are widely used. To a greater or lesser extent, these models are based on the premise that the SVC may be represented as a synchronous generator, i.e. synchronous condenser, behind an inductive reactance.

The simplest model represents the SVC as a generator with zero active power output and reactive power limits. The node at which the *generator* is connected is represented as a PV node. This assumption may be justified as long as the SVC operates within limits. However, gross errors may result if the SVC operates outside limits (Ambriz-Perez et al., 2000). An additional drawback of the SVC models based on the *generator* principle is that it assumes that the SVC draws constant reactive power in order to keep the voltage magnitude at the target value whereas, in practice, the SVC is an adjustable reactance, which is a function of voltage magnitude.

A simple and efficient way to model the SVC in a Newton–Raphson power flow algorithm is described in this section (Fuerte-Esquivel and Acha, 1997). It is based on the use of the variable susceptance concept, which it is adjusted automatically in order to achieve a specified voltage magnitude. The shunt susceptance represents the total SVC susceptance necessary to maintain the voltage magnitude at the specified value.

Its implementation in a Newton–Raphson power flow algorithm requires the introduction of an additional type of node, namely PVB (where P relates to active power, Q to reactive power and B to shunt susceptance). It is a controlled node where the nodal voltage magnitude and the nodal active and reactive powers are specified while the SVC's variable susceptance B_{SVC} is handled as state variable. If B_{SVC} is within limits, the specified voltage is attained and the controlled node remains PVB type. However, if B_{SVC} goes out of limits, B_{SVC} is fixed at the violated limit and the node becomes PQ type in the absence of any other regulating equipment connected to the node and capable of achieving voltage control.

As discussed in Section 4.2.1, the active and reactive powers drawn by a variable shunt compensator connected at node *l* are

$$P_l = 0$$
$$Q_l = -|V_l|^2 B_{SVC} \tag{4.65}$$

The linearized SVC equation is given below, where the variable susceptance B_{SVC} is taken to be the state variable

$$\begin{bmatrix} \Delta P_l \\ \Delta Q_l \end{bmatrix} = \begin{bmatrix} 0 & 0 \\ 0 & \frac{\partial Q_l}{\partial B_{SVC}} \end{bmatrix} \begin{bmatrix} \Delta \theta_l \\ \Delta B_{SVC} \end{bmatrix} \tag{4.66}$$

At the end of iteration (r), the variable shunt susceptance B_{SVC} is updated

$$B_{SVC}^{(r+1)} = B_{SVC}^{(r)} + \Delta B_{SVC}^{(r)} \tag{4.67}$$

4.5.3 Numerical example 5

The five-node network detailed in Section 4.4.6 is modified to include one SVC connected at node Lake to maintain the nodal voltage magnitude at 1 p.u. Convergence is obtained in four iterations to a power mismatch tolerance of $\varepsilon \leq 10^{-12}$ using an OOP Newton–Raphson power flow program (Fuerte-Esquivel et al., 1988). The power flow solution is shown in Figure 4.18 whereas the nodal voltage magnitudes and phase angles are given in Table 4.5.

The power flow result indicates that the SVC generates 20.5 MVAr in order to keep the voltage magnitude at 1 p.u. voltage magnitude at Lake node. The SVC installation results in an improved network voltage profile except in Elm, which is too far away from Lake node to benefit from the SVC influence.

The Slack generator reduces its reactive power generation by almost 6% compared to the base case and the reactive power exported from North to Lake reduces by more than 30%. The largest reactive power flow takes place in the transmission line connecting North and South, where 74.1 MVAr leaves North and 74 MVAr arrives at South. In general, more reactive power is available in the network than in the base case and the generator connected at South increases its share of reactive power

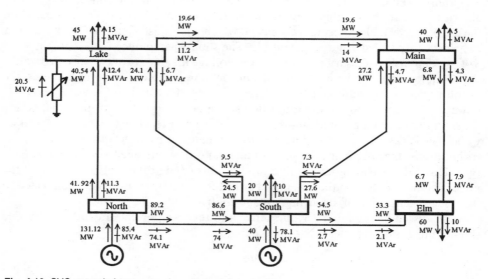

Fig. 4.18 SVC upgraded test network and power flow results.

Table 4.5 Nodal complex voltages of SVC upgraded network

Voltage information	System nodes				
	North	South	Lake	Main	Elm
$|V|$ (p.u.)	1.06	1	1	0.994	0.975
θ (degrees)	0	−2.05	−4.83	−5.11	−5.80

absorption compared to the base case. As expected, active power flows are only marginally affected by the SVC installation.

4.5.4 STATCOM power flow modelling

The STATCOM operational characteristic resembles that of an ideal synchronous machine that generates balanced, three-phase voltages with rapidly controllable amplitude and phase angle. Such a characteristic enables the STATCOM to be well represented in positive sequence power flow studies as a synchronous generator with zero active power generation and reactive power limits (IEEE/CIGRE, 1995).

The node at which the STATCOM is connected is represented as a PV node, which may change to a PQ node in the event of limits being violated. In such a case, the generated/absorbed reactive power would correspond to the violated limit. Contrary to the SVC, the STATCOM is represented as a voltage source for the full range of operation, enabling a more robust voltage support mechanism.

An alternative way to model the STATCOM in a Newton–Raphson power flow algorithm is described in this section. It is a simple and efficient model based on the use of a variable voltage source, which adjusts automatically in order to achieve a specified voltage magnitude. In this case, the node at which the STATCOM is connected is a controlled node where the nodal voltage magnitude and the nodal active and reactive powers are specified while the source voltage magnitude is handled as a state variable.

Based on the representation given in Figure 4.4, the following equation can be written

$$I_{vR} = Y_{vR}(V_{vR} - V_l) \tag{4.68}$$

where

$$Y_{vR} = \frac{1}{Z_{vR}} = G_{vR} + jB_{vR} \tag{4.69}$$

The active and reactive powers injected by the source may be derived using the complex power equation

$$S_{vR} = V_{vR}I_{vR}^* = V_{vR}Y_{vR}^*(V_{vR}^* - V_l^*) \tag{4.70}$$

Taking the variable voltage source to be $V_{vR} = |V_{vR}|(\cos\theta_{vR} + j\sin\theta_{vR})$, and after performing some complex operations, the following active and reactive power equations are obtained

$$P_{vR} = |V_{vR}|^2 G_{vR} - |V_{vR}||V_l|\{G_{vR}\cos(\theta_{vR} - \theta_l) + B_{vR}\sin(\theta_{vR} - \theta_l)\} \tag{4.71}$$

$$Q_{vR} = -|V_{vR}|^2 B_{vR} - |V_{vR}||V_l|\{G_{vR}\sin(\theta_{vR} - \theta_l) - B_{vR}\cos(\theta_{vR} - \theta_l)\} \tag{4.72}$$

If the STATCOM is connected at node l and it is assumed that its conductance is negligibly small and that there is no active power exchanged with the AC system, i.e. $G_{vR} = 0$ and $\theta_{vR} = \theta_l$

$$P_{vR} = 0$$
$$Q_{vR} = -|V_{vR}|^2 B_{vR} + |V_{vR}||V_l|B_{vR}$$
(4.73)

Based on these equations, the linearized STATCOM equation is given below, where the variable voltage magnitude $|V_{vR}|$ is taken to be the state variable

$$\begin{bmatrix} \Delta P_l \\ \Delta Q_{vR} \end{bmatrix} = \begin{bmatrix} \frac{\partial P_l}{\partial \theta_l} & \frac{\partial P_l}{\partial |V_{vR}|} \\ \frac{\partial Q_{vR}}{\partial \theta_l} & \frac{\partial Q_{vR}}{\partial |V_{vR}|} \end{bmatrix} \begin{bmatrix} \Delta \theta_l \\ \Delta |V_{vR}| \end{bmatrix}$$
(4.74)

At the end of iteration (r), the variable voltage magnitude $|V_{vR}|$ is updated

$$|V_{vR}|^{(r+1)} = |V_{vR}|^{(r)} + \Delta|V_{vR}|^{(r)}$$
(4.75)

The SVC in the modified five-node network used in Example 5 was replaced with a STATCOM to maintain nodal voltage magnitude at Lake node at 1 p.u. In this case the power flow solution is identical to the case when the SVC is used. It should be remarked that this is a special case, which yields the same result whether the shunt controller is an SVC or a STATCOM. At regulated voltage magnitudes different from 1 p.u. the results will not coincide. This is better appreciated from Figure 4.19 where the performance of an ideal reactive power controller, e.g. STATCOM, is compared against the performance of an ideal variable susceptance controller, e.g. SVC.

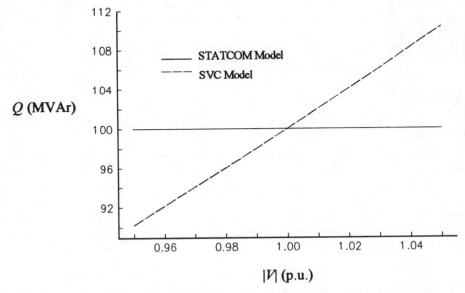

Fig. 4.19 Reactive powers injected by a STATCOM and an SVC as a function of voltage magnitude.

4.6   Active power control

4.6.1   General aspects

A well-established method to increase the transmission line capability is to install series compensation in order to reduce the transmission line's net series impedance. From the control point of view there is great incentive to provide compensation by electronic means. For instance, the TCSC enables effective active power flow regulation in the compensated transmission line. The TCSC has the ability to operate in both the inductive and the capacitive regions. TCSC operation in the inductive region will increase the electrical length of the line thereby reducing the line's ability to transfer power. Conversely, TCSC operation in the capacitive region will shorten the electrical length of the line, hence increasing power transfer margins.

The structure of a modern series compensator may consist of a large number of small inductive-capacitive parallel branches connected in tandem and each branch having independent control. Nevertheless, for the purpose of fundamental frequency, power flow studies, a variable series reactance provides a simple and very efficient way to model the TCSC. The changing reactance adjusts automatically to constrain the power flow across the branch to a specified value. The amount of reactance is determined efficiently by means of Newton's algorithm. The changing reactance X_{TCSC} represents the total equivalent reactance of all the TCSC modules connected in series.

Active power flow can also be controlled by adjusting the phase angle difference across a series connected impedance. As outlined in Section 4.2.3, this is the power transmission characteristic exploited by mechanically controlled phase shifting transformers and by electronic phase angle controllers. The latter has an almost instantaneous speed of response and it achieves its objective of controlling active power flow by inserting a variable quadrature voltage in series with the transmission line. The effectiveness of traditional phase shifters in performing this function has been well demonstrated in practice over many years (IEEE/CIGRE, 1995).

4.6.2   TCSC power flow modelling

For inductive operation the TCSC power equations at node l are

$$P_l = \frac{|V_l||V_m|}{X_{TCSC}} \cdot \sin(\theta_l - \theta_m) \tag{4.76}$$

$$Q_l = \frac{|V_l|^2}{X_{TCSC}} - \frac{|V_l||V_m|}{X_{TCSC}} \cdot \cos(\theta_l - \theta_m) \tag{4.77}$$

For capacitive operation, the signs of the equations are reversed. Also, for the power equations corresponding to node m the subscripts l and m are exchanged in equations (4.76)–(4.77).

For the case when the TCSC is controlling active power flowing from nodes l to m at a value P_{lm}^{reg} the set of linearized power flow equations are

$$
\begin{bmatrix}
\Delta P_l \\
\Delta P_m \\
\Delta Q_l \\
\Delta Q_m \\
\Delta P_{lm}
\end{bmatrix}
=
\begin{bmatrix}
\frac{\partial P_l}{\partial \theta_l} & \frac{\partial P_l}{\partial \theta_m} & \frac{\partial P_l}{\partial |V_l|} & \frac{\partial P_l}{\partial |V_m|} & \frac{\partial P_l}{\partial X_{TCSC}} \\
\frac{\partial P_m}{\partial \theta_l} & \frac{\partial P_m}{\partial \theta_m} & \frac{\partial P_m}{\partial |V_l|} & \frac{\partial P_m}{\partial |V_m|} & \frac{\partial P_m}{\partial X_{TCSC}} \\
\frac{\partial Q_l}{\partial \theta_l} & \frac{\partial Q_l}{\partial \theta_m} & \frac{\partial Q_l}{\partial |V_l|} & \frac{\partial Q_l}{\partial |V_m|} & \frac{\partial Q_l}{\partial X_{TCSC}} \\
\frac{\partial Q_m}{\partial \theta_l} & \frac{\partial Q_m}{\partial \theta_m} & \frac{\partial Q_m}{\partial |V_l|} & \frac{\partial Q_m}{\partial |V_m|} & \frac{\partial Q_m}{\partial X_{TCSC}} \\
\frac{\partial P_{lm}}{\partial \theta_l} & \frac{\partial P_{lm}}{\partial \theta_m} & \frac{\partial P_{lm}}{\partial |V_l|} & \frac{\partial P_{lm}}{\partial |V_m|} & \frac{\partial P_{lm}}{\partial X_{TCSC}}
\end{bmatrix}
\begin{bmatrix}
\Delta \theta_l \\
\Delta \theta_m \\
\Delta |V_l| \\
\Delta |V_m| \\
\Delta X_{TCSC}
\end{bmatrix}
\tag{4.78}
$$

The active power flow mismatch equation in the TCSC is,

$$
\Delta P_{lm} = P_{lm}^{reg} - P_{lm}^{calc}
\tag{4.79}
$$

and the state variable X_{TCSC} of the series controller is updated at the end of iteration (r) using the following equation

$$
X_{TCSC}^{(r+1)} = X_{TCSC}^{(r)} + \Delta X_{TCSC}^{(r)}
\tag{4.80}
$$

4.6.3   Numerical example 6

The original network has been modified to include one TCSC to compensate the transmission line connecting nodes Lake and Main. The TCSC is used to maintain active power flow towards Main at 21 MW. The initial condition of the TCSC is set at 50% of the transmission line inductive reactance given in Table 4.2, i.e. $X = 1.5\%$. Convergence was obtained in five iterations to a power mismatch tolerance of $\varepsilon \leq 10^{-12}$. The power flow results are shown on Figure 4.20 and the nodal voltage magnitudes and phase angles are given in Table 4.6.

Since the TCSC cannot generate active power, there is an increase in active power flowing towards Lake node, through the transmission lines connecting North to Lake and South to Lake, in order to meet the increase in active power specified at the sending end of the TCSC. In the transmission line South–Lake, the active power flow increases from 24.47 MW in the original network to 25.5 MW at the sending end of the line whereas in the transmission line North–Lake, the increase is from 41.79 MW to 42.43 MW.

It should be remarked that transmission line Lake–Main was series compensated to increase the active power flow from 19.38 MW to 21 MW, which is just under 8% active power increase. The nodal voltage magnitudes do not change compared to the base case but the voltage phase angles do change; particularly at Lake node where there is a negative increase of almost one degree to enable increases in active power flows.

4.6.4 SPS power flow modelling

The active and reactive powers injected at nodes l and m by the SPS shown in Figure 4.3 are

$$
P_l = |V_l|^2 G_{ll} + |V_l||V_m|(G_{lm} \cos(\theta_l - \theta_m) + B_{lm} \sin(\theta_l - \theta_m))
\tag{4.81}
$$

$$
Q_l = -|V_l|^2 B_{ll} - |V_l||V_m|(B_{lm} \cos(\theta_l - \theta_m) - G_{lm} \sin(\theta_l - \theta_m))
\tag{4.82}
$$

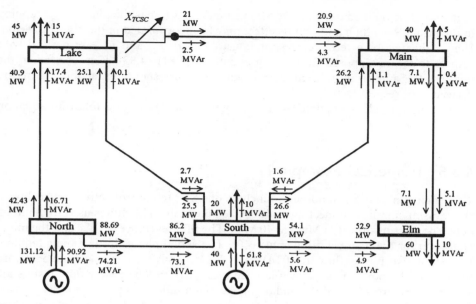

Fig. 4.20 TCSC upgraded test network and power flow results.

Table 4.6 Nodal complex voltages of TCSC upgraded network

Voltage information	System nodes				
	North	South	Lake	Main	Elm
$\|V\|$ (p.u.)	1.06	1	0.987	0.984	0.972
θ (degrees)	0	−2.04	−4.73	−4.81	−5.7

For equations corresponding to node m the subscripts l and m are exchanged in equations (4.81)–(4.82).

For the case when the SPS is controlling active power flowing from nodes l to m at a value P_{lm}^{reg} the set of linearized power flow equations are

$$
\begin{bmatrix}
\Delta P_l \\
\Delta P_m \\
\Delta Q_l \\
\Delta Q_m \\
\Delta P_{lm}
\end{bmatrix}
=
\begin{bmatrix}
\frac{\partial P_l}{\partial \theta_l} & \frac{\partial P_l}{\partial \theta_m} & \frac{\partial P_l}{\partial |V_l|} & \frac{\partial P_l}{\partial |V_m|} & \frac{\partial P_l}{\partial \phi} \\
\frac{\partial P_m}{\partial \theta_l} & \frac{\partial P_m}{\partial \theta_m} & \frac{\partial P_m}{\partial |V_l|} & \frac{\partial P_m}{\partial |V_m|} & \frac{\partial P_m}{\partial \phi} \\
\frac{\partial Q_l}{\partial \theta_l} & \frac{\partial Q_l}{\partial \theta_m} & \frac{\partial Q_l}{\partial |V_l|} & \frac{\partial Q_l}{\partial |V_m|} & \frac{\partial Q_l}{\partial \phi} \\
\frac{\partial Q_m}{\partial \theta_l} & \frac{\partial Q_m}{\partial \theta_m} & \frac{\partial Q_m}{\partial |V_l|} & \frac{\partial Q_m}{\partial |V_m|} & \frac{\partial Q_m}{\partial \phi} \\
\frac{\partial P_{lm}}{\partial \theta_l} & \frac{\partial P_{lm}}{\partial \theta_m} & \frac{\partial P_{lm}}{\partial |V_l|} & \frac{\partial P_{lm}}{\partial |V_m|} & \frac{\partial P_{lm}}{\partial \phi}
\end{bmatrix}
\begin{bmatrix}
\Delta \theta_l \\
\Delta \theta_m \\
\Delta |V_l| \\
\Delta |V_m| \\
\Delta \phi
\end{bmatrix}
\tag{4.83}
$$

The active power flow mismatch equation in the SPS is,

$$
\Delta P_{lm} = P_{lm}^{\text{reg}} - P_{lm}^{\text{calc}}
\tag{4.84}
$$

where equation (4.5) in Section 4.2.3 may be used for the purpose of calculating P_{lm}^{calc} and to derive the relevant Jacobian terms in equation (4.83).

It should be pointed out that the SPS in Figure 4.3(b) has the phase angle tapping in the primary winding and that its effect may be incorporated in the phase angle θ_m. Hence, the Jacobian terms corresponding to P_l, Q_l, P_m and Q_m are derived with respect to θ_m, as opposed to ϕ, using equations (4.81)–(4.82). For cases when the phase shifter angle is in the secondary winding the corresponding Jacobian terms are derived with respect to θ_l.

The state variable ϕ is updated at the end of iteration (r) using the following equation

$$\phi^{(r+1)} = \phi^{(r)} + \Delta\phi^{(r)} \tag{4.85}$$

4.6.5 Numerical example 7

The original network is modified to include one SPS to control active power flow in the transmission line connecting nodes Lake and Main. The SPS is used to maintain active power flow towards Main at 40 MW. The SPS reactance is 10% and the initial condition for the phase shifting angle is 0°. The actual phase shifting angle required to keep active power flow at 40 MW is −5.83°. Convergence is obtained in four iterations to a power mismatch tolerance of $\varepsilon \leq 10^{-12}$. The power flow results are shown on Figure 4.21 and the nodal voltage magnitudes and phase angles are given in Table 4.7.

Since the SPS cannot generate active power, there is a large increase in active power, compared to the base case, flowing towards Lake node through the transmission lines connecting North to Lake and South to Lake. In the transmission line North–Lake, the active power flow increases from 41.79 MW to 50.3 MW at the sending end of the line whereas in the transmission line South–Lake, the increase is from 24.47 MW to 37.6 MW.

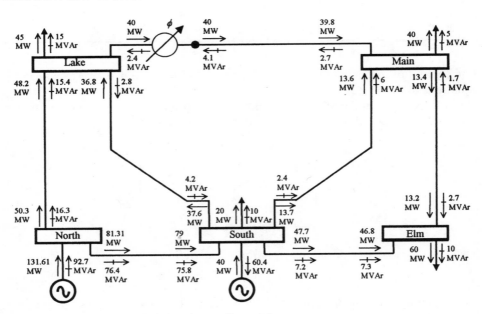

Fig. 4.21 SPS upgraded test network and power flow results.

Table 4.7 Nodal complex voltages of SPS upgraded network

Voltage information	System nodes				
	North	South	Lake	Main	Elm
$\|V\|$ (p.u.)	1.06	1	0.984	0.984	0.972
θ (degrees)	0	−1.77	−5.80	−3.06	−4.95

It should be noticed that the upgrade in transmission line Lake–Main has enabled very substantial increases in active power flow through this line, e.g. from 19.38 MW to 40 MW. The nodal voltage magnitudes do not change much compared to the base case but the phase angles do change; particularly at nodes Lake and Main where the absolute phase angle difference between the two nodes increases from 0.32° in the original case to 2.74° in the modified case of this example.

4.7 Combined active and reactive power control

4.7.1 General aspects

Simultaneous active and reactive power control is a new reality in high-voltage transmission and low-voltage distribution networks due to recent developments in power electronics technology and powerful digital control techniques. Such technological advances are embodied in the new generation of FACTS and Custom Power equipment, such as the UPFC, the DVR and the HVDC light. They are based on new power electronic converters using GTO and IGBT switches and PWM control techniques.

4.7.2 Simple UPFC power flow modelling

The UPFC can be modelled very simply by resorting to only conventional power flow concepts, namely the use of a PV type node and a PQ type node. Figure 4.22(a) shows the schematic representation of a UPFC connected between nodes *l* and *m* of a large power system. Figure 4.22(b) shows the equivalent circuit representation using the power flow terminology.

This simple way of modelling the UPFC was first reported by (Nabavi-Niaki and Iravani, 1996). This is an effective and elegant model but care should be exercised with its use because the model may lack control flexibility. For instance, the model only works if one wishes to exert simultaneous control of nodal voltage magnitude, active power flowing from nodes *l* to *m* and reactive power injected at node *l*. As illustrated in Figure 4.22, the UPFC is modelled by transforming node *l* into a PQ type node and node *m* into a PV type node. The UPFC active power flow is assigned to both the fictitious generator connected at node *m* and to the fictitious load connected at node *l*. The UPFC reactive power injected at node *l* is also assigned to the fictitious load. Furthermore, the UPFC voltage magnitude at node *m* is assigned to the newly created PV type node. It should be remarked that the implementation of this model in a computer program requires no modification of the code.

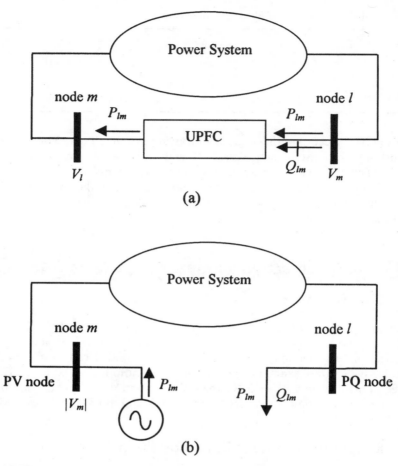

Fig. 4.22 UPFC model based on conventional power flow concepts.

4.7.3 Advanced UPFC power flow modelling

A more flexible UPFC power flow model is derived below starting from first principles. The UPFC model comes in the form of two coordinated voltage sources: one representing the fundamental component of the Fourier series of the switched voltage waveform at the AC terminals of the shunt connected converter, and the other representing a similar parameter at the AC terminals of the series connected converter. It should be noticed that the behaviour of these two voltage sources is not independent from each other but, rather, they satisfy a common active power exchange with the external power network. The equivalent circuit representation is shown in Figure 4.6(b).

As far as the power flow solution is concerned, the only restriction that this model may have is that the UPFC converter valves are taken to be lossless. However, active power losses in the converter valves are expected to be small and this is a reasonable assumption to make in power flow studies. In this situation, the active power supplied to the shunt converter, $\text{Re}\{V_{vR} \cdot I_{vR}^*\}$ satisfies the active power demanded by the series converter, $\text{Re}\{V_{cR} \cdot I_m^*\}$. The impedance of the series and shunt transformers, Z_{cR} and Z_{vR}, are included explicitly in the model. The ideal voltage sources and the constraint power equation given in equations (4.9)–(4.11) are used to derive this UPFC model.

Based on the equivalent circuit shown in Figure 4.6(b), the following transfer admittance equation can be written

$$
\begin{bmatrix} I_l \\ I_m \end{bmatrix} = \begin{bmatrix} (Y_{cR} + Y_{vR}) & -Y_{cR} & -Y_{cR} & -Y_{vR} \\ -Y_{cR} & Y_{cR} & Y_{cR} & 0 \end{bmatrix} \begin{bmatrix} V_l \\ V_m \\ V_{cR} \\ V_{vR} \end{bmatrix}
\tag{4.86}
$$

The injected active and reactive powers at nodes l and m may be derived using the complex power equation

$$
\begin{bmatrix} S_l \\ S_m \end{bmatrix} = \begin{bmatrix} V_l & 0 \\ 0 & V_m \end{bmatrix} \begin{bmatrix} I_l^* \\ I_m^* \end{bmatrix}
$$

$$
= \begin{bmatrix} V_l & 0 \\ 0 & V_m \end{bmatrix} \begin{bmatrix} (Y_{cR}^* + Y_{vR}^*) & -Y_{cR}^* & -Y_{cR}^* & -Y_{vR}^* \\ -Y_{cR}^* & Y_{cR}^* & Y_{cR}^* & 0 \end{bmatrix} \begin{bmatrix} V_l^* \\ V_m^* \\ V_{cR}^* \\ V_{vR}^* \end{bmatrix}
\tag{4.87}
$$

$$
= \begin{bmatrix} V_l & 0 \\ 0 & V_m \end{bmatrix} \begin{bmatrix} G_{ll} - jB_{ll} & G_{lm} - jB_{lm} & G_{lm} - jB_{lm} & G_{l0} - jB_{l0} \\ G_{ml} - jB_{ml} & G_{mm} - jB_{mm} & G_{mm} - jB_{mm} & 0 \end{bmatrix} \begin{bmatrix} V_l^* \\ V_m^* \\ V_{cR}^* \\ V_{vR}^* \end{bmatrix}
$$

After some straightforward but arduous algebra, the following active and reactive power equations are obtained

$$
\begin{aligned}
P_l = {} & |V_l|^2 G_{ll} + |V_l||V_m|\{G_{lm}\cos(\theta_l - \theta_m) + B_{lm}\sin(\theta_l - \theta_m) \\
& + |V_l||V_{cR}|\{G_{lm}\cos(\theta_l - \theta_{cR}) + B_{lm}\sin(\theta_l - \theta_{cR})\} \\
& + |V_l||V_{vR}|\{G_{l0}\cos(\theta_l - \theta_{vR}) + B_{l0}\sin(\theta_l - \theta_{vR})\}
\end{aligned}
\tag{4.88}
$$

$$
\begin{aligned}
Q_l = {} & -|V_l|^2 B_{ll} + |V_l||V_m|\{G_{lm}\sin(\theta_l - \theta_m) - B_{lm}\cos(\theta_l - \theta_m)\} \\
& + |V_l||V_{cR}|\{G_{lm}\sin(\theta_l - \theta_{cR}) - B_{lm}\cos(\theta_l - \theta_{cR})\} \\
& + |V_l||V_{vR}|\{G_{l0}\sin(\theta_l - \theta_{vR}) - B_{l0}\cos(\theta_l - \theta_{vR})\}
\end{aligned}
\tag{4.89}
$$

$$
\begin{aligned}
P_m = {} & |V_m|^2 G_{mm} + |V_m||V_l|\{G_{ml}\cos(\theta_m - \theta_l) + B_{ml}\sin(\theta_m - \theta_l)\} \\
& + |V_m||V_{cR}|\{G_{mm}\cos(\theta_m - \theta_{cR}) + B_{mm}\sin(\theta_m - \theta_{cR})\}
\end{aligned}
\tag{4.90}
$$

$$
\begin{aligned}
Q_m = {} & -|V_m|^2 B_{mm} + |V_m||V_l|\{G_{ml}\sin(\theta_m - \theta_l) - B_{ml}\cos(\theta_m - \theta_l)\} \\
& + |V_m||V_{cR}|\{G_{mm}\sin(\theta_m - \theta_{cR}) - B_{mm}\cos(\theta_m - \theta_{cR})\}
\end{aligned}
\tag{4.91}
$$

The active and reactive powers for the series converter are derived as follows:

$$S_{cR} = P_{cR} + jQ_{cR} = V_{cR}I_m^* = V_{cR}\{Y_{ml}^*V_l^* + Y_{mm}^*V_m^* + Y_{mm}^*V_{cR}^*\} \tag{4.92}$$

$$P_{cR} = |V_{cR}|^2 G_{mm} + |V_{cR}||V_l|\{G_{ml}\cos(\theta_{cR} - \theta_l) + B_{ml}\sin(\theta_{cR} - \theta_l)\} \\ + |V_{cR}||V_m|\{G_{mm}\cos(\theta_{cR} - \theta_m) + B_{mm}\sin(\theta_{cR} - \theta_m)\} \tag{4.93}$$

$$Q_{cR} = -|V_{cR}|^2 B_{mm} + |V_{cR}||V_l|\{G_{ml}\sin(\theta_{cR} - \theta_l) - B_{ml}\cos(\theta_{cR} - \theta_l)\} \\ + |V_{cR}||V_m|\{G_{mm}\sin(\theta_{cR} - \theta_m) - B_{mm}\cos(\theta_{cR} - \theta_m)\} \tag{4.94}$$

The active and reactive powers for the shunt converter are derived as follows

$$S_{vR} = P_{vR} + jQ_{vR} = V_{vR}I_{vR}^* = V_{vR}Y_{vR}^*\{V_{vR}^* - V_l^*\} \tag{4.95}$$

$$P_{vR} = -|V_{vR}|^2 G_{l0} + |V_{vR}||V_l|\{G_{l0}\cos(\theta_{vR} - \theta_l) + B_{l0}\sin(\theta_{vR} - \theta_l) \tag{4.96}$$

$$Q_{vR} = |V_{vR}|^2 B_{l0} + |V_{vR}||V_l|\{G_{l0}\sin(\theta_{vR} - \theta_l) - B_{l0}\cos(\theta_{vR} - \theta_l)\} \tag{4.97}$$

Assuming lossless converters, the UPFC neither absorbs nor injects active power with respect to the AC system. Hence, the following constraint equation must be satisfied

$$P_{vR} + P_{cR} = 0 \tag{4.98}$$

This is a complex model, which imposes severe demands on the numerical algorithms used for its solution. Since in power systems planning and operation reliability towards the convergence is the main concern, it is recommended that the Newton–Raphson algorithm be used for its solution (Fuerte-Esquivel et al., 2000). In this method the UPFC state variables are combined with the network nodal voltage magnitudes and phase angles in a single frame-of-reference for a unified, iterative solution. The UPFC state variables are adjusted automatically in order to satisfy specified power flows and voltage magnitudes.

Following the general principles laid out in Section 4.4.4, the relevant equations in (4.88)–(4.98) are derived with respect to the UPFC state variables. Equation (4.44) is suitably modified to incorporate the linearized equation representing the UPFC contribution. The UPFC is a very flexible controller and its linearized system of equations may take several possible forms. For instance, if nodes l and m are the nodes where the UPFC and the power network join together and the UPFC is set to control voltage magnitude at node l, active power flowing from node m to node l and reactive power injected at node m, then the following linearized equation shows the relevant portion of the overall system of equations

$$\begin{bmatrix} \Delta P_l \\ \Delta P_m \\ \Delta Q_l \\ \Delta Q_m \\ \Delta P_{ml} \\ \Delta Q_{ml} \\ \Delta P_{bb} \end{bmatrix} = \begin{bmatrix} \frac{\partial P_l}{\partial \theta_l} & \frac{\partial P_l}{\partial \theta_m} & \frac{\partial P_l}{\partial |V_{vR}|} & \frac{\partial P_l}{\partial |V_m|} & \frac{\partial P_l}{\partial \theta_{cR}} & \frac{\partial P_l}{\partial |V_{cR}|} & \frac{\partial P_l}{\partial \theta_{vR}} \\ \frac{\partial P_m}{\partial \theta_l} & \frac{\partial P_m}{\partial \theta_m} & 0 & \frac{\partial P_m}{\partial |V_m|} & \frac{\partial P_m}{\partial \theta_{cR}} & \frac{\partial P_m}{\partial |V_{cR}|} & 0 \\ \frac{\partial Q_l}{\partial \theta_l} & \frac{\partial Q_l}{\partial \theta_m} & \frac{\partial Q_l}{\partial |V_{vR}|} & \frac{\partial Q_l}{\partial |V_m|} & \frac{\partial Q_l}{\partial \theta_{cR}} & \frac{\partial Q_l}{\partial |V_{cR}|} & \frac{\partial Q_l}{\partial \theta_{vR}} \\ \frac{\partial Q_m}{\partial \theta_l} & \frac{\partial Q_m}{\partial \theta_m} & 0 & \frac{\partial Q_m}{\partial |V_m|} & \frac{\partial Q_m}{\partial \theta_{cR}} & \frac{\partial Q_m}{\partial |V_{cR}|} & 0 \\ \frac{\partial P_{ml}}{\partial \theta_l} & \frac{\partial P_{ml}}{\partial \theta_m} & 0 & \frac{\partial P_{ml}}{\partial |V_m|} & \frac{\partial P_{ml}}{\partial \theta_{cR}} & \frac{\partial P_{ml}}{\partial |V_{cR}|} & 0 \\ \frac{\partial Q_{ml}}{\partial \theta_l} & \frac{\partial Q_{ml}}{\partial \theta_m} & 0 & \frac{\partial Q_{ml}}{\partial |V_m|} & \frac{\partial Q_{ml}}{\partial \theta_{cR}} & \frac{\partial Q_{ml}}{\partial |V_{cR}|} & 0 \\ \frac{\partial P_{bb}}{\partial \theta_l} & \frac{\partial P_{bb}}{\partial \theta_m} & \frac{\partial P_{bb}}{\partial |V_{vR}|} & \frac{\partial P_{bb}}{\partial |V_m|} & \frac{\partial P_{bb}}{\partial \theta_{cR}} & \frac{\partial P_{bb}}{\partial |V_{cR}|} & \frac{\partial P_{bb}}{\partial \theta_{vR}} \end{bmatrix} \begin{bmatrix} \Delta\theta_l \\ \Delta\theta_m \\ \Delta|V_{vR}| \\ \Delta|V_m| \\ \Delta\theta_{cR} \\ \Delta|V_{cR}| \\ \Delta\theta_{vR} \end{bmatrix} \tag{4.99}$$

where it is assumed that node m is PQ type. Also, ΔP_{bb} is the power mismatch given by equation (4.98).

Good starting conditions for all the UPFC state variables are mandatory to ensure a reliable iterative solution. It has been found that for the series voltage source such initial conditions may be obtained by assuming lossless coupling transformers together with null voltage phase angles in equations (4.88)–(4.91). For the shunt voltage source the exercise involves equations (4.93), (4.96) and (4.98) (Fuerte-Esquivel et al., 2000).

It should be remarked that the power flow equations for the DVR become readily available from the above equations by eliminating the contribution of the shunt voltage source from equations (4.88)–(4.94). Notice that equations (4.95)–(4.98) do not form part of the DVR power flow model. The linearized equation for the DVR has the voltage magnitudes and phase angles at nodes l and m and the series voltage source as state variables.

4.7.4 Numerical example 8

The five-node network is modified to include one UPFC to provide power and voltage control in the transmission line connected between nodes Lake and Main. The UPFC is used to maintain active and reactive powers leaving the UPFC towards Main at 40 MW and 2 MVAr, respectively. Moreover, the UPFC's shunt converter is set to regulate nodal voltage magnitude at Lake at 1 p.u.

The shunt and series voltage sources are taken to be limitless and to have the following reactance values: $X_{cR} = X_{vR} = 0.1$ p.u. The initial conditions of the voltage sources, as calculated by using the relevant equations in (4.88)–(4.98) with null phase angles, are given in Table 4.8.

Convergence was obtained in four iterations to a power mismatch tolerance of $\varepsilon \leq 10^{-12}$. The nodal voltage magnitudes and phase angles are given in Table 4.9 and the power flow results are shown in Figure 4.23.

It should be noticed that in this example the UPFC was set to exert its full control potential and that it operated within its design limits. In this case, a power flow solution using the simple model described in Section 4.7.2, where the UPFC is modelled as a combination of a PV node and a PQ node, yields the same result.

The objective to control active and reactive powers and voltage magnitude at the target values was achieved with the following voltage magnitudes and phase angles of the series and shunt sources: $|V_{cR}| = 0.101$ p.u., $\theta_{cR} = -92.73°$, $|V_{vR}| = 1.017$ p.u. and $\theta_{vR} = -6°$.

As expected, the UPFC improved the voltage profile when compared to the original network. It is worth noticing that major changes in the redistribution of

Table 4.8 UPFC initial conditions

Voltage information	Voltage sources	
	Series	Shunt
$|V|$ (p.u.)	0.04	1
θ (degrees)	−87.13	0

Table 4.9 Nodal complex voltages of UPFC upgraded network

Voltage information	System nodes				
	North	South	Lake	Main	Elm
$\|V\|$ (p.u.)	1.06	1	1	0.992	0.975
θ (degrees)	0	−1.77	−6.02	−3.19	−5.77

active power flow have taken place, particularly in the powers flowing towards Lake node through transmission lines connected between North–Lake and South–Lake. The resulting power flows satisfy the power consumed by the load at Lake node (45 MW) and the active power demanded by the UPFC series converter, which is set to control active power flow at 40 MW as opposed to the 19.38 MW that existed in the original network. The maximum amount of active power exchanged between the UPFC and the AC system will depend on the robustness of the UPFC shunt node, i.e. Lake node. Since the UPFC generates its own reactive power, the generator connected at North node decreases its reactive power generation and the generator connected at South node increases its absorption of reactive power.

As a further exercise, we look at the characteristics of the DVR as a steady state controller. The UPFC model is replaced with a DVR model and the complex voltages are shown in Table 4.10.

The Newton–Raphson algorithm converges in five iterations to a mismatch power tolerance of $\varepsilon \leq 10^{-12}$. The DVR also controls active and reactive power flows through transmission line Lake–Main at 40 MW and 2 MVAr, respectively. The voltage magnitude and phase angle of the series voltage source are: $|V_{cR}| =$

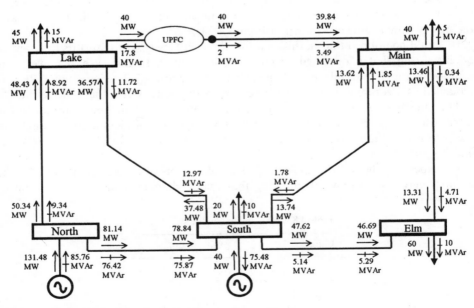

Fig. 4.23 UPFC upgraded test network and power flow results.

Table 4.10 Nodal complex voltages of DVR upgraded network

Voltage information	System nodes				
	North	South	Lake	Main	Elm
$\|V\|$ (p.u.)	1.06	1	0.987	0.994	0.976
θ (degrees)	0	−1.75	−5.72	−3.18	−4.96

0.059 p.u. and $\theta_{cR} = -115.2°$. Apart from the voltage magnitude at Lake node dropping to 0.987 p.u., the voltage magnitudes at the other nodes do not change noticeably. It is worth noticing that for the conditions set in this example the magnitude of the DVR series voltage source is considerably smaller than the UPFC series voltage source.

4.7.5 HVDC Light power flow modelling

The power flow equations of the HVDC light are closely related to equations (4.71)–(4.72), which are the power flow equations of the STATCOM. The HVDC light comprises two VSCs which are linked to the AC system via shunt connected transformers. Furthermore, the two VSCs are connected in series on the DC side, either back-to-back or through a DC cable (Asplund et al., 1998).

If it is assumed that power flows from nodes l to m, the active and reactive power injections at these nodes are

$$P_l = |V_l|^2 G_{vR1} - |V_l||V_{vR1}|\{G_{vR1}\cos(\theta_l - \theta_{vR1}) + B_{vR1}\sin(\theta_l - \theta_{vR1}) \qquad (4.100)$$

$$Q_l = -|V_l|^2 B_{vR1} - |V_l||V_{vR1}|\{G_{vR1}\sin(\theta_l - \theta_{vR1}) - B_{vR1}\cos(\theta_l - \theta_{vR1}) \qquad (4.101)$$

$$P_m = |V_m|^2 G_{vR2} - |V_m||V_{vR2}|\{G_{vR2}\cos(\theta_m - \theta_{vR2}) + B_{vR2}\sin(\theta_m - \theta_{vR2})\} \qquad (4.102)$$

$$Q_m = -|V_m|^2 B_{vR2} - |V_m||V_{vR2}|\{G_{vR2}\sin(\theta_m - \theta_{vR2}) - B_{vR2}\cos(\theta_m - \theta_{vR2})\} \qquad (4.103)$$

In this situation the rectifier is connected to node l and the inverter to node m. Hence, active and reactive powers for the rectifier are readily available by exchanging subscripts l and $vR1$ in the voltage magnitudes and phase angles in equations (4.100)–(4.101). By the same token, active and reactive powers for the inverter are derived by exchanging subscripts m and $vR2$ in the voltage magnitudes and phase angles in equations (4.102)–(4.103).

An active power constraint equation, similar to equation (4.98) for the UPFC, is also required for the HVDC light. For the case of a back-to-back connected HVDC Light

$$\text{Re}\{V_{vR1}I_l^* - V_{vR2}I_m^*\} = 0 \qquad (4.104)$$

Similarly to the STATCOM model presented in Section 4.5.4, it may be assumed that the conductances of the two converters are negligibly small, i.e. $G_{vR1} = 0$ and $G_{vR2} = 0$, but contrary to the STATCOM model, in this case there is active power exchanged with the AC system, hence, $\theta_{vR1} \neq \theta_l$ and $\theta_{vR2} \neq \theta_m$.

Based on equations (4.100)–(4.104), the linearized equation for the HVDC light is given below for the case when nodal voltage magnitude is controlled at node m by the inverter and active power flow is controlled by the rectifier at node l (Acha, 2002)

$$
\begin{bmatrix} \Delta P_l \\ \Delta Q_l \\ \Delta P_m \\ \Delta Q_m \\ \Delta P_{bb} \end{bmatrix} = \begin{bmatrix} \frac{\partial P_l}{\partial \theta_l} & \frac{\partial P_l}{\partial |V_l|} & 0 & 0 & \frac{\partial P_l}{\partial \theta_{vR1}} \\ \frac{\partial Q_l}{\partial \theta_l} & \frac{\partial Q_l}{\partial |V_l|} & 0 & 0 & \frac{\partial Q_l}{\partial \theta_{vR1}} \\ 0 & 0 & \frac{\partial P_m}{\partial \theta_m} & \frac{\partial P_m}{\partial |V_{vR2}|} & 0 \\ 0 & 0 & \frac{\partial Q_m}{\partial \theta_m} & \frac{\partial Q_m}{\partial |V_{vR2}|} & 0 \\ \frac{\partial P_{bb}}{\partial \theta_l} & \frac{\partial P_{bb}}{\partial |V_l|} & \frac{\partial P_{bb}}{\partial \theta_m} & \frac{\partial P_{bb}}{\partial |V_{vR2}|} & \frac{\partial P_{bb}}{\partial \theta_{vR1}} \end{bmatrix} \begin{bmatrix} \Delta \theta_l \\ \Delta |V_l| \\ \Delta \theta_m \\ \Delta |V_{vR2}| \\ \Delta \theta_{vR1} \end{bmatrix}
\tag{4.105}
$$

The variable voltage magnitude $|V_{vR2}|$ and the voltage phase angle θ_{vR1} are selected to be the state variables. Also, ΔP_{bb} is the power mismatch given by equation (4.104), which corresponds to the case when the converters are connected back-to-back. If this is not the case and the converters are connected in series via a DC cable then the voltage drop across the cable would be included in the constraint equation. Additional equations become necessary to cater for the increased number of state variables, with the DC equations being used to this end. At the end of iteration (r), the voltage magnitude $|V_{vR2}|$ and phase angle θ_{vR1} are updated

$$
|V_{vR2}|^{(r+1)} = |V_{vR2}|^{(r)} + \Delta |V_{vR2}|^{(r)}
\tag{4.106}
$$

$$
\theta_{vR1}^{(r+1)} = \theta_{vR1}^{(r)} + \Delta \theta_{vR1}^{(r)}
\tag{4.107}
$$

If the converters are connected back-to-back, a simple model based on the concept of PV and PQ nodes may be used instead. For the control case considered in equation (4.105), the rectifier is modelled as a PQ node and the inverter as a PV node. However, it should be noticed that this model may lack control flexibility.

The UPFC in the modified five-node network used in Example 8 was replaced with an HVDC light system to enable 40 MW and 2 MVAr to be transmitted towards Main via the transmission line Lake–Main. Moreover, the rectifier is set to control nodal voltage magnitude at Lake node at 1 p.u. As expected, the power flow solution agrees with the solution given in Example 8.

4.7.6   Numerical example 9

A further power flow solution is carried out for the case when the HVDC light replaces the UPFC in the five-node network. In this example, the active power generated by the generator in South node is specified to increase from 40 to 88.47 MW and the nodal voltage magnitudes at North and South are fixed at 1.036 p.u. and 1.029 p.u., respectively. The active power leaving the HVDC Light towards Main is set at 25 MW. The inverter is set to absorb 6 MVAr and the rectifier to regulate nodal voltage magnitude at Lake at 1 p.u. The nodal voltage magnitudes and phase angles are given in Table 4.11 and the power flow results are shown in Figure 4.24.

The objective to control active and reactive powers and voltage magnitude at the target values is achieved with the following voltage magnitudes and phase angles of

Table 4.11 Nodal complex voltages of HVDC light upgraded network

Voltage information	System nodes				
	North	South	Lake	·Main	Elm
$|V|$ (p.u.)	1.036	1.029	1	1.006	0.999
θ (degrees)	0	−1.402	−4.685	−3.580	−4.722

the rectifier and inverter sources: $|V_{vR1}| = 1.005$ p.u., $\theta_{vR1} = 6.11°$, $|V_{vR2}| = 1.001$ p.u. and $\theta_{vR2} = 1.71°$.

As expected, the HVDC Light improved the voltage profile when compared to the original network but this is also in part due to the higher voltage magnitude specified at South node. It should be noted that the generator in this node is now contributing reactive power to the system and that the generator in North node is absorbing reactive power. In general, the new operating conditions enable a better distribution of active power flows throughout the network. For instance, the largest active power flow in the network decreases from 89.33 MW in the original network to 43.2 MW in this example. The generators share, almost equally, the power demands in Lake node to satisfy a load of 45 MW and the 25 MW required by the HVDC light. Furthermore, the largest reactive power flow in the original network decreases from 73.99 MVAr to 7.75 MVAr in this example. This enables better utilization of transmission assets and reduces transmission losses. The power flow solution presented in this example is based on an optimal power flow solution (Ambriz-Perez, 1998) where generator fuel costs and transmission losses are minimized.

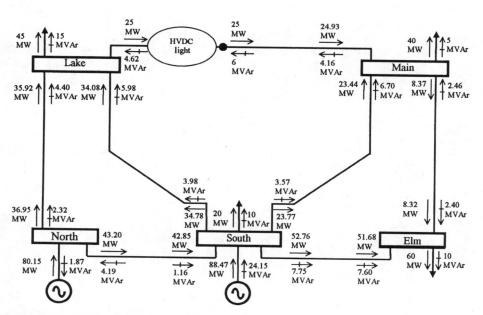

Fig. 4.24 HVDC Light upgraded test network and power flow results.

4.8 Conclusion

This chapter has presented the mathematical modelling of plant components used to control active and reactive power flows and voltage magnitude in high-voltage transmission networks. The emphasis has been on positive sequence power flow modelling of both conventional equipment and modern power systems controllers. The main steady state characteristics of the most prominent FACTS and Custom Power controllers were discussed with a view to developing simple and yet comprehensive power flow models for this new generation of power systems equipment. The following FACTS controllers received attention in this chapter: the SVC, the STATCOM, the SPS, the TCSC, the DVR, the UPFC, and the HVDC Light.

The theory of power flows and the fundamental equations used in electrical power circuits have been covered in depth, with plenty of detailed numerical examples. The Newton–Raphson power flow algorithm has been singled out for full treatment due to its high reliability towards the convergence. Numerical methods with strong convergence characteristics are mandatory when solving FACTS upgraded power systems networks. This is due to the difficulty involved in solving the highly non-linear equations used to represent such equipment and the very large-scale system that the power network represents.

5

Power semiconductor devices and converter hardware issues

5.1 Introduction

The advances of high voltage/current semiconductor technology directly affect the power electronics converter technology and its progress. The 'perfect' high-power semiconductor is yet to be fully developed and become commercially available. However, new semiconductors have changed the way that power switches are protected, controlled and used and an understanding of the device characteristics is needed before a system is developed successfully.

Technological progress in the power electronics area over the last twenty years or so has been achieved due to the advances in power semiconductor devices. In this chapter, these devices are presented and current developments are discussed.

5.2 Power semiconductor devices

The various semiconductor devices can be classified into three categories with respect to the way they can be controlled:

1. *Uncontrolled*. The diode belongs to this category. Its on or off state is controlled by the power circuit.
2. *Semi-controlled*. The thyristor or silicon controlled rectifier (SCR) is controlled by a gate signal to turn-on. However, once it is on, the controllability of the device is lost and the power circuit controls when the device will turn-off.
3. *Fully-controlled*. Over the last twenty years a number of fully controlled power semiconductors have been developed. This category includes the main kind of

transistors such as the bipolar junction transistor (BJT) and the metal oxide semiconductor field effect transistor (MOSFET). New hybrid devices such as the insulated gate bipolar transistor (IGBT), the gate turn-off thyristor (GTO), the mos-controlled thyristor (MCT), and many others have recently been introduced.

In the next sections the various power semiconductors are presented.

5.2.1   Diode

The circuit symbol of the diode is shown in Figure 5.1(a). The diode as mentioned earlier belongs to the family of uncontrolled devices that allow the current to flow in one direction only, that is from the anode (A) to the cathode (K).

The diode's typical steady-state i–v characteristics along with the ideal ones are depicted in Figure 5.1(b) and (c) respectively. The operation of the device can be described in a simplified way as follows. When the voltage across the diode from the anode to the cathode v_{AK} ($v_{AK} = v_D$) with the polarity shown in Figure 5.1(a) is positive (forward biased), the diode starts to conduct current whose value is controlled by the circuit itself. Furthermore, a small voltage drop appears across the diode. When the voltage across the diode v_{AK} becomes negative, the device stops conducting with a small current (leakage current) flowing from the cathode to the anode. It should be noted that the ideal i–v characteristics should not be used as part of a design procedure but only to explain the operation of a given circuit.

The typical two-layer structure of the diode is shown in Figure 5.1(d). It is a single junction device with two layers in a silicon wafer, a p-layer lacking electrons and an n-layer doped with a surplus of electrons.

If a diode is conducting and a reverse bias voltage is applied across, it turns off as soon as the forward current becomes zero. However, the process of a diode turning off is not a straightforward one. The extended time required for a diode to turn off and the phenomena happening during such time are known as *diode reverse recovery*. Practically, the time required for a diode to turn off ranges from between a few nanoseconds to a few microseconds. This depends on the technology used to manufacture the device and on the power ratings of the device.

A basic explanation of the reverse recovery phenomena can be given with the assistance of Figure 5.2. The reverse recovery current reaches its maximum value (I_{RM}) after a time interval t_r from the zero crossing point. By then, sufficient carriers have been swept out and recombined and therefore current cannot continue to increase. It starts then to fall during the interval t_f. The sum of the two intervals t_r and t_f is also known as *reverse recovery time* t_{rr}. It is also known as the storage time because it is the required time to sweep out the excess charge from the silicon Q_{rr} due to reverse current. This phenomenon can create large voltage overshoots and losses in inductive circuits. The time t_{rr} characterises the diodes as fast recovery, ultra fast recovery and line frequency diodes. Proper design of the power circuit can influence the behaviour of the device during reverse recovery and limit the negative effect of the described problem.

The diode has no low power control terminal like other semiconductors and therefore is less susceptible to electronic noise problems. However, it still must be protected against overcurrent, overvoltage and transients. For overvoltages, snubber

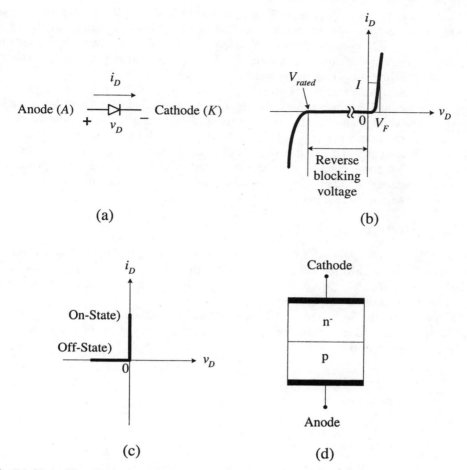

Fig. 5.1 Diode: (a) circuit symbol; (b) typical *i–v* characteristics; (c) ideal *i–v* characteristics; and (d) typical structure.

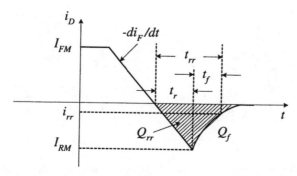

Fig. 5.2 Diode reverse recovery parameters and definitions.

circuits must be used in general to suppress transients which may result in high voltages and ensure that the breakdown voltage (V_{BR}) is not exceeded as shown in Figure 5.1(b). For current, usually the average value, the rms value and the peak value for a given duration are considered. Due to thermal effect on these values, typically the diodes operate below their rated value.

If the circuit requirements for voltage and current are higher than the ratings of a given individual diode, a number of diodes may be connected in series and/or parallel to share the voltage and/or current respectively. Exact voltage and current sharing is not always feasible, since it is impossible that two similar devices exhibit the exact same characteristics. To avoid problems of unequal sharing of voltage and/or current, which in some cases may result in thermal differences and other problems, external resistors or other devices may be used to ensure that the voltage and/or current are shared as required.

5.2.2   Thyristor

The SCR, simply referred to as thyristor is a semi-controlled four-layer power semiconductor with three electrodes, namely, the anode (A), the cathode (K) and the gate (G). The circuit symbol of the thyristor and its structure are shown in Figures 5.3(a) and (b) respectively.

Since it is a four-layer device, it possesses three junctions. A two-transistor based analogy can be used to explain the operating characteristics of the device as shown in Figures 5.3(c) and (d).

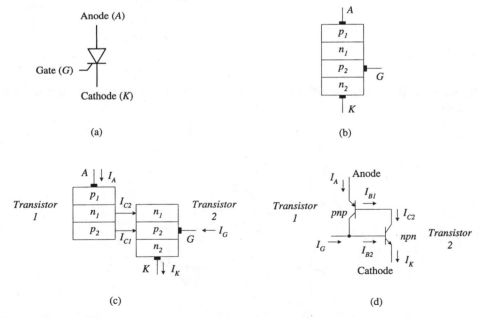

Fig. 5.3 Thyristor: (a) circuit symbol; (b) structure; (c) schematic structure of the two-transistor model; and (d) two transistor equivalent circuit.

An ideal thyristor exhibits infinite resistance to positive anode current unless a positive current pulse I_G is supplied through the gate. Then, the thyristor enters its on state and its resistance becomes zero. It remains at this state till the anode current becomes zero. If the gate current pulse I_G is then zero, the thyristor resumes its initial state of having infinite resistance from the anode to the cathode to positive anode current. However, it should be noted that the anode current does not become zero even when the gate pulse current I_G becomes zero when the thyristor is on. This is the most significant difference between the thyristor and the other fully controlled semiconductors, which will be presented later in this chapter.

The ideal i–v characteristics of the thyristor are plotted in Figure 5.4(a). The current in the thyristor flows from the anode (A) to the cathode (K), like the ordinary diode when it is turned on. Using the two-transistor equivalent circuit shown in Figure 5.3(d), the triggering and the operation of the thyristor can be further explained as follows. When a positive gate current pulse I_G is applied to the p_2 base of the npn transistor (Figure 5.1(c)), the transistor starts to conduct. Negative current flowing through the base of the pnp transistor, also turns the other transistor on. The current flowing through the pnp transistor becomes the base current now of the npn transistor and the whole process described above continues to occur. The regenerative effect turns the thyristor on with a very low forward voltage across. It also leads the two transistors into saturation with all the junctions being forward biased. If the gate pulse is removed, this situation will not change, i.e. the two transistors will remain on. The current flowing through the thyristor is limited only by the external power circuit. Once the thyristor is on, the device behaves as a single junction (although as it was mentioned earlier, there are three junctions). The only way then to turn the thyristor off is to make the anode to cathode current virtually zero.

The operation of the thyristor can be explained with the assistance of the non-ideal i–v characteristics of the device shown in Figure 5.4(b). When the thyristor is in its off state, it can block a positive (forward) polarity voltage from the anode to the

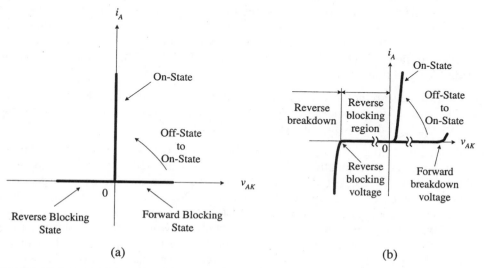

Fig. 5.4 Thyristor i–v characteristics: (a) ideal; and (b) non-ideal.

cathode. There is a need for two conditions to be present simultaneously to turn on the thyristor:

1. forward voltage from the anode (A) to the cathode (K)
2. positive gate current to be applied for a short time.

When the two conditions are met, the thyristor can be triggered or as also referred the thyristor can be fired into its on state. It then behaves almost as a short circuit with a low voltage drop across (typically few Volts depending upon the type of the thyristor and its power ratings). Once the thyristor enters its on state, the controllability of the device through the gate circuit is lost and the thyristor behaves as an ordinary diode. This happens even if the gate current is removed. The thyristor cannot be turned off through the gate. Only if, due to the operation of the power circuit, the current from the anode to the cathode tries to change direction (becomes negative or else flows from the cathode to the anode), the thyristor turns off and the anode to the cathode current becomes eventually zero. This happens under certain conditions and the circuit design must ensure that while the anode to the cathode current is negative and finally becomes zero, a negative voltage must be present across the thyristor to ensure that it turns off completely. Manufacturers' data sheets specify times and requirements for the thyristor to turn off. When the voltage across the thyristor is negative (reverse bias) a very small current (leakage current) flows from the cathode to the anode.

5.2.3   Light-triggered thyristor (LTT)

The thyristor represents a mature technology and is already the most widely used device especially in high and very-high power applications for decades. However, there are a number of developments happening in order to further improve the performance characteristics of the device.

In the early 1970s the electrically triggered thyristor (ETT) was developed. However, when such devices are used in series in large numbers to develop a high-voltage valve, the electrical triggering and the required insulation were complex making the hardware equipment expensive. In the late 1970s, a light-sensitive gating method was developed and the associated amplifying layers were built integrally into the power thyristor to facilitate the light-triggering concept (EPRI, 1978). The main reasons of using LTT technology are as follows:

- Light signals are not affected by ElectroMagnetic Interference (EMI).
- The optical fibre provides one of the best available electrical isolation and transmits the light directly into the gate of the device.

The blocking voltage of the initial devices was relatively low (Temple, 1980; Temple, 1981). Since then continually new devices were manufactured that were able to block higher voltages (Tada et al., 1981; Katoh et al., 1997). Another important aspect was the protection of the device against dv/dt and di/dt (Przybysz et al., 1987). This resulted in the development of the self-protected LTT (Cibulka et al., 1990; Aliwell et al., 1994).

Today, research and development aims mainly at reducing the complexity of the device itself while improving its reliability. Each valve in high-power applications is built with a number of thyristors and work in recent years has resulted in an increase of the blocking voltage level so that the number of thyristors required to build the

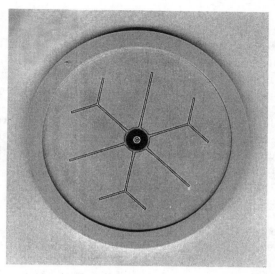

Fig. 5.5 Photograph of a 5-inch light-triggered thyristor with integrated breakover diode. (Courtesy of Siemens and EUPEC.)

same valve from the blocking voltage point of view can be reduced. It is widely accepted by manufacturers that the highest blocking voltage that results in optimized device as far as cost, power losses, reliability and fabrication process are concerned is about 8-kV (Ruff et al., 1999; Asano et al., 1998).

Today, manufacturers try to integrate the drive and protection circuitry within the device. Specifically, the light and overvoltage triggering functions have been integrated with the device. When compared with the ETT, the component count of the drive circuit is reduced substantially (Lips et al., 1997). Furthermore, the overvoltage protection is also integrated into the device which further reduces the complexity of the circuitry arrangement required to ensure safe operating conditions and risk of failure reduction. An improved 8-kV LTT with the overvoltage protection developed by Siemens and EUPEC has become available (Schulze et al., 1996; Schulze et al., 1997; Ruff et al., 1999). An 8-kV LTT with integrated diode (Niedernostheide et al., 2000) is shown in Figure 5.5.

Many LTT devices have been successfully used in Japan (Asano et al., 1998). The recently developed 8-kV LTT by Siemens, AG was tested as commercial product at Bonneville Power Administration's (BPAs), Celilo Converter Station at The Dalles, Oregon, USA in 1997. Celilo is the northern end of BPAs 3.1-MW HVDC line from the Columbia River system to Southern California.

Current R&D work aims at developing fully self-protected devices with break over diode (BOD), forward recovery protection (FRP) and dv/dt protection as a high-power LTT (Ruff et al., 1999).

5.2.4 Desired characteristics of fully-controlled power semiconductors

In switch-mode solid-state converters, the fully controlled power semiconductors can be turned on and off with control signals applied to a third terminal and can be broadly classified as voltage controlled or current controlled. In the first case, and in simple terms, a voltage signal between two terminals controls the on and off state, whereas in the second case, the injection of current through the third terminal provides such control.

Simplified and linearized voltage and current waveforms during the turn-on and turn-off interval are shown in Figure 5.6. In reality, these waveforms are shaped with snubber networks added in the power circuit to protect the main semiconductor device and to reduce or minimize the switching losses. The overlap between the voltage and current waveforms therefore is greatly dependent upon not only the switching characteristics of the device itself but also on the way the power circuit is designed and controlled.

For instance, there is a family of converters based on resonant concepts where the voltage and current waveforms not only have the shape of sinusoidal signals as opposed to linear waveforms shown in Figure 5.6 but also the overlap is minimal and the respective switching losses quite low.

In the last fifteen years such resonant concepts have been extensively applied in the converter technology and many ideas from the thyristor converters have been used to control the shape of the switching waveforms and reduce the losses. This way the switching frequency of the system can be increased with a number of benefits attached to such improvement. The new family of converters known as *soft-switching* converters or *quasi-resonant* converters with control techniques modified or based on PWM concepts have been the focus of R&D (Divan, 1989; Divan, 1991; Divan et al., 1989; Divan et al., 1993). There are already many products in this area in the market mainly for adjustable speed motor drives and medium power converters for power systems applications.

It is beyond the scope of this book to provide further information on such technology. A review paper of the developments of this technology has been recently written by Bellar et al., 1998.

Before presenting the main semiconductor devices, we will discuss the desired characteristics of the power switches.

The 'perfect' fully controlled power switch would have the following characteristics:

1. *High forward and reverse voltage blocking ratings.* In order to achieve higher power ratings for a given converter, many switches are connected in series to build a

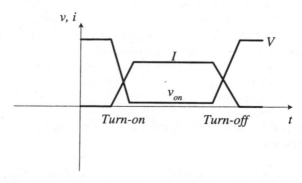

Fig. 5.6 Linear switching voltage and current waveforms for a semiconductor switch.

valve especially for high and ultra-high power applications. If new devices become available with higher voltage ratings, the number of the required switches connected in series to produce the same valve will be reduced. This will minimize the problems with the voltage sharing of the various switches in series, will increase the reliability of the overall system and will minimize the problems with their protection.

2. *High current during conduction state.* At the moment, when the current ratings of a given converter must be met, a number of switches are connected in parallel. If a device is available with high current ratings, the need for parallel connection as well as the problem of current sharing can be eliminated.

3. *Low off-state leakage current.* In most cases such a requirement is not significant as the already available switches exhibit almost negligible off-state leakage current.

4. *Low on-state voltage drop across the switch.* Even a relatively low voltage drop of a few volts across the device at significant current flowing through the device can result in high conduction losses. It is therefore important that such an on-state voltage drop is as low as possible. This becomes more important when a number of switches are connected in series to increase the power handling capability of the converter, as the load current flows through a number of switches generating high conduction losses.

5. *Low turn-on and turn-off losses.* The ability to switch from on to off state and vice versa with minimum overlap between the current and voltage waveforms means that the switching turn-on and off losses are low. When such characteristics are combined with the low conduction losses, cooling requirements and other auxiliary components may be reduced or even eliminated in certain applications making the converter simpler, smaller, more efficient and simply less expensive.

6. *Controlled switching characteristics during turn-on and turn-off.* This means that overcurrent control becomes simpler and easier, the stresses on the device and other parts of the converter such as load, transformers, etc. can be reduced along with EMI generation, the need for filters and snubber circuits.

7. *Capability to handle its rated voltage and current at the same time without the need for derating.* This will mean snubberless design, i.e. the required extra snubber components (resistor–inductor–capacitor–diode) to protect the switch and shape its switching waveforms, can be eliminated. Therefore, if the design does not require all these components, a simpler configuration, more efficient and more reliable will result.

8. *High dv/dt and di/dt ratings.* This will eliminate or reduce the size of the snubber circuits. Of course EMI generation will limit how fast the current and voltage waveforms can change but it is desirable that the switch has large dv/dt and di/dt ratings to eliminate the previously mentioned snubber circuitry.

9. *Ability to operate in high temperatures.* This will also eliminate the cooling requirements and simplify the converter's structure.

10. *Short-circuit fault behaviour.* This will mean that the converter will still be able to operate when a number of switches are connected in series allowing designs that have redundancy factors especially in high and ultra-high power applications.

11. *Light triggering and low power requirements to control the switch.* This will allow fibre optics to be used to control the switch. In most cases the power to drive the switch is taken from the power circuit itself and the low power requirements will minimize the losses of the system.

Having discussed the desired characteristics, we consider the various fully controlled power semiconductors and their realistic characteristics in the next sections.

5.2.5 Gate-turn-off thyristor

This semiconductor device, as the name implies, is a hybrid device that behaves like a thyristor. However, it has an added feature that the provided gate control allows the designer to turn the device on and off if and when desired. It became commercially available during the late 1980s although it was invented a long time ago (Van Ligten et al., 1960). Recently it has undergone a number of improvements and in the next few years may be able to replace the thyristor in the really high power area of applications.

The GTO thyristor is a device similar to the conventional thyristor. However, it is not just a latch-on device but also a latch-off one. The circuit symbol along with the layers are shown in Figures 5.7(a) and (b). The equivalent circuit is depicted in Figure 5.7(c). Its ideal and non-ideal i–v characteristics are plotted in Figures 5.7(d) and (e) respectively.

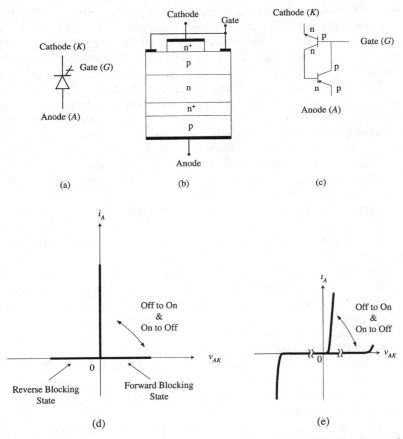

Fig. 5.7 GTO: (a) circuit symbol; (b) device structure; (c) equivalent circuit; (d) ideal i–v characteristics; and (e) non-ideal i–v characteristics.

It should be noted that although the GTO can be turned on like a thyristor, with a low positive gate current pulse, a large negative pulse is required to turn it off. These are relatively slow devices when compared with other fully controlled semiconductors. The maximum switching frequency attainable is in the order of 1 kHz. The voltage and current ratings of the commercially available GTOs are comparable to the thyristors approaching 6.5 kV, 4.5 kA and are expected to increase to cover completely the area occupied by thyristors as shown in Figure 5.12.

5.2.6 Metal-oxide-semiconductor field effect transistor

The metal-oxide semiconductor field effect transistor (MOSFET) is a transistor device capable of switching fast with low switching losses. It cannot handle high power and is mostly suited for low-power applications. These include switch-mode power supplies (SMPS) and low voltage adjustable speed motor drives used in copier machines, facsimiles and computers to name a few. In fact for very low

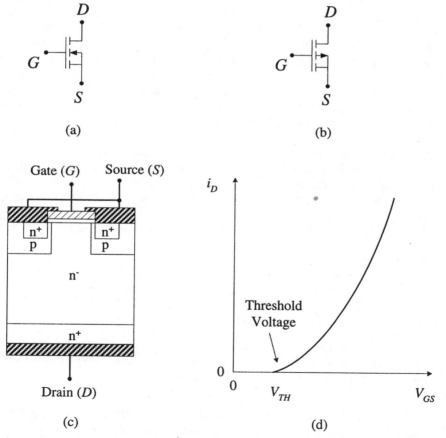

Fig. 5.8 Power MOSFET: (a) circuit symbol for an *n*-channel; (b) circuit symbol for a *p*-channel; (c) basic structure of an *n*-channel device; and (d) voltage signal control of a typical *n*-channel device.

power it is possible to operate the converter in switching frequencies in the MHz region.

This is by far the fastest switching power semiconductor device and this is due to the gate-controlled electric field required to turn the device on and off. In the case of a BJT, a current pulse is required to control it. It is also a slower device when compared with the MOSFET. Although its applications are limited with the lower power handling capability, it is important to understand its operation and structure as many of the new popular devices commercially available are based on MOSFET technology. Figures 5.8(a) and (b) show the circuit symbol for an *n*-channel and a *p*-channel MOSFET. The device is controlled by a voltage signal between the gate (G) and the source (S) that should be higher than the threshold voltage as shown in Figure 5.8(d).

5.2.7 Insulated-gate bipolar transistor

The IGBT is the most popular device for AC and DC motor drives reaching power levels of a few hundred kW. It has also started to make its way in the high voltage converter technology for power system applications. It is a hybrid semiconductor device that literally combines the advantages of MOSFETs and BJTs. Specifically, it has the switching characteristics of the MOSFET with the power handling capabilities of the BJT. It is a voltage-controlled device like the MOSFET but has lower conduction losses. Furthermore, it is available with higher voltage and current ratings. There are a number of circuit symbols for the IGBT with the most popular shown in Figure 5.9(a). The equivalent circuit is shown in Figure 5.9(b). The basic structure is then shown in Figure 5.9(c). The typical *i–v* characteristics are plotted in Figure 5.9(d).

The IGBTs are faster switching devices than the BJTs but not as fast as the MOSFETs. The IGBTs have lower on-state voltage drop even when the blocking voltage is high. Their structure is very similar to the one of the vertical diffused MOSFET, except the p+ layer that forms the drain of the device. This layer forms a junction (p–n).

Most of the IGBTs available on the market are two types as follows:

1. Punch-through IGBTs (PT-IGBTs).
2. Non-punch-through IGBTs (NPT-IGBTs).

Figure 5.10 shows the two basic structures of the two kinds of devices mentioned above.

When comparing the two kinds of devices the following observations can be made.

1. The PT-IGBTs do not have reverse blocking voltage capability.
2. The NPT-IGBTs have better short circuit capability but higher on-state voltage drop. They also have a positive temperature coefficient, which is a great benefit when paralleling devices.

There exist vertically optimized NPT structure based IGBT modules with $6.5\,\mathrm{k}V_{dc}$ blocking voltage with rated currents up to 600 A. They have positive temperature coefficient of the on-state voltage, short circuit capability and high ruggedness against overcurrent.

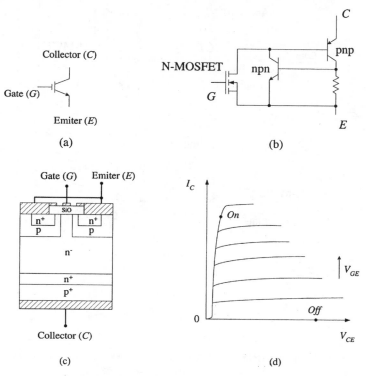

Fig. 5.9 IGBT features: (a) circuit symbol; (b) equivalent circuit; (c) device layer structure; and (d) i–v characteristics.

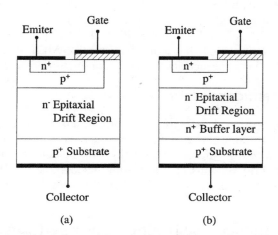

Fig. 5.10 Types of IGBTs: (a) punch-through IGBT; and (b) non-punch-through IGBT.

5.2.8 MOS-controlled thyristor

The MCT is a hybrid device that combines characteristics of two families of technologies, namely MOS and thyristor.

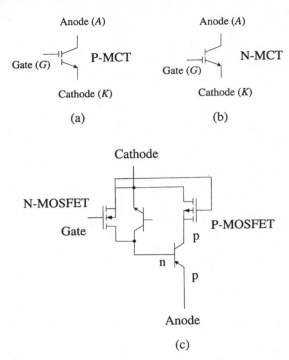

Fig. 5.11 MCT: (a) circuit symbol for a P-MCT; (b) circuit symbol for an N-MCT; and (c) equivalent circuit of an N-MCT.

The basic difference between the previously presented GTO and the MCT is that the second is turned on and off by short pulses of voltage between the gate and anode terminals rather than current pulse used to control the first one. The circuit symbol is shown in Figures 5.11(a) and (b) for a P-MCT and N-MCT respectively. The equivalent circuit is presented in Figure 5.11(c). The MCT exhibits capability to operate at high switching frequencies with low conduction losses.

5.2.9 Other semiconductor devices

There are also many other devices available in the market as a product or at R&D level. Many different names are given to them such as integrated gate-commutated thyristor (IGCT or GCT), emitter turn-off thyristor (ETO) and others. All of them are more or less hybrid versions of the existing devices and effort is spent to make them with higher ratings, better switching characteristics and with reduced conduction and switching losses.

5.2.10 Semiconductor switching-power performance

The power frequency range of the various semiconductors discussed in the previous sections are summarized in Figure 5.12. It is clear that the thyristor dominates the ultra-high power region for relatively low frequencies. The GTO is the next device when it comes to power handling capabilities extending to frequencies of a few hundred Hz. The IGBT occupies the area of medium power with the ability to

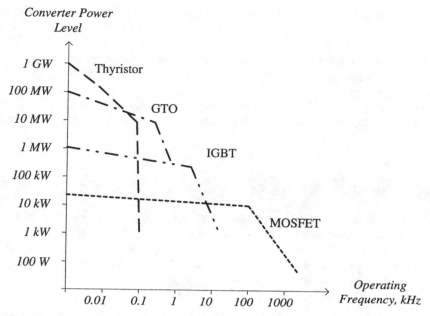

Fig. 5.12 Converter power level and frequency for various semiconductor devices.

operate at relatively higher frequencies, and finally the MOSFET extends its operation to high frequency regions for relatively low power levels. The tendency over the next few years is to have the GTO extend its power area towards the thyristor level. At the same time, the IGBT will also extend its power ability towards the GTO with higher switching frequency.

5.3   Power modules

Manufacturers of high power semiconductor devices offer power modules, which are easy to use to build a power electronics converter. Power modules offer two or more devices typically of the same type interconnected in a certain way to facilitate building a given converter topology. The power modules also naturally have increased voltage and/or current ratings due to internal series and/or parallel connection of several semiconductors. Converter legs for a single-phase and three-phase converter are also available and in many cases a modular converter including not only the three-phase inverter legs, but also the front-end three-phase diode rectifier and other integrated components.

5.4   Passive components

Many other components must be used to make a converter topology function properly to shape the voltage and current supplied from the source to the ones required by the load in a regulated manner and in many cases allow the power flow to be bidirectional. Components such as inductors, capacitors and resistors must be used not only as part of protection devices in the case of snubbers, but also as filter elements.

Different technologies are available depending upon the power level and the function of the component. For instance, electrolytic, paper, paper–film, film, ceramic, mica, aluminium electrolytic, and oil filled capacitors are widely used in power electronics systems.

In the case of resistors, carbon composition, metal film, low voltage resistors, high voltage resistors, wire-wound resistors, and resistance wire materials are used in various ways and cases.

5.5   Ancillary equipment

A number of ancillary equipment is also used to build power electronics systems. These include support equipment as many of the components of the system are quite heavy. Also included are cabinets, copper bars, heat sinks, drive and control circuits as appropriate, isolation equipment, protection systems, diagnostics, fuses, information and display boards to name a few.

5.6   Cooling systems

Power losses associated with the operation of the semiconductors reduce their thermal capacity. High temperatures of the wafers drastically reduce the electrical characteristics of the devices, namely their maximum blocking voltage, switching times, etc. In order to increase the life expectancy and the reliability of power electronic equipment, adequate cooling means must be provided. Needless to say that overheating may cause total destruction of the device and the converter at large.

The temperature of the semiconductor junction T_j determines its reliability performance. Its maximum allowable value is specified by the manufacturer in the data sheets. It is therefore necessary to keep this temperature within a certain limit and for that reason, depending upon the application, a number of cooling mechanisms are available to the design engineer.

There exist three different mechanisms of heat transfer as follows:

- *Conduction.* The mode of heat transfer in solids or fluids, that are in conduct with one another, and heat can be transferred from the warm object to the cooler one.
- *Convection.* The mode of heat transfer between a solid object and the surrounding air. These mechanisms can be further divided into two subcategories, namely the natural convection and the forced one. The first one occurs naturally when a cooler non-moving air surrounds a warm object. The second one occurs when the air flow around the warm object is forced by a fan or other mechanical means. This method is more efficient and faster when compared with the natural convection. Of course other means such as liquid, i.e. oil or water can be used to remove heat from a given object.
- *Radiation.* The mode of heat transfer due to electromagnetic emission when a transparent medium surrounds a warm object.

The energy flow per unit time by conduction is given by the following formula:

$$P_{conduction} = \frac{\lambda}{d} \cdot A \cdot (T_1 - T_2) \tag{5.1}$$

where

λ is the thermal conductivity of the material in $[W/m \cdot {}^\circ C]$
T_1, T_2 are the temperatures in $[{}^\circ C]$
A is the surface area in $[m^2]$
d is the length in $[m]$
The energy flow per unit time by convection is

$$P_{convection} = \alpha \cdot A \cdot (T_1 - T_2) \tag{5.2}$$

where

α is the convection coefficient $[\frac{W}{m^2 \cdot {}^\circ C}]$
A is the surface area in $[m^2]$
T_1, T_2 are the temperatures in $[{}^\circ C]$
Finally, the energy flow per unit time by radiation is

$$P_{radiation} = S \cdot E \cdot A \cdot (T_1^4 - T_2^4) \tag{5.3}$$

where

S is the Stefan–Boltzmann constant $[5.67 \cdot 10^{-8} \frac{W}{m^2 \cdot K^4}]$
E is the emissivity of the material
A is the area in $[m^2]$
T_1, T_2 are the temperatures in $[{}^\circ K]$
In all previously mentioned cases, the heat transfer is dependent upon the surface area of the object. To increase the surface area, a heat sink is used to mount the device. The heat generated in the device is transferred first from the semiconductor to the heat sink and then to the ambient air if no other means are provided. In heat sinks all modes of heat transfer exist, namely, conduction between the semiconductor, and the heat sink, convection between the heat sink and the air, and radiation from the heat sink and semiconductor to the air. The efficiency of the transfer mode also depends upon the medium used for cooling when forced mechanisms are used. To improve the heat transfer due to conduction, the contact pressure between the semiconductor and the heat sink surface may be increased and conductive grease or soft thermal padding may also be used.

However, in most cases of low power electronic equipment a fan is placed at the bottom of the enclosure and slotted openings are provided to allow circulation of the air. In converters of significant power level and when the power-to-weight-ratio is very high, other means of forced cooling are used. For instance, oil similar to the one used in transformers is used to remove the heat from the converter.

In many cases water forced through hollow pipes is used as a cooling means. The heat-pipe coolers are composed of

- An aluminium base with elements clamped to conduct heat.
- Cooling plates composed of copper or aluminium with surfaces.
- Heat pipes that provide the thermal link between the aluminium base and the plates.

Another kind of heat pipe may include insulation between the evaporator and the condenser allowing water as a coolant or water and glycol and not necessarily chlorofluorocarbons (CFCs).

Figure 5.13 shows some heat sinks with power semiconductors mounted on them to illustrate the previously discussed points.

Fig. 5.13 Heat sinks: (a) air cooled extruded heat sink (velocity = 5 m/s, Rsa = 0.2 C/W, weight = 2.6 lb/ft); (b) air cooled fabricated heat sink (velocity = 5 m/s, Rsa = 0.02 C/W, weight = 21 lb/ft); and (c) liquid cooled heat sink (flow rate = 5 lt/s, Rsa = 0.002 C/W, weight = 4.5 lb/ft). (Courtesy of R-Theta, Inc., Mississauga, Ontario, Canada.)

5.7 Component layout

The layout of the converter is very important as high voltage and current are switched at high frequencies. This generates a great deal of EMI and voltage spikes, and care should be taken to minimize the inductance so that the electric noise effect is also kept to the minimum. Of course the worst-case scenario would be wrong triggering of a device that may result in short circuit, which will probably cause destruction of the system.

5.8 Protection of semiconductors – snubber circuits

Proper use of the devices presented so far requires determination of semiconductor losses since adequate cooling means have to be provided to keep the device temperature within rated values.

Generally, the semiconductor losses are grouped into three categories (Rockot, 1987):

1. conduction (on-state and dynamic saturation)
2. switching (turn-on and turn-off)
3. off-state.

The relative magnitudes of the conduction and switching losses are greatly dependent on the type of the converter (i.e. resonant, quasi-resonant, PWM, etc.), the operating frequency, the type of the load (i.e. linear or non-linear, resistive or inductive), and certain characteristics of the switch itself (i.e. turn-on time, turn-off time, etc.). Off-state losses are generally a very small portion of the total losses and are considered negligible.

Snubber circuits are a typical way to minimize switching losses in converters (McMurray, 1972; 1980; 1985). In general, snubber circuits are used for the reduction of switching losses and associated stresses (i.e. protection against high dv/dt and di/dt) of power semiconductor devices. The turn-on and turn-off circuits are placed in series/parallel to the power switching devices, respectively. For instance, one major purpose of using such circuits, especially for BJTs and GTOs is to keep the power device within its safe operating area (SOA).

Two different types of snubber circuits can be considered as follows:

1. dissipative
2. non-dissipative (low-loss snubber).

The basic difference between them is as follows:

- In dissipative snubber circuits, the energy stored in reactive elements (limiting di/dt inductor and limiting dv/dt capacitor) is dissipated in resistors and converted into heat. This type is certainly not the best choice to achieve high switching frequencies and/or high power levels.
- In non-dissipative (low-loss) snubber circuits, there are no substantial losses due to resistors. In this case, losses are only caused by non-ideal device properties, such as conduction and transient switching losses of the switching devices contained in the snubber circuits.

Snubber circuits are employed for the modern semiconductor devices such as power BJTs, MOSFETs, IGBTs, and GTOs. Figure 5.14 shows the conventional dissipative snubber circuits. Specifically, the turn-on snubber R_s–L_s to control the rate of rise of the switch current during turn-on and the turn-off snubber R_s–C_s to control the rise rate of the switch voltage during turn-off are shown. The polarized snubber circuits (turn-on/turn-off) are included. The combined polarized complete turn-on/turn-off snubber circuit is also depicted. The transistor S in each case is the respective semiconductor device that is being protected by the passive snubber components R_s, L_s, C_s and D_s.

With the use of a combined snubber circuit (Figure 5.14), the interaction between the semiconductor device and the snubber circuit is as follows:

- During turn-on the voltage fall is a linear time function completely dictated by the switch characteristics, while the series snubber inductor L_s dictates the current rise.
- During turn-off, the current fall is a linear time function completely determined by the switch characteristics, while the voltage rise is determined by the shunt (parallel) snubber capacitor C_s.

The operation of the combined snubber circuit (Figure 5.14) is described as follows:

After switch turn-on, the snubber capacitor C_s, discharges via the semiconductor device through the C_s–R_s–L_s loop. The discharge current is superimposed on the load current. The snubber capacitor C_s voltage reaches zero afterwards, at which moment the snubber polarizing diode D_s begins to conduct and the remaining overcurrent in the inductor L_s decays exponentially through the L_s–R_s loop. Then after switch turn-off, the series snubber inductor L_s begins to discharge and the snubber diode D_s conducts thus connecting C_s in parallel with the semiconductor device. The discharge voltage of the inductor is superimposed over the input voltage already present across the switch. The discharge circuit consists of the branch L_s–C_s–R_s. The inductor current reaches zero afterwards at which moment the snubber polarizing diode D_s blocks and the remaining overvoltage decays exponentially through the C_s–R_s loop.

The advantages of the conventional dissipative snubber circuits can be summarized as follows:

- Transfer of the switching losses from the semiconductor device to an external resistor;
- Suppression of high voltage transients;
- Control of the rise rate of the current during turn-on and the rise rate of the voltage during turn-off;
- Reduction of the generated 'noise' and the electromagnetic interference;
- Avoidance of the second breakdown in BJT based transistor inverters.

On the other hand, the following disadvantages associated with these snubber circuits can be identified:

- The energy stored in the reactive elements is dissipated in external resistors, thus decreasing overall converter efficiency;
- Overvoltages can still occur as a result of resonances between snubber or stray inductances and snubber or parasitic capacitors;

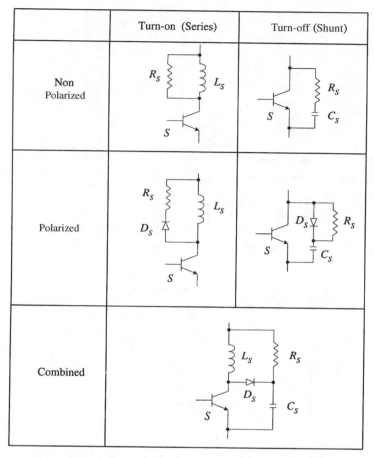

	Turn-on (Series)	Turn-off (Shunt)
Non Polarized		
Polarized		
Combined		

Fig. 5.14 Conventional dissipative snubber circuits.

- Extra components are required, thus increasing power circuit complexity;
- The power losses also complicate the thermal layout and the heat sink design thus leading to an increase in cost.

At higher power levels and switching frequencies, it is more desirable to use non-dissipative (low loss) snubber circuits. The snubber circuits previously presented (Figure 5.14) can be used for each switching device separately. However, it is more efficient to combine components and to use for instance one reactive element (inductor/capacitor) for both switches of a PWM inverter leg.

There are various snubber configurations that improve the overall component count by reducing the number of snubber elements (Undeland, 1976; Undeland et al., 1983; 1984; Zach et al., 1986). In many cases and depending upon the application of the converters, its power level, etc. the snubber circuits maybe more or less complicated. Some snubber configurations proposed for converters are shown in Figures 5.15, 5.16 and 5.17 showing increased complexity and different arrangements

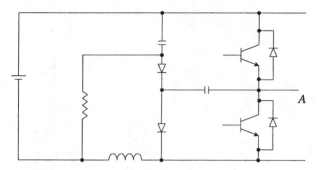

Fig. 5.15 An inverter leg with the improved dissipative snubber circuit.

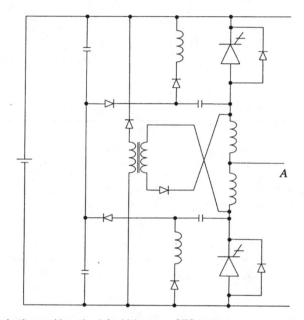

Fig. 5.16 A non-dissipative snubber circuit for high power GTO inverter.

in trying to recover the high energy associated with the operation of the snubber circuit (Holtz et al., 1988; 1989).

5.9 Current trends in power semiconductor technology

In recent years, reports have shown that improvements in the performance of the semiconductors can be achieved by replacing silicon with the following:

- silicon carbide (SiC)
- semiconducting diamond
- gallium arsenide.

The first group of devices is the most promising technology (Palmour et al., 1997).

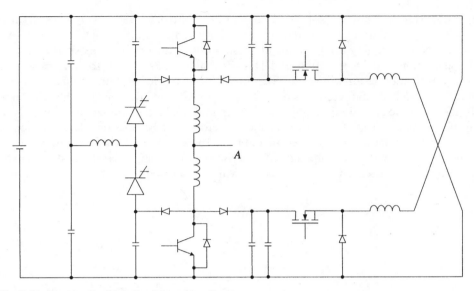

Fig. 5.17 A lossless snubber circuit for an inverter leg.

These new power semiconductor materials offer a number of interesting characteristics, which can be summarized as follows:

- large band gap
- high carrier mobility
- high electrical and thermal conductivity.

Due to the characteristics mentioned above, this new class of power device offers a number of positive attributes such as:

- high power capability
- operation at high frequencies
- relatively low voltage drop when conducting
- operation at high junction temperatures.

Such devices will be able to operate at temperatures up to approximately 600 °C. It is anticipated that this technology will probably offer semiconductors with characteristics closer to the desired ones discussed in the previous section.

Another important development is associated with the matrix converter (direct AC–AC conversion without a DC-link stage). For this converter bidirectional self-commutated devices are needed to build the converter. At the moment research efforts show some promising results (Heinke et al., 2000). However, a commercial product is probably not going to be available before the next decade or so.

5.10 Conclusion

Progress in semiconductor devices achieved over the last twenty years and anticipated developments and improvements promise an exciting new era in power electronic systems. Snubberless operation of fully controlled semiconductors at high values of current and voltage and their rates of change will be realizable in the near future. New emerging applications of these semiconductors in areas such as Power Transmission and Distribution and High Voltage Industrial Motor Drives will be possible. The thyristor will remain the only component for certain applications, due to its unmatched characteristics. However, expected improvements of the GTO and IGBT technology and emerging new devices may replace it sooner than later. New applications and use of improved semiconductors may be possible. The next ten to twenty years will therefore see design and use of power electronic systems towards the 'silicon only' with 'no impedance' reactive power compensators and a totally electronically controlled power system as will be discussed in the following chapters.

6

Power electronic equipment

6.1 Introduction

Reactive power compensation in electric power systems is very important as explained in earlier chapters. In this chapter, we examine closer how compensators are realized in practice using the semiconductors and associated technology presented in Chapter 5.

In the first part of the chapter, the *static* compensators are presented. This kind of equipment belongs to the class of active compensators. Furthermore, *static* means that, unlike the synchronous condenser, they have no moving parts. They are used for surge-impedance compensation and for compensation by sectioning in long-distance, high-voltage transmission systems. In addition they have a variety of load-compensating applications. Their practical applications are listed in greater detail in Table 6.1. The main headings in Table 6.1 will be recognized as the fundamental requirements for operating an AC power system, as discussed in previous chapters. Other applications not listed in Table 6.1, but which may nevertheless

Table 6.1 Practical applications of static compensators in electric power systems

---

Maintain voltage at or near a constant level
- under slowly varying conditions due to load changes
- to correct voltage changes caused by unexpected events (e.g. load rejections, generator and line outages)
- to reduce voltage flicker caused by rapidly fluctuating loads (e.g. arc furnaces).

Improve power system stability
- by supporting the voltage at key points (e.g. the mid-point of a long line)
- by helping to improve swing damping.

Improve power factor

Correct phase unbalance

---

be very beneficial, include the control of AC voltage near conventional HVDC converter terminals, the minimization of transmission losses resulting from local generation or absorption of reactive power, and the suppression of subsynchronous resonance. Some types of compensators can also be designed to assist in the limitation of dynamic overvoltages.

In later parts of the chapter some widely used thyristor based controllers, namely the TCR, the thyristor-controlled transformer (TCT), and the TSC are introduced. We then discuss the conventional switch-mode voltage-source converters (VSCs). Some new topologies incorporating solid-state technology to provide multilevel waveforms for high power applications are also presented. Finally, the chapter discusses applications of such technology in energy storage systems, HVDC power transmission systems and active filtering.

6.2 Thyristor-controlled equipment

6.2.1 Thyristor-controlled reactor (TCR)

In this chapter, the IEEE terms and definitions for the various power electronic based controllers are used throughout.

Thyristor-controlled reactor (TCR) is defined as: a shunt-connected thyristor-controlled inductor whose effective reactance is varied in a continuous manner by partial conduction control of the thyristor valve.

Thyristor-switched reactor (TSR) is defined as: a shunt-connected, thyristor-switched inductor whose effective reactance is varied in a stepwise manner by full- or zero-conduction operation of the thyristor valve.

6.2.1.1 *Principles of operation of the TCR*

The basis of the TCR is shown in Figure 6.1. The controlling element is the thyristor controller, shown here as two back-to-back thyristors which conduct on alternate half-cycles of the supply frequency. If the thyristors are gated into conduction precisely at the peaks of the supply voltage, full conduction results in the reactor, and the current is the same as though the thyristor controller were short-circuited. The current is essentially reactive, lagging the voltage by nearly 90°. It contains a small in-phase component due to the power losses in the reactor, which may be of the order of 0.5–2% of the reactive power. Full conduction is shown by the current waveform in Figure 6.2(a).

If the gating is delayed by equal amounts on both thyristors, a series of current waveforms is obtained, such as those in Figure 6.2(a) through (d). Each of these corresponds to a particular value of the gating angle α, which is measured from the zero-crossing of the voltage. Full conduction is obtained with a gating angle of 90°. Partial conduction is obtained with gating angles between 90° and 180°. The effect of increasing the gating angle is to reduce the fundamental harmonic component of the current. This is equivalent to an increase in the inductance of the reactor, reducing its reactive power as well as its current. So far as the fundamental component of current is concerned, the TCR is a controllable susceptance, and can therefore be applied as a static compensator.

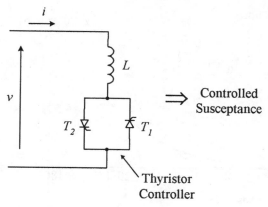

Fig. 6.1 Basic thyristor-controlled reactor.

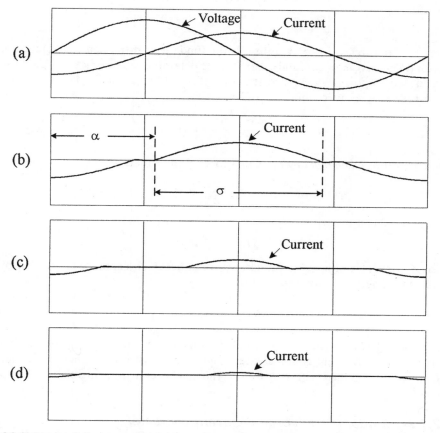

Fig. 6.2 Voltage and line current waveforms of a basic single-phase TCR for various firing angles. (a) $\alpha = 90°$, $\sigma = 180°$; (b) $\alpha = 100°$, $\sigma = 160°$; (c) $\alpha = 130°$, $\sigma = 100°$; (d) $\alpha = 150°$, $\sigma = 60°$.

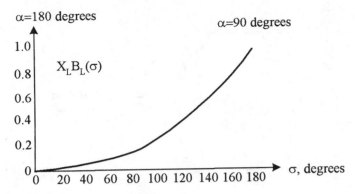

Fig. 6.3 Control law of a basic TCR.

The instantaneous current i is given by

$$i = \begin{cases} \dfrac{\sqrt{2}V}{X_L}(\cos a - \cos \omega t), & a < \omega t < a + \sigma \\ 0, & a + \sigma < \omega t < a + \pi \end{cases} \tag{6.1}$$

where V is the rms voltage; $X_L = \omega L$ is the fundamental-frequency reactance of the reactor (in Ohms); $\omega = 2\pi f$; and α is the gating delay angle. The time origin is chosen to coincide with a positive-going zero-crossing of the voltage. The fundamental component is found by Fourier analysis and is given by

$$I_1 = \frac{\sigma - \sin \sigma}{\pi X_L} V \text{ A rms} \tag{6.2}$$

where σ is the *conduction angle*, related to α by the equation

$$a + \frac{\sigma}{2} = \pi \tag{6.3}$$

Equation 6.2 can be written as

$$I_1 = B_L(\sigma)V \tag{6.4}$$

where $B_L(\sigma)$ is an adjustable fundamental-frequency susceptance controlled by the conduction angle according to the law

$$B_L(\sigma) = \frac{\sigma - \sin \sigma}{\pi X_L} \tag{6.5}$$

This control law is shown in Figure 6.3. The maximum value of B_L is $1/X_L$, obtained with $\sigma = \pi$ or $180°$, that is, full conduction in the thyristor controller. The minimum value is zero, obtained with $\sigma = 0$ ($\alpha = 180°$). This control principle is called *phase control*.

6.2.1.2 *Fundamental voltage/current characteristic*
The TCR has to have a control system that determines the gating instants (and therefore σ), and that issues the gating pulses to the thyristors. In some designs the

control system responds to a signal that directly represents the desired susceptance B_L. In others, the control algorithm processes various measured parameters of the compensated system (e.g. the voltage) and generates the gating pulses directly without using an explicit signal for B_L. In either case the result is a voltage/current characteristic of the form shown in Figure 6.4. Steady-state operation is shown at the point of intersection with the system load line. In the example, the conduction angle is shown as 130°, giving a voltage slightly above 1.0 p.u., but this is only one of an infinite number of possible combinations, depending on the system load line, the control settings, and the compensator rating. The control characteristic in Figure 6.4 can be described by the equation

$$\mathbf{V} = \mathbf{V}_k + jX_S\mathbf{I}_1 \quad 0 < I_1 < I_{max} \tag{6.6}$$

where I_{max} is normally the rated current of the reactors shown here as 1 p.u.

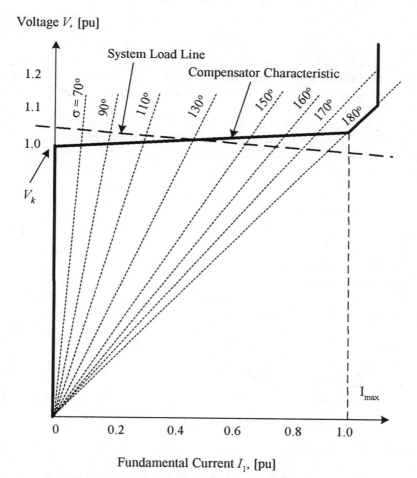

Fig. 6.4 Fundamental voltage/current characteristic in the TCR compensator.

6.2.1.3 *Harmonics*

Increasing the gating angle (reducing the conduction angle) has two other important effects. First, the power losses decrease in both the thyristor controller and the reactor. Second, the current waveform becomes less sinusoidal; in other words, the TCR generates harmonic currents. If the gating angles are balanced, (i.e. equal for both thyristors), all odd order harmonics are generated, and the rms value of the nth harmonic component is given by

$$I_n = \frac{4}{\pi} \frac{V}{X_L} \left[\frac{\sin(n+1)\alpha}{2(n+1)} + \frac{\sin(n-1)\alpha}{2(n-1)} - \cos\alpha \frac{\sin n\alpha}{n} \right] \quad n = 3, 5, 7\dots \quad (6.7)$$

Figure 6.5(a) shows the variation of the amplitudes of some of the major (lower-order) harmonics with the conduction angles, and Figure 6.5(b) the variation of the total harmonic content.

Table 6.2 gives the maximum amplitudes of the harmonics down to the 37th. (Note that the maxima do not all occur at the same conduction angle.)

The TCR described so far is only a single-phase device. For three-phase systems the preferred arrangement is shown in Figure 6.6; i.e. three single-phase TCRs connected in delta. When the system is balanced, all the triplen harmonics circulate in the closed delta and are absent from the line currents. All the other harmonics are present in the line currents and their amplitudes are in the same proportions as shown in Figure 6.5 and Table 6.2. However, the waveforms differ from those ones presented in Figure 6.2.

It is important in the TCR to ensure that the conduction angles of the two back-to-back thyristors are equal. Unequal conduction angles would produce even harmonic components in the current, including DC. They would also cause unequal thermal stresses in the thyristors. The requirement for equal conduction also limits σ to a

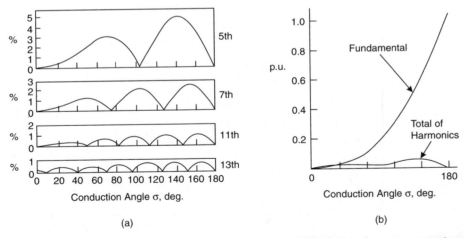

(a)   (b)

Fig. 6.5 TCR Harmonics. (a) major harmonic current components of TCR. Each is shown as a percentage of the fundamental component at full conduction. The percentages are the same for both phase and line currents; and (b) total harmonic content of TCR current, as a fraction of the fundamental component at full conduction. The percentages are the same for both phase and line currents.

Table 6.2 Maximum amplitudes of harmonic currents in TCR[a]

Harmonic order	Percentage
1	100.00
3	(13.78)[b]
5	5.05
7	2.59
9	(1.57)
11	1.05
13	0.75
15	(0.57)
17	0.44
19	0.35
21	(0.29)
23	0.24
25	0.20
27	(0.17)
29	0.15
31	0.13
33	(0.12)
35	0.10
37	0.09

[a] Values are expressed as a percentage of the amplitude of the fundamental component at full conduction.
[b] The values apply to both phase and line currents, except that triplen harmonics do not appear in the line currents. Balanced conditions are assumed.

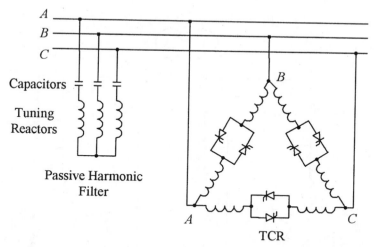

Fig. 6.6 Three-phase TCR with shunt capacitors. The split arrangement of the reactors in each phase provides extra protection to the thyristor controller in the event of a reactor fault.

maximum of 180°. However, if the reactor in Figure 6.1 is divided into two separate reactors (Figure 6.7), the conduction angle in each leg can be increased to as much as 360°. This arrangement has lower harmonics than that of Figure 6.1, but the power losses are increased because of currents circulating between the two halves.

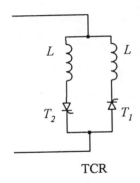

TCR

Fig. 6.7 TCR with more than 180° of conduction in each leg to reduce harmonic currents.

As already noted, TCR harmonic currents are sometimes removed by filters (Figure 6.6). An alternative means for eliminating the 5th and 7th harmonics is to split the TCR into two parts fed from two secondaries on the step-down transformer, one being in wye and the other in delta, as shown in Figure 6.8. This produces a 30° phase shift between the voltages and currents of the two TCRs and virtually eliminates the 5th and 7th harmonics from the primary-side line current. It is known as a 12-pulse arrangement because there are 12 thyristor gatings every period. The same phase-multiplication technique is used in conventional HVDC rectifier transformers

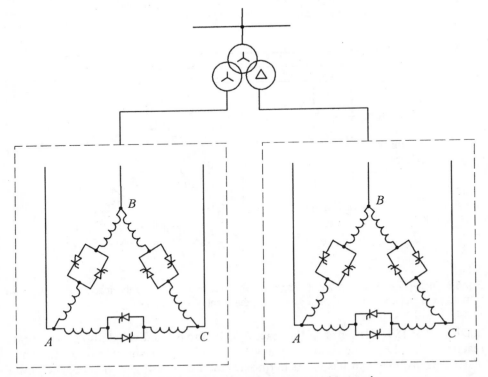

Fig. 6.8 Arrangement of 12-pulse TCR configuration with double-secondary transformer.

for harmonic cancellation. With the 12-pulse scheme, the lowest-order characteristic harmonics are the 11th and 13th. It can be used without filters for the 5th and 7th harmonics, which is an advantage when system resonances occur near these frequencies. For higher-order harmonics a plain capacitor is often sufficient, connected on the low-voltage side of the step-down transformer. Otherwise a high-pass filter may be used. The generation of third-harmonic currents under unbalanced conditions is similar to that in the six-pulse arrangement (Figure 6.6).

With both 6-pulse and 12-pulse TCR compensators, the need for filters and their frequency responses must be evaluated with due regard to the possibility of unbalanced operation. The influence of other capacitor banks and sources of harmonic currents in the electrical neighbourhood of the compensator must also be taken into account. For this purpose, several software packages are available and some examples with a specific one will be provided in Chapter 8.

The 12-pulse connection has the further advantage that if one half is faulted the other may be able to continue to operate normally. The control system must take into account the 30° phase shift between the two TCRs, and must be designed to ensure accurate harmonic cancellation. A variant of the 12-pulse TCR uses two separate transformers instead of one with two secondaries.

6.2.2 The thyristor-controlled transformer (TCT)

Another variant of the TCR is the TCT (Figure 6.9). Instead of using a separate step-down transformer and linear reactors, the transformer is designed with very high

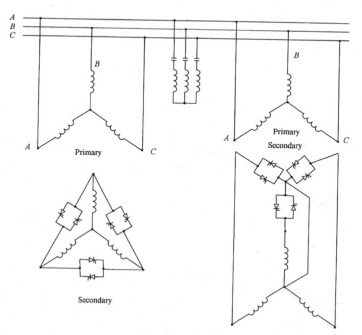

Fig. 6.9 Alternative arrangements of thyristor-controlled transformer compensator. (a) with wye-connected reactors and delta-connected thyristor controller; and (b) wye-connected reactors and thyristor controller (four-wire system).

leakage reactance, and the secondary windings are merely short-circuited through the thyristor controllers. A gapped core is necessary to obtain the high leakage reactance, and the transformer can take the form of three single-phase transformers. With the arrangements in Figure 6.9 there is no secondary bus and any shunt capacitors must be connected at the primary voltage unless a separate step-down transformer is provided. The high leakage reactance helps protect the transformer against short-circuit forces during secondary faults. Because of its linearity and large thermal mass the TCT can usefully withstand overloads in the lagging (absorbing) regime.

6.2.3 The TCR with shunt capacitors

It is important to note that the TCR current (the compensating current) can be varied *continuously*, without steps, between zero and a maximum value corresponding to full conduction. The current is always lagging, so that reactive power can only be absorbed. However, the TCR compensator can be biased by shunt capacitors so that its overall power factor is leading and reactive power is generated into the external system. The effect of adding the capacitor currents to the TCR currents shown in Figure 6.4 is to bias the control characteristic into the second quadrant, as shown in Figure 6.10. In a three-phase system the preferred arrangement is to connect the capacitors in wye, as shown in Figure 6.6. The current in Figure 6.10 is, of course, the fundamental positive sequence component, and if it lies between $I_{C\,max}$ and $I_{L\,max}$ the control characteristic is again represented by equation (6.6). However, if the voltage regulator gain is unchanged, the slope reactance X_s will be slightly increased when the capacitors are added.

As is common with shunt capacitor banks, the capacitors may be divided into more than one three-phase group, each group being separately switched by a circuit

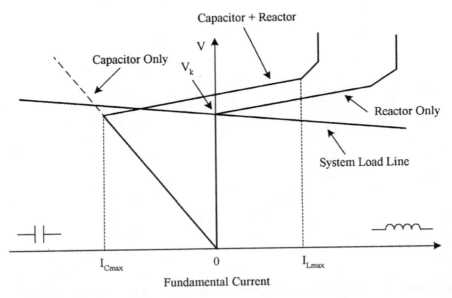

Fig. 6.10 Voltage/current characteristics of TCR.

breaker. The groups can be tuned to particular frequencies by small series reactors in each phase, to filter the harmonic currents generated by the TCR and so prevent them from flowing in the external system. One possible choice is to have groups tuned to the 5th and 7th harmonics, with another arranged as a high-pass filter. The capacitors arranged as filters, and indeed the entire compensator, must be designed with careful attention to their effect on the resonances of the power system at the point of connection.

It is common for the compensation requirement to extend into both the lagging and the leading ranges. A TCR with fixed capacitors cannot have a lagging current unless the TCR reactive power rating exceeds that of the capacitors. The net reactive power absorption rating with the capacitors connected equals the difference between the ratings of the TCR and the capacitors. In such cases the required TCR rating can be very large indeed (up to some hundreds of MVAr in transmission system applications). When the net reactive power is small or lagging, large reactive current circulates between the TCR and the capacitors without performing any useful function in the power system. For this reason the capacitors are sometimes designed to be switched in groups, so that the degree of capacitive bias in the voltage/current characteristic can be adjusted in steps. If this is done, a smaller 'interpolating' TCR can be used.

An example is shown schematically in Figure 6.11, having the shunt capacitors divided into three groups. The TCR controller is provided with a signal representing the number of capacitors connected, and is designed to provide a continuous overall voltage/current characteristic. When a capacitor group is switched on or off, the conduction angle is immediately adjusted, along with other reference signals, so that the capacitive reactive power added or subtracted is exactly balanced by an equal

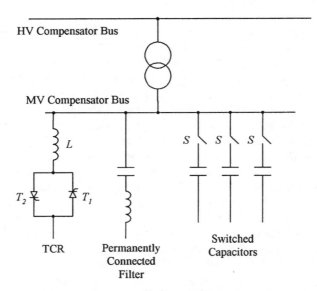

Fig. 6.11 Hybrid compensator with switched capacitors and 'interpolating' TCR. The switches S may be mechanical circuit breakers or thyristor switches.

change in the inductive reactive power of the TCR. Thereafter the conduction angle will vary continuously according to the system requirements, until the next capacitor switching occurs.

The performance of this hybrid arrangement of a TCR and switched shunt capacitors depends critically on the method of switching the capacitors, and the switching strategy. The most common way to switch the capacitors is with conventional circuit breakers. If the operating point is continually ranging up and down the voltage/current characteristic, the rapid accumulation of switching operations may cause a maintenance problem in the circuit breakers. Also, in transmission system applications there may be conflicting requirements as to whether the capacitors should be switched in or out during severe system faults. Under these circumstances repeated switching can place extreme duty on the capacitors and circuit breakers, and in most cases this can only be avoided by inhibiting the compensator from switching the capacitors. Unfortunately this prevents the full potential of the capacitors from being used during a period when they could be extremely beneficial to the stability of the system.

In some cases these problems have been met by using thyristor controllers instead of circuit breakers to switch the capacitors, taking advantage of the virtually unlimited switching life of the thyristors. The timing precision of the thyristor switches can be exploited to reduce the severity of the switching duty, but even so, during disturbances this duty can be extreme. The number of separately switched capacitor groups in transmission system compensators is usually less than four.

6.2.4 The thyristor-switched capacitor (TSC)

Thyristor switched capacitor is defined as 'a shunt-connected, thyristor-switched capacitor whose effective reactance is varied in a stepwise manner by full- or zero-conduction operation of the thyristor valve'.

6.2.4.1 Principles of operation

The principle of the TSC is shown in Figures 6.12 and 6.13. The susceptance is adjusted by controlling the number of parallel capacitors in conduction. Each capacitor always conducts for an integral number of half-cycles. With k capacitors in parallel, each controlled by a switch as in Figure 6.13, the total susceptance can be equal to that of any combination of the k individual susceptances taken $0, 1, 2 \ldots$ or k at a time. The total susceptance thus varies in a stepwise manner. In principle the steps can be made as small and as numerous as desired, by having a sufficient number of individually switched capacitors. For a given number k the maximum number of steps will be obtained when no two combinations are equal, which requires at least that all the individual susceptances be different. This degree of flexibility is not usually sought in power-system compensators because of the consequent complexity of the controls, and because it is generally more economic to make most of the susceptances equal. One compromise is the so-called binary system in which there are $(k - 1)$ equal susceptances B and one susceptance $B/2$. The half-susceptance increases the number of combinations from k to $2k$.

The relation between the compensator current and the number of capacitors conducting is shown in Figure 6.14 (for constant terminal voltage). Ignoring switching transients, the current is sinusoidal, that is, it contains no harmonics.

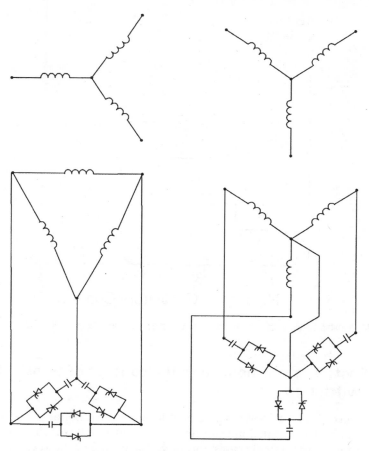

Fig. 6.12 Alternative arangements of three-phase thyristor-switched capacitor. (a) delta-connected secondary, Delta-connected TSC; and (b) wye-connected secondary, wye-connected TSC (four-wire system).

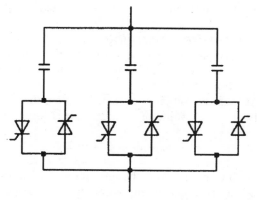

Fig. 6.13 Principles of operation of TSC. Each phase of Figure 6.12 comprises of parallel combinations of switched capacitors of this type.

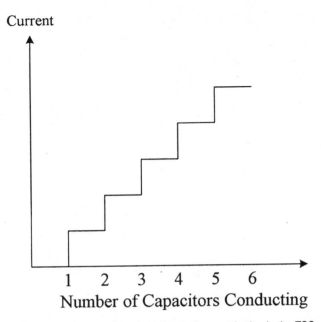

Current

Number of Capacitors Conducting

Fig. 6.14 Relationship between current and number of capacitors conducting in the TSC.

6.2.5　Switching transients and the concept of transient-free switching

When the current in an individual capacitor reaches a natural zero-crossing, the thyristors can be left ungated and no further current will flow. The reactive power supplied to the power system ceases abruptly. The capacitor, however, is left with a trapped charge (Figure 6.15(a)). Because of this charge, the voltage across the thyristors subsequently alternates between zero and twice the peak-phase voltage. The only instant when the thyristors can be gated again without transients is when the voltage across them is zero (Figure 6.15(b)). This coincides with peak-phase voltage.

6.2.5.1　Ideal transient-free switching

The simple case of a switched capacitor, with no other circuit elements than the voltage supply, is used first to describe the important concept of transient-free switching. Figure 6.16 shows the circuit.

With sinusoidal AC supply voltage $v = \hat{v}\sin(\omega_0 t + \alpha)$, the thyristors can be gated into conduction only at a peak value of voltage, that is, when

$$\frac{dv}{dt} = \omega_0\hat{v}\cos(\omega_0 t + \alpha) = 0 \tag{6.8}$$

Gating at any other instant would require the current $i = C\,dv/dt$ to have a discontinuous step change at $t = 0^+$. Such a step is impossible in practice because of inductance, which is considered in the next section. To permit analysis of Figure 6.16, the gating must occur at a voltage peak, and with this restriction the current is given by

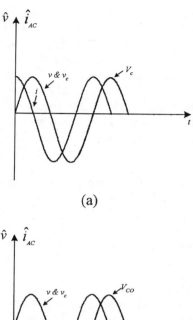

(a)

(b)

Fig. 6.15 Ideal transient-free switching waveforms. (a) switching on; and (b) switching off.

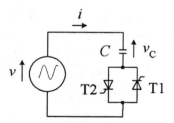

Fig. 6.16 Circuit for analysis of transient-free switching.

$$i = C\frac{\mathrm{d}v}{\mathrm{d}t} = \hat{v}\omega_0 C \cos{(\omega_0 t + \alpha)} \tag{6.9}$$

where $\alpha = \pm\pi/2$. Now $\omega_0 C = B_c$ is the fundamental-frequency susceptance of the capacitor, and $X_c = 1/B_c$ its reactance, so that with $\alpha = \pm\pi/2$

$$i = \pm\hat{v}B_c \sin{(\omega_0 t)} = +\hat{i}_{AC} \sin{(\omega_0 t)} \tag{6.10}$$

where $\hat{i}_{AC}$ is the peak value of the AC current, $\hat{i}_{AC} = \hat{v}B_C = \hat{v}/X_C$.

In the absence of other circuit elements, we must also specify that the capacitor be precharged to the voltage $V_{C0} = \pm\hat{v}$, that is, it must hold the prior charge $\pm\hat{v}/C$. This is because any prior DC voltage on the capacitor cannot be accounted for in the simple circuit of Figure 6.16. In practice this voltage would appear distributed across series inductance and resistance with a portion across the thyristor switch.

With these restrictions, that is, $dv/dt = 0$ and $V_{C0} = \pm\hat{v}$ at $t = 0$, we have the ideal case of transient-free switching, as illustrated in Figure 6.15. This concept is the basis for switching control in the TSC. In principle, once each capacitor is charged to either the positive or the negative system peak voltage, it is possible to switch any or all of the capacitors on or off for any integral number of half-cycles without transients.

6.2.5.2 *Switching transients in the general case*

Under practical conditions, it is necessary to consider inductance and resistance. First consider the addition of series inductance in Figure 6.16. In any practical TSC circuit, there must always be at least enough series inductance to keep di/dt within the capability of the thyristors. In some circuits there may be more than this minimum inductance. In the following, resistance will be neglected because it is generally small and its omission makes no significant difference to the calculation of the first few peaks of voltage and current.

The presence of inductance and capacitance together makes the transients oscillatory. The natural frequency of the transients will be shown to be a key factor in the magnitudes of the voltages and currents after switching, yet it is not entirely under the designer's control because the total series inductance includes the supply-system inductance which, if known at all, may be known only approximately. It also includes the inductance of the step-down transformer (if used), which is subject to other constraints and cannot be chosen freely.

It may not always be possible to connect the capacitor at a crest value of the supply voltage. It is necessary to ask what other events in the supply-voltage cycle can be detected and used to initiate the gating of the thyristors, and what will be the resulting transients.

The circuit is that of Figure 6.17. The voltage equation in terms of the Laplace transform is

$$V(s) = \left[L \cdot s + \frac{1}{C \cdot s}\right] I(s) + \frac{V_{C0}}{s} \tag{6.11}$$

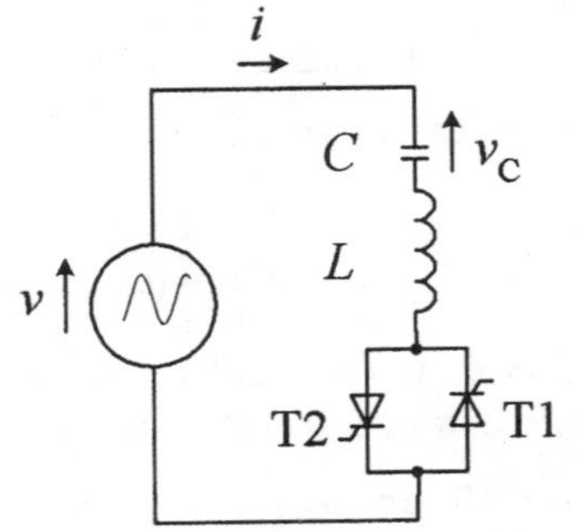

Fig. 6.17 Circuit for analysis of practical capacitor switching.

The supply voltage is given by $v = \hat{v}\sin(\omega_0 t + \alpha)$. Time is measured from the first instant when a thyristor is gated, corresponding to the angle α on the voltage waveform. By straightforward transform manipulation and inverse transformation we get the instantaneous current expressed as

$$i(t) = \hat{i}_{AC}\cos(\omega_0 t + \alpha) - nB_C\left[V_{C0} - \frac{n^2}{n^2-1}\hat{v}\sin\alpha\right]\sin(\omega_n t) - \hat{i}_{AC}\cos\alpha\cos(\omega_n t)$$

(6.12)

where ω_n is the natural frequency of the circuit

$$\omega_n = \frac{1}{\sqrt{LC}} = n\omega_0$$

(6.13)

and

$$n = \sqrt{\frac{X_C}{X_L}}$$

(6.14)

n is the per-unit natural frequency.

The current has a fundamental-frequency component i_{AC} which leads the supply voltage by $\pi/2$ radians. Its amplitude $\hat{i}_{AC}$ is given by

$$\hat{i}_{AC} = \hat{v}B_C\frac{n^2}{n^2-1}$$

(6.15)

and is naturally proportional to the fundamental-frequency susceptance of the capacitance and inductance in series, that is, $B_c n^2/(n^2-1)$. The term $n^2/(n^2-1)$ is a magnification factor, which accounts for the partial series-tuning of the L–C circuit. If there is appreciable inductance, n can be as low as 2.5, or even lower, and the magnification factor can reach 1.2 or higher. It is plotted in Figure 6.18.

The last two terms on the right-hand side of equation (6.12) represent the expected oscillatory components of current having the frequency ω_n. In practice, resistance

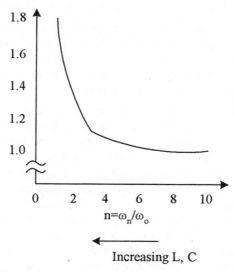

Fig. 6.18 Voltage and current magnification factor $n^2/(n^2-1)$.

causes these terms to decay. The next section considers the behaviour of the oscillatory components under important practical conditions.

1. *Necessary condition for transient-free switching.* For transient-free switching, the oscillatory components of current in equation (6.12) must be zero. This can happen only when the following two conditions are simultaneously satisfied:

$$\cos \alpha = 0 \quad (i.e. \sin \alpha = \pm 1) \tag{6.16}$$

$$V_{C0} = \pm \hat{v} \frac{n^2}{n^2 - 1} = \pm X_c \hat{i}_{AC} \tag{6.17}$$

The first of these equations means that the thyristors must be gated at a positive or negative crest of the supply voltage sinewave. The second one means that the capacitors must also be precharged to the voltage $\hat{v}n^2/(n^2 - 1)$ with the same polarity. The presence of inductance means that for transient-free switching the capacitor must be 'overcharged' beyond $\hat{v}$ by the magnification factor $n^2/(n^2 - 1)$. With low values of n, this factor can be appreciable (Figure 6.18).

Of the two conditions necessary for transient-free switching, the precharging condition expressed by equation (6.17) is strictly outside the control of the gating-control circuits because V_{C0}, n, and $\hat{v}$ can all vary during the period of non-conduction before the thyristors are gated. The capacitor will be slowly discharging, reducing V_{C0}; while the supply system voltage and effective inductance may change in an unknown way, changing n. In general, therefore, it will be impossible to guarantee perfect transient-free reconnection.

In practice the control strategy should cause the thyristors to be gated in such a way as to keep the oscillatory transients within acceptable limits. Of the two conditions given by equations (6.16) and (6.17), the first one can in principle always be satisfied. The second one can be approximately satisfied under normal conditions. For a range of system voltages near 1 p.u., equation (6.17) will be nearly satisfied if the capacitor does not discharge (during a non-conducting period) to a very low voltage: or if it is kept precharged or 'topped up' to a voltage near $\pm \hat{v}n^2/(n^2 - 1)$.

2. *Switching transients under non-ideal conditions.* There are some circumstances in which equations (6.16) and (6.17) are far from being satisfied. One is when the capacitor is completely discharged, as for example when the compensator has been switched off for a while. Then $V_{C0} = 0$. There is then no point on the voltage wave when both conditions are simultaneously satisfied.

In the most general case V_{C0} can have any value, depending on the conditions under which conduction last ceased and the time since it did so. The question then arises, how does the amplitude of the oscillatory component depend on V_{C0}? How can the gating instants be chosen to minimize the oscillatory component? Two practical choices of gating are: (a) at the instant when $v = V_{C0}$, giving $\sin \alpha = V_{C0}/\hat{v}$; and (b) when $dv/dt = 0$, giving $\cos \alpha = 0$. The first of these may never occur if the capacitor is overcharged beyond $\hat{v}$. The amplitude $\hat{i}_{osc}$ of the oscillatory component of current can be determined from equation (6.12) for the two alternative gating angles. In Figures 6.19 and 6.20 the resulting value of $\hat{i}_{osc}$ relative to $\hat{i}_{AC}$ is shown as a function of V_{C0} and n, for each of the two gating angles.

From these two figures it is apparent that if V_{C0} is exactly equal to $\hat{v}$, the oscillatory component of current is non-zero and has the same amplitude for both gating angles,

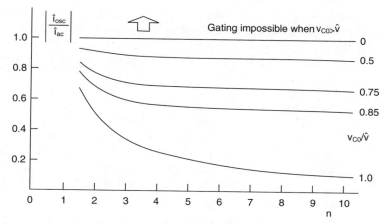

Fig. 6.19 Amplitude of oscillatory current component. Thyristors gated when $v = v_{C0}$.

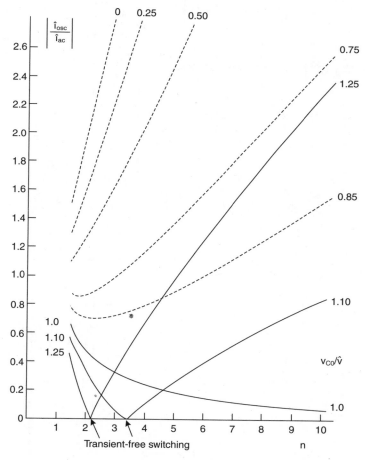

Fig. 6.20 Amplitude of oscillatory current component. Thyristors gated when $dv/dt = 0$.

whatever the value of the natural frequency n. For any value of V_{c0} less than $\hat{v}$, gating with $v = V_{C0}$ always gives the smaller oscillatory component whatever the value of n.

The conditions for transient-free switching appear in Figure 6.20 in terms of the precharge voltage required for two particular natural frequencies corresponding to $n = 2.3$ and $n = 3.6$.

6.2.5.3 Switching a discharged capacitor

In this case $V_{C0} = 0$. The two gating angles discussed were: (a) when $v = V_{C0} = 0$; and (b) when $dv/dt = 0$ ($\cos \alpha = 0$). In the former case only equation (6.17) is satisfied. From equation (6.12) it can be seen that in the second case (gating when $dv/dt = 0$) the oscillatory component of current is greater than in the first case (gating when $v = V_{C0} = 0$). An example is shown in Figure 6.21 and Figure 6.22.

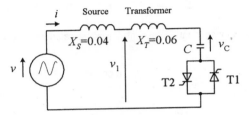

Fig. 6.21 Switching a discharge capacitor; circuit diagram.

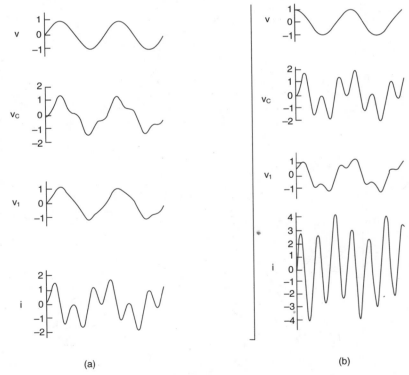

(a)   (b)

Fig. 6.22 Switching transients with discharge capacitor. (a) gating when $v = v_{C0} = 0$; (b) gating when $dv/dt = 0$.

The reactances are chosen such at $\hat{i}_{AC} = 1$ p.u. and the natural frequency is given by $n = X_C/(X_S + X_T) = 3.6$ p.u. In case (a), the amplitude of the oscillatory component of current is exactly equal to $\hat{i}_{AC}$. In case (b), the oscillatory component has the amplitude $n\hat{i}_{AC}$ and much higher current peaks are experienced. The capacitor experiences higher voltage peaks and the supply voltage distortion is greater.

6.3 Voltage-source converters (VSCs) and derived controllers

The solid-state DC–AC power electronic converters can be classified into two categories with respect to the type of their input source on the DC side being either a voltage- or a current-source:

1. Voltage-source converters or else voltage-source inverters (VSIs): the DC bus input is a voltage source (typically a capacitor) and its current through can be either positive or negative. This allows power flow between the DC and AC sides to be bidirectional through the reversal of the direction of the current.
2. Current-source converters (CSCs) or else current-source inverters (CSIs): the DC bus input is a current source (typically an inductor in series with a voltage source, i.e. a capacitor) and its voltage across can be either positive or negative. This also allows the power flow between the DC and AC sides to be bidirectional through the reversal of the polarity of the voltage.

The conventional phase-controlled thyristor-based converters can only be current source systems. The modern converters based on fully controlled semiconductors can be of either type. In most reactive power compensation applications, when fully controlled power semiconductors are used, the converters then are voltage-source based. However, the conventional thyristor-controlled converters are still used in high power applications and conventional HVDC systems.

In the following sections, we discuss first the half-bridge and the full-bridge single-phase VSC topologies. It is important to understand the operation principles of these two basic converters to fully understand and appreciate all the other derived topologies, namely the conventional six-switch three-phase VSC and other multilevel topologies.

6.3.1 Single-phase half-bridge VSC

Let us consider first the simplest and basic solid-state DC–AC converter, namely the single-phase half-bridge VSC. Figure 6.23 shows the power circuit. It consists of two switching devices (S_1 and S_2) with two antiparallel diodes (D_1 and D_2) to accommodate the return of the current to the DC bus when required. This happens when the load power factor is other than unity. In order to generate a mid-point (O) to connect the return path of the load, two equal value capacitors (C_1 and C_2) are connected in series across the DC input. The result is that the voltage V_{dc} is split into two equal sources across each capacitor with voltage of $V_{dc}/2$. The assumption here is

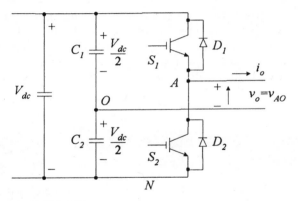

Fig. 6.23 Single-phase half-bridge VSC.

that the value of the capacitors is sufficiently large to ensure a stiff DC voltage source. This simply means that their voltage potential remains unchanged during the operation of the circuit. This also means that the potential of the mid-point (O) is constant with respect to both positive and negative DC bus rails at all times ($V_{dc}/2$ and $-V_{dc}/2$ respectively).

Let us now examine the operation of this circuit. It can be explained in combination with Figure 6.24. The two control signals for turning on and off the switches S_1 and S_2 are complementary to avoid destruction of the bridge. This would happen due to the throughput of high current coming from the low impedance DC voltage sources, if both switches were turned on simultaneously. When the switch S_1 is turned on ($t_3 < t < t_5$), the output voltage $v_o = v_{AO}$ is equal to the voltage $V_{dc}/2$ of the capacitor C_1. The mode of operation of the switching block (S_1 and D_1) is then controlled by the polarity of the output current i_o. If the output current is positive, with respect to the direction shown in Figure 6.23, then the current is flowing through switch S_1 ($t_4 < t < t_5$, Figure 6.24). If the output current is negative, the diode D_1 is conducting, although switch S_1 is turned on ($t_3 < t < t_4$). Similarly, if the switch S_2 is turned on ($t_1 < t < t_3$), the output voltage is equal to the voltage $V_{dc}/2$ of the capacitor C_2 with the polarity appearing negative this time. The output current i_o once again determines the conduction state of the switch and diode. If the output current is positive, the diode D_2 is conducting ($t_1 < t < t_2$). If the output current is negative, the current flows through switch S_2 ($t_2 < t < t_3$). Such states of switches and diodes are clearly marked in the waveforms of Figure 6.24 for the various time intervals. The modes of operation of the half-bridge single-phase VSC are also summarized in Table 6.3.

Figure 6.24(a) shows the output voltage waveform $v_o = v_{AO}$ generated by the converter operation as previously explained. Due to the square-wave generated by the converter, the output voltage waveform is rich in harmonics. Specifically, as shown in Figure 6.24(c) all odd harmonics are present in the spectrum of the output voltage. The fact that the converter cannot control the rms value of the output voltage waveform at fundamental frequency is also a limitation. A separate arrangement must be made to vary the DC bus voltage V_{dc} in order to vary and control the output voltage v_o.

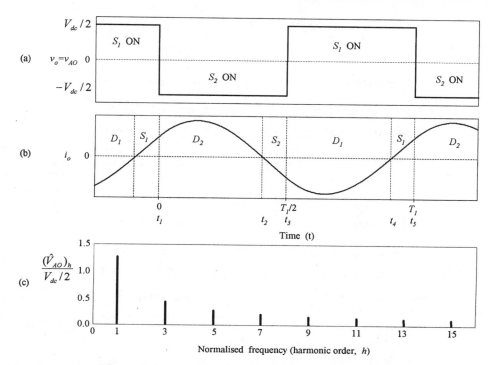

Fig. 6.24 Key waveforms of the single-phase half-bridge VSC circuit operation. (a) output voltage $v_o = v_{AO}$; (b) output current i_o; and (c) harmonic spectrum of the output voltage $v_o = v_{AO}$.

Table 6.3 Modes of operation of the single-phase half-bridge VSC

Switching device state		Output voltage $v_o = v_{AO}$	Output current i_o	Conducting semiconductor	Power transfer
S_1	S_2				
1*	0	$V_{dc}/2$	Positive	S_1 $t_4 < t < t_5$	DC → AC
1	0	$V_{dc}/2$	Negative	D_1 $t_3 < t < t_4$	AC → DC
0	1	$-V_{dc}/2$	Positive	D_2 $t_1 < t < t_2$	AC → DC
0	1	$-V_{dc}/2$	Negative	S_2 $t_2 < t < t_3$	DC → AC

* The switch is ON when its state is 1 (one) and is OFF when its state is 0 (zero).

The amplitude of the fundamental component of the output voltage square-wave v_o shown in Figure 6.24(a) can be expressed using Fourier series as follows

$$(\hat{V}_o)_1 = (\hat{V}_{AO})_1 = \frac{4 \cdot V_{dc}}{2 \cdot \pi} \tag{6.18}$$

The amplitude of all the other harmonics is given by

$$(\hat{V}_o)_h = (\hat{V}_{AO})_h = \frac{4 \cdot V_{dc}}{2 \cdot \pi \cdot h} = \frac{(\hat{V}_o)_1}{h} \qquad h = 3, 5, 7, 9, \dots \tag{6.19}$$

where h is the order of the harmonic.

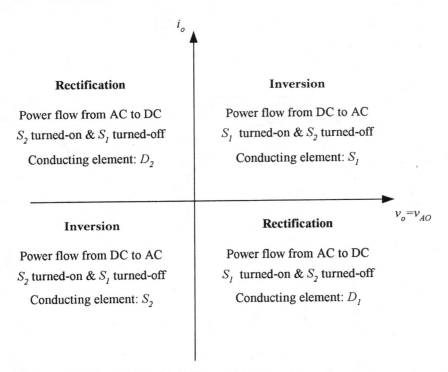

Fig. 6.25 Quadrants of operation of the single-phase half-bridge VSC.

The converter discussed here operates in all four quadrants of output voltage and current as shown in Figure 6.25. There are two distinct modes of operation associated with the transfer of power from the DC to the AC side. When the power flows from the DC bus to the AC side, the converter operates as an inverter. The switches S_1 and S_2 perform this function. In the case that the power is negative, which means power is returned back to the DC bus from the AC side, the converter operates as a rectifier. The diodes D_1 and D_2 perform this function.

The capability of the converter to operate in all four quadrants (Figure 6.25) means that there is no restriction in the phase relationship between the AC output voltage and the AC output current. The converter can therefore be used to exchange leading or lagging reactive power. If the load is purely resistive and no filter is attached to the output the diodes do not take part in the operation of the converter and only real power is transferred from the DC side to the AC one. Under any other power factor, the converter operates in a sequence of modes between a rectifier and an inverter. The magnitude and angle of the AC output voltage with respect to the AC output current control in an independent manner the real and reactive power exchange between the DC and AC sides.

This converter is also the basic building block of any other switch-mode VSC. Specifically, the combination of the switching blocks (S_1 and the antiparallel diode D_1) and (S_2 and D_2) can be used as a leg to build three-phase and other types of converters with parallel connected legs and other topologies. These types of converters will be described in later sections of this chapter.

6.3.2 Single-phase full-bridge VSC

In this section we will examine in detail the single-phase full-bridge VSC. Its power circuit is shown in Figure 6.26. It consists of two identical legs like the half-bridge single-phase converter (Figure 6.23) discussed in Section 6.3.1. Specifically, there are four switching elements (S_1, S_2, S_3, S_4), four antiparallel diodes (D_1, D_2, D_3, D_4) and a DC bus voltage source V_{dc} that can be a single capacitor. The other leg provides the return path for the current this time and the DC bus mid-point does not need to be available to connect the load. The output voltage v_o appears across the two points A and B as shown in Figure 6.26.

The control restriction discussed for the single-phase half-bridge topology (Figure 6.23) applies to this converter as well. Clearly the control signals for the switch pairs (S_1, S_2) and (S_3, S_4) must be complementary to avoid any bridge destruction due to shoot through of infinite current (at least theoretically).

There are two control methods for this topology. The first one treats the switches (S_1, S_4) and (S_2, S_3) as a pair. This means that they are turned on and off at the same time and for the same duration. For square-wave operation the switches S_1 and S_4 are on for half of the period. For the other half, the pair of S_2, S_3 is turned on. Like the single-phase half-bridge VSC, the direction of the output current i_o determines the conduction state of each semiconductor.

When the two switches S_1 and S_4 are turned on, the voltage at the output is equal to the DC bus voltage V_{dc}. Similarly, when the switches S_2 and S_3 are turned on the output voltage is equal to $-V_{dc}$. Such circuit operation is illustrated in Figure 6.27. In the first case, when the direction of the output current i_o is positive as shown in Figure 6.26, the current flows through switches S_1 and S_4 and the power is transferred from the DC side to the AC one ($t_4 < t < t_5$). When the current becomes negative, although the switches S_1 and S_4 are turned on, the diodes D_1 and D_4 conduct the current and return power back to the DC bus from the AC side ($t_3 < t < t_4$). For the other half of the period, when the switches S_2 and S_3 are turned on and the current is positive, the diodes D_2 and D_3 conduct ($t_1 < t < t_2$). In this

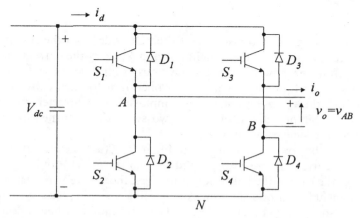

Fig. 6.26 Single-phase full-bridge VSC.

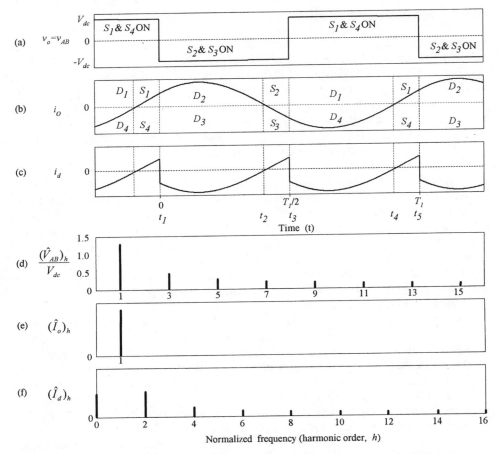

Fig. 6.27 Key waveforms of the single-phase full-bridge VSC circuit operation. (a) output voltage $v_o = v_{AB}$; (b) output current i_o; (c) input DC bus current i_d; (d) harmonic spectrum of the output voltage $v_o = v_{AB}$; (e) harmonic spectrum of the output current i_o; and (f) harmonic spectrum of the input DC bus current i_d.

instance, power is transferred also back to the DC side from the AC side. Finally, when the current is negative, the switches S_2 and S_3 carry the current and assist the converter to transfer power from the DC bus to the AC side ($t_2 < t < t_3$). In summary, there are four distinct modes of operation for this converter when the control method shown in Figure 6.27 is employed (two inverter modes and two rectifier modes). Simply said, at all times two switches are turned on and the legs are controlled in a synchronized way.

The output voltage $v_o = v_{AB}$ is shown in Figure 6.27(a). The output current i_o and the input DC current i_d are also plotted in Figures 6.27(b) and (c) respectively. Similarly, like the case of the half-bridge topology, the square-wave generated across the AC side includes all odd harmonics and being a single-phase system, the third harmonic is also present (Figure 6.27(d)). These harmonics when reflected back to the DC side source include all even harmonics (Figure 6.27(f)).

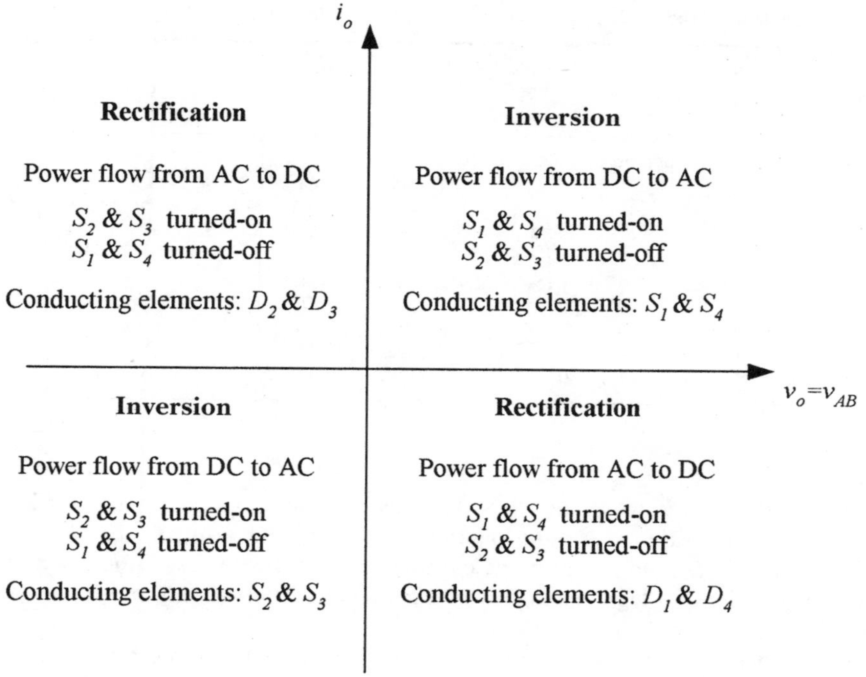

Rectification	**Inversion**
Power flow from AC to DC	Power flow from DC to AC
S_2 & S_3 turned-on S_1 & S_4 turned-off	S_1 & S_4 turned-on S_2 & S_3 turned-off
Conducting elements: D_2 & D_3	Conducting elements: S_1 & S_4
Inversion	**Rectification**
Power flow from DC to AC	Power flow from AC to DC
S_2 & S_3 turned-on S_1 & S_4 turned-off	S_1 & S_4 turned-on S_2 & S_3 turned-off
Conducting elements: S_2 & S_3	Conducting elements: D_1 & D_4

Fig. 6.28 Quadrants of operation of the single-phase full-bridge VSC.

The fundamental component of the output voltage v_o waveform has an amplitude value of

$$(\hat{V}_o)_1 = (\hat{V}_{AB})_1 = \frac{4 \cdot V_{dc}}{\pi} \qquad (6.20)$$

And its various harmonics are given by

$$(\hat{V}_o)_h = (\hat{V}_{AB})_h = \frac{4 \cdot V_{dc}}{\pi \cdot h} = \frac{(\hat{V}_o)_1}{h} \qquad h = 3, 5, 7, 9, \ldots \qquad (6.21)$$

where h is the order of the harmonic.

The converter is capable of operating in all four quadrants of voltage and current as shown in Figure 6.28. The various modes and their relationship to the switching and/or conduction state of the semiconductors are also summarized in Table 6.4 for further clarity. The phase relationship between the AC output voltage and AC output current does not have to be fixed and the converter can provide real and reactive power at all leading and lagging power factors. However, the converter itself cannot control the output voltage if the DC bus voltage V_{dc} remains constant. There is a need to adjust the level of the DC bus voltage if one wants to control the rms value of the output voltage v_o.

There is however a way to control the rms value of the fundamental component of the output voltage as well as the harmonic content of the fixed waveform shown in Figure 6.27(a). In this method, the control signals of the two legs are not

Table 6.4 Modes of operation of the single-phase full-bridge VSC

S_1	S_2	S_3	S_4	Output voltage $v_o = v_{AB}$	Output current i_o	Conducting semiconductor	Power transfer
Switching device state							

S_1	S_2	S_3	S_4	$v_o = v_{AB}$	i_o		
Square-wave method or Phase-shifted method							
1	0	0	1	V_{dc}	Positive	$S_1\ S_4\ t_4 < t < t_5$	DC → AC
1	0	0	1	V_{dc}	Negative	$D_1\ D_4\ t_3 < t < t_4$	AC → DC
0	1	1	0	$-V_{dc}$	Negative	$S_2\ S_3\ t_2 < t < t_3$	DC → AC
0	1	1	0	$-V_{dc}$	Positive	$D_2\ D_3\ t_1 < t < t_2$	AC → DC
Phase-shifted method only (extra modes – free-wheeling modes)							
1	0	1	0	0	Positive	$S_1\ D_3$	None
1	0	1	0	0	Negative	$S_3\ D_1$	None
0	1	0	1	0	Positive	$S_4\ D_2$	None
0	1	0	1	0	Negative	$S_2\ D_4$	None

synchronized in any way and the switches are not treated as pairs like previously. For the safe operation of the converter, the control signals between (S_1 and S_2) and (S_3 and S_4) must be complementary. In this case, there is a phase-shift between the two legs and this way a zero volts interval can appear across the output.

For instance, if switches S_1 and S_3 are turned on at the same time, the output voltage (v_{AB}) will be zero. The current in the case of other than unity power factor must keep flowing. There is no power exchange between the DC side and the AC one (free-wheeling mode). If the current is positive, the current flows through S_1 and D_3. If the current is negative, it flows through D_1 and S_3. Similarly, when the two bottom switches S_2 and S_4 are turned on at the same time, the output voltage (v_{AB}) is zero and the output current once again determines which element conducts and allows the output current to continue flowing. Specifically, if the current is positive, the diode D_2 and the switch S_4 are conducting. In the case that the current is negative, the switch S_2 and diode D_4 provide a path for the output current. These extra modes of operation for the single-phase full-bridge topology (Figure 6.26) are also included in Table 6.4 as the free-wheeling modes.

For a given phase-shift (α degrees) between the control signals of the two legs, the waveforms are shown in Figure 6.29. It is clear that the output voltage waveform is a three-level one, being able to have the values of V_{dc}, 0 and $-V_{dc}$ as shown in Figure 6.29(a). The control signals are shown in Figures 6.29(b)–(d). It is also clear that between the top and bottom switches of each leg complementary control signals are used. It should be noted that for $\alpha = 0$, the output voltage becomes similar to the previously presented control method (square-wave, Figure 6.27(a)).

The output voltage v_o (v_{AB}) is shown in Figure 6.30(a) along with the output current i_o and the DC bus current i_d in Figures 6.30(b) and (c) respectively. Therefore, by controlling the phase-shift between the two legs (α degrees), the rms value of the fundamental component can be controlled. The amplitude of all odd harmonics, as shown in Figure 6.30(d) for the output voltage, can also be controlled. The output current has only a fundamental component as shown in Figure 6.30(e), where the DC bus current has a DC component and all even harmonics as shown in Figure 6.30(f).

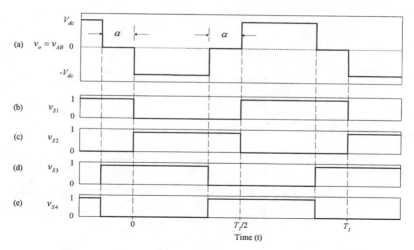

Fig. 6.29 Key waveforms of the single-phase full-bridge phase-shifted controlled VSC circuit operation. (a) output voltage $v_o = v_{AB}$; (b) control signal for switch S_1; (c) control signal for switch S_2; (d) control signal for switch S_3; and (e) control signal for switch S_4.

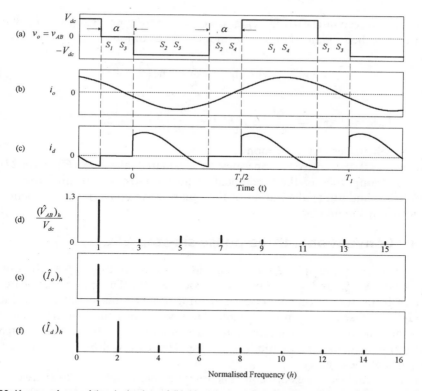

Fig. 6.30 Key waveforms of the single-phase full-bridge phase-shifted controlled VSC circuit operation. (a) output voltage $v_o = v_{AB}$; (b) output current i_o; (c) DC bus current i_d; (d) harmonic spectrum of the output voltage $v_o = v_{AB}$; (e) harmonic spectrum of the output current i_o; and (f) harmonic spectrum of the input DC bus current i_d.

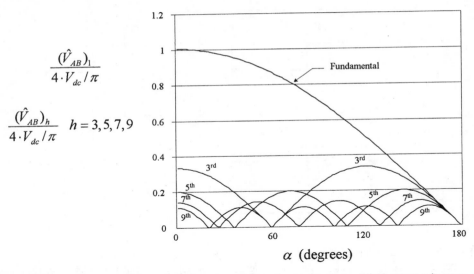

$$\frac{(\hat{V}_{AB})_1}{4 \cdot V_{dc}/\pi}$$

$$\frac{(\hat{V}_{AB})_h}{4 \cdot V_{dc}/\pi} \quad h = 3,5,7,9$$

Fig. 6.31 Normalized amplitudes of fundamental and harmonics for the phase-shifted output voltage as a function of α (zero volts interval in degrees).

For a given zero interval α in degrees, as shown in Figures 6.29(a) and 6.30(a), the amplitude of the fundamental and harmonics are as follows

$$(\hat{V}_o)_1 = (\hat{V}_{AB})_1 = \frac{4 \cdot V_{dc}}{\pi} \sin\left[\left(\frac{\pi - \alpha}{2}\right)\right] \tag{6.22}$$

and

$$(\hat{V}_o)_h = (\hat{V}_{AB})_h = \frac{4 \cdot V_{dc}}{\pi \cdot h} \sin\left[h \cdot \left(\frac{\pi - \alpha}{2}\right)\right] \quad h = 3, 5, 7, 9, \ldots \tag{6.23}$$

where h is the order of the harmonic.

When $\alpha = 0$ the converter operates as a square-wave one (Figure 6.27). The normalized amplitude of the fundamental and the most significant harmonics, i.e. 3rd, 5th, 7th and 9th to the output of the square-wave converter as a function of α, are plotted in Figure 6.31.

6.3.3 Conventional three-phase six-step VSC

The conventional three-phase six-switch VSC is shown in Figure 6.32. It consists of six switches S_1–S_6 and six antiparallel diodes D_1–D_6. The number indicates their order of being turned on. A fictitious neutral (O) as a mid-point is also included although in most cases is not available. However, when the converter under consideration is used as an active filter in the case of a four-wire three-phase system, this point (O) is used to connect the fourth-wire. This case will be discussed further in later parts of the chapter.

The three converter legs are controlled with a phase-shift of $120°$ between them. The basic way to control the three-phase six-switch VSC is to turn on each switch for half of the period ($180°$) with a sequence 1, 2, 3, ... as they are numbered and shown in Figure 6.32.

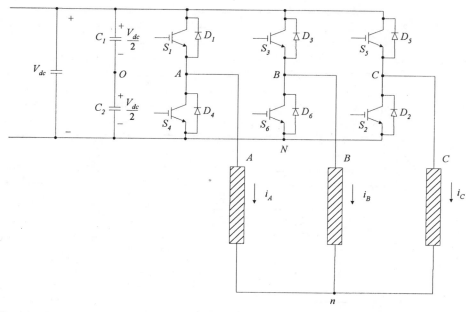

Fig. 6.32 Conventional three-phase six-switch VSC.

The operation of the converter can be explained with the assistance of Figure 6.33. Specifically, the control signals for each of the six switches are shown in Figure 6.33(a). Clearly, each switch remains on for 180° and every 60° a new switch is turned on and one of the previous group is turned off. At any given time therefore, one switch of each leg is on. Assuming that the fictitious mid-point (O) is available, three square-type waveforms for the voltages v_{AO}, v_{BO}, and v_{CO} can be drawn as shown in Figure 6.33(b). Each of the voltage waveforms has two peak values of $V_{dc}/2$, and $-V_{dc}/2$, and they are displaced by 120° from each other.

From the three waveforms v_{AO}, v_{BO}, and v_{CO}, the line-to-line voltage waveforms can be drawn since

$$v_{AB} = v_{AO} - v_{BO}$$
$$v_{BC} = v_{BO} - v_{CO} \qquad (6.24)$$
$$v_{CA} = v_{CO} - v_{AO}$$

The three resultant line-to-line voltage waveforms are then shown in Figure 6.33(c). It is clear that each waveform takes three values (V_{dc}, 0, $-V_{dc}$) and there is a 120° phase-shift between them. These waveforms have a 60° interval when they are zero for each half of the period, a total of 120° per period. As explained earlier, each leg can handle current in both directions at any time, since either the turned on switch or the antiparallel diode of the other switch can be the conducting element depending upon the polarity of the output line current.

The potential of the load neutral point (n) shown in Figure 6.32 with respect to the mid-point of the DC bus (O) is drawn in Figure 6.33(d). It can be seen that such a waveform has frequency three times the output frequency and the two peak values

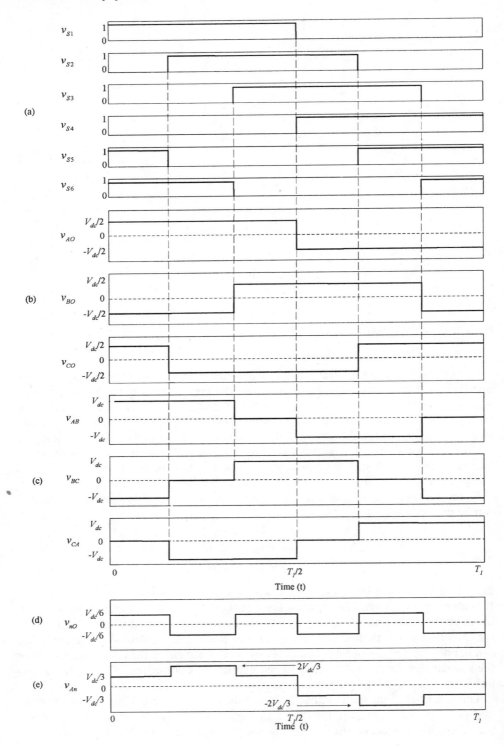

v_{S1}

v_{S2}

v_{S3}

(a)

v_{S4}

v_{S5}

v_{S6}

(b) v_{AO}

v_{BO}

v_{CO}

v_{AB}

(c) v_{BC}

v_{CA}

Time (t)

(d) v_{nO}

(e) v_{An}

Time (t)

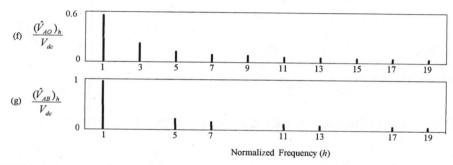

(f) $\dfrac{(\hat{V}_{AO})_h}{V_{dc}}$

(g) $\dfrac{(\hat{V}_{AB})_h}{V_{dc}}$

Normalized Frequency (h)

Fig. 6.33 Key waveforms of the three-phase six-step VSC circuit operation. (a) control signals for switches S_1 S_2, S_3, S_4, S_5, S_6; (b) voltage waveforms v_{AO}, v_{BO}, and v_{CO}; (c) output line-to-line voltage waveforms v_{AB}, v_{BC}, v_{CA}; (d) voltage waveform between the load neutral point (n) and the DC bus mid-point (O); (e) voltage waveform between the line point A and the load neutral point n; (f) harmonic spectrum of the line-to-DC bus mid-point; and (g) harmonic spectrum of the line-to-line voltage v_{AB}.

are between $V_{dc}/6$ and $-V_{dc}/6$. Finally, the line-to-load neutral point (n) voltage waveform is illustrated in Figure 6.33(e). Such a voltage waveform has two positive values ($V_{dc}/3$ and $2V_{dc}/3$) and two negative ones ($-V_{dc}/3$ and $-2V_{dc}/3$).

The harmonics of the various waveforms can be calculated using Fourier series. The fundamental amplitude of the voltage waveforms v_{AO}, v_{BO}, and v_{CO} is

$$(\hat{V}_{AO})_1 = (\hat{V}_{BO})_1 = (\hat{V}_{CO})_1 = \frac{4 \cdot V_{dc}}{2 \cdot \pi} \tag{6.25}$$

$$(\hat{V}_{AO})_h = (\hat{V}_{BO})_h = (\hat{V}_{CO})_h = \frac{4 \cdot V_{dc}}{2 \cdot \pi \cdot h} \quad h = 3, 5, 7, \ldots \tag{6.26}$$

where h is the order of the harmonic.

For the line-to-line voltage waveforms v_{AB}, v_{BC}, and v_{CA} then the fundamental amplitude is

$$\hat{V}_{AB1} = \frac{2\sqrt{3}}{\pi} \cdot V_{dc} \tag{6.27}$$

and therefore the rms value of the fundamental component is then

$$V_{AB1,rms} = \frac{2\sqrt{3}}{\pi\sqrt{2}} \cdot V_{dc} = \frac{\sqrt{6}}{\pi} \cdot V_{dc} = 0.78 \cdot V_{dc} \tag{6.28}$$

Similarly, the amplitude of the harmonic voltages is

$$(\hat{V}_{AB})_h = \frac{2\sqrt{3}}{\pi \cdot h} \cdot V_{dc} \quad h = 5, 7, 11, 13, \ldots \tag{6.29}$$

The rms value of the line-to-line voltage including all harmonics is

$$V_{AB,rms} = \sqrt{\frac{1}{\pi} \int_{-\pi/3}^{\pi/3} V_{dc}^2 \, d\omega t} = \frac{\sqrt{2}}{\sqrt{3}} \cdot V_{dc} = 0.816 \cdot V_{dc} \tag{6.30}$$

The normalized spectrum of the line-to-DC bus mid-point and the line-to-line voltage waveforms are plotted in Figures 6.33(f) and (g) respectively. It can be seen that the voltage waveforms v_{AO}, v_{BO}, and v_{CO} contain all odd harmonics. The load connection as shown in Figure 6.32 does not allow 3rd harmonic and all multiples to flow, and this is confirmed with the spectrum of the line-to-line voltage waveform v_{AB} where 3rd, 9th and 15th harmonics are eliminated as shown in Figure 6.33(g).

6.3.4 Single-phase half-bridge neutral-point-clamped (NPC) VSC

For single-phase applications, so far the half-bridge and the full-bridge conventional topologies have been discussed in detail. These converters have the capability to generate two-level voltage waveforms in both cases where only frequency control is possible and a separate control of the DC bus voltage must be employed to control the output AC voltage waveform (when square-wave control method is considered). Except of course for the case where a phase-shifted control method is used for the single-phase full-bridge VSC topology. In this case, the converter is capable of generating a three-level waveform and with controlled amplitude.

However, there exists a topology that is capable of generating a three-level voltage waveform at the output with a half-bridge version. Such a converter leg has made a significant contribution in the general area of converters, as a building block, especially for high power applications. We present this VSC topology in this section.

A three-level half-bridge VSC based on the NPC topology is shown in Figure 6.34 (Nabae et al., 1981). In this version the neutral point is clamped with diodes.

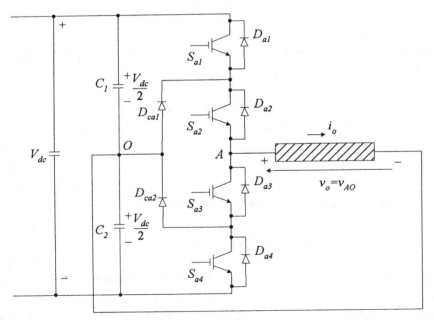

Fig. 6.34 Three-level single-phase half-bridge NPC VSC.

Specifically, the converter consists of four switches (S_{a1}, S_{a2}, S_{a3}, S_{a4}) and the antiparallel diodes (D_{a1}, D_{a2}, D_{a3}, D_{a4}). Due to the nature of the leg being able to generate a three-level voltage waveform between the points A and O, two DC bus voltage sources of equal value are required. This can be accomplished with two equal value capacitors C_1 and C_2 where the initial DC bus voltage V_{dc} is split across to make two voltage sources of $V_{dc}/2$ value available.

In previous sections, the phase-shifted control method (Figures 6.29 and 6.30) for a single-phase full-bridge VSC shown in Figure 6.26 was explained. The interesting point of such a technique is the ability to control the output voltage and its harmonics contents by adjusting the angle α (degrees) where the line-to-line waveform becomes zero.

It has been introduced in the technical literature that the number of levels of the voltage between the mid-point of the converter leg and the DC bus mid-point (line-to-neutral voltage waveform) is used to classify a given multilevel topology. The conventional three-phase VSC as shown in Figure 6.32 is then a two-level converter since it is capable of producing a two-level waveform between the two points mentioned above.

To clamp the voltage, two extra clamping diodes D_{ca1} and D_{ca2} as shown in Figure 6.34 are required to connect the DC bus mid-point to the load applying zero volts. They also allow the current to flow in either direction when the converter operates in the free-wheeling mode (zero volts at the output). For this case the load can be connected between the points A and O like the case of the single-phase half-bridge VSC shown in Figure 6.23.

The control for the three-level half-bridge VSC is slightly different and will be explained next. It can be confirmed with the assistance of Figures 6.34 and 6.35 that

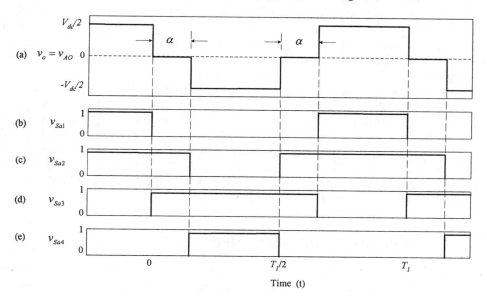

Fig. 6.35 Key waveforms of the three-level single-phase half-bridge NPC VSC circuit operation. (a) output voltage $v_o = v_{AO}$; (b) control signal for the switch S_{a1}; (c) control signal for the switch S_{a2}; (d) control signal for switch S_{a3}; and (e) control signal for switch S_{a4}.

Table 6.5 Modes of operation of the three-level half-bridge NPC VSC

Switching device state				Output voltage $v_o = v_{AO}$	Output current i_o	Conducting semiconductor	Power transfer
S_{a1}	S_{a2}	S_{a3}	S_{a4}				
Square-wave method							
1	1	0	0	$V_{dc}/2$	Positive	$S_{a1}\ S_{a2}$	DC → AC
1	1	0	0	$V_{dc}/2$	Negative	$D_{a1}\ D_{a2}$	AC → DC
0	0	1	1	$-V_{dc}/2$	Negative	$S_{a3}\ S_{a4}$	DC → AC
0	0	1	1	$-V_{dc}/2$	Positive	$D_{a3}\ D_{a4}$	AC → DC
0	1	1	0	0	Positive	$S_{a2}\ D_{ca1}$	None
0	1	1	0	0	Negative	$S_{a3}\ D_{ca2}$	None

when switches S_{a1} and S_{a2} are turned on at the same time, the voltage of the capacitor C_1 ($V_{dc}/2$) will be applied across the load. When this pair of switches is turned on, the other pair of switches (S_{a3}, S_{a4}) must be turned off to avoid destruction of the bridge. Similarly when the switches S_{a3} and S_{a4} are turned on simultaneously the output voltage $v_o = v_{AO}$ becomes negative ($-V_{dc}/2$) due to the voltage of capacitor C_2 being applied across the load. Now, in order for the converter to generate zero voltage across the output (the third level of the output voltage waveform), the two switches S_{a2} and S_{a3} are turned on simultaneously and the other two switches S_{a1} and S_{a4} are turned off. This way, through the assistance of the two clamping diodes D_{ca1} and D_{ca2}, the potential of the DC bus mid-point O is across the load generating zero volts in the voltage waveform v_{AO} as shown in Figure 6.35(a). The control signals for the four switches S_{a1}, S_{a2}, S_{a3}, and S_{a4} are plotted in Figures 6.35(b)–(e) respectively. It is clear that the switches S_{a1} and S_{a3} have complementary signals, and the same applies for the control signals between the switches S_{a4} and S_{a2}. The duration that the switch S_{a1} is on simultaneously with S_{a2} controls the length of the output voltage that is positive as explained earlier. The same applies for the interval that the output voltage is negative when the switch S_{a4} is on simultaneously with S_{a3}.

Table 6.5 summarizes the modes of operation of the three-level single-phase half-bridge VSC based on the NPC topology with clamping diodes. This converter is also capable of operating in all four quadrants, since both the output voltage and current can be both positive and negative (bidirectional VSC topology). These quadrants of operation of the three-level single-phase half-bridge NPC VSC are indicated in Figure 6.36.

It should be noted that the waveform generated by the three-level converter (Figure 6.35(a)) and the single-phase full-bridge VSC with the phase-shifted method (Figure 6.29(a)) are identical. Therefore the harmonic content is also identical as analysed in Section 6.3.2 and plotted in a normalized form in Figure 6.31.

6.3.5 Single-phase full-bridge NPC VSC

The converter leg presented in Section 6.3.4 can be used to build full-bridge single-phase and three-phase VSC topologies with the capability of generating three or higher-level voltage waveforms. In this case, the line-to-line voltage waveform will be of a higher than three level. However, the converter in the technical literature is called a three-level one since the number of levels of the line-to-line voltage waveform is *not*

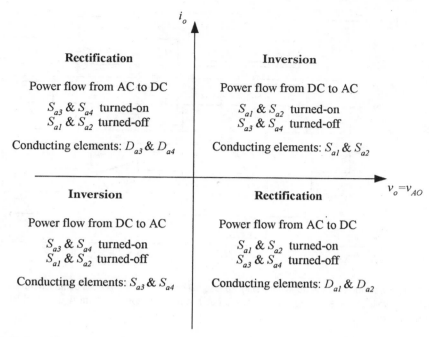

Fig. 6.36 Quadrants of operation of the three-level single-phase half-bridge NPC VSC.

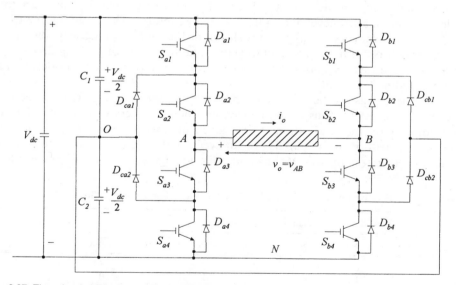

Fig. 6.37 Three-level single-phase full-bridge NPC VSC.

used to name the level of the topologies but rather the line to the DC bus mid-point voltage waveform (line-to-neutral).

A three-level single-phase full-bridge VSC is shown in Figure 6.37. Each leg generates a three-level voltage waveform when it is referred to the mid-point of the

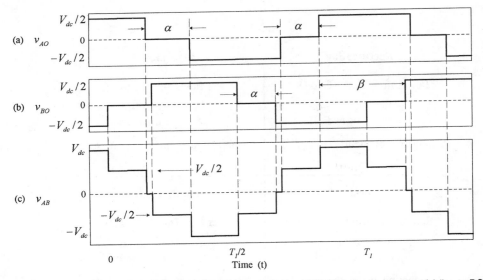

Fig. 6.38 Key waveforms of the three-level single-phase full-bridge NPC VSC circuit operation. (a) line-to-DC bus mid-point voltage waveform v_{AO}; (b) line-to-DC bus mid-point voltage waveform v_{BO}; and (c) line-to-line voltage waveform v_{AB}.

DC bus as shown in Figures 6.38(a) (voltage v_{AO}) and 6.38(b) (voltage v_{BO}). There is a phase-shift between the output voltage waveforms of the two legs in order to be able to generate a five-level line-to-line voltage waveform. The resultant line-to-line voltage waveform ($v_{AB} = v_{AO} - v_{BO}$) is shown in Figure 6.38(c). Clearly, the line-to-line voltage waveform is a five-level waveform, taking values of V_{dc}, $V_{dc}/2$, 0, $-V_{dc}/2$ and $-V_{dc}$. The various modes of operation for the converter under consideration are summarized in Table 6.6.

Higher-level legs can be built in a similar way, which would, of course, require a higher number of DC bus sources. Even and odd numbers of levels can be built depending upon the application. For a given number of levels m, $m-1$ DC bus sources (capacitors) are required. For an even number of levels, the zero level will be missing from the line-to-DC bus mid-point voltage waveform. A five-level leg is

Table 6.6 Modes of operation of the three-level single-phase full-bridge NPC VSC

			Switching device state					Output voltage $v_o = v_{AB}$
S_{a1}	S_{a2}	S_{a3}	S_{a4}	S_{b1}	S_{b2}	S_{b3}	S_{b4}	
1	1	0	0	0	0	1	1	V_{dc}
0	0	1	1	1	1	0	0	$-V_{dc}$
1	1	0	0	0	1	1	0	$V_{dc}/2$
0	1	1	0	0	0	1	1	$V_{dc}/2$
0	1	1	0	1	1	0	0	$-V_{dc}/2$
0	0	1	1	0	1	1	0	$-V_{dc}/2$
0	1	1	0	0	1	1	0	0
1	1	0	0	1	1	0	0	0 (possible)
0	0	1	1	0	0	1	1	0 (possible)

shown in Figure 6.39. Clearly, as described above, four DC bus sources are used and this time more clamping diodes are required.

For the five-level half-bridge leg shown in Figure 6.39, there exist switch pairs that require complementary control signals. These pairs are: (S_{a1}, S_{a5}), (S_{a2}, S_{a6}), (S_{a3}, S_{a7}), and (S_{a4}, S_{a8}). Moreover, the various switches do not have the same switching frequency and as the number of levels increases such a problem becomes more of a drawback.

The states of the switching devices of a five-level single-phase half-bridge VSC as shown in Figure 6.39 are summarized in Table 6.7.

One significant drawback of the NPC topology is the unequal distribution of switching losses among the switches and also the unequal load distribution among the various capacitors. This problem becomes more serious as the number of levels of the converter increases.

6.3.6   Other multilevel converter topologies

So far many power electronics based circuits have been presented which are capable of generating more than two-level voltage waveforms. There is however another converter topology, which is also capable of producing multilevel voltage waveforms. This topology contains two legs per phase as shown in the single-phase version in Figure 6.40. Each phase leg consists of two legs similar to the half-bridge explained earlier and shown in Figure 6.23. Each leg is controlled independently and with a specific phase-shift is able to generate a three-level voltage waveform between the phase point A and the mid-point of the DC bus O. In order to be able to add the waveforms generated by the two legs, an inductor-based configuration is used as shown in Figure 6.40.

For square-wave operation, the voltage waveform between the point A_1 and the DC bus mid-point is a two-level waveform taking values between $V_{dc}/2$ and $-V_{dc}/2$. The same applies for the voltage waveform between the other point of the phase leg A_2 and the point O. These two signals are phase-shifted accordingly and are drawn in Figures 6.41(a) and (b). The potential of point A referred to the point O is the sum of the two waveforms v_{A1O}, and v_{A2O}. This voltage waveform is shown in Figure 6.41(c). It is a three-level waveform taking values of V_{dc}, 0 and $-V_{dc}$. Finally, the voltage across the inductor, that is the potential difference between the two points A_1 and A_2, is illustrated in Figure 6.41(d). Similar arrangements can be used for the other two-phase legs to build a three-phase converter. Furthermore, more legs per phase can be used and more inductor arrangements can be used to sum even more voltage waveforms so that higher numbers of levels for the phase voltage waveform can be generated. This depends upon the application of course. Such arrangements can also offer opportunities to cancel more harmonics with appropriate phase-shifting.

Another circuit to obtain multilevel systems is of course the combination of the NPC converter and the arrangement with inductors to add voltage waveforms. The converter then is three-level with respect to one-phase leg, and becomes a five-level one with respect to the phase. Such a five-level circuit based on inductor summing and the NPC converter is shown in Figure 6.42. In this case appropriate phase-shifted PWM techniques can be used to take advantage of the topology and position the first significant harmonics of the resultant output voltage waveforms to higher frequencies.

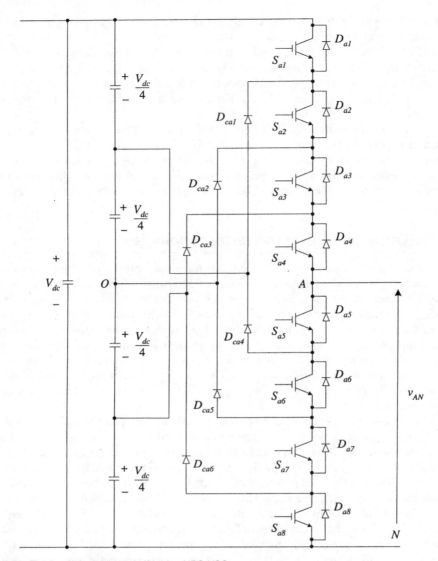

Fig. 6.39 Five-level single-phase half-bridge NPC VSC.

Table 6.7 Modes of operation of the five-level single-phase half-bridge NPC VSC

			Switching device state					Output voltage
S_{a1}	S_{a2}	S_{a3}	S_{a4}	S_{a5}	S_{a6}	S_{a7}	S_{a8}	$v_o = v_{AN}$
1	1	1	1	0	0	0	0	V_{dc}
0	1	1	1	1	0	0	0	$3V_{dc}/4$
0	0	1	1	1	1	0	0	$V_{dc}/2$
0	0	0	1	1	1	1	0	$V_{dc}/4$
0	0	0	0	1	1	1	1	0

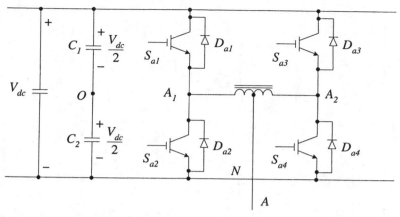

Fig. 6.40 Three-level converter with parallel legs and a summing inductor to generate multilevel voltage waveforms.

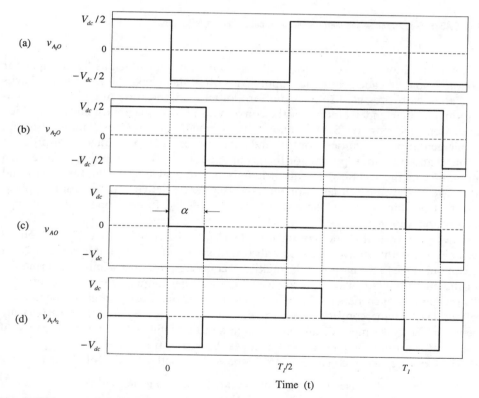

Fig. 6.41 Key waveforms of the three-level converter with parallel legs and a summing inductor circuit operation. (a) voltage waveform between the mid-point of the left phase leg A_1 and the DC bus mid-point O, v_{A10}; (b) voltage waveform between the mid-point of the right phase leg A_2 and the DC bus mid-point O, v_{A20}; (c) voltage waveform between the phase point and the DC bus mid-point, v_{AO}; and (d) voltage waveform across the inductor v_{A1A2}.

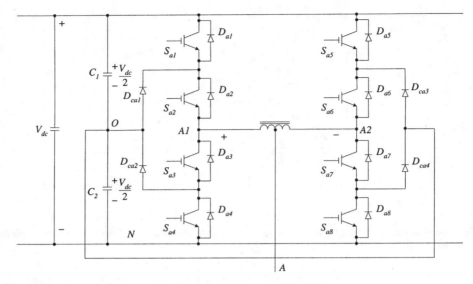

Fig. 6.42 Five-level phase leg with parallel legs based on the NPC VSC.

There are however two other multilevel configurations known as flying capacitor topology and cascaded converter topology. Both of them have merits and drawbacks like all circuits presented so far. And for a different application in reactive compensation a further understanding of the converter and its applicability must be studied and well understood. Switch and other element ratings, cost, and hardware implementation difficulties, control and other issues must be evaluated in order to achieve an optimum topology for the given application. These topologies have been presented in the technical literature mainly as adjustable speed motor drives and they are at the research level for the power system reactive compensation applications. They are presented here due to their possible future applicability in high power applications.

The flying capacitor topology and one of its legs is shown in Figure 6.43. The control technique for this converter is described as follows. It uses a phase-shifted PWM technique. Due to the nature of the multilevel converter, the most significant harmonics of the output voltage waveform are located at a higher frequency typically controlled by the number of carriers used (the harmonic multiplying factor is equal to the number of the level of the converter minus one). For an N-level system, $N-1$ carriers are required. Then the most significant harmonics in the unfiltered output voltage signal are located around frequencies $(N-1)$ times the carrier frequency.

The flying capacitor converter seems to be very attractive for the following reasons:

- A simple PWM phase-shifted technique can be used to generate the control signals for the semiconductors.
- The voltages of the capacitors are automatically balanced under ideal conditions.
- For a more sophisticated system, the capacitor voltages can be actively monitored and controlled by an appropriate DC shifting of the signal generator.

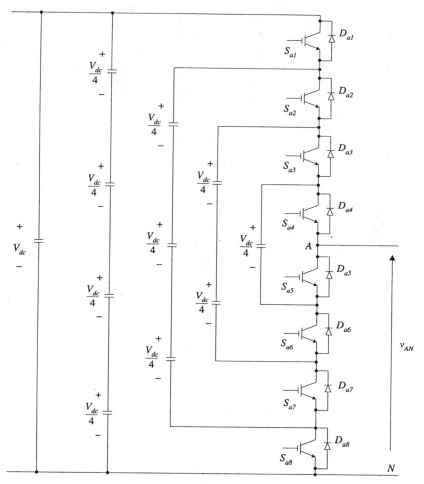

Fig. 6.43 Five-level flying capacitor converter phase leg.

- All semiconductors have equal switching frequency which is equal to the carrier frequency.
- The topology is modular.

However, a number of issues must be resolved in order for such a topology to become a commercially viable alternative to conventional VSC topologies for high power applications. These issues can be summarized as follows:

- The number of high voltage capacitors is considered quite high. Furthermore, taking into account that they need to conduct the full load current at least part of the switching cycle makes them very expensive with high values.
- The topology is subject to faults and does not have tolerance to them, therefore appropriate control and monitoring is required.
- The flying capacitors initially have zero charge and starting the converter is not a trivial issue. This needs to be seriously addressed.

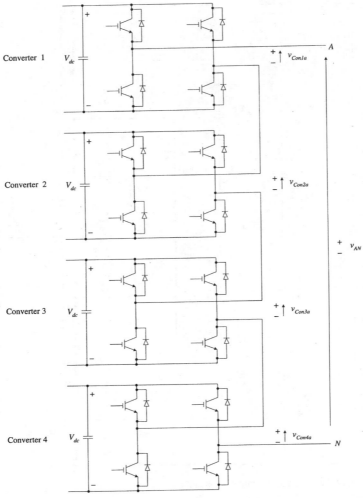

Fig. 6.44 Nine-level cascaded multilevel converter topology based on the single-phase full-bridge VSC.

Finally, the cascaded converter topology is presented in Figure 6.44. This topology offers significant advantages. The first one is the equal switching frequency of each switch. The second one is its ability to employ the phase-shifted control technique, which allows cancellation of more harmonics. This becomes more important when PWM is considered even at a low frequency. The number of the legs is the direct multiple of the carrier frequency to obtain the location of the significant harmonics. This will become clear when the various PWM schemes are introduced in detail.

For fundamental frequency operation, i.e. switches are turned on and off once per cycle, each converter is capable of generating a three-level voltage waveform across the two mid-point legs using the phase-shifted square-wave control method. Due to the nature of the converter phase leg, the phase voltage will be the sum of all converter voltages as follows:

$$v_{AN} = v_{con1a} + v_{con2a} + v_{con3a} + v_{con4a} \qquad (6.31)$$

Therefore, the phase voltage v_{AN} will have a total of eight-levels plus the zero level (overall nine-levels converter). For the leg shown in Figure 6.44, the voltage v_{AN} will have values of $4V_{dc}$, $3V_{dc}$, $2V_{dc}$, V_{dc}, 0 and $-V_{dc}$, $-2V_{dc}$, $-3V_{dc}$, and $-4V_{dc}$. Generally speaking, for an m-level converter we need to use $(m-1)/2$ single-phase full-bridge circuits. The line-to-line voltage waveform will have higher numbers of levels. The key waveforms for the nine-level circuit shown in Figure 6.44 are shown in Figure 6.45. Specifically, each converter generates a three-level square-wave signal with a different angle α. The effect of that is that when the four voltage waveforms of each of the four converters are added, a higher level staircase voltage waveform is obtained as shown in Figure 6.45(e). This generates a phase voltage waveform that approaches a sinusoidal looking waveform with minimum harmonic distortion although each individual voltage waveform has a relatively high harmonic distortion (modified square wave).

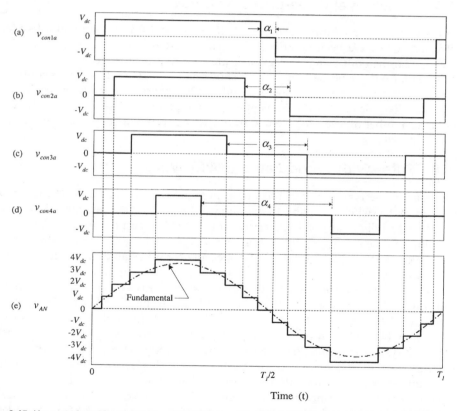

Fig. 6.45 Key waveforms for the nine-level cascaded multilevel converter topology based on the single-phase full-bridge VSC circuit operation. (a) output voltage of converter 1, v_{con1a}; (b) output voltage of converter 2, v_{con2a}; (c) output voltage of converter 3, v_{con3a}; (d) output voltage of converter 4, v_{con4a}; and (e) converter phase voltage v_{AN}.

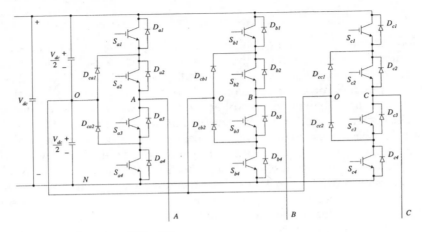

Fig. 6.46 Three-level three-phase NPC VSC.

6.3.7 Three-level three-phase NPC VSC

So far the operation of three-level legs (half-bridge and full-bridge) and a five-level half-bridge one have been described. It is easy therefore to see how a three-phase converter can be built using the legs presented in the previous sections.

A three-level three-phase NPC VSC is shown in Figure 6.46. Each leg is controlled in a similar way as explained before and a 120° phase-shift between each leg is introduced like the case of the conventional three-phase VSC shown in Figure 6.32. Again the number of levels for the line-to-line waveforms will be higher than the level of the converter.

6.3.8 Pulse-width modulated (PWM) VSCs

The square-wave type of control has been presented so far for the VSC topologies. However, if the switch is capable of operating at higher frequencies, which is typically the case with fully controlled semiconductors, PWM concepts can be applied. This control technique is quite an old and proven concept and has dominated the industry since the early 1960s (Schönung, 1964) especially for adjustable speed motor drives.

The thyristor technology was not used with PWM techniques but rather fundamental frequency control based on the square-wave control was used for high power applications. The availability of the GTO and IGBT technology has made it possible for the PWM concepts and topologies known from the adjustable speed motor drives area to now be applied in the reactive power control area and other applications in the power system for energy storage and power quality. These applications will be discussed in detail in later sections of this chapter. In this section, the PWM concepts will be introduced in combination with the VSC topologies presented so far.

The single-phase half-bridge VSC (Figure 6.23) can be controlled using the two-level PWM. As previously discussed, the half-bridge single-phase VSC is a two-level converter as it generates a two-level voltage waveform between the mid-point of the leg and the mid-point of the DC bus (line-to-neutral). Therefore, the two-level PWM method can be used.

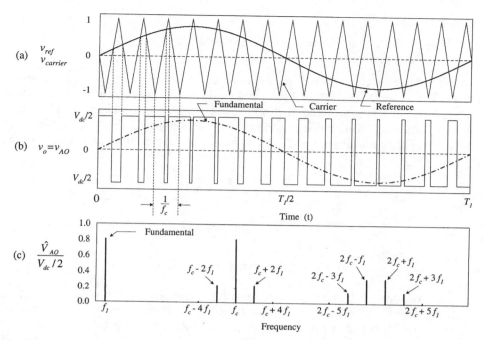

Fig. 6.47 Two-level sinusoidal PWM method. (a) reference (sinusoidal) and carrier (triangular) signals ($f_c = 15 \cdot f_1$ and $M_a = 0.8$); (b) voltage waveform v_{AO}; and (c) normalized harmonic amplitude of the voltage waveform v_{AO}.

The two-level PWM method can be described with the assistance of Figure 6.47. The method is based on the comparison between a reference signal (sinusoidal) having the desired frequency (f_1) and a carrier signal (triangular) with a relatively higher frequency f_c. These signals are shown in Figure 6.47(a). For illustrative purposes, a carrier frequency f_c of 15 times the desired frequency f_1 has been chosen. By varying the amplitude of the sinusoidal signal against the fixed amplitude of the triangular signal kept at 1 p.u. value, the amplitude of the fundamental component at f_1 can be controlled in a linear fashion. This comparison generates a modulated square-wave signal that can be used to control the switches of a given converter topology.

For instance if a leg is considered similar to the converter shown in Figure 6.23, a two-level voltage waveform can be generated between the mid-point of the leg A, and the mid-point of the DC bus O. This waveform has therefore two-levels of $V_{dc}/2$ and $-V_{dc}/2$. Figure 6.47(b) shows the respective waveform. Clearly, the width of the square-wave is modulated in a sinusoidal way and the fundamental component superimposed on Figure 6.47(b) can be extracted with the use of a particular filter. The waveform also contains harmonics associated with the carrier frequency f_c and its multiples, and related sidebands.

It is necessary to define the following amplitude modulation ratio M_a.

$$M_a = \frac{\hat{A}_s}{\hat{A}_c} \tag{6.32}$$

where

$\hat{A}_s$ is the amplitude of the sinusoidal signal and
$\hat{A}_c$ is the amplitude of the triangular signal.

The PWM method shown in Figure 6.47 is presented for an amplitude modulation ratio of 0.8 ($\hat{A}_s = 0.8$ p.u., $\hat{A}_c = 1$ p.u.). When the harmonic content of the resultant voltage waveform is considered, the following observations can be made. The waveform v_{AO} contains a fundamental component with amplitude equal to M_a on a per unit basis as shown in Figure 6.47(c). The harmonics are positioned as sidebands as follows

$$f_h = k \cdot f_c \pm m \cdot f_1 \qquad (6.33)$$

where

$$k = 1, 3, 5, \ldots \text{ when } m = 0, 2, 4, 6, \ldots$$

and

$$k = 2, 4, 6, \ldots \text{ when } m = 1, 3, 5, \ldots$$

When the two-level PWM method is used with a single-phase full-bridge VSC (Figure 6.26), the waveforms are shown in Figure 6.48. When comparing the waveforms of Figure 6.48 with the ones presented earlier in Figure 6.47 for a half-bridge leg, the

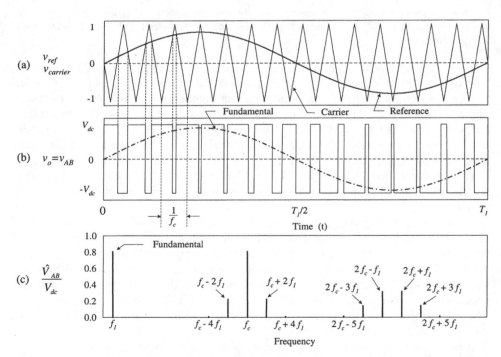

Fig. 6.48 Two-level sinusoidal PWM with a single-phase full-bridge VSC. (a) reference (sinusoidal) and carrier (triangular) signals ($f_c = 15 \cdot f_1$ and $M_a = 0.8$); (b) voltage waveform v_{AB}; and (c) normalized harmonic amplitude of the voltage waveform v_{AB}.

only difference is that the output voltage v_o is taken across points A and B in this case. Therefore, the two-levels of the output waveform take V_{dc} and $-V_{dc}$ values. The control method for the single-phase full-bridge VSC assumes that the switches (S_1, S_4) and (S_2, S_3) are treated as pairs and obviously in a complementary manner (Figure 6.26). The normalized amplitude values of the fundamental and the various harmonics are identical as confirmed with the Figure 6.48(c).

In a previous section, two control methods were presented for a single-phase full-bridge VSC, namely the square-wave method and the phase-shifted square-wave method. The second control method can be extended to include PWM methods.

The phase-shifted PWM method is also known as a three-level PWM method since is it capable of generating a three-level line-to-line voltage waveform. It is also known as unipolar PWM since the line-to-line voltage waveform is either positive and zero or negative and zero for each half of the period.

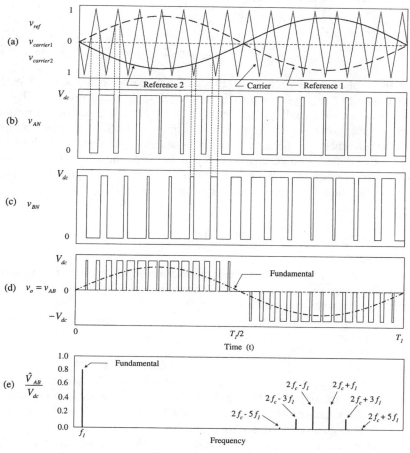

Fig. 6.49 Three-level sinusoidal PWM method for single-phase full-bridge VSC. (a) two reference signals (sinusoidal) and carrier (triangular) signal ($f_c = 15 \cdot f_1$ and $M_a = 0.8$); (b) voltage waveform v_{AN}; (c) line-to-line voltage waveform v_{AB}; and (d) normalized harmonic amplitude of the voltage waveform v_{AB}.

This technique is shown in Figure 6.49. Specifically, in this method two reference signals are used with 180° phase shift as shown in Figure 6.49(a). The same carrier is used to generate the modulated square-waveforms. The direct comparison of the triangular signal with the reference one is used to control one leg. The direct comparison between the other reference and the triangular signal is used to control the other leg. The two voltage waveforms between the mid-point of the leg, say A and B and the negative DC rail point N are shown in Figure 6.49(b) and (c) respectively. The output voltage waveform v_o defined as v_{AB} is drawn in Figure 6.49(d). It can be seen that such voltage waveform has three-levels, namely V_{dc}, 0, and $-V_{dc}$. The frequency of the resultant line-to-line voltage waveform is also twice the carrier frequency. The output voltage waveform contains a fundamental component shown in Figure 6.49(d) as a superimposed waveform and can also be extracted with the appropriate filtering arrangement. The harmonics shown in Figure 6.49(e) are improved when compared with the two-level PWM method shown in Figure 6.48(c). The harmonic components are positioned as follows

$$f_h = k \cdot f_c \pm m \cdot f_1 \qquad (6.34)$$

where

$$k = 2, 4, 6, \ldots \text{ when } m = 1, 3, 5, \ldots$$

For a three-phase six-switch VSC (Figure 6.32) the basic sinusoidal PWM technique is illustrated in Figure 6.50. In this case, since there are three legs, three reference (sinusoidal) signals phase-shifted by 120° from one another are used with one carrier (triangular) signal as shown in Figure 6.50(a). The direct comparison between the reference and the carrier generates square-wave signals which are used to drive the six switches. The voltage waveforms between the leg mid-points A and B with respect to the negative DC bus rail point N are given in Figure 6.50(b) and (c). The line-to-line voltage waveform can be simply drawn since

$$v_{AB} = v_{AN} - v_{BN}$$
$$v_{BC} = v_{BN} - v_{CN} \qquad (6.35)$$
$$v_{CA} = v_{CN} - v_{AN}$$

The resultant line-to-line voltage waveform has three-levels, namely V_{dc}, 0, and $-V_{dc}$.

It should be noted that for as long as the amplitude of the sinusoidal signal remains within the 1 p.u. range, the converter operates in a linear mode. Once the amplitude of the sinusoidal signal becomes higher than 1 p.u., the converter operates in the overmodulation region and certain low order harmonics start to appear in the output voltage waveforms.

In the case of multilevel NPC converter topology, the PWM technique must be adjusted in order to provide the appropriate control. Specifically, for the three-level single-phase half-bridge NPC VSC topology, two carriers are needed. The simple relation between the phase-shift between them is 180° phase shift. This is shown in Figure 6.51(a). Two triangular carriers are used and the comparison between them and the sinusoidal reference generates the control signals for the various switches. The control signals between S_{a1} and S_{a3}, and S_{a2} and S_{a4} must be complementary as discussed earlier. These control signals are plotted in Figure 6.51(b)–(e). The resultant line-to-neutral voltage waveform is then shown in Figure 6.51(g). It is clear that due to

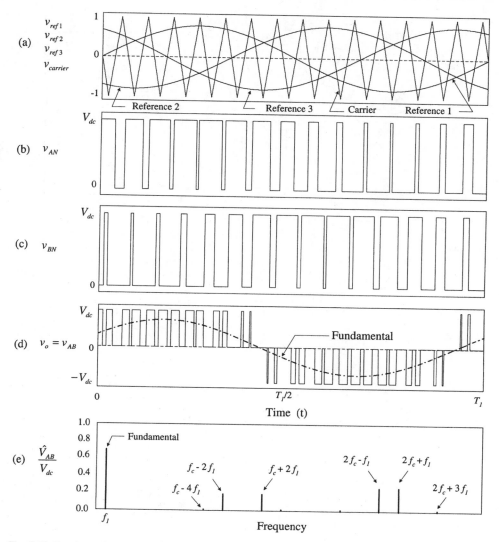

Fig. 6.50 Two-level sinusoidal PWM method for the conventional six-switch three-phase VSC. (a) reference signals and carrier signal (triangular) ($f_c = 15 \cdot f_1$ and $M_a = 0.8$); (b) voltage waveform v_{AN}; (c) voltage waveform v_{BN}; (d) line-to-line output voltage waveform v_{AB}; and (e) normalized harmonic amplitude of the voltage waveform v_{AB}.

PWM operation, the line-to-neutral voltage waveform has three levels, namely, V_{dc}, 0, and $-V_{dc}$. To illustrate the effect of the PWM operation, the harmonic spectrum of the line-to-neutral voltage waveform is given in Figure 6.51(f). The first significant harmonics are located around the carrier frequency as the PWM theory presented in the previous section suggests and as sidebands of that frequency as well.

Based on the PWM operation of the previous converter, a full-bridge version can be built. The PWM control is illustrated in Figure 6.52. Specifically, the two line-to-neutral voltage waveforms as obtained with the previous described method are plotted

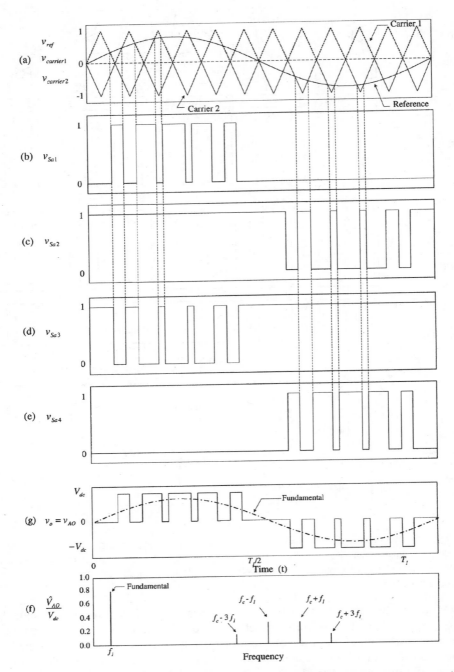

Fig. 6.51 Sinusoidal PWM for the three-level single-phase half-bridge NPC VSC. (a) reference and two carrier waveforms phase-shifted by 180°; (b) control signal for switch S_{a1}; (c) control signal for switch S_{a2}; (d) control signal for switch S_{a3}; (e) control signal for switch S_{a4}; (g) resultant line-to-neutral voltage waveform v_{AO}; and (f) harmonic spectrum of the line-to-neutral voltage waveform v_{AO}.

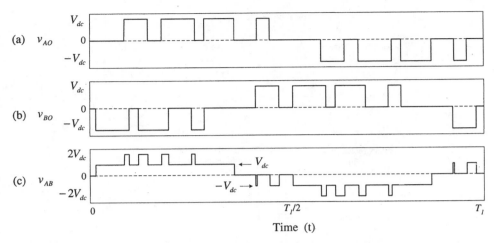

Fig. 6.52 Sinusoidal PWM for the three-level single-phase full bridge NPC VSC. (a) line-to-neutral voltage waveform v_{AO}; (b) line-to-neutral voltage waveform v_{BO}; and (c) resultant line-to-line voltage waveform v_{AB}.

in Figures 6.52(a) and (b) respectively. It is then easy to obtain the resultant line-to-line voltage waveform shown in Figure 6.52(c). It can be observed that this waveform is a multilevel waveform taking five values, namely $2V_{dc}$, V_{dc}, 0, $-V_{dc}$, and $-2V_{dc}$.

Finally it should be added that all these basic topologies presented in this section could be used along with appropriate connections of transformers to generate multilevel voltage waveforms of higher number than the individual converter.

6.4 Uninterruptible Power Supplies (UPSs)

Although the outage of the electricity supply rarely occurs in most developed countries, there exist cases and critical loads that must be protected against such event. The majority of the events that happen are due to extreme weather conditions. Furthermore, the trend is that the average outage times for customers connected to the low voltage levels have been reducing over the last 50 years continually.

However, there are other problems associated with the electricity network such as power line disturbances, namely, voltage spikes, surges and dips, harmonics, and electromagnetic interference. There are critical loads such as computer or information systems which process key data for organizations, medical apparatus, military and government systems that are necessary to be supplied by very high quality of electricity with the highest possible availability factor. For this kind of loads a UPS system is needed.

Large power UPS systems with more than 1 MVA rating are used in large computer rooms by many organizations processing critical data such as banks, government agencies, airlines, and transport and telecommunications companies.

Earlier UPS systems were of rotary design based on DC and AC motor/alternator respectively with a battery for back up. With the advent of the thyristor in the 1960s, static converter based equipment UPS appeared. A block diagram of a basic UPS system is shown in Figure 6.53. The AC mains voltage through a rectifier is converted

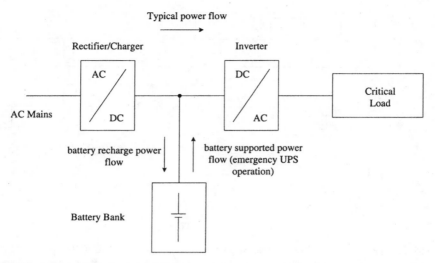

Fig. 6.53 Block diagram of a basic UPS system.

into DC providing a stiff DC bus voltage as an input to the inverter if it is of a voltage source type. A battery is connected across the DC bus to provide the back up power when the AC mains fail through the inverter. When the AC supply becomes available again, power flows through the rectifier/charger to the battery to recharge it and to the critical load via the inverter.

To increase the reliability of the UPS system, the power line can be used as a separate bypass input power supply. In this case, a static transfer switch changes over the power supply to the load from the UPS to the power line. Figure 6.54 shows the circuit arrangement.

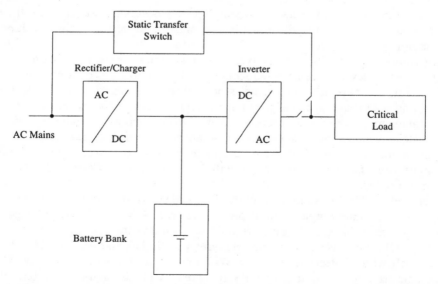

Fig. 6.54 Complementary functions for the UPS and the power line through a static transfer switch arrangement.

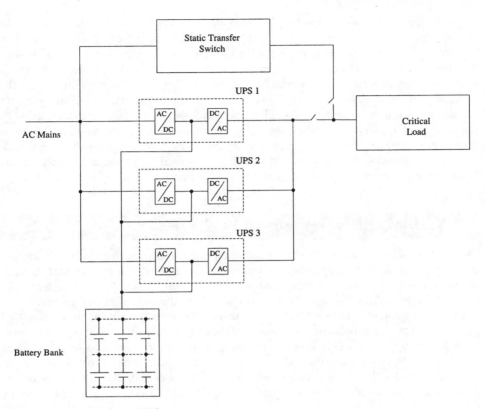

Fig. 6.55 Multi-module based UPS system.

To increase the reliability of a single module UPS system, a redundant system may be considered. It can be designed with the $(N - 1)$ concept. Simply said, the total kVA ratings of the overall system with $(N - 1)$ units should be equal to the load kVA rating. In this case, the loss of any one UPS unit does not create a problem since the rest of them remaining in service can still supply the load in a satisfactory way. Such a redundant system is shown in Figure 6.55.

For a low kVA rating, the UPS system can be an on-line or an off-line one. In the on-line case, the load is typically supplied through the UPS. If there is a fault with the converter of the UPS system, the AC mains supplies direct the load through the by-pass configuration. In the off-line case, the AC mains supplies the load and the UPS system is on-line when the AC mains fail or under circumstances that the quality of the supply is very low (i.e. under disturbances).

Today, PWM inverters of high frequency are mainly used especially in low and medium power levels. Such systems based on the converter and the technology previously presented in this chapter, have a number of advantages when compared with the thyristor based UPS systems. They include reduced size and weight mainly due to the smaller size of the filter required to meet the THD requirements for the generated supply, lower or even no acoustic noise if the frequencies used are higher than the ones within the audible range (approximately >18 kHz). Such frequencies are feasible with the use of IGBTs and MOSFETs presented in Chapter 5.

Uninterruptible power supplies systems require an energy storage device to be able to supply the load under power line failure. In most cases, a battery bank is used. The selection of battery is not a hard task although many technologies are available. Specifically, alkaline batteries of the nickel–cadmium type, lead–acid and other more exotic technologies can be theoretically considered. However, the high cost of all the technologies previously mentioned make the lead–acid battery the most common choice for commercial applications. There are a number of drawbacks associated with the lead–acid battery technology including maintenance requirements and environmental concerns. In recent years, new systems based on technologies such as flywheels have been commercially developed even for relatively medium power level applications. These systems are presented in further detail in Section 6.6.1.

6.5 Dynamic voltage restorer (DVR)

Over the last decade and in the twenty-first century, the electricity sector has been going and will go through further deregulation and privatization in the developed world. Competition therefore amongst electricity suppliers with the increased use of power electronics in everyday activities has resulted in increased attention to the issue of power quality.

In Section 6.4, the UPS systems were discussed. In this section, the concept of custom power (CP), proposed to ensure high quality of power supply will be presented briefly. The DVR is such an example. It can be designed to have excellent dynamic performance capable of protecting critical and/or sensitive load against short duration voltage dips and swells. The DVR is connected in series with the distribution line as shown in Figure 6.56. It typically consists of a VSC, energy

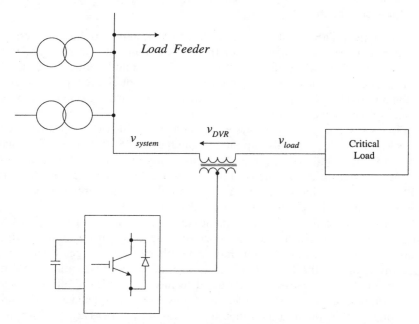

Fig. 6.56 Schematic representation of a dynamic voltage restorer (DVR).

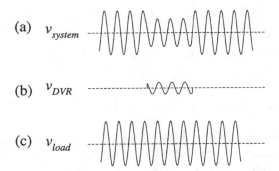

Fig. 6.57 Key waveforms of the DVR operation.

storage capacitor bank, harmonic filters and a connecting transformer. Protection equipment and instrumentation is also part of the system.

But how does the DVR work? The DVR, connected in series as mentioned earlier, injects AC voltage in series with the incoming network voltages. Due to the presence of a PWM VSC, real and reactive power can be exchanged with the system since all DVR injected voltages can be controlled with respect to their amplitude and phase (PWM operation).

When everything is fine with the line voltages, the DVR operates in a standby mode with very low losses. Since no switching takes place and the voltage output is zero (the connecting transformer is seen as a short circuit by the network), the losses in the DVR are conduction losses and relatively very low. If there is a voltage dip, the DVR injects a series voltage to compensate for the dip and restore the required level of the voltage waveform. Such key waveforms are shown in Figure 6.57. In Chapter 8, this system will be further discussed and a simulation example will be provided.

6.6 Energy storage systems

Electrical energy unfortunately is one of the few products, which must be produced almost when it is required for consumption and has no inherent self-life. However, there are a number of energy storage schemes for various purposes and these are discussed in this section.

The continuous demand for uninterrupted and quality power has resulted in a number of smart and alternative energy storage systems. Therefore, some exciting new systems will be introduced first. These include flywheels and superconducting materials. Conventional systems such the hydroelectric pumped storage, batteries and other new technologies with a promising future will also be presented. Some of them may be used in electric utilities applications and some may be more suitable for low power levels such as an electric or hybrid vehicle and other low power demand management applications.

6.6.1 Flywheel energy storage systems

A flywheel energy storage system is an old idea gaining more attention due to technological advances making it a commercially viable solution for the industry.

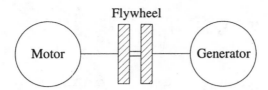

Fig. 6.58 A block diagram of a conventional flywheel system.

Although as previously mentioned, the flywheel is one of the oldest technologies for energy storage – Greek potters still use them today – modern systems based on the same idea incorporate high-tech composite material based wheels and low-friction bearings that operate in extremely high rotational speeds which may reach 100 000 rpm. Of course conventional systems which couple to existing rotating machines are still available.

Electric energy in the form of kinetic energy is stored in a flywheel comprising of a spinning disc, wheel or cylinder. This efficient and quiet way of storing energy offers a reliable source of power which can be accessed to provide an alternative source during electrical outages as a UPS system. A block diagram of a conventional flywheel is shown in Figure 6.58. The two concentric rotating parts of the flywheel are where the energy is stored and retrieved when needed.

In power utility applications, its commercially important application includes peak electricity demand management. Flywheels can be used to store energy generated during periods that electricity demand is low and then access that energy during high peak. The applications of flywheels extend to areas of electric vehicles and satellite control and gyroscopic stabilization.

Modern flywheels use composite materials and power electronics. The ultra-high rotational speeds require magnetic bearings, where magnetic forces are used to 'levitate' the rotor minimizing frictional losses. Such systems operate in partial vacuum which makes the control of the system quite sophisticated.

For power quality applications, cost is a very important consideration and hybrid solutions between the conventional systems and the modern highly sophisticated ones are available. Figure 6.59 shows an exploded view of a modern flywheel motor/generator structure.

Figure 6.60 shows a flywheel system controlled via an IGBT converter. The flywheel absorbs power to charge from the DC bus and when required, power is transferred back to the DC bus since the inverter can operate in the regenerative mode, slowing down the flywheel. Such decision can be based on a minimum acceptable voltage across the DC bus below which the flywheel can start discharging. Like a battery, when the flywheel is fully charged, its speed becomes constant. When the flywheel is discharged, the DC bus voltage is held constant and the flywheel behaves as a generator, transferring power back to the DC bus at an independent rotor speed.

A commercially available flywheel energy storage system of 240 kW for utility applications operating at approximately 7000 rpm is shown in Figure 6.61.

A number of UPS configurations can be considered with the use of flywheels. For instance, in case of critical loads and the availability of a generator, a flywheel system may be used to supply the critical load until the starting and synchronization of the

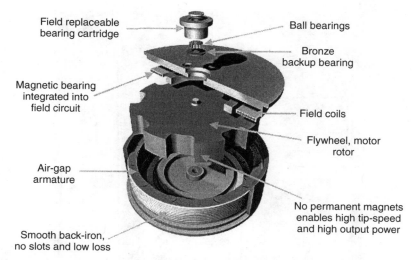

Field replaceable
bearing cartridge

Ball bearings

Bronze
backup bearing

Magnetic bearing
integrated into
field circuit

Field coils

Flywheel, motor
rotor

Air-gap
armature

No permanent magnets
enables high tip-speed
and high output power

Smooth back-iron,
no slots and low loss

Fig. 6.59 Exploded view of a modern flywheel motor/generator structure. (Courtesy of Active Power Inc., USA.)

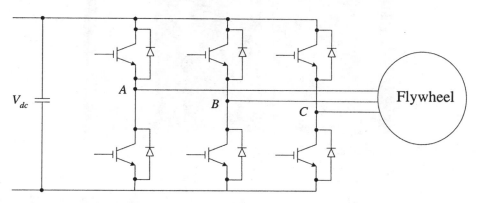

V_{dc}

A

B

C

Flywheel

Fig. 6.60 Modern flywheel energy storage system based on VSC.

generator as shown in Figure 6.62. Such a system is called continuous power supply (CPS). It differs from the conventional UPS system as the critical load is connected to the AC mains used as a primary source of power. The static UPS systems use backup battery power and the CPS uses a dynamic energy storage system, a flywheel for example. Finally CPS systems condition the power coming from the utility or in case of emergency from a diesel generator providing also power factor correction and reduction in current harmonics.

A flywheel may be part of a power quality system or else power conditioning system used to eliminate network problems associated with voltage sags, short notches and swells, harmonic distortion and power factor. Figure 6.63 shows a block diagram of a typical configuration based on a flywheel.

Finally in case of a UPS system requiring a battery bank, in order to extend the life of the battery arrangement, a flywheel system maybe used as shown in Figure 6.64. Uninterruptible power supplies systems are designed and used to provide the

Fig. 6.61 A 240 kW flywheel system. (Courtesy of Active Power Inc., USA.)

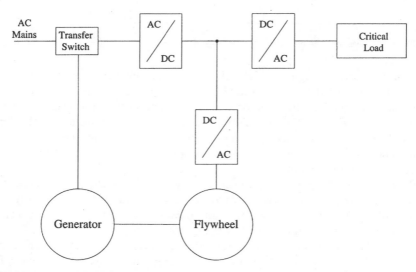

Fig. 6.62 Flywheel based continuous power system.

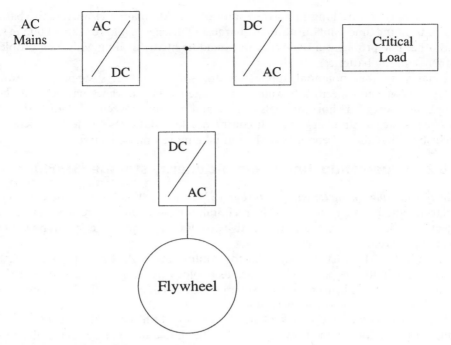

Fig. 6.63 Flywheel based power quality system.

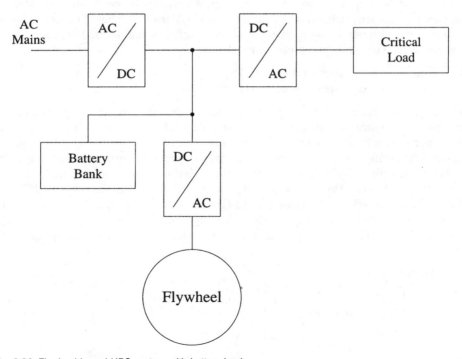

Fig. 6.64 Flywheel based UPS system with battery bank.

power supply during long non-availability of the AC mains. However, the battery depends on the times and duration of charge and discharge and for short voltage sags and other line problems a flywheel can extend its life by dealing with such problems rather than the batteries.

Finally, another potential application for small flywheel systems is renewable energy systems and specifically wind power systems. The flywheel may act as a buffer supplying energy for short intervals of time and mainly between wind gusts since the flywheel systems can charge and discharge quickly. Batteries cannot compete with such short demands of energy supply and take more time to charge.

6.6.2 Superconducting magnetic energy storage (SMES)

Superconducting magnetic energy storage (SMES) is defined as: a superconducting electromagnetic energy storage system containing electronic converters that rapidly injects and/or absorbs real and/or reactive power or dynamically controls power flow in an AC system.

A typical SMES system connected to a utility line is shown in Figure 6.65. But before explaining the power electronics technology available for such systems, let's examine first the phenomenon of superconductivity, a natural phenomenon and probably one of the most unusual ones.

Superconductivity is the lack of resistance in certain materials at extremely low temperatures allowing the flow of current with almost no losses. Specifically, super-conductors demonstrate no resistance to DC current and very low to AC current. They also exhibit quite strong diamagnetism, which simply means they are strongly repelled by magnetic fields. The levitating MAGLEV trains are based on this principle. The materials known today as superconductors must be maintained at relatively low temperature. There are two kinds of materials:

1. low temperature superconductor (LTS)
2. high temperature superconductor (HTS).

The latter has been discovered recently and has opened up new opportunities for commercial applications of the SMES systems. Applications of such material range from the microelectronics area such as radio frequency circuits to highly efficient power lines, transformers, motors, and magnetic levitating trains just to name a few.

The Dutch physicist H.K. Onnes first discovered superconductivity in 1911 at the University of Leiden. Progress was made later by others, but it was only in 1957 when the American physicists J. Bardee, L.N. Cooper and J.R. Schrieffer introduced the BCS theory named after their initials which explained the phenomenon for the first time in history. This theory provided the first complete physical description of the

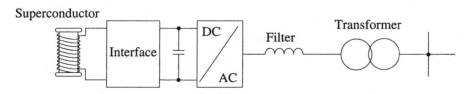

Fig. 6.65 A typical SMES system connected to a power network.

phenomenon known as a quantum phenomenon, in which conduction electrons happen to move in pairs thus showing no electrical resistance. For their work they won the Nobel Prize in 1972. However, until 1985, the highest temperature superconductor was niobium germanium at 23 K (23 K or 418 °F). The temperature of 23 K was very difficult to achieve, as liquid helium is the only gas that can be used to cool the material to that temperature. Due to its nature, liquid helium is very expensive and inefficient and that was the main obstacle for commercial applications of superconductors. In 1986, K.A. Miller and J.G. Bednorz discovered a superconducting oxide material at temperatures higher than ones which had been thought possible. For their discovery they won the Nobel Prize in physics in 1987. They had effectively raised the temperature for a superconductor to 30 K (−406 F). In 1987, P. Chu announced the discovery of a compound (Yttrium Barium Copper Oxide) that became superconducting at 90 K. Even higher temperatures were achieved in later times with bismuth compounds at 110 K and thallium compounds at 127 K. When materials were discovered that their critical temperature to become superconductors was raised above 77 K, the low cost and readily available liquid nitrogen could be used to cool the superconductor. This made some products and applications commercially viable.

Superconductivity offers two interesting and different ways of energy storage, namely SMES systems and flywheels based on superconductive magnetic bearings as presented in the previous section (Hull, 1997).

The characteristics of an SMES system can be summarized as follows:

- Very quick response time (six cycles or simply 100 ms for a 50 Hz system, for large-scale systems, and fewer cycles for smaller-scale units).
- High power (multi-MW systems are possible, for instance 50–200 MW with 30–3000 MJ capacity).
- High efficiency (since no conversion of energy from one form to another, i.e. from mechanical or chemical to electrical and vice versa does not occur, the round trip efficiency can be very high).
- Four quadrant operation.

The above mentioned attributes can provide significant benefits to a utility for a number of cases as follows:

- load levelling
- improve the stability and reliability of the transmission line
- enhance power quality
- extend line transmission capacity
- provide voltage and reactive power control
- spinning reserve.

A SMES system belongs to FACTS, which can exchange both real and reactive power with the grid. Therefore, it can be used successfully to manage the performance of the grid at a given point. It is based on a well-known concept of DC current flowing through a coiled wire (Figure 6.65). However, the wire is not a typical type which has losses through the conduction of current. The wire is made of a superconducting material. An important part of any SMES system is the required cryocooling. A highly efficient cryostat containing the superconductor

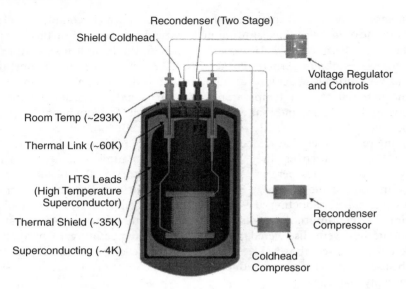

Shield Coldhead

Recondenser (Two Stage)

Voltage Regulator
and Controls

Room Temp (~293K)

Thermal Link (~60K)

HTS Leads
(High Temperature
Superconductor)

Thermal Shield (~35K)

Superconducting (~4K)

Recondenser
Compressor

Coldhead
Compressor

Fig. 6.66 A high efficiency cryostat containing the superconductor magnet. (Courtesy of American Superconductor Inc.)

magnet is shown in Figure 6.66. The three-phase VSC topology (Figure 6.32) can be used to transfer power between the superconductor and the power system/load.

6.6.3 Other energy storage systems

There are a number of other energy storage systems. A hydroelectric pumped-storage plant for instance is a quite popular one with power utilities. It works like the conventional hydroelectric station, except for the fact that the same water is used over and over again to produce electricity. There are two reservoirs at different altitudes. When power from the plant is needed, water from the upper reservoir is released driving the hydro turbines. The water is then stored in the lower reservoir. A pump is used then to pump the water back from the lower reservoir to the upper one, so that it can be used again to generate electricity. Pumped-storage plants generate electricity during peak load demand. The water is generally pumped back to the upper reservoir at night and/or weekends when the demand is lower and hence the operating costs of the plant can be reduced to meet the economics of the method. Of course the advantage of using the water again and again requires the building of a second reservoir therefore increasing the cost of the overall plant. Since the plant uses electricity when the water is pumped into the upper reservoir, the concept behind the development of such plants is based on the conversion of relatively low cost, off-peak electricity generated by thermal plants into high value on-peak electricity when the hydroelectric plant generates electricity to assist with demand management for utilities.

Another energy storage system may be based on batteries. Such a system of course requires a great deal of maintenance and periodic replacement. Furthermore, supercapacitors represent a state-of-the-art technology with potential applications in power quality. When compared with the lead–acid batteries a supercapacitor is capable of releasing energy a lot more rapidly and can address energy storage applications in the milliseconds to approximately 100 s. The energy storage capability per volume unit is also higher than a conventional capacitor.

Finally, there exist systems based on hydrogen storage and technology associated with double-layer capacitors. All these systems can offer a solution for different energy storage needs and power requirements.

6.7 HVDC

High voltage direct current power transmission, although not part of the grid to distribute power to customers, is a significant technology used successfully to transmit power in a more economic way over long distances, to connect two asynchronous networks and in many other cases. The idea and the relevant technology were under development for many years and started as early as in the late 1920s. However, the application became commercially possible in 1954 when an HVDC link was used to connect the island of Götland and the mainland of Sweden. The power of that project was 20 MW and the DC voltage was 100 kV. At the time, mercury arc valves were used to convert the AC into DC and vice versa. The control equipment used vacuum tubes.

Since then of course, the semiconductor field went through a revolution mainly due to the development of the thyristor and other devices as presented in Chapter 5. It is these continuous developments that drive the changes and the improvements in the HVDC technology.

The thyristor or SCR was developed by General Electric and became commercially available in the early 1960s in ratings of approximately 200 A and 1 kV. However, it took more than a decade for the device to mature and be used successfully in commercial high-power applications such as HVDC. The mercury arc valves then were replaced by thyristor valves, which reduced the complexity and size of the HVDC converter stations a great deal. The introduction of digital control and microcomputers has also made its contribution to the further development of the technology.

Today, further improvements can be expected and some are already in place with the availability of the IGBT to build HVDC systems based on the VSC topologies discussed in an earlier section of this chapter. These state-of-the-art developments will be discussed in the following sections of this chapter.

In simple terms HVDC is the conversion of AC into DC using a phase-controlled converter with thyristors and then transfer the power as DC into the other side which again converts the DC into an AC with a similar converter. A simple diagram representing an HVDC system and its major equipment is shown in Figure 6.67.

There are two AC systems interchanging their role of a sending and receiving end power system shown as *AC System 1* and *AC System 2* (Figure 6.67). These systems are connected through a transformer with the power electronics converter based on thyristor technology. These converters (*Converter 1* and *Converter 2*) operate as a line

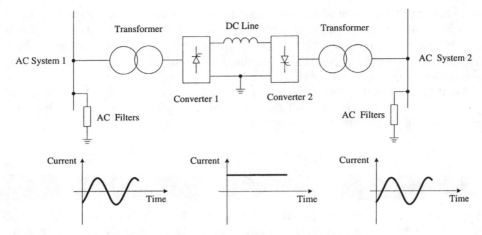

Fig. 6.67 Simple representation of a conventional HVDC power transmission system.

commutated inverter or as a line-commutated rectifier depending upon the way the power flows interchanging their role as well. The AC current is rectified into a DC quantity and the power is transmitted in DC form via a conducting medium. The DC line can be a short length of a busbar if the HVDC system is a back-to-back one, or a long cable or overhead line if the two converters are physically located within some distance between them. On the other end, the DC current is inverted with the assistance of the other converter into an AC waveform. The fundamental frequency switching of the thyristors and the associated phase-control generates waveforms which are rich in low frequency harmonics on the AC side current and on the DC side voltage. These harmonics must be filtered to meet the requirements of specific standards.

It is however very hard to filter such low frequency harmonics and due to the nature of the high power involved, higher order pulse converters are used. If one converter is supplied by voltages generated by a star-connected transformer and the other one by a delta-connected one, the phase-shift of the transformer voltages can suppress the harmonics around the 6th per unit frequency (5th and 7th). This will result in first significant harmonic frequencies around the 12th harmonic (11th and 13th). This converter arrangement is shown in Figure 6.68 and is known as a 12-pulse converter.

Even though the harmonics are shifted at higher frequencies, there is still a need to filter them with appropriate filters on the AC side. These filters are connected in shunt configuration and are built with resistors, capacitors and inductors. They are designed to have the appropriate impedance at specific frequencies. The converters draw from the AC system reactive power and such power must be compensated. Therefore, the filters must have capacitive behaviour at the fundamental frequency to be able to supply and thus compensate the reactive power required by the converter.

Each thyristor as shown in Figure 6.68 drawn as a single one may be built with a number of them in series to be able to block high voltages. The DC voltage levels are not fixed and most projects commissioned today use different voltage levels. For

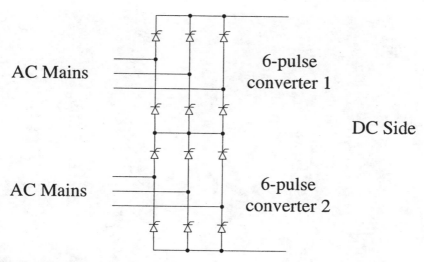

Fig. 6.68 Circuit configuration of a 12-pulse thyristor converter.

instance DC voltage levels as high as 600 kV have been used in projects and taking into account that the thyristor blocking voltage is approximately today 8 kV, one can clearly see that a number of them must be used in series to achieve the required blocking voltage mentioned earlier. A thyristor module based on a LTT device (presented in Chapter 5) is shown in Figure 6.69.

For reliable operation of the HVDC system under all conditions, switchgears are used. These assist the system to clear faults and to re-configure the station to operate in a different way if required. The reliability and the ability to operate in many cases under extreme weather conditions are very important. For instance the design temperature of the AC breakers and the installation at Radisson converter station, James Bay, Canada needs to be −50 °C. Figure 6.70 shows this installation.

Fig. 6.69 A light triggered thyristor (LTT) valve for conventional HVDC applications. (Courtesy of Siemens.)

Fig. 6.70 AC breakers and current transformers at Radisson converter station, James Bay, Canada. Design temperature is −50 °C. (Courtesy of ABB, Sweden.)

6.7.1 HVDC schemes and control

Depending upon the function and location of the converter stations, various schemes and configurations of HVDC systems can be identified as follows:

1. *Back-to-back HVDC system*. In this case the two converter stations are located at the same site and there is no transmission of power with a DC link over a long distance. A block diagram of a back-to-back system is shown in Figure 6.71. The two AC systems interconnected may have the same or different frequency, i.e. 50 Hz and 60 Hz (asynchronous interconnection). There are examples of such systems in Japan and South America. The DC voltage in this case is quite low (i.e. 50 kV–150 kV) and the converter does not have to be optimized with respect to the DC bus voltage and the associated distance to reduce costs, etc. Furthermore, since both converters are physically located in the same area, the civil engineering costs of the project are lower when compared with a similar HVDC power transmission system where two stations at two different locations must be built.

A 1000 MW back-to-back HVDC link is shown in Figure 6.72. The scheme comprises of two 500 MW poles each operating at 205 kV DC, 2474 A together with conventional switchgears at each end of the link. Fifty-four thyristors, each rated at

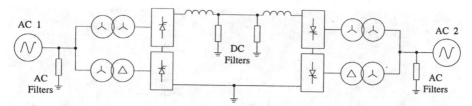

Fig. 6.71 Back-to-back HVDC power system with 12-pulse converters.

Fig. 6.72 A 1000 MW back-to-back HVDC link, Chandrapur, India. (Courtesy of ALSTOM, Transmission and Distribution, Power Electronic Systems, Stafford, England, UK.)

5.2 kV, are connected in series to form a valve and four valves stacked vertically form a 'quadrivalve' tower. One 'quadrivalve' is approximately 3.8 × 3.8 × 6.2 m high and weighs around 14 tonnes. The six 'quadrivalve' towers are shown in Figure 6.73.

The quadrivalves are arranged in the valve hall with space around them for maintenance access, electrical clearance and connections. The valve hall is designed to provide a temperature and humidity controlled environment and the screened walls contain the radio frequency interference generated by the valve-switching transients.

2. *Monopolar HVDC system.* In this configuration, two converters are used which are separated by a single pole line and a positive or a negative DC voltage is used. Many of the cable transmissions with submarine connections use monopolar systems. The ground is used to return current. Figure 6.74 shows a block diagram of a monopolar HVDC power transmission system with 12-pulse converters.

3. *Bipolar HVDC system.* This is the most commonly used configuration of an HVDC power transmission system in applications where overhead lines are used to transmit power. In fact the bipolar system is two monopolar systems. The advantage of

Fig. 6.73 Inside the valve hall, showing its six 'quadrivalve' towers. (Courtesy of ALSTOM, Transmission and Distribution, Power Electronic Systems, Stafford, England, UK.)

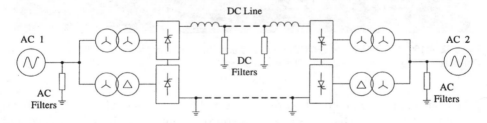

Fig. 6.74 Monopolar HVDC power transmission system based on 12-pulse converters.

such a system is that one pole can continue to transmit power in the case that the other one is out of service for whatever reason. In other words, each system can operate on its own as an independent system with the earth as a return path. Since one is positive and one is negative, in the case that both poles have equal currents, the ground current is zero theoretically, or in practice within a 1% difference. The 12-pulse based bipolar HVDC power transmission system is depicted in Figure 6.75.

4. *Multi-terminal HVDC system*. In this configuration there are more than two sets of converters like the bipolar version (Figure 6.75). A multi-terminal HVDC system with 12-pulse converters per pole is shown in Figure 6.76. For example a large multi-terminal HVDC system is the 2000 MW Quebec–New England power transmission system. In this case, converters 1 and 3 can operate as rectifiers while converter 2

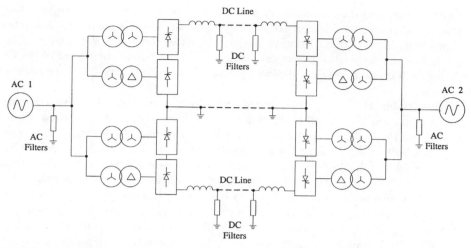

Fig. 6.75 Bipolar HVDC power transmission system based on 12-pulse converter for each pole.

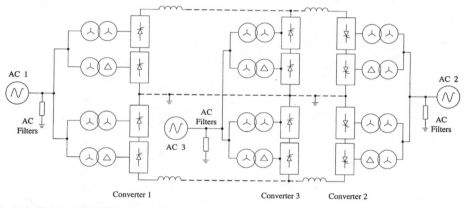

Fig. 6.76 Multi-terminal HVDC power transmission system with 12-pulse converter for each pole parallel connected.

operates as an inverter. Working in the other order, converter 2 can operate as a rectifier and converters 1 and 3 as an inverter. By mechanically switching the connections of a given converter other combinations can be achieved. For example, converters 2 and 3 can operate as an inverter and converter 1 as a rectifier and vice versa.

There is a breakeven point for which the transmission of bulk power with HVDC as opposed to HVAC becomes more economical. Although the projects are evaluated on their own economic terms and conditions, it is widely accepted by industry that the distance that makes HVDC more competitive than HVAC is about 800 km or greater in the case of overhead lines. This distance becomes a lot shorter if submarine or underground cables are used for the transmission bringing it down to approximately 50 km or greater. This allows of course not only the trading of electricity between two networks but also economic exploitation of remote site power generation.

Other advantages include increased capacity for power transmission within a fixed corridor and power transfer between two AC networks that is frequency and phase independent. Finally, due to non-mechanical parts in the power conversion, a fast modulation and reversal of power can be achieved, and due to the nature of the DC link, the fault currents between the two systems are not transferred from one network to another.

Higher order HVDC systems based on 24-pulse or even 48-pulse converter arrangements are also possible. In this case the harmonics can be shifted around the 24th and the 48th harmonics respectively. This means the most significant harmonics will be the 23rd and the 25th harmonics for the 24-pulse converter and 47th and 49th for the 48-pulse one. Clearly such harmonics are easier to filter when compared with the 11th and 13th harmonics of the 12-pulse system. However, in this case, the transformer must be designed to have phase-shifting properties other than the star–delta connection (30°). Being a high voltage transformer, this makes it quite costly to the point that AC side and DC side filters are an easier and cheaper way to use to filter the low order harmonics (at least the 11th and the 13th harmonics due to the 12-pulse converter). A bipolar HVDC system based on 24-pulse converters per pole is drawn in Figure 6.77.

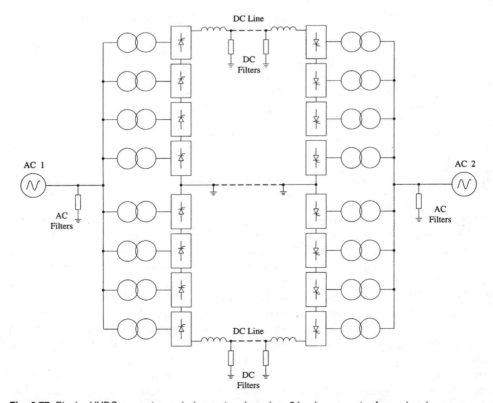

Fig. 6.77 Bipolar HVDC power transmission system based on 24-pulse converter for each pole.

6.7.2   Advanced concepts in conventional HVDC applications

Although thyristor-based HVDC systems represent mature technology, there are still exciting developments worth mentioning such as (Arrillaga, 1998):

- active AC and DC filtering (Figure 6.79)
- capacitor commutated converter (CCC) based systems
- air-insulated outdoor thyristor valves
- new and advanced cabling technology
- direct connection of generators to HVDC converters.

In the case of a thyristor-based converter for HVDC, series capacitors can be used to assist the commutations. Such a single-line diagram of a monopolar converter HVDC system is shown Figure 6.78. Such capacitors are placed between the converter valves and the transformer. A major advantage for using such approach is that the reactive power drawn by the converter is not only lower when compared with conventional line commutated converters but also fairly constant over the full load range. Furthermore, such HVDC system can be connected to networks with a much lower short-circuit capacity. Finally, Figure 6.79 shows an active DC filter installation.

6.7.3   HVDC based on voltage-source converters

The HVDC systems presented in the previous section were based on thyristor technology. The phase-controlled converters require reactive power which flows in one direction only. This is shown in Figure 6.80(a). The flow of the real power across the DC bus can be potentially in both directions.

HVDC systems based on the technology of VSCs described earlier in this chapter is also possible with the use of IGBT or GTO switches. In this case the real power flow remains unchanged and is in both directions like before. This is shown

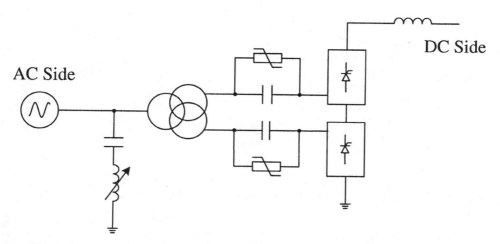

Fig. 6.78 Single-line diagram of a monopolar HVDC power transmission system with capacitor commutated converter (CCC).

Fig. 6.79 Active DC filter at the Swedish terminal of the Baltic cable link. (Courtesy of ABB, Sweden.)

(a)

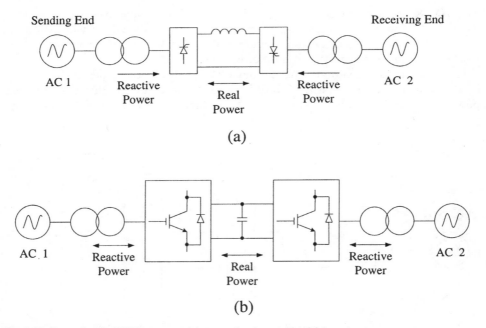

(b)

Fig. 6.80 Power flow in HVDC systems. (a) conventional; and (b) VSC based.

in Figure 6.80(b). However, the reactive power flow is improved and can be in both directions mainly due to the independent control of the amplitude and phase of the converter output voltage due to PWM operation.

There are a number of significant advantages gained from the application of PWM VSC technology into the HVDC transmission systems. These can be summarized as follows:

1. Independent control of both real and reactive power almost instantaneously.
2. Minimum contribution of the converter to the short-circuit power.
3. Transformerless applications may be possible if the voltage handling capacity of the semiconductors is high enough to be connected directly to the AC system.
4. The system can be connected to an AC weak grid without the presence of generators, as the voltages are not required for the commutation of the thyristors which are replaced by fully controlled devices.
5. Reduction of the size of the installation since the AC filters are smaller, and the reactive power compensators are not required.

The converter is a typical six-switch three-phase VSC as shown in Figure 6.32 where transistors are used to represent the switches. A number of IGBTs of course are connected in series to make up one switch.

There are a number of potential applications for the HVDC systems based on IGBT or similar technology to build the converter. For instance with the continuous push for renewable technology systems, it is important that these applications are exploited further. Wind farms can be located either off-shore or away from communities for various reasons including minimum environmental impact on local communities, maximization of the resource available, building of large plants, etc. Such relatively large-scale power generation can be connected to the grid via an HVDC system with VSCs. This will potentially reduce the cost of the investment by cutting down transmission costs. Of course the same concept can be applied to other sources of power such as hydro. In the case of small islands, like Greece for instance, where diesel generators are used, VSC-based HVDC technology can be used to connect them to the mainland's grid and this way the dependency on non-renewable energy sources can be eliminated.

Moreover, upgrading AC lines for the same power capacity can be difficult these days mainly for environmental reasons. The AC cables from existing transmission lines can be replaced by DC cables to increase the transmission capability of the line without adding extra cable towers that would be difficult to build. Furthermore, upgrading AC lines into cities' centres is costly and permits for the right of way may be difficult to obtain. If more high-rise buildings cause power demand increases, HVDC can be used as an alternative in competitive terms against AC power transmission.

This technology is relatively new. Specifically, the first VSC based PWM HVDC system has been in operation since March 1997 (Helljsön project, Sweden, 3 MW, 10 km distance, ±10 kV). The installation of this project is shown in Figure 6.81. Another one is the Götland project (Sweden) commissioned recently (50 MW, 70 km distance, ±80 kV).

There are currently three similar projects under construction or just completed recently as follows:

1. The HVDC connection between Texas and Mexico at Eagle Pass.
2. The DirectLink between Queensland and New South Wales in Australia (180 MW, 65 km distance).

Fig. 6.81 The Hellsjön VSC-based HVDC system. (HVDC light, Courtesy of ABB, Sweden.)

3. The cross-sound cable subsea power interconnection linking Connecticut and Long Island in New York, USA.

As the ratings of the IGBTs increase further and the technology of connecting these devices in series improves, it is likely that most HVDC links will be based on VSCs.

6.7.4 Multilevel VSCs and HVDC

The multilevel VSC topologies have been successfully investigated and developed for adjustable speed electric motor drives of high power (Holtz et al., 1988), and AC heavy traction drives (Ghiara et al., 1990) and mainly as three-level systems.

It is only natural that such topologies and concepts can be extended to use them as a basic block in a multilevel HVDC system with VSCs. The main obstacles are always cost and reliability and when these factors are addressed the technology can be developed commercially. Such a system has been proposed and studied (Lipphardt, 1993).

The advantage of such an approach would be the use of lower voltage switches to handle higher power. An important advantage of course would be the benefit of shifting the harmonics of the output of the converter at higher frequencies without having to operate the PWM controller at high frequencies. It is simply the same advantage of shifting the harmonics by transformers as in the old systems. The only difference here would be that the PWM controllers will be able to do that within the converter and the summation of the waveforms will be done again by reactive elements whose size will be a lot smaller.

6.8   Active filters (AFs)

The solid-state power electronic converters can be used as part of an apparatus to control electric loads such as adjustable speed electric motor drives, to create regulated power supplies, etc. The same equipment however generates harmonics and the currents drawn from the AC mains are highly reactive. The harmonics injected back into the AC system create serious problems and the 'pollution' of the supply networks has become a major concern for all utilities and power engineers.

There are ways to rectify the problems associated with 'polluted' power networks. Filtering or power conditioning which may include other more sophisticated functions for the equipment used is therefore not only required in electric power systems but is also considered a mature technology as far as passive elements are concerned.

A combination of inductive–capacitive networks has been used successfully in most cases to filter harmonics and capacitor banks have been employed to improve the power factor of a plant. Such conventional solutions have fixed levels of performance, are usually bulky and create resonance phenomena.

The requirements for harmonics and reactive power compensation along with the continuous development of power electronics have resulted in dynamic and adjustable solutions for the pollution of the AC networks. Such equipment is based on power electronic converters. The converters interacting with the network to filter harmonics or compensate for reactive/real power they are known as active filters or power conditioners or power quality equipment.

In this section we present the various converter-based topologies used as active filters or power conditioners in schematic form only. It is beyond the scope of this book to provide any more detailed information on this subject, but rather show the potential of the VSC technology for power system applications.

Converter based active filtering topologies are used to provide compensation for:

- harmonics
- reactive power
- neutral currents
- unbalanced loads.

The applications include different cases such as:

- single-phase
- three-phase with floating neutral (three wires only)
- three-phase with neutral (four wire).

A number of topologies are used as active filters in series or shunt connection along with a combination of them as well in series/shunt configuration. The series topologies are normally used to deal with:

- voltage harmonics
- spikes
- sags
- notches

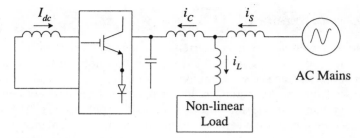

Fig. 6.82 CSC based shunt connected active filter.

The shunt topologies are normally used to deal with:

- current harmonics
- reactive power compensation.

There are two types of topologies used as AFs, namely the current-source and the voltage-source based. Figure 6.82 shows a current-source single-phase inverter in shunt connection used as an active filter.

The voltage-source converter based shunt-connected active filter is shown in Figure 6.83. This topology typically has a large DC capacitor and it can be used in expandable multilevel or multistep versions to increase power ratings or improve the performance operating at lower switching frequency and in many cases with fundamental frequency modulation. The same hardware can be used as an active filter connected in series as shown in Figure 6.84. The next step is a natural extension of the two systems previously mentioned to arrive at the unified series/shunt

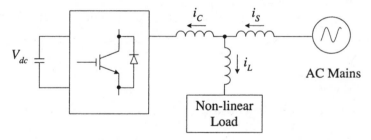

Fig. 6.83 VSC based shunt connected active filter.

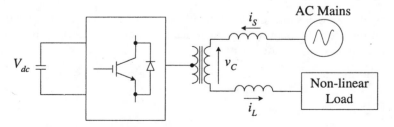

Fig. 6.84 VSC based series connected active filter.

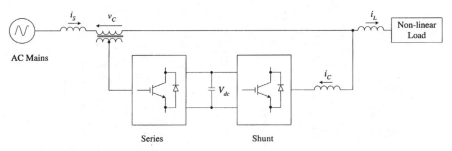

Fig. 6.85 VSC based series/shunt combined active filter.

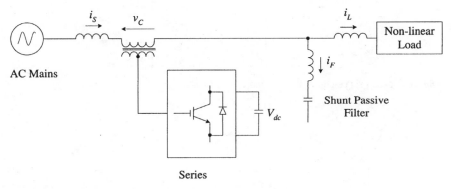

Fig. 6.86 VSC based series active filter combined with shunt passive one.

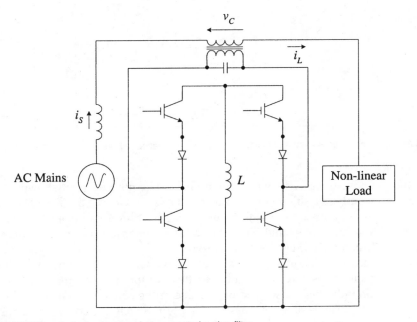

Fig. 6.87 CSC based single-phase series connected active filter.

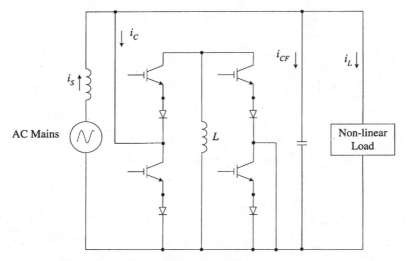

Fig. 6.88 CSC based single-phase shunt connected active filter.

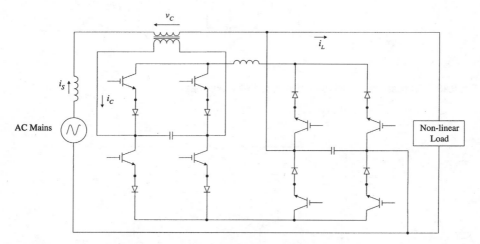

Fig. 6.89 CSC based single-phase combined series/shunt connected active filter.

VSC-based active filter as shown in Figure 6.85. The power circuit shown in Figure 6.83 is used mainly as a shunt compensator and it is known as a STATCOM. Its basic function in utility applications is to provide reactive power compensation, eliminate the line current harmonics and balance the three-phase loads in a three-phase configuration. It can be used to restore the voltage in a series connection as a DVR shown in Figure 6.84. In all figures where a converter is used as an active filter, the AC mains is shown as a voltage source with series inductance, and at the point of connection, an inductor is also used on the side of the converter. The only difference is that if the converter is of a current-source type, a capacitor is connected prior to the inductor as square-wave currents are generated at the output of the converter which

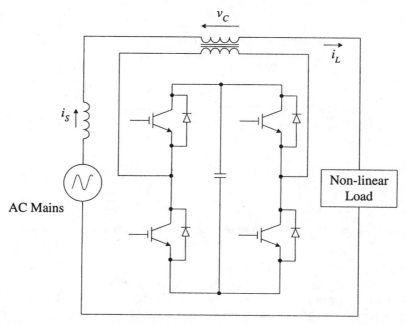

Fig. 6.90 VSC based single-phase series connected active filter.

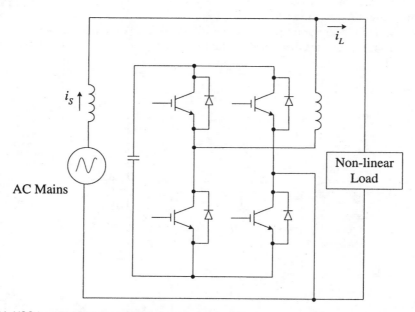

Fig. 6.91 VSC based single-phase shunt connected active filter.

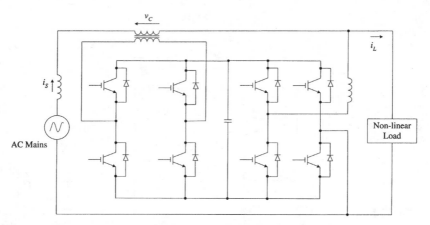

Fig. 6.92 VSC based single-phase combined series/shunt connected active filter.

need to be filtered and become sinusoidal waveforms. Furthermore, in the case of a voltage-source type converter being used, the inductor is connected at the output of the converter as the voltage waveforms created are of a square-wave type and also need to be filtered and become sinusoidal prior to being fed into the line.

In the case of the converter being connected in series, a transformer is used to connect the output of the converter in series with the line. Once again both load and mains have an inductor in series.

The unified active filter that has a series and shunt connected VSCs is shown in Figure 6.85. The two converters share the same DC bus and the same rules to connect them into the line are followed.

The next step is to combine the active filters with passive ones as a series and/or parallel. These filters are discussed in the following section (Figures 6.93–6.95).

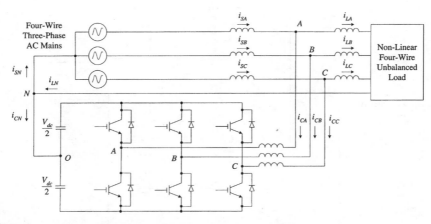

Fig. 6.93 Four-wire three-phase VSC based shunt connected active filter.

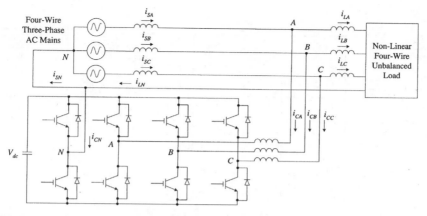

Fig. 6.94 Four-wire four-pole VSC based shunt connected active filter.

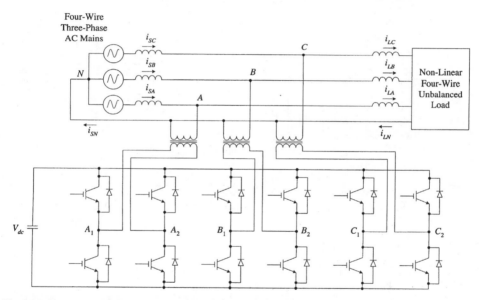

Fig. 6.95 Four-wire three-phase three bridge VSC shunt connected active filter.

6.9   Combined active and passive filters

In high power applications with DC and AC motor drives, DC power supplies or HVDC conventional thyristor-based systems 12-pulse rectifier loads are widely used. Such configurations are typically used because they generate significantly lower harmonic currents when compared to a six-pulse rectifier circuit.

In order to meet harmonic requirements (i.e. IEEE 519) although the 12-pulse system offers improved harmonics it still requires filtering. Only an 18-pulse rectifier circuit can meet IEEE 519 requirements without any additional filtering. In conventional

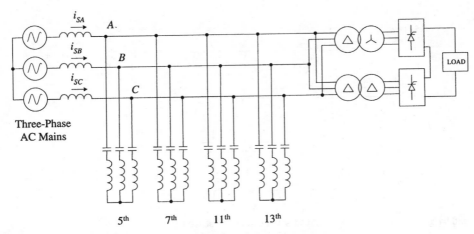

Fig. 6.96 Typical passive filter based arrangement for a 12-pulse rectifier system.

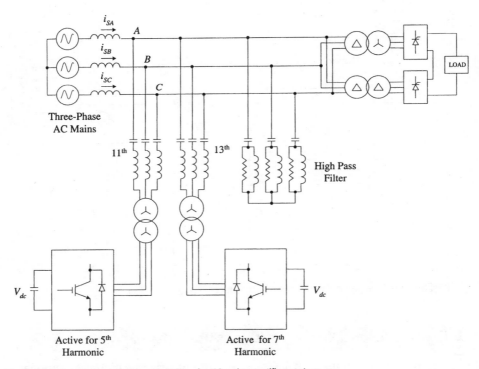

Fig. 6.97 Hybrid active/passive shunt filter for 12-pulse rectifier system.

filtering arrangements, *L–C* tuned filters at 5th, 7th, 11th, and 13th harmonic frequencies are employed. The 12-pulse rectifier does not generate significant 5th and 7th harmonics. However, one cannot ignore them as resonances between passive filter components and line impedances are likely to increase the amplitude of the harmonics at 5th and 7th frequencies. Moreover, 11th and 13th harmonic frequencies must be dealt with via the design of tuned passive filters. Figure 6.96 shows a typical passive filter configuration for a 12-pulse rectifier with shunt filters tuned at 5th, 7th, 11th, and 13th harmonics.

The application of active filtering as shunt configuration based on a VSC technology has the advantage of low converter ratings and simplicity. Such systems of course for high power applications are not feasible, as most active filtering schemes presented in the previous section require high bandwidth PWM converters to successfully eliminate harmonics below the 13th. Simply said such a solution is also not cost effective for high power applications (>10 MW).

Hybrid topologies can be considered. The main motivation to use hybrid solution is to reduce the ratings of the active filter. Figure 6.97 shows a hybrid active/passive shunt filter system suitable for 12-pulse rectifiers. Specifically, two VSC based active filters for the 5th and 7th harmonics are used in combination with series connected passive filters tuned at 11th and 13th harmonic frequencies. Because the application involves high power, six-step three-phase inverters can be employed. The rating for the inverters is no more than approximately 2% of the load kVA rating.

6.10 Advanced concepts in reactive power control equipment

Many new reactive power control equipment based on the VSC topologies presented earlier have been under research and development over the last decade. A number of them have been developed and successfully implemented. These include the UPFC, and the interline power flow controller (IPFC). The UPFC is not discussed in this chapter, but it is treated in other parts of the book.

6.11 Conclusion

In this chapter, the conventional thyristor-controlled equipment for reactive power control in power systems has been presented first. The voltage source converter topologies were then presented in detail including multilevel converter topologies. Such topologies will have a major impact on the applications of reactive control and power quality equipment in the industry. New systems based on energy storage, namely the flywheel technology and superconductor energy storage systems were then briefly discussed to highlight the potential of this technology. HVDC systems with conventional technology and using VSC technology and PWM systems were also presented as a significant application area of high power electronics in the electric power systems. Finally, active and hybrid filters based on active and passive technologies were also discussed where the VSC technology will have a major impact and significant improvements in performance. Many new applications will become possible in the near future once the limitations of fully controlled devices such as the IGBT are overcome. This will potentially allow the full replacement of the thyristor in the future systems even in very high power applications. This may seem quite speculative today, but if one looks back at the developments that have happened in the semiconductor area in the last 40 years one can hopefully visualize that such advancements may only be a matter of time.

7

Harmonic studies of power compensating plant

7.1 Introduction

The use of power electronics-based equipment in high-voltage power transmission and in low-voltage distribution has increased steadily over the last three decades. Notwithstanding their great many operational benefits, they also have increased the risk of introducing harmonic distortion in the power system because several of these devices achieve their main operating state at the expense of generating harmonic currents. In the early days, most applications of this technology were in the area of HVDC transmission (Arrillaga, 1999). However, the SVC which is a more recent development, has found widespread use in the area of reactive power management and control (Miller, 1982). In the last 20 years or so, a substantial number of SVCs have been incorporated into existing AC transmission systems (Erinmez, 1986; Gyugyi, 1988). Many utilities worldwide now consider the deployment of the newest and most advanced generation of power electronics-based plant components, FACTS and Custom Power equipment (Hingorani, 1993; 1995), a real alternative to traditional equipment based on electromechanical technologies (IEEE/CIGRE, 1995).

Over the years, many adverse technical and economic problems have been traced to the existence of harmonic distortion. Professional bodies have long recognized harmonics as a potential threat to continuity of supply and have issued guidelines on permissible levels of harmonic distortion (IEEE IAS/PES, 1993). However, it is generally accepted that this problem, if left unchecked, could get worse. Hence, great many efforts are being directed at finding new measuring, simulation and cancellation techniques that could help to contain harmonic distortion within limits. Substantial progress has been made in the development of accurate instrumentation to monitor the harmonic behaviour of the network at the point of measurement (Arrillaga et al., 2000). However, in planning and systems analysis the problem must be addressed differently because measurements may not be economic or the network may not exist. In such cases, digital simulations based on mathematical modelling provide a viable alternative to actual measurements (Dommel, 1969). Research efforts worldwide have produced accurate and reliable models for predicting power systems harmonic distortion. Time and frequency domain solutions have been used for such a purpose. Owing to its popularity, most frequency domain techniques use Fourier's transform (Semlyen et al., 1988) but alternative transforms such as Hartley (Acha et al., 1997), Walsh (Rico and Acha, 1998) and Wavelets can also be used for alternative harmonic solutions.

The thrust of this chapter is to present harmonic models of power plant compensation equipment, but it is useful to set the scene by first examining some of the adverse effects caused by the existence of harmonics and the potential harmonic magnification problems which may be introduced by a bank of capacitors, together with the beneficial effects brought about by the use of tuning reactors.

Models of TCR, SVC and TCSC are presented in Sections 7.4, 7.5 and 7.6, respectively. These models use Fourier's transform and are used to solve harmonic distortion problems in power systems containing electronic compensation. They come in the form of harmonic admittance and impedance matrices, respectively. In the absence of harmonics build up due to, for instance, resonance conditions, these plant components may be considered linear, time-variant. The harmonic admittance and impedance models are derived by 'linearizing' the TCR equations, in a manner that resembles the linearization exercise associated with, say, the non-linear equations of magnetic iron cores (Semlyen and Rajakovic, 1989).

It should be noted that linear, time-invariant components generate no harmonic distortion whereas non-linear and linear, time-variant components do generate harmonic distortion. Examples of linear, time-invariant components are banks of capacitors, thyristor-switched capacitors, air-core inductors, transmission lines and cables. Examples of non-linear components are, saturated transformers and rotating machinery, salient pole synchronous generators feeding unbalanced systems, electric arc furnaces, fluorescent lamps, microwave ovens, computing equipment and line commutated AC–DC converters (Acha and Madrigal, 2001). Time-variant components are, for instance, SVCs and TCSCs operating under medium to low harmonic voltage distortion, VSC-based equipment with PWM control, e.g. STATCOM, DVR, UPFC and HVDC light.

7.2 Effect of harmonics on electrical equipment

In industrial installations, the first evidence of excessive harmonic levels is blown capacitor fuses or failed capacitors in capacitor banks. Current standards cover the characteristics of shunt power capacitors (IEEE IAS/PES, 1993). It is well known that continuous operation with excessive harmonic current leads to increased voltage stress and excessive temperature rises, resulting in a much reduced power plant equipment's useful life. For instance, a 10% increase in voltage stress will result in 7% increase in temperature, reducing the life expectancy to 30% (Miller, 1982). More severe capacitor failure may be initiated by dielectric corona, which depends on both intensity and duration of excessive peak voltages.

Harmonic currents are also known to cause overheating in rotating machinery, particularly synchronous generators. This applies to both solid-rotor synchronous generators and salient-pole synchronous generators feeding unbalanced networks. Harmonic currents produce an electromagnetic force that causes currents to flow in the rotor adding to the heating. Positive sequence harmonics, e.g. 7th, 13th, rotate in the same direction as the fundamental frequency and induce harmonic orders 6th, 8th, 12th, 14th, in the rotor. Negative sequence harmonics, e.g. 5th, 11th, rotate against the direction of the rotor and produce harmonic orders 4th, 6th, 10th, 12th, and so on, in the rotor. The resulting pulsating magnetic fields caused by the opposing rotating pairs, e.g. 6th and 12th, may require a derating of the machine. To illustrate the point, the derating of a synchronous generator operating near a six-pulse rectifier, can be quite considerable, depending on the particular machine design. On the other hand, derating for balanced 12-pulse rectifier operation is, on average, minimal (Miller, 1982).

Induction motors are much less affected by harmonics than are synchronous generators. However, excessive harmonic currents can lead to overheating, particularly in cases when they are connected to systems where capacitors in resonance with the system are aggravating one or more harmonics.

Harmonic currents carried by transformers will increase the load loss, I^2R, by a factor greater than the mere increase in RMS current. The increase depends on the proportion of I^2R loss proportional to frequency squared (eddy current loss), and the amount proportional to the first power of frequency (stray load loss). The same rule-of-thumb holds for current limiting and tuning reactors. Precise information about the amount and order of each significant harmonic is mandatory in reactor design practise.

7.3   Resonance in electric power systems

Banks of capacitors are very often added to power systems to provide reactive power compensation, with voltage support and power factor correction being two popular applications. An issue of great importance to bear in mind is that the capacitor bank and the inductance of the system will be in parallel resonance in one or more frequency points, and that harmonics injected into the system at coincident frequencies will be amplified.

The small system shown in Figure 7.1 is used to illustrate the principle of harmonic current flow and resonance. To simplify the explanation, it is assumed that the harmonic source generates constant harmonic currents. The one-line diagram of Figure 7.1(a) may be represented on a per-phase basis by the equivalent circuit in Figure 7.1(b).

The n-th harmonic current divides between the capacitor and the supply according to the equation

$$I_n = I_{sn} + I_{fn} \tag{7.1}$$

The impedance of the capacitor branch at any frequency is given by

$$Z_f = Z_{fc} + Z_{fl} \tag{7.2}$$

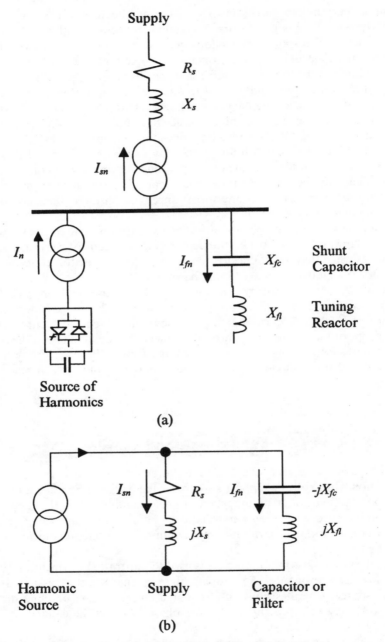

Fig. 7.1 (a) One-line diagram of small system; and (b) per-phase equivalent circuit.

where Z_{fc} is the impedance of the capacitor and Z_{fl} is the impedance of a tuning reactor. The subscript f alludes to the filtering action of the capacitor branch.

The harmonic current I_n divides between the capacitor and the supply in proportion to the admittance of these parallel branches. If Z_s is the equivalent impedance of the supply, including the transformer, then the following relations will apply

$$I_{fn} = \frac{Z_s}{Z_f + Z_s} I_n = \rho_f I_n \tag{7.3}$$

$$I_{sn} = \frac{Z_f}{Z_f + Z_s} I_n = \rho_s I_n \tag{7.4}$$

From these equations, it is not difficult to see that if the distribution factor ρ_s is large at a particular harmonic frequency coincident with one of the harmonics generated by a harmonic source, then amplification of the harmonic current will occur and the currents in the capacitor and the supply may become excessive. This would particularly be the case if $Z_f + Z_s \to 0$ at some harmonic frequency. Hence, ρ_s must be kept low at these frequencies if excited by coincident harmonic currents.

The function of the tuning reactor shown in series with the capacitor in Figure 7.1(a) is to form a series-resonant branch or filter, for which $Z_f \to 0$ at the resonant frequency. As a result, $\rho_s \to 0$ thus minimizing the possibility of harmonic currents flowing into the utility network. The ideal outcome is when $\rho_f \to 1$ so that $I_{fn} = I_n$, meaning that all the harmonic current generated enters the filter.

7.3.1 Numerical example 1

A simple numerical example may be used to illustrate the performance of a detuned and a tuned capacitor filter. Assume that the step-down transformer impedance is much greater than the source impedance so that for a narrow range of frequencies the approximation $X_s/R_s = $ constant may be used. Assume the following parameters

Bus voltage = 13.8 kV
Short circuit MVA = 476
Capacitor reactive power = 19.04 MVAr
$X_s/R_s = 10$

Knowing that inductive reactance is directly proportional to frequency and that capacitive reactance is inversely proportional to frequency

$$X_s = \frac{n(13.8)^2}{476} = 0.4n \tag{7.5}$$

$$X_{fc} = \frac{(13.8)^2}{19.04n} = \frac{10}{n} \tag{7.6}$$

$$R_s = \frac{X_s}{10} = 0.04n \tag{7.7}$$

$$\rho_f = \frac{0.04 + j0.4}{0.04 + j(0.4 - 10/n^2)} \tag{7.8}$$

In Figure 7.2, ρ_f and ρ_s are plotted against the harmonic order n. There is a parallel resonance between the capacitor and the supply at the 5th harmonic. It should be noted that at that point $\rho_s \approx \rho_f$.

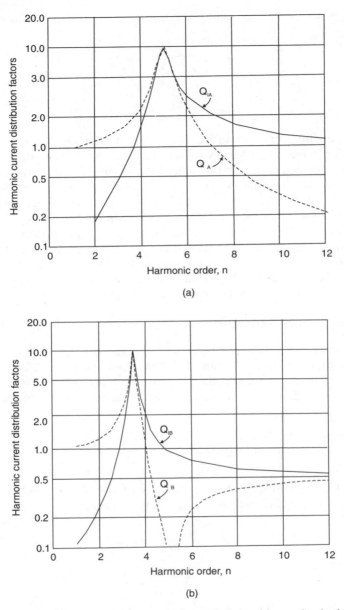

Fig. 7.2 Harmonic current distribution factors versus harmonic order: (a) capacitor bank with no tuning reactor; and (b) capacitor bank with tuning reactor.

If a tuning reactor X_{fl} is added to the capacitor to form a series 5th harmonic filter, and if the resistance of the reactor is considered negligible in comparison with the system resistance, then at 60 Hz

$$X_{fl} = \frac{X_{fc}}{5^2} = \frac{10}{25} = 0.4\,\Omega \tag{7.9}$$

The equation for ρ_f becomes

$$\rho_f = \frac{R_s + jX_s}{R_s + j(X_s + X_{fl} - X_{fc})} \qquad (7.10)$$

Figure 7.2(b) shows the response in terms of ρ_f and ρ_s with the tuning reactor. Note that $\rho_f = 1$ at the 5th harmonic, i.e. $\rho_s = 0$, and is maximum (parallel resonance) at a lower harmonic order, about 3.54.

7.4 Thyristor-controlled reactors

7.4.1 TCR periodic characteristics

The instantaneous v–i characteristics exhibited by a TCR acting under sinusoidal AC excitation voltage are a family of ellipses, which are a function of the conduction angle σ, as shown in Figure 7.3.

The firing angle δ can be controlled to take any value between 90° and 180° corresponding to values of σ between 180° and 0°. The former case corresponds to the TCR in a fully conducting state whilst the latter corresponds to the TCR in a completely non-conducting state. Both operating conditions are free from harmonics, whereas any other condition in between will be accompanied by the generation of harmonics.

For the case, when the TCR is fully conducting and driven by a periodic voltage source the relationship between the excitation voltage and TCR current can be written as

$$\frac{d}{dt} i_R(t) = \frac{1}{L_R} v(t) \qquad (7.11)$$

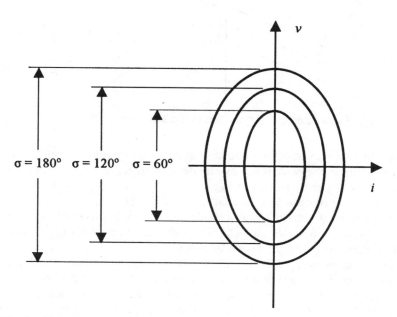

Fig. 7.3 A family of instantaneous v–i characteristics of a single-phase TCR.

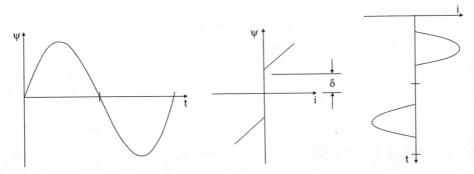

Fig. 7.4 A full cycle of the TCR current and flux excitation.

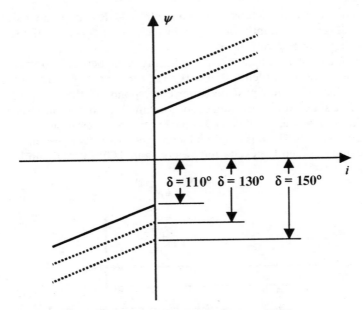

Fig. 7.5 A family of instantaneous $\psi - i$ characteristics of a single-phase TCR.

However, this relationship does not hold at conduction angles σ smaller than 180°. In such a situation, the current will exhibit dead-band zones and becomes non-sinusoidal. This effect is clearly shown in Figure 7.4, where the $\psi - i$ characteristic relates a full cycle of the excitation flux to a full cycle of the TCR current.

More generally, the characteristics exhibited by a single-phase TCR, acting under a sinusoidal AC excitation flux, are a family of straight lines which are a function of the flux-based firing angle δ_ψ, as shown in Figure 7.5.

Furthermore, numeric differentiation can be used to obtain a full cycle of the derivative of the TCR current with respect to the flux with respect to time.

It is noted from Figure 7.6 that when the TCRs are conducting the magnitude of the derivative is inversely proportional to the reactor's inductance L_R and it is zero if no conduction takes place. Also, the conduction angles σ_1 and σ_2 may differ.

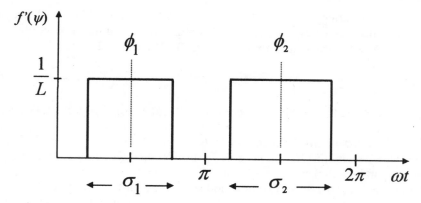

Fig. 7.6 A full cycle of derivative $f'(\psi)$.

In a thyristor-controlled, inductive circuit the flux-based relationship between the firing angle and the conduction angle is given by the following expression

$$\sigma = \pi - 2\delta_\psi \tag{7.12}$$

It should be noted that this expression differs from the conventional voltage-based relation (Miller, 1982)

$$\sigma = 2(\pi - \delta) \tag{7.13}$$

In equation (7.12), the flux-based firing angle δ_ψ can be controlled to take any value between $0°$ and $90°$, corresponding to values of σ between $180°$ and $0°$.

7.4.2 TCR currents in harmonic domain

Early representations of the TCR involved simple harmonic currents injections. They were a function of the firing angle, and were made to include imbalances, but no voltage dependency was accounted for (Mathur, 1981).

A more realistic representation in the form of a voltage-dependent harmonic currents injection was derived to account for the facts that TCRs are not always connected to strong network points and that both, network and TCR imbalances, may be an important part of the problem under study (Yacamini and Resende, 1986). A more advanced model is derived below, it comes in the form of a harmonic admittance matrix, which shows to be a special case of the harmonic Norton equivalent normally associated with non-linear plant component representation (Semlyen et al., 1988). The derivation follows similar principles as the work presented in (Bohmann and Lasseter, 1989).

Currents exhibiting dead-band zones, such as the one shown in Figure 7.4, can be conveniently expressed by the time convolution of the switching function, $s_R(t)$, with the excitation flux, $\psi(t)$

$$i_R(t) = \frac{1}{L_R} \int_0^T s_R(\tau)\psi(\tau)d\tau \tag{7.14}$$

The function $s_R(t)$ takes values of one whenever the thyristor is on and zero whenever the thyristor is off. Like the TCR derivative shown in Figure 7.6, $s_R(t)$ is also a function of the conduction periods σ_1 and σ_2.

Applying a Fourier transform to both sides of equation (7.14), and taking the Integration and Frequency Convolution theorems into account, it is possible to write an expression in the frequency domain for the TCR current, $\mathbf{I_R}$

$$\mathbf{I_R} = \frac{1}{L_R}\mathbf{S_R}\mathbf{\Psi} \tag{7.15}$$

where $\mathbf{S_R}$ and $\mathbf{\Psi}$ are the switching function and the excitation flux vectors, respectively.

7.4.2.1　Harmonic switching vectors

One way to obtain the harmonic coefficients of the switching vector, $\mathbf{S_R}$, is by drawing a fundamental frequency cycle of the derivative of the TCR current with respect to the flux with respect to time and then using an FFT routine (Acha, 1991). The harmonic content of $\mathbf{S_R}$ would then be obtained by multiplying this result by L_R, the inductance of the linear reactor. However, this is an inefficient and error prone option. A more elegant and efficient alternative to determine the harmonic coefficients of the switching function was put forward by Rico et al. (1996).

The more efficient formulation uses a periodic train of pulses to model the switching function $s_R(t)$, which in the frequency domain is well represented by a complex harmonic vector, $\mathbf{S_R}$, with the following structure

$$\mathbf{S_R} = \begin{bmatrix} \frac{a_h}{2} - j\frac{b_h}{2} \\ \vdots \\ \frac{a_1}{2} - j\frac{b_1}{2} \\ a_0 \\ \frac{a_1}{2} + j\frac{b_1}{2} \\ \vdots \\ \frac{a_h}{2} + j\frac{b_h}{2} \end{bmatrix} \tag{7.16}$$

where the vector accommodates the complex harmonic coefficients from $-h$ to $+h$. Also, the generic coefficient S_h is

$$S_h = \frac{a_h}{2} + j\frac{b_h}{2} = \frac{1}{\pi}\int_{-\pi}^{\pi} s(t)e^{-jh\omega t}d\omega t \tag{7.17}$$

The Fourier coefficients a_h and b_h are calculated from equations (7.18) to (7.20), which take into account the fact that the switching function has a value of one in the following intervals $[-\pi/2 - \sigma_1/2, -\pi/2 + \sigma_1/2]$ and $[\pi/2 - \sigma_2/2, \pi/2 + \sigma_2/2]$

$$a_0 = \frac{1}{\pi}\left[\int_{-\frac{\pi}{2}-\frac{\sigma_1}{2}}^{-\frac{\pi}{2}+\frac{\sigma_1}{2}} d\omega t + \int_{\frac{\pi}{2}-\frac{\sigma_2}{2}}^{\frac{\pi}{2}+\frac{\sigma_2}{2}} d\omega t\right] = \frac{\sigma_1 + \sigma_2}{2\pi} \tag{7.18}$$

$$\begin{aligned} a_h &= \frac{1}{\pi}\left[\int_{-\frac{\pi}{2}-\frac{\sigma_1}{2}}^{-\frac{\pi}{2}+\frac{\sigma_1}{2}} \cos(h\omega t)d\omega t + \int_{\frac{\pi}{2}-\frac{\sigma_2}{2}}^{\frac{\pi}{2}+\frac{\sigma_2}{2}} \cos(h\omega t)d\omega t\right] \\ &= \frac{2}{h\pi}\left[\sin\left(\frac{h\sigma_2}{2}\right) + \sin\left(\frac{h\sigma_1}{2}\right)\right]\cos\left(\frac{h\pi}{2}\right) \end{aligned} \tag{7.19}$$

$$b_h = \frac{1}{\pi} \left[\int_{-\frac{\pi}{2}-\frac{\sigma_1}{2}}^{-\frac{\pi}{2}+\frac{\sigma_1}{2}} \sin(h\omega t)\mathrm{d}\omega t + \int_{\frac{\pi}{2}-\frac{\sigma_2}{2}}^{\frac{\pi}{2}+\frac{\sigma_2}{2}} \sin(h\omega t)\mathrm{d}\omega t \right]$$

$$= \frac{2}{h\pi} \left[\sin\left(\frac{h\sigma_2}{2}\right) - \sin\left(\frac{h\sigma_1}{2}\right) \right] \sin\left(\frac{h\pi}{2}\right)$$

(7.20)

The harmonic switching vector can handle asymmetrically gated, reverse-parallel thyristors since the conduction angles σ_1 and σ_2 can take independent values. Hence, equation (7.15), incorporating the switching vector, as given in equation (7.16), provides an effective means of calculating TCR harmonic currents for cases of both equal and unequal conduction angles. This is a most desirable characteristic in any TCR model, since TCRs are prone to exhibit imbalances due to manufacturing tolerances in their parts.

7.4.2.2 Harmonic admittances

Similarly to the harmonic currents, the TCR harmonic admittances are also a function of the conduction angles σ_1 and σ_2. In cases when the TCR is fully conducting, i.e. $\sigma_1 = \sigma_2 = 180°$, only the DC term exists. Smaller values of conduction angles lead to the appearance of harmonic admittance terms: the full harmonic spectrum is present when $\sigma_1 \neq \sigma_2$ but only even harmonics and the DC term appear in cases when $\sigma_1 = \sigma_2$.

The TCR harmonic admittances, when combined with the admittances of the parallel capacitor and suitably inverted, provide a means for assessing SVC resonant conditions as a function of firing angle operation. As an extension, the SVC harmonic admittances can be combined with the admittances of the power system to assess the impact of the external network on the SVC resonant characteristics.

The current derivative, with respect to the flux, is expressed as follows

$$\mathbf{f}'(\mathbf{\Psi}) = \frac{1}{L_R} \mathbf{S_R}$$

(7.21)

In the time domain, the magnitude of the derivative is inversely proportional to the reactor's inductance L_R during the conduction period and it is zero when no conduction takes place. In the frequency domain, the harmonic admittances are inversely proportional to the magnitude of the harmonic terms contained in the switching vector.

7.4.2.3 Harmonic Norton and Thévenin equivalent circuits

An incremental perturbation of equation (7.15) around a base operating point $\mathbf{\Psi_b, I_b}$ leads to the following linearized equation (Semlyen et al., 1988),

$$\Delta \mathbf{I_R} = \mathbf{f}'(\mathbf{\Psi}) \cdot \Delta \mathbf{\Psi}$$

(7.22)

where $\mathbf{f}'(\mathbf{\Psi})$ is a harmonic vector of first partial derivatives.

The evaluation of the rhs term in equation (7.22) may be carried out in terms of conventional matrix operations, as opposed to convolutions operations, if the harmonic vector $\mathbf{f}'(\mathbf{\Psi})$ is expressed as a band-diagonal Toeplitz matrix, $\mathbf{F_R}$, i.e.

$$
\begin{bmatrix}
\vdots \\
\varphi_{-2} \\
\varphi_{-1} \\
\varphi_0 \\
\varphi_1 \\
\varphi_2 \\
\vdots
\end{bmatrix}
\Rightarrow
\begin{bmatrix}
\ddots & \ddots & & \ddots & & \\
\ddots & \varphi_0 & \varphi_{-1} & \varphi_{-2} & & \\
\ddots & \varphi_1 & \varphi_0 & \varphi_{-1} & \varphi_{-2} & \\
 & \varphi_2 & \varphi_1 & \varphi_0 & \varphi_{-1} & \varphi_{-2} \\
 & & \varphi_2 & \varphi_1 & \varphi_0 & \varphi_{-1} & \ddots \\
 & & & \varphi_2 & \varphi_1 & \varphi_0 & \ddots \\
 & & & & \ddots & \ddots & \ddots
\end{bmatrix}
\tag{7.23}
$$

The alternative harmonic domain equation

$$
\Delta \mathbf{I_R} = \mathbf{F_R} \Delta \mathbf{\Psi} \tag{7.24}
$$

is well suited to carry out power systems harmonic studies. This expression may also be written in terms of the excitation voltage as opposed to the excitation flux

$$
\Delta \mathbf{I_R} = \mathbf{H_R} \Delta \mathbf{V} \tag{7.25}
$$

The following relationship exists between $\mathbf{F_R}$ and $\mathbf{H_R}$

$$
\mathbf{H_R} = \mathbf{F_R} D\left(\frac{1}{j\omega h}\right) \tag{7.26}
$$

where $D(\,\cdot\,)$ is a diagonal matrix with entries $1/j\omega h$.

By incorporating the base operating point $\mathbf{V_b}, \mathbf{I_b}$ in equation (7.24), the resultant equation may be interpreted as a harmonic Norton equivalent

$$
\mathbf{I_R} = \mathbf{H_R} \mathbf{V} + \mathbf{I_N} \tag{7.27}
$$

where $\mathbf{I_N} = \mathbf{I_b} - \mathbf{H_R} \mathbf{V_b}$.

Alternatively, a representation in the form of a harmonic Thévenin equivalent may be realized from the Norton representation

$$
\mathbf{V} = \mathbf{Z_R} \mathbf{I_R} + \mathbf{V_T} \tag{7.28}
$$

where $\mathbf{V_T} = \mathbf{V_b} - \mathbf{Z_R} \mathbf{I_b}$ and $\mathbf{Z_R} = 1/\mathbf{H_R}$.

7.4.2.4   *Constraint equations*

In the presence of low to moderate levels of harmonic voltage distortion, the TCR is a linear plant component, albeit a time-variant one, and the harmonic Norton current source in equation (7.27) will have null entries, i.e. the TCR is represented solely by a harmonic admittance matrix. Likewise, if the TCR is represented by a Thévenin equivalent, equation (7.28), the harmonic Thévenin source does not exist. The engineering assumption here is that the TCR comprises an air-core inductor and a phase-locked oscillator control system to fire the thyristors. In such a situation, the reactor will not saturate and the switching function will be constant.

For TCR operation under more pronounced levels of distortion, the switching function can no longer be assumed to remain constant, it becomes voltage dependent instead. This dependency is well represented by the periodic representation of equation (7.11), beginning at the time when the thyristor is turned on, at $\phi_1 - \sigma_1/2$, and with an initial condition that the current is zero

$$I_R(\omega t) = \frac{1}{L_R} \int_{\phi_1 - \frac{\sigma_1}{2}}^{t} V(\omega t) d\omega t \tag{7.29}$$

If the voltage is assumed to be a harmonic series then the current will have a similar representation

$$I_R(\omega t) = \sum_{-\infty}^{\infty} \frac{1}{h\omega L_R} V \left(\frac{e^{jh\omega t} - e^{-jh\omega t}}{j2} \right) \Big|_{\phi_1 - \frac{\sigma_1}{2}}^{t} \tag{7.30}$$

This equation describes the current until the thyristor turns off. Just after the first zero crossing, at $\phi_1 + \sigma_1/2 \rightarrow I_R(\omega t) = 0$

$$0 = \sum_{-\infty}^{\infty} \frac{2V}{h\omega L_R} e^{jh\phi_1} \sin\left(\frac{h\sigma_1}{2}\right) \tag{7.31}$$

Similarly

$$0 = \sum_{-\infty}^{\infty} \frac{2V}{h\omega L_R} e^{jh\phi_2} \sin\left(\frac{h\sigma_2}{2}\right) \tag{7.32}$$

The constrained equations (7.31) and (7.32) are solved by iteration. Each is dependent on two angles, σ_1 and ϕ_1 for equation (7.30) and σ_2 and ϕ_2 for equation (7.31). The angles σ_1 and σ_2 may be used to determine the switching vector in equation (7.16).

7.4.3 Three-phase TCRs

A three-phase TCR normally consists of three delta connected, single-phase TCRs in order to cancel out the 3rd, 9th and 15th harmonic currents. Banks of capacitors and TSCs produce no harmonic distortion and there is no incentive for them to be connected in delta. The admittance matrix of equation (7.27) can be used as the basic building block for assembling three-phase TCR models. Linear transformations can be used for such a purpose.

The combined harmonic equivalent of three single-phase TCRs is

$$\begin{pmatrix} I_{R,1} \\ I_{R,2} \\ I_{R,3} \end{pmatrix} = \begin{pmatrix} H_{R,1} & 0 & 0 \\ 0 & H_{R,2} & 0 \\ 0 & 0 & H_{R,3} \end{pmatrix} \begin{pmatrix} V_1 \\ V_2 \\ V_3 \end{pmatrix} \tag{7.33}$$

In a power invariant, delta connected circuit the relationships between the unconnected and connected states are

$$\begin{pmatrix} I_A \\ I_B \\ I_C \end{pmatrix} = \frac{\angle 30°}{\sqrt{3}} \begin{pmatrix} 1 & 0 & -1 \\ -1 & 1 & 0 \\ 0 & -1 & 1 \end{pmatrix} \begin{pmatrix} I_1 \\ I_2 \\ I_3 \end{pmatrix} \tag{7.34}$$

and

$$\begin{pmatrix} V_1 \\ V_2 \\ V_3 \end{pmatrix} = \frac{\angle -30°}{\sqrt{3}} \begin{pmatrix} 1 & -1 & 0 \\ 0 & 1 & -1 \\ -1 & 0 & 1 \end{pmatrix} \begin{pmatrix} V_A \\ V_B \\ V_C \end{pmatrix} \tag{7.35}$$

Premultiplying equation (7.33) by the matrix term of equation (7.34), suitably modified to account for the higher order dimensions associated with the harmonic problem, and substituting equation (7.35) into the intermediate result, the following solution is arrived at

$$\begin{pmatrix} I_{R,A} \\ I_{R,B} \\ I_{R,C} \end{pmatrix} = \frac{1}{3} \begin{pmatrix} H_1 + H_2 & -H_2 & -H_1 \\ -H_2 & H_2 + H_3 & -H_3 \\ -H_1 & -H_3 & H_3 + H_1 \end{pmatrix} \begin{pmatrix} V_A \\ V_B \\ V_C \end{pmatrix} \tag{7.36}$$

7.4.3.1 Numerical example 2

The three-phase TCR harmonic model is used to calculate the harmonic currents drawn by a TCR installed in a 400 kV substation. The static compensator draws a net $35 + 10\%$ MVAr inductive at the tertiary terminal of a 240 MVA, 400/230/33 kV autotransformer.

The network is assumed to have 2% negative sequence voltage unbalance and the average system frequency is taken to be 50 Hz. The three-phase fault level at the 400 kV side is 11 185 MVA, while that on the 230 kV side is 6465 MVA. The short-circuit parameters of the transformer are 12.5%, 81.2% and 66.3% for the HV/MV, HV/LV and MV/LV sides, respectively. The TCR inductance per phase is $L = 90$ mH.

Norton equivalent representations that vary linearly with frequency are used for both the 400 kV network and the 230 kV network, A T-representation is used for the three-winding transformer. The linear Norton equivalents and the transformer admittances are combined with the harmonic domain admittance of the TCR. The overall representation is a nodal admittance matrix that contains information for the nodes, phases, harmonics and cross-couplings between harmonics. Table 7.1 gives the magnitudes of the harmonic current (rms values) drawn by the delta connected TCR when conduction angles of 120° are applied to all six thyristors.

It should be noted that the 2% negative sequence in the excitation voltage leads to unequal current magnitudes in phase A from those in phases B and C. Also, the delta

Table 7.1 Harmonic currents drawn by the TCR

Harmonic	Phase A (A rms)	Phase B (A rms)	Phase C (A rms)
1	268.79	260.81	260.81
3	5.54	3.20	3.20
5	17.63	18.91	18.91
7	6.93	6.30	6.30
9	1.59	0.81	0.81
11	2.86	3.56	3.56
13	2.05	1.81	1.81
15	0.85	0.43	0.43
17	0.98	1.53	1.53
19	0.84	0.77	0.77
21	0.49	0.25	0.25
23	0.39	0.93	0.93
25	0.33	0.36	0.36

connected TCR does not prevent completely the third harmonic currents and their multiples from reaching the network. It should be remarked that under balanced operation, these harmonic currents should be confined within the delta connected circuit. Also, as expected, TCR currents above the 13th harmonic term are quite small and may be ignored in most network harmonic studies.

Sometimes it is useful to use simplified expressions to check the sanity of the results. In this case, we shall calculate the fundamental frequency, positive sequence component of the TCR current by using the following equation (Miller, 1982)

$$I_1 = \frac{(\sigma - \sin \sigma)}{\pi} \cdot \frac{V}{X_L} \text{ A rms} \tag{7.37}$$

which gives the following result

$$I_1 = \frac{(120° \times \frac{\pi}{180°}) - \sin 120°}{\pi(2\pi \cdot 50 \times 0.09)} \times \frac{33 \times 10^3}{\sqrt{3}} = 263.48 \text{ A rms} \tag{7.38}$$

This value agrees rather well with the positive sequence value derived from applying symmetrical components to the fundamental frequency three-phase currents given in Table 7.1, i.e. 263.47 A rms.

7.4.3.2 Numerical example 3

A portion of a 220-kV power system for which complete information exists in the open literature (Acha et al., 1989) is used to illustrate the results produced by the three-phase TCR model. The system is shown in Figure 7.7. This is a well-studied test network, which shows a parallel resonance laying between the 4th and 5th harmonic frequencies, i.e. 200–250 Hz, as shown by the frequency response impedance in Figure 7.8.

A delta connected three-phase TCR is connected at busbar 1. Transmission lines are modelled with full frequency-dependence, geometric imbalances and long-line effects. Generators, transformers and loads have been assumed to behave linearly.

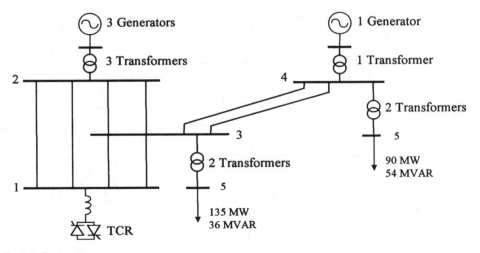

Fig. 7.7 Test system.

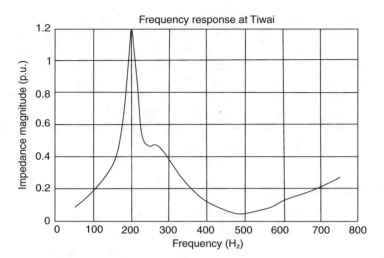

Fig. 7.8 Frequencey response impedance as seen from node 1.

It is well known that the TCRs will inject maximum 5th harmonic current when the conduction angle is 140° (Miller, 1982). In the case being analysed, this condition is compounded with the parallel resonance at near the 5th harmonic frequency exhibited by the network to give rise to a distorted voltage waveform at busbar 1. Figures 7.9(a) and (b) show the voltage waveform and the harmonic content for the three phases. Large harmonic voltage imbalances are shown in this result where the percentage of the 5th harmonic reaches almost 8% for phase B and 12% for phase C. The remaining harmonic voltages are well below recommended limits and are cause

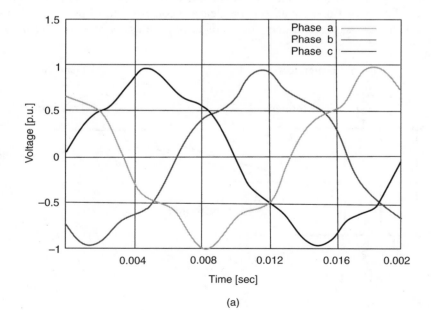

(a)

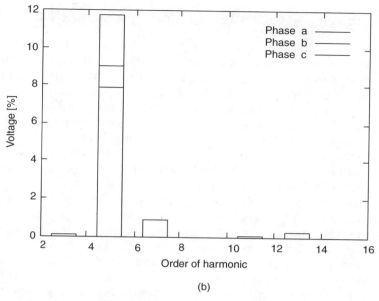

(b)

Fig. 7.9 Voltage waveform and harmonic content at the TCR.

of no concern. However, filtering equipment would have to be connected at busbar 1 to provide a low impedance path for the 5th harmonic current.

Alternatively, the 5th and 7th TCR harmonic currents can be removed very effectively from the high voltage side of the network by employing two identical half-sized TCR units and a three phase transformer with two secondary windings.

7.5   SVC representations

The model of a single-phase SVC is readily assembled by adding up the harmonic admittance of the TCR in equation (7.27) and the harmonic admittance of the capacitor, Y_C. The latter is a diagonal matrix with entries $j\omega hC$ and will hold for both banks of capacitors and thyristor-switched capacitors

$$\mathbf{I}_{SVC} = (\mathbf{H}_R + \mathbf{Y}_C)\mathbf{V} = \mathbf{Y}_{SVC}\mathbf{V} \tag{7.39}$$

where $\mathbf{Y}_{SVC}$ and $\mathbf{I}_{SVC}$ are the equivalent admittance and the current drawn by the SVC, respectively. It should be noted that $\mathbf{Y}_{SVC}$ is a function of the conduction angles σ via $\mathbf{H}_R$.

Since the three-phase banks of capacitors, or thyristor-switched capacitors, are effectively connected in a grounded star configuration, the harmonic admittance model of the three-phase SVC is easily obtained

$$\begin{pmatrix} \mathbf{I}_{SVC,A} \\ \mathbf{I}_{SVC,B} \\ \mathbf{I}_{SVC,C} \end{pmatrix} = \frac{1}{3} \begin{pmatrix} \mathbf{H}_1 + \mathbf{H}_2 + 3\mathbf{Y}_{C,1} & -\mathbf{H}_2 & -\mathbf{H}_1 \\ -\mathbf{H}_2 & \mathbf{H}_2 + \mathbf{H}_3 + 3\mathbf{Y}_{C,2} & -\mathbf{H}_3 \\ -\mathbf{H}_1 & -\mathbf{H}_3 & \mathbf{H}_3 + \mathbf{H}_1 + 3\mathbf{Y}_{C,3} \end{pmatrix} \begin{pmatrix} \mathbf{V}_A \\ \mathbf{V}_B \\ \mathbf{V}_C \end{pmatrix} \tag{7.40}$$

7.6 Thyristor-controlled series compensation

The TCSC steady-state response may be calculated by solving the TCSC differential equations using a suitable numeric integration method or by expressing the TCSC equations in algebraic form and then using a phasorial method. The former approach involves the integration of the differential equations over many cycles until the transient response dies out. This solution method is rich in information since the full evolution of the response is captured, from transient inception to steady-state operation, but problems may arise when solving lightly damped circuits because of the low attenuation of the transient response. Two different solution flavours emerge from the phasor approach: (i) A non-linear equivalent impedance expression is derived for the TCSC and solved by iteration. The solution method is accurate and converges very robustly towards the convergence, but it only yields information about the fundamental frequency, steady-state solution; and (ii) Alternatively, the TCSC steady-state operation may be determined by using fundamental and harmonic frequency phasors leading to non-iterative solutions in the presence of low to moderate harmonic voltage distortion. The solution takes place in the harmonic domain and this is the approach presented in Section 7.6.2. The method yields full information for the fundamental and harmonic frequency TCSC parameters but no transient information is available.

7.6.1 Main parameters and operating modes

A basic TCSC module consists of a single-phase TCR in parallel with a fix capacitor. An actual TCSC comprises one or more modules. Figure 7.10 shows the layout of one phase of the TCSC installed in the Slatt substation (Piwko et al., 1996).

As previously discussed in Section 7.4.1, the TCR achieves its fundamental frequency operating state at the expense of generating harmonic currents, which are a function of the thyristor's conduction angle. Nevertheless, contrary to the SVC application where the harmonic currents generated by the TCR tend to escape towards the network, in the TCSC application the TCR harmonic currents are trapped inside the TCSC due to the low impedance of the capacitor, compared to

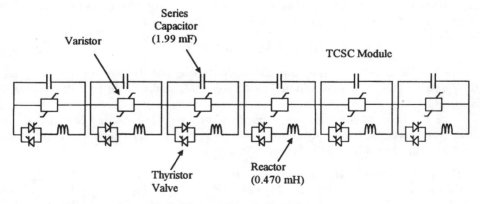

Fig. 7.10 Layout of one phase of the ASC installed in the Slatt substation.

the network equivalent impedance. This is at least the case for well-designed TCSCs operating in capacitive mode. Measurements conducted in both the Slatt and the Kayenta TCSC systems support this observation. For instance, the Kayenta system generates at its terminals, a maximum THD voltage of 1.5% when operated in capacitive mode and firing at an angle of 147° (Christl et al., 1991). It should be noted that there is little incentive for operating the TCSC in inductive mode since this would increase the electrical length of the compensated transmission line, with adverse consequences on stability margins and extra losses.

By recognizing that the thyristor pair in the TCSC module has two possible operating states, namely off and on (Helbing and Karady, 1994) developed equations for the TCSC voltage and current:

1. Thyristors off:

$$V_C^{\text{off}}(t, \alpha) = \frac{I_M \sin \alpha}{\omega C}[1 - \sin(\omega t + \alpha)] - \frac{I_M \cos \alpha}{\omega C}\cos(\omega t + \alpha) + V_{\text{st}'} \tag{7.41}$$

where I_M is the peak line current and $V_{\text{st}'}$ is the voltage across the capacitor at thyristor commutation time.

$$I_C^{\text{off}}(t, \alpha) = I_M \sin \omega t \tag{7.42}$$

In this situation, the inductor and thyristor current are zero, and the capacitor current equals the load current.

2. Thyristors on:

During conduction the inductor voltage equals the capacitor voltage.

$$V_C^{\text{on}}(t, \alpha) = I_M \frac{\omega_0^2 L \cos \alpha}{\omega^2 - \omega_0^2}\left\{\omega \cos(\omega t - \alpha) - \omega_0 \sin\left[\omega_0 t - \frac{\omega_0}{\omega}\left(\alpha - \frac{\pi}{2}\right)\right]\right\}$$

$$- I_M \frac{\omega_0^2 \omega L \cos \alpha}{\omega^2 - \omega_0^2}\left\{\sin(\omega t - \alpha) + \cos\left[\omega_0 t - \frac{\omega_0}{\omega}\left(\alpha - \frac{\pi}{2}\right)\right]\right\} \tag{7.43}$$

$$+ V_{\text{st}''}\cos\left[\omega_0 t - \frac{\omega_0}{\omega}\left(\alpha - \frac{\pi}{2}\right)\right]$$

where $V_{\text{st}''}$ is the capacitor voltage at the time of thyristor firing.

$$I_L^{\text{on}}(t, \alpha) = I_M \frac{\omega \omega_0^2 \sin \alpha}{\omega^2 - \omega_0^2}\left\{\frac{\sin\left(\omega_0 t - \frac{\omega}{\omega_0}\left(\alpha - \frac{\pi}{2}\right)\right)}{\omega_0} - \frac{\cos(\omega t - \alpha)}{\omega}\right\}$$

$$- I_M \frac{\omega_0^2 \cos \alpha}{\omega^2 - \omega_0^2}\left\{\cos\left(\omega_0 t - \frac{\omega}{\omega_0}\left(\alpha - \frac{\pi}{2}\right)\right) + \sin(\omega t - \alpha)\right\} \tag{7.44}$$

where $\omega_0 = \frac{1}{\sqrt{LC}}$.

The capacitor current comprises the line current plus the inductor current

$$I_C^{\text{on}}(t, \alpha) = I_L^{\text{on}}(t, \alpha) + I_M \sin \omega t \tag{7.45}$$

These equations are useful for calculating on a cycle-by-cycle basis the currents and voltages in the inductor, thyristor and capacitor. For instance (Helbing and Karady,

1994), give results for a TCSC module with the following parameters, $C = 212\,\mu F$ and $L = 15\,\text{mH}$, a line current of 2000 A and a firing angle of 133°.

The steady-state waveforms of the voltages and currents associated with the various TCSC components are shown in Figures 7.11, 7.12 and 7.13. Figure 7.11 shows the voltage and current waveforms in the capacitor, whereas Figures 7.12 and 7.13 show similar information in the inductor and in the bidirectional thyristors, respectively.

Figure 7.14(a) and (b) give information of the harmonic behaviour of the TCSC module under analysis. The result shows that the only harmonic of concern is the third harmonic as the firing angle decreases, i.e. the conduction angle increases. Careful design should ensure that the third harmonic voltage is kept at manageable levels.

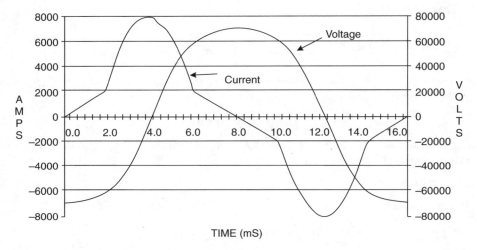

Fig. 7.11 Voltage and current waveforms in the TCSC capacitor.

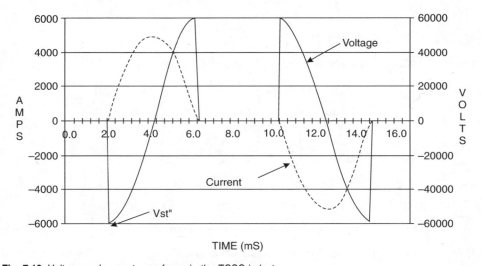

Fig. 7.12 Voltage and current waveforms in the TCSC inductor.

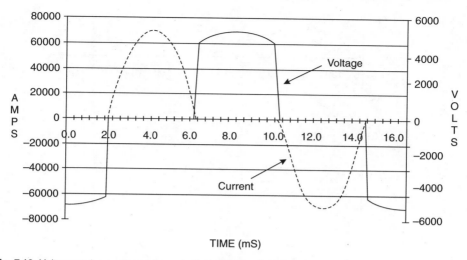

Fig. 7.13 Voltage and current waveforms in the bidirectional thyristors.

The TCSC has three basic operating modes: (i) the thyristor blocked mode; (ii) the thyristor bypassed mode; and (iii) the thyristor vernier mode. In (i), the thyristors do not conduct at all, and the transmission line current follows exclusively the TCSC capacitive path. The condition in (ii) corresponds to the case when the thyristors are conducting current continuously, with most of the transmission line current flowing through the thyristors. The TCSCs with realistic inductive and capacitive parameters have a small, net inductive reactance when operated in bypassed mode. In (iii), the thyristors are operated with phase control delay, leading to partial thyristor conduction. Two distinct operating characteristics will result from operating the TCSC in vernier mode, one inductive and one capacitive. In TCSCs with realistic LC parameters, low levels of thyristor conduction, i.e. large firing angle delays, will establish a net capacitive reactance making the TCSC to operate in the capacitive operating region. Conversely, high levels of thyristor conduction, i.e. low firing angle delays, will result in a net inductive reactance leading to TCSC operation in the inductive

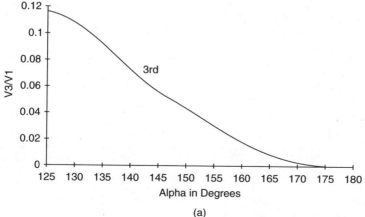

(a)

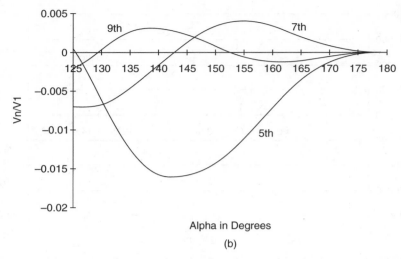

Fig. 7.14 Harmonic generation in per unit of fundamental frequency voltage as a function of firing angle.

region. For the case of the TCSC Kayenta scheme, with $X_C = 15\,\Omega$ and $X_L = 2.6\,\Omega$, firing angles of $90°$ to approximately $139°$ will lead to operation in the inductive region. On the other hand, firing angles of approximately $147°$ to $180°$ will lead to operation in the capacitive region. As shown in Figure 7.15, the fundamental frequency resonant point is centred at around $143°$.

The TCSC impedance of the Kayenta scheme is also used to emphasize the importance of including all the relevant harmonic terms in the calculations, in

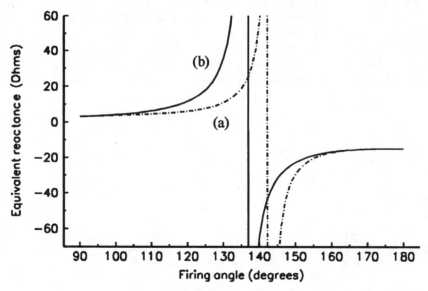

Fig. 7.15 TCSC impedance characteristic as a function of firing angle: (a) correct steady-state impedance; and (b) *understated* steady-state impedance.

addition to the fundamental frequency component. Figure 7.15(a) corresponds to the accurate solution whereas the result in Figure 7.15(b) was obtained by using only the fundamental frequency component, i.e. the harmonic terms were neglected.

Figure 7.16 shows the voltage across the TCSC capacitor for different values of firing angles. From Figure 7.16(a) and (b), it is observed that the distortion in the capacitor voltage waveform is larger when the TCSC operates in the inductive region of vernier operation. As expected the voltage magnitude increases as the resonant point is approached. The voltage across the capacitor is sinusoidal when the TCSC is operating in both thyristor bypassed mode, i.e. $\alpha = 90°$, and thyristor blocked mode, i.e. $\alpha = 180°$. Figures 7.17 and 7.18 show the current through the TCR and capacitor for different values of firing angles, respectively. The value of firing angle determines the direction of the current through the TCR and capacitor. Both plots show that the current magnitude increases as the resonant point is approached. As shown in

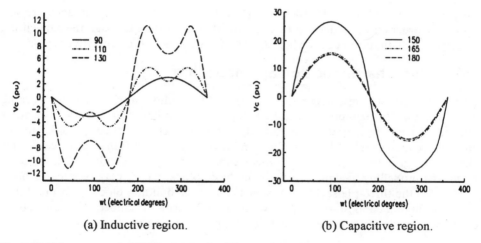

(a) Inductive region.　　　　(b) Capacitive region.

Fig. 7.16 Voltage across the TCSC capacitor for different values of firing angle.

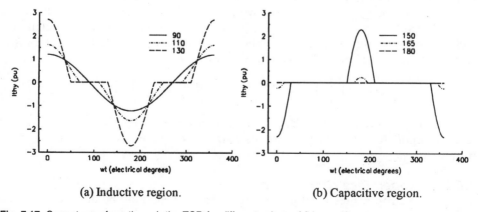

(a) Inductive region.　　　　(b) Capacitive region.

Fig. 7.17 Current waveform through the TCR for different values of firing angle.

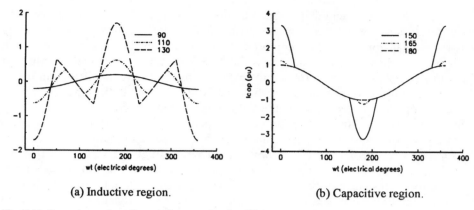

(a) Inductive region.   (b) Capacitive region.

Fig. 7.18 Current waveform through the capacitor for different values of firing angle.

Figures 7.17(a) and (b) and 7.18(a) and (b), TCSC operation in the inductive region produces larger currents flowing through the thyristors than through the capacitors. The opposite situation occurs when the TCSC operates in the capacitive region.

7.6.2   TCSC harmonic domain modelling

Due to the circulating currents inside the TCSC module, intrinsic in the working mechanism of this equipment, the TCR representation based on harmonic currents injections is of limited use. Instead, the TCR is well modelled by a harmonic admittance matrix, which can then be combined with the admittance of the capacitive element to give the overall admittance representation of a single TCSC module. From the modelling viewpoint, this is the basic block, which may be used to build models for the three-phase TCSC systems. The basic building block is also useful to conduct fundamental studies of how the TCSC harmonic impedances and cross-coupling impedances vary as a function of the conduction angle.

7.6.2.1   Single-phase TCSC representation

In principle, equation (7.39) is valid for both the single-phase SVC and the TCSC, but the latter is better represented as a two-port circuit because it is a series connected element, that would be interfaced at both ends with transmission network plant, i.e. high-voltage transmission lines. Using the result in equation (7.39), the nodal transfer admittance matrix of the TCSC is built with ease

$$\begin{pmatrix} \mathbf{I_s} \\ \mathbf{I_r} \end{pmatrix} = \begin{pmatrix} \mathbf{Y_{TCSC}} & -\mathbf{Y_{TCSC}} \\ -\mathbf{Y_{TCSC}} & \mathbf{Y_{TCSC}} \end{pmatrix} \begin{pmatrix} \mathbf{V_s} \\ \mathbf{V_r} \end{pmatrix} \tag{7.46}$$

where $\mathbf{Y_{TCSC}} = \mathbf{Y_{SVC}} = (\mathbf{H_R} + \mathbf{Y_C})$, $\mathbf{V_s}$ and $\mathbf{V_r}$ are the voltages at the sending and receiving ends, $\mathbf{I_s}$ and $\mathbf{I_r}$ are the currents at the sending and receiving ends, respectively.

7.6.2.2   Impedance characteristics

The voltage drop expression for the single-phase TCSC may be derived using the result in equation (7.39)

$$\Delta V = (H_R + Y_C)^{-1} I_{TCSC} = Z_{TCSC} I_{TCSC} \tag{7.47}$$

where the voltage drop is $\Delta V = V_s - V_r$. Also, Z_{TCSC} and I_{TCSC} are the equivalent impedance and the current across the TCSC, respectively. It should be noted that Z_{SVC} is a function of the conduction angle σ via H_R.

7.6.2.3 Three-phase TCSC representation

Equation (7.46) represents a single-phase TCSC in harmonic domain. However, expanding this model to encompass three-phase TCSCs is straightforward because of the decoupled nature of the three phases

$$
\begin{pmatrix} I_{A,s} \\ I_{B,s} \\ I_{C,s} \\ I_{A,r} \\ I_{B,r} \\ I_{C,r} \end{pmatrix}
=
\left(
\begin{array}{ccc|ccc}
Y_{TCSC,A} & 0 & 0 & -Y_{TCSC,A} & 0 & 0 \\
0 & Y_{TCSC,B} & 0 & 0 & -Y_{TCSC,B} & 0 \\
0 & 0 & Y_{TCSC,C} & 0 & 0 & -Y_{TCSC,C} \\
-Y_{TCSC,A} & 0 & 0 & Y_{TCSC,A} & 0 & 0 \\
0 & -Y_{TCSC,B} & 0 & 0 & Y_{TCSC,B} & 0 \\
0 & 0 & -Y_{TCSC,C} & 0 & 0 & Y_{TCSC,C}
\end{array}
\right)
\begin{pmatrix} V_{A,s} \\ V_{B,s} \\ V_{C,s} \\ V_{A,r} \\ V_{B,r} \\ V_{C,r} \end{pmatrix}
\tag{7.48}
$$

7.7 TCSC systems

Equation (7.46) represents one single-phase TCSC module in the harmonic domain. If the TCSC comprises more than one module, or if the TCSC module is part of a series compensation scheme comprising conventional capacitor banks, then two-port representations may be used instead. The former case corresponds to the series compensation scheme found in the Slatt substation, where six identical TCSC modules are used (Piwko et al., 1996). This compensating scheme has been dubbed, Advanced Series Compensator (ASC). The latter compensation scheme is found in the Kayenta substation, where one $15\,\Omega$ TCSC module is connected in tandem with two capacitor banks, with values of $40\,\Omega$ and $55\,\Omega$, respectively (Christl et al., 1991).

The two-port, ABCD representation of a generic transmission element connected between nodes s and r is

$$
\begin{pmatrix} V_s \\ I_s \end{pmatrix} = \begin{pmatrix} A & B \\ C & D \end{pmatrix} \begin{pmatrix} V_r \\ -I_r \end{pmatrix}
\tag{7.49}
$$

Due to the lumped nature of the TCSC module, as opposed to a transmission line or a cable, where the distributed inductive and capacitive effects are very pronounced, the ABCD representation of one TCSC module is very simple

$$
\begin{pmatrix} V_s \\ I_s \end{pmatrix} = \begin{pmatrix} 1 & Z_{TCSC} \\ 0 & 1 \end{pmatrix} \begin{pmatrix} V_r \\ -I_r \end{pmatrix}
\tag{7.50}
$$

where 1 and 0 are the unity and null matrices, respectively.

A similar representation exists for the conventional series capacitor bank in this frame of reference, i.e.

$$
\begin{pmatrix} V_s \\ I_s \end{pmatrix} = \begin{pmatrix} 1 & Z_{SC} \\ 0 & 1 \end{pmatrix} \begin{pmatrix} V_r \\ -I_r \end{pmatrix}
\tag{7.51}
$$

where Z_{SC} is the impedance of the series capacitor.

For completeness, the ABCD parameters of a transmission line with long-line effects, i.e. distributed parameters, are given below

$$A = T_i \times D(\cos h(\gamma_m l)) \times T_v^{-1}$$

$$B = T_v \times D(z_{0m} \times \sin h(\gamma_m l)) \times T_i^{-1}$$

$$C = -T_i \times D\left(\frac{1}{z_{0m}} \times \sin h(\gamma_m l)\right) \times T_i^{-1}$$
(7.52)

$$D = A^t$$

where T_v and T_i are linear transformation matrices that require the eigen-solution of the products ZY and YZ, respectively. Z and Y are the series impedance and the shunt admittance of the pi-nominal circuit per-unit length of a transmission line. As an extension, $Z_m = T_v^{-1}ZT_i$ and $Y_m = T_i^{-1}YT_v$. Also, l is the length of the line and $D(\cdot)$ is a diagonal matrix. $\gamma_m = \sqrt{z_m y_m}$ and $z_{0m} = \sqrt{z_m/y_m}$ are the propagation constant and the characteristic impedance of the transmission line, where $z_m \epsilon Z_m$ and $y_m \sin Y_m$. This model includes full frequency dependence and long-line effects.

For the case when n TCSC modules are connected in tandem, such as the Slatt compensation scheme, which comprises six modules, the equivalent TCSC system is

$$\begin{pmatrix} V_s \\ I_s \end{pmatrix} = \begin{pmatrix} 1 & Z_{TCSC,1} \\ 0 & 1 \end{pmatrix} \times \begin{pmatrix} 1 & Z_{TCSC,2} \\ 0 & 1 \end{pmatrix} \times \cdots \times \begin{pmatrix} 1 & Z_{TCSC,6} \\ 0 & 1 \end{pmatrix} \begin{pmatrix} V_r \\ -I_r \end{pmatrix}$$

$$= \begin{pmatrix} 1 & Z_{TCSC,1} + Z_{TCSC,2} + \cdots + Z_{TCSC,6} \\ 0 & 1 \end{pmatrix} \begin{pmatrix} V_r \\ -I_r \end{pmatrix}$$
(7.53)

The case of the Kayenta compensation scheme consists of three modules, of which only one module is TCSC and the other two are conventional capacitor banks, i.e.

$$\begin{pmatrix} V_s \\ I_s \end{pmatrix} = \begin{pmatrix} 1 & Z_{TCSC} \\ 0 & 1 \end{pmatrix} \times \begin{pmatrix} 1 & Z_{SC,1} \\ 0 & 1 \end{pmatrix} \times \begin{pmatrix} 1 & Z_{SC,2} \\ 0 & 1 \end{pmatrix} \begin{pmatrix} V_r \\ -I_r \end{pmatrix}$$

$$= \begin{pmatrix} 1 & Z_{TCSC} + Z_{SC,1} + Z_{SC,2} \\ 0 & 1 \end{pmatrix} \begin{pmatrix} V_r \\ -I_r \end{pmatrix}$$
(7.54)

The attractiveness of the ABCD representation is that it is quite compact, compared to say, network nodal analysis, and it still allows each individual TCSC module to incorporate its own firing angle. Moreover, the approach allows for a direct incorporation of the compensated transmission line and the external network, albeit in equivalent form, e.g. Norton and Thévenin equivalents.

Some application studies require information of the voltages at intermediate points of the compensation scheme, and nodal analysis provides a systematic tool for achieving such a result. For instance, for the case of the Kayenta scheme, the nodal admittance matrix equation is

$$\begin{pmatrix} I_s \\ 0 \\ 0 \\ I_r \end{pmatrix} = \begin{pmatrix} Y_{TCSC} & -Y_{TCSC} & 0 & 0 \\ -Y_{TCSC} & Y_{TCSC} + Y_{SC,1} & -Y_{SC,1} & 0 \\ 0 & -Y_{SC,1} & Y_{SC,1} + Y_{SC,2} & -Y_{SC,2} \\ 0 & 0 & -Y_{SC,2} & Y_{SC,2} \end{pmatrix} \begin{pmatrix} V_s \\ V_1 \\ V_2 \\ V_r \end{pmatrix}$$
(7.55)

where V_1 and V_2 are the nodal voltages at the junctions of the TCSC module and the capacitor bank 1, and the capacitor banks 1 and 2, respectively.

7.8 Conclusion

This chapter has discussed the main adverse effects caused by harmonics in electrical equipment, in particular in industrial installations where capacitors used for power-factor correction become severely affected by the presence of harmonics. The all-important problem of parallel resonances caused when banks of capacitors are combined with the inductance of the AC system, is discussed in some detail. Simple equations are used to examine this problem from the quantitative point of view and a numerical example is presented.

Comprehensive harmonic domain models are presented for the TCR, the SVC and the TCSC. The SVC achieves fast and accurate voltage magnitude control at its point of connection with the AC network due to the TCR, which can be set to absorb a variable amount of reactive power with very little delay. However, an operational drawback of this scheme is that the TCR achieves its main operating point at the expense of generating harmonic currents. The order and magnitude of these harmonics being a function of the thyristors' firing angles. The harmonic domain models presented in this chapter enable realistic studies of both TCR and SVC equipment connected to AC networks of any size and complexity. The models are developed in the phase domain to incorporate frequency dependent, multiphase transmission systems, which may be very unbalanced at harmonic frequencies. Furthermore, the three-phase SVC representation also caters for TCR imbalances in either its firing angle control or in the linear inductors or capacitors. Numerical examples are provided to illustrate the usefulness of these models in power systems harmonic studies.

The discussion also applies to the TCSC, where the fast acting, regulating characteristic of the TCR enables the TCSC to shorten or to lengthen the electrical distance of the compensated transmission line with almost no delay. This characteristic of the TCSC is being exploited in high-voltage transmission installations to provide instantaneous active power flow regulation. However, TCSC harmonic generation and the existence of resonant conditions inside the TCSC call for accurate and comprehensive analysis tools. The harmonic domain models presented in this chapter are suitable to study such complex phenomena.

8

Transient studies of FACTS and Custom Power equipment

8.1 Introduction

Electromagnetic transient studies have always played an essential role in the analysis of electrical power systems. They provide priceless information relating to the behaviour of the system in the event of different forms of transient phenomena, which can hardly be achieved by other means. This chapter addresses the transient studies of electrical networks with embedded, power electronics-based, FACTS and Custom Power (CP) controllers. The FACTS controllers considered here are:

- SVC
- TCSC
- STATCOM.

The CP controllers include:

- D-STATCOM
- DVR
- PFC
- Shunt-Connected VSC-based AF
- Solid-State Transfer Switch (SSTS).

The transient analysis and modelling is performed with the state-of-the-art digital simulator PSCAD/EMTDC v2.00 (Manitoba, 1996) for UNIX, unless otherwise stated. The appendix at the end of this chapter presents the settings of the most relevant blocks used in the digital implementations developed in PSCAD/EMTDC, for each of the FACTS and CP controllers considered here.

8.2   Electromagnetic transient analysis

The transient response of any natural system is the way in which the response of the system behaves as a function of time. Mathematically, the transient behaviour of a given system is modelled by differential equations. However, this approach can be reasonably applied to systems where the underlying principles are clear and where the system is sufficiently elementary, so that a 'basic' approach can be used. Due to the high complexity involved in the solution of differential equations by hand-methods, it has been imperative to develop efficient and reliable numerical techniques implemented on digital computers, which reproduce confidently the transient response of almost every system provided that these are modelled appropriately.

Electrical power networks like other physical systems are exposed to various forms of transient phenomena; nowadays, fast variations of electrical parameters such as voltage or current are very common due to the elaborated equipment and configurations used in the power systems. Bearing this in mind, digital tools have become an invaluable resource when the transient response of the electrical network is required. When used for this purpose, digital tools are commonly labelled as electromagnetic transient simulators.

A considerable percentage of power systems studies rely on electromagnetic transient simulations. They provide substantial information associated with the performance of the network under any operating condition and enable the user to identify and assess the interaction between the various elements encompassing the network. This information can be used for miscellaneous purposes such as evaluation, planning, operation, design, commissioning, characterization, etc.

Generally, power networks are very complex all around the world. The enhancement of transmission and distribution systems by means of high-power electronics technology, such as FACTS and CP controllers has increased considerably the complexity of electrical networks. Consequently, the development of power systems studies has become more difficult. Moreover, in some cases the only possible way to carry out the analysis of a given network is by means of electromagnetic transient simulators. Fortunately, for the electricity supply industry, digital simulators have equally been developing in order to meet the new system requirements. They are powerful and provide the user with friendly interface environments. Some of them have already incorporated models of power electronics-based controllers so that transient analysis results can be achieved accurately and with high reliability. Some of the most popular electromagnetic transient simulators currently available are as follows:

- EMTP/ATP (Electromagnetic Transient Program)
- PSCAD/EMTDC (Power Systems Computer Aided Design/Electromagnetic Transient Direct Current)
- NETOMAC
- SPICE
- SABER

These simulators provide built-in models for a wide variety of power system components, which assist users to easily study electrical networks. Although all the above simulators can be used to model a power system network, different difficulty in developing appropriate models for the system can be experienced. The reason being that they have been designed for various purposes. For instance, some have been designed for electronic circuits and their models for the various semiconductors can be more sophisticated (i.e. SPICE) than the ones provided by other simulators specifically designed for power system simulations (i.e. PSCAD/EMTDC).

As mentioned before, PSCAD/EMTDC has been used here to carry out the transient analysis of FACTS and CP controllers. Therefore, in the following subsection we present a tutorial-like introduction to this digital tool in order to familiarize the reader with it and thus, facilitate the understanding of models and analysis presented in this chapter.

8.3 Electromagnetic transient simulator PSCAD/EMTDC

PSCAD/EMTDC is a general-purpose time domain simulation tool for examining the transient behaviour of electrical networks. Since it was first developed in 1976, the EMTDC simulation program has constantly been evolving in its scope and capabilities. PSCAD provides a flexible user interface to make use of EMTDC, enabling an integrated visual environment that supports all aspects associated with the simulation, including circuit assembly, run-time control, analysis and reporting (Gole, Nayak et al., 1996; Manitoba, 1994).

The following list summarizes the main studies that can be conducted with EMTDC:

- contingency studies of AC networks containing rotating machines, exciters, governors, turbines, transformers, transmission lines and cables
- sub-synchronous resonance studies of networks with rotating machines, controls, transmission lines and HVDC systems
- design and evaluation of filter performance and harmonic analysis
- control system design and co-ordination of HVDC, FACTS and CP controllers
- optimal design of controller parameters
- investigation of new circuits and control concepts.

PSCAD/EMTDC has a comprehensive palette of components. Circuits are built by dragging and dropping the appropriate model block onto the drawing canvas, and using drag and stretch wires to connect it to the circuit under construction. The process of circuit construction is thus similar to that of drawing a schematic diagram of the power circuit under study. The main components available in PSCAD/EMTDC are as follows:

- resistors (R), inductors (L), capacitors (C)
- single-phase transformers, i.e. mutually coupled windings
- transmission lines and cables
- current and voltage sources
- switches and circuit breakers
- diodes, thyristors and GTOs

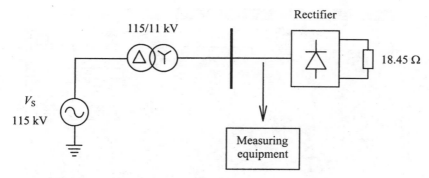

Fig. 8.1 Test circuit to be built in PSCAD.

- analogue and digital control functions
- AC machines, exciters, governors, stabilizers and inertial models
- meters and measuring functions
- generic DC and AC controls
- HVDC, SVC and other FACTS and CP controllers.

Once the construction of the circuit schematic diagram has been completed, it is run using the module RunTime Executive. The simulation results to be captured are selected using the RunTime Executive module. It is possible to observe these results as the simulation progresses. This module allows for the use of sliders, push buttons, dials and meters that permit the user to control the program in an interactive manner. The process required for graphically building a circuit and simulating its transient response in PSCAD/EMTDC is explained next in a very illustrative and comprehensive fashion.

Figure 8.1 shows the one-line diagram of the electrical circuit used in this tutorial. It comprises of a three-phase AC voltage source feeding into a six-pulse diode rectifier, via a delta–star connected transformer.

The process may be divided into four major steps:

1. creation of a new project and data entry
2. generation of the circuit schematic diagram using Draft
3. transient simulation using RunTime Executive
4. plotting and analysis of results using MultiPlot.

8.3.1   Creation of a new project and data entry

1. Start the PSCAD graphical user interface by typing PSCAD in the shell command. A window like the one shown in Figure 8.2 appears. At this point a new project is created using the CREATE PROJECT option under the File Manager. Figure 8.2 already shows this project which in this exercise is called 'ACSYSTEM'.
2. The next step is to create a study case that will contain all the files relating to the circuit. Open the project 'ACSYSTEM' by choosing the OPEN option under the pull down menu in the 'ACSYSTEM' icon. Using the CREATE CASE option under

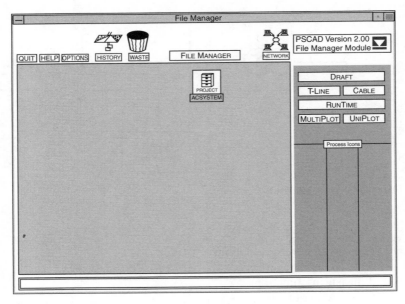

Fig. 8.2 PSCAD window appearing once the project 'ACSYSTEM' has been created.

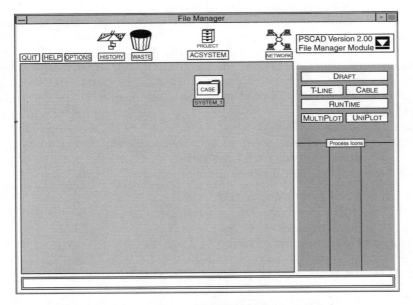

Fig. 8.3 PSCAD window appearing once the case 'SYSTEM_1' has been created.

the pull down menu in the project icon create a case called 'SYSTEM_1'. The window looks like the one shown in Figure 8.3.

3. The Draft tool is used to create the circuit file. The 'SYSTEM_1' case is opened using the OPEN option from the pull down menu of the project icon. The procedure is

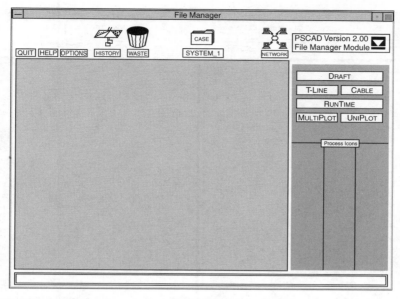

Fig. 8.4 PSCAD window appearing once the case 'SYSTEM_1' has been opened.

the same as in step 2. Once the case is opened, the window looks like the one shown in Figure 8.4. Now we proceed to draw the schematic diagram of the model circuit.

8.3.2 Generation of the circuit schematic diagram using Draft

The process required for drawing the circuit schematic diagram is as follows:

1. Select the action box labelled Draft to start the module. A window similar to the one shown in Figure 8.5 appears. This window shows the Draft module bar of menus, part of the drawing canvas and the library of components.
2. There is a pull down menu for each component in the library located at the right-hand side of the screen. Select the COPY option under the pull down menu of the required library component and drag it on to the work sheet. For this example, it is necessary to copy the components shown in Figure 8.6 to the drawing canvas. These include:
   - *Three-phase source* model with built-in controls for adjusting the magnitude and/or phase of the source.
   - *Three-phase, two-winding transformer model* with built-in controls to define transformer parameters such as capacity, operating frequency, winding data, and saturation among others.
   - *Real/Reactive power meter* that measures the three-phase real and/or reactive power flow into three nodes from three network branches. The instantaneous power signals are smoothed through a first order lag to simulate transducer delays.
   - *Signal plotting block* that causes Draft to add code to the EMTDC program which will record the signal flowing into the component.
   - *Wire connectors* and *label,* a *diode and a resistor.*

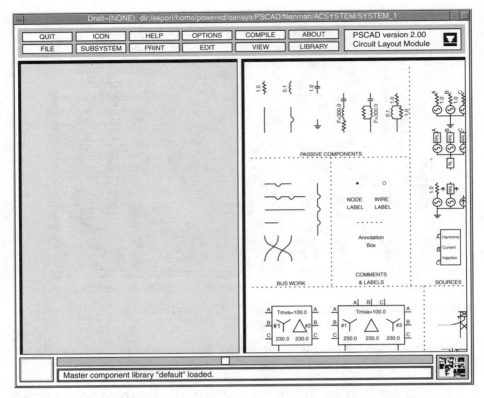

Fig. 8.5 Draft tool window.

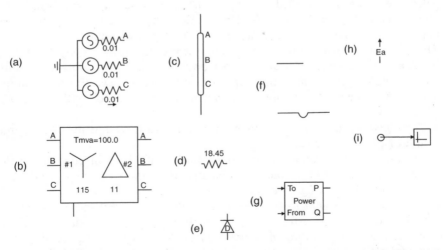

Fig. 8.6 Set of components required for the circuit of the example: (a) three-phase voltage source; (b) three-phase wye–delta transformer; (c) three-phase voltage signal sensor; (d) resistor; (e) diode; (f) wires; (g) active and reactive power meter; (h) voltage signal meter; and (i) signal plotting block.

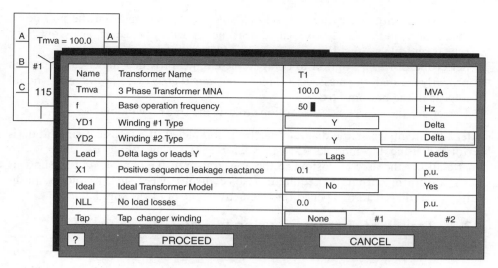

Name	Transformer Name	T1		
Tmva	3 Phase Transformer MNA	100.0		MVA
f	Base operation frequency	50 ▊		Hz
YD1	Winding #1 Type	Y		Delta
YD2	Winding #2 Type	Y		Delta
Lead	Delta lags or leads Y	Lags		Leads
X1	Positive sequence leakage reactance	0.1		p.u.
Ideal	Ideal Transformer Model	No		Yes
NLL	No load losses	0.0		p.u.
Tap	Tap changer winding	None	#1	#2

?		PROCEED		CANCEL

Fig. 8.7 Window to enter the parameters of the two-winding transformer model.

3. Select suitable parameters for each component. Choose the EDIT option in the pull down menu of each selected component and set the appropriate parameters. Figure 8.7 shows the window menu for the two-winding transformer.
4. Connect the components using the stretching wires. After completing the schematic drawing, the circuit must look like the one shown in Figure 8.8.

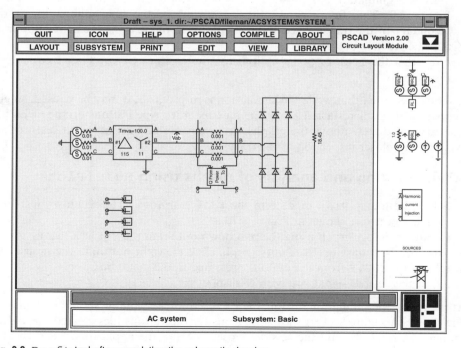

Fig. 8.8 Draft tool after completing the schematic drawing.

5. To save the circuit just created, select the SAVE AS option from the pull down menu found in the FILE box located near the top left of the Draft window. Save the current file as 'sys_1'.
6. Select the COMPILE option to compile the circuit. Provided the circuit has been properly created, the message: *Compile complete 0 error(s), 0 warning(s)* should appear in the bottom box.
7. Use either the QUIT or ICON options to exit the Draft window.

After the circuit schematic diagram has been completed, the transient simulation is performed using the module RunTime Executive. The RunTime Executive palette allows the user to customize the appearance of the console and to show as many waveform outputs as required. Also, control devices such as sliders, push-buttons and dials, can be opened for interactive control of the simulation.

8.3.3 Transient simulation using RunTime Executive

1. Start the RunTime Executive by selecting it from the corresponding box in the File Manager.
2. Use the LOAD option in the BATCH pull down menu to load the file 'sys_1'.
3. Select the PLOT option in the CREATE pull down menu to create the plots. Use graph 1 to display the line voltage, graph 2 to display the load current and graphs 3 and 4 to display the active and reactive power respectively.
4. Push the PLAY button to start the simulation. While the simulation is running, it is possible to click the [A/S] icon at the right-hand side of the plot to auto scale the graph.
5. Once the simulation has finished the window looks similar to the one shown in Figure 8.9. This figure shows the waveforms of the line voltage V_{ab} at the secondary of the transformer, the line current in phase a, I_a, the active power P, and the reactive power Q.
6. Use either the ICON or QUIT options to minimize or exit RunTime Executive respectively.

It should be noted that while the simulation is in progress, it may be paused, single-stepped through or restarted, using the tape recorder type buttons on the menu bar located immediately above the graphs. Also, cursors and zoom in-out features are available for closer inspection of the traces.

8.3.4 Plotting and analysis of results using MultiPlot

1. Select the MultiPlot module in the File Manager. The window must look similar to the one shown in Figure 8.10.
2. Create an empty graph using the pull down option in the CREATE menu.
3. Position the mouse on the empty graph, click the right button in the mouse and select ADD CURVE from the options presented in the menu box.
4. Select the desired signal you wish to display.

At the end of the simulation session, the File Manager window should look like the one shown in Figure 8.11. It shows the icons for the various files created for a given simulated circuit. To end the session, close down all the applications, e.g. Draft, RunTime Executive and MultiPlot, and then press the QUIT button.

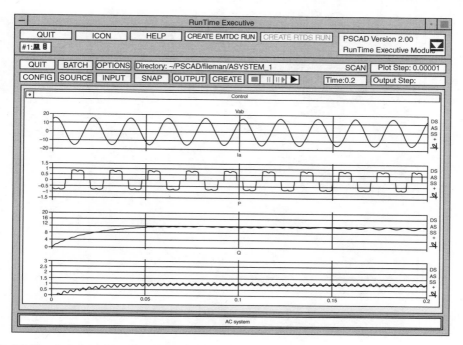

Fig. 8.9 Transient simulation using `RunTime Executive`.

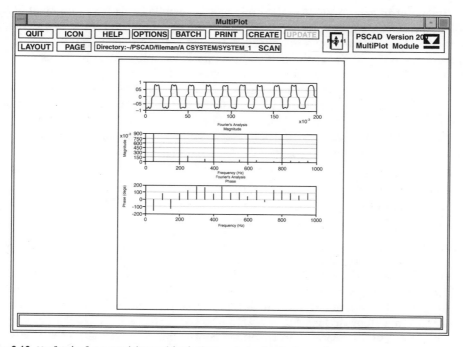

Fig. 8.10 `Multiplot` module used for further analysis of output waveforms.

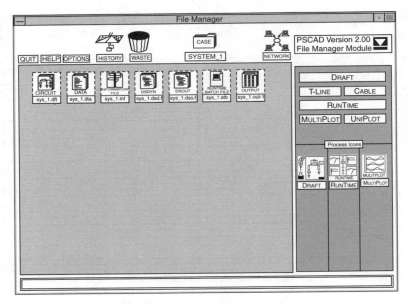

Fig. 8.11 File Manager window and files created for a given simulated circuit.

8.4   Static Var Compensator (SVC)

At this point in time, SVCs are the most widely installed FACTS equipment. They mimic the working principles of a variable shunt susceptance and use fast thyristor controllers with settling times of only a few fundamental frequency periods. From the operational point of view, the SVC adjusts its value automatically in response to changes in the operating conditions of the network. The SVC has the ability to either draw capacitive or inductive current from the network. By suitable control of this equivalent reactance, it is possible to regulate the voltage magnitude at the SVC point of connection, thus enhancing significantly the power system's performance.

More specifically, as discussed in Chapter 3, voltage regulation at a key location of the transmission system should provide the following benefits:

- prevention of large voltage variations
- prevention of voltage instability (voltage collapse)
- enlargement of transient (first swing) stability limits
- provision of power oscillations damping.

The SVC may be designed in many different ways. Figure 8.12 shows the schematic diagrams of the most typical arrangements for continuously controlled SVCs i.e. fixed capacitors (FC) with TCR and TSC with TCR. The thyristors are the controllable elements enabling smooth control of the TCR when operated in the range of 90–180°. On the other hand, the TSC is a fast-switched element that achieves voltage regulation in a stepwise fashion.

When the SVC is operated in a voltage control mode, it is the fastest thyristor-controlled FACTS controller, with settling times of almost one period in the case of

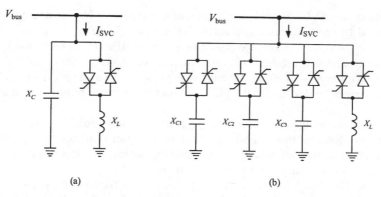

Fig. 8.12 Typical SVC's structures: (a) a TCR with a fixed capacitor; and (b) a TCR with a TSC.

the FC/TCR arrangement. In the case of switched elements (TSC/TCR), the response time is usually 30–60 μs depending upon the SVC configuration and system strength. In order to achieve such a high-speed response, it is necessary to properly assess the type and size of the power components as well as the control scheme according to the specific network configuration and operation requirements.

Figure 8.13 shows a simplified block diagram of a voltage control scheme for a typical SVC application (Tyll, 1992; Shen, 1998). Essential elements in this control scheme are: the measuring circuits, the voltage regulator, the allocator, the linearizer, and the TCR and TSC firing circuits.

Measuring circuits. The main function of these circuits is to measure the voltages and currents at different points of the power network, which provide relevant

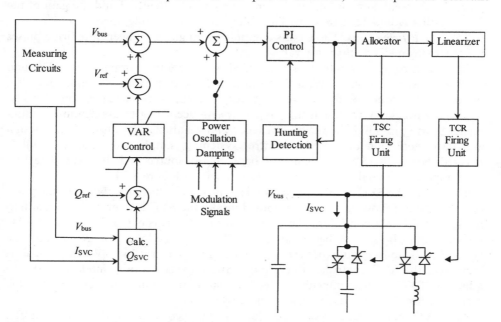

Fig. 8.13 Simplified voltage control block diagram of a typical SVC application.

information for SVC control and protection purposes. The measured signals are conditioned to provide suitable control to the other blocks of the control system.

Voltage regulator. The voltage regulator performs the closed loop voltage control. The difference between the voltage reference and the voltage measured at the point of connection of the SVC is fed as the control error signal to a PI (proportional-integral) regulator that provides the total SVC susceptance reference required to minimize the error.

Power oscillation damping. When a power modulation control circuit is included in the SVC controller, this high-level control function utilizes the power system response as the input and acts on the voltage regulation to provide damping for slow electro-mechanical swings in the power system.

Allocator. This block has the function of converting the susceptance reference from the voltage regulator into specific information which is then processed in order to determine the number of reactive banks that must be switched on and the required firing angle.

Linearizer. The linearizer converts the susceptance from the allocator to a firing angle α. To maintain the same control response over the entire SVC operating range, the angle α is determined as a non-linear function of the susceptance reference order. This function is normally given as a table that is derived from the following formula

$$1 - X_L B(\alpha) = \alpha + \frac{\sin(\pi\alpha)}{\pi} \tag{8.1}$$

where $B(\alpha)$ is the susceptance of the TCR fired at the angle α.

Hunting detection and gain adjustment. The stability controller supervises the operation of the voltage controller. Unstable operation (hunting), which may take place during weak system operating conditions, will be detected and the gain of the PI controller would be reduced by half to try to achieve stable operation.

TSC–TCR firing units. These units compute the angles α and generate firing pulses for the TSC and TCR thyristor valves.

Other control elements that can be added to the control circuit are the DC and reactive power controllers. With the addition of these elements the control system becomes more robust and efficient; however, its complexity increases considerably. Then, it is necessary to design the control system according to application requirements bearing in mind simplicity, efficiency and reliability. To illustrate the design and implementation of the SVC control system, a simple single-phase circuit is selected, where the SVC is connected between the source and the load. The FC/TCR topology is used as shown in the test system in Figure 8.14.

The aim of the SVC in this application is to provide voltage regulation at the point of connection, following load variations. Initially the SVC is operated in open-loop mode and for this condition, the power exchange between the SVC and the AC system should be zero. When breaker *Brk* is closed, the load is increased and the voltage at the load point experiences a voltage sag of nearly 16%. When the load is increased, the SVC controller operation changes to closed-loop mode in order to adjust the SVC effective impedance X_{SVC} so that it injects capacitive current into the system to restore the voltage back to the target value.

The SVC parameters have been determined according to the compensation requirements for the case when the second load is connected. Based on the reactive

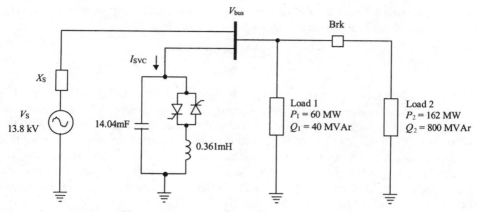

Fig. 8.14 Test system implemented to carry out time domain analysis of the SVC.

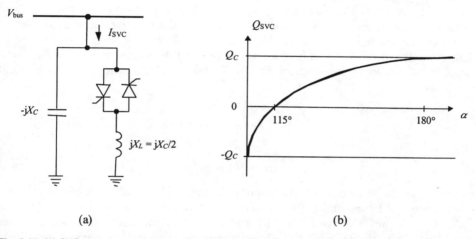

(a)   (b)

Fig. 8.15 (a) SVC capacitance and inductances values; and (b) characteristic plot $Q_{SVC}(\alpha)$.

power required by *Load* 2, the SVC is sized with enough capacity to supply at least this reactive power in order to drive the voltage V_{bus} back to the reference, that is

$$Q_{SVC} > 800 \, \text{MVAr} \tag{8.2}$$

In this example, the maximum reactive capacity of the SVC is set at $Q_{SVC} = 840 \, \text{MVAr}$. The values for the capacitance and the TCR inductance are then calculated based on this setting.

With reference to Figure 8.15(a)

$$X_C = \frac{(V_{bus})^2}{Q_{SVC}} = \frac{(13.8 \, \text{kV})^2}{840 \, \text{MVAr}} = 0.226714 \, \Omega \tag{8.3}$$

and

$$X_L = \frac{X_C}{2} \tag{8.4}$$

From Equations 8.3 and 8.4 and considering a fundamental frequency of $f = 50$ Hz, the capacitance and inductance values are

$$C = 14.04 \, \text{mF}$$

$$L = 0.361 \, \text{mH}$$

Once the capacitance and inductance have been sized, it is necessary to determine the initial operating condition of the SVC. Initially, *Brk* is open and there is no need for the SVC to be in operation. However, it is already connected and interacting with the AC system. Then the selection of the initial firing angle α must be such that under this operating condition the SVC does not exchange any power with the AC system.

This firing angle corresponds to the case when the effective reactances X_C and X_L cancel each other out. In this case, the SVC effective reactance X_{SVC} is infinite and there is no current leaving or entering the SVC, i.e. the power exchange between the SVC and the AC system is zero.

According to the inductive and capacitive reactances, each SVC has its own firing angle-reactive power characteristic, $Q_{SVC}(\alpha)$ which is a function of the inductive and capacitive reactances. The firing angle initial condition may be determined using a graph similar to that shown in Figure 8.15(b). The following steps may be used to determine this plot. Firstly, it is necessary to obtain the effective reactance X_{SVC} as a function of the firing angle α, using the fundamental frequency TCR equivalent reactance X_{TCR}

$$X_{TCR} = \frac{\pi X_L}{\sigma - \sin \sigma} \tag{8.5}$$

and

$$\sigma = 2(\pi - \alpha) \tag{8.6}$$

where X_L is the reactance of the linear inductor, and σ and α are the thyristors' conduction and firing angles, respectively.

At $\alpha = 90°$ the TCR conducts fully and the equivalent reactance X_{TCR} becomes X_L. At $\alpha = 180°$, the TCR is blocked and its equivalent reactance becomes extremely large, i.e. infinite.

The total effective reactance of the SVC, including the TCR and capacitive reactances, is determined by the parallel combination of both components

$$X_{SVC} = \frac{X_C X_{TCR}}{X_C + X_{TCR}} \tag{8.7}$$

which as a function of the conduction angle σ becomes

$$X_{SVC} = \frac{\pi X_C X_L}{X_C(\sigma - \sin \sigma) - \pi X_L} \tag{8.8}$$

And finally as a function of the firing angle α becomes

$$X_{SVC} = \frac{\pi X_C X_L}{X_C[2(\pi - \alpha) + \sin 2\alpha] - \pi X_L} \tag{8.9}$$

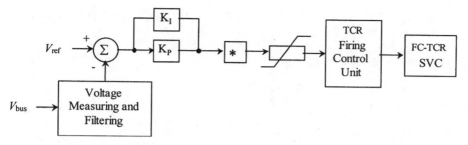

Fig. 8.16 Basic control scheme designed for the FC/TCR topology of the example.

As expected, the effective reactance of the SVC is a function of the firing angle α. Equation 8.9 may be used to plot $Q_{SVC}(\alpha)$ and to determine the angle α for which $Q_{SVC}(\alpha) \approx 0$, using the following fundamental relationship

$$Q_{SVC} = V_{bus}^2 \cdot \frac{X_C[2\pi - \alpha + \sin 2\alpha] - \pi X_L}{\pi X_C X_L} \tag{8.10}$$

As indicated by Equation 8.10, Q_{SVC} takes a value of zero when the effective reactance X_{SVC} is extremely large, i.e. infinite. This condition is satisfied when the following relationship approaches zero

$$X_C[2(\pi - \alpha) + \sin 2\alpha] - \pi X_L \to 0 \tag{8.11}$$

With the SVC parameters used in this example, the value of the firing angle α that satisfies Equation 8.11 is found to be $\alpha \approx 115°$. This angle is used as the initial condition for α in the open-loop control of the SVC.·

To illustrate the SVC's ability to provide voltage regulation at the point of connection, a simplified control scheme has been implemented for the single-phase SVC circuit shown in Figure 8.14. The block diagram is shown in Figure 8.16. This control scheme works as follows: The amplitude of the bus voltage V_{bus} is measured and filtered. Then it is compared against the voltage reference V_{ref}. The voltage difference (error) between the two signals is processed by a PI controller which causes a corresponding change in the firing angle α. The value provided by the PI controller is used as the input to the TCR firing angle control unit where the firing pulse is calculated. The zero-crossing of the V_{bus} voltage signal is taken as the reference for the firing angle. Figures 8.17 and 8.18 show the digital implementation of the power circuit and control scheme respectively. Both diagrams were developed using PSCAD/EMTDC v3.04 for PCs.

Two experiments are carried out as follows:
In experiment 1 the constant AC voltage source V_S feeds *Load 1* only. The SVC is connected in parallel with the load and it is controlled in open-loop mode. The firing angle α for the thyristors is set at $115°$. As mentioned above, with $\alpha = 115°$ the power exchange between the SVC and the AC system is close to zero for the SVC parameters and load conditions shown in Figure 8.17. The voltage V_{rms} at the load point is close to 0.96 p.u. At a time $t = 0.6$ s, *Load 2* is switched on by closing *Brk*, with the load overall increasing. Under the new load conditions the voltage at the load point drops by as much as 16%, giving a V_{rms} value equal to 0.8 p.u., as shown in Figure 8.19(a).

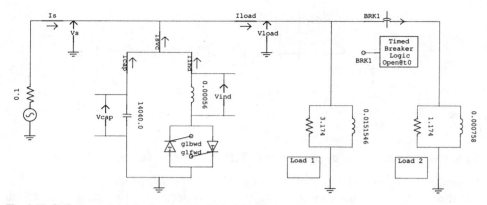

Fig. 8.17 SVC power circuit implemented in PSCAD/EMTDC.

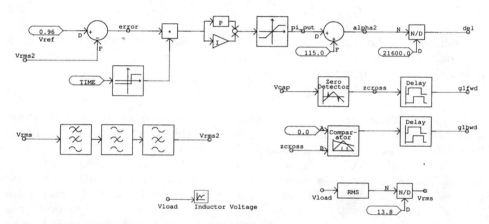

Fig. 8.18 SVC control scheme implemented in PSCAD/EMTDC.

In experiment 2, the SVC is controlled in closed-loop mode, in order to restore the voltage back to the original value of 0.96 p.u. At $t = 0.6$ s, the SVC begins to control the firing angle α of the back-to-back thyristors, changing the effective reactance X_{SVC} in such a way that the SVC injects capacitive current into the AC system. By using this reactive compensation control scheme the voltage is regulated and driven back to the original value as shown in Figure 8.19(b).

Figure 8.20 shows the voltage V_{load} waveform at the load point for both operating conditions, with no reactive compensation (Figure 8.20(a)) and with the SVC injecting capacitive current (Figure 8.20(b)). It can be observed that when the SVC is operating in closed-loop mode the voltage is kept constant, at the reference value, even when the load has increased. A delay of almost two cycles due to the parameters selected for the controller can be seen in the response.

The waveform of the SVC current I_{SVC} is shown in Figure 8.21. It should be noted that the current I_{SVC} increases considerably when the SVC starts voltage regulation. Due to variations in the firing angle α, the effective impedance X_{SVC} changes and

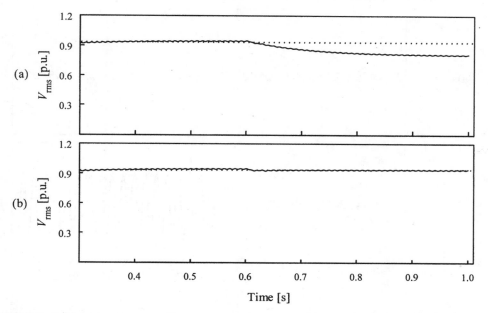

Fig. 8.19 Voltage V_{rms} at the load point: (a) with SVC operating in open-loop mode; and (b) with SVC operating in closed-loop mode.

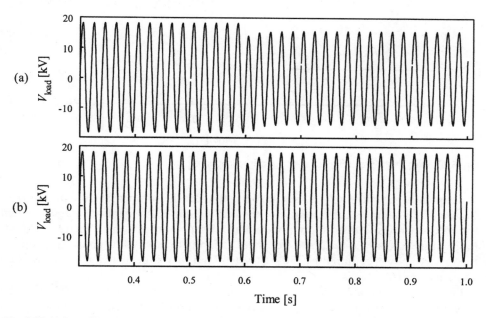

Fig. 8.20 Voltage V_{load} at the load point: (a) with SVC operating in open-loop mode; and (b) with SVC operating in closed-loop mode.

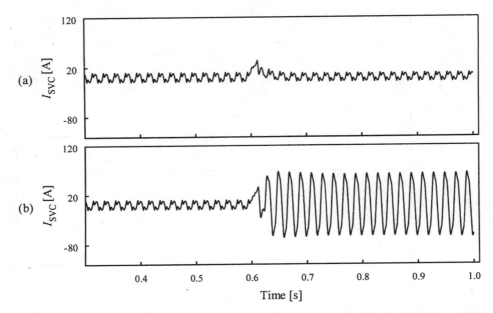

Fig. 8.21 SVC current I_{SVC}: (a) with the SVC operating in open-loop mode; and (b) with the SVC operating in closed-loop mode.

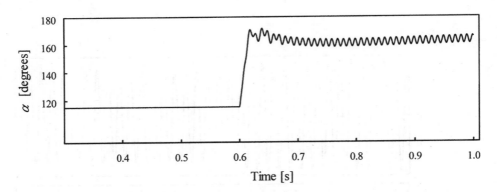

Fig. 8.22 Firing angle α with SVC operating in closed-loop mode.

consequently the current I_{SVC} rises abruptly to meet the compensation requirements. Figure 8.22 illustrates the response of the firing angle α. As mentioned above, when the SVC operates in open-loop mode α has a fixed value of 115°. When the closed-loop control is enabled the angle α changes abruptly to nearly 170° in order to supply the reactive power required by the AC system and then it decreases to a steady state value of $\alpha \approx 162°$.

Figures 8.23 and 8.24 show the waveforms in each element of the SVC, with the SVC controller in open-loop and in closed-loop modes, respectively. These figures show the behaviour of the currents and voltages in both the TCR and in the capacitor for the two different operating conditions. Specifically, in Figure 8.23, when the SVC

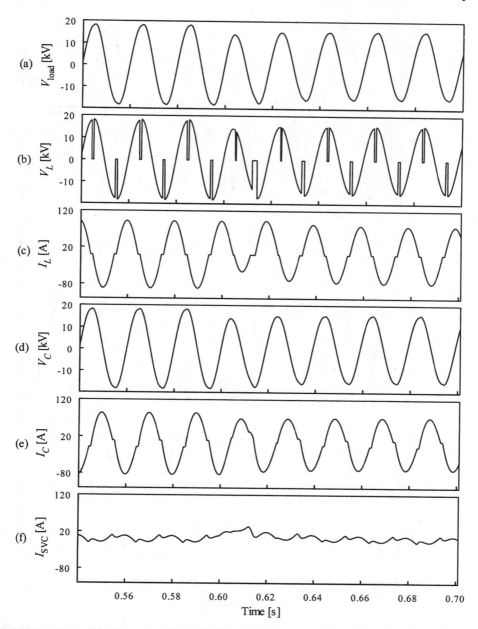

Fig. 8.23 SVC characteristic waveforms in open-loop mode: (a) voltage V_{load} at the load point; (b) voltage V_L at the SVC inductor; (c) current I_L through the SVC inductor; (d) voltage V_C through the SVC capacitor; (e) current I_C through the SVC capacitor; and (f) total current I_{SVC} through the SVC.

is in open-loop mode, the currents and voltages in the SVC decrease in response to an increase in load. However, after a small transient period, the current I_{SVC} recovers to the same wave shape that it had before the load change at $t = 0.6\,\text{s}$. On the other

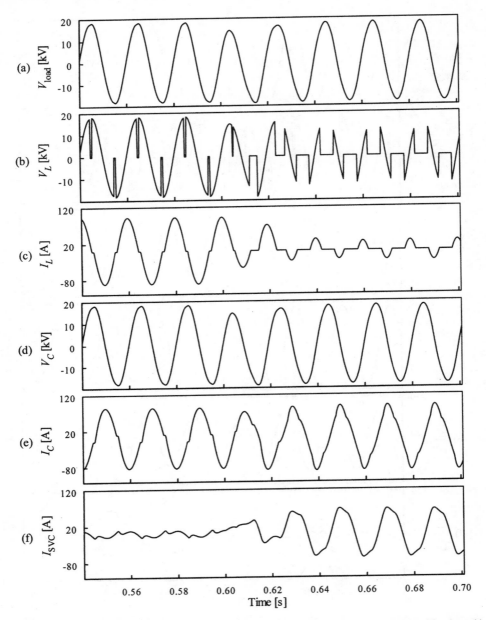

Fig. 8.24 SVC characteristic waveforms in closed-loop mode: (a) voltage V_{load} at the load point; (b) voltage V_L at the SVC inductor; (c) current I_L through the SVC inductor; (d) voltage V_C at the SVC capacitor; (e) current I_C through the SVC capacitor; and (f) total current I_{SVC} through the SVC.

hand, when the SVC is in closed-loop mode, the current through the reactor decreases considerably to the point that most of the SVC current flows through the capacitive element, as shown in Figure 8.24.

It is clear from these results that the SVC is an effective system controller which may be used to provide voltage regulation at the point of connection and to improve substantially the voltage quality in power systems. In most three-phase applications the SVC uses symmetrical voltage control (average value of 3 phases). However, the SVC can also be used to provide compensation to unbalanced three-phase loads and, at the same time, to restore voltage balance. This is achieved with a more sophisticated SVC control module.

8.5 Thyristor-Controlled Series Compensator (TCSC)

This section presents time domain simulations of the TCSC circuit and its implementation in PSCAD/EMTDC v3.04 for PCs. Two examples are presented:

1. Firstly, the basic model of the TCSC is implemented in PSCAD/EMTDC in order to identify its main characteristics.
2. Secondly, a test system representing a transmission network with an embedded TCSC system is implemented to show the effectiveness of the TCSC to provide line impedance compensation.

The TCSC is a key member of the FACTS family of power electronic controllers that provides smooth, rapid and continuous adjustment of the transmission line impedance. Figure 8.25 shows the equivalent circuit representation of the basic TCSC scheme, where a TCR is placed in parallel with a fixed capacitor. The controlling elements are the two back-to-back thyristors, connected in series with the linear reactor.

The TCSC has three fundamental modes of operation as follows:

1. thyristor-blocked mode
2. thyristor-bypassed mode
3. thyristor operating in phase-controlled mode.

In thyristor-blocked mode, the current through the TCR is zero and the TCSC functions as a capacitive reactance X_C. In thyristor-bypassed mode, the thyristor valves are fired with no delay and the TCSC has small inductive impedance. When the thyristor operates in phase-controlled mode, the value of the firing angle

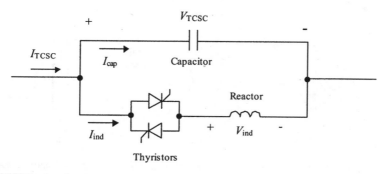

Fig. 8.25 TCSC basic scheme.

determines the direction of the current through the TCR and the capacitor, enabling the TCSC to work as either a capacitive or an inductive reactance. In this mode, the thyristor firing mechanism is controlled to vary the amount of effective reactance connected to the system (Jalali et al., 1994; Helbing and Karaday, 1994; Zhou, Liang, 1999).

The series capacitive compensation is bypassed during minimum loading in order to avoid transmission line overvoltages resulting from excessive capacitive effects in the system. Conversely, series capacitive compensation is fully utilized during maximum loading. The purpose of this operating strategy is to increase the transfer of power from generating sites to load centres, without overloading transmission lines.

8.5.1 Example 1

From the operational point of view, the TCSC shown in Figure 8.25 may be interpreted as a variable impedance which is a function of the thyristor firing angle α. In most applications, the voltage across the capacitor V_{TCSC} is taken as the reference voltage for the purpose of determining the thyristor firing angle α. The thyristors are fired when the capacitor voltage and current are opposite in polarity. This gives a range of 90–180° for the firing angle of the forward-connected thyristor. Firing the thyristors in this range results in a current flow through the inductor that opposes that in the capacitor, creating a loop flow. This loop current increases the voltage across the capacitor and the overall series compensation. This loop current increases as α decreases from 180 to 90°.

The main characteristics and waveforms of each element of the TCSC are obtained for the circuit shown in Figure 8.26. For the purpose of the simulation, a constant AC voltage source $V_S = 1\,kV$ is used to supply a series R–L load.

In order to perform the time domain analysis the circuit shown in Figure 8.26 is implemented in PSCAD/EMTDC, as shown in Figure 8.27. This figure shows both the power circuit and the open-loop control of the TCSC. The controller generates the firing signals for the thyristors based on a zero-crossing detector and a delay function block. In this case the TCSC is only connected between the constant AC voltage source and the linear series R–L load. The source voltage signal V_S provides a

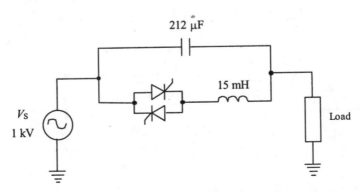

Fig. 8.26 Single-phase diagram used to simulate the operation of the TCSC and identify its main characteristics.

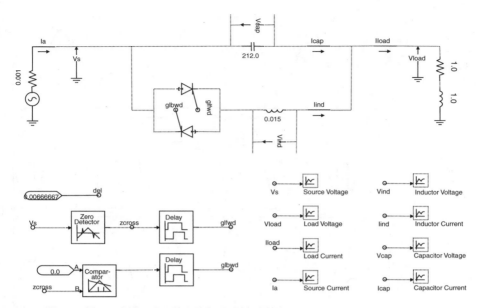

Fig. 8.27 TCSC basic circuit implemented in PSCAD/EMTDC.

constant and stable reference and it is taken as the input signal to the zero-crossing detector. Taking a fundamental frequency of $f = 50$ Hz, the delay function in the controller is adjusted in order to obtain a firing angle of $\alpha = 130°$.

The waveforms of the simulated TCSC model are shown in Figure 8.28 for a firing angle of $\alpha = 130°$ and a fundamental frequency of $f = 50$ Hz. Specifically, Figure 8.28(a) shows the source voltage and Figures 8.28(b) and 8.28(c) show the inductor voltage and current, respectively. Figures 8.28(d) and 8.28(e) show the voltage and current of the capacitor respectively. Note that the voltages V_S, V_L and V_C are in phase. It should also be noted that the zero-crossing of the source voltage V_S coincides with the negative peak of the inductor current I_L and with the positive peak of the capacitor current I_C.

The characteristic waveforms shown in Figure 8.28 can be obtained for any firing angle α in the range $90° < \alpha < 180°$. It is important to mention that in general the TCSC performance in the inductive region is not as smooth as in the capacitive region. In inductive operation conduction, the inductive current and the active losses are greater than in the capacitive region. Also, the capacitor current and voltage waveforms present higher harmonic distortion.

8.5.2 Example 2

The test system used in the example 2 is shown in Figure 8.29. Only one phase of the test system is used. It comprises of a constant AC voltage source feeding a linear series R–L load through three parallel branch transmission circuits. The equivalent impedance of each transmission path is adjusted to be equal, with one of them including a TCSC. As shown in Figure 8.29, the top branch contains a breaker, *Brk*, which is used to simulate the opening of this branch at a given point in time of

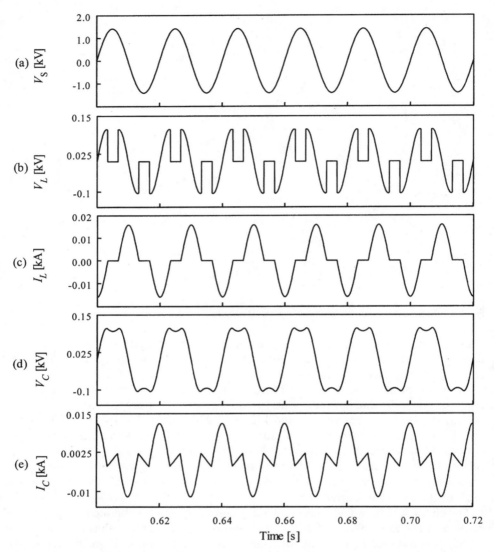

Fig. 8.28 TCSC characteristic waveforms for the model circuit with $\alpha = 130°$. (a) voltage V_S of the source; (b) voltage V_L at the TCSC inductor; (c) current I_L through the TCSC inductor; (d) voltage V_C at the TCSC capacitor; and (e) current I_C through the TCSC capacitor.

the transient simulation and to analyse the dynamic performance of the TCSC under the new operating condition. When *Brk* opens the equivalent impedance of the transmission system increases and consequently the current supplied to the load drops. Thus, the aim of the TCSC and its controller is to provide capacitive compensation to the remaining circuit consisting of two parallel inductive branches in such a way that the power flows and the current fed to the load remains at the same level as before.

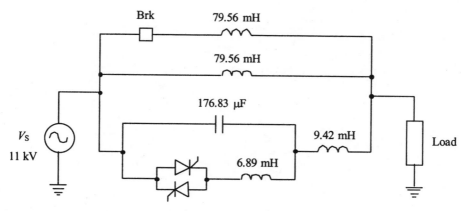

Fig. 8.29 Test system used to simulate the transient response of the TCSC in a medium-voltage transmission system.

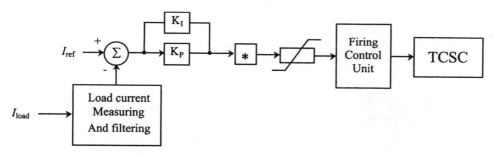

Fig. 8.30 A typical PI controller for a TCSC.

This application requires the TCSC to be controlled in a closed-loop fashion. For the purposes of this example the TCSC is operated by means of the control scheme shown in Figure 8.30. This particular scheme is based on measurements of the *rms* load current I_{load} which is compared against a reference value I_{ref} in order to obtain an error signal. Before the comparison is carried out, the *rms* current is filtered to eliminate any high-order harmonic which may exist in the signal and that may lead to the controller's spurious operation. The error signal is then processed by a PI controller that generates the appropriate thyristor's firing angle required to adjust the equivalent impedance of the TCSC and to drive the load current back to the reference or prefault value.

Before the firing signals are sent to the thyristors, the output of the PI controller is converted to angle units and properly conditioned to keep this angle within the limits. This is also required to avoid operation near resonant points. The firing control unit shown in Figure 8.30 includes the zero-crossing and delay functions. Also, the initial condition for the firing angle α may be set in this unit. In these simulations the thyristors are initially operated at a firing angle of $\alpha = 130°$, with no closed-loop control. Once the system reaches steady state, an electrical disturbance is created by opening *Brk*. Following this condition, the TCSC is operated with the closed-loop

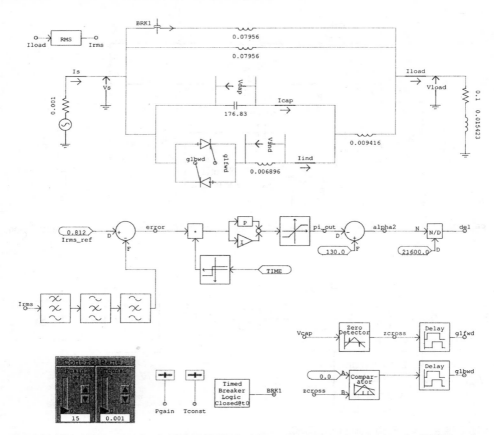

Fig. 8.31 Digital implementation in PSCAD/EMTDC of the test system used to simulate the TCSC in a line-impedance compensation application.

control mentioned above. PSCAD/EMTDC is used to implement the test system and the TCSC controller, resulting in the digital implementation shown in Figure 8.31.

The results of the simulation for this test system are presented in several figures as follows: Figure 8.32 shows the *rms* load current $I_{\text{load, rms}}$. Its steady-state value is approximately 0.8 p.u. Specifically, Figure 8.32(a) shows the *rms* load current $I_{\text{load, rms}}$ for the case when the TCSC is operated with open-loop control. Its new steady-state value drops to nearly 70% when *Brk* is opened at $t = 1.8$ s. Figure 8.32(b) shows once again the load current when the TCSC controller is in operation. It can be seen that the equivalent impedance of the transmission system is rapidly adjusted by the TCSC and that the load current is driven back to the reference value with almost no delay. The TCSC control scheme is shown to be effective for the requirements of this example. The waveforms of the load current and voltage at the load point are shown in Figures 8.33 and 8.34 for both operating conditions.

Figure 8.35 shows the characteristic of the firing angle α generated by the control scheme. It can be seen that before *Brk* opens the TCSC operates with a firing angle of $\alpha = 130°$ in open-loop fashion. At $t = 1.8$ s, when *Brk* opens and the TCSC

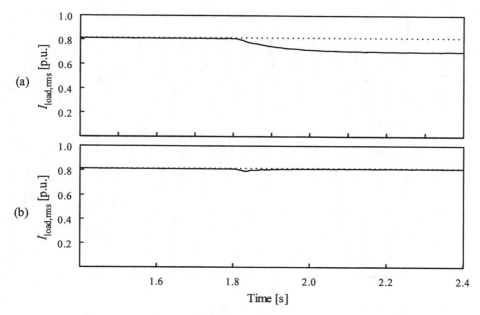

Fig. 8.32 Current $I_{load,\,rms}$ supplied to the load: (a) with TCSC in open-loop mode; and (b) with TCSC in closed-loop mode.

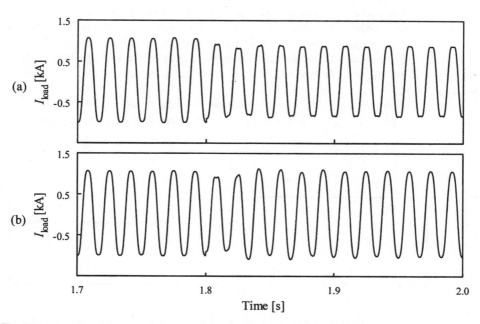

Fig. 8.33 Waveform of the current I_{load} supplied to the load: (a) with TCSC in open-loop mode; and (b) with TCSC in closed-loop mode.

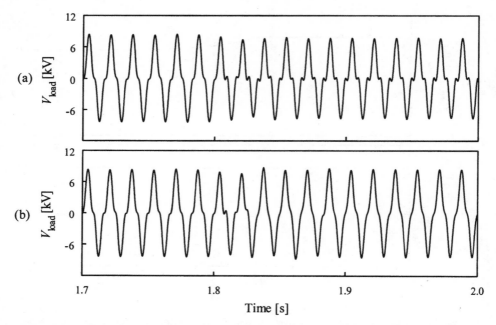

Fig. 8.34 Waveform of the voltage V_{load} at the load point: (a) with TCSC in open-loop mode; and (b) TCSC in closed-loop mode.

controller is set in operation, the angle α decreases from 130° to nearly 113° and it then settles down to a new steady-state value of approximately 117°.

By decreasing α the equivalent impedance of the TCSC becomes more capacitive thus reducing the inductive impedance of the overall transmission circuit.

Figure 8.36 shows the TCSC waveforms when it is operated in open-loop fashion. As a result of the rise in equivalent reactance both the capacitor and inductor voltages increase.

Figure 8.37 shows the TCSC waveforms operating in closed-loop mode. It can be seen in this figure that just after the disturbance has occurred, the capacitor and

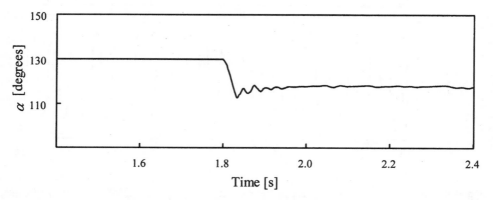

Fig. 8.35 Firing angle α processed by the TCSC closed-loop controller.

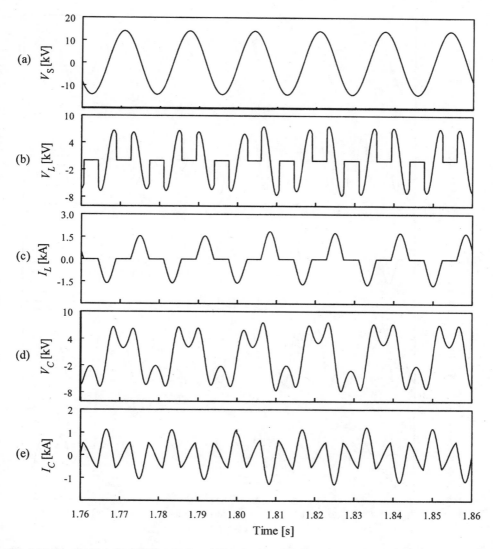

Fig. 8.36 Waveforms in the TCSC operating with open-loop control. Disturbance occurs at $t = 1.8$ s: (a) voltage V_S of the source; (b) voltage V_L at the TCSC inductor; (c) current I_L through the TCSC inductor; (d) voltage V_C at the TCSC capacitor: and (e) current I_C through the TCSC capacitor.

inductor voltages start to decrease and have no longer half- and quarter-wave symmetry. This is mainly due to the sudden change in firing angle value from 130° to 113°. Nevertheless, as the system reaches the new steady-state condition, these voltages waveforms recover their symmetry.

These time-domain results show the effectiveness of the TCSC circuit to improve the transmission branch performance by means of rapid and smooth adjustment of the effective transmission circuit impedance. The main factors that affect the TCSC

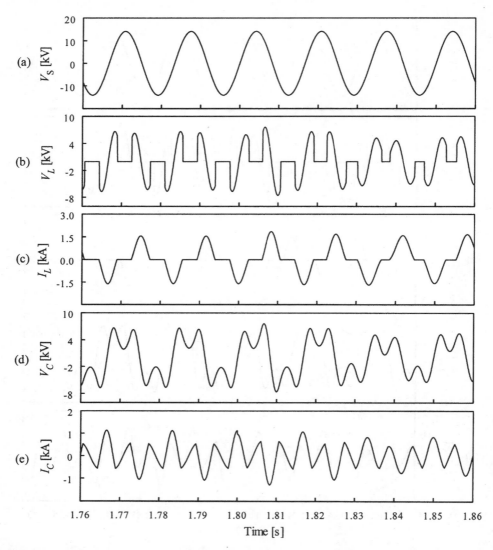

Fig. 8.37 Waveforms in the TCSC operating with closed-loop control. Disturbance occurs at $t = 1.8$ s: (a) voltage V_S of the source; (b) voltage V_L at the TCSC inductor; (c) current I_L through the TCSC inductor; (d) voltage V_C at the TCSC capacitor; and (e) current I_C through the TCSC capacitor.

response are the initial operating point for the firing angle α, the amount of change required, and the amount of net series compensation involved between operating points.

8.6   Static Compensator (STATCOM)

The STATCOM belongs to a family of power electronics controllers that base their operation on the VSC principle. These converter topologies have been presented in

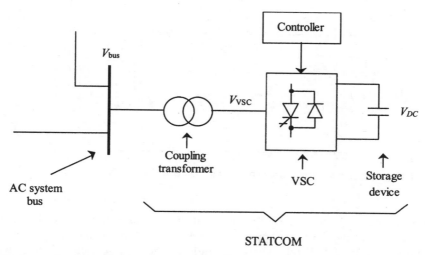

Fig. 8.38 Connection of the STATCOM with the AC system.

Chapter 6. Its performance is analogous to that of the rotating synchronous condenser. It may be used for the dynamic compensation of power transmission systems, providing voltage support and increased transient stability margins (Zhuang et al., 1996).

This section presents the modelling of the STATCOM used in both, transmission (FACTS) and distribution (CP) systems applications to provide reactive power compensation and voltage regulation at the point of connection. The principle of operation and main characteristics of the STATCOM are described followed by particular example cases of its use as a FACTS and CP controller.

The most basic configuration of the STATCOM consists of a two-level VSC with a DC energy storage device, a coupling transformer connected in shunt with the AC system, and the associated control circuits. Figure 8.38 depicts the schematic diagram of the STATCOM. The DC energy storage device may be a battery, whose output voltage remains constant, or it may be a capacitor, whose terminal voltage can be raised or lowered by inverter control, in such a way that its stored energy is either increased or decreased.

The VSC converts the DC voltage across the storage device into a set of three-phase AC output voltages that are in phase and coupled with the AC system through the reactance of the coupling transformer, discussed in detail in Chapter 6. A key characteristic of this controller is that the active and reactive powers exchanged between the converter and the AC system, can be controlled by changing the phase angle between the converter output voltage and the bus voltage at the point of common coupling (PCC) (Ma et al., 1997; Han et al., 1998).

The single-phase equivalent circuit of a power system with a STATCOM controller is shown in Figure 8.39. If the magnitude of V_{VSC} is greater than that of V_{bus} then the STATCOM supplies reactive power to the AC system, and it draws reactive power from the AC system if the magnitude of V_{bus} is greater than that of V_{VSC}. With suitable variation of the phase angle between the STATCOM output voltage and the AC system voltage, the STATCOM can exchange active power with the AC system.

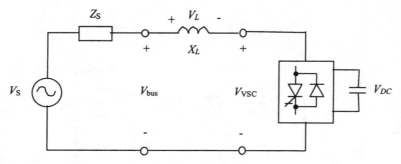

Fig. 8.39 Single-phase equivalent circuit of a power system with a STATCOM controller.

This exchange can be used to replenish the internal losses of the VSC and to keep the DC capacitor charged to the appropriate DC voltage, or to increase/decrease the capacitor voltage and thereby the magnitude of the output voltage of the STAT-COM.

Figure 8.40 shows the steady state vector representation at the fundamental frequency for capacitive and inductive modes, and for the transition states from capacitive to inductive and vice versa. The terminal voltage V_{bus} is equal to the sum of the inverter voltage V_{VSC} and the voltage across the coupling transformer reactance V_L in both capacitive and inductive modes. The transition from capacitive to

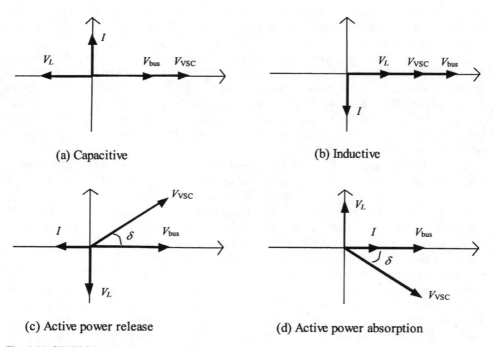

Fig. 8.40 STATCOM vector representation.

inductive mode occurs by changing the angle δ from zero to a positive value. The active power is transferred from the DC capacitor to the AC terminal and causes the DC link voltage to drop. The transition from inductive to capacitive mode occurs by changing the angle δ from zero to a negative value. The active power is transferred from the AC terminal to the DC capacitor and causes the DC link voltage to rise.

With reference to Figure 8.39 and Figure 8.40, the active and reactive power may be expressed by the following equations

$$P = \frac{V_{bus} V_{VSC}}{X_L} \sin \delta \tag{8.12}$$

$$Q = \frac{V_{bus}^2}{X_L} - \frac{V_{bus} V_{VSC}}{X_L} \cos \delta \tag{8.13}$$

In any practical STATCOM there are losses in the transformer windings and in the converter switches. These losses consume active power from the AC terminals. Accordingly, a small phase difference always exists between the VSC voltage and the AC system voltage. A summary of the power exchanges between the STATCOM and the AC system as a function of the STATCOM output voltage V_{VSC} and the AC system voltage V_{bus} is presented in Table 8.1.

From the analysis shown above it can be seen that the STATCOM can be controlled essentially by a single parameter: the phase angle between the VSC output voltage and the AC system voltage. Moreover, if the converter is restricted to reactive power exchange, then the AC output voltage is governed by only controlling the magnitude of the DC link voltage. This is possible due to the fact that the magnitude of the AC output voltage is directly proportional to the DC capacitor voltage.

The DC capacitor size may be selected by analytical methods (Moran et al., 1989) considering DC voltage ripple constraints and power rating. The use of analytical equations to determine the most appropriate DC capacitor size may be an involved task. Moreover, the DC capacitor size has a direct impact on the performance of the closed-loop controller and there will always exist a compromise between the VSC harmonic generation and the controller's speed of response (Xu et al., 2001). It is in this respect that electromagnetic transient simulators are very useful, providing an alternative way to select the size of the capacitor. This involves a straightforward trial and error process where the ripple constraint and the speed of response required in the controller are taken into account. The capacitor size is determined below using the transient simulator.

Table 8.1 Power exchange as a function of STATCOM voltage V_{VSC} and the AC system voltage V_{bus}

Voltage relation	Power exchange		
	STATCOM	⇔	AC system
$\|V_{VSC}\| > \|V_{bus}\|$	Q	⇒	
$\|V_{VSC}\| < \|V_{bus}\|$		⇐	Q
$\delta < 0$	P	⇒	
$\delta > 0$		⇐	P

The switching control of the VSC valves can be executed using two different techniques:

1. *Fundamental frequency switching (FFS)*, where the switching of each semiconductor device is limited to one turn-on and one turn-off per cycle. With this technique the conventional six-pulse VSC produces a quasi-square-wave output with the inherent high harmonic content, as previously discussed in Chapter 6. As will be described later, when FFS is chosen, several six-pulse units are combined to form a multi-pulse structure in order to achieve better waveform quality and higher power ratings.
2. *Pulse-width-modulation (PWM)*, where the semiconductor switches are turned on and off at a rate considerably higher than the power frequency. The output waveform is chopped and the width of the resulting pulses is modulated. This shifts the undesirable harmonics in the output to higher frequencies and filtering is possible with smaller components as was also illustrated in Chapter 6.

Both, the fundamental frequency and PWM switching approaches suffer from certain drawbacks for utility applications:

- The fundamental frequency switching approach requires complex transformer configurations to achieve low waveform distortion. In addition, the low switching frequency constrains the response rate and precludes incorporation of active harmonic filtering. Nevertheless, this is currently the preferred approach because of lower losses and higher semiconductor switch utilization. Present implementations of the STATCOM in high-voltage applications employ fundamental frequency switching.
- The PWM approach results in high switching losses and the fundamental frequency output obtainable is somewhat reduced. Consequently, at present PWM is less attractive for utility applications that require high efficiency and large power ratings. However, it has certain advantages such as faster response and capability for harmonic elimination, which could be exploited in the future with semiconductor switch improvements. However, PWM is preferred for CP low-voltage applications.

In low-to-medium voltage CP applications of VSC, PWM is widely used for suppression of harmonics and control of DC to AC voltage ratio. However, for FACTS applications, the high ratings of the converter will require valves of high power ratings, dictating slow switching speed and increased switching losses. With regards to the VSC electronic valves, VSCs using GTOs as the power devices are preferred for FACTS applications whereas VSCs using IGBTs are preferred for low-voltage CP applications (Zaho and Iravani, 1994; Edwards and Nannery, 1998; Raju et al., 1997).

8.6.1   STATCOM used as a FACTS controller

The output voltage waveform of the conventional six-pulse VSC contains harmonic components with frequencies of $[6k \pm 1]\,f$ (and its input current has related harmonic components with frequencies of $6kf$), where f is the fundamental output frequency and $k = 1, 2, 3, \ldots$ The high harmonic content of the output voltage makes this simple inverter impractical for high-power applications.

Using the principle of *harmonic reduction*, the input and output of *n* basic six-pulse inverters (which are operated with appropriate relative phase-displacements) can be combined so as to obtain an overall $P = 6n$ multipulse structure. The frequencies of the harmonics present in the output voltage and input current of this *P-pulse* inverter are $[Pk \pm 1]f$ and Pkf, respectively. As can be seen, the harmonic spectrum improves rapidly with increasing pulse number. In addition, the amplitude of these harmonics is inversely related to the pulse number; that is, the amplitude of the *k-th* harmonic of the output voltage waveform is proportional to $1/[Pk \pm 1]$ and that of the DC supply current to $1/Pk$ (Gyugyi, 1994).

Consequently, the FACTS STATCOM uses many six-pulse VSCs, appropriately phase shifted, with their output combined electromagnetically to produce a nearly sinusoidal resultant waveform. The pulse number of such an arrangement is generally quoted as six times the number of basic inverters used, and provides an indication of the level of harmonic reduction achieved. For transmission line applications, a pulse number of 24 or higher is required to achieve adequate waveform quality without large passive filters. A single line diagram of a STATCOM system is shown in Figure 8.41. The VSC combines eight three-phase inverters into a 48-pulse

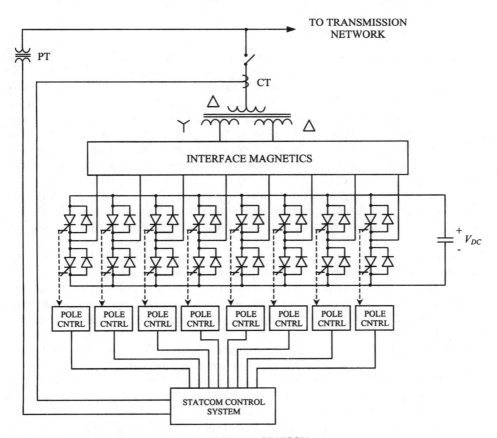

Fig. 8.41 Single-line diagram of a 48-pulse VSC-based STATCOM.

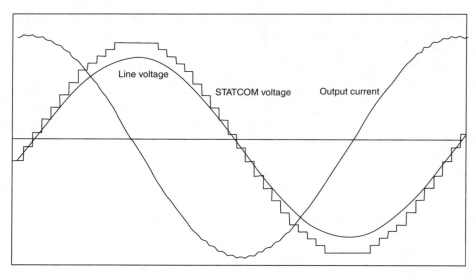

Fig. 8.42 Output voltage and current waveforms for a 48-pulse STATCOM generating reactive power.

configuration. The eight-inverter poles comprising sixteen GTO valves, depicted symbolically, are associated with one of the three output phases the STATCOM generates. Each inverter pole produces a square voltage waveform, progressively phase-shifted from one pole to the next by an appropriately chosen angle. These eight square-wave pole voltages are combined by magnetic summing circuits into two voltage waveforms displaced by 30°. One of these waveforms feeds the wye and the other the delta secondary of the main coupling transformer. The final 48-pulse output voltage waveform is obtained at the transformer primary. The voltage and current output waveforms are shown in Figure 8.42 (Schauder, 1997).

A simplified block diagram of the control system used for the 48-pulse STATCOM is shown in Figure 8.43. An inner feedback loop is used to regulate the STATCOM instantaneous reactive current. Note that this control is achieved by varying the phase angle α, of the inverter output voltage relative to the transmission line voltage. This technique makes it possible to maintain a constant maximum ratio between the converter output voltage and the DC capacitor voltage. The reference value for the reactive current control loop is generated by an outer loop responsible for the system voltage control. This outer control loop is similar to that used in conventional static var compensators, and includes an adjustable slope setting that defines the voltage error at full STATCOM reactive output.

A simple example is presented in this section where a 12-pulse STATCOM is implemented in PSCAD/EMTDC to illustrate the waveforms generated by the multipulse topology. The circuit used for this purpose is shown in Figure 8.44. The PSCAD/EMTDC implementations of this circuit and the switching controller are shown in Figures 8.45 and 8.46 respectively.

Figure 8.47 shows the output voltage and current waveforms generated by the 12-pulse VSC-based STATCOM of the example.

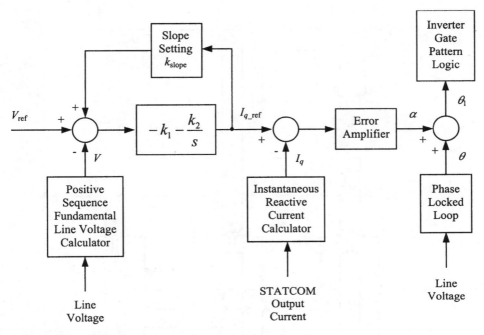

Fig. 8.43 Simplified block diagram of a typical STATCOM control system.

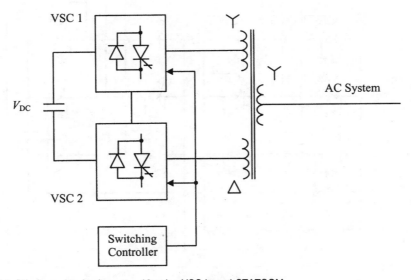

Fig. 8.44 Circuit used to implement a 12-pulse VSC-based STATCOM.

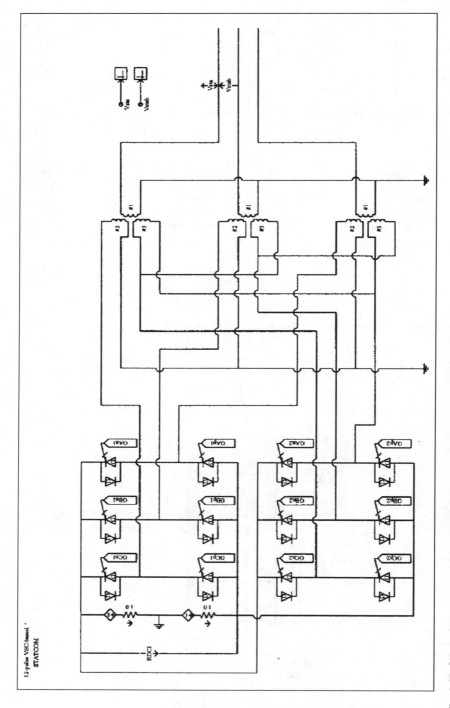

Fig. 8.45 Circuit of a 12-pulse VSC-based STATCOM implemented in PSCAD/EMTDC.

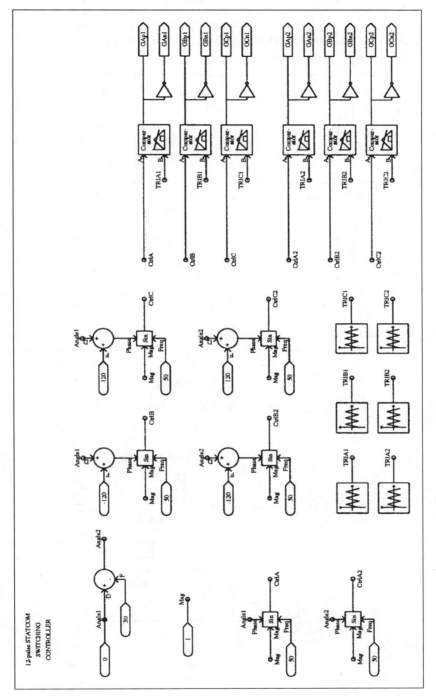

Fig. 8.46 Switching controller for the 12-pulse STATCOM implemented in PSCAD/EMTDC.

8.6.2   Distribution Static Compensator (D-STATCOM)

When used in low-voltage distribution systems the STATCOM is normally identified as Distribution STATCOM (D-STATCOM). It operates in a similar manner as the

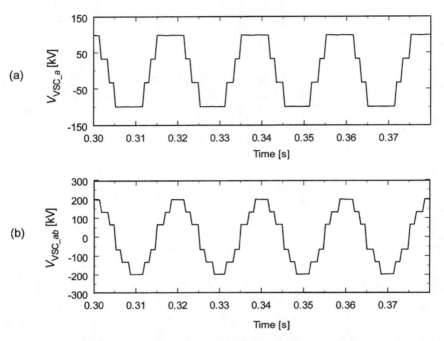

Fig. 8.47 Voltage generated by the 12-pulse VSC-based STATCOM: (a) phase voltage V_{VSC_a}; and (b) line voltage V_{VSC_ab}.

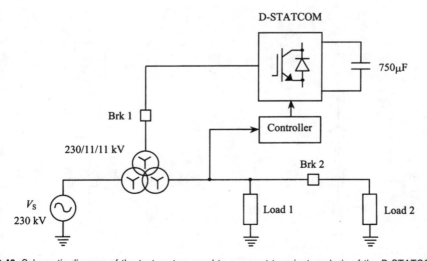

Fig. 8.48 Schematic diagram of the test system used to carry out transient analysis of the D-STATCOM.

STATCOM (FACTS controller), with the active power flow controlled by the angle between the AC system and VSC voltages and the reactive power flow controlled by the difference between the magnitudes of these voltages. As with the STATCOM, the capacitor acts as the energy storage device and its size is chosen based on power ratings, control and harmonics considerations. The D-STATCOM controller continuously monitors the load voltages and currents and determines the amount of compensation required by the AC system for a variety of disturbances. In this section, the D-STATCOM is modelled using the digital simulator PSCAD/EMTDC.

Figure 8.48 shows the schematic diagram of the test system used to carry out the transient modelling and analysis of the D-STATCOM. The test system comprises of a 230 kV three-phase transmission system, represented by a Thévenin equivalent feeding into the primary side of a three-winding transformer. A varying load is connected into the 11 kV, secondary side of the transformer. A two-level VSC-based D-STATCOM is connected to the 11 kV tertiary winding to provide instantaneous voltage support at the load point. A 750 µF capacitor on the DC side provides the D-STATCOM energy storage capabilities. Breaker *Brk1* is used to control the period of operation of the D-STATCOM and *Brk2* controls the connection of *Load 2* to the system.

In this particular example the aim of the D-STATCOM is to provide voltage regulation at the load point and mitigate the voltage sag generated when the load is increased. The system is considered to be operating under balanced conditions and both loads are linear. The D-STATCOM structure is based on a simple two-level VSC which is controlled using conventional sinusoidal PWM. Filtering equipment is not included in the design.

A block diagram of the control scheme designed for the DSTATCOM is shown in Figure 8.49. It is based only on measurements of the voltage V_{rms} at the load point. The voltage error signal is obtained by comparing the measured V_{rms} voltage against a reference voltage, V_{rms_ref}. The difference between these two signals is processed by a PI controller in order to obtain the phase angle δ required to drive the error to zero. The angle δ is used in the PWM generators as the phase angle of the sinusoidal control signal. The switching frequency used in the sinusoidal PWM generators is $f_{sw} = 1050$ Hz and the modulation index is $M_a \approx 1$. The digital implementation in PSCAD/EMTDC of the power system and D-STATCOM controller for this example are shown in Figures 8.50 and 8.51.

Simulations were carried out for both cases where the D-STATCOM was connected into the system and not. In the simulation interval 0.8–1.0 s the load is increased by closing *Brk2*.

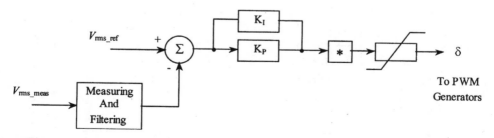

Fig. 8.49 Control scheme designed for the D-STATCOM.

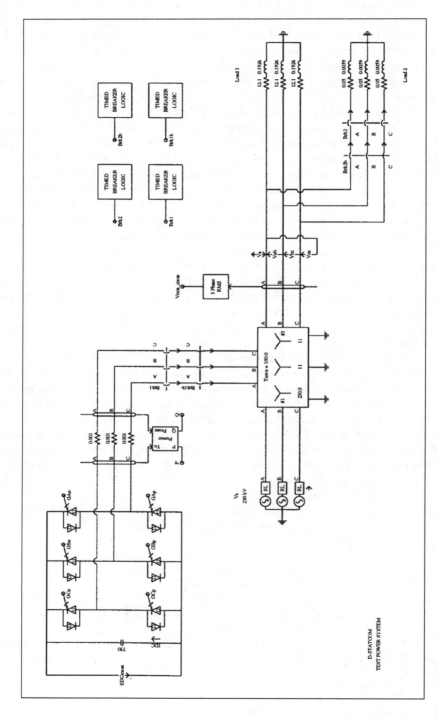

Fig. 8.50 D-STATCOM test system implemented in PSCAD/EMTDC.

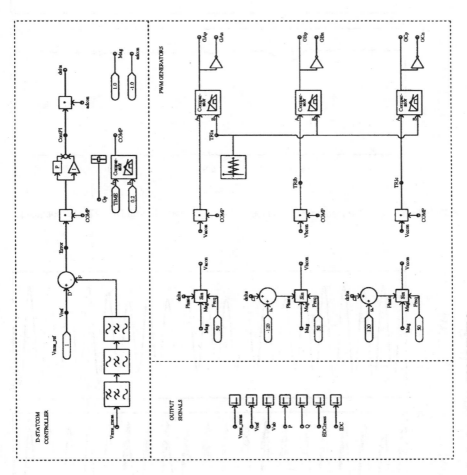

Fig. 8.51 D-STATCOM controller implemented in PSCAD/EMTDC.

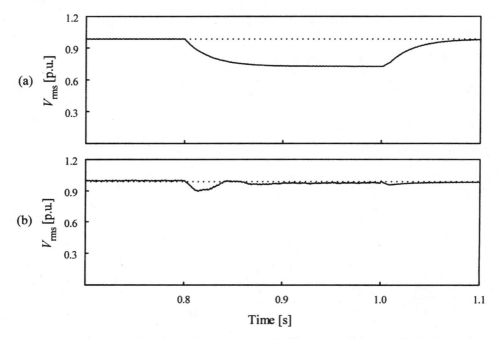

Fig. 8.52 Voltage V_{rms} at the load point: (a) without D-STATCOM; and (b) with D-STATCOM operating.

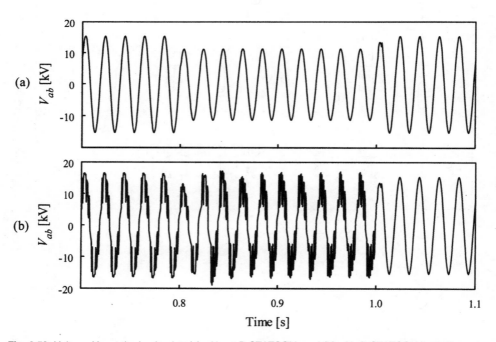

Fig. 8.53 Voltage V_{ab} at the load point: (a) without D-STATCOM; and (b) with D-STATCOM operating.

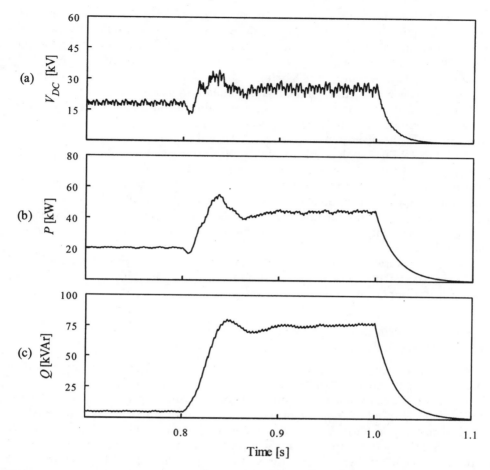

Fig. 8.54 (a) DC link voltage. Power exchange between the AC system and the D-STATCOM: (b) active power; and (c) reactive power.

Under this new operating condition the voltage at the load point experiences a voltage sag of 26% with respect to the reference value which is adjusted to be unity. In this same interval *Brk1* is closed and the D-STATCOM starts operating to mitigate the voltage sag and restore the voltage back to the reference value. Figure 8.52(a) shows the voltage V_{rms} at the load point without D-STATCOM and Figure 8.52(b) with the D-STATCOM in operation. It is possible to observe that the voltage sag is being minimized almost completely.

The regulated V_{rms} voltage shows a reasonably smooth profile. Figure 8.53 shows the line voltage V_{ab} at the load point for both operating conditions. As mentioned before, no filtering equipment has been used throughout the simulation. Figure 8.54(a) shows the DC voltage of the VSC. Before the D-STATCOM starts operating the capacitor is charged to a steady state voltage level of approximately 19 kV. This initial condition of the capacitor improves the response of the D-STATCOM and simplifies the requirements of the control system.

When the D-STATCOM is in full operation, the DC voltage increases to nearly 28 kV. As shown in Figure 8.54(b), in this period the D-STATCOM absorbs active power from the AC system to charge the capacitor and maintain the required DC link voltage level. The reactive power exchange between the AC system and the compensator is shown in Figure 8.54(c).

The results achieved through the digital simulations clearly show the capability of the D-STATCOM to mitigate voltage sags providing a continuously variable level of shunt compensation. The response of the controller is fast, and even when simple, it is effective for the operating conditions considered in the example.

The D-STATCOM has plenty of applications in low-voltage distribution systems aimed to improve the quality and reliability of the power supplied to the end-user. It can be used to prevent non-linear loads from polluting the rest of the distribution system. The rapid response of the D-STATCOM makes it possible to provide continuous and dynamic control of the power supply including voltage and reactive power compensation, harmonic mitigation and elimination of voltage sags and swells.

There are several factors that must be considered when designing the STATCOM and associated control circuits. In relation to the power circuit the following issues are of major importance:

- DC link capacitor size
- coupling transformer reactance and transformation ratio
- output filter equipment.

These elements must be properly selected bearing in mind the application's requirements, voltage regulation and power compensation. The DC capacitor has direct influence on the harmonic distortion of the output voltage generated by the STATCOM and the speed of response of the controller. If the capacitor is undersized the controller's response will be fast but the DC link voltage will have excessive ripple and consequently the output voltage will contain high levels of harmonic distortion. Moreover, high transient overshoots will exist. On the other hand, an oversized capacitor will improve the output voltage waveform shape and reduce the transient overshoots but at the expense of a sluggish controller's response. Besides, some oscillations will appear in the STATCOM response and if care is not taken in the adjustment of the PI parameters, the system may become unstable.

The selection of the coupling transformer parameters has a large impact on the performance of the STATCOM. It plays an important role in the value of voltage regulation and power compensation that the STATCOM can provide. In essence, the amplitude and the phase angle of the voltage drop across the transformer reactance define the active and reactive power flows between the STATCOM and the AC system. This reactance can be seen as a smoothing reactor that will attenuate medium and high order harmonics in the STATCOM output voltage.

8.7 Dynamic Voltage Restorer (DVR)

Similarly to the D-STATCOM, the DVR consists of a VSC, a switching control scheme, a DC energy storage device and a coupling transformer that in this case, is

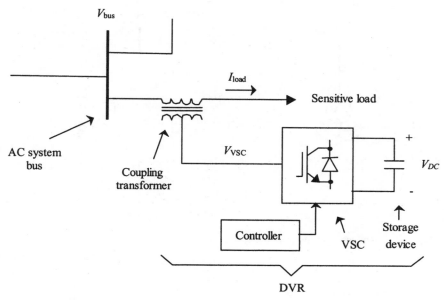

Fig. 8.55 Schematic representation of the DVR.

connected in series with the AC system, as illustrated in Figure 8.55. This controller is suited for solving a variety of power quality and reliability problems including (Osborne et al., 1995; Taylor, 1995; Chan and Kara, 1998):

- voltage sags and swells
- voltage unbalances
- voltage harmonics
- power factor correction
- outages.

The DVR injects a set of three-phase AC voltages in series and synchronized with the distribution feeder voltages of the AC system. The amplitude and phase angle of the injected voltages are variable thereby allowing control of the active and reactive power exchanges between the DVR and the AC system within predetermined positive (power supply), and negative (power absorption) limits.

This section presents the time domain analysis of the DVR for the case when it is used to maintain constant voltage at the point of connection. The test system used to carry out the transient studies is shown in Figure 8.56. The DVR is connected in series with *Load 1* in order to protect this load against any disturbance that could appear in the system. In this example, the DVR must keep the voltage at *Load 1* point constant under a three-phase fault at point A. The DVR coupling transformer is connected in delta in the DVR side. It has a leakage reactance of 10% and unity turns ratio (no booster capabilities exist). The DC link voltage is assumed to be 2.5 kV.

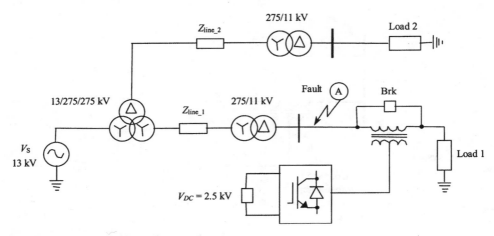

Fig. 8.56 Test system used to carry out the DVR transient analysis.

The simulation scenarios are as follows:

(i) In the first simulation the DVR is disconnected and a three-phase short-circuit fault is applied at point A, via a fault resistance of $0.66\,\Omega$, during the interval $0.8\text{--}1.0\,\text{s}$. The voltage sag at the load point is 25% with respect to the reference value.

(ii) The second simulation is carried out using the same scenario as above but now with the DVR in operation.

Figures 8.57 and 8.58 show the digital implementation in PSCAD/EMTDC of the power system and the DVR controller. Using the facilities available in the simulator, the DVR is simulated to be in operation only for the duration of the fault, as it is expected in a practical situation. The results for both simulations are shown in Figure 8.59. When the DVR is in operation, the voltage sag is mitigated almost completely, and the voltage V_{rms} at the load point is driven back to the reference as shown in Figure 8.59(b). The PWM control scheme controls the magnitude and the phase of the injected voltages, restoring V_{rms}. The sag mitigation is performed with a smooth, stable and rapid DVR response; acceptable overshoots are observed when the DVR comes in and out of operation. Figure 8.60 shows the V_a voltage at the sensitive load point. Figure 8.60(a) shows the voltage V_a when the DVR is not in operation (*Brk1* open). When *Brk1* is closed and the DVR is connected in series with *Load* 1 the voltage sag is mitigated as shown in Figure 8.60(c). A slight increase in the peak value of the waveform is observed compared to the case when the DVR is not in operation.

This effect is purely due to the harmonic distortion generated by the DVR. However, the rms voltage is kept very close to the reference value as shown in Figure 8.59(b). The voltage injected by the DVR in phase a is shown in Figure 8.60(b). It should be noted that no filters are used in the simulations with a switching frequency of $f_{\text{sw}} = 450\,\text{Hz}$.

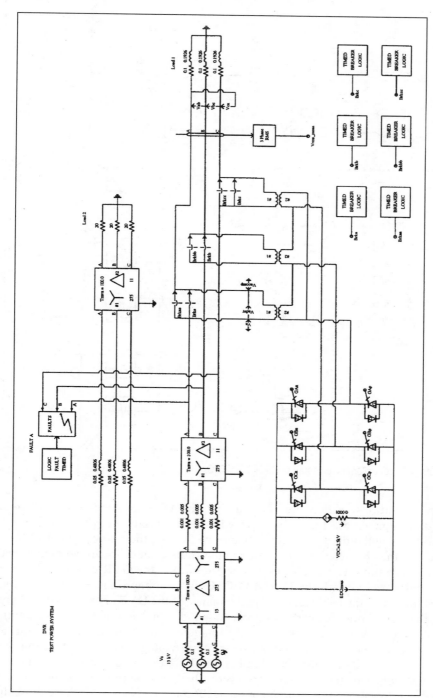

Fig. 8.57 DVR test system implemented in PSCAD/EMTDC.

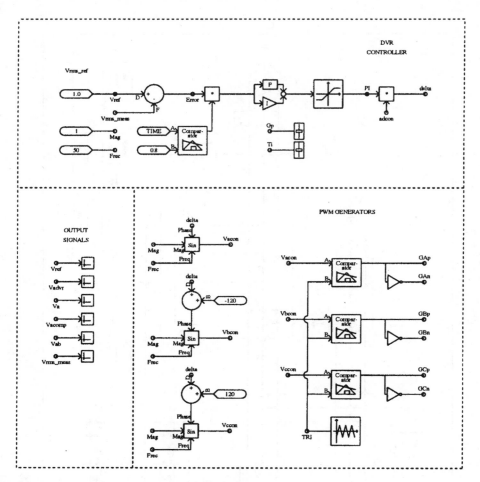

Fig. 8.58 DVR controller implemented in PSCAD/EMTDC.

The simulations carried out showed that the DVR provides excellent voltage regulation capabilities. It must be observed that its capacity for power compensation and voltage regulation depends mainly on two factors: the rating of the DC storage device and the characteristics of the coupling transformer. These two factors determine the maximum value of series compensation that the DVR can provide.

In similar way as with the D-STATCOM, the coupling transformer plays a very important role in the behaviour and performance of the DVR. Thus, it is necessary to select the transformer properly. In order to avoid saturation under every condition, the coupling transformer must be sized to handle at least twice the normal steady-state flux requirement at maximum *rms* injection voltage, without saturation. Normally a high reactance is necessary to filter out the harmonic distortion introduced by the PWM action of the inverter. However, a high reactance of the coupling transformer will slow down the response of the DVR and fast transients will be difficult to identify and correct.

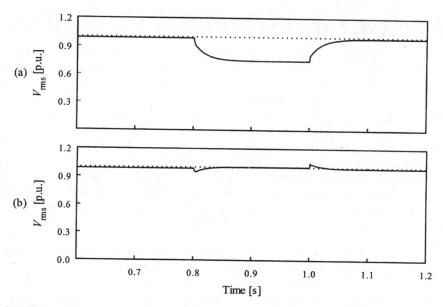

Fig. 8.59 Voltage V_{rms} at the load point: (a) without the DVR; and (b) with the DVR operating.

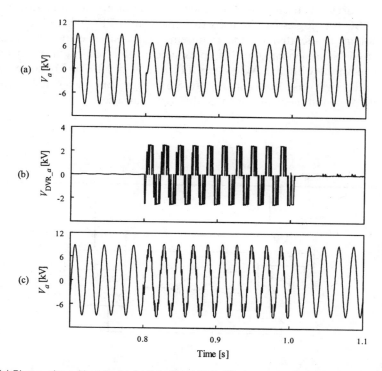

Fig. 8.60 (a) Phase voltage V_a at the load point without DVR; (b) phase voltage supplied by the DVR in phase a; and (c) phase voltage V_a at the load point with the DVR operating.

8.8　Power Factor Corrector (PFC)

Power factor correction usually means the practice of generating reactive power as close as possible to the load that requires it, rather than supplying it from a remote power station. Most industrial loads have lagging power factors; that is, they absorb reactive power. The load current therefore tends to be larger than is required to supply the real power alone. Only the real power is ultimately useful in energy conversion and the excess load current represents a waste to the consumer, who has to pay not only for the excess cable capacity to carry it but also for the excess heat loss produced in the supply cables. The supply utilities also have good reasons for not transmitting unnecessary reactive power from generators to loads: their generators and distribution networks cannot be used at full capacity, and the control of voltage in the supply system can become more difficult. Supply tariffs to industrial customers almost always penalize low power factor loads, and have done so for many years (Miller, 1982).

These aspects and the current power quality regulations have led to the extensive development of power factor correction systems which have lately been an active research topic in power electronics. Conventional techniques for power factor correction involve the use of fixed capacitor banks and reactors with electromechanical controllers. However, the advances in the power electronics technology have enabled the development of new techniques and systems to improve the power factor. In this point the research has been heavily focused on inverter applications (Mao, 1997).

Several VSC topologies can be used to implement a PFC where the most appropriate topology is dictated by the requirements of the specific application. The topology used to implement the PFC presented in this section is based on a VSC connected in shunt with the AC system (Tepper et al., 1996; Moran et al., 1995; Zargari et al., 1995) as shown in Figure 8.61. This topology can be used either individually or simultaneously for three different purposes:

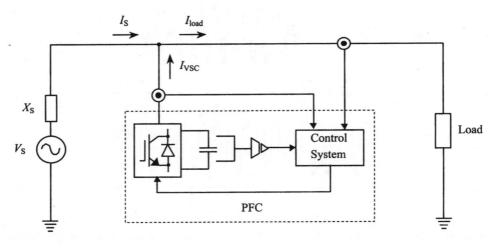

Fig. 8.61 Schematic diagram of the PFC.

1. voltage regulation and compensation of reactive power (STATCOM)
2. correction of power factor (PFC)
3. elimination of undesirable current harmonics (shunt active filter).

The design approach of the control system determines the priorities and functions developed by the shunt-connected VSC in each case. In section 8.4 this topology was used as a STATCOM to provide voltage regulation and compensation of reactive power at the point of connection. In that case a simple control strategy based on voltage measurements was implemented to control the operation of the shunt-connected VSC. However, for the PFC model the implementation of the control strategy is based on a current-controlled VSC scheme. The VSC is controlled as a current source using PWM. Controlled in this way the VSC injects the proper amount of reactive current required by the load so that the main supply delivers only the required active current thus improving the power factor.

The principle of operation of the PFC can be explained using the schematic diagram of Figure 8.61. Without compensation the load current I_{load} is commonly made up of the following terms:

$$I_{load} = I_{load\_0} + I_{load\_p} + I_{load\_q} + I_{load\_h} \tag{8.14}$$

where

I_{load_0} DC component
I_{load_p} in-phase line current
I_{load_q} reactive current
I_{load_h} harmonic currents.

Normally, the DC component is very small or it does not exist at all, then I_{load_0} is excluded from Equation 8.14. For the specific case of power factor correction and assuming a linear load, the term I_{load_h} can be considered zero and Equation 8.14 finally reduces to

$$I_{load} = I_{load\_p} + I_{load\_q} \tag{8.15}$$

In order to achieve unity power factor operation the mains supply must only deliver I_{load_p} in Equation 8.15. This can be achieved if the PFC is controlled to generate and inject into the system the reactive current I_{load_q} required by the load. From Equation 8.15 the reactive current I_{load_q} is calculated by subtracting the active current component I_{load_p} from the measured current I_{load} as

$$I_{load\_q} = I_{load} - I_{load\_p} \tag{8.16}$$

In order to generate I_{load_q} the VSC must be provided with an appropriate current control loop. At present there are several current control techniques available such as hysteresis, predictive and indirect current control techniques which are implemented using a stationary (*abc*) frame of reference. These techniques can be further explained as follows:

1. Hysteresis current control keeps the error within a specified band. The advantages of this technique are simplicity, good accuracy, and high robustness. The major drawback is that the switching frequency varies within one load cycle; this results

in a higher switching frequency than other techniques and the average varies with operating conditions, thus resulting in additional stresses on switching devices and difficulties in designing the appropriate filtering equipment.

2. Predictive current control with fixed switching frequency is based on prediction of the current error from a load model. The advantages are speed and accuracy in tracking the reference waveform; however, it is sensitive to parameter variations, inaccuracies, and delays.

3. Indirect current control eliminates the need for current transducers and employs a standard sinusoidal PWM pattern. However, system parameter values are required and the stability region is more restricted as compared to the hysteresis controller.

The current controller designed for the PFC presented in this section is developed using a rotating ($dq0$) frame of reference that offers higher accuracy than the stationary frame techniques. The block diagram of the overall control system is shown in Figure 8.62.

As illustrated in the block diagram of Figure 8.62 the inputs to the control system are the load currents I_{load_a}, I_{load_b} and I_{load_c}, the converter currents I_{VSC_a}, I_{VSC_b} and I_{VSC_c}, and the voltage V_{DC} of the DC link.

Two control loops are used in this controller, a current control loop and a voltage control loop for the DC link voltage. The measured DC link voltage is first filtered and then compared with a voltage reference. The error is fed to a PI controller in order to reduce the steady-state error. The load and inverter currents are transformed to the rotating ($dq0$) frame and filtered to extract the fundamental components. The currents are transformed to the ($dq0$) frame using the following transformation

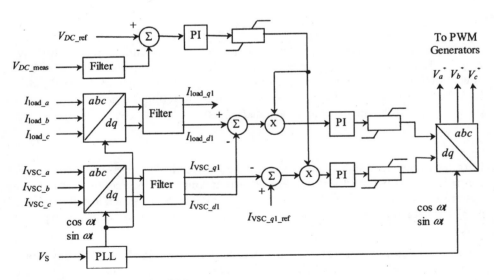

Fig. 8.62 Current controller in the $dq0$ frame.

$$\begin{bmatrix} f_\alpha \\ f_\beta \end{bmatrix} = \frac{2}{3} \begin{bmatrix} 1 & -1/2 & -1/2 \\ 0 & \sqrt{3}/2 & -\sqrt{3}/2 \end{bmatrix} \begin{bmatrix} f_a \\ f_b \\ f_c \end{bmatrix}$$ (8.17)

where the function f in this case represents the instantaneous current. The transformation from the $\alpha\beta$ reference frame to the rotating $(dq0)$ frame is achieved by means of the following transformation

$$\begin{bmatrix} f_d \\ f_q \end{bmatrix} = \begin{bmatrix} \cos \omega t & \sin \omega t \\ -\sin \omega t & \cos \omega t \end{bmatrix} \begin{bmatrix} f_\alpha \\ f_\beta \end{bmatrix}$$ (8.18)

where ω is the synchronous angular frequency of the mains supply. The DC components in the rotating $(dq0)$ frame f_d and f_q correspond to the positive sequence fundamental components of f_α and f_β. Since the dq transformation is one that converts frequency dependant signals into ones with constant value, an ideal three-phase system yields constant f_d and f_q. The relation between the dq and active and reactive components depends on the frame of reference selected.

The rotating frame of reference can be chosen arbitrarily. However, once it is chosen every following calculation must be done with respect to the selected frame. As an example, Figure 8.63 shows two different rotating frames; any of these can be selected as the reference. In this example, the rotating frame is selected such that the q-axis is in phase with the phase a as shown in Figure 8.63(b). The reference signals are the load current dq components that are compared with the measured converter currents. The error signals are then fed to the PI controllers and the output is used as the control signals in the PWM generators. Before the control signals are sent to the PWM generators they are converted back into the stationary (abc) frame of reference using the inverse transformation of Equations 8.17 and 8.18 in the following way

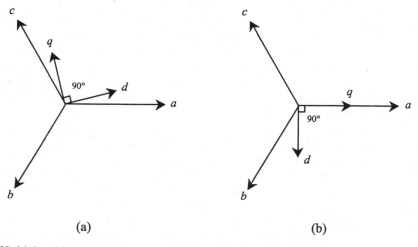

(a) (b)

Fig. 8.63 (a) An arbitrary rotating frame; and (b) chosen rotating frame of reference.

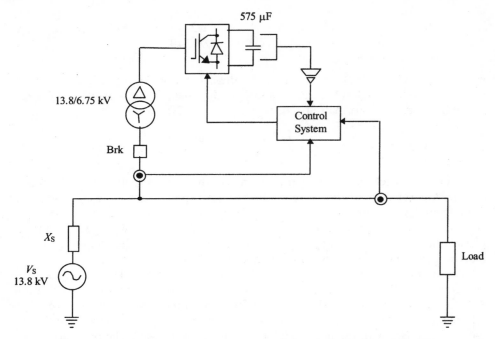

Fig. 8.64 Schematic diagram of the test system used to carry out transient analysis of the PFC.

$$
\begin{bmatrix} f_a^* \\ f_b^* \\ f_c^* \end{bmatrix} = \begin{bmatrix} 1 & 0 \\ -1/2 & \sqrt{3}/2 \\ -1/2 & -\sqrt{3}/2 \end{bmatrix} \begin{bmatrix} \cos\omega t & -\sin\omega t \\ \sin\omega t & \cos\omega t \end{bmatrix} \begin{bmatrix} f_d^* \\ f_q^* \end{bmatrix} \tag{8.19}
$$

where f_a^*, f_b^*, f_c^* are the commands in the PWM generators.

The electrical system used to carry out the transient simulations of the PFC is shown in Figure 8.64. It comprises of a simple three-phase system where an AC constant source is supplying a linear R–L load. The PFC is connected in shunt with the AC system between the source and the *load* through the reactance of a Y–Δ coupling transformer. The breaker *Brk* controls the connection of the PFC to the AC system. The PFC is provided with a control system that measures the load current I_{load}, the VSC output current I_{VSC}, and the voltage of the DC link V_{DC}. The control logic is then derived based on these measurements as previously explained. A 575 μF is connected on the DC side of the VSC to provide the energy storage capability. Figure 8.65 illustrates the digital implementation developed in PSCAD/EMTDC of the test system. The controller is shown in Figures 8.66 and 8.67.

Under normal operating conditions the power factor of the load is at an extremely low value of 0.35 lagging. The PFC is connected to raise the power factor and bring the whole system into unity power factor operation. The simulations were run for a long period of time but only a few cycles are presented for clarity.

Figure 8.68 shows the source current I_S, the load current I_{load}, and the converter output current I_{VSC}. These waveforms are plotted together with the source voltage V_S. The simulation begins with the PFC disconnected from the network and both, I_S

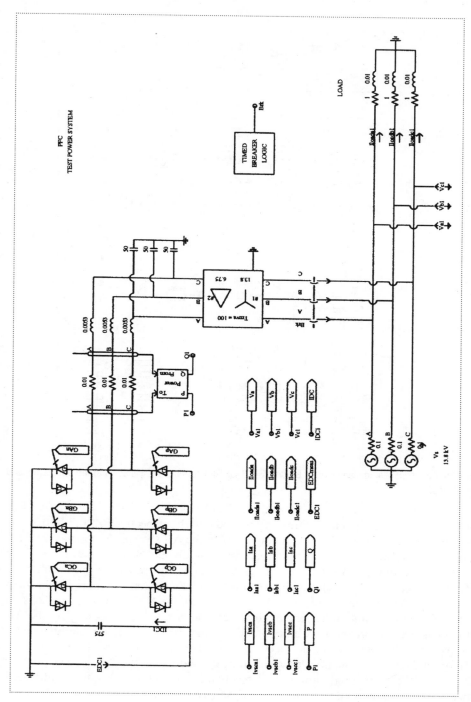

Fig. 8.65 PFC test system implemented in PSCAD/EMTDC.

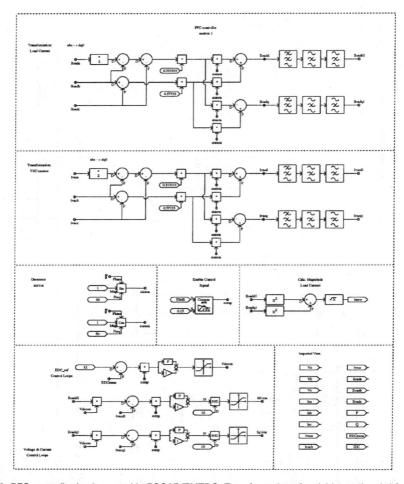

Fig. 8.66 PFC controller implemented in PSCAD/EMTDC: Transformation of variables to the *dq0* frame, and control loops.

and I_{load} lag V_S as shown in Figures 8.68(a) and 8.68(b) respectively. At $t = 0.15$ s the breaker *Brk* is closed and the PFC is connected to the AC system. As soon as the PFC starts operating the power factor increases very rapidly and it only takes a couple of cycles until the input power factor is driven to unity as illustrated in Figure 8.68(a).

Observe that the phase relation between I_{load} and V_S remains unaltered even when the PFC is in operation. As shown in Figure 8.68(b), the load current I_{load} keeps on lagging V_S by the same initial angle. However, the power factor as seen by the AC source has been improved to a unity value, i.e. the AC source is not supplying any reactive power to the load, as it is seen by the source as a purely resistive one.

In order to improve the power factor to the desired value, the PFC injects into the AC system the appropriate amount of reactive power required by the load which otherwise, has to be delivered by the AC source. As mentioned before, the PFC controller splits the load current into its active and reactive components by

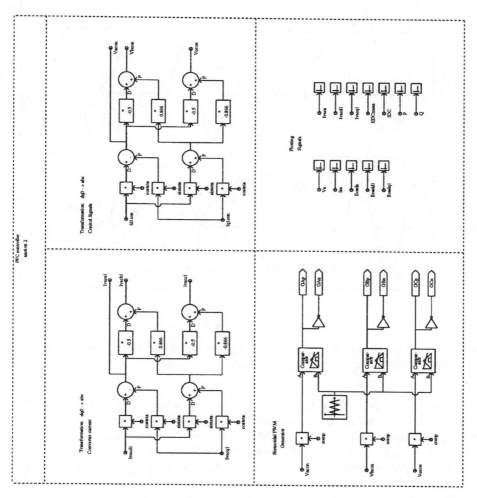

Fig. 8.67 PFC controller implemented in PSCAD/EMTDC: Transformation of command signals back to the *abc* frame, and PWM generators.

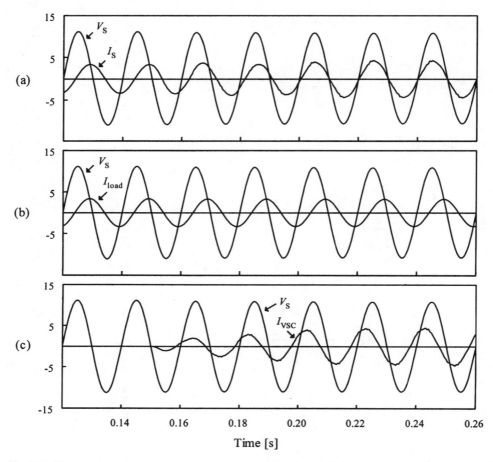

Fig. 8.68 Key waveforms for the PFC circuit: (a) source voltage V_S and current I_S; (b) source voltage V_S and load current I_{load}; and (c) source voltage V_S and converter current I_{VSC}.

a transformation into the rotating $dq0$ frame. These dq-components are used as reference input values in the closed loop control scheme. According to the selected rotating $dq0$ frame shown in Figure 8.63 the reactive components of I_{load}, I_S and I_{VSC} are shown in Figure 8.69. At $t = 0.15$ s the PFC is connected to the network and the reactive current required by the load is supplied by the PFC as shown in Figure 8.69(c). Figure 8.69(b) shows the reactive current supplied by the source which decreases rapidly very close to zero. In this way, the power factor increases significantly and becomes practically unity.

Figure 8.70 shows the corresponding DC link voltage V_{DC} which is maintained at 33 kV. The response of the controller can be appreciated in this plot, and it can be seen that it takes almost two cycles before the DC voltage is driven from an initial zero value to the required 33 kV. The size of the DC capacitance is selected sufficiently large to minimize the DC voltage ripple without slowing the response of the controller. The DC voltage ripple can be further reduced by connecting an appro-

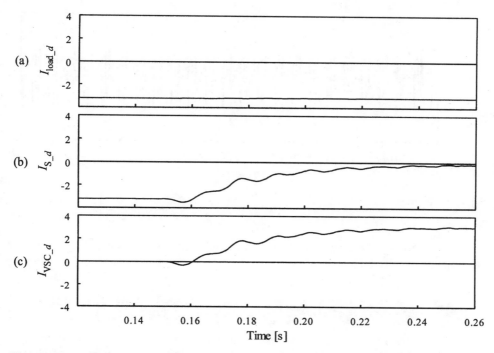

Fig. 8.69 Reactive components in the rotating frame: (a) load current I_{load_d}; (b) source current I_{S_d}; and (c) converter current I_{VSC_d}.

priate filter at the VSC output terminals. However, for the purpose of this example filtering has not been included.

Figure 8.71 shows the current through the DC link capacitor, I_{DC}. The current I_{DC} has the typical pattern for the case of lagging power factor compensation. When the compensation is for a leading power factor the orientation of the waveform is in the opposite direction. It shows low current harmonic distortion that is reflected in the

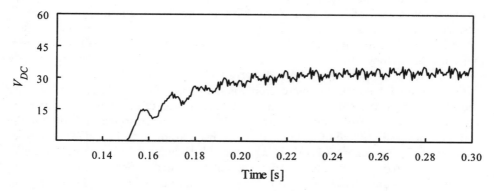

Fig. 8.70 DC link voltage V_{DC}.

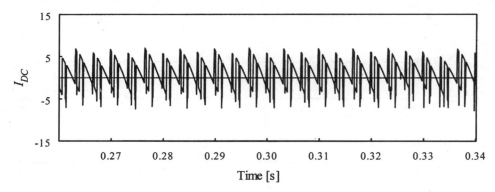

Fig. 8.71 DC link current I_{DC}.

current injected by the converter I_{VSC}, and the resulting compensated source current I_S shown in Figure 8.68.

8.9   Active Filters (AFs)

In Chapter 6, various converter topologies have been introduced as a way to improve the quality of the power supply. The reason being that the composition of electric utility systems' elements has gone through a gradual change from being largely linear to partially or dominantly non-linear during the past 30 years or so. The proliferation of non-linear loads and sources, such as power electronic based equipment, has led to a serious problem of power quality for both, utilities and customers, as these non-linear elements are the main contributors of harmonic pollution in the system.

This situation has become a major concern for power system specialists due to the effects of non-sinusoidal voltages and currents on sensitive loads and on the overall distribution system. For example, harmonic current components increase power system losses, cause excessive heating in rotating machinery, create significant inter-ference with communication circuits that shared common right-of-ways with AC power lines, and can generate noise on regulating and control circuits causing erroneous operation of such equipment. On the other hand, among other compon-ents, rotating machinery can be significantly impacted by the harmonic voltage distortion as it translates into harmonic fluxes that induce additional losses. Decreased efficiency, along with heating, vibration, and high-pitched noises, are clear symptoms of harmonic voltage distortion (Singh et al., 1999).

A common source of harmonic currents is the phase-controlled thyristor rectifier where the current waveform distortion, i.e. the generation of harmonics, results from the phase delay control method. The details of these harmonics depend on the rectifier's firing angle, the inductance of the power supply, the DC load, and other circuit parameters. Figure 8.72(a) shows a typical thyristor rectifier and Figure 8.73 shows the source voltage and rectifier current waveforms. Because the harmonic current contents and characteristics are less dependent upon the AC side, this type of harmonic source behaves like a current source. Therefore, they are called harmonic

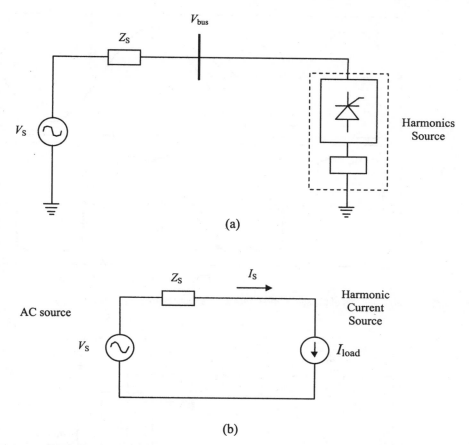

Fig. 8.72 Typical type of harmonic current source: (a) phase-controlled thyristor rectifier; and (b) single-phase equivalent circuit.

current source and represented as a current source shown in Figure 8.72(b). Other common sources of periodic, non-sinusoidal signals, and hence harmonics, are adjustable speed drives, inverters, and compact fluorescent lamps (Peng, 1998).

At present, another common harmonic source is that of diode rectifiers with 'smoothing' DC capacitors as shown in Figure 8.74(a). Figure 8.75 shows the current and voltage waveforms. Although the current is highly distorted, its harmonic amplitude is greatly affected by the impedance of the AC side whereas the voltage at the rectifier's input terminals is characteristic and less dependent upon the AC impedance.

Therefore, a diode rectifier with a 'smoothing' capacitor behaves like a voltage source rather than a current source. Figure 8.74(b) shows the equivalent circuit of the diode rectifier system, where the diode rectifier is represented as a harmonic voltage source. Accordingly, the harmonic current originates from the rectifier voltage, and its content is determined by, and dependent, upon the rectifier voltage and the AC impedance. Conventionally, passive L–C filters have been used to eliminate line

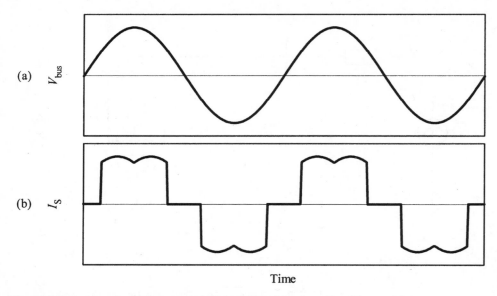

Fig. 8.73 Typical waveforms of phase-controlled rectifiers: (a) voltage V_{bus}; (b) current I_S.

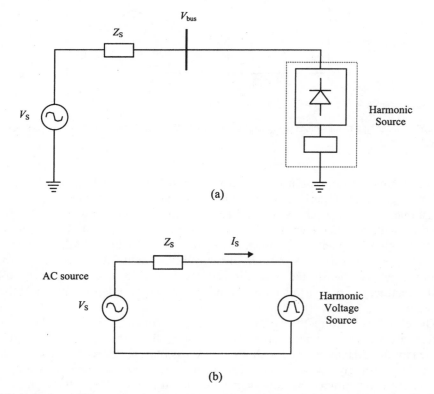

Fig. 8.74 Typical type of harmonic voltage source: (a) diode rectifier; and (b) single-phase equivalent circuit.

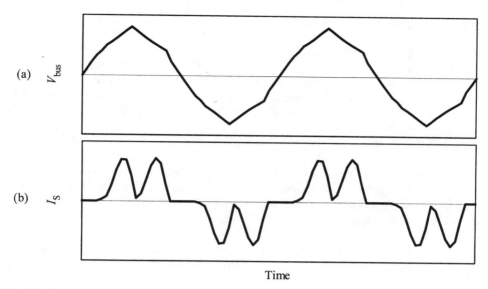

Fig. 8.75 Typical waveforms of diode rectifiers: (a) voltage V_{bus}; and (b) current I_S.

harmonic pollution and to increase the line power factor. However, in practical applications passive filters have the demerits of fixed compensation, being relatively bulky, and resonating with other system elements. The increased severity of harmonic pollution in power networks has attracted the attention of power electronics and power system engineers to develop dynamic and adjustable solutions to the power quality problems giving rise to the active power filters technology.

Active filtering provides compensation for harmonics, reactive power, and/or neutral current in AC networks. It is also used to eliminate voltage harmonics, to regulate terminal voltage, to suppress voltage flicker, and to improve voltage balance in three-phase systems. This wide range of objectives is achieved either individually or in combination, depending upon the requirements and control strategy and configuration that have to be selected appropriately.

Active filters are based on sophisticated power electronics and can be much more expensive than passive filters depending upon the application. However, they have the distinctive advantage that they do not resonate with the system. They can be used in very difficult circumstances where passive filters cannot operate successfully due to parallel resonance complications. They can also address more than one harmonic at a time and combat other power quality problems such as flicker. They are particularly useful for large, distorting loads fed from relatively weak points on the power system. The basic idea behind the active power filters is to replace the portion of the sine waveform that is missing in the current and/or voltage in a non-linear load. An electronic control monitors the line voltage and/or current, switching the power electronics very precisely to track the load current or voltage and force it to be sinusoidal. Many circuit topologies for series and/or shunt active filtering exist and have been presented in Chapter 6.

8.9.1 Shunt active filter

The topology of a VSC connected in shunt with the AC system was used in previous sections as a STATCOM and PFC for power factor improvement. This section presents the time domain analysis of this topology when used as shunt active filter for the elimination of current harmonics. A simple control scheme is developed to regulate the operation of the active filter and transient simulations are carried out in PSCAD/EMTDC.

As mentioned above the shunt AF is a PWM VSC that is placed in shunt with a load (or a harmonic current source) and has the capability to inject into the AC system a harmonic current with the same amplitude but opposite phase than that of the load. Figure 8.76 illustrates the schematic representation of the shunt AF. The principal components are the VSC, a DC energy storage device that in this case is a capacitor, a coupling transformer (not shown in the Figure) and associated control circuits.

The control scheme developed for the shunt AF is based on the determination of the load current harmonic components. With this information the control system drives the VSC in such a way that it generates and injects into the AC system a current with the appropriate harmonic content to neutralize the current harmonics due to the load. Without compensation the load current I_{load} can be split into two terms as

$$I_{load} = I_{load\_1} + I_{load\_h} \tag{8.20}$$

where I_{load_1} and I_{load_h} represent the fundamental and harmonic components of the load current respectively. The controller developed for the shunt AF is very similar to the one used for the PFC. In the last section the control scheme of the PFC was focussed on controlling the active and reactive parts of the fundamental component. For the shunt AF the control scheme concentrates on the harmonic component of the load current that can be obtained from Equation 8.20 as

$$I_{load\_h} = I_{load} - I_{load\_1} \tag{8.21}$$

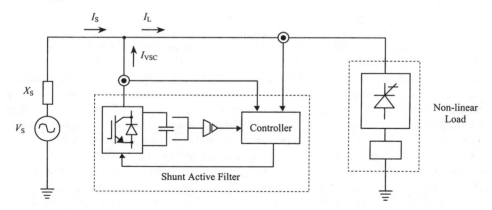

Fig. 8.76 Schematic diagram of a shunt AF and associated control circuit.

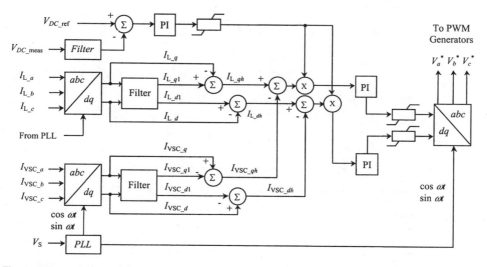

Fig. 8.77 Block diagram of the control scheme designed for the shunt AF.

Equation 8.21 implies first the determination of the fundamental component I_{load_1} and then the subtraction of I_{load_1} from the total load current I_{load} in order to isolate the harmonic component I_{load_h}. Figure 8.77 shows the block diagram of the shunt AF controller. As can be seen in this figure, two control loops are used i.e. a DC link voltage control loop and a current loop in a similar way as with the PFC.

Direct generation of a VSC 'average voltage' reference for current regulation can also be achieved by stationary or rotating frame PI-based current controllers. This last option was selected in this example.

Figure 8.78 shows the schematic diagram of the test system used to carry out the time domain analysis of the shunt AF. The system comprises of a three-phase system where a constant AC source is supplying a non-linear load represented by a phase-controlled rectifier. The shunt AF is connected with the AC system between the source and the non-linear load through the reactance of a Y–Δ coupling transformer. The connection of the shunt AF to the AC system is controlled by means of breaker *Brk*. The shunt AF is provided with a control system that measures the load current I_{load}, the VSC output current I_{VSC}, and the DC link voltage V_{DC}. The control logic is then derived based on these measurements. A 175 µF capacitor is connected in the DC side of the VSC to provide the energy storage capability. A firing angle control scheme was designed for the operation of the phase-controlled rectifier. By controlling the instant at which the thyristors are gated, the average current in the rectifier can be controlled in a continuous manner. The control is based on comparison of a saw-tooth waveform V_{st} (synchronized with the AC source voltage) against a control signal $V_{control}$. The thyristor firing angle α with respect to the positive zero crossing of the AC source voltage is obtained in terms of $V_{control}$ and the peak of the saw-tooth waveform V_{st_peak} as (Mohan et al., 1995)

$$\alpha° = 180° \frac{V_{control}}{V_{st\_peak}} \tag{8.22}$$

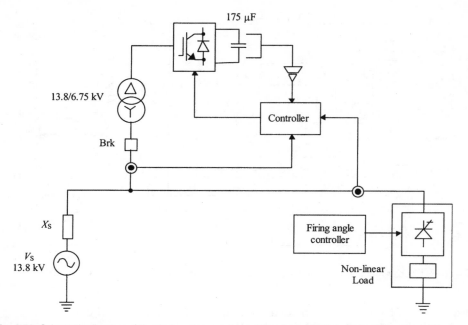

Fig. 8.78 Schematic diagram of the test system used to carry out transient analysis of the shunt AF.

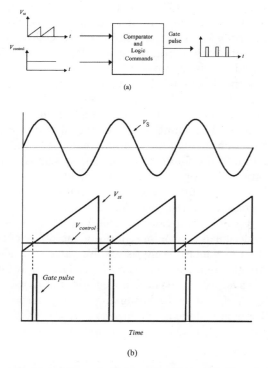

Fig. 8.79 Firing angle control of the phase-controlled rectifier; (a) block diagram; and (b) control signals.

Another gate trigger signal can be obtained, delayed with respect to the zero crossing of the AC source voltage. The control scheme diagram is shown in Figure 8.79.

The implementation of the test power system in PSCAD/EMTDC is shown in Figures 8.80–8.84.

The results obtained through the transient simulation are presented for the time interval of 0.06–0.18 s. At the beginning of the simulation the shunt AF is disconnected from the AC system, i.e. *Brk* is in the open state. At $t = 0.1$ s *Brk* is closed and the active filter is connected to the AC system and starts operating. Figure 8.85 shows the source current I_S, the load current I_L and the VSC current I_{VSC} for both operating conditions. It can be seen in Figure 8.85(a) that when the shunt AF starts operating at $t = 0.1$ s the source current recovers its sinusoidal waveform as the shunt AF is blocking properly the low order current harmonics generated by the load.

It is important to observe in Figure 8.85(b), that the line current drawn by the load remains unchanged even when the filter operates. The effect of the filter is to block the line current harmonics generated by the load from flowing back into the distribution network and disturb other network components in the vicinity.

Figure 8.86 shows the harmonic spectrum of the source current I_S before and after the shunt AF operates. Without filtering, I_S has a current total harmonic distortion ITHD = 30.52% with high contents of low order harmonics such as the 5th, 7th, 11th and 13th. With the shunt AF in operation, the total harmonic distortion of the source current decreases to ITHD = 8.73% as the content of the low order harmonics is significantly reduced as shown in Figure 8.86(b). It must be observed that the fundamental component of the source current is different before and after the filter operation. The fundamental component value is greater when the filter is in operation. This can be explained bearing in mind that the VSC of the active filter has a DC link capacitor whose voltage must be kept constant for the correct operation of the filter. That is, the source current increases as the active filter is drawing active power from the AC system to charge the capacitor and maintain constant DC link voltage.

Figure 8.87 shows the harmonic current component of the load current I_L, the active filter VSC current I_{VSC} and the source current I_S. It can be clearly appreciated in this figure how the harmonic current component generated by the active filter and the harmonic current component due to the load have the same wave shape but opposite direction. The response of the filter controller is fast and it only needs half a cycle to start tracking the reference currents and drive the filter to generate the appropriate harmonic currents to cancel those of the load current. Figures 8.88 and 8.89 show the harmonic current components of the load, filter and source currents in the rotating $dq0$ frame.

Specifically, the harmonic current components in the rotating frame q-axis are shown in Figure 8.88 and the harmonic current components in the d-axis are shown in Figure 8.89. Once again, it can be seen that the harmonic current dq components generated by the active filter and the harmonic current dq components due to the load have the same wave shapes but opposite directions.

The voltage V_{DC} through the DC link capacitor of the active filter is shown in Figure 8.90(a) and the active and reactive powers absorbed by the shunt AF are shown in Figures 8.90(b) and 8.90(c) respectively. After the transient period when the filter is connected to the network, the shunt AF absorbs active power to

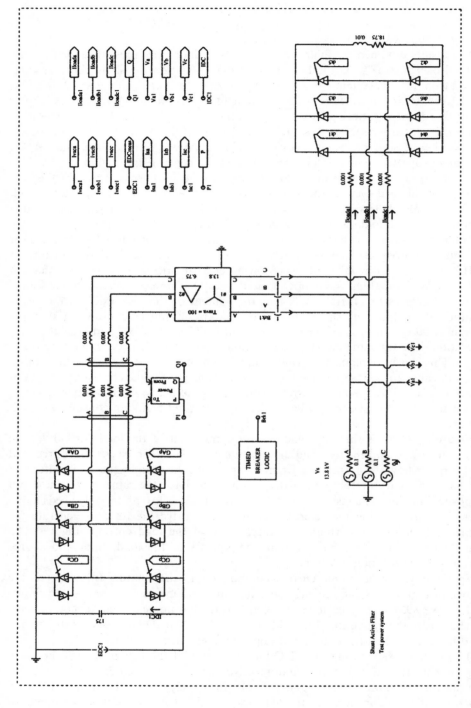

Fig. 8.80 Test system implemented in PSCAD/EMTDC to carry out transient analysis of the shunt AF.

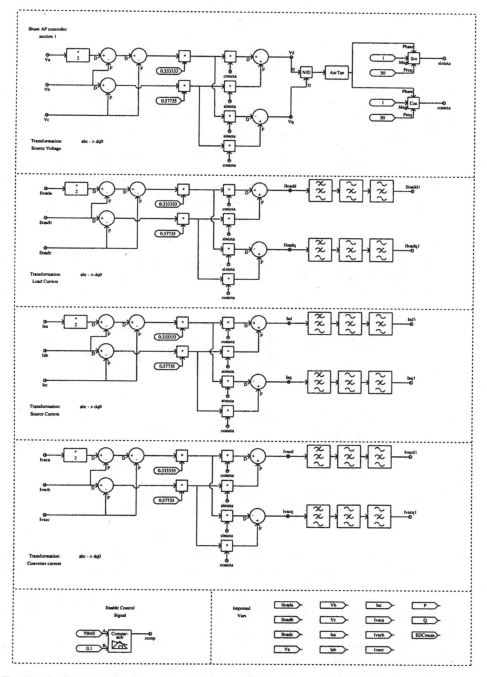

Fig. 8.81 Shunt AF controller implemented in PSCAD/EMTDC: Transformation of variables to the *dq0* frame.

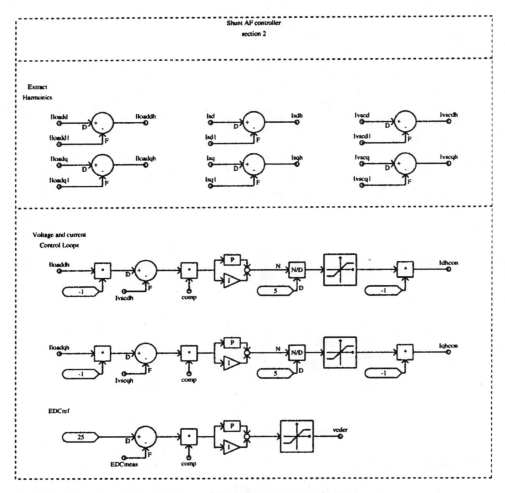

Fig. 8.82 Shunt AF controller implemented in PSCAD/EMTDC: Control loops.

charge the capacitor to a constant value of almost 33 kV for the rest of the simulations. The DC link voltage is not completely constant and presents significant ripple
component.

In order to decrease the DC voltage ripple, it is possible to select a larger value for
the DC capacitance but this compromises the controller response, as a larger DC
capacitance will result in a more sluggish system. Another solution to minimize the
DC voltage ripple is the use of switching ripple filter topology at the output of the
shunt active filter in order to provide a sink for the dominant inverter switching
frequencies that cause the DC voltage ripple. If properly designed, switching ripple
filters can also provide attenuation for higher harmonic supply currents that are
above the current regulator bandwidth of shunt AF inverter (Bhattacharya et al.,
1998).

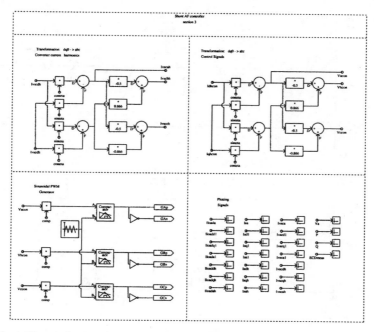

Fig. 8.83 Shunt AF controller implemented in PSCAD/EMTDC: Transformation of command signals back to the *abc* frame, and PWM generators.

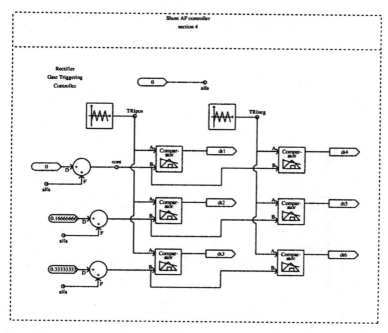

Fig. 8.84 Shunt AF controller implemented in PSCAD/EMTDC: Firing angle module of the phase-controlled rectifier.

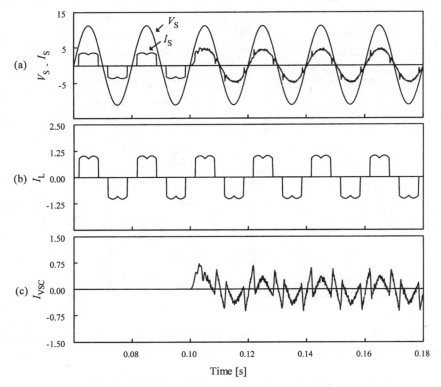

Fig. 8.85 Current waveforms in the shunt AF model circuit: (a) source voltage V_S and current I_S; (c) current I_L; and (c) converter current I_{VSC}.

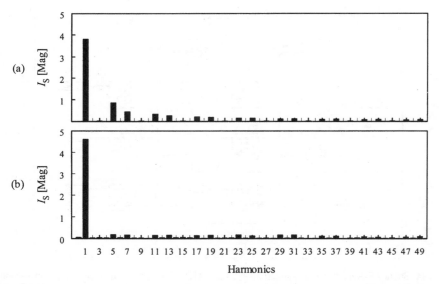

Fig. 8.86 Harmonic spectrum of the source current I_S: (a) without shunt AF; and (b) with shunt AF operating.

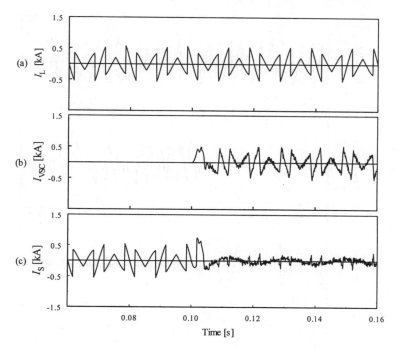

Fig. 8.87 Current harmonic components: (a) current I_L; (b) converter current I_{VSC}; and (c) source current I_S.

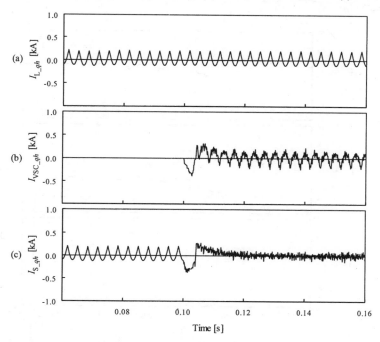

Fig. 8.88 Current harmonic components in the q-axis: (a) current I_{L_qh}; (b) converter current I_{VSC_qh}; and (c) source current I_{S_qh}.

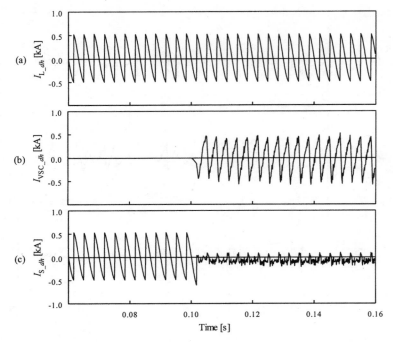

Fig. 8.89 Current harmonic components in the d-axis: (a) current I_{L_dh}; (b) converter current I_{VSC_dh}; and (c) source current I_{S_dh}.

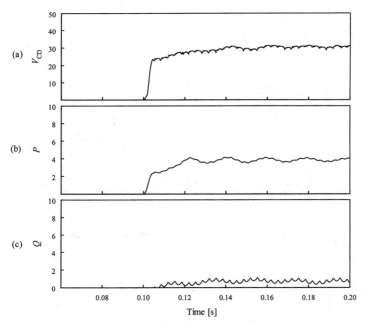

Fig. 8.90 (a) DC link voltage V_{DC}. Power exchange between the AC system and the shunt AF; (b) active power P; and (c) reactive power Q.

8.10   Solid-State Transfer Switch (SSTS)

The SSTS is a high-speed, open-transition switch that enables the transfer of electrical loads from one AC power source to another within a few milliseconds. It is designed to replace the mechanical auto-transfer equipment currently used to switch major industrial and commercial facilities from one feeder to another. The open-transition property of the SSTS means that the switch breaks contact with one source before it makes contact with the other source.

The advantage of this transfer scheme over the closed-transition mechanical switch is that the electrical sources are never cross-connected unintentionally. The cross connection of independent AC sources, with the alternate source switching on to a faulted system is discouraged by electrical utilities (Chan, Kara and Kieboom, 1998). The SSTS can be used very effectively to protect sensitive loads against voltage sags, swells and other electrical disturbances. The basic configuration of this device consists of two three-phase solid-state switches, one for the main feeder and one for the backup feeder. These switches have an arrangement of back-to-back connected thyristors, as illustrated in the one-line diagram shown in Figure 8.91. If a voltage sag or interruption is detected on the main feeder that is supplying the load, then that switch is opened and the load is transferred to the backup feeder within a very short time (Gole and Palav, 1998).

This section presents the time domain analysis of the SSTS system using the electromagnetic transient simulator PSCAD/EMTDC. The test system shown in Figure 8.92 is used in order to carry out transient analysis of the SSTS. The system comprises of two identical feeders feeding into a 13 kV-bus. A sensitive load is connected to the bus.

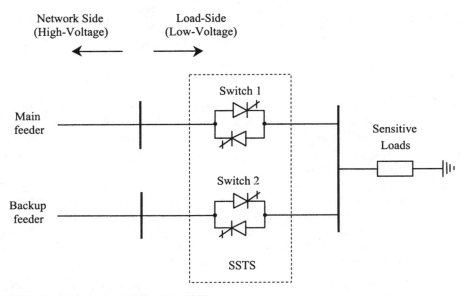

Fig. 8.91 Schematic representation of the SSTS.

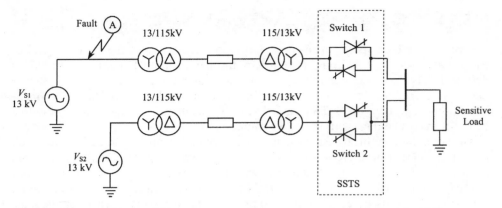

Fig. 8.92 Schematic diagram of the test system used to carry out transient analysis of the SSTS.

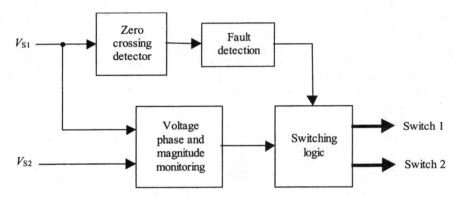

Fig. 8.93 Control circuit designed for the SSTS.

Figure 8.93 shows the block diagram of a simple control strategy that can be used to operate the SSTS for the application illustrated in the example. Each time a fault condition is detected in the main feeder, the control system swaps the firing signals to the thyristors in both switches, *Switch 1* in the main feeder is deactivated and *Switch 2* in the backup feeder is activated.

The control system measures the peak value of the voltage waveform at every half-cycle and checks whether or not it is within a prespecified range. If it is outside limits, an abnormal condition is detected and the firing signals to the thyristors are changed to transfer the load to the healthy feeder. The digital implementation in PSCAD/EMTDC of the test system is shown in Figure 8.94. The following simulations were carried out to perform the time domain analysis of the SSTS:

- In the first experiment the SSTS is disconnected and a three-phase fault is applied at the main feeder in point A as shown in Figure 8.92. The fault is applied at a time

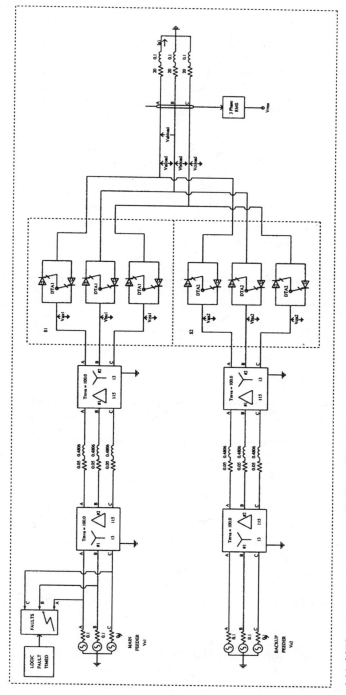

Fig. 8.94 SSTS test system implemented in PSCAD/EMTDC.

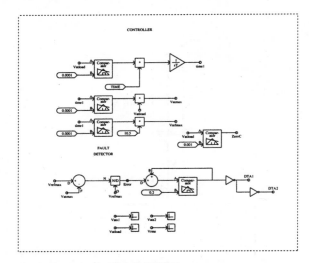

Fig. 8.95 SSTS controller implemented in PSCAD/EMTDC.

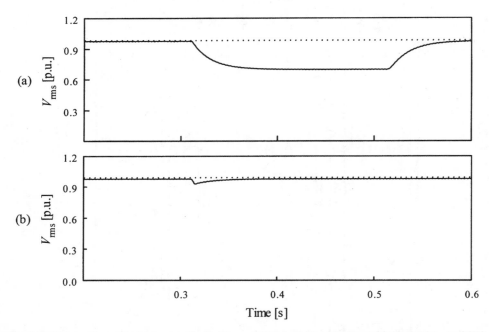

Fig. 8.96 Voltage V_{rms} at the load point. The fault is applied at $t = 0.31$s: (a) without SSTS; and (b) with SSTS operating.

0.31 s with fault duration of 0.2 s. The magnitude of the voltage sag due to the fault is 30%, as seen from the voltage V_{rms} shown in Figure 8.96(a).

- A second experiment was carried out using a similar scenario as above but now with the SSTS in operation. The voltage V_{rms} at the load point is shown in Figure 8.96(b).

As mentioned before, the control system monitors the maximum and minimum values of the voltage waveform at the load point every half-cycle. Whenever a faulted condition in the electrical supply is detected, the triggering signals to both switches are reversed. Figure 8.96(b) shows that after the disturbance has occurred the *rms* voltage at the load point is driven back to the prefault value very rapidly.

It should be noted that the SSTS does not regulate voltage neither generate or absorb reactive power. Its only function is to deactivate a faulty feeder in favour of a fault-free one. The waveform of the voltage V_a at the load point for both operating conditions is shown in Figure 8.97.

It can be seen that when the faulted condition is registered, it only takes a fraction of a cycle (less than 4 ms at 50 Hz fundamental frequency) for the SSTS to perform the transfer of load to the backup feeder, and restore the voltage to the prefault condition. Figure 8.98 shows a few cycles of the voltage waveform to observe in detail the moment of the load transfer between the faulty feeder and the healthy one.

Arguably, there is always a load transfer delay associated with SSTS applications which is a function of the fault detection technique used. In this example, the quality of the voltage waveform is checked at every peak and trough, with respect to a reference voltage value, e.g. 90% of rated value. Besides, monitoring the voltage at peak values reduces the possibility of the control scheme being adversely affected by the presence of large harmonic distortion.

The circuit configurations of an SSTS installation are dependent on several factors such as the availability of an existing alternate source, the size of critical loads, and the need to protect single or several separate critical loads among others. The dual

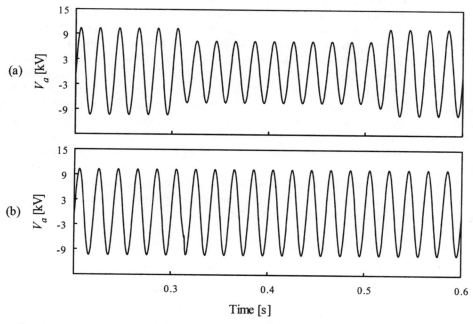

Fig. 8.97 Phase voltage V_a at the load point. The fault is applied at $t = 0.31$s: (a) without SSTS; and (b) with SSTS operating.

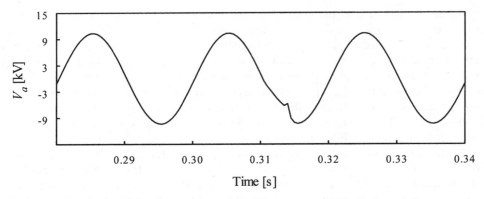

Fig. 8.98 Waveform of the phase voltage V_a at the load point. The fault is applied at $t = 0.31$s.

service circuit configuration shown in Figure 8.91 is the most widely used implementation of the SSTS system. In some application the SSTS is used in conjunction with the D-STATCOM in order to provide sag and swell protection, as well as supply continuous power in the presence of an upstream fault.

8.11 Conclusion

The use of computer programs in the simulation of FACTS and CP controllers, including their controls, is extremely important for the development and understanding of this power electronics-based technology. They yield key information relating to the performance of the system under any operating condition, which is not possible to achieve by analytical means. They allow to identify and to assess the interaction between the various elements in the network. This chapter has presented time-domain results for several FACTS and CP controllers. The highly developed graphics facilities available in the electromagnetic transient simulator PSCAD/EMTDC were used to conduct all aspects of model implementation and to carry out simulation studies.

The basic control schemes presented in this chapter are simple and easy to implement in any transient simulator. Of course, they may be made to operate more efficiently but this will be at the expense of added control complexity. The reader should have no difficulties in exploring more advanced control aspects in the superb environment afforded by PSCAD/EMTDC.

9

Examples, problems and exercises

1. Draw a diagram of a transmission tower for a high-voltage overhead transmission line.
2. What is the function of a transformer?
3. What parameters are used to describe 'power quality'?
4. What is the minimum number of conductors required for a three-phase overhead transmission line?
5. How is *power factor* defined when the voltage or current is not sinusoidal?
6. Thomas Edison is credited with the invention of 'the electric light bulb'. In the early days of the electricity supply industry (roughly 100 years ago), when the new electric companies were expanding and promoting the use of electric power, Edison believed that DC was superior to AC. On the other hand, George Westinghouse took the opposite view. For low-voltage (i.e. residential) and medium-voltage (industrial) supplies, the argument is obviously well settled in favour of AC, but for very high voltage transmission it is not always a straightforward choice.

   Moreover, in the case of small isolated power systems such as the power system of a *car* or an *aircraft*, the argument is being re-opened. Whereas most cars use 12 VDC and most commercial aircraft use 115-V three-phase AC at 400 Hz, these standards may be replaced within the next decade or two.

   Table 9.1 summarizes some of Edison's and Westinghouse's arguments, along with some additional ones that are relevant today. An additional column is provided for you to add your own comments.

---

[1] The exercises in this section can be used for classwork, either with a whole class or in small groups.

Table 9.1 AC vs. DC: some points for argument and discussion

DC (Edison)	AC (Westinghouse)	Your opinion (DC or AC)
	AC is more 'natural' than DC because it is what you get when you rotate a magnet inside a coil, and that is really what you have in a power-station generator.	
	It is easier to make switchgear (especially contactors and circuit-breakers) for AC, because you have a natural current-zero every half-cycle, where the current can be interrupted easily without striking a massive arc.	
DC requires only two conductors, and in certain cases you can even use a single conductor with 'ground return'. This is obviously cheaper.	Westinghouse has Stanley's patents on the transformer, and GE doesn't.[a]	
AC can be easily 'transformed' from low-voltage to high-voltage and back again. This is an advantage in long-distance transmission, or in transmitting high power levels, because you can use a lower current and therefore thinner conductors (and less copper or aluminium).	DC is perfectly smooth.	
DC is perfectly smooth and, unlike AC, does not produce 'lamp flicker' or 'AC hum' in telephone and signalling circuits.	AC is better for supplying industry with motive power, because you can use induction motors which are self-starting, highly efficient, and very inexpensive and rugged. Besides, Westinghouse has Tesla's patents on the induction motor, and GE doesn't.	
DC is better for lighting, especially public lighting with arc lamps.	With modern field-oriented AC drives, the torque control with AC motors is as good as it is with DC motors.	
DC is better for supplying electric railways, because the traction motors are DC motors with very smooth torque control and torque/speed characteristics ideally suited to traction requirements.	With polyphase AC (i.e. two or three phases) you can run different loads off different phases, so the security of supply is better.	
DC is better for connecting two large power networks together (e.g. Britain and France, or USA and Canada), because you don't need to synchronize the two networks.	With AC you have reactance in the circuit, and when there is a fault, the reactance limits the fault current.	
With AC you have reactance in the circuit, and therefore a larger voltage drop in the cables or overhead lines.	With DC motors you need a commutator and brushes, which need frequent maintenance and cause radio interference.	
With DC and modern power electronics you can create a power supply of any voltage waveform (including sinewave AC, if that is what you want).		

[a] GE was founded by Thomas Edison.

9.2 A basic worked example – leading and lagging loads

Figure 9.1 shows a circuit with a supply system whose open-circuit voltage is $\mathbf{E}$ and short-circuit impedance is $\mathbf{Z}_s = 0 + jX_s$, where $X_s = 0.1\,\Omega$. The load impedance is $Z = 1\,\Omega$ but the power factor can be unity, 0.8 lagging, or 0.8 leading. For each of these three cases, the supply voltage E must be adjusted to keep the terminal voltage $V = 100\,\text{V}$. For each case determine E, the power-factor angle ϕ, the load angle δ, the power P, the reactive power Q, and the volt-amperes S.

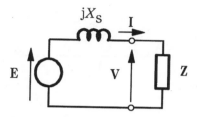

Fig. 9.1 Simple AC circuit.

Unity power-factor. Referring to Figure 9.2, we have $E \cos\delta = V = 100$ and $E \sin\delta = X_s I = 0.1 \times 100/1 = 10\,\text{V}$. Therefore $\mathbf{E} = 100 + j10 = 100.5e^{j5.71°}\,\text{V}$. The power-factor angle is $\phi = \cos^{-1}(1) = 0$, $\delta = 5.71°$, and $\mathbf{S} = P + jQ = \mathbf{VI}^* = 100 \times 100e^{j0} = 10\,\text{kVA}$, with $P = 10\,\text{kW}$ and $Q = 0$.

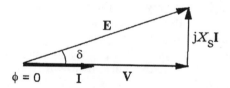

Fig. 9.2 Unity PF.

Lagging power-factor. Referring to Figure 9.3, the current is rotated negatively to a phase angle of $\phi = \cos^{-1}(0.8) = -36.87°$. Although $I = 100\,\text{A}$ and $X_s I$ is still $10\,\text{V}$, its new orientation 'stretches' the phasor $\mathbf{E}$ to a larger magnitude: $\mathbf{E} = \mathbf{V} + jX_s\mathbf{I} =$

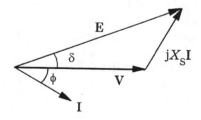

Fig. 9.3 Lagging PF.

$(100 + j0) + j0.1 \times 100e^{-j36.87°} = 106.3e^{j4.32°}$ V. Note that the supply voltage E has to be higher to achieve the same load voltage when the power-factor is lagging. The load angle is $\delta = 4.32°$ and $\mathbf{S} = \mathbf{V}\mathbf{I}^* = 100 \times 100e^{+j36.87°} = 8000 + j6000$ VA. Thus $S = 10\,\mathrm{kVA}$, $P = 8\,\mathrm{kW}$ and $Q = +6\,\mathrm{kVAr}$ (absorbed).

Leading power-factor. The leading power-factor angle causes a reduction in the value of E required to keep V constant: $\mathbf{E} = 100 + j0.1 \times 100e^{+j36.87°} = 94.3e^{j4.86°}$ V. The load angle is $\delta = 4.86°$, and $\mathbf{S} = 10\,000e^{-j36.87°} = 8000 - j6000$; i.e. $P = 8\,\mathrm{kW}$ and $Q = 6\,\mathrm{kVAr}$ (generated).

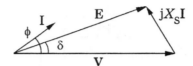

Fig. 9.4 Leading PF.

We have seen that even though the power and the current are the same in all cases, the inductive load with its lagging power factor requires a higher source voltage E. The capacitive load with its leading power factor requires a lower source voltage.

If the source voltage E were kept constant, then the inductive load would have a lower terminal voltage V and the capacitive load would have a higher terminal voltage. As an exercise, repeat the calculations for $E = 100\,\mathrm{V}$ and determine V in each case, assuming that $Z = 1\,\Omega$ with each of the three different power-factors.

We can see from this that power-factor correction capacitors (connected in parallel with an inductive load) will not only raise the power factor but will also increase the voltage. On the other hand, if the voltage is too high, it could conceivably be reduced by connecting inductors in parallel. In modern high-voltage power systems at locations far from the generating stations, it is possible to control the voltage by varying the amount of inductive or capacitive current drawn from the system at the point where the voltage needs to be adjusted. This is called *reactive compensation* or *static VAr control*. In small, isolated power systems (such as an automotive or aircraft power system supplied from one or two generators) this is not generally necessary because the open-circuit voltage of the generator E can be varied by field control, using a *voltage regulator*.

9.3   Simple basic problems

1. A single-phase power system has an open-circuit voltage $E = 6.35\,\mathrm{kV}$ and a fault level of 16 MVA. Calculate the short-circuit current I_{sc} in kA, and the Thévenin internal reactance X_s in ohms. (See Figures 2.1 and 9.1).
2. What value of resistance R would draw 1.5 MW when connected to the power system of Question 1? (See Figures 2.1 and 9.2). Calculate also the terminal voltage V, the voltage drop X_sI, and the load angle δ.
3. What value of inductive reactance X_L would be needed to reduce the voltage by 3% in the power system of Question 1 (assuming that no other loads are

connected)? (See Figures 2.3 and 9.3). Express the answer in ohms and also *per unit* of X_s (i.e. the ratio X_L/X_s).

4. What value of capacitive reactance X_C would be needed to raise the voltage by 3% in the power system of Question 1 (assuming that no other loads are connected)? (See Figures 2.4 and 9.4). Express the answer in ohms and also *per unit* of X_s (i.e. the ratio X_C/X_s).

5. In the symmetrical power system shown in Figure 2.5a, $E_s = E_r = 6.35\,\text{kV}$ and $X = 2.52\,\Omega$. If the voltage-drop XI is 40% of E_s, calculate the current I, the power transmitted, the power factor at both ends of the line, and the load angle δ between $\mathbf{E}_s$ and $\mathbf{E}_r$.

6. A three-phase delta-connected induction motor is fed from a supply of 440 V line–line, and delivers 225 kW to a water pump. Calculate the line current, assuming 90% for the efficiency and 85% for the power factor.

7. Each phase of a three-phase delta-connected load comprises a capacitor of 40 μF in series with a resistor of 100 Ω. This load is connected to a three-phase supply at 440 V and 50 Hz. Calculate (a) the rms phase current in the load; (b) the line current; and (c) the total power taken from the supply.

8. The load of Question 7 is to be dismantled and shipped to a far-off country, where the local power company has declared that all electrical goods of foreign origin must be connected in star (i.e. wye). Calculate the new line currents and the power taken from the supply, if the phases that were originally connected in delta are reconnected in star. Comment on the result. The supply is still 440 V at 50 Hz.

9. Three impedances, each comprising a resistance of 40 Ω in series with an inductance of 95.5 mH, are connected in wye to a 400 V, 50 Hz, three-phase AC supply. Calculate (a) the supply line current; and (b) the resistance R and inductance L (in series) of a balanced delta-connected load that takes the same line current at the same power factor.

10. Three identical inductive impedances are connected in delta to a 415 V, 50 Hz, three-phase supply of sequence RYB. The current in the R *line* is 4.8 A and it leads the voltage $\mathbf{V}_{YB}$ by 53°. Determine (a) the rms phase current; and (b) the resistance and inductance of each phase-impedance. (*Do* be careful with subscripts, arrows, etc. in this one.)

11. Three single-phase loads are connected to a 250 V, three-phase, three-wire supply of sequence RYB:

   6 kW at unity PF between R and Y;
   4 kW at 0.8 PF leading between Y and B;
   2 kW at 0.5 PF lagging between B and R.

Taking $\mathbf{V}_{RY}$ as reference phasor, calculate all three line-currents. (*Hint:* use $\mathbf{S} = \mathbf{VI}^*$ and calculate the phase currents first. Watch the asterisks as well as the subscripts and arrows.)

9.3.1 Answers to problems in Section 9.3

1. 2.52 kA; 2.52 Ω.
2. $R = 26.643\,\Omega$ or $0.238\,\Omega$; $V = 6.322\,\text{kV}$ or $0.5979\,\text{kV}$; $X_sI = 0.5979\,\text{kV}$ or $6.322\,\text{kV}$; and $\delta = 5.403°$ or $84.597°$.

3. 81.48 Ω; 32.33 p.u.
4. 86.52 Ω; 34.33 p.u.
5. 1.008 kA; 6.271 MW; 0.980 lagging at the sending end (E_s); 0.980 leading at the receiving end (E_r).
6. 386 A.
7. (a) $I_{phase} = 3.44$ A; (b) $I_{line} = 5.96$ A; (c) $P = 3.56$ kW.
8. $I_{line} = 1.99$ A; $P = 1.19$ kW (*both reduced to one-third*).
9. (a) 4.62 A; (b) 120 Ω; 286 mH.
10. (a) 2.77 A; (b) 120 Ω; 286 mH.
11. $\mathbf{I_R} = 16.0 - j13.9$ A; $\mathbf{I_Y} = -21.6 - j19.9$ A; $\mathbf{I_B} = 5.6 + j33.7$ A.

9.4   Worked examples

1. An inductive three-phase wye-connected load is supplied at 4160 V and takes 1400 kW of real power and 700 kW of reactive power. The supply system impedance is j0.9 Ω/phase. Calculate

   (i) the current;
   (ii) the power factor;
   (iii) the open-circuit voltage (i.e. the supply voltage E) if the load voltage $V = 4160$ V;
   (iv) the ratio of the open-circuit voltage E to the load voltage V; and
   (v) the load angle (i.e. the phase angle between **E** and **V**).

   (i) $P + jQ = \sqrt{3} V_L I_L^*$

   (ii) $\therefore I_L = (1400 + j700) \times 10^3 / (\sqrt{3} \times 4160) = 217.23 e^{j26.56°}$ A

   (iii) $\Delta V = \dfrac{X_s Q}{V} + j\dfrac{X_s P}{V} = \dfrac{0.9 \times 700/3}{4160/\sqrt{3}} + j\dfrac{0.9 \times 1400/3}{4160/\sqrt{3}}$

   $= 87.435 + j174.87 = 195.51 e^{j63.43°}$ V.

   (iv) $\mathbf{E} = (4160/\sqrt{3} + j87.435) + j174.87 = 2489.2 + j174.87 = 2495.3 e^{j4.02°}$ V.

   (v) $\dfrac{E}{V} = \dfrac{2495.3}{4160/\sqrt{3}} = 1.039$

2. For the system in Problem 1, use the equation $V = E(1 - Q/S)$ to estimate the ratio E/V, where S is the short-circuit level.

   $S = 2495^2 / 0.9 = 6917$ kVA/phase, so

   $$V = E\left(1 - \frac{Q}{S}\right) = E\left(1 - \frac{700/3}{6917}\right) = 0.9663$$

   whence $E/V = 1/0.9663 = 1.035$ (Unlike the result of Problem 1, this result is only approximate).

3. For the system in Problem 1, find the capacitance/phase and the total reactive power of a capacitor that will make $E = V = 4160$ V, if the load is constant at $1400 + j700$ kVA. The frequency is 50 Hz.

With $E = V$

$$V^2 = \left(V + \frac{X_s Q}{V}\right)^2 + \left(\frac{X_s P}{V}\right)^2$$

$$V^4 = (V^2 + X_s Q)^2 + (X_s P)^2$$

$$\therefore \quad Q^2 + \frac{2V^2}{X_s} Q + P^2 = 0$$

whence $Q = -S \pm \sqrt{S^2 - P^2}$

Now $S = 4.16^2/0.9 = 19.288$ MVA (all three phases) and $P = 1.40$ MVA, so the net reactive power required to make $E = V$ is

$$Q = Q_{load} + Q_\gamma = -19.2884 \pm \sqrt{19.2884^2 - 1.40^2}$$

$$= -19.2884 \pm 19.2375 = -38.5259 \quad \text{or} \quad -0.0509 \text{ MVA}$$

The correct solution is -0.0509 MVA so that with $Q_{load} = 0.70$ MVAr we get $Q_\gamma = -0.7509$ MVAr. Then the capacitor current is

$$I_\gamma = \frac{0.7509 \times 10^6}{\sqrt{3} \times 4160} = 104.2 \text{ A}$$

The capacitor reactance must be $(4160/\sqrt{3})/104.2 = 23.047 \,\Omega$/phase (assuming wye connection), and therefore at 50 Hz the required capacitance is $10^6/(2\pi \times 50 \times 104.2) = 138 \,\mu\text{F}$.

4. An unbalanced delta-connected load draws the following power and reactive power from a three-phase supply whose line–line voltage is 560 V:

   200 kW between lines a, b
   170 kW at 0.85 power-factor lagging between lines b, c
   170 kW at 0.85 power-factor leading between lines c, a.

   Determine the susceptances of a purely reactive delta-connected compensating network that will balance this load and correct its power factor to unity. Also determine the resulting line currents.

   General result is

   $$B_{\gamma ab} = -B_{ab} + (G_{ca} - G_{bc})/\sqrt{3}$$
   $$B_{\gamma bc} = -B_{bc} + (G_{ab} - G_{ca})/\sqrt{3}$$
   $$B_{\gamma ca} = -B_{ca} + (G_{bc} - G_{ab})/\sqrt{3}$$

   leaving $G = G_{ab} + G_{bc} + G_{ca}$ in each phase of a wye-connected resulting network. In each phase $P + jQ = VI^* = V^2 Y^*$ so $Y = (P - jQ)/V^2$ so

   in phase ab, $Y_{ab} = (200 - j0) \times 10^3/560^2 = 0.638 + j0 \text{ S}$
   in phase bc, $Y_{bc} = (170 - j105.357)/560^2 = 0.542 - j0.336 \text{ S}$
   in phase ca, $Y_{ca} = (170 + j105.357)/560^2 = 0.542 + j0.336 \text{ S}$

$$B_{\gamma ab} = -0 + (0.542 - 0.542)/\sqrt{3} = 0$$
$$B_{\gamma bc} = -(-0.336) + (0.638 - 0.542)/\sqrt{3} = 0.391 \text{ S (capacitor)}$$
$$B_{\gamma ca} = -0.336 + (0.542 - 0.638)/\sqrt{3} = -0.391 \text{ S (inductor)}$$

The resulting impedance in each phase is $0.638 + 0.542 + 0.542 = 1.722\,\Omega$, so the line current is $(560/\sqrt{3})/1.722 = 187.8\,\text{A}$.

5. A transmission cable has a sending-end voltage $E_s = 345\,\text{kV}$ line–line. Losses may be neglected. The cable has an inductive reactance per unit length of $0.60\,\Omega/\text{km}$ and a capacitive admittance of $50.0\,\mu\text{S/km}$ at 50 H, and its length is $a = 54.8\,\text{km}$. Assuming that the receiving-end is open-circuited, calculate

   (i) the surge impedance Z_0;
   (ii) the electrical length θ in degrees;
   (iii) the receiving-end voltage expressed in per-unit with E_s as reference;
   (iv) the sending-end current;
   (v) the reactive power at the sending end, in MVAr; and
   (vi) the reactive power at the sending end, expressed as a fraction of the surge-impedance loading.

   (i) $Z_o = \sqrt{(x_L \cdot x_C)} = \sqrt{(x_L/y_C)} = \sqrt{(0.60/50 \times 10^{-6})} = 109.55\,\Omega$
   (ii) $\beta = \sqrt{(x_L/x_C)} = \sqrt{(x_L \cdot y_C)} = \sqrt{(0.60 \times 50 \times 10^{-6})} = 5.477 \times 10^{-3}$ radians/km
     $= 0.3138°/\text{km}$, so $\theta = \beta a = 0.3138 \times 54.8 = 17.2°$
   (iii) $\mathbf{V_r} = \dfrac{\mathbf{E_s}}{\cos\theta} = \dfrac{1.0}{\cos 17.2°} = 1.0468$
   (iv) $\mathbf{I_s} = j\dfrac{\mathbf{E_s}}{Z_o}\tan\theta = \dfrac{345/\sqrt{3}}{109.55}\tan 17.2°\,\text{kA} = j563\,\text{A}$
   (v) $Q_s = \sqrt{3} \times 345 \times 0.563 = 336\,\text{MVAr}$
   (vi) $P_o = 345^2/109.55 = 1086.5\,\text{MVA}$, so $Q_s/P_o = 336/1086.5 = 0.309$ p.u.

6. A transmission cable has a receiving end voltage $V_r = 345\,\text{kV}$ line–line. The load is 900 MVA with a lagging power factor of 0.88, and is wye-connected. Find the value of the line current, expressed as a phasor. Take $\mathbf{V_r}$ as reference. The cable may be assumed lossless.

$$P = 900 \times 0.88/3 = 264\,\text{MW/phase}$$
$$Q = 300 \times \sin(\cos^{-1}(0.88)) = 300 \times \sin 28.3576° = 142.492\,\text{MVAr}$$
Load is lagging or inductive, so $Q > 0$.

$$\mathbf{I_r} = (P - jQ)/\mathbf{V_r} = (264 - 142.492)/(345/\sqrt{3})$$
$$= 1.32540 - j0.71537 = 1.50613e^{-j28.3576°}\,\text{kA}$$

7. The cable in Problem 6 has an inductive reactance per unit length of $0.60\,\Omega/\text{km}$ and a capacitive admittance of $50.0\,\mu\text{S/km}$ at 50 Hz. The cable length is $a = 14.8\,\text{km}$. Calculate

   (i) the surge impedance Z_0;
   (ii) the electrical length θ in radians and degrees;

(iii) the sending end voltage when the load is 900 MVA with a lagging power factor of 0.88;

(iv) the transmission angle δ in degrees;

(v) the sending-end current;

(vi) the power and reactive power at the sending end; and

(vii) draw the phasor diagram showing the phase voltage and current at both ends.

$$\omega\ell = 0.60 \ \Omega/\text{km} \text{ and } \omega c = 50 \times 10^{-6} \ \text{S/km}$$

(i) $Z_o = \sqrt{(\ell/c)} = \sqrt{(\omega\ell/\omega c)} = \sqrt{(0.60/(50 \times 10^{-6}))} = 109.545 \ \Omega$

(ii) $\beta = \sqrt{(\omega\ell \times \omega c)} = \sqrt{(0.60 \times 50 \times 10^{-6})} = 0.005477 \ \text{radians/km}$
$= 0.31382°/\text{km}$
$\theta = \beta a = 0.005477 \times 14.8 = 0.08106 \ \text{radians} = 4.64456°$

(iii) $\mathbf{E_s} = \mathbf{V_r} \cos\theta + j Z_o \mathbf{I_r} \sin\theta$
From Question 6, $\mathbf{I_r} = 1.50613 e^{-j28.3576°} \ \text{kA}$

$\therefore \mathbf{E_s} = (345/\sqrt{3})\cos 4.64456° + j109.545 \times \sin 4.64456° \times 1.50613 e^{-j28.3576°} \ \text{kV}$

$= 198.532 + 13.35984 \ e^{j(90 - 28.3576)°}$

$= 198.532 + 6.34556 + j11.757 = 204.878 + j11.757$

$= 205.214 e^{j3.2843°} \ \text{kV} \ 1\text{-n}$, i.e. $355.442 \ \text{kV}$ line–line

Thus if $V_r = 1.0 \ \text{p.u}$, $E_s = 205.215/(345/\sqrt{3}) = 1.0303 \ \text{p.u.}$

(iv) Transmission angle $\delta = 3.2843°$.
Check the power transmission: $Z_o \sin\theta = 109.545 \ \sin 4.64456° = 8.87031$
$P = (205.215 \times 345\sqrt{3}/8.87031)\sin 3.2843° = 264.0 \ \text{MW/phase.}$

(v) $\mathbf{I_s} = j(\mathbf{V_r}/Z_o)\sin\theta + \mathbf{I_r}\cos\theta$

$= j(345/\sqrt{3})/109.545 \sin 4.64456° + 1.50613 e^{-j28.3576°} \times \cos 4.64456°$

$= 1.32104 - j0.56579 \ \text{kA} = 1.43710 e^{-j23.1850°} \ \text{kA}$

(vi) $P_s + jQ_s = \mathbf{E_s}\mathbf{I_s^*} = 3 \times 205.214 e^{j3.2843°} \times 1.43710 e^{j23.1850°}$
$= 792.0 + j394.3 \ \text{MVA.}$

(vii)

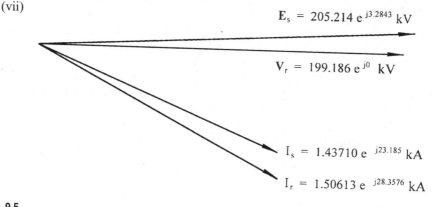

$E_s = 205.214 \ e^{\ j3.2843} \ \text{kV}$

$V_r = 199.186 \ e^{\ j0} \ \text{kV}$

$I_s = 1.43710 \ e^{\ j23.185} \ \text{kA}$

$I_r = 1.50613 \ e^{\ j28.3576} \ \text{kA}$

Fig. 9.5

8. If the load in Problem 7 is disconnected, and no change is made to the sending-end voltage, what will be the value of the receiving-end voltage? Also calculate the charging current and the charging MVAr at the sending end.

   With $I_r = 0, E_s = V_r \cos\theta$ so $V_r = 355.442/\cos 4.64456° = 356.613 \text{ kV} = 1.03366 \text{ p.u.}$ Charging current is $I_s = j(E_s/Z_o) \tan\theta = j(205.214/109.545) \tan 4.64456° = j0.15219 \text{ kA}$. Charging MVAr $= \sqrt{3} \times 355.442 \times 0.15219 = 93.695 \text{ MVAr}$.

9. A 29.6-km lossless transmission cable has synchronous machines at both ends, which maintain the terminal voltages at 345 kV line–line. If the inductive reactance per unit length is 0.60 Ω/km and the capacitive admittance is 50.0 µS/km at 50 Hz, calculate

   (i) the Surge Impedance Load P_0;
   (ii) the maximum transmissible power P_{max};
   (iii) the reactive power requirements at both ends, when the load power is $0.23P_0$ and the mid-point voltage is held at 1.0 p.u. by adjusting the sending- and receiving-end voltages; and
   (iv) the values of the sending- and receiving-end voltages required to maintain 1.0-p.u. voltage at the mid-point.

   The surge impedance Z_0 is the same as the cable in Question 7, i.e. $Z_0 = 109.545 \, \Omega$.

   (i) $P_0 = V_0^2/Z_0 = 345^2/109.545 = 1086.54 \text{ MW}$
   (ii) Electrical length $\theta = 2 \times 4.64456° = 9.28912°$ $P_{max} = P_0/\sin\theta = 1086.54/\sin 9.28912° = 6731.28 \text{ MW}$

   (iii) $Q_s = P_0 \left[\dfrac{P^2 V_o^2}{P_o^2 V_m^2} - \dfrac{V_m^2}{V_o^2}\right] \dfrac{\sin\theta}{2} = 1086.54 \times [0.23^2 - 1]\dfrac{\sin 9.28912°}{2} = -83.054 \text{ MVA}$

   $Q_s < 0$, i.e. absorbing reactive power. At the receiving end $Q_r = -Q_s$, also absorbing.

   (iv) $E_s = E_r = \sqrt{1 - \left[1 - \dfrac{P^2}{P_o^2}\right]\sin^2\dfrac{\theta}{2}} = \sqrt{1 - [1 - 0.23^2]\sin^2 4.64456°} = 0.99689 \text{ p.u.}$

10. (i) Define the terms *surge impedance loading, transmission angle and electrical length* in relation to an electrical transmission line or cable.
    (ii) Write an equation for the phasor voltage $\mathbf{E}_s$ at the sending end of a lossless cable, in terms of the voltage $\mathbf{V}_r$, power P_r and reactive power Q_r at the receiving-end, if the electrical length is θ radians. Include the transmission angle δ in the expression for $\mathbf{E}_s$, and use it to derive an equation for the reactive power requirements Q_s and Q_r in terms of the transmission angle δ, the electrical length θ, and the voltages E_s and E_r.
    (iii) A cable having an electrical length of 8.7° has a rated voltage of 500 kV line–line, and a surge impedance $Z_0 = 50.4 \, \Omega$. (i) Determine the maximum transmissible power P_{max} when it is operated as a symmetrical line with $E_s = E_r = 500 \text{ kV}$; and (ii) Determine the transmission angle δ and the reactive power requirements at both ends of the cable when the power transmission is 47% of the surge impedance load.

    (i) Surge impedance load $=$ that load which produces a flat voltage profile, i.e. V_0^2/Z_0.
    Transmission angle $\delta =$ angle between E_s and E_r.

Electrical length θ = phase angle between E_s and E_r at the surge-impedance load.

(ii) $\mathbf{E_s} = \mathbf{E_s}e^{j\delta} = V_r\cos\theta + jZ_0\dfrac{P_r - jQ_r}{V_r}\sin\theta$

... use this to derive

$$Q_s = -Q_r = -\frac{E_s^2(\cos\delta - \cos\theta)}{Z_0\sin\theta}$$

(iii) (a) Surge impedance load $P_0 = V_0^2/Z_0 = 500^2/50.4 = 4960\,\text{MW}$ $P_{max} = P_0/\sin\theta = 4960/\sin 8.7° = 32\,793\,\text{MW}$.

(b) $P/P_0 = \sin\delta/\sin\theta = 0.47$, so $\sin\delta = 0.47 \times \sin 8.7°$, i.e. $\delta = 4.07674°$.
$Q_s = -Q_r = -500^2(\cos 4.07674° - \cos 8.7°)/(50.4\sin 8.7°)$
$= -294.3\,\text{MVAr}$ – absorbing at both ends.

11. (i) What are the functions of *reactive compensation* applied to electrical transmission systems?
(ii) What are the differences between *passive* and *active* compensators? Give examples of both.
(iii) By means of a sketch showing V_r/E_s vs. P/P_0, illustrate how the receiving-end voltage of a transmission cable can be maintained within a narrow range near 1.0 p.u. by means of switched shunt compensating devices. E_s is the sending-end voltage, P is the power transmission, and P_0 is the natural load.

(i) (a) to produce a flat voltage profile at all levels of power transmission;
(b) to improve stability by increasing the maximum transmissible power P_{max}; and
(c) to provide the most economical means for meeting the reactive power requirements.

(ii) Passive compensation = fixed or switched reactors and capacitors
Active compensation = continuously variable devices: e.g. thyristor-controlled reactors, synchronous condensers, AVRs used with turbine-generators; 'FACTS' devices.

(iii)

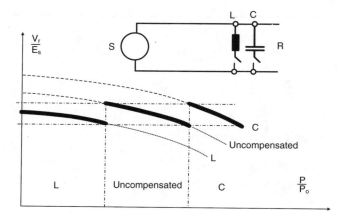

Fig. 9.6

12. (i) Write an equation for the phasor voltage $\mathbf{E}_s$ at the sending end of a lossless cable, in terms of the voltage $\mathbf{V}_r$, power P_r and reactive power Q_r at the receiving end, if the electrical length is θ radians. Use this equation to derive an expression for the reactance X required to make the no-load voltage at the receiving end of a radial transmission cable equal to the sending-end voltage.

   (ii) Using the theory of part (i) and any necessary development thereof, determine the values of four reactors equally spaced along a 500 kV, 80-km symmetrical line such that the no-load voltage profile is substantially flat. Of the four reactors, one is at the sending end and one at the receiving end, and the synchronous machines at the two ends contribute no reactive power. The line series inductive reactance is $0.60\,\Omega/\text{km}$ and shunt capacitive susceptance is $50.0\,\mu\text{S/km}$.

   (iii) What is the maximum voltage in the compensated line of part (b) at no-load, and where does it occur?

   (iv) What is the total combined reactive power of the four reactors at no-load and rated voltage?

   (i) $\mathbf{E}_s = \mathbf{V}_r \cos\theta + jZ_o\mathbf{I}_r \sin\theta = \mathbf{V}_r\left[\cos\theta + \dfrac{Z_o}{X}\sin\theta\right]$

   so that for $E_s = V_r$

   $$X = Z_o \frac{\sin\theta}{1 - \cos\theta}$$

   (ii) $\theta = 80 \times \sqrt{(0.60 \times 50 \times 10^{-6})} = 0.43818$ radians $= 25.1°$

   $Z_0 = \sqrt{(0.60/(50 \times 10^{-6}))} = 109.545\ \Omega$

   (iii) $2X$ at the ends and X at two intermediate locations (26.7 km from each end).

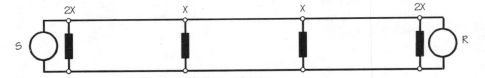

Fig. 9.7

$$X = \frac{Z_0}{2}\frac{\sin(\theta/n)}{1 - \cos(\theta/n)} = \frac{109.545}{2}\frac{\sin(25.1/3)}{1 - \cos(25.1/3)} = 748\ \Omega$$

   Maximum voltage is at the mid-point and at $80/6 = 13.3$ km from each end: $V_m = E_s/\cos(\theta/2n)$ with $n = 3$; i.e. $V_m = 500/\cos(25.1/6) = 500 \times 1.00267$ kV line–line or 1.00267 p.u.

   (iv) Total compensating reactive power $= (500/\sqrt{3})^2/748 \times 3 \times (1 + 1 + 1/2 + 1/2) = 1.003$ MVAr.

13. A 500-kV cable is 80 km long and has a mid-point dynamic shunt compensator that maintains the voltage at its terminals equal to 1.0 p.u. under all loading

conditions. The series inductive reactance of the line is $X_L = 48.0\,\Omega$ and the shunt capacitive susceptance is $B_c = 4000\,\mu S$. Calculate

(i) the transmission angle δ when the load is 1540 MW;
(ii) the value of the compensating susceptance B_γ and reactance X_γ at this load.

(i) $P = \dfrac{2E^2}{X_L}\sin\dfrac{\delta}{2} = 1540 = \dfrac{2 \times 500^2}{48}\sin\dfrac{\delta}{2}$

so $\delta = 17.0°$.

(ii) $B_\gamma = \dfrac{B_c}{2} - \dfrac{4}{X_L}\left[1 - \dfrac{E}{E_m}\cos\dfrac{\delta}{2}\right]$

$= \dfrac{4000 \times 10^{-6}}{2} - \dfrac{4}{48}\left[1 - \cos\dfrac{17°}{2}\right] = 0.00108\ S$

so $X_\gamma = 1/0.00108 = 922\,\Omega$.

Problem 13 – alternative solution (i)
In this solution, we represent the inductance and capacitance of the line by 'lumped parameters' distributed as shown in Fig. 9.8. The phasor diagram is shown in Fig. 9.9. Note the extensive use of symmetry in drawing these diagrams. Each half of the line is represented by a π equivalent circuit. The phasor diagram emphasizes the sending-end half of the line, with $\mathbf{E}_s$ at one end and $\mathbf{V}_m$ at the other; the receiving-end

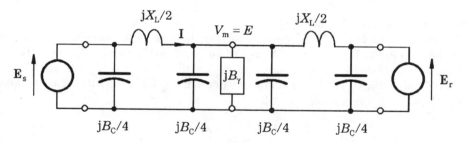

Fig. 9.8 Lumped-parameter representation of line with mid-point compensator.

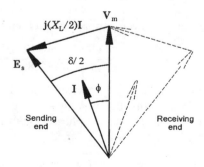

Fig. 9.9 Phasor diagram.

half is similar, with V_m at one end and E_r at the other. The voltages E_s and E_r are both equal to E and the reactive compensator maintains $V_m = E$.

For the sending-end half of the line we can write

$$P = \frac{E^2}{X_L/2} \sin \frac{\delta}{2}$$

so that $1540 = 500^2/24 \sin (\delta/2)$, giving $\delta/2 = 8.50177°$. This is the transmission angle over each half of the line, so the total transmission angle is $\delta = 17.0°$. By symmetry, the current phasor is at right-angles to the voltage-drop phasor joining V_m and E_s, so that the power-factor angle between I and V_m is $\phi = \delta/4 = 4.25089°$. The same power-factor angle is between E_s and I, but it is a lagging angle at the sending end and leading at the mid-point. This indicates that the line inductance is absorbing reactive power at both points. The reactive power absorbed by $X_L/2$ is $I^2 X_L/2$/phase. Since $\quad P = \sqrt{3} V_{LL} I_L \cos \phi, \quad I_L = 1540/(\sqrt{3} \times 500 \times \cos 4.25089°) = 1.78314\,\text{kA}$, so that the total reactive power absorbed is $3 I^2 X_L/2 = 228.93143\,\text{MVAr}$ in each half of the line, or $457.86286\,\text{MVAr}$ over the whole line. Of this, 25% is absorbed at the two ends and 50% $(228.93143\,\text{MVAr})$ at the mid-point. However, the shunt capacitance at the mid-point is *generating* $2 \times E^2 B_c/4 = 2 \times 500^2 \times (4000 \times 10^{-6}/4) = 500\,\text{MVAr}$. Therefore, the *net* reactive power at the mid-point is $500 - 228.93143 = 271.06857\,\text{MVAr}$, and this must be *absorbed* by the compensator. The compensator must therefore have an inductive susceptance $B_\gamma = 271.06857/500^2 = 0.00108\,\text{S}$, or a reactance $X_\gamma = 922.2\,\Omega$. At the sending end, the generator absorbs $271.06857/2 = 135.5\,\text{MVAr}$, and the same at the receiving end.

Problem 13 – alternative solution (ii)
We can treat the line as a 'long line' and use the distributed-parameter equations based on Z_0, θ, etc. Thus, $Z_0 = \sqrt{(X_L X_C)}$ where $X_L = 48\,\Omega$ and $X_C = 1/4000 \times 10^{-6} = 250\,\Omega$, so $Z_0 = 109.545\,\Omega$.[2] Also the electrical length is $\theta = \sqrt{(X_L/X_C)} = \sqrt{(48/250)} = 0.43818$ radians $= 25.10575°$. Taking just one half of the line, with equal voltages at both ends, we can use the equation

$$P = \frac{E^2}{Z_0 \sin \dfrac{\theta}{2}} \sin \frac{\delta}{2}$$

i.e. $1540 = 500^2/(109.545 \sin 25.10575°/2) \sin (\delta/2)$, giving $\delta = 16.87°$. (Note the slight difference from the $17.0°$ obtained with the 'lumped-parameter' method in solution (i) above.)

We can now find the reactive power required at each end of each half of the line:

$$Q_s = -\frac{E^2(\cos \delta - \cos \theta)}{Z_0 \sin \theta} = \frac{500^2(\cos 8.43346° - \cos 12.55288°)}{109.545 \sin 12.55288°} = -137.46\,\text{MVAr}$$

with the same at the receiving end and twice this value at the mid-point, i.e. $274.93\,\text{MVAr}$. The compensator must have a susceptance equal to $274.93/500^2 = 0.00110\,\text{S/phase}$, i.e. a reactance of $909.35\,\Omega/\text{phase}$. Again note the slight difference from the $922.2\,\Omega/\text{phase}$ calculated with the lumped-parameter model.

---

[2] Note that X_L is proportional to the line length, whereas X_C is inversely proportional to the line length, so that $Z_0 = \sqrt{(X_L X_C)} = \sqrt{(x_L x_C)}$, where X is total reactance and x is reactance per unit length.

In this solution, the line capacitance and inductance do not appear explicitly since they are incorporated in the constants Z_0 and θ.

The two ends of the line and the compensator in the middle are all absorbing reactive power, indicating that the line is working below its surge impedance loading. To check this, note that $P_0 = 500^2/109.545 = 2282$ MW, which is indeed greater than the power transmission of 1540 MW.

14. (i) What is meant by the *system load line* in relation to the voltage at a busbar in a power transmission system?

(ii) A power transmission system with a high $X{:}R$ ratio has a short-circuit level of 14 500 MVA. What is slope of the system load line in p.u./MVAr?

(i) The system load line shows the relation between V/E and Q/S, where V is the actual bus voltage, E is the no-load voltage, Q is the reactive power drawn from the bus, and S is the short-circuit level. The equation of the load line is approximately $V/E = 1 - Q/S$.

(ii) Slope of load-line $= \mathrm{d}(V/E)/\mathrm{d}(Q/S) = -1$.

15. An unbalanced three-phase load is delta-connected to a balanced power supply at 415 V line–line. The impedances are $Z_{ab} = 0.9584\,\Omega$ at unity power-factor; $Z_{bc} = 0.9584\,\Omega$ at 0.9 power-factor leading; and $Z_{ca} = 0.9584\,\Omega$ at 0.7 power-factor lagging. Determine the impedances of three reactive compensating capacitors or reactors connected in parallel with the three load impedances, such that the resulting load is balanced and has unity power factor. What is the line current of the compensated load?

$$Y_{ab} = G_{ab} + jB_{ab} = 1/0.9584 = 1.04341\ \text{S}$$

$$Y_{bc} = G_{bc} + jB_{bc} = 1/[0.9584e^{-j\,\text{Arc}\cos(0.9)}] = 0.93907 + j0.45481\ \text{S}$$

$$Y_{ca} = G_{ca} + jB_{ca} = 1/[0.9584e^{j\,\text{Arc}\cos(0.7)}] = 0.73038 - j0.74514\ \text{S}$$

$$B_{\gamma ab} = -B_{ab} + (G_{ca} - G_{bc})/\sqrt{3} = (0.73038 - 0.93907)/\sqrt{3}$$
$$= -0.12049\ \text{(inductive)}$$

$$B_{\gamma bc} = -B_{bc} + (G_{ba} - G_{ca})/\sqrt{3} = -0.45481 + (1.04341 - 0.73038)/\sqrt{3}$$
$$= -0.27408\ \text{(inductive)}$$

$$B_{\gamma ca} = -B_{ca} + (G_{bc} - G_{ab})/\sqrt{3} = 0.74514 + (0.93907 - 1.04341)/\sqrt{3}$$
$$= 0.68490\ \text{(capacitive)}$$

$$Z_{\gamma ab} = 1/(-j0.12049) = j8.30\,\Omega\ \text{(inductive)}$$
$$Z_{\gamma bc} = 1/(-j0.27408) = j3.65\,\Omega\ \text{(inductive)}$$
$$Z_{\gamma ca} = 1/(j0.68490) = -j1.46\,\Omega\ \text{(capacitive)}$$

Line current $I_L = (V_{LL}/\sqrt{3})/G$
where $G = G_{ab} + G_{bc} + G_{ca} = 1.04341 + 0.93907 + 0.73038 = 2.71286$.
Thus $I_L = (415/\sqrt{3})/2.71286 = 88.3$ A.

16. (i) Explain the difference between a *wye* connection and a *delta* connection, and mention one advantage of each connection.

(ii) Draw the circuit diagram of a wye-connected supply with a delta-connected load. Also draw two separate phasor diagrams, one for the voltages and currents of the supply, and the other for the voltages and currents of the load. Use the phasor diagrams to show that under balanced conditions

$$V_{LL} = \sqrt{3}V_{ph} \quad \text{and} \quad I_L = I_{ph} \text{ at the supply, and}$$

$$V_{LL} = V_{ph} \quad \text{and} \quad I_L = \sqrt{3}I_{ph} \text{ at the load;}$$

where I_L is the line current, I_{ph} is the phase current, V_{LL} is the line–line voltage, and V_{ph} is the phase voltage.

(iii) A 415-V, three-phase, three-wire supply has phase sequence RYB, with the following loads:

6.0 kW at unity power-factor between lines R,Y;
4.5 kW at 0.8 power-factor lagging between lines Y,B;
2.7 kW at 0.5 power-factor leading between lines B,R.

Taking $\mathbf{V_{RY}}$ as reference phasor, calculate all three-phase currents and all three-line currents. Hence, calculate the ratio of the average-line current to the average-phase current.

(i) Advantage of wye: provides earthing point. If three-wire, it suppresses tri-plen-harmonic currents and permits two-wattmeter method to be used. Advantage of delta: provides path for triplen currents.

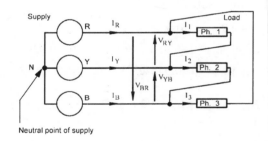

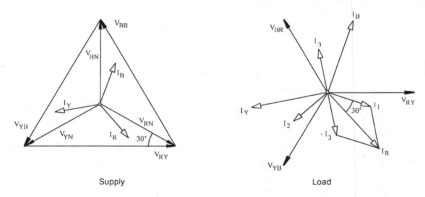

Fig. 9.10

(ii) From supply diagram, $I_L = I_{ph}$ in all three lines/phases. From the voltage diagram, $V_{RY} = 2\cos 30° \times V_{RN} = \sqrt{3}V_{RN}$; other lines/phases likewise. From load diagram, $I_R = I_1 - I_3$ and if balanced, $I_L = 2 \times \cos 30°$ $I_{ph} = \sqrt{3}I_{ph}$.

(iii) $6000 + j0 = V_{RY}I_{RY}^* = 415e^{j0}I_{RY}^*$ so $I_{RY} = 14.458A = I_1$

$(4500/0.8)e^{j\cos^{-1}(0.8)} = 415e^{-j120°}I_{YB}^*$ so $I_{YB} = 13.554e^{-j156.87°}A = -12.464 - j5.324A = I_2$

$(2700/0.5)e^{-j\cos^{-1}(0.5)} = 415e^{j120°}I_{BR}^*$ so $I_{BR} = -13.012A = I_3$

$I_R = I_1 - I_3 = 27.470A$

$I_Y = I_2 - I_1 = -26.922 - j5.324A = 27.444e^{-j168.813°}A$

$I_B = I_3 - I_2 = -0.548 - j5.324A = 5.352e^{j95.877°}A$

Average line current/Average phase current $= (27.470 + 27.444 + 5.352)/(14.458 + 13.554 + 13.012) = 1.469$.

17. (i) Draw a circuit diagram showing the connection of two wattmeters to measure the power in a three-wire supply to a three-phase load.

(ii) Using a suitable phasor diagram for the two-wattmeter connection, prove that the power-factor angle ϕ of a balanced load can be determined from the equation

$$\tan \phi = \sqrt{3}\frac{P_1 - P_2}{P_1 + P_2}$$

where P_1 and P_2 are the readings on the individual wattmeters.

(iii) A three-phase AC motor draws balanced currents from a three-phase supply. Its power factor is 0.85 lagging. The output power of the motor is 9.7 kW and the efficiency is 92%. Determine the individual readings P_1 and P_2 of two wattmeters measuring the input power to the motor in the two-wattmeter connection.

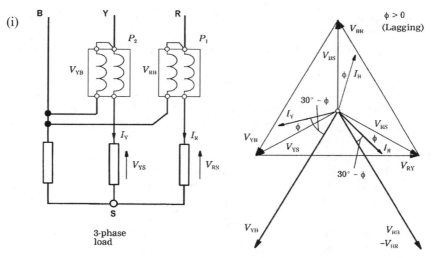

(i)

Fig. 9.11

(ii) $P_1 = V_{RB}I_R \cos(30° - \phi) = V_{LL}I_L(\cos 30° \cos \phi + \sin 30° \sin \phi)$
$P_2 = V_{YB}I_Y \cos(30° + \phi) = V_{LL}I_L(\cos 30° \cos \phi - \sin 30° \sin \phi)$
$P_1 + P_2 = V_{LL}I_L \times 2 \cos 30° \cos \phi = \sqrt{3}V_{LL}I_L \cos \phi = P$ (total power)
$P_1 - P_2 = V_{LL}I_L \times 2 \sin 30° \sin \phi = V_{LL}I_L \sin \phi$

Hence

$$\tan \phi = \sqrt{3}\frac{P_1 - P_2}{P_1 + P_2}$$

(iii) $P = 9700/0.92 = 10\,543\text{W} = P_1 + P_2$
$\tan \phi = \tan(\text{arc cos}(0.85)) = 0.620$

$\therefore P_1 - P_2 = 0.620/\sqrt{3} \times 10\,543 = 3.773\text{W}$
$P_1 + P_2 = 10\,543\text{W}$
$2P_1 = 10\,543 + 3773 = 14\,316$ so $P_1 = 7158\text{W}$
$2P_2 = 10\,543 - 3773 = 6770$ so $P_2 = 3385\text{W}.$

18. (i) State four distinct functions of power transformers.
   (ii) Draw the equivalent circuit of one phase of a three-phase power transformer, with all impedances referred to the HV (high-voltage) side.
   (iii) A 250-kVA, 10-kV/400-V, three-phase Yy0 transformer gave the following standard test data for the line–line voltage, line current, and total three-phase input power:

   Input to HV winding; LV short-circuited : $V_{LL} = 1005\,\text{V}$, $I_L = 14.4\,\text{A}$, $P = 2.49\,\text{kW}$.
   Input to LV winding; HV open-circuited: $V_{LL} = 400\,\text{V}$, $I_L = 3.886\,\text{A}$, $P = 2.50\,\text{kW}$.

   Make a neat sketch of an approximate equivalent circuit for one phase of this transformer, in which all the impedances R_1, R_2', jX_{L1}, jX_{L2}', R_c and jX_m are referred to the HV winding. Determine the values of these parameters.

(i)
• Transform voltage level for optimum transmission
• Transform current level for measurement (C.T.); or voltage (P.T. or V.T.)
• Isolate coupled circuits
• Impedance matching
• Introduce series impedance (to limit fault current)
• Create a neutral point (e.g. ground connection remote from power station)
• Suppress harmonics (especially triplen harmonics)
• Provide tappings for loads along a transmission line
• Produce phase shift or multiple phases (e.g. for multiple-pulse converters)
• Produce frequency-multiplication (saturated core)
• Constant-voltage reactive compensation (saturated core).

(ii)

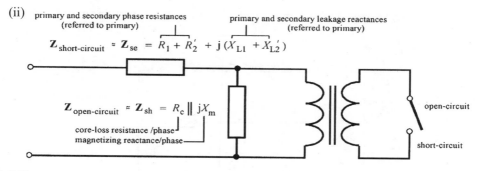

Fig. 9.12

(iii) In short-circuit test: $2490 = \sqrt{3} \times 1005 \times 14.4 \cos \phi$, so $\phi = 84.299°$ (current lags voltage). Neglecting $\mathbf{Z}_{sh}$, $\mathbf{Z}_{se} = (1005/\sqrt{3})/(14.4e^{-84.299°}) = 40.294e^{j84.299°}$ $\Omega = 4.00 + j40.0\,\Omega$ (referred to HV).

In open-circuit test: $2500 = \sqrt{3} \times 400 \times 3.886 \cos \phi$, so $\phi = 21.786°$
$\mathbf{Z}''_{sh} = (400/\sqrt{3})/(3.886e^{-21.786°}) = 59.429e^{j21.786°}$ ohm ($''$ means referred to LV)
$\mathbf{Z}_{sh} = (10\,000/400)^2 \mathbf{Z}''_{sh} = 37\,143e^{j21.786°}$ (referred to HV)
$\mathbf{Y}_{sh} = 1/\mathbf{Z}_{sh} = (1/37\,143)e^{-j21.786°} = 0.000025 - j0.00000992\,\text{S}$

$\therefore R_c = 1/0.000025 = 40\,000\,\Omega$;
$X_m = 1/0.00000992 = 100\,000\,\Omega$,
both referred to HV.

19. (i) Draw a circuit diagram *and* a phasor diagram showing how third-harmonic voltages cause oscillation of the star point in a three-phase electrical network.
   (ii) A delta-connected three-phase load has the following harmonic components of voltage and current in each phase:

Harmonic	rms voltage, V	rms current, A	Phase angle (deg.)
1	220	12.5	15
3	0	11.5	–
5	19	4.5	21
7	15	6	−26.0

Calculate

(a) the rms line current;
(b) the rms line–line voltage;
(c) the total mean power supplied; and
(d) the ratio of the actual I^2R losses to the I^2R losses that are attributable to the fundamental alone.

(i) Oscillation of the star point when the neutral is not connected

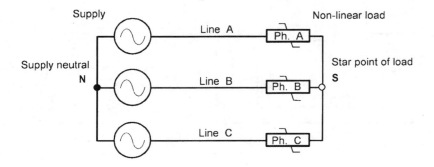

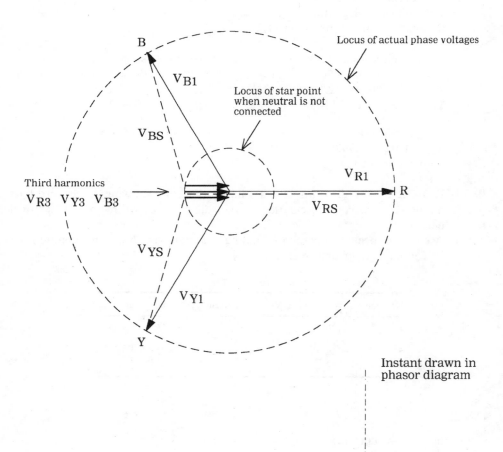

Fig. 9.13

(ii) (a) $I_{L(rms)} = \sqrt{[(\sqrt{3} \times 12.5)^2 + 0 + (\sqrt{3} \times 4.5)^2 + (\sqrt{3} \times 3.0)^2]}$
$= \sqrt{[468.75 + 0 + 60.75 + 27.0]}$
$= 23.59 \text{A(rms)}$

(b) $V_{L(rms)} = \sqrt{[220^2 + 19.0^2 + 15.0^2]}$
$= 221.33 \text{ V(rms)}$

(c) $P = 3 \times [220 \times 12.5 \cos 15.0° + 19.0 \times 4.5 \cos 21.0°$
$+ 15.0 \times 6.0 \cos(-26.0°)]$
$= 2656.30 + 79.82 + 80.89$
$= 2817.00 \text{ W}$

(d) Cable loss ratio $= I_{L(rms)}^2 / I_{1(rms)}^2 = 23.59^2 / (\sqrt{3} \times 12.5)^2 = 1.187$

20. (i) Draw the EMF phasor diagram for a Yd1 transformer. Also draw the configuration of the primary and secondary windings on a three-limb core. Include all internal connections and correct terminal labels.

(ii) A 230/66-kV Yd1 transformer gave the following test results:

Test	Line Current, A	Power factor	Condition
Open circuit	20	0.45	HV winding open 25% voltage on LV winding
Short circuit	120	0.08	LV winding shorted 2% voltage on HV winding

Draw an equivalent circuit for one phase and calculate the series impedance $\mathbf{Z}_{se} = R_e + jX_e$ and shunt admittance $\mathbf{Y}_{sh} = 1/R_c + 1/jX_m$, both referred to the HV side.

(i)

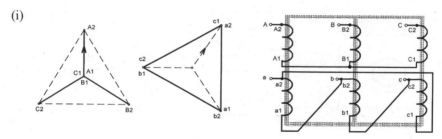

Fig. 9.14

(ii)

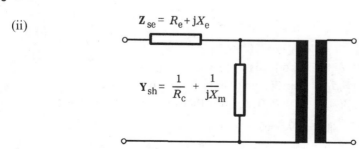

Fig. 9.15

From open-circuit test

$$Y_{sh} = \frac{20e^{-j\arccos(0.5)}}{0.25 \times \dfrac{66}{\sqrt{3}} \times 10^3} \times \left[\frac{230}{66}\right]^2 = 0.01148 - j0.02276S$$

giving $R_c = 87.11\,\Omega$ and $X_m = 43.94\,\Omega$.
From short-circuit test

$$Z_{se} = \frac{0.02 \times \dfrac{230}{\sqrt{3}}}{120} e^{j\arccos(0.08)} = 0.02213e^{j85.411°} = 0.00177 + j0.02206\,\Omega$$

giving $R_e = 0.00177\,\Omega$ and $X_e = 0.002206\,\Omega$.

21. (i) Draw a circuit diagram and a phasor diagram showing the use of two wattmeters to measure the total power in a three-phase three-wire AC load.
   (ii) Derive an expression for the power factor of a balanced three-phase AC load in terms of the wattmeter readings P_1 and P_2.
   (iii) An unbalanced delta-connected load on a three-phase 415-V 50-Hz supply has the following impedances in each phase:

   $$Z_{ab} = 15 + j0\,\Omega \quad Z_{bc} = 1.2 + j16.5\,\Omega \quad Z_{ca} = -j18.2\,\Omega.$$

   Determine the three-line currents in magnitude and phase, and the readings of two wattmeters connected such that P_1 measures I_a and V_{ac}, while P_2 measures I_b and V_{bc}. Take $\mathbf{V}_{ab}$ as reference phasor.

(i)

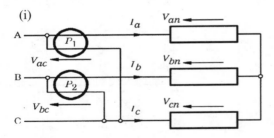
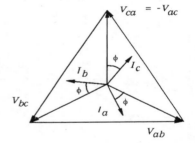

Fig. 9.16

(ii) $P_1 = \mathrm{Re}\{\mathbf{V}_{ac}\mathbf{I}_a^*\} = V_L I_L \cos(30° - \phi)$

$P_2 = \mathrm{Re}\{\mathbf{V}_{bc}\mathbf{I}_b^*\} = V_L I_L \cos(30° + \phi)$
$P_1 + P_2 = V_L I_L \times 2\cos 30° \cos(-\phi) = \sqrt{3}V_L I_L \cos\phi$
$P_1 - P_2 = -V_L I_L \times 2\sin 30° \sin(-\phi) = V_L I_L \sin\phi$
$\therefore \tan\phi = \sqrt{3}(P_1 - P_2)/(P_1 + P_2)\ldots.$ then power factor $= \cos\phi$.

(iii) $\mathbf{I}_{ab} = 415/(15 + j0) = 27.6667 + j0\,A$

$\mathbf{I}_{bc} = 415e^{-j120°}/(1.2 + j16.5) = 415e^{-120°}/16.54e^{j85.84°} = 25.085e^{-j205.84°}\,A$
$\mathbf{I}_{ca} = 415e^{j120°}/(-j18.2) = 22.80e^{j210°} = -19.75 - j11.40A$

$$\mathbf{I_a} = \mathbf{I_{ab}} - \mathbf{I_{ca}} = 47.41 + j11.40 = 48.76e^{j13.52°}\,\text{A}$$
$$\mathbf{I_b} = \mathbf{I_{bc}} - \mathbf{I_{ab}} = -50.24 + j10.94 = 51.42e^{j167.72°}\,\text{A}$$
$$\mathbf{I_c} = \mathbf{I_{ca}} - \mathbf{I_{bc}} = 2.83 - j22.33 = 22.51e^{-j82.78°}\,\text{A}$$

$$P_1 = \text{Re}\{\mathbf{V_{ac}I_a^*}\} = 415e^{-j60°} \times 48.76e^{-j13.52°} = 5741\text{W}$$
$$P_2 = \text{Re}\{\mathbf{V_{bc}I_b^*}\} = 415e^{-j120°} \times 51.42e^{-j167.72°} = 6496\text{W}$$

Check: $P_1 + P_2 = 12\,237\,\text{W}$

$$|\mathbf{I_{ab}}|^2 R_{ab} + |\mathbf{I_{bc}}|^2 R_{bc} + |\mathbf{I_{ca}}|^2 R_{ca} = 27.6667^2 \times 15 + 25.085^2 \times 1.2 = 12\,237\,\text{W}.$$

22. (i) What are the main disadvantages of *single-phase* distribution of AC electric power?
   (ii) Explain the methods used to reduce or eliminate the following harmonics in AC power systems:

   (i) odd triplen harmonics, i.e. 3rd, 9th, 15th etc.
   (ii) odd non-triplen harmonics, i.e. 5th, 7th, 11th, 13th etc.

   (iii) A star-connected, three-phase AC load is supplied with 415 V three-phase sinewave AC power at a frequency f Hz, and the star point is solidly connected to the supply neutral. The load impedances at 50 Hz (in ohms) are as follows:

   $$\mathbf{Z_a} = 9.184 + j0 \quad \mathbf{Z_b} = 3 + j17 \quad \mathbf{Z_c} = 3 - j17.$$

   Calculate the rms values and phase angles of the line currents and the neutral current when the frequency f is

   (a) 50 Hz
   (b) 150 Hz

(i) Unbalance; 100-Hz oscillation in the power flow causes vibration, noise, and lamp flicker. Single phase cannot by itself produce a rotating ampere-conductor distribution in electric motors (it needs a capacitor and a split-phase winding).
(ii) (a) Triplen harmonics are suppressed by star connection or trapped by delta connection; or taken by neutral wire.
   (b) Non-triplen harmonics. In electric machines, they are minimized by winding design (harmonic winding factors) and by having a sine-distributed magnetic flux around the airgap. In transformers, they are minimized by limiting the flux to a level below saturation. In non-linear power-electronic loads such as rectifiers, the 5th and 7th can be cancelled by using a 12-pulse rather than 6-pulse circuit. This requires a transformer with two secondaries, one wye and the other delta. Otherwise, the 5th and 7th can be filtered by damped or tuned filters built up from L, C and R elements.
(iii) (a) $\mathbf{I_a} = 415/\sqrt{3}/9.184 = 26.088\,\text{A}$
   $\mathbf{I_b} = 415/\sqrt{3}e^{-j120°}/(3 + j17) = 415/\sqrt{3}e^{-j120°}/17.263e^{j80°}$
   $\quad = 13.880e^{-j200.0°} = -13.044 + j4.745\,\text{A}$
   $\mathbf{I_c} = 415/\sqrt{3}e^{j120°}/(3 - j17) = 415/\sqrt{3}e^{j120°}/17.263e^{-j80°}$
   $\quad = 13.880e^{j200.0°} = -13.044 - j4.745\,\text{A}$
   $\mathbf{I_n} = \mathbf{I_a} + \mathbf{I_b} + \mathbf{I_c} = 0$

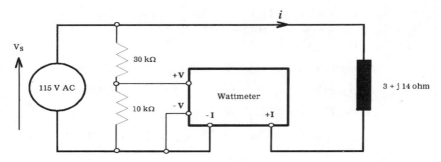

Fig. 9.17

(b) $I_a = 415/\sqrt{3}/9.184 = 26.088$ A (unchanged)

$I_b = 415/\sqrt{3}e^{-j120°}/(3 + j17 \times 150/50) = 415/\sqrt{3}e^{-j120°}/51.088e^{j86.634°}$

$= 4.690e^{-j206.634°} = -4.192 + j2.102$ A

$I_c = 415/\sqrt{3}e^{j120°}/(3 - j17 \times 50/150) = 415/\sqrt{3}e^{j120°}/6.412e^{-j62.103°}$

$= 37.369e^{j182.103°} = -37.344 - j1.371$ A

$I_n = I_a + I_b + I_c = -15.448 + j0.731 = 15.465e^{j177.29°}$ A.

23. (i) Draw a circuit diagram and a phasor diagram showing the two-wattmeter method of measuring power in a three-phase system.

 (ii) Prove from first principles that the two-wattmeter method is valid for instantaneous power and not just for average power.

 (iii) Figure 9.17 shows a single-phase load of $3 + j14\,\Omega$ supplied from a sinusoidal voltage source of rms value 115 V and frequency 50 Hz. A single-phase wattmeter is connected with its current coil in series with the load. The voltage coil is connected via a voltage divider circuit comprising resistors of $10\,k\Omega$ and $30\,k\Omega$ as shown.

Calculate

 (a) the current
 (b) the real and reactive power $P + jQ$ at the terminals
 (c) the reading W on the wattmeter
 (d) the wattmeter reading if the $10\,k\Omega$ resistor is replaced by a capacitor whose impedance at 50 Hz is $-j6.429\,k\Omega$.

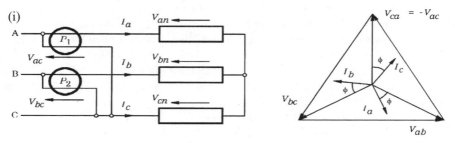

Fig. 9.18

 (ii) Total instantaneous power $p = v_a i_a + v_b i_b + v_c i_c$

With three-wire connection, $i_a + i_b + i_c = 0$

$$\therefore p = v_a i_a + v_b i_b - v_c(i_a + i_b)$$
$$= (v_a - v_c)i_a + (v_b - v_c)i_b$$
$$= v_{ab}i_a + v_{bc}i_b$$

(iii) (a) $\mathbf{I} = 115/(3 + j14) = 115/(14.318e^{j77.905°}) = 8.032e^{-j77.905°}$ A

(b) $P + jQ = \mathbf{VI}^* = 115 \times 8.032e^{j77.905°} = 193.537 + j903.171$ VA

(c) Wattmeter voltage coil reads only 1/4 of the load voltage, so the reading is
$W = 193.537/4 = 48.38$ W.

(d) Wattmeter voltage coil voltage is

$$115 \times \frac{-j6.429}{30 - j6.429} = 24.097e^{-j77.904°} \text{ V}$$

Wattmeter coil current is $8.032e^{-j77.905°}$ A.

$\therefore$ Wattmeter reads Re $\{\mathbf{VI}^*\} = $ Re$\{24.097e^{-j77.904°} \times 8.032e^{j77.905°}\}$
$$= 193.55 \text{ W}$$

24. (i) Draw the phasor diagram of induced voltages for a Yd11 transformer. Also draw the configuration of the primary and secondary windings on a three-limb core. Include all internal connections and correct terminal labels.

(ii) Draw the equivalent circuit for one phase of a three-phase transformer, including the total series resistance R_e and total series leakage reactance X_e referred to the primary, and the core-loss resistance R_c and magnetizing reactance X_m, also referred to the primary.

(iii) A 400-MVA, 230/66-kV Yy6 transformer has series impedances of $R_e = 2.0\,\Omega$/phase, and shunt impedances of $X_e = 20.0\,\Omega$/phase, $R_c = 13\,000\,\Omega$/phase and $X_m = 6\,500\,\Omega$/phase, all referred to the high-voltage winding. Calculate the three-phase power and reactive power supplied under the following test conditions:

Test	Condition
Open circuit	HV winding open
	25% voltage on LV winding
Short circuit	LV winding shorted
	2% voltage on HV winding

(i)

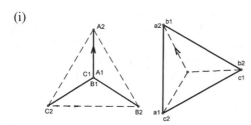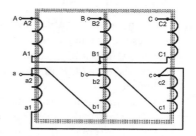

Fig. 9.19

(ii)

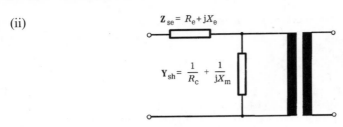

$Z_{se} = R_e + jX_e$

$Y_{sh} = \dfrac{1}{R_c} + \dfrac{1}{jX_m}$

Fig. 9.20

(iii) In the *open-circuit test* with no current at the HV terminals, the impedance looking in to the LV terminals is $[(R_e + jX_e) + (R_c \| jX_m)] \times (66/230)^2$, i.e.

$$\begin{aligned}
\mathbf{Z}_{LV} &= [2 + j20 + 13\,000 \times j6500/(13\,000 + j6500)] \times (66/230)^2 \\
&= 214.259 + j429.836\,\Omega \\
&= 480.277e^{j63.505°}\,\Omega/\text{phase(equivalent star)}
\end{aligned}$$

The line current is $\mathbf{I} = 0.25 \times 66 \times 10^3/\sqrt{3}/480.277e^{j63.505°} = 19.835e^{-j63.505°}$ A.

$\therefore P + jQ = 0.25 \times \sqrt{3} \times 66 \times 10^3 \times 19.835e^{j63.505°} = 252.886 + j507.326\,\text{kVA}$.

In the *short-circuit test* the impedance looking in at the HV terminals is
$(R_e + jX_e) \| (R_c \| jX_m) = (2 + j20) \| (13\,000 \| j6500) = 20.035e^{j84.219°}\,\Omega$
The current is $\mathbf{I} = 0.02 \times 230/\sqrt{3}/20.035e^{j84.219°} = 132.559e^{-j84.219°}$ A.

$\therefore P + jQ = 0.02 \times \sqrt{3} \times 230 \times 132.559e^{j84.219°} = 106.38 + j1050.8\,\text{kVA}$.

25. (i) Define the *surge impedance* of a transmission line or cable.
    Describe the operation of a power transmission cable under the following conditions:

    (a) when the load is *less than* the surge impedance load; and
    (b) when the load *exceeds* the surge impedance load.

    Assume that the voltage is maintained constant at rated value at both ends, and make particular reference to the voltage profile and the reactive power requirements at the ends.

    (ii) A transmission cable has a sending-end voltage $E_s = 245\,\text{kV}$ line–line. Losses may be neglected. The cable has an inductive reactance per unit length of $0.60\,\Omega/\text{km}$ and a capacitive admittance of $50.0\,\mu\text{S/km}$ at 60 Hz, and its length is $a = 74.8\,\text{km}$. Assuming that the receiving end is open-circuited, calculate
    (a) the surge impedance Z_0;
    (b) the electrical length θ in degrees;
    (c) the receiving-end voltage expressed in per-unit with E_s as reference;
    (d) the sending-end current;

(e) the reactive power at the sending end, in MVAr; and

(f) the reactive power at the sending end, expressed as a fraction of the surge-impedance loading.

(i) The surge impedance load P_0 is equal to V_0^2/Z_0 where $Z_0 = \sqrt{(l/c)} = \sqrt{(x_L x_C)}$, l being the inductance per unit length, c the capacitance per unit length, x_L the series inductive reactance per unit length, and x_C the shunt capacitive reactance per unit length along the line; and V_0 is the rated voltage. If V_0 is the line–line voltage, P_0 is the total power over all three phases. If V_0 is the line-neutral voltage, it is the power per phase. When the transmitted power P is equal to the surge impedance load, the voltage profile is flat and the reactive power requirements at the ends are zero.

(a) When $P < P_0$ the voltage rises towards the mid-point and reactive power must be absorbed at both ends to maintain the voltage equal to V_0.

(b) When $P > P_0$ the voltage falls towards the mid-point and reactive power must be generated at both ends to maintain the voltage equal to V_0.

(ii) (a) $Z_0 = \sqrt{(x_L \cdot x_C)} = \sqrt{(x_L/y_C)} = \sqrt{(0.60/50 \times 10^{-6})} = 109.55\,\Omega$

(b) $\beta = \sqrt{(x_L/x_C)} = \sqrt{(x_L \cdot y_C)} =$
$\sqrt{(0.60 \times 50 \times 10^{-6})} = 5.477 \times 10^{-3}$ radians/km $= 0.3138°$/km
so $\theta = \beta a = 0.3138 \times 74.8 = 23.47°$

(c) $V_r = \dfrac{E_s}{\cos\theta} = \dfrac{1.0}{\cos 23.47°} = 1.0902\,\text{p.u.} = 267\,\text{kV}$

(d) $I_s = j\dfrac{E_s}{Z_0}\tan\theta = \dfrac{245/\sqrt{3}}{109.55}\tan 23.47°\,\text{kA} = j561\,\text{A}$

(e) $Q_s = \sqrt{3} \times 245 \times 0.561 = 238\,\text{MVAr}$

(f) $P_0 = 245^2/109.55 = 548\,\text{MVA}$, so $Q_s/P_0 = 238/548 = 0.434\,\text{p.u.}$

26. (i) Explain why the TCR is preferred over the TSC when it is desired to have a reactive compensator with continuous control of the current.

(ii) Draw the complete power circuit diagram for a three-phase TCR, including shunt capacitors/filters, and a step-down transformer.

(iii) Draw the phase current waveform in relation to the phase voltage waveform, for a typical conduction angle of, say, $\sigma = 120°$.

(iv) A delta-connected TCR is connected to a 400-kV transmission line through a 7:1 step-down transformer. Its maximum reactive power at rated voltage is 100 MVAr. For a conduction angle of 115°, calculate

(a) the rms fundamental component of the line current at the high-voltage terminals of the transformer; and

(b) the peak current in each thyristor.

(i) The TCR permits continuous control of the fundamental component of line current by phase control, whereas the TSC can only adjust the current by switching between discrete values.

(ii)

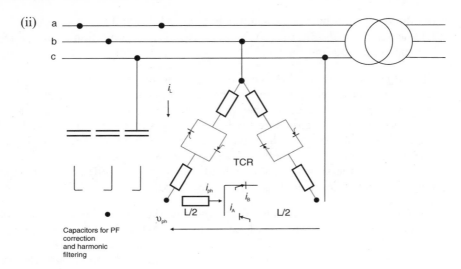

Capacitors for PF
correction
and harmonic
filtering

Fig. 9.21

(iii)

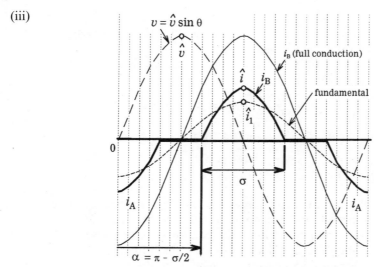

Phase voltage and current waveforms

Fig. 9.22

(iv) (a) First calculate X_L: $100 \times 10^6 = \sqrt{3} \times (400 \times 10^3/7) \times I_L$ so $I_L = 1010$ A
and $I_{ph} = 583.3$ A.

$\therefore X_L = (400 \times 10^3/7)/583.3 = 97.96\,\Omega$ in each phase.

$$I_{1L} = \sqrt{3} \times I_1 ph = \sqrt{3} \times \frac{V_{ph}}{X_L} \frac{\sigma - \sin \sigma}{\pi}$$

$$= \sqrt{3} \times \frac{400 \times 10^3}{7 \times 97.96} \times \frac{115 \times \dfrac{\pi}{180} - \sin 115°}{\pi} = 354\,\text{A}$$

at the low-voltage terminals of the transformer, i.e. $354/7 = 50.6\,A$ at the high-voltage terminals. (Note that this gives a total reactive power of $\sqrt{3} \times 400 \times \quad 0.506 = 35.0\,MVAr$, which corresponds to the fraction $(\sigma - \sin\sigma)/\pi$ of the rated MVAr, since $(\sigma - \sin\sigma)/\pi = 0.350$.)

(b) The phase delay angle is $\alpha = 180° - \sigma/2 = 122.5°$, so the peak phase current (occurring at $180°$) is

$$\hat{i} = \frac{\sqrt{2} \times V_{LLrms}}{X_L} \times (\cos\alpha - \cos\pi) = \frac{\sqrt{2} \times 400 \times 10^3}{7 \times 97.96}$$
$$\times (\cos 122.5° + 1) = 382\,A$$

27. (i) Explain with your own words and diagrams how the *frequency* and the *voltage* are controlled in an isolated power plant with a local load. Assume that the generator is a conventional wound-field synchronous machine driven by a diesel engine.

   (ii) Prove by means of a series of diagrams, or otherwise, that an unbalanced linear ungrounded three-phase load can be transformed into a balanced, real three-phase load without changing the power exchange between source and load, by connecting an ideal reactive compensating network in parallel with it. Assuming a delta-connected unbalanced load $Y_{ab} = G_{ab} + jB_{ab}$, $Y_{bc} = G_{bc} + jB_{bc}$, $Y_{ca} = G_{ca} + jB_{ca}$, derive expressions for the susceptances of the compensating network.

   (iii) An unbalanced delta-connected load draws the following power and reactive power from a three-phase supply whose line–line voltage is 560 V:

   200 kW between lines a, b
   170 kW at 0.85 power-factor lagging between lines b, c
   170 kW at 0.85 power-factor leading between lines c, a.

   Determine the susceptances of a purely reactive delta-connected compensating network that will balance this load and correct its power factor to unity. Also determine the resulting line currents.

   (i) Frequency is controlled by the speed governor on the prime mover. Voltage is controlled by the excitation in the generator.
   (ii) See Figure 9.23. General result is

$$B_{\gamma ab} = -B_{ab} + (G_{ca} - G_{bc})/\sqrt{3}$$
$$B_{\gamma bc} = -B_{bc} + (G_{ab} - G_{ca})/\sqrt{3} \qquad (9.23)$$
$$B_{\gamma ca} = -B_{ca} + (G_{bc} - G_{ab})/\sqrt{3}$$

   leaving $G = G_{ab} + G_{bc} + G_{ca}$ in each phase of a wye-connected resulting network.
   (iii) In each phase $P + jQ = VI^* = V^2 Y^*$ so $Y = (P - jQ)/V^2$ so

   in phase ab, $Y_{ab} = (200 - j0) \times 10^3/560^2 = 0.638 + j0\,S = G_{ab} + jB_{ab}$
   in phase bc, $Y_{bc} = (170 - j105.537) \times 10^3/560^2 = 0.542 - j0.336\,S = G_{bc} + jB_{bc}$

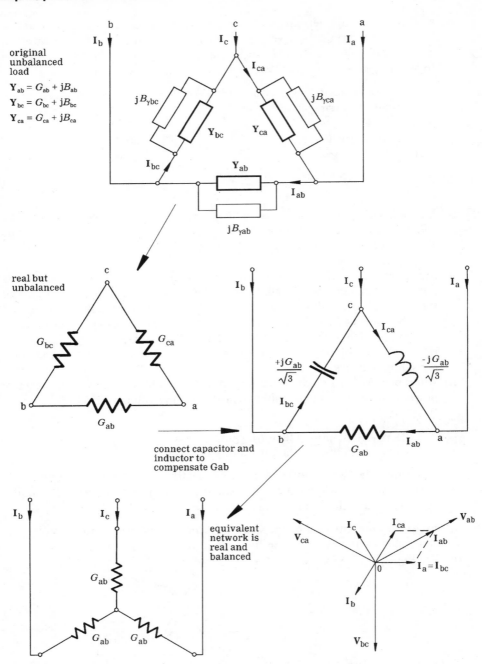

original unbalanced load

$\mathbf{Y}_{ab} = G_{ab} + jB_{ab}$

$\mathbf{Y}_{bc} = G_{bc} + jB_{bc}$

$\mathbf{Y}_{ca} = G_{ca} + jB_{ca}$

real but unbalanced

connect capacitor and inductor to compensate Gab

equivalent network is real and balanced

Fig. 9.23

in phase ca, $\mathbf{Y}_{ca} = (170 + j105.537) \times 10^3/560^2 = 0.542 + j0.336\,\mathrm{S} = G_{ca} + jB_{ca}$

$$B_{\gamma ab} = -0 + (0.542 - 0.542)/\sqrt{3} = 0\,\mathrm{S}$$

$$B_{\gamma bc} = -(-0.336) + (0.638 - 0.542)/\sqrt{3} = 0.391\,\mathrm{S}$$

$$B_{\gamma ca} = -0.336 + (0.542 - 0.638)/\sqrt{3} = -0.391\,\mathrm{S}$$

The resultant $G_{ph} = G_{ab} + G_{bc} + G_{ca} = 0.638 + 0.542 + 0.542 = 1.722\,\mathrm{S}$

$$I_{ph} = I_L = (560/\sqrt{3}) \times 1.722 = 556.75\,\mathrm{A}$$

and the total power is $\sqrt{3} \times 560 \times 556.75 = 540\,\mathrm{kW}$ (same as original unbalanced load).

28. (i) Write down the equations for the voltage and current profiles of a lossless power transmission line in terms of the receiving-end voltage $\mathbf{E}_r$, the receiving-end current $\mathbf{I}_r$, the surge impedance Z_0, and the wavenumber β. Also give formulas for β and Z_0 in terms of x_L, the series inductive reactance per unit length, and x_C the shunt capacitive reactance per unit length.

(ii) Using the equations in part (a), prove that the current at the sending-end of a symmetrical line is given by

$$\mathbf{I}_s = j\frac{\mathbf{E}_s}{Z_0}\frac{\sin\theta}{1 + \cos\theta}$$

where $\theta = \beta a$ is the electrical length of the line and a is the actual length. Also derive an equation for the mid-point voltage $\mathbf{V}_m$ in terms of $\mathbf{E}_s$ and θ. Sketch the profiles of $|\mathbf{V}(x)|$ and $|\mathbf{I}(x)|$ for $0 \leq x \leq a$, where x is distance along the line measured from the sending end.

(iii) A symmetrical cable line operates at no load with terminal voltages of 345 kV line–line. It has an inductive reactance of $0.56\,\Omega/\mathrm{km}$ and a capacitive admittance of $50.0\,\mu\mathrm{S/km}$ at 50 Hz. The cable length is $a = 19.8\,\mathrm{km}$. Calculate and draw to scale the phasor diagrams of line-to-neutral voltage and current

   (a) at the sending end;
   (b) at the mid-point; and
   (c) at the receiving end.

   Use the sending-end voltage $\mathbf{E}_s$ as the reference phasor for all three cases, in order to show the relative phase angles of the voltages and currents at the three positions.

(i) $\mathbf{V}(x) = \mathbf{V}_r \cos\beta(a - x) + jZ_0\mathbf{I}_r \sin\beta(a - x)$

$\mathbf{I}(x) = j\dfrac{\mathbf{V}_r}{Z_0}\sin\beta(a - x) + \mathbf{I}_r \cos\beta(a - x)$

where $\beta = \omega\sqrt{(lc)} = \sqrt{(x_L/x_C)}$ and $Z_0 = \sqrt{(l/c)} = \sqrt{(x_L x_C)}$.

(ii) From equations (a) with $x = 0$, using the symbol $\mathbf{E}$ for terminal (fixed) voltages

$$\mathbf{E}_s = \mathbf{E}_r \cos \theta + j Z_0 \mathbf{I}_r \sin \theta$$

$$\mathbf{I}_s = j\frac{\mathbf{E}_r}{Z_0} \sin \theta + \mathbf{I}_r \cos \theta$$

By symmetry $\mathbf{I}_s = -\mathbf{I}_r$ and from the equation for $\mathbf{E}_s$ we get

$$-\mathbf{I}_r = j\frac{\mathbf{E}_r}{Z_0}\frac{\sin \theta}{1 + \cos \theta} = j\frac{\mathbf{E}_r}{Z_0} \tan \frac{\theta}{2}$$

[Note the alternative form using $\tan (\theta/2)$]. With $\mathbf{E}_s = \mathbf{E}_r$ we get

$$\mathbf{I}_s = j\frac{\mathbf{E}_s}{Z_0}\frac{\sin \theta}{1 + \cos \theta}$$

Also the mid-point voltage is given by

$$\mathbf{V}_m = \mathbf{V}_r \cos \theta/2 + j Z_0 \mathbf{I}_r \sin \theta/2$$

$$= \mathbf{E}_s(\cos \theta/2 + \sin \theta/2 \tan \theta/2) = \mathbf{E}_s\left(\cos \theta/2 + \frac{\sin^2 \theta/2}{\cos \theta/2}\right) = \frac{\mathbf{E}_s}{\cos \frac{\theta}{2}}$$

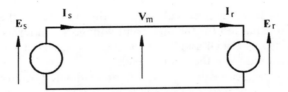

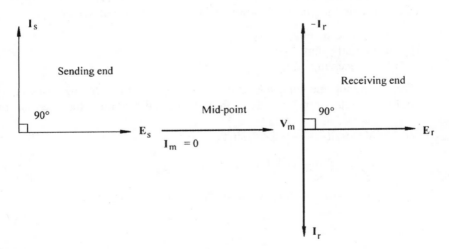

Fig. 9.24

(iii) We have $\mathbf{E}_s = 345/\sqrt{3} = 199.2e^{j0°}$ kV line-neutral and $\theta = \beta a = \sqrt{(0.56 \times 50 \times 10^{-6})} \times 19.8 = 0.105$ radians $= 6.003°$, and $Z_0 = \sqrt{(0.56/50 \times 10^{-6})} = 105.83\,\Omega$, so

$$\mathbf{I}_s = -\mathbf{I}_r = j\frac{345 \times 10^3/\sqrt{3}}{105.83} \times \frac{e^{j0} \sin 6.003°}{1 + \cos 6.003°} = j98.7\,A$$

At the mid-point, $\mathbf{V}_m = 199.2e^{j0°}/\cos(6.003/2°) = 199.46$ kV line-neutral, hardly changed from the sending-end and receiving-end values, since this is quite a short line. Also $\mathbf{I}_m = 0$.

Supplementary problems (no solutions)
29. (i) What are the functions of reactive compensation applied to electrical transmission systems? Distinguish between active and passive compensation.

(ii) By means of a sketch showing V_r/E_s vs. P/P_0, illustrate how the receiving-end voltage of a transmission cable can be maintained within a narrow range near 1.0 p.u. by means of switched shunt compensating devices. E_s is the sending-end voltage, P is the power transmission, and P_0 is the natural load.

(iii) Write an equation for the phasor voltage $\mathbf{E}_s$ at the sending end of a lossless cable, in terms of the voltage $\mathbf{V}_r$, power P_r and reactive power Q_r at the receiving end, if the electrical length is θ radians. Use this equation to derive an expression for the reactance X required to make the no-load voltage at the receiving end of a radial transmission cable equal to the sending-end voltage.

(iv) (a) Determine the value of a reactor placed at the mid-point of a 500 kV, 80-km symmetrical line such that the mid-point voltage is 1.0 p.u. The synchronous machines at the two ends maintain the voltage equal to 1.0 p.u. at both ends. The line series inductive reactance is $0.60\,\Omega/$km and shunt capacitive susceptance is $50.0\,\mu S/$km.

(b) What is the maximum voltage in the compensated line at no-load, and where does it occur?

(c) What is the reactive power of the mid-point reactor?

30. (i) Define the term *surge impedance* as used with electrical power transmission lines and cables. Briefly describe the properties of the voltage and current along a line that is operating at the so-called *surge-impedance load*.

(ii) Write down an equation for the sending-end voltage of a transmission line in terms of the receiving-end voltage $\mathbf{V}_r$, the receiving-end current $\mathbf{I}_r$, the surge impedance Z_0, and the electrical length of the line θ.

(iii) A transmission cable has a receiving end voltage $V_r = 345$ kV line–line. The load is wye-connected and is $264 + j142.5$ MVA/phase. Losses may be neglected. The cable has an inductive reactance per unit length of $0.60\,\Omega/$km and a capacitive admittance of $50.0\,\mu S/$km at 50 Hz. The cable length is $a = 14.8$ km. Calculate

(a) the receiving-end current, expressed as a phasor with $\mathbf{V}_r$ as reference;
(b) the surge impedance Z_0;

(c) the electrical length θ in radians and degrees;
(d) the sending-end voltage expressed as a phasor with $\mathbf{V}_r$ as reference;
(e) the sending-end current, expressed as a phasor with $\mathbf{V}_r$ as reference; and
(f) the power and reactive power at the sending end.

Appendix

This appendix presents the settings of the most relevant blocks used in the digital implementations developed in PSCAD/EMTDC, for each of the FACTS and Custom Power controllers considered in Chapter 8.

SVC

TITLE: SVC_FACTS
TIME-STEP: 3.5e-05
FINISH-TIME: 0.4
PRINT-STEP: 0.0005
RTDS-RACK: 0
RTDS REAL-TIME: Yes

SVC test power circuit (Figure 8.17)

Single-Phase Source
Mag	: 13.8 kV
f	: 50
Initial Phase	: 0.0
Ramp up time	: 0.0001 [sec]

Timed Breaker Logic
Initial State	: Open
Time of First Breaker Operation	: 0.6 [sec]

SVC controller (Figure 8.18)

PI Controller
Gp	: 2500
Ti	: 0.001

Hard Limiter
Upper limit	: 65.0
Lower limit	: −20

Filtering Blocks

NAME	: FIL1
G	: 1.0
DR	: 0.7
F	: 90
HP	: No
MP	: No
LP	: Yes

NAME	: FIL2
G	: 1.0
DR	: 0.16
F	: 120
HP	: Yes
MP	: No
LP	: Yes

NAME	: FIL3
G	: 1.0
DR	: 0.16
F	: 60
HP	: Yes
MP	: No
LP	: Yes

END

TCSC

TITLE: TCSC_FACTS
TIME-STEP: 3.5e-05
FINISH-TIME: 0.4
PRINT-STEP: 0.0005
RTDS-RACK: 0
RTDS REAL-TIME: Yes

TCSC test circuit example 1 (Figure 8.27)

Single-Phase Source

Mag	: 1 kV
f	: 50
Initial Phase	: 0.0
Ramp up time	: 0.0001 [sec]

TCSC test circuit example 2 (Figure 8.31)

Single-Phase Source

Mag	: 11 kV
f	: 50

Initial Phase   : 0.0
Ramp up time   : 0.0001 [sec]

PI Controller
Gp   : 15
Ti   : 0.001

Hard Limiter
Upper limit   : 38.0
Lower limit   : 0

Filtering Blocks
NAME   : FIL1
G   : 1.0
DR   : 0.7
F   : 90
HP   : No
MP   : No
LP   : Yes

NAME   : FIL2
G   : 1.0
DR   : 0.16
F   : 120
HP   : Yes
MP   : No
LP   : Yes

NAME   : FIL3
G   : 1.0
DR   : 0.16
F   : 60
HP   : Yes
MP   : No
LP   : Yes

Timed Breaker Logic
Initial State   : Open
Time of First Breaker Operation   : 1.8 [sec]

END

STATCOM

XDRAFT Version 4.2.2
EMTDC
TITLE: STATCOM_FACTS
TIME-STEP: 3.5e-05
FINISH-TIME: 0.4
PRINT-STEP: 0.0005

RTDS-RACK: 0
RTDS REAL-TIME: Yes

12-Pulse vsc-based STATCOM: power circuit (Figure 8.45)

Three-Phase Three-Winding Transformer (3)

Tmva	: 5
f	: 50
Xl12	: 0.1
Xl13	: 0.1
Xl23	: 0.1
V1	: 115
V2	: 115
V3	: 115

GTOs

RD	: 5000.0
CD	: 0.05
RON	: 0.01
ROFF	: 1.0E6
EFVD	: 0.001
EBO	: 1.0E5

Freewheeling Diodes

RD	: 5000.0
CD	: 0.05
RON	: 0.01
ROFF	: 1.0E6
EFVD	: 0.001
EBO	: 1.0E5

DC Voltage Source (2)

Ctrl	: RunTime
Vm	: 66
F	: 60.0
Tc	: 0.05
Imp	: RRL Values
ACDC	: DC

12-Pulse VSC-based STATCOM: switching controller (Figure 8.46)

Sine Modulators (6)

Type	: Sin
FMod	: Hertz
PMod	: Degrees

Triangle Generator TRIB1

F	: 50
P	: −210
Type	: Triangle
Duty	: 50
Max	: 1
Min	: −1

Triangle Generator TRIC1

F	: 50
P	: 30
Type	: Triangle
Duty	: 50
Max	: 1
Min	: −1

Triangle Generator TRIA1

F	: 50
P	: −90
Type	: Triangle
Duty	: 50
Max	: 1
Min	: −1

Triangle Generator TRIA2

F	: 50
P	: −120
Type	: Triangle
Duty	: 50
Max	: 1
Min	: −1

Triangle Generator TRIB2

F	: 50
P	: −240
Type	: Triangle
Duty	: 50
Max	: 1
Min	: −1

Triangle Generator TRIC2

F	: 50
P	: 0
Type	: Triangle
Duty	: 50
Max	: 1
Min	: −1

Comparators (6)

Pulse	: Level
OPos	: 1
ONone	: 0
ONeg	: 1
OHi	: 1
OLo	: 0

END

D-STATCOM

XDRAFT Version 4.2.2
EMTDC
TITLE: DSTATCOM_CUSTOM POWER
TIME-STEP: 5e-05
FINISH-TIME: 1.4
PRINT-STEP: 0.0005
RTDS-RACK: 0
RTDS REAL-TIME: Yes

D-STATCOM test power system (Figure 8.50)

Three-phase Voltage Source
Type	: R//L
Ctrl	: RunTime
MVA	: 100.0
Vm	: 230.0
F	: 50
Tc	: 0.0001
ZSeq	: No
Imp	: RRL Values
NHarm	: 0
R1s	: 26.45
R1p	: 1.0
L1p	: 0.1

Three-phase three-winding transformer
Tmva	: 100.0
f	: 50
YD1	: Y
YD2	: Y
YD3	: Y
Lead	: Leads
Xl12	: 0.1
Xl13	: 0.1
Xl23	: 0.1
V1	: 230.0
V2	: 11
V3	: 11

Breakers
NAME	: Brk1
OPEN	: Open
ROFF	: 1.0E6
RON	: 0.005

NAME	: Brk1b
OPEN	: Closed
ROFF	: 1.0E6
RON	: 0.005

```
NAME      : Brk2
OPEN      : Open
ROFF      : 1.0E6
RON       : 0.01

NAME      : Brk2b
OPEN      : Closed
ROFF      : 1.0E6
RON       : 0.01
```

Timed Breaker Logic
```
NAME      : Brk1
TO        : 0
TC        : 5

NAME      : Brk1b
TO        : 1.0
TC        : 5

NAME      : Brk2
TO        : 0.0
TC        : 0.8

NAME      : Brk2b
TO        : 1.0
TC        : 5
```

Active/Reactive Power meter
```
P     : Yes
Q     : Yes
TS    : 0.02
```

Three-phase rms calculator
```
Ts       : 0.025
Scale    : 11
```

GTOs
```
RD        : 5000.0
CD        : 0.05
RON       : 0.01
ROFF      : 1.0E6
EFVD      : 0.001
EBO       : 1.0E5
```

Freewheeling Diodes
```
RD        : 5000.0
CD        : 0.05
RON       : 0.01
ROFF      : 1.0E6
EFVD      : 0.001
EBO       : 1.0E5
```

D-STATCOM controller (Figure 8.51)

Filtering Blocks

NAME	: FIL1
G	: 1.0
DR	: 0.7
F	: 90
HP	: No
MP	: No
LP	: Yes

NAME	: FIL2
G	: 1.0
DR	: 0.16
F	: 120
HP	: Yes
MP	: No
LP	: Yes

NAME	: FIL3
G	: 1.0
DR	: 0.16
F	: 60
HP	: Yes
MP	: No
LP	: Yes

PI Controller

GP	: Gp
TI	: 0.001
YHI	: 50
YLO	: −10
YINIT	: 5

Proportional Gain Gp

Desc	: Gp
Value	: 350
Max	: 6000
Min	: 0.0

Sine Modulator

Type	: Sin
FMod	: Hertz
PMod	: Degrees

Triangle Generator

F	: 450
P	: −95
Type	: Triangle
Duty	: 50

```
Max      : 1
Min      : -1
```

END

DVR

XDRAFT Version 4.2.2
EMTDC
TITLE: DVR_CUSTOM POWER
TIME-STEP: 5e-05
FINISH-TIME: 1.4
PRINT-STEP: 0.0005
RTDS-RACK: 0
RTDS REAL-TIME: Yes

DVR test power system (Figure 8.57)

Three-Phase Voltage Source
```
Type      : R
Ctrl      : RunTime
MVA       : 100.0
Vm        : 13.0
F         : 50.0
Tc        : 0.02
ZSeq      : No
Imp       : RRL Values
NHarm     : 0
R1s       : 0.1
R1p       : 1.0
L1p       : 0.1
Z1        : 1.0
```

DC Voltage Source
```
Ctrl      : RunTime
Vm        : 2.5
F         : 0.0
Tc        : 0.05
Imp       : RRL Values
ACDC      : DC
```

Three-Phase Three-Winding Transformer
```
Tmva      : 100.0
f         : 50.0
YD1       : Y
YD2       : Delta
YD3       : Y
Lead      : Lags
Xl12      : 0.1
```

```
Xl13      : 0.1
Xl23      : 0.1
V1        : 13
V2        : 275
V3        : 275
```

Three-phase Two-Winding Transformers (2)
```
Tmva      : 100.0
f         : 50
YD1       : Y
YD2       : Delta
Lead      : Lags
Xl        : 0.1
V1        : 275
V2        : 11
```

Single-Phase Transformers (3)
```
Tmva      : 100
f         : 50
Xl        : 0.10
V1        : 11
V2        : 11
```

Breakers
```
NAME      : Brka, Brkb, Brkc
OPEN      : Closed
ROFF      : 1.E6
RON       : 0.005

NAME      : Brkaa, Brkbb, Brkcc
OPEN      : Open
ROFF      : 1.E6
RON       : 0.005
```

Timed Breaker Logic
```
NAME      : Brka, Brkb, Brkc
TO        : 0.8
TC        : 5

NAME      : Brkaa, Brkbb, Brkcc
TO        : 0
TC        : 1.0
```

Logic Faulted Timed
```
TF        : 0.8
DF        : 0.2
```

Fault Specifications
```
RON       : 1.6
ROFF      : 1.0E6
A         : Yes
B         : Yes
C         : Yes
G         : Yes
```

Three-Phase RMS calculator
Ts   : 0.02
Scale   : 11

GTOs
RD   : 5000.0
CD   : 0.05
RON   : 0.01
ROFF   : 1.0E6
EFVD   : 0.001
EBO   : 1.0E5

Freewheeling Diodes
RD   : 5000.0
CD   : 0.05
RON   : 0.01
ROFF   : 1.0E6
EFVD   : 0.001
EBO   : 1.0E5

DVR controller (Figure 8.58)

PI Controller
GP   : Gp
TI   : Ti
YHI   : 100
YLO   : −100
YINIT   : 85

Proportional Gain Gp
Desc   : Gp
Value   : 350
Max   : 6000
Min   : 0.0

Sine Modulator
Type   : Sin
FMod   : Hertz
PMod   : Degrees

Triangle Generator
F   : 1250
P   : −95
Type   : Triangle
Duty   : 50
Max   : 1
Min   : −1

Comparators (3)
Pulse   : Level
OPos   : 1
ONone   : 0
ONeg   : 1

OHi   : 1
OLo   : 0

END

PFC

XDRAFT Version 4.2.2
EMTDC
TITLE: PFC_CUSTOM POWER
TIME-STEP: 5e-05
FINISH-TIME: 0.35
PRINT-STEP: 5e-05
RTDS-RACK: 0
RTDS REAL-TIME: Yes

PFC test power system (Figure 8.65)

Three-Phase Voltage Source
    Ctrl   : RunTime
    MVA   : 100
    Vm   : 13.8
    F   : 50
    Tc   : 0.0001
    ZSeq   : No
    Imp   : RRL Values
    NHarm   : 0
    R1s   : 0.1
    R1p   : 10
    L1p   : 0.001
    Z1   : 1.0

Three-Phase Two-Winding Transformer
    Tmva   : 100
    f   : 50
    YD1   : Y
    YD2   : Delta
    Lead   : Leads
    Xl   : 0.1
    V1   : 13.8
    V2   : 6.75

Breakers
    NAME   : Brk
    OPEN   : Open
    ROFF   : 1.0E6
    RON   : 0.08

Timed Breaker Logic
    NAME   : Brk
    TO   : 0
    TC   : 0.15

Active/Reactive Power Meter
    P   : Yes
    Q   : Yes
    TS   : 0.02

GTOs
    RD   : 5000.0
    CD   : 0.05
    RON   : 0.01
    ROFF   : 1.0E6
    EFVD   : 0.001
    EBO   : 1.0E5

Freewheeling Diodes
    RD   : 5000.0
    CD   : 0.05
    RON   : 0.01
    ROFF   : 1.0E6
    EFVD   : 0.001
    EBO   : 1.0E5

PFC controller: transformation abc → dq0 and control loops (Figure 8.66)

Filtering Blocks (3)
    NAME   : Fil1
    G   : 1.0
    DR   : 0.7
    F   : 85
    HP   : No
    MP   : No
    LP   : Yes

    NAME   : Fil2
    G   : 1.0
    DR   : 0.16
    F   : 100
    HP   : Yes
    MP   : No
    LP   : Yes

    NAME   : Fil3
    G   : 1.0
    DR   : 0.16
    F   : 50
    HP   : Yes
    MP   : No
    LP   : Yes

Modulators

Type	: Cos
FMod	: Hertz
PMod	: Degrees

Type	: Sin
FMod	: Hertz
PMod	: Degrees

PI Controller d

GP	: 0.8
TI	: 0.001
YHI	: 25
YLO	: −25
YINIT	: 25

PI Controller q

GP	: 0.8
TI	: 0.0001
YHI	: 24
YLO	: −24
YINIT	: 25

PI Controller DC

GP	: 0.8
TI	: 0.01
YHI	: 10
YLO	: −10
YINIT	: 0.0

PFC controller: transformation dq0 → abc and PWM generators (Figure 8.67)

Triangle Generator

F	: 1050
P	: 35
Type	: Triangle
Duty	: 50
Max	: 1
Min	: −1

Comparators (3)

Pulse	: Level
OPos	: 1
ONone	: 0
ONeg	: 1
OHi	: 1
OLo	: 0

END

SHUNT AF

XDRAFT Version 4.2.2
EMTDC
TITLE: Shunt AF_Custom Power
TIME-STEP: 5e-05
FINISH-TIME: 0.4
PRINT-STEP: 0.0001
RTDS-RACK: 0
RTDS REAL-TIME: Yes

Shunt AF test power system (Figure 8.80)

Three-Phase Voltage Source

Ctrl	: RunTime
MVA	: 100
Vm	: 13.8
F	: 50
Tc	: 0.0001
ZSeq	: No
Imp	: RRL Values
NHarm	: 0
R1s	: 0.1
R1p	: 10
L1p	: 0.001
Z1	: 1.0

Three-Phase Two-Winding Transformer

Tmva	: 100
f	: 50
YD1	: Y
YD2	: Delta
Lead	: Leads
Xl	: 0.1
V1	: 13.8
V2	: 6.75

Breaker

NAME	: Brk1
OPEN	: Open
ROFF	: 1.0E6
RON	: 0.08

Timed Breaker Logic

NAME	: Brk1
TO	: 0
TC	: 0.1

Active/Reactive Power Meter

P	: Yes
Q	: Yes
TS	: 0.02

GTOs

RD	: 5000.0
CD	: 0.05
RON	: 0.01
ROFF	: 1.0E6
EFVD	: 0.001
EBO	: 1.0E5

Thyristors

RD	: 5000.0
CD	: 0.05
RON	: 0.01
ROFF	: 1.0E6
EFVD	: 0.001
EBO	: 1.0E5

Freewheeling Diodes

RD	: 5000.0
CD	: 0.05
RON	: 0.01
ROFF	: 1.0E6
EFVD	: 0.001
EBO	: 1.0E5

Shunt AF controller: transformation abc → dq0 (Figure 8.81)

Modulators

Type	: Cos
FMod	: Hertz
PMod	: Degrees
Type	: Sin
FMod	: Hertz
PMod	: Degrees

Filtering Blocks (6)

G	: 1.0
DR	: 0.7
F	: 85
HP	: No
MP	: No
LP	: Yes
G	: 1.0
DR	: 0.16
F	: 100
HP	: Yes
MP	: No
LP	: Yes
G	: 1.0
DR	: 0.16
F	: 50

HP : Yes
MP : No
LP : Yes

Shunt AF controller: control loops (Figure 8.82)

PI Controller d
GP : 80
TI : 0.0001
YHI : 25
YLO : −25
YINIT : −10

PI Controller q
GP : 80
TI : 0.000075
YHI : 25
YLO : −25
YINIT : −10

PI Controller CD
GP : 1
TI : 0.001
YHI : 10
YLO : −10
YINIT : 0.0
COM : PI Controller

Shunt AF controller: PWM generators (Figure 8.83)

Triangle Generator
F : 1050
P : 35
Type : Triangle
Duty : 50
Max : 1
Min : −1

Comparators (3)
Pulse : Level
OPos : 1
ONone : 0
ONeg : 1
OHi : 1
OLo : 0

Shunt AF controller: rectifier firing angle control (Figure 8.84)

Triangle Generator Pos
F : 50
P : 0.0

```
        Type     : Triangle
        Duty     : 99.5
        Max      : 1
        Min      : 0
```

Comparator Pos
```
        Pulse    : Level
        OPos     : 1
        ONone    : 0
        ONeg     : 0
        OHi      : 1
        OLo      : 0
```

Triangle Generator Neg
```
        F        : 50
        P        : 180
        Type     : Triangle
        Duty     : 99.5
        Max      : 1
        Min      : 0
```

Comparator Neg
```
        Pulse    : Level
        OPos     : 1
        ONone    : 0
        ONeg     : 1
        OHi      : 1
        OLo      : 0
```

END

SSTS

XDRAFT Version 4.2.2
EMTDC
TITLE: SSTS_CUSTOM POWER
TIME-STEP: 5e-05
FINISH-TIME: 0.7
PRINT-STEP: 0.0005
RTDS-RACK: 0
RTDS REAL-TIME: Yes

SSTS test power system (Figure 8.94)

Three-Phase Voltage Source (2)
```
        Ctrl     : RunTime
        MVA      : 100.0
        Vm       : 13
        F        : 50
        Tc       : 0.0
```

```
ZSeq      : No
Imp       : RRL Values
NHarm     : 0
R1s       : 0.1
R1p       : 1.0
L1p       : 0.1
Z1        : 1.0
```

Transformers

Step-Up Three-Phase Three-Winding (2)
```
Tmva      : 100.0
f         : 50.0
YD1       : Y
YD2       : Delta
Lead      : Lags
Xl        : 0.1
V1        : 13
V2        : 115
```

Step-Down Three-Phase Three-Winding (2)
```
Tmva      : 100.0
f         : 50.0
YD1       : Delta
YD2       : Y
Lead      : Lags
Xl        : 0.1
V1        : 115
V2        : 13
```

Fault Specifications
```
RON       : 1.0
ROFF      : 1.0E6
A         : Yes
B         : Yes
C         : Yes
G         : Yes
```

Logic Fault Timed
```
TF        : 0.3108
DF        : 0.2
```

Three-Phase RMS Meter
```
Ts        : 0.02
Scale     : 13
```

Thyristors
```
RD        : 5000.0
CD        : 0.05
RON       : 0.01
ROFF      : 1.0E6
EFVD      : 0.001
EBO       : 1.0E5
```

SSTS controller (Figure 8.95)

Integrator

Extrn	: Internal
Reset	: No
COM	: Integrator
T	: 0.0001
Yo	: 0.01
YRst	: 0.0
YHi	: 10
YLo	: -10

Comparator time1

Pulse	: Pulse
OPos	: 1
ONone	: 0
ONeg	: 1
OHi	: 1
OLo	: 0

Comparator Vatmax

Pulse	: Level
OPos	: 1
ONone	: 0
ONeg	: 1
OHi	: 1.0
OLo	: -1.0

Comparator Vrefmax

Pulse	: Pulse
OPos	: 1
ONone	: 0
ONeg	: 1
OHi	: 1.0
OLo	: 1.0

Comparator ZeroC

Pulse	: Pulse
OPos	: 1
ONone	: 0
ONeg	: -1
OHi	: 1.0
OLo	: -1

Comparator DTA1

Pulse	: Level
OPos	: 1
ONone	: 0
ONeg	: 1
OHi	: 1
OLo	: 0

END

Bibliography

Acha, E., Harmonic Domain Representation of Thyristor Controlled Reactors, *Proceedings of the IEE 5th International Conference on AC and DC Power Transmission*, London, UK, pp. 404–406, 17–20 September 1991.

Acha, E., Flexible HVDC Light Model for Large Scale Power Flows. *Internal Report*, University of Glasgow, Glasgow, UK, 2001.

Acha, E. and Abur, A., Flexible HVDC Light Model for Large Scale Power Flows and State Estimation Studies, to be presented at *5th International Conference on Power System Management and Control*, London, UK, 16–19 April 2002.

Acha, E., Ambriz-Perez, H. and Fuerte-Esquivel, C.R., Advanced Transformer Control Modelling in an Optimal Power Flow Using Newton's Method, *IEEE Transactions on Power Systems*, Vol. 15, No. 1, pp. 290–298, February 2000.

Acha, E., Arrillaga, J., Medina, J.A. and Semlyen, A., A General Frame of Reference for the Analysis of Harmonic Distortion with Multiple Transformer Non-Linearities, *IEE Proceedings on Generation, Transmission and Distribution*, Part C, Vol. 136, No. 5, pp. 271–278, September 1989.

Acha, E., Rico, J.J., Acha, S. and Madrigal, M., Harmonic Modelling in Hartley's Domain with Particular Reference to Three Phase Thyristor-Controlled Reactors, *IEEE Transactions on Power Delivery*, Vol. 12, No. 4, pp. 1622–1628, October 1997.

Acha, E. and Madrigal, M., *Power Systems Harmonics: Computer Modelling and Analysis*, John Wiley & Sons, Chichester, England, 2001.

Agelidis, V.G. and Calais, M., Application Specific Harmonic Performance Evaluation of Multicarrier PWM Techniques, *IEEE Power Electronics Specialists Conference*, Fukuoka, Japan, pp. 172–178, June 1998.

Agelidis, V.G., Keerthipala, W.W.L. and Lawrance, W.B., Multi-Modular Multilevel PWM Converter Systems, *Nordic Workshop on Power and Industrial Electronics*, Espoo, Finland, pp. 56–60, August 1998.

Agelidis, V.G. and Xu, L., A Novel HVDC System Based on Flying Capacitor Multilevel PWM Converters, *Paper presented at the International Conference on Power Systems 2001, Organised by CIGRE Study Committee 14*, Wuhan, China, September 2001.

Agrawal, B. and K. Shenoi, Design Methodology for $\Sigma\Delta M$, *IEEE Transactions on Communications*, Vol. 31, No. 3, pp. 360–370, March 1983.

Akagi, H., Utility Applications of Power Electronics in Japan. *Proceedings of IEEE Industrial Electronics Conference (IECON)*, Vol. 2, pp. 409–416, 1997.

Akagi, H., New Trends in Active Filters for Power Conditioning, *IEEE Transactions on Industry Applications*, Vol. 32, No. 6, November–December 1996.

Aliwell, R.W. and Crees, D.E., Development of a Self-Protected Light-Triggered Thyristor. *Proceedings of IEE Colloquium No. 104*, 7.1–7.3, April 1994.

Ambriz-Perez, H., Flexible AC Transmission Systems Modelling in Optimal Power Flows Using Newton's Method, PhD Thesis, The University of Glasgow, Glasgow, UK, December 1998.

Ambriz-Perez, H., Acha, E. and Fuerte-Esquivel, C.R., Advanced SVC Models for Newton-Raphson Load Flow and Newton Optimal Power Flow Studies, *IEEE Transactions on Power Systems*, Vol. 15, No. 1, pp. 129–136, February 2000.

Anderson, P.M., *Analysis of Faulted Power Systems*, the Iowa State University Press, 1973.

Anderson, P.M. and Fouad, A.A., *Power System Control and Stability*, the Iowa State University Press, 1977.

Aree, P., Small-Signal Stability Analysis of Electronically Controlled Power Networks, PhD Thesis, The University of Glasgow, Glasgow, UK, April 2000.

Arrillaga, J., *HVDC Transmission*, IEE Publications, London, 1999.

Arrillaga, J. and Watson, N.R., *Computer Modelling of Electrical Power Systems*, John Wiley & Sons, 2nd edition, Chichester, England, 2001.

Arrillaga, J., Watson, N.R. and Chan, S., *Power System Quality Assessment*, Wiley & Sons, Chichister, England, 2000.

Asano, K. and Sugawara, Y., Unified Evaluation and Figure of Merit for 8-kV 3.5-kA Light-Triggered Thyristor. *Proceedings of International Symposium on Power Semiconductors and Devices (ISPSD)*, Kyoto, Japan, 229, 1998.

Asplund, G., Application of HVDC Light to Power System Enhancement, *IEEE Winter Meeting, Session: Development and Application of Self-Commutated Converters in Power Systems*, Singapore, January 2000.

Asplund, G., Eriksson, K. and Svensson, K., HVDC Light – DC Transmission Based on Voltage Sourced Converters, *ABB Review*, No. 1, pp. 4–9, 1998.

Baliga, B.J., Power Semiconductor Devices for Variable Frequency Drives. Chapter 1, *Power Electronics and Variable Frequency Drives – Technology and Applications*, edited by B.K. Bose, IEEE Press, New York, NY, USA, 1997.

Bellar, M.D., Wu, T.S., Tchamdjou, A., Mahdavi, J. and Ehsani, M., A Review of Soft-Switched DC–AC Converters. *IEEE Transactions on Industry Applications*, Vol. 34, No. 4, pp. 847–860, July/August 1998.

Bhagwat, P.M. and Stefanovic, V.R., Generalised Structure of a Multilevel PWM Inverter, *IEEE Transactions on Industry Applications*, Vol. 19, No. 6, pp. 1057–1069, November/December, 1983.

Blaabjerg, F., Snubbers in PWM-VSI-Inverter, *Proceedings of IEEE Power Electronics Specialists Conference* (PESC), pp. 104–111, 1991.

Blackburn, D.L., Status and Trends in Power Semiconductor Devices, *Record of IEEE Conference on Industrial Electronics, Control and Instrumentation* (IECON), Vol. 2, pp. 619–625, 1993.

Bohmann, L. and Lasseter, R.H., Harmonic Interactions in Thyristor Controlled Reactor Circuits, *IEEE Transactions on Power Delivery*, Vol. 4, No. 3, pp. 1919–1926, July 1989.

Borgard, L., Grid Voltage Support. *Transmission & Distribution World*, October 1999.

Bornhardt, K., Novel Modulation Techniques for DC-Side Commutated Inverters, *Record of European Power Electronics Conference* (EPE), pp. 92–97, 1987.

Bornhardt, K., New Possibilities for DC-Side Commutated Inverter Circuits, *Record of European Power Electronics Conference* (EPE), pp. 549–554, 1989.

Bornhardt, K., Novel Soft-Switched GTO Inverter Circuits, *Record of IEEE Industry Applications Society Annual Meeting*, pp. 1222–1227, 1990.

Bose, B.K., Power Electronics: A Technology Review, *Proceedings of the IEEE*, Vol. 80, No. 8, pp. 1303–1334, August 1992.

Bose, B.K. (ed.), *Power Electronics and Variable frequency Drives: technology and Applications*, IEEE Press, 1997.

Bose, B.K., Evaluation of Modern Power Semiconductor Devices and Future Trend of Converters, *Record of IEEE Industry Applications Society Annual Meeting*, pp. 790–797, 1989.

Bose, B.K., Power Electronics: An Emerging Technology, *IEEE Transactions on Industrial Electronics*, Vol. 36, No. 3, pp. 403–412, August 1989.

Bose, B.K., Evaluation of Modern Power Semiconductor Devices and Future Trends of Converters, *IEEE Transactions on Industry Applications*, Vol. 28, No. 2, pp. 403–413, 1992.

Bose, B.K., Power Electronics and Motion Control – Technology Status and Recent Trends, *Proceedings of IEEE Power Electronics Specialists Conference (PESC)*, pp. 3–10, 1992.

Bose, B.K., Recent Advances in Power Electronics, *IEEE Transactions on Power Electronics*, Vol. 7, No. 1, pp. 2–16, January 1992.

Bose, B.K., Power Electronics and Motion Control – Technology Status and Recent Trends, *IEEE Transactions on Industry Applications*, Vol. 29, No. 5, pp. 902–909, September/October 1993.

Bowes, S.R., Advanced Regular-Sampled PWM Control Techniques for Drives and Static Power Converters, *IEEE Transactions Industrial Electronics*, Vol. 42, No. 4, pp. 367–373, August 1995.

Bowes, S.R. and Clark, P.R., Regular-Sampled Harmonic-Elimination PWM Control of Inverter Drives, *IEEE Transactions on Power Electronics*, Vol. 10, No. 5, pp. 521–531, September 1995.

Bowes, S.R. and Grewal, S., Novel Harmonic Elimination PWM Control Strategies for Three-Phase PWM Inverters Using Space Vector Techniques, *IEE Proceedings: Electric Power Applications*, Vol. 146, No. 5, pp. 495–514, 1999.

Bowes, S.R. and Lai, Y.S., Investigation into Optimising High Switching Frequency Regular Sampled PWM Control for Drives and Static Power Converters, *IEE Proceedings: Electric Power Applications*, Vol. 143, No. 4, pp. 281–293, July 1996.

Bowes, S.R. and Lai, Y.S., The Relationship between Space-Vector Modulation and Regular-Sampled PWM, *IEEE Transactions on Industrial Electronics*, Vol. 44, No. 5, pp. 670–679, October 1997.

Bremner, J.J., Torque Coefficient Analysis of Multi-Device Power Systems, PhD Thesis, The University of Glasgow, Glasgow, UK, September 1996.

Brown, H.E., *Solution of Large Networks by Matrix Methods*, John Wiley & Sons, New York, 1975.

Calais, M., Agelidis, V.G. and Meinhardt, M., Multilevel Converters for Single-Phase Grid-Connected Photovoltaic Systems: An Overview. *Solar Energy*, Vol. 66, No. 5, pp. 325–335, 1999.

Carrera, G., Marchesoni, M., Salutari, R. and Sciutto, G., A New Multilevel PWM Method: A Theoretical Analysis, *IEEE Transactions Power Electronics*, Vol. 7, No. 3, pp. 497–505, July 1992.

Chen, Y., Mwinyiwiwa, B., Wolanski, Z. and Ooi, B.T., Unified Power Flow Controller (UPFC) based on Chopper Stabilised Diode-Clamped Multilevel Converters, *IEEE Transactions on Power Electronics*, Vol. 15, No. 2, pp. 258–267, March 2000.

Chen, Y. and Ooi, B.T., Advanced Static Var-Compensator using Multimodules of Multilevel Converters with Equalisation Control of DC Voltage Levels, *Proceedings of IEEE PESC '96*, Baveno, pp. 747–752, Italy, 1996.

Chen, Y., Mwinyiwiwa, B., Wolanski, Z. and Ooi, B.T., A Regulating and Equalising DC Capacitor Voltages in Multilevel Advanced Static VAR Compensator, *IEEE Transactions on Power Delivery*, Vol. 12, pp. 901–907, April 1997.

Cheng, P.T., Bhattacharya, S. and Divan, D.M., Application of Dominant Harmonic Active Filter System with 12 Pulse Nonlinear Loads. *IEEE Transactions on Power Delivery*, Vol. 14, No. 2, pp. 642–647, April 1999.

Cho, J.G., Kim, H.S. and Cho, G.H., Novel Soft Switching PWM Converter using a New Parallel Resonant DC-Link, *Record of IEEE Power Electronics Specialists Conference (PESC)*, pp. 241–247, 1991.

Choi, J.W. and Sul, S.K., Resonant Link Bidirectional Power Converter without Electrolytic Capacitor, *Record of IEEE Power Electronics Specialists Conference (PESC)*, pp. 293–299, 1993.

Choi, N.S., Cho, G.C. and Cho, G.H., Modelling and Analysis of a Static Var Compensator using Multilevel Voltage Source Inverter, *Proceedings of IEEE Industry Applications Annual Meeting*, pp. 901–908, 1993.

Christl, N., Hedin, R., Johnson, R., Krause P. and Montoya, A., Power System Studies and Modelling for Kayenta 230 kV Substation Advanced Series Compensation, *Proceedings of the IEE 5th International Conference on AC and DC Power Transmission*, London, UK, pp. 33–37, 17–20, September 1991.

Cibulka, Frank, Crane, Lynn, Marks and John, Field Evaluation of Industry's First Self-Protected Light-Triggered Thyristor. *IEEE Transactions on Power Delivery*, Vol. 5, No. 1, pp. 110–116, January 1990.

Dehmlow, M., Heumann, K. and Sommer, R., Losses in Active Clamped Resonant DC-Link Inverter Systems, *Record of IEEE Power Electronics Specialists Conference (PESC)*, pp. 496–502, 1993.

de Mello, F.P., Power System Dynamics Overview, IEEE 75 CH070-4-PWR, Winter Power Meeting, 1975.

Dewan, S.B. and Straughen, A., Power Semiconductor Circuits, J. Wiley & Sons, Inc., 1975.

Dewinkel, C. and Lamoree, J.D., Storing Power for Critical Loads, *IEEE Spectrum*, Vol. 30, No. 6, pp. 38–42, June 1993.

Divan, D.M., Inverter Topologies and Control Techniques for Sinusoidal Output Power Supplies, *Record of IEEE Applied Power Electronics Conference and Exposition (APEC)* pp. 81–87, 1991.

Divan, D.M., The Resonant DC Link Converter – A New Concept in Static Power Conversion, *IEEE Transactions on Industry Applications*, Vol. 25, No. 2, pp. 317–325, March/April 1989.

Divan, D.M. and Skibinski, G., Zero-Switching-Loss Inverters for High Power Applications, *IEEE Transactions on Industry Applications*, Vol. 25, No. 4, pp. 634–643, July/August 1989.

Divan, D.M., Venkataramanan, G. and De Doncker, R.W., Design Methodologies for Soft Switched Inverters, *IEEE Transactions on Industry Applications*, Vol. 29, No. 1, pp. 126–135, January/February 1993.

Divan, D.M., Malesani, L., Tenti, P. and Toigo, V., A Synchronised Resonant DC Link Converter for Soft-Switched PWM, *IEEE Transactions on Industry Applications*, Vol. 29, No. 5, pp. 940–948, September/October 1993.

Divan, D.M., Venkataramanan, V., Malesani, L. and Toigo, V., Control Strategies for Synchronized Resonant Link Inverters, *Record of International Power Electronics Conference (IPEC)*, pp. 338–345, 1990.

Dommel, H.W., Digital Computer Solution of Electromagnetic Transients in Single and Multiphase Networks, *IEEE Transactions on Power Apparatus and Systems*, Vol. PAS-88, pp. 388–399, April 1969.

Edris, A., FACTS Technology Development: An Update, *IEEE Power Engineering Review*, Vol. 20, No. 3, pp. 4–9, March 2000.

Ekanayake, J.B. and Jenkins, N., Selection of Passive Elements for a Three-Level Inverter Based Static Synchronous Compensator, *IEEE Transactions on Power Delivery*, Vol. 14, No. 2, pp. 655–661, April 1999.

Ekanayake, J.B. and Jenkins, N., A Three-Level Advanced Static Var Compensator, *IEEE Transactions on Power Delivery*, Vol. 11, No. 1, pp. 540–545, January 1996.

Ekanayake, J.B. and Jenkins, N., Mathematical Models of a Three-Level Advanced Static Var Compensator, *IEE Proceedings, Generation, Transmission and Distribution*, Vol. 144, No. 2, pp. 201–206, March 1997.

EPRI, Light-Triggered Thyristors for Electric Power Systems, 932, November 1978.

Erinmez, I.A. (ed.), Static Var Compensators, Working Group 38-01, Task Force No. 2 on SVC, *CIGRE*, 1986.

Evans, P.D. and Mestha, L.K., Analysis of Conventional Snubber Circuits for PWM Inverters using Bipolar Transistors, *IEE Proceedings*, Vol. 135, Part. B, No. 4, pp. 180–192, July 1988.

Fairnley, W., Myles, A., Whitelegg, T.M. and Murray, N.S., Low Frequency Oscillations on the 275 kV Interconnectors between Scotland and England, *CIGRE Conference*, Paper 31-08, 1982.

Ferraro, A., An Overview of Low-Loss Snubber Technology for Transistor Converters, *Record of IEEE Power Electronics Specialists Conference (PESC)*, pp. 466–477, 1982.

Finney, S.J., Green, T.C. and Williams, B.W., Spectral Characteristics of Resonant Link Inverters, *Record of IEEE Power Electronics Specialists Conference (PESC)* 1992, pp. 607–614.

Fitzgerald, A.E., Kingsley, C. and Umans, S.D., *Electrical Machinery*, 4th edition, McGraw-Hill, New York, 1983.

Freris, L.L. and Sasson, A.M., Investigation of the Load Flow Problem, *Proceedings of IEE*, Vol. 115, No. 10, pp. 1459–1470, October 1968.

Fuerte-Esquivel, C.R., Modelling and Analysis of Flexible AC Transmission Systems, PhD Thesis, The University of Glasgow, Glasgow, UK, September 1997.

Fuerte-Esquivel, C.R. and Acha, E., A Newton-Type Algorithm for the Control of Power Flow in Electrical Power Networks, *IEEE Transactions on Power Systems*, Vol. 12, No. 4, pp. 1474–1480, November 1997.

Fuerte-Esquivel, C.R., Acha, E. and Ambriz-Perez, H., A Comprehensive UPFC Model for the Quadratic Load Flow Solution of Power Networks, *IEEE Transactions on Power Systems*, Vol. 15, No. 1, pp. 102–109, February 2000.

Ghiara, T., Marchesoni, M. and Sciutto, G., High Power Factor Control System in Multilevel Converters for AC Heavy Traction Drives. *Proceedings of IEEE Applied Power Electronics Conference*, pp. 672–680, 1990.

Gönen, T., *Electric Power Distribution System Engineering*, McGraw-Hill, New York, 1986.

Grant, D.A. and Gowar, J., *Power MOSFETs: Theory and Applications*, John Wiley & Sons, Inc., 1989.

Gross, G. and Galiana, F.D., Short-Term Load Forecasting, *Proceedings of the IEEE*, Vol. 75, No. 12, pp. 1558–1572, December 1987.

Gyugyi, L., Power Electronics in Electric Utilities: Static Var Compensators, *Proceedings of the IEE*, Vol. 76, No. 4, pp. 483–494, April 1988.

Gyugyi, L., A Unified Power Flow Control Concept for Flexible AC Transmission Systems, *IEE Proceedings*, Part C, Vol. 139, No. 4, pp. 323–331, July 1992.

Gyugyi, L., Schauder, S.L., Williams, S.L., Rietmann, T.R., Torgerson, D.R. and Edris, A., The Unified Power Flow Controller: A New Approach to Power Transmission Control, *IEEE Transactions on Power Delivery*, Vol. 10, pp. 1085–1097, April 1995.

Gyugyi, L. and Schauder, C., US Patent, 5, 343, 139, August 30, 1994.

Habelter, T. and Divan, D.M., Performance Characterization of a New Discrete Pulse Modulated Current Regulator, *Record of IEEE Industry Applications Society Annual Meeting*, pp. 395–405, 1988.

Hansen, A. and Havemann, H., Design of Snubber Circuits for a Transistor-Inverter using a Minimum Number of Components, *Record of IFAC Control in Power Electronics and Electrical Drives*, Lausanne, Switzerland, pp. 165–171, 1983.

Hasegawa, T., Yamaji, K., Irokawa, H., Shirahama, H., Tanaka, C. and Akabane, K., Development of a Thyristor Value for Next Generation 500-kV HVDC Transmission Systems, *IEEE Transactions on Power Delivery*, Vol. 11, No. 4, pp. 1783–1788, October 1996.

Hayashi, T. and Takasaki, M., Transmission Capability Enhancement using Power Electronics Technologies for the Future Power System in Japan, *Electric Power Systems Research*, 44, pp. 7–14, (1998).

He, J., Mohan, N. and Wold, B., Zero-Voltage-Switching PWM Inverter for High-Frequency DC–AC Power Conversion, *IEEE Transactions on Industry Applications*, Vol. 29, No. 5, pp. 959–968, September/October 1993.

Heier, S., *Grid Integration of Wind Energy Conversion Systems*, John Wiley & Sons, Chichester, England, 1998.

Heinke, F. and Sittig, R., Monolithic Bidirectional Switch, MBS, *International Symposium on Semiconductor Power Devices & ICs, ISPSD*, Toulouse, May 22–26, 2000.

Helbing, S.G. and Karady, G.G., Investigation of an Advanced Form of Series Compensation, *IEEE Transactions on Power Delivery*, Vol. 9, No. 2, pp. 939–947, April 1994.

Heumann, K., Power Electronics – State of the Art, *Record of International Power Electronics Conference (IPEC)*, pp. 1–10, 1990.

Hingorani, N.G., Power Electronics in Electric Utilities: Role of Power Electronics in Future Power Systems, *Proceedings of the IEEE*, Vol. 76, No. 4, pp. 481–482, April 1998.

Hingorani, N.G., High Power Electronics and Flexible AC Transmission System, *IEEE Power Engineering Review*, pp. 3–4, July 1998.

Hingorani, N.G., Flexible AC Transmission Systems, *IEEE Spectrum*, Vol. 30, No. 4, pp. 41–48, April 1993.

Hingorani, N.G., Introducing Custom Power, *IEEE Spectrum*, Vol. 32, No. 6, pp. 41–48, June 1995.

Hingorani, N.G., High-Voltage DC Transmission: A power electronics workhorse, *IEEE Spectrum*, Vol. 33, No. 4, pp. 63–72, April 1996.

Hingorani, N.G. and Gyugyi, L., *Understanding FACTS: Concepts and Technology of Flexible AC Transmission Systems*, The Institute of Electrical and Electronics Engineers, Inc., New York, 2000.

Hochgraf, C., Lasseter, R., Divan, D. and Lipo, T.A., Comparison of Multilevel Inverters for Static Var Compensation, *Proceedings of IEEE Industry Applications Annual Meeting* pp. 921–928, 1994.

Hoft, R.G., Semiconductor Power Electronics, Van Nostrand Reinhold, 1986.

Holtz, J. and Salama, S.F., Megawatt GTO-Inverter with Three-Level PWM Control and Regenerative Snubber Circuits, *Proceedings of IEEE Power Electronics Specialists Conference*, pp. 1263–1270, 1988.

Holtz, J., Salama, S. and Werner, K.H., A Nondissipative Snubber Circuit for High-Power GTO Inverters, *IEEE Transactions on Industry Applications*, Vol. 25, No. 4, pp. 620–626, July/August, 1989.

Hull, J.R., *IEEE Spectrum*, Vol. 20, July 1997.

IEEE Power Engineering Society, FACTS Overview, *International Conference on Large High Voltage Electric Systems*, 1995.

IEEE/CIGRE Working Group, FACTS Overview, *IEEE PES Special Publication* 95-TP-108, 1995.

IEEE/CIGRE, FACTS Overview, Special Issue, 95-TP-108, *IEEE Service Center*, Piscataway, NJ, 1995.

IEEE Industry Applications Society/Power Engineering Society, IEEE Recommended Practices and Requirements for Harmonic Control in Electrical Power Systems, *IEEE Std 519–1992*, April 1993.

IEEE Special Stability Controls Working Group, Static Var Compensator Models for Power Flow and Dynamic Performance Simulation, *IEEE Transactions on Power Systems*, Vol. 9, No. 1, pp. 229–240, February 1995.

Kassakian, J.G., Schlecht, M.F. and Verghese, G.V., *Principles of Power Electronics*, Addison-Wesley, 1991.

Katoh, S., Choi, J.H., Yokota, T., Watanabe, A., Yamaguchi, T. and Saito, K., 6-kV, 5.5-kA Light-Triggered Thyristor, *Proceedings of IEEE International Symposium on Power Semiconductor Devices (ISPSD)*, pp. 73–76, 1997.

Kheraluwala, M. and Divan, D.M., Delta Modulation Strategies for Resonant Link Inverters, *Record of IEEE Power Electronics Specialists Conference (PESC)*, pp. 271–278, 1987.

Kimbark, E.W., *Power System Stability. Volume III: Synchronous Machines*, IEEE Press Power Systems Engineering Series, The Institute of Electrical and Electronic Engineers, New York, 1995.

Kinney, S.J., Mittelstadt, W.A. and Suhrbier, R.W., The Results and Initial Experience for the BPA 500 kV Thyristor Controlled Series Capacitor Unit at Slatt Substation, Part I – Design, Operation and Fault Test Results, *Flexible AC Transmission Systems: The Future in High Voltage Transmission Conference, EPRI*, Baltimore, Maryland, October 1994.

Kundur, P., *Power Systems Stability and Control*, the EPRI Power System Engineering Series, McGraw-Hill, New York, 1994.

Lai, J. and Peng, F.Z., Multilevel Converters – A New Breed of Power Converters. *IEEE Transactions on Industry Applications*, Vol. 32, No. 3, pp. 509–517, May/June 1996.

Lai, J.S. and Bose, B.K., High Frequency Quasi-Resonant DC Voltage Notching Inverter for AC Motor Drives, *Record of IEEE Industry Applications Society Annual Meeting*, pp. 1202–1207, 1990.

Lai, Y.S. and Bowes, S.R., New Suboptimal Pulse-Width Modulation technique for Per-Phase Modulation and Space Vector Modulation, *IEEE Transactions on Energy Conversion*, Vol. 12, No. 4, pp. 310–316, December 1997.

Lander, C.W., Power Electronics, McGraw Hill, 1993.

Larsen, E.V., Bowler, C., Damsky, B. and Nilsson, S., Benefits of Thyristor Controlled Series Compensation, *International Conference on Large High Voltage Electric Systems (CIGRE)*, Paper 14/37/38-04, Paris, September 1992.

Ledu, A., Tontini, G. and Winfield, M., Which FACTS Equipment for Which Need?, *International Conference on Large High Voltage Electric Systems (CIGRE)*, Paper 14/37/38-08, Paris, September 1992.

Lipo, T.A., Recent Progress in the Development of Solid-State AC Motor Drives, *IEEE Transactions on Power Electronics*, Vol. 3, No. 2, pp. 105–117, April 1988.

Lipphardt, G., Using a Three-Level GTO Voltage Source Inverter in a HVDC Transmission System, *Proceedings of European Power Electronics and Applications Conference*, pp. 151–155, 1993.

Lips, H.P., Matern, R., Neubert, R., Popp, L. and Uder, M., Light-Triggered Thyristor Valve for HVDC Application, *Proceedings of 7th European Conference on Power Electronics and Applications EPE97*, Trondheim, Norway, Vol. 1, No. 287, 1997.

Lorenz, R.D. and Divan, D.M., Dynamic Analysis and Experimental Evaluation of Delta Modulators for Field Oriented AC Machine Regulators, *Record of IEEE Industry Applications Society Annual Meeting*, pp. 196–201, 1987.

Lund, R., Manjrekar, M.D., Steimer, P. and Lipo, T.A., Control Strategies for a Hybrid Seven-Level Inverter, *Conference Record of EPE*, pp. 1–10, 1999.

Malesani, L., Tenti, P., Divan, D.M. and Toigo, V., A Synchronized Resonant DC Link Converter for Soft-Switched PWM, *Record of IEEE Industry Applications Society Annual Meeting*, pp. 1037–1044, 1989.

Malesani, L., Tomasin, P. and Toigo, V., Modulation Techniques for Quasi Resonant DC Link PWM Converters, *Record of IEEE Industry Applications Society Annual Meeting*, pp. 789–795, 1992.

Manias, S. and Ziogas, P.D., A Novel Current Impulse Commutation Circuit for Thyristor Inverters, *IEEE Transactions on Industry Applications*, Vol. IA-19, No. 2, pp. 244–249, March/April, 1983.

Manjrekar, M. and Venkataramaan, G., Advanced Topologies and Modulation Strategies for Multilevel Inverters, *Conference Proceedings of IEEE PESC*, Vol. 2, pp. 1013–1018, 1996.

Manjrekar, M.D. and Lipo, T.A., A Hybrid Multilevel Inverter for Drive Applications, *Conference Record of IEEE Applied Power Electronics Conference*, pp. 523–529, 1998.

Marchesoni, M., High Performance Current Control Techniques for Applications to Multilevel High-Power Voltage Source Inverters, *IEEE Transactions on Power Electronics*, Vol. 7, No. 1, pp. 189–204, January 1992.

Martinez, S. and Aldana, F., Current-Source Double DC-Side Forced Commutated Inverter, *IEEE Transactions on Industry Applications*, Vol. IA-14, No. 6, pp. 581–593, November/December 1978.

Mathur, R.M., A Study of Noncharacteristic Harmonics Generated by Thyristor Phase Controlled Reactors, *IEE Conference Publication 205*, pp. 117–120, 1981.

Matthias, J., Improved Snubber for GTO Inverters With Energy Recovery by Simple Passive Network, *Record of European Power Electronics Conference (EPE)*, pp. 15–20, 1987.

Mazda, F.F., *Power Electronics Handbook, Components, Circuits and Applications*, Butterworth, 1993.

McHattie, R., Dynamic Voltage Restorer: The Customer's Perspective, *IEE Colloquium on Dynamic Voltage Restorers*, Digest No. 98/189, Glasgow, Scotland, UK, 1998.

McMurray, W., Feasibility of GTO Thyristors in a HVDC Transmission System, EPRI EL-5332, Project 2443-5, Final Report, August 1987.

McMurray, W., Optimum Snubbers for Power Semiconductors, *IEEE Transactions on Industry Applications*, Vol. IA-8, No. 5, pp. 593–600, September/October 1972.

McMurray, W., Selection of Snubbers and Clamps to Optimize the Design of Transistor Switching Converters, *IEEE Transactions on Industry Applications*, Vol. IA-16, No. 4, pp. 513–523, July/August 1980.

McMurray, W., Efficient Snubbers for Voltage-Source GTO Inverters, *Record of IEEE Power Electronics Specialists Conference (PESC)*, pp. 20–27, 1985.

Menzies, R.W. and Zhuang, Y., Advanced Static Compensation using a Multilevel GTO Thyristor Inverter, *IEEE Transactions on Power Delivery*, Vol. 10, pp. 732–738, April 1995.

Mertens, A. and Divan, D.M., A High Frequency Resonant DC Link Inverter using IGBT's, *Record of International Power Electronics Conference (IPEC)*, pp. 152–160, 1990.

Mertens, A. and Skudelny, H.Ch., Calculations on the Spectral Performance of Discrete Pulse Modulation Strategies, *Record of IEEE Power Electronics Specialists Conference (PESC)*, pp. 357–365, 1991.

Mestha, L.K. and Evans, P.D., Analysis of On-State Losses in PWM Inverters, *IEE Proceedings*, Vol. 136, Part B, No. 4, pp. 189–195, July 1989.

Meynard, T., Fadel, M. and Aouda, N., Modelling of Multilevel Converters, *IEEE Transactions on Industrial Electronics*, Vol. 44, No. 3, pp. 356–364, 1997.

Meynard, T.A. and Foch, H., Multilevel Conversion: High Voltage Choppers and Voltage Source Inverters. *IEEE Transactions on Power Electronics*, No. 3, pp. 397–403, 1992.

Miller, T.J.E. (ed.), *Reactive Power Control in Electric Systems*, John Wiley & Sons, New York, 1982.

Mohan, N., Undeland, T.M. and Robbins, W.P., *Power Electronics: Converters, Applications and Design*, 2nd edition, John Wiley & Sons, 1995.

Mwinyiwiwa, B., Wolanski, Z. and Ooi, B.T., Current Equalisation in SPWM FACTS Controllers at Lowest Switching Rates, *IEEE Transactions on Power Electronics*, Vol. 14, No. 5, pp. 900–905, 1999.

Mwinyiwiwa, B., Wolanski, Z., Chen, Y. and Ooi, B.T., Multimodular Multilevel Converters with Input/Output Linearity, *IEEE Transactions on Industry Applications*, Vol. 33, No. 5, pp. 1214–1219, September/October 1997.

Nabae, A., Takahashi, I. and Akagi, H., A New Neutral-Point-Clamped PWM Inverter. *IEEE Transactions on Industry Applications*, Vol. 17, No. 5, pp. 518–523, September/October 1981.

Nabavi-Niaki, A. and Iravani, M.R., Steady-State and Dynamic Models of Unified Power Flow Controller (UPFC) for Power System Studies, IEEE Transactions on Power Systems, Vol. 11, No. 4, pp. 1937–1943, November 1996.

Newton, C. and Sumner, M., Neutral Point Control for Multi-Level Inverters: Theory, Design and Operational Limitations, *Proceedings of the IEEE Industry Applications Annual Meeting*, pp. 1336–1343, 1997.

Newton, C., Sumner, M. and Alexander, T., The Investigation and Development of a Multi-Level Voltage Source Inverter, *Conference Proceedings of IEE/PEVD '96*, Nottingham, UK, pp. 317–321, September 1996.

Niedernostheide, F.J., Schulze, H.-J., Dorn, J., Kellner-Werdehausen, U. and Westerholt, D., Light-Triggered Thyristors with Integrated Protection Functions, *Proceedings of the ISPSD 2000*, Toulouse, May 22–25, in press.

Niedernostheide, F.J., Schulze, H.J. and Kellner-Werdehausen, U., High-Power Thyristors with Integrated Functions, *Proceedings of the ISPSD 2000*, Prague, August 30–September 1.

Nishihara, M., Power Electronics Diversity, *Record of International Power Electronics Conference (IPEC)*, 21–28, 1990.

Noroozian, M. and Andersson, G., Power Flow Control by Use of Controllable Series Components, *IEEE Transactions on Power Delivery*, Vol. 8, No. 3, pp. 1420–1429, July 1993.

Ohno, E., The Semiconductor Evolution in Japan – A Four Decade Long Maturity Thriving to an Indispensable Social Standing, *Record of International Power Electronics Conference (IPEC)*, 11–20, 1990.

Ooi, B.T., Dai, S.Z. and Galiana, F.D., A Solid-State PWM Phase Shifter, *IEEE Transactions on Power Delivery*, Vol. 8, pp. 573–579, April 1993.

Ooi, B.T., Joos, G. and Huang, X., Operating Principles of Shunt STATCOM based on 3-Level Diode-Clamped Converters, *Proceedings of IEEE PES Winter Meeting*, New York, February 1999.

Paice, D.A., *Power Electronic Converter Harmonics: Multipulse Methods for Clean Power*. IEEE Press, 1996.

Palmour, J.W., Singh, R., Glass, R.C., Kordina, O. and Carter, C.H. Jr., Silicon Carbide for Power Devices, *IEEE ISPSD 1997*, Weimar, pp. 25–32, May 26–29.

Peng, F.Z., Lai, J., McKeever, J.W. and VanCoevering, J., A Multilevel Voltage-Source Inverter with Separate DC Sources for Static Var Generation, *IEEE Transactions on Industry Applications*, Vol. 32, No. 5, pp. 1130–1138, September/October 1996.

Peng, F.Z., McKeever, J.W. and Adams, D.J., Cascade Multilevel Inverters for Utility Applications, *IEEE IECON Proceedings of 1997*, pp. 437–442.

Peng, F.Z., McKeever, J.W. and Adams, D.J., Power Line Conditioner using Cascade Multilevel Inverters for Distribution Systems, *IEEE Transactions on Industry Applications*, Vol. 34, No. 6, pp. 1293–1298, November/December 1998.

Peng, F.Z., McKeever, W. and Adams, D.J., A Power Line Conditioner using Cascade Multilevel Inverter for Distribution Systems, *IEEE Transactions on Industry Applications*, Vol. 34, No. 6, pp. 1293–1298, November/December 1998.

Peterson, N.M. and Scott-Meyer, W., Automatic Adjustment of Transformer and Phase Shifter Taps in the Newton Power Flow, *IEEE Transactions on Power Apparatus and Systems*, Vol. PAS-90, No. 1, pp. 103–108, January/February 1971.

Piwko, R.J., Wegner, C.A., Kinney, S.J. and Eden, J.D., Subsynchronous Resonance Performance Test of the Slatt Thyristor-Controlled Series Capacitor, *IEEE Transactions on Power Delivery*, Vol. 11, No. 2, pp. 1112–1119, April 1996.

Przybysz, J.X., Miller, D.L., Leslie, S.G. and Kao, Y.C., High di/dt Light-Triggered Thyristors. *IEEE Transactions on Electron Devices*, ED-34, 10, pp. 2192–2199, October 1987.

Rice, J.B., Design of Snubber Circuits for Thyristor Converters, *Record of IEEE Industry General Applications Annual Meeting*, pp. 485–589, 1969.

Rico, J.J. and Acha, E., The Use of Switching functions and Walsh Series to Calculate Waveform Distortion in Thyristor Controlled Compensated Power Circuits, *IEEE Transactions on Power Delivery*, Vol. 13, No. 4, pp. 1370–1377, October 1998.

Rico, J.J., Acha, E. and Miller, T.J.E., Harmonic Domain Modelling of Three Phase Thyristor-Controlled Reactors by Means of Switching Vectors and Discrete Convolutions, *IEEE Transactions on Power Delivery*, Vol. 11, No. 3, pp. 1678–1684, July 1996.

Rockot, J.H., Losses in High-Power Bipolar Transistors, *IEEE Transactions on Power Electronics*, Vol. PE-2, No. 1, pp. 72–80, January 1987.

Rohas, R., Ohnishi, T. and Suzuki, T., An Improved Voltage Vector Control Method for Neutral Point Clamped Inverters, *IEEE Transactions on Power Electronics*, Vol. 10, No. 6, pp. 666–672, November 1995.

Ruff, M., Schulze, H.J. and Kellner, U., Progress in the Development of an 8-kV Light-Triggered Thyristor with Integrated Protection Functions. *IEEE Transactions on Electron Devices*, Vol. 46, No. 8, pp. 1768–1774, 1999.

Schauder, C., Gernhardt, M., Stacey, E., Lemak, T., Gyugyi, L., Cease, T.W. and Edris, A Development of a ±100 MVAR Static Condenser for Voltage Control of Transmission Systems, *IEEE Transactions on Power Delivery*, Vol. 10, No. 3, pp. 1486–1493, July 1995.

Schauder, C., Gyugyi, L., Lund, M.R., Hamai, D.M., Rietman, T.R., Torgerson, D.R. and Edris, A., Operation of the Unified Power Flow Controller (UPFC) under Practical Constraints, *IEEE Transactions on Power Delivery*, Vol. 13, pp. 630–639, April 1998.

Schibli, N.P., Nguyen, T. and Rufer, A.C., Three-Phase Multilevel Converter for High-Power Induction Motors. *IEEE Transactions on Power Electronics*, Vol. 13, No. 5, pp. 978–985, September 1998.

Schönung, A. and Stemmler, H., Static Frequency Changers with Subharmonic Control in Conjunction with reversible Variable-Speed AC-Drives. Brown Boveri Review, Vol. 51, 1964.

Schulting, L., A 100-kVA Resonant DC Link Inverter with GTO's – Design Consideration and First Practical Experience, *Record of IEEE Industry Applications Society Annual Meeting*, 729–736, 1992.

Schulze, H.J., Ruff, M., Baur, B., Pfirsch, F., Kabza, H. and Kellner, U., *Proceedings of International Symposium on Power Semiconductor Devices and Ics.*, pp. 197–200, 1996.

Schulze, H.J., Ruff, M., Baur, B., Pfirsch, F., Kabza, H., Kellner, U. and Voss, P., Light-Triggered 8-kV Thyristor with a New Integrated Breakover Diode. *Electronic Engineering* (London), Vol. 69, No. 848, pp. 24–28, August 1997.

Semlyen, A., Acha, E. and Arrillaga, J., Newton-Type Algorithms for the Harmonic Phasor Analysis of Non-Linear Power Circuits in Periodical Steady State with Special Reference to Magnetic Non-Linearities, *IEEE Transactions on Power Delivery*, Vol. 3, No. 3, pp. 1090–1098, July 1988.

Semlyen, A. and Rajakovic, N., Harmonic Domain Modelling of Laminated Iron Cores, *IEEE Transactions on Power Delivery*, Vol. 4, No. 1, pp. 382–390, January 1989.

Shipley, R.B., *Introduction to Matrices and Power Systems*, John Wiley & Sons, New York, 1976.

Singh, B., Al-Haddad, K. and Chandra, A., A Review of Active Filters for Power Quality Improvement. *IEEE Transactions on Industrial Electronics*, Vol. 46, No. 5, pp. 960–971, October, 1999.

Sinha, G. and Lipo, T.A., A Four-Level Rectifier Inverter System for Drive Applications, *Proceedings IEEE Industry Applications Society Annual Meeting*, pp. 980–987, 1996.

Sood, P. and Lipo, T.A., Power Conversion Distribution System using a Resonant High Frequency AC Link, *Record of IEEE Industry Applications Society Annual Meeting*, pp. 533–541, 1986.

Stagg, G.W. and El-Abiad, A.H., *Computer Methods in Power System Analysis*, McGraw-Hill Series in Electronic Systems, McGraw-Hill, 1968.

Stefanovic, V.R., Current Developments in AC Drives, *Record of International Power Electronics Conference (IPEC)*, 382–390, 1991.

Steinke, J.K., Switching Frequency Optimal PWM Control of a Three-Level Inverter, *IEEE Transactions on Power Electronics*, Vol. 7, No. 3, pp. 487–496, July 1992.

Stemmler, H. State of the Art and Future Trends in High Power Electronics, *Proceedings of International Power Electronics Conference (IPEC)*, Tokyo, Vol. 1, pp. 4–14, April 3–7, 2000.

Steyn, C.G., Analysis and Optimization of Regenerative Linear Snubbers, *IEEE Transactions on Power Electronics*, Vol. 4, No. 3, pp. 362–370, July 1989.

Stoll, H.G., *Least-Cost Electric Utility Planning*, John Wiley & Sons, New York, 1989.

Stott, B., Review of Load-Flow Calculations Methods, *IEEE Proceedings*, Vol. 62, pp. 916–929, July 1974.

Suh, B.S. and Hyun, D.S., A New N-Level High Voltage Inversion System, *IEEE Transactions on Industrial Electronics*, Vol. 44, No. 1, pp. 107–115, February 1997.

Tada, Akiharu, Kawakami, Akira, Miyazima, Tatsuo, Nakagawa, Tsutomu, Yamanaka, Kenichi, Ohtaki and Kaname, 4-kV, 1500-A Light Triggered Thyristor, *Proceedings, Solid State devices*, pp. 99–104, 1981.

Tadros, Y. and Salama, S., Three Level IGBT Inverter, *IEEE Transactions on Power Electronics*, No. 3, pp. 6–52, 1992.

Temple, V.A.K., Development of a 2.6-kV Light-Triggered Thyristor for Electric Power systems, *IEEE Transactions on Electron Devices*, ED-27, No. 3, pp. 583–591, March 1980.

Temple, V.A.K., Comparison of Light Triggered and Electrically Triggered Thyristor Turn-On. *IEEE Transactions on Electron Devices*, ED-28, No. 7, pp. 860–865, July 1981.

Teodorescu, R., Blaabjerg, F., Pedersen, J.K., Cengelci, E., Sulistijo, S.U., Woo, B.O. and Enjeti, P., Multilevel Converters – A Survey, *Proceedings of the European Power Electronics Conference*, pp. 2–11, 1999.

Tinney, W.F. and Hart, C.E., Power Flow Solutions by Newton's Method, *IEEE Transactions on Power Apparatus and Systems*, Vol. PAS-96, No. 11, pp. 1449–1460, November 1967.

Tolbert, L. Peng, F. and Habetler, T., Multilevel Converters for Large Electric Drives, *IEEE Transactions on Industry Applications*, Vol. 35, No. 1, pp. 36–44, January/February 1999.

Tolbert, L.M. and Habetler, T.G., Novel Multilevel Inverter Carrier-Based PWM Method, *IEEE Transactions on Industry Applications*, Vol. 35, No. 5, pp. 1098–1107, September–October 1999.

Tolbert, L.M. and Habetler, T.G., A Multilevel Converter-Based Universal Power Conditioner, *IEEE Power Electronics Specialists Conference 1999*, pp. 393–399.

Tolbert, L.M., Peng, F.Z. and Habetler, T.G., Multilevel Converters for Large Electric Drives, *IEEE Transactions on Industry Applications*, Vol. 35, No. 1, pp. 36–44, January–February 1999.

Tolbert, L.M., Peng, F.Z. and Habetler, T.G., Multilevel PWM Methods at Low Modulation Indices, *IEEE Applied Power Electronics Conference 1999*, pp. 1032–1038.

Trzynadlowski, A.M., Introduction to Modern Power Electronics, John Wiley & Sons, Inc., 1998.

Undeland, T.M., Switching Stress Reduction in Power Transistor Converters, *Record of IEEE Industry Applications Society Annual Meeting*, pp. 383–392, 1976.

Undeland, T.M., Snubbers for Pulse Width Modulated Bridge Converters with Power Transistors or GTOs, *Record of International Power Electronics Conference (IPEC)*, pp. 313–323, 1983.

Undeland, T.M., Jenset, F., Steinbakk, A., Rogne, T. and Hernes, M., A Snubber Configuration for both Power Transistors and GTO PWM Inverters, *Record of IEEE Power Electronics Specialists Conference (PESC)*, pp. 42–53, 1984.

Van Ligten, H. and Navon, D. Basic Turn-off of GTO Switches, *IRE Wescon Convention Record, Part 3 on Electron Devices*, pp. 49–52, August 1960.

Venkataramanan, G., and Divan, D.M., Pulse Width Modulation with Resonant DC Link Converters, *IEEE Transactions on Industry Applications*, Vol. 29, No. 1, pp. 113–120, January/February 1993.

Venkataramanan, G., Divan, D.M. and Jahns, T.M., Discrete Pulse Modulation Strategies for High-Frequency Inverter Systems, *IEEE Transactions on Power Electronics*, Vol. 8, No. 3, pp. 279–287, July 1993.

Walker, G. and Ledwich, G., Bandwidth Considerations for Multilevel Converters, *IEEE Transactions on Power Electronics*, Vol. 14, No. 1, pp. 74–81, January 1999.

Weedy, B.M., *Electric Power Systems*, 3rd edition, John Wiley & Sons, 1987.

Woo, B.O. and Cho, G.H., Soft Switching AC/DC/AC Converter with Current Freewheeling Circuit, *Record of IEEE Power Electronics Specialists Conference (PESC)*, pp. 31–38, 1991.

Wood, A.J. and Wollenberg, B.F., Power Generation Operation & Control, John Wiley & Sons, 1984.

Xu, L. and Agelidis, V.G., A Flying Capacitor Multilevel PWM Converter based UPFC, Paper presented at the *IEEE PESC '01*, Vancouver, Canada, June 2001.

Xu, L., Agelidis, V.G. and Acha, E., Development Considerations of a DSP-Controlled PWM VSC-Based STATCOM, *IEE Proceedings, Electric Power Applications*, September 2001.

Yacamini, R. and Resende, J.W., Thyristor Controlled Reactors as Harmonic Sources in HVDC Converters Stations and AC Systems, *IEE Proceedings*, Part B, Vol. 133, No. 4, pp. 263–269, July 1986.

Zach, F., Kaiser, K., Kolar, J. and Haselsteiner, F., New Lossless Turn-On and Turn-Off (Snubber) Networks for Inverters, Including Circuits for Blocking Voltage Limitation, *IEEE Transactions on Power Electronics*, Vol. PE-1, No. 2, April 1986.

Zhang, H., VonJouanne, A. and Wallace, A., Multilevel Inverter Modulation Schemes to Eliminate Common-Mode Voltages, *IEEE IAS Annual Meeting 1998*, pp. 752–758.

Zollenkopf, K., Bifactorization – Basic Computational Algorithm and Programming Techniques, *Conference on Large Sets of Sparse Linear Equations*, Oxford, pp. 75–96, 1970.

Index